KT-457-632

Visual Basic .NET

A Complete Object-Oriented Programming Course

Including Unified Modelling Language (UML)

Phil Jones

Foreword by Tim Sneath

continuum
LONDON · NEW YORK

Dedicated to
Rita, all my love, Philip

Continuum
The Tower Building
11 York Road
London SE1 7NX

370 Lexington Avenue
New York
NY 10017-6503

© Philip Jones 2003

All rights reserved. No part of this publication may be reproduced or transmitted in any form or by any means, electronic or mechanical, including photocopying, recording, or any information storage or retrieval system, without prior permission in writing from the publishers.

British Library Cataloguing-in-Publishing Data
A catalogue record for this book is available from the British Library.

ISBN: 0-8264-5714-2

Typeset by AMA DataSet Limted
Printed and bound in Great Britain by Biddles Ltd, Guildford and King's Lynn

Contents

Contents

Foreword

Trying to predict the future is hard.

You're likely to be wrong, for one thing.

When Microsoft began work on the .NET vision, it was intended to mark a seismic shift away from a monolithic model of computing towards a new distributed approach that placed the Internet at the centre, rather than at the periphery. The vision defined a brand new application development tool suite, a radical revision to the widely used Visual Basic programming language and, most significantly, a new application platform for building applications called the .NET Framework, comprising an execution environment and over 2000 pre-built classes to help developers be more productive.

At last, with the launch of Visual Studio .NET in February 2002, the first part of the .NET vision is complete; the platform is now ready and it's possible to start building applications that target the .NET Framework. Part of Visual Studio .NET is the Visual Basic .NET language and compiler, for which this book is your tutorial and guide.

We've come a long way over the eleven years since Visual Basic 1.0 was launched, when it was limited to creating small-scale, forms-based applications. Indeed, the language itself is unrecognisable from the original BASIC over thirty years ago, with a full range of object-orientated features including class and interface inheritance, encapsulation and polymorphism[1]. Visual Basic is now a fully mature language with the power to tackle pretty much anything from a command-line utility to the most demanding enterprise system.

Learning Visual Basic .NET can be a daunting task at first. There seems so much to take on board, and it can be difficult to know where to start. That's where this book comes in. Phil Jones has written a clear and practical guide that will give you everything you need to become an expert in Visual Basic .NET. I'm impressed with this book: the tutorial sections strike an excellent balance between ease of reading and comprehensive coverage of object-orientated terminology, and the practical exercises are both fun and thought-provoking. In combination with websites such as http://msdn.microsoft.com and http://www.gotdotnet.com, you'll be able to pick up the skills you need to master Visual Basic .NET quickly and with little pain.

Microsoft has spent over £5 billion to invest in the success of .NET. Whilst predicting the future trends in technology is a risky business, there is little doubt that we are living in exciting times where connecting devices from mobile phones to PCs to large application servers using the Internet will allow a huge variety of applications that have not even been conceived of yet. If you take the time to master the skills in Visual Basic .NET development taught by this book, you'll be one of a growing community of developers who have all the skills necessary to participate in this connected world.

Tim Sneath (tims@microsoft.com)

.NET Principal Systems Engineer

Microsoft Ltd.

---

[1] Don't worry if these terms don't make sense: they're all explained later in the book!

Preface

Who is this book for?

This book will teach its readers how to code object-oriented programs, and it introduces design techniques. It is aimed at four main types of reader:

1. Those who wish to learn how to program through individual study.

2. Students attending a formal course of study in how to program using Visual Basic .NET.

3. Lecturers and teachers who require a course text that supplies a carefully graded course supported by in-text questions and practical activities designed for students to complete during lectures and lessons.

4. Programmers already familiar with previous versions of Visual Basic who need assistance in understanding how to code VB .NET programs using object-oriented techniques.

> **NOTE TO LECTURERS AND TEACHERS:** There is extra support material to assist with your lectures and practical sessions when you adopt this book as your course text. This material can be located on the web at the following URL: http://business-sciences. cant.ac.uk/computing/visualbasicnet/

The emphasis of the book

Visual Basic .NET, compared with previous versions of Visual Basic, is now a 'fully fledged' object-oriented programming language, and the emphasis of this book is to cover the features of the language that support object-oriented programming (OOP).

Unified Modelling Language (UML)

Programming with objects requires that you 'think in objects'. An extremely useful technique that supports a programmer in this aim is the **UML collaboration diagram.** This diagram is introduced in Chapter 7 and used throughout the book where it helps with an understanding of how objects communicate with one another when a program executes.

How to use this book

It is not possible to learn a programming language by just reading a textbook. To learn a programming language requires that you practice what you have just read, at the computer. This textbook introduces you to aspects of programming then advises that you practice them at the computer before moving on.

I have introduced new aspects of programming though a *specification* that defines a problem to be solved. The text then describes a solution to this problem and you are then directed to implement this solution at the computer. As you progress through the book the specifications become more involved and difficult. You should not move on until you have implemented (and understood) the solution to the specification at the computer.

Directed study

The book supports **student-centred learning** by using icons to direct student activities, and as such, would make an ideal course text for degree, foundation degree, HND/HNC, GNVQ Advanced and related A level courses in Computing, Software Engineering and Information Technology.

The book has also been developed with the sole reader in mind. Individuals who wish to learn about Visual Basic .NET, without attending a course, will find the material useful and the layout of the book will encourage an interactive approach that is ideal for learning a programming language.

To assist in directing your study are:

- Revision questions
- Development questions
- Practical activities

Every question will be numbered. A revision and development question will be specifically identified by the words revision or development appearing in brackets after the question number. Two examples are shown below.

QUESTION 8.2 (DEVELOPMENT)

Use the VB .NET on line help to discover the difference between passing a parameter by value and passing a parameter by reference as represented by the keywords ByVal and ByRef.

QUESTION 15.1 (REVISION)

What would happen if you altered the following line of the program shown in Figure 15.3 in the way indicated below?

divider = potentialPrime \ 2

Change to:

divider = potentialPrime / 2

A revision question is designed to test the readers' understanding of what they have just read, or it will test their understanding of a Practical Activity they have just completed.

A development question differs from a revision question in that it is not designed to check the readers understanding of what they have just done. Instead, a Development Question is designed to encourage the reader to develop a further understanding of the subject by utilizing the Visual Basic .NET comprehensive help database.

A practical activity directs the reader (or student) to perform a practical task at the computer. The activity usually follows a section of text that shows the steps involved in performing a practical task with Visual Basic .NET.

An example of a practical activity is shown below.

PRACTICAL ACTIVITY 14.3

Rewrite the event handling procedure shown in Listing 14.1 so that it performs in the same way but using the *Do .. Loop While* construct **instead** of the *Do .. Loop Until* construct.

Enter and run your solution.

HINT: While **Not** (conditional test)

Appendix

The Appendix deals with the fundamental knowledge required by a computer programmer. If you are new to programming or new to programming in objects then you should read this appendix **before** starting Chapter 1.

1 The Visual Basic Environment

> **NOTE**: If you are new to object-oriented computer programming you would benefit from reading the appendix before you start working your way through the chapters.

To open VB .NET the user issues appropriate mouse moves and clicks as illustrated by Figure 1.1 (which shows a typical Windows environment).

Figure 1.1 Click as shown by the callout label. What you see on your VDU screen will be dependent upon the applications installed on your system. Consequently, it may not be exactly as shown here.

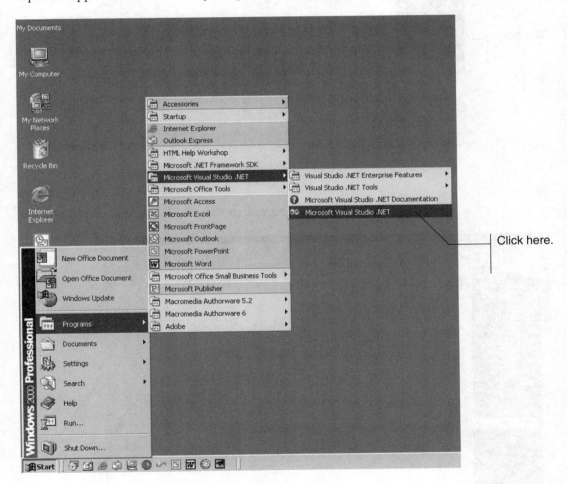

After clicking you should see something similar to the illustration shown in Figure 1.2: this is the VB .NET Integrated Development Environment (IDE).

Click on *My Profile* as shown by the callout label in Figure 1.2 and something similar to that shown in Figure 1.3 will appear.

Figure 1.2 This illustrates the start page for the Integrated Development Environment.

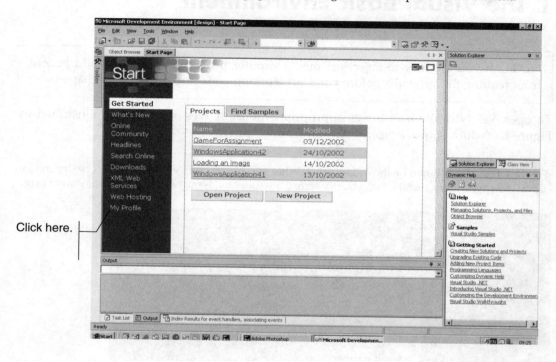

Figure 1.3 Setting your profile.

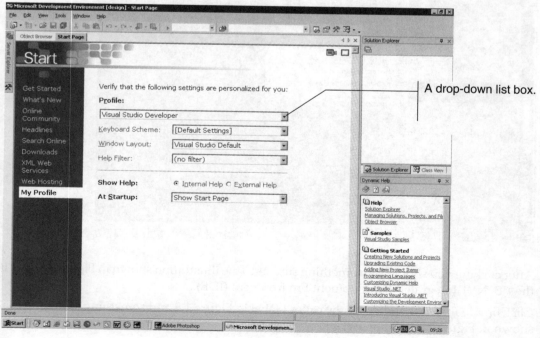

The IDE is used for developing applications in numerous languages (such as C++ and C #). The profile page allows you to set the environment to match your requirements. To set it up for developing an application using VB .NET is achieved by selecting from the appropriate drop-down list boxes (as shown by the callout labels in Figure 1.3).

Figure 1.4 shows how to set the help filter to Visual Basic Documentation. Naturally, you would choose to view the help files associated with Visual Basic, because this is the language you are using to develop your application.

Figure 1.4 Setting the Help Filter.

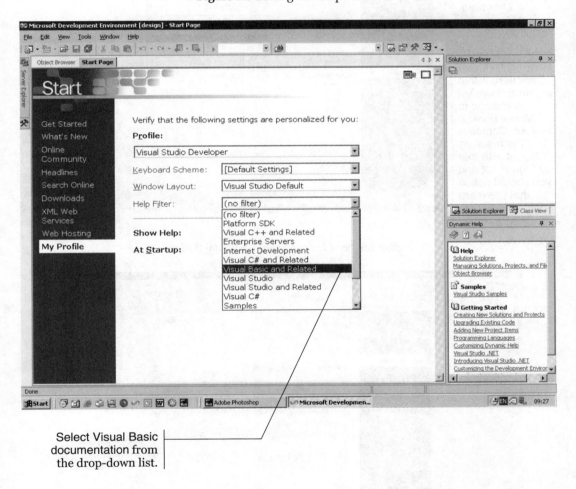

Select Visual Basic documentation from the drop-down list.

The Window Layout is set to *Visual Studio Default*. If you are familiar with Visual Basic 6 you may prefer to set this to *Visual Basic 6*, as shown in Figure 1.5.

Once your profile has been set, click on *Get Started* (as shown by the callout label in Figure 1.5) and this will return you to the screen shown in Figure 1.6.

Figure 1.5 Setting the Window Layout to Visual Basic 6.

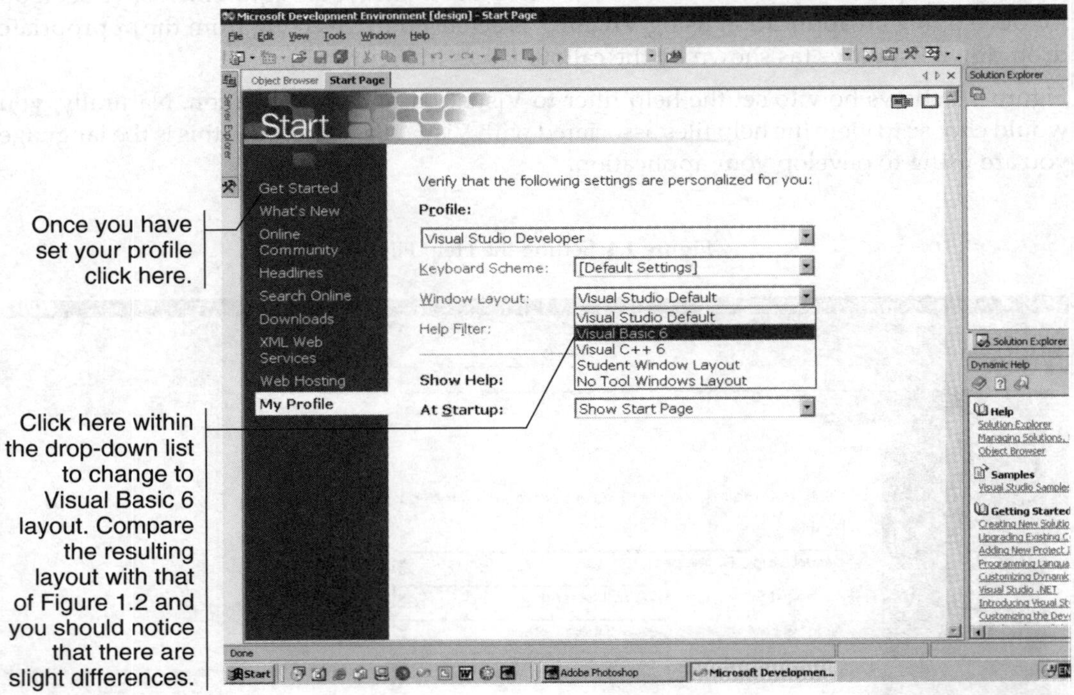

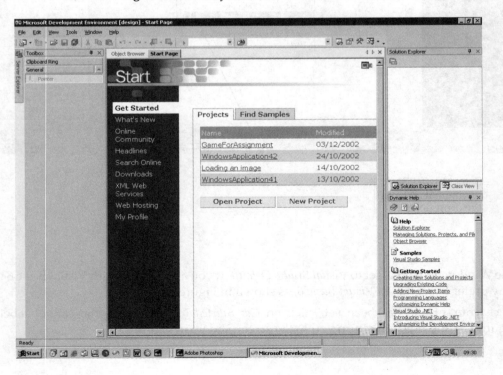

Once you have set your profile click here.

Click here within the drop-down list to change to Visual Basic 6 layout. Compare the resulting layout with that of Figure 1.2 and you should notice that there are slight differences.

Figure 1.6 New layout based on Visual Basic 6.

Starting a Windows application

The following sequence of screenshots (Figures 1.7–1.10) and associated callout labels show the steps involved in starting a Windows application.

> **NOTE**: A callout label contains text that points to a particular region of a screenshot, used throughout the book to highlight features and to guide you in developing an application. On many occasions the callout labels will be numbered and the numbered sequence should be followed when you attempt to perform the task shown in the figure. Each screenshot shows how an element of the VB .NET environment and an application runtime looks on the visual display unit (VDU).

Figure 1.7 Step 1.

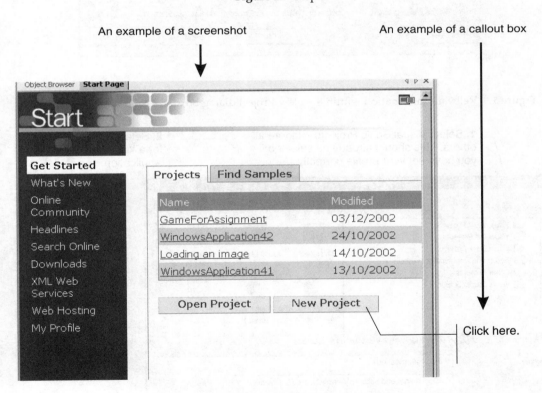

An example of a screenshot

An example of a callout box

Click here.

Once you have clicked *New Project* you will be presented with the dialog box shown in Figure 1.8.

This dialog box presents the programmer (i.e. you) with a vast array of information. Fortunately, at this stage you only need to consider some of the information presented. Figure 1.9 uses callout labels to indicate the relevant information. Every callout label is numbered to indicate the sequence of actions necessary to create a new project.

Figure 1.8 The New Project dialog box.

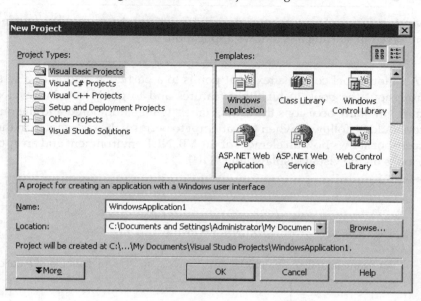

Figure 1.9 Relevant information within the New Project dialog box for Visual Basic developers.

1. Select Visual Basic Projects – ignore all others. This should already be selected if you have set your profile correctly.

2. Select this **template** for a Windows Application.

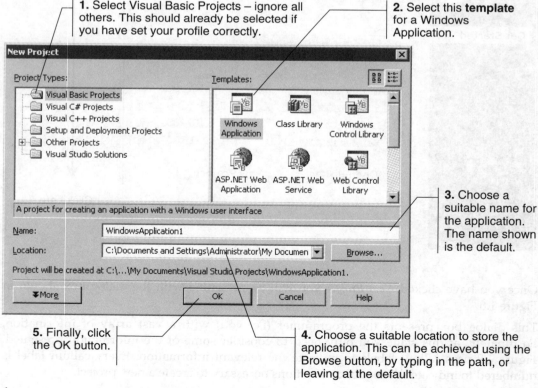

3. Choose a suitable name for the application. The name shown is the default.

5. Finally, click the OK button.

4. Choose a suitable location to store the application. This can be achieved using the Browse button, by typing in the path, or leaving at the default.

If you have followed the sequence of actions shown in Figure 1.9 then you will be presented with a screen that looks similar to Figure 1.10. This is the design time IDE, which is the environment in which you build software applications (i.e. programs).

Figure 1.10 The design time Integrated Design Environment (IDE).

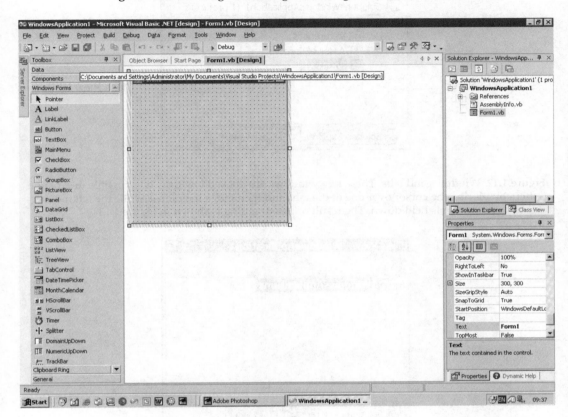

IDE Windows

As the previous figures show, the layout of the Visual Basic .NET environment can be tailored to the programmer's requirement. Figure 1.11 shows a segment of Figure 1.10. This segment shows the Solution Explorer and Class View and how to access them via the tabs.

The process described by Figure 1.12 can be applied to all the windows within the Visual Basic .NET environment. Consequently, you can tailor the environment to your own preference. Figures 1.14 and 1.15 show tailored views of the VB .NET environment.

Figure 1.11 Windows and Tabs. The view here shows the Solution Explorer to the foreground. Clicking on the Class View tab will bring the Class View to the foreground, as shown in Figure 1.12.

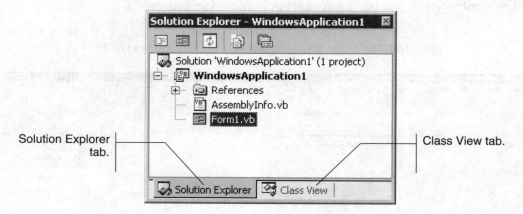

Solution Explorer tab.

Class View tab.

Figure 1.12 Windows and tabs. These two windows are docked together. It is possible to separate them by placing the cursor over one of the tabs and then move the mouse while the left mouse button is held down. The result of this **dragging** is shown in Figure 1.13.

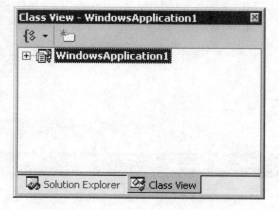

Figure 1.13 Separated windows.

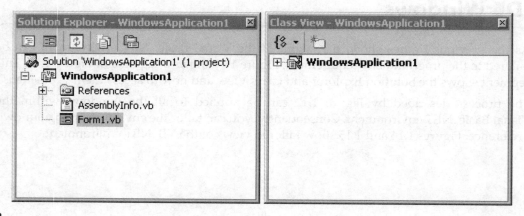

Figure 1.14 A tailored VB .NET environment.

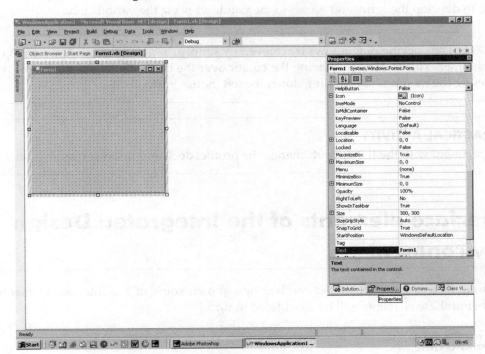

Figure 1.15 Another tailored VB .NET environment.

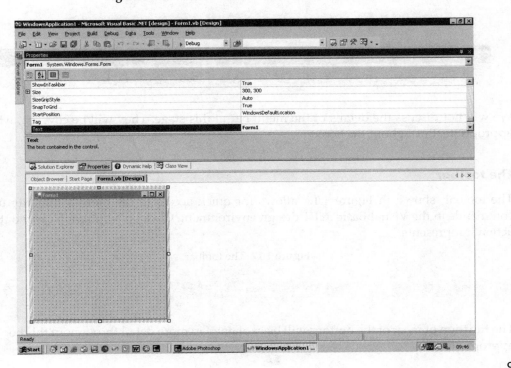

My preference, for what it is worth, is the layout shown in Figure 1.10, as it gives plenty of space to develop the form, and access to the windows is via the various tabs.

NOTE: The docking of windows is achieved by simply dragging the windows on top of each other. This is done by placing the cursor over the bar at the top of a window and moving the mouse while holding down the left mouse button.

PRACTICAL ACTIVITY 1.1

Experiment with the IDE layout: change the profile; dock and undock windows, etc.

Interface elements of the Integrated Design Environment

Previous figures have illustrated the IDE and shown some of the interface elements. A number of these elements will be considered in turn.

The menu bar

The menu bar, shown in Figure 1.16, displays the commands used to build an application. There are nine main menu headings, from File through to Help.

Figure 1.16 The menu bar.

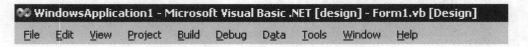

We will not discuss the details of the menu bar at this stage. They will be covered, where appropriate, throughout the book.

The toolbar

The toolbar, shown in Figure 1.17, allows for quick access to the more commonly used commands in the Visual Basic .NET design environment. Click on a button to carry out the action it represents.

Figure 1.17 The toolbar.

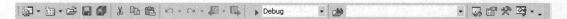

The function of most of the buttons will be explained in more detail throughout this book as appropriate.

PRACTICAL ACTIVITY 1.2

Allow the cursor to 'rest' on each of the buttons in turn and wait a short while. A label (tool tip) will appear to indicate the function of the button. An example of this is illustrated in Figure 1.18.

Figure 1.18 Illustrating the automatic appearance of a tool tip.

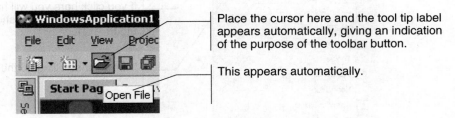

Place the cursor here and the tool tip label appears automatically, giving an indication of the purpose of the toolbar button.

This appears automatically.

The toolbox

Figure 1.19 illustrates the Visual Basic .NET toolbox. The toolbox provides a set of tools that the programmer can use when designing the graphical user interface for an application. These tools can be used to draw controls on a form, such as buttons, labels, text boxes, etc.

Figure 1.19 The toolbox. All controls are suitably labelled with their Visual Basic control name.

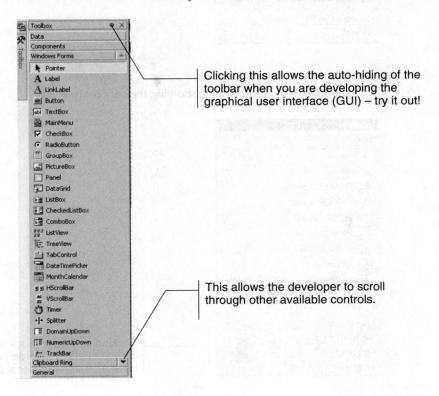

Clicking this allows the auto-hiding of the toolbar when you are developing the graphical user interface (GUI) – try it out!

This allows the developer to scroll through other available controls.

11

Another view of the toolbox is shown in Figure 1.20 after the developer has scrolled down the list of controls.

Figure 1.20 Another view of the toolbox **after** scrolling down the list.

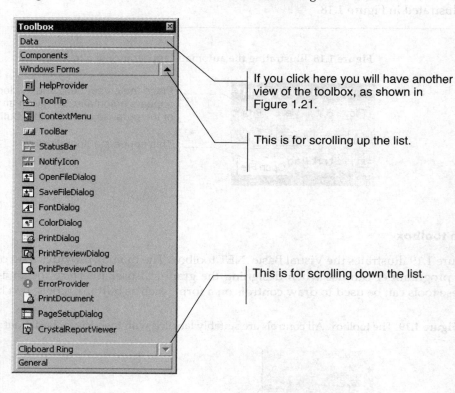

If you click here you will have another view of the toolbox, as shown in Figure 1.21.

This is for scrolling up the list.

This is for scrolling down the list.

Figure 1.21 Another view showing the data components.

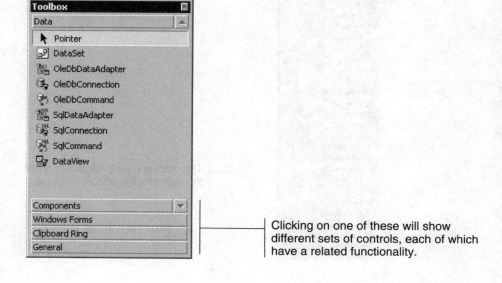

Clicking on one of these will show different sets of controls, each of which have a related functionality.

The function of most of the controls will be explained in more detail throughout the book as appropriate. However, three of the most frequently used controls are described next.

A Label   **The label control**.

A label is a graphical control you can use to display text that the user **cannot** change directly. However, code can be written that changes a label in response to events at runtime. For example, if an application takes a while to process data you could display a processing-status message.

> **NOTE**: Events are used to inform applications that something important has happened. For example, when you click a control on a form, a click event is raised that can call an event handling procedure. The moving of the cursor over a particular control on a form can raise a mouse move event, to which an event handler procedure is attached. There are many more examples of events and they will be covered as appropriate throughout the book.

PictureBox   The PictureBox control.

A PictureBox can display a graphic from a number of formats, such as:

- Bitmap (*.BMP)
- Icon (*.ICO)
- Metafile (*.WMF).

ab Button   **A Button**.

A user can click a button to begin, interrupt or end a process. When chosen, a button appears to be pushed in, consequently, it is often called a push button.

Form

Figure 1.22 illustrates a form that acts as a window within the application developed by the Visual Basic programmer. A programmer customizes this form to produce the graphical user interface (GUI) for the application.

Forms have properties that determine aspects of their appearance, such as position, size and background colour. Forms also have behaviour (methods), such as *ResetBackColor*, which resets the background colour of a form to its default value. Forms can also respond to events initiated by the user or triggered by the system.

> **NOTE**: The method *ResetBackColor* sets the *BackColor* property of the form to the default colour for a form. Properties and methods are often related in this way.

Figure 1.22 A form acts as a window that makes up part of an application's interface.

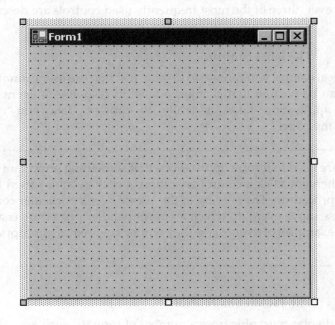

NOTE: A user event is an action initiated by the user of the application (program) such as clicking onto a control. A system event is an event triggered by the computer hardware. A typical system event is when the computer clock indicates a specific time to perform an operation, e.g. at midnight backup the server.

Solution explorer

When an application (program) is being developed (i.e. a solution) it will be made up of many files. The Solution Explorer enables the programmer (i.e. you) to manage these files.

Figure 1.23 show a typical Solution Explorer for a recently created project. This window conveys a considerable amount of information. However, for the time being most of this information can be ignored. The information of importance at the moment is the fact that this

Figure 1.23 A Solution Explorer window.

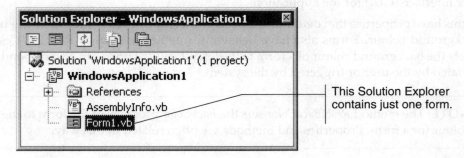

This Solution Explorer contains just one form.

Windows application has just one form, as shown by the callout label. If you were to add more forms then the Solution Explorer would look as shown in Figure 1.24.

Figure 1.24 A Solution Explorer, showing that the current solution has three forms.

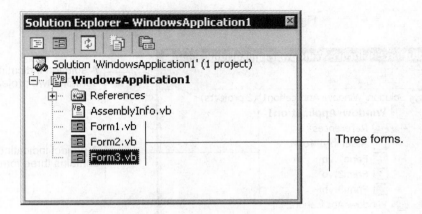

For every form within the Solution Explorer there is a corresponding file saved in a folder. So, for example, Figure 1.24 has three Form entries (Form1, Form2 and Form3). Consequently, there will be three files with a **vb** extension. Therefore, the filenames will be Form1.**vb**, Form2.**vb** and Form3.**vb**.

NOTE: It is usual to rename a form to reflect its purpose within an application. The filename for a renamed form takes the new name and adds the .vb extension. Filenames are prefixed with the three letters frm – this makes it easier to identify a form when it is referred to in program code.

The additional facilities offered by the Solution Explorer will be introduced throughout the book as appropriate.

A project and a solution

A project is a collection of files that can be compiled to create a component (e.g. a calendar) or an application suitable for distribution. Whereas a solution is a collection of projects and other files that together form a component or application (e.g. a database for a doctors surgery).

NOTE: The project is a folder-based model where all project items are placed in the project folder hierarchy. When you add a file, a copy of the file is placed in the project folder; when the project is built, the file is loaded from that copy of the file.

Solutions can be complex consisting of many projects and files. Ultimately, a solution is a way of organizing numerous projects and files that are part of an overall solution. Figure 1.25 shows a solution consisting of two projects. The first project consists of three window forms, whereas the second project consists of one window form and a class (more on classes later).

Figure 1.25 An example of a solution.

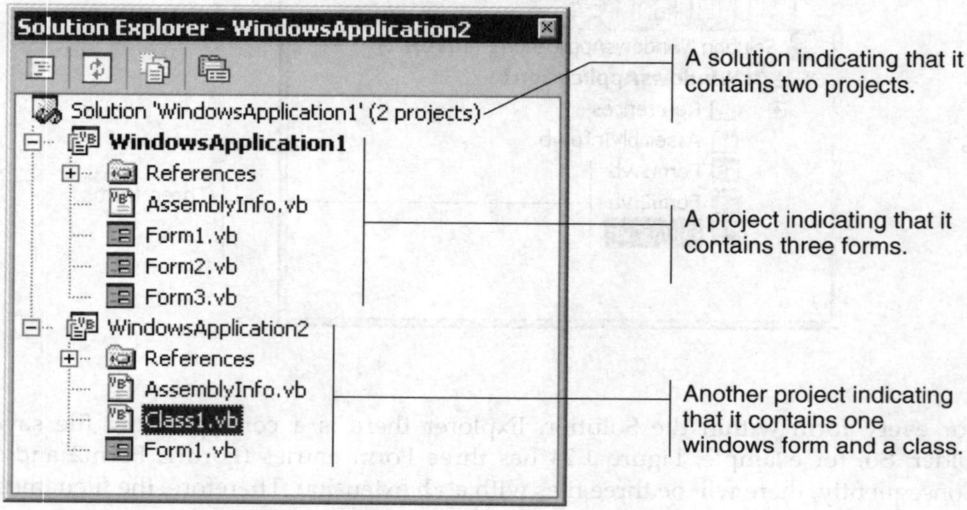

A solution indicating that it contains two projects.

A project indicating that it contains three forms.

Another project indicating that it contains one windows form and a class.

NOTE: Everything has to be part of a solution. A solution holds all the information needed to compile code.

Class View

The Class View window is similar to the Solution Explorer, in that it gives a view of a solution and a project. However, whereas the Solution Explorer gives a view of files, the Class View gives a view of classes and their members (e.g. methods, properties and events). This is an essential view for the object-oriented features of VB .NET. Figure 1.26 illustrates a typical example of a Class View window.

NOTE: Other languages, notably Java, use the term attributes instead of properties. However, VB .NET with its use of the property procedure makes it appropriate to use the term properties. VB .NET has other members of a class referred to as class variable (or fields) that are hidden within the class (or should be hidden) – more on this later.

Figure 1.26 A Class View window.

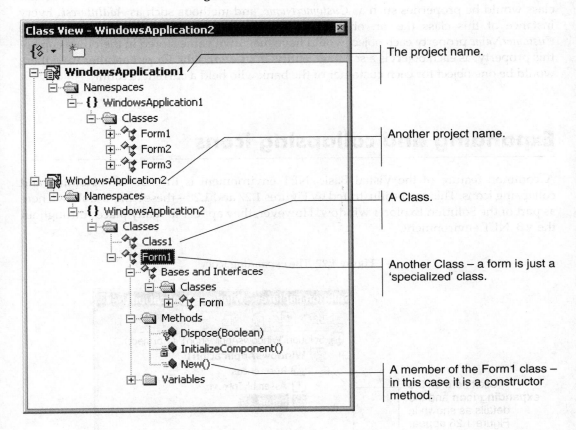

The project name.

Another project name.

A Class.

Another Class – a form is just a 'specialized' class.

A member of the Form1 class – in this case it is a constructor method.

NOTE: Classes, class members (i.e. methods, properties and events) and objects (instances of classes) will be covered later in the book. However, a simple description of some of these terms follow.

Classes, objects and members

A class is a template from which objects are made. A class is an abstraction that is used to represent a 'real life' object. Consequently, a class could be used to define the template for a bank account, or a die or a car.

An object is an instance of a class, i.e. the object is made from the class, rather like a scone is made from a pastry cutter.

Members are the values (properties) that can be held by an object (more accurately instances of class level variables – fields – hold the values and they are accessed via property procedures) and the behaviours (methods) carried out by the object.

For example, suppose you were developing an application for a bank then you would most probably have a class called *CurrentAccount*. Each instance of this class would be an object

17

that corresponds to a specific customer current account. The members of the *CurrentAccount* class would be properties such as *CustomerName*, and methods such as *AddInterest*. Every instance of this class (i.e. an object) would have these members. In the case of the *CustomerName* property each object would have their own value stored in their own copy of this property, as each object is a separate 'entity' in its own right. Or put another way, there would be one object for each customer of the bank who held a current account.

Expanding and collapsing icons

A common feature of the Visual Basic .NET environment is the use of expanding and collapsing icons. This can be illustrated by Figures 1.27 and 1.28 – these icons are shown here as part of the Solution Explorer window. However, they appear in many places throughout the VB .NET environment.

Figure 1.27 The expanding icon.

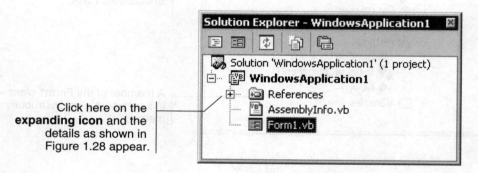

Click here on the **expanding icon** and the details as shown in Figure 1.28 appear.

Figure 1.28 The collapsing icon.

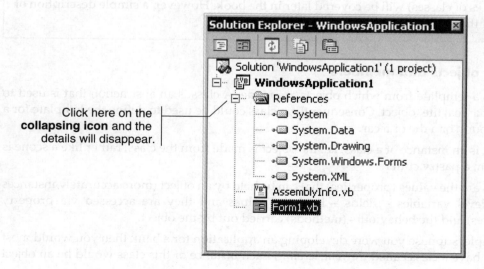

Click here on the **collapsing icon** and the details will disappear.

Properties window

Figure 1.29 shows two views of the Properties Window for a form. The programmer sets the properties of the form (and other controls) during design time by using the Properties Window. Properties specify the initial values for such characteristics as font appearance and background colour.

> **NOTE:** Design time is the time when the programmer is building the graphical user interface, drawing controls, setting properties and typing in the code.

Figure 1.29 Two views of a Properties Window for a form.

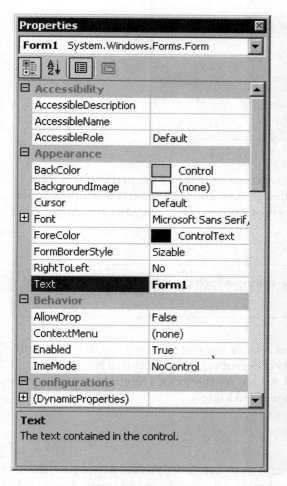

The categorized view

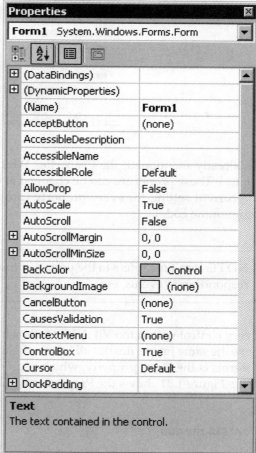

The alphabetic view

It is possible to toggle between both views by clicking on to one of the icons as shown in Figure 1.30.

Figure 1.30 Toggling between views.

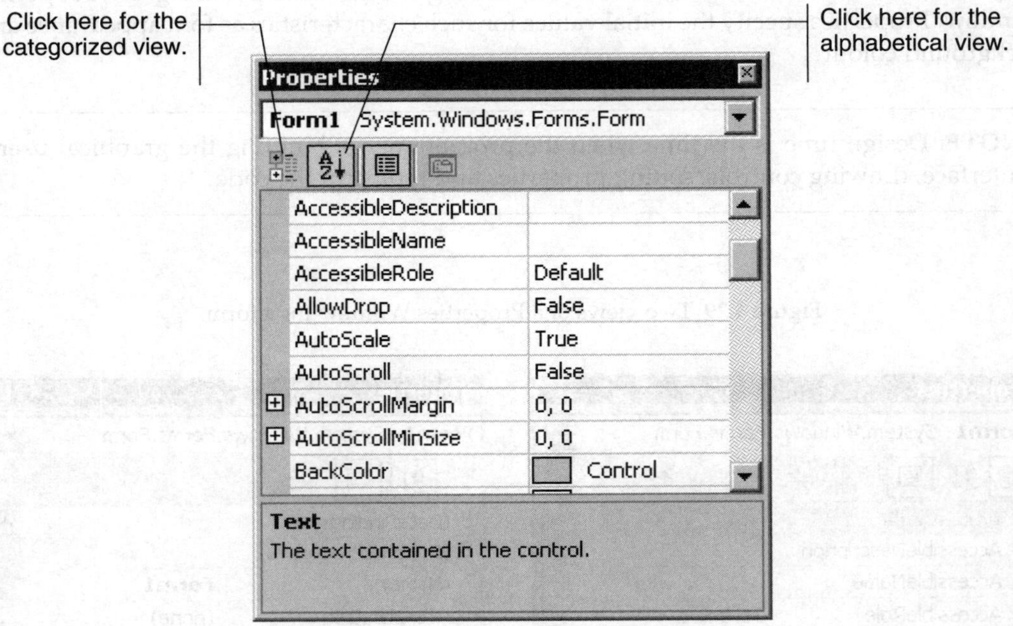

Click here for the categorized view.

Click here for the alphabetical view.

As already mentioned, the Properties Window contains a list of properties for a form or control. These properties can be changed at design time and the Properties Window shows the current setting for every property (properties can also be changed at run time by the programme code).

NOTE: Run time refers to the period of time during which the program is executing and responding to events, etc.

Every control within the VB .NET toolbox has a set of associated properties. Many controls have the same properties but all have a slightly different set. A property that is common to all controls is the *Name* property, which is used to identify the control (object) in the program code. Figure 1.31 shows the Properties Window for a button.

Context menus

Visual Basic provides context menus that contain short cuts to frequently performed actions during design time. Clicking the right mouse button activates a context menu. Figure 1.32 shows the context menu activated when a form is being developed. Figure 1.33 shows the context menu associated with the toolbox.

Figure 1.31 The Properties window for a button.

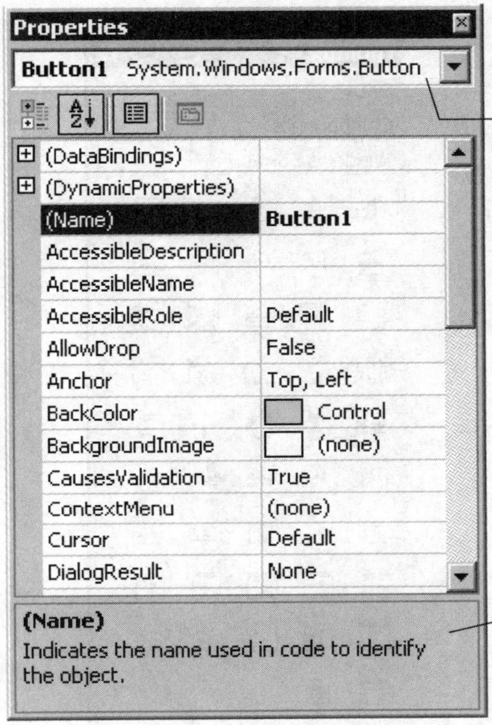

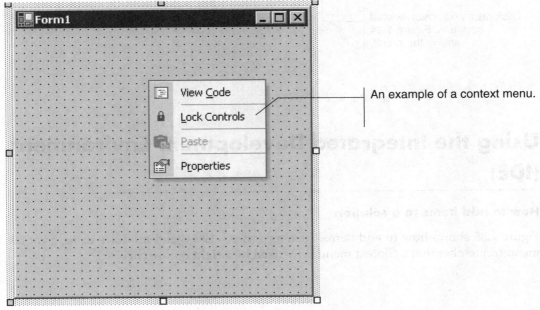

This entry informs the developer that the Properties window is displaying a list of properties associated with a button.

Compare this with the entry shown in Figure 1.29 for a form.

Also compare the list of properties for a form and for a button and you should see that there are differences.

This entry also shows the hierarchy chain for the Button class more on this later.

NOTE: A brief description appears here for whatever is highlighted in the list.

Figure 1.32 The context menu for a Visual Basic form. This menu lists the frequently used actions performed during design time by a Visual Basic programmer.

An example of a context menu.

Figure 1.33 An example of another context menu.

Figure 1.34 An alternative view of the components.

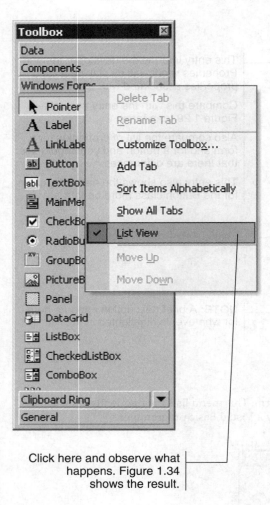

Click here and observe what happens. Figure 1.34 shows the result.

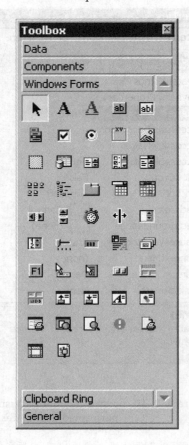

Using the Integrated Development Environment (IDE)

How to add items to a solution

Figure 1.35 shows how to add items, such as, forms, classes and modules using a context menu (remember that a context menu is invoked by a right mouse click).

Figure 1.35 Adding items to a solution.

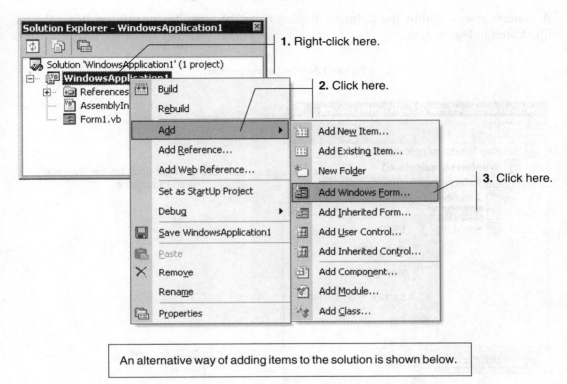

1. Right-click here.

2. Click here.

3. Click here.

An alternative way of adding items to the solution is shown below.

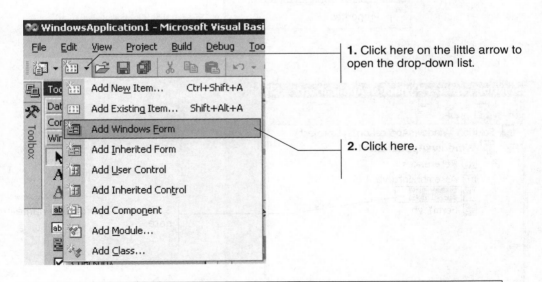

1. Click here on the little arrow to open the drop-down list.

2. Click here.

NOTE: there are other ways to add items to a solution – you are left to discover these.

How to rename an item

A context menu within the Solution Explorer can be used to rename an item; this is illustrated in Figure 1.36.

Figure 1.36 Renaming an item.

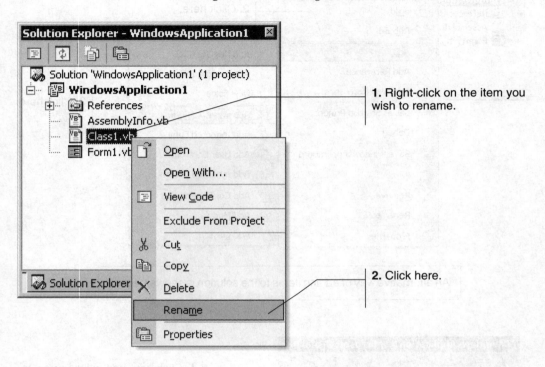

1. Right-click on the item you wish to rename.

2. Click here.

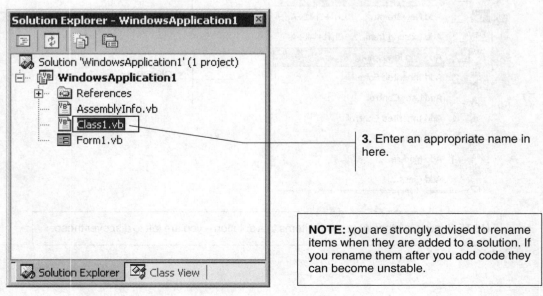

3. Enter an appropriate name in here.

NOTE: you are strongly advised to rename items when they are added to a solution. If you rename them after you add code they can become unstable.

Saving items within a solution

Figure 1.37 shows how to save items within a solution.

Figure 1.37 Saving a solution. It can be seen that this solution has two forms (Form1.vb, Form2.vb), a class module (Class1.vb), and a module (Module1.vb).

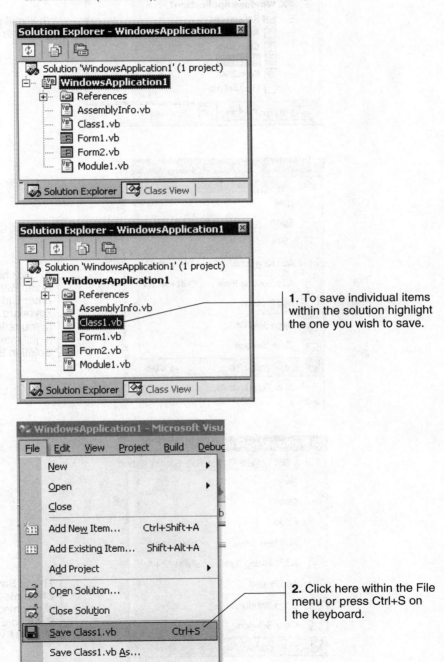

1. To save individual items within the solution highlight the one you wish to save.

2. Click here within the File menu or press Ctrl+S on the keyboard.

Figure 1.37 (cont.)

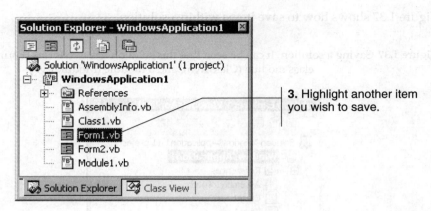

3. Highlight another item you wish to save.

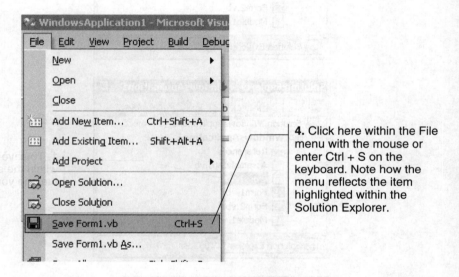

4. Click here within the File menu with the mouse or enter Ctrl + S on the keyboard. Note how the menu reflects the item highlighted within the Solution Explorer.

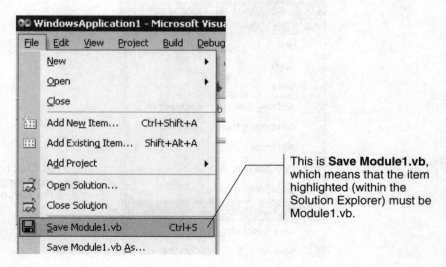

This is **Save Module1.vb**, which means that the item highlighted (within the Solution Explorer) must be Module1.vb.

Figure 1.37 (cont.)

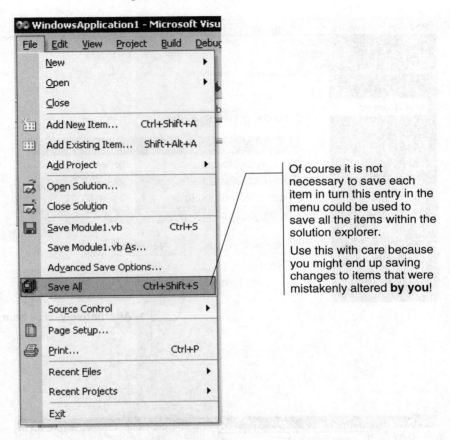

Of course it is not necessary to save each item in turn this entry in the menu could be used to save all the items within the solution explorer.

Use this with care because you might end up saving changes to items that were mistakenly altered **by you**!

Loading a project

Loading a project can be achieved from the start page and from the menu bar; both approaches are illustrated in Figure 1.38.

Figure 1.38 Loading a project.

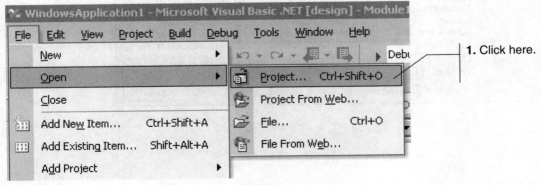

1. Click here.

Figure 1.38 (cont.)

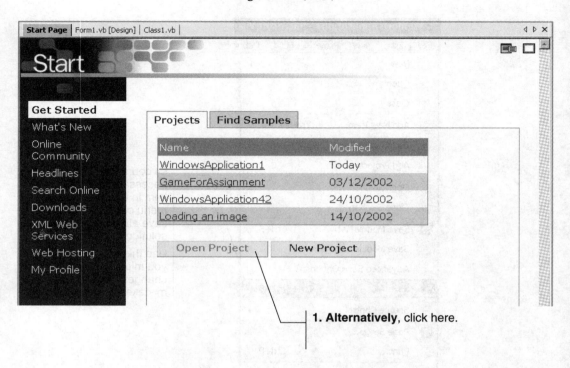

1. Alternatively, click here.

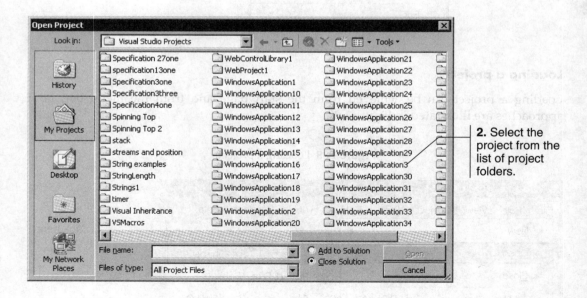

2. Select the project from the list of project folders.

Figure 1.38 (cont.)

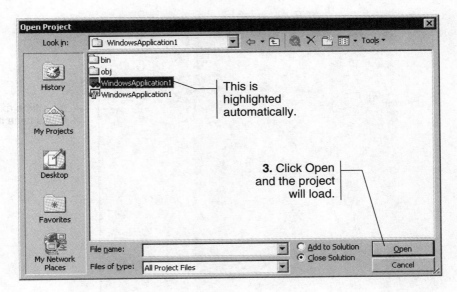

Running your code

This is illustrated in Figure 1.39.

Figure 1.39 Running your code.

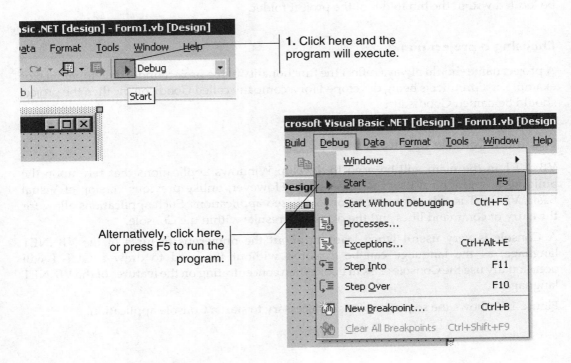

Figure 1.39 (cont.)

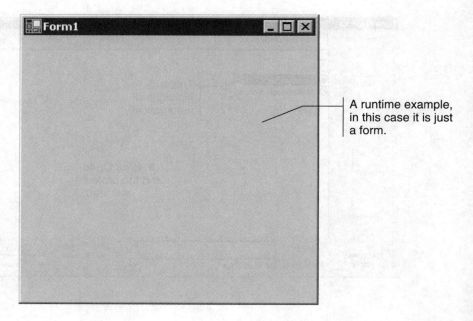

A runtime example, in this case it is just a form.

The executable file

Once your program has been fully tested it is ready for the customer. The executable file can be located within the bin folder of the project folder.

Choosing a project name

A project name should always reflect the functionality of the project under development. For example, if a product is being developed for a company called Goodison plc then the project should be named Goodison.

Starting a Console application

VB .NET in the main will be used to develop Windows applications that rely upon the building of a graphical user interface (GUI). However, unlike previous version of Visual Basic, VB .NET is able to produce **Console**-based applications. Such applications allow for the entry of command lines and the display of results within the Console.

A Console is very useful when learning about the numerous features of the VB .NET language, as the language can be explored without the need to draw a GUI. I will occasionally use the Console class in book when concentrating on the features of the VB .NET language.

Figure 1.40 shows the sequence of tasks necessary to start a Console application.

Figure 1.40 Starting a Console application.

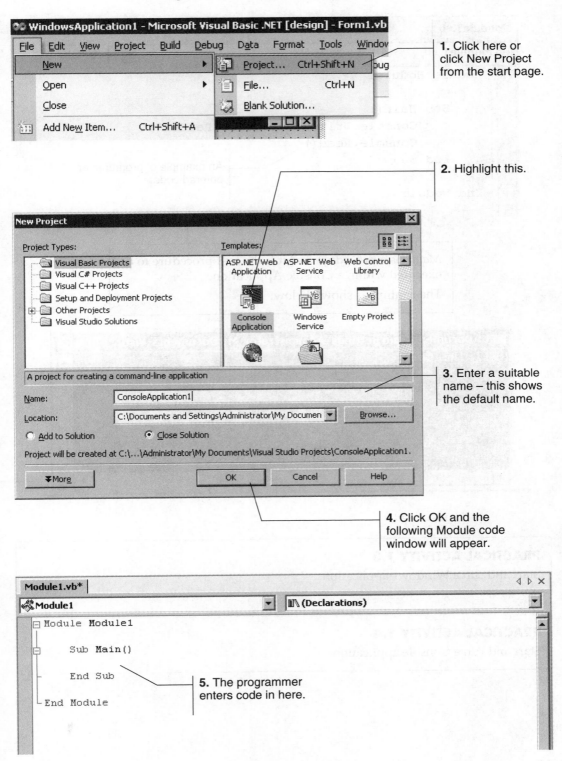

1. Click here or click New Project from the start page.

2. Highlight this.

3. Enter a suitable name – this shows the default name.

4. Click OK and the following Module code window will appear.

5. The programmer enters code in here.

Figure 1.40 (cont.)

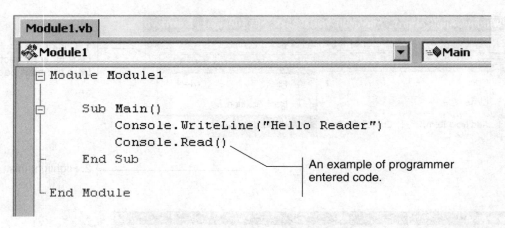

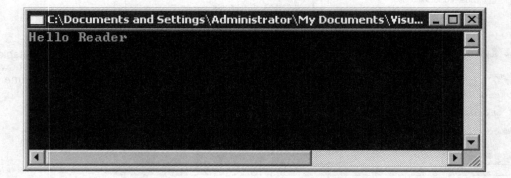

Main() is a procedure and it is the first procedure to be executed within a Console Application.

The runtime is shown below.

PRACTICAL ACTIVITY 1.3

Start and run a Windows application.

PRACTICAL ACTIVITY 1.4

Start and run a Console application.

QUESTION 1.1 (DEVELOPMENT)

Learn how to run the executable files, produced during Practical Activity 1.4 from the Windows operating system, i.e. run them outside the Visual Basic environment.

QUESTION 1.2 (REVISION)

Suggest suitable project names for the following examples:

1. A database being developed for a local hospital.
2. A multimedia CD produced for a local football club that charts their history during the last decade.

---

2 Creating the user interface

All programs receive, process and output data. This data can be input and output in numerous ways. When developing a Windows-based program the best practice is to obtain the data from the graphical user interface (GUI) and pass it to program variables. The data within these variables then processed with the results of the processing stored in variables. Once the results are ready they are transferred from the variables to the GUI. This approach to developing an application is illustrated by Figure 2.1.

Figure 2.1 Best practice when developing a Windows program.

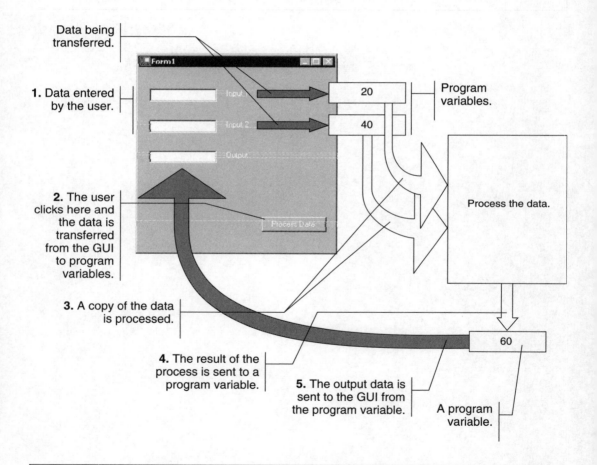

NOTE: A program variable is a named area of computer memory used to store data.

This chapter deals with how to create the GUI using the available interface controls. Processing data and the use of program variables are covered in later chapters.

The Visual Basic form

Forms are fundamental to the development of Windows applications using VB .NET. They are the foundation for creating the GUI. A form can act as a window, a dialog box or as a container for 'storing' objects to be used in other windows. Controls (objects) from the toolbox are drawn onto forms to create the desired user interface.

Properties of a form

Figure 1.29 from Chapter 1 shows two views of a Properties window for a form. It can be seen from these views that a form has many properties. It is not possible to explain the purpose and function of all these properties within one relatively small book. However, some of the more frequently used properties will be discussed and you are left to explore the other properties using the comprehensive on-line dynamic help facility provided with VB .NET.

> **NOTE**: Using the on-line help is an essential skill for a programmer. I strongly recommend that you use it frequently.

How to change the state of a property at design time

Changing the *WindowState* property

Figure 2.2 shows the sequence of actions that are needed to change the *WindowState* property of a form.

Figure 2.2 Changing the setting of the *WindowState* property.

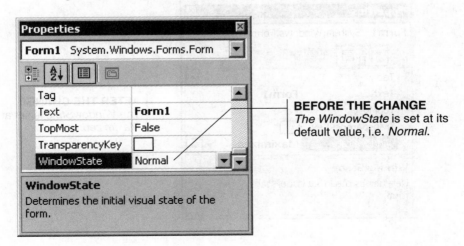

BEFORE THE CHANGE
The WindowState is set at its default value, i.e. *Normal*.

35

Figure 2.2 (cont.)

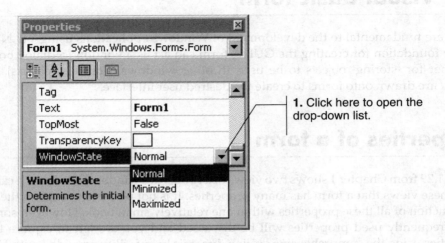

1. Click here to open the drop-down list.

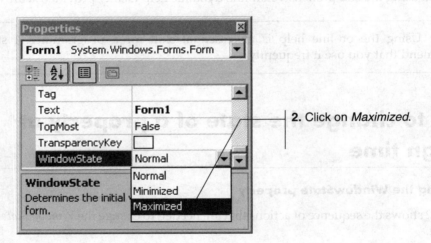

2. Click on *Maximized*.

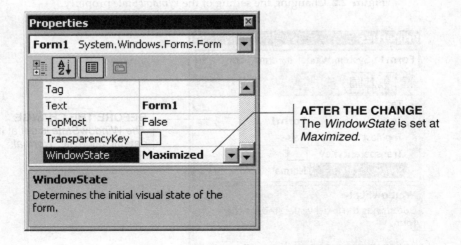

AFTER THE CHANGE
The *WindowState* is set at *Maximized*.

The *WindowState* property of a form has three possible values: *Normal, Minimized* and *Maximized* (note the American spelling). Another way to alter the setting of the property is to double-click onto the property identifier in the first column of the properties window – each double-click will cycle onto the next setting of the property. This is illustrated in Figure 2.3.

Figure 2.3 Cycling through the settings of the *WindowState* property.

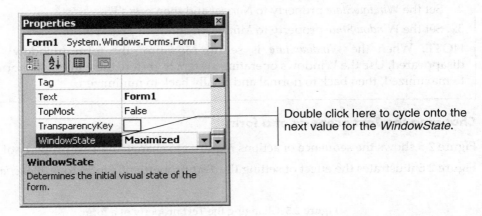

Double click here to cycle onto the next value for the *WindowState*.

Figure 2.4 illustrates the runtime of a form with its *WindowState* property set at *Maximized*.

Figure 2.4 The runtime for a *Maximized* form – it fills up the entire VDU screen.

PRACTICAL ACTIVITY 2.1

Start a new project and change the *WindowState* setting as indicated below; then run the project from the design environment and observe the effect of each change on the *WindowState*.

1. Set the *WindowState* property to *Maximized* and then press F5.

2. Set the *WindowState* property to *Normal* and then press F5.

3. Set the *WindowState* property to *Minimized* and then press F5.

NOTE: When the *WindowState* is set to *Minimized* the form (window) has **not** disappeared. Use the Windows operating system to restore the window to normal, then to maximized, then back to normal and finally back to minimized.

Changing the *Text* property of a form

Figure 2.5 shows the sequence of actions required to change the Text property of a form.

Figure 2.6 illustrates the effect of setting the *Text* property of a form to *Introduction*.

Figure 2.5 Changing the *Text* property of a form.

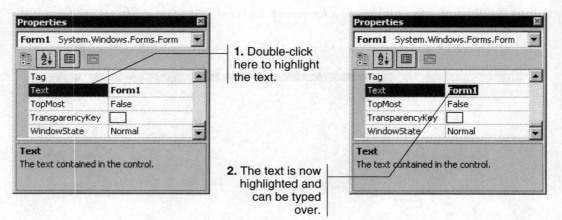

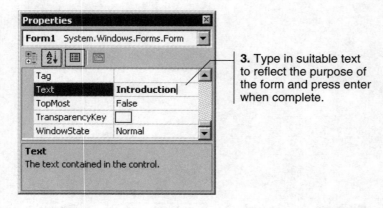

Figure 2.6 The effect of setting the *Text* property to *Introduction*.

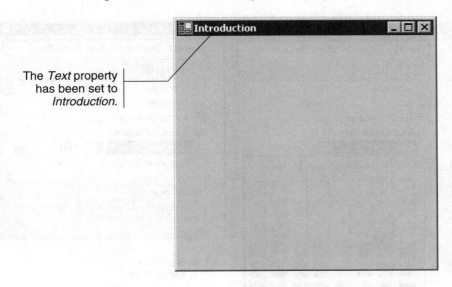

The *Text* property has been set to *Introduction*.

Changing the *BackColor* property of a form

A form can have its background colour altered by setting its *BackColor* property (note the American spelling of colour). Figure 2.7 illustrates the sequence of actions required to change the background colour to red.

Figure 2.7 Setting the background colour of a form.

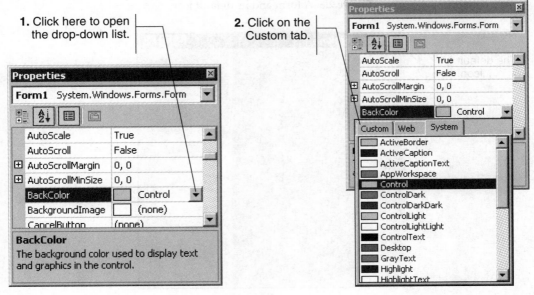

1. Click here to open the drop-down list.

2. Click on the Custom tab.

Figure 2.7 (cont.)

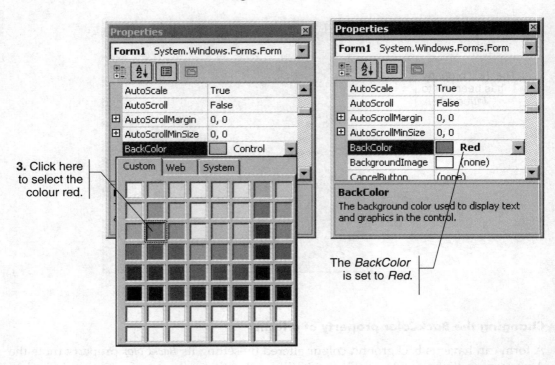

3. Click here to select the colour red.

The *BackColor* is set to *Red*.

Changing the *Icon* property of a form

The *Icon* property is used to assign a unique icon to a form to help indicate the form's purpose. Figure 2.8 illustrates the default icon associated with every Visual Basic form.

Figure 2.8 A form and its default icon.

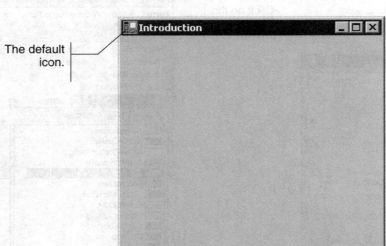

The default icon.

Figure 2.9 illustrates the sequence of actions required to change the *Icon* property of a form.

Figure 2.9 Setting the *Icon* property of a form.

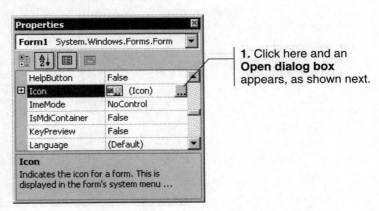

1. Click here and an **Open dialog box** appears, as shown next.

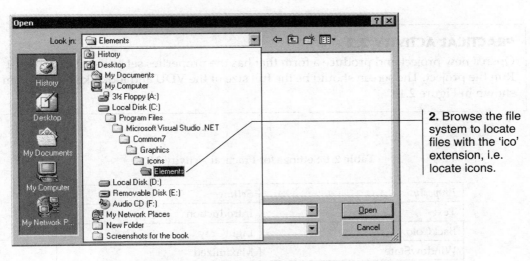

2. Browse the file system to locate files with the 'ico' extension, i.e. locate icons.

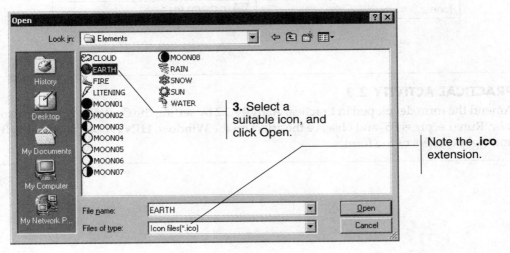

3. Select a suitable icon, and click Open.

Note the **.ico** extension.

Figure 2.9 (cont.)

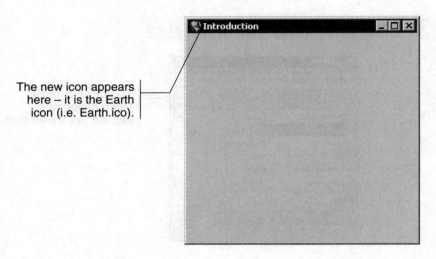

The new icon appears here – it is the Earth icon (i.e. Earth.ico).

PRACTICAL ACTIVITY 2.2

Open a new project and produce a form that has the properties set as listed in Table 2.1. Run the project. The screen should be the full size of the VDU and look like the diagram shown in Figure 2.10.

Table 2.1 Settings for Practical Activity 2.2.

Property	Setting
Text	Introduction
BackColor	LightGray
WindowState	Maximized
Icon	(CDROM01.ico)

PRACTICAL ACTIVITY 2.3

Amend the form developed in Practical Activity 2.2 by setting the *ControlBox* property to *false*. Run (i.e. press F5) and observe the affect on the Window. **HINT**: Look at the top left and right corners of the form.

Figure 2.10 The diagram referred to in Practical Activity 2.2.

How to draw a control on a form

A button will be used to demonstrate the drawing of a control on a form. Figure 2.11 illustrates the sequence of actions required to draw a control using the drag method.

Figure 2.11 Drawing a control on to a form.

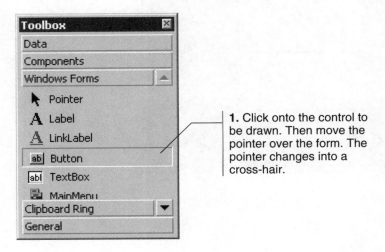

1. Click onto the control to be drawn. Then move the pointer over the form. The pointer changes into a cross-hair.

Figure 2.11 (cont.)

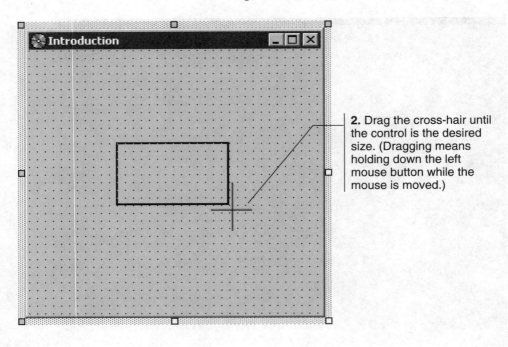

2. Drag the cross-hair until the control is the desired size. (Dragging means holding down the left mouse button while the mouse is moved.)

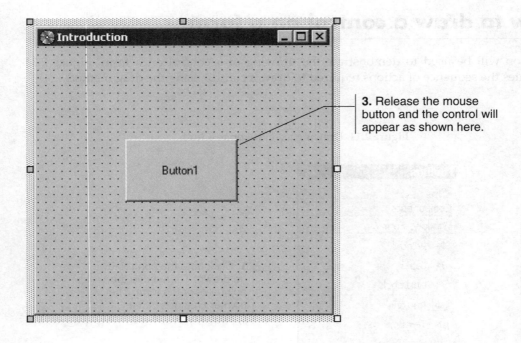

3. Release the mouse button and the control will appear as shown here.

An alternative method for drawing a control onto a form is to double-click the required control. This will create a default size control on the form. This can then be re-sized and moved as required.

Another method is simply to drag a control from the toolbox to the form.

NOTE: At this point it is worth reflecting upon the contents of the toolbox. Each of the controls within the toolbox can be used to place an **instance** of 'themselves' upon a form. In other words they are classes with members (methods, properties and events) and each instance of the control on the form is an object of the control type. For example you can place numerous buttons on to a form and each button is a separate 'entity'. Consequently, each button will have all the members of the button class and each button will be an instance of the button class.

NOTE: Furthermore, as you draw controls on to a form the VB .NET IDE is 'writing code behind the scenes'. This code can be observed by clicking onto the expanding icon within the code window as illustrated in Figure 2.12. At this stage however just accept that this code is generated for you. Although you can alter this code it is not advisable, and I strongly recommend that you keep the code hidden 'behind' the expanding icon. However, there is no harm in looking at it.

Figure 2.12 Looking at the 'behind the scenes' code.

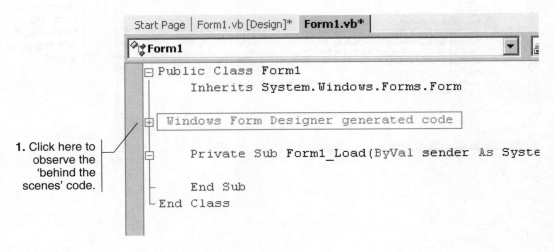

Figure 2.12 (cont.)

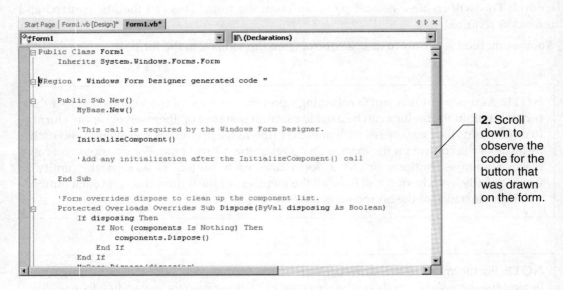

2. Scroll down to observe the code for the button that was drawn on the form.

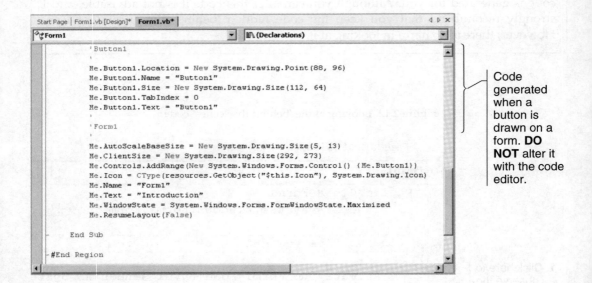

Code generated when a button is drawn on a form. **DO NOT** alter it with the code editor.

Resizing a control

Figure 2.13 illustrates how to resize a control.

Figure 2.13 How to resize a control.

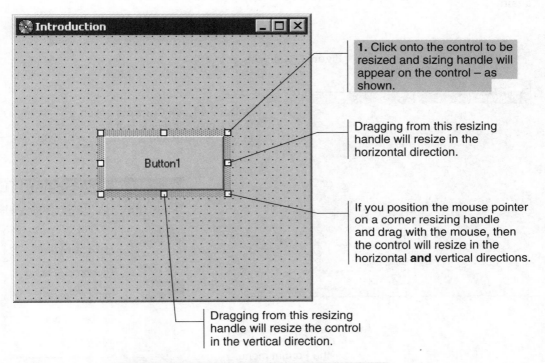

1. Click onto the control to be resized and sizing handle will appear on the control – as shown.

Dragging from this resizing handle will resize in the horizontal direction.

If you position the mouse pointer on a corner resizing handle and drag with the mouse, then the control will resize in the horizontal **and** vertical directions.

Dragging from this resizing handle will resize the control in the vertical direction.

2. Once the control is dragged to the required size release the mouse button.

Repositioning a control

Place the cursor over the control to be moved and the *SizeAll* cursor (insert icon) will appear. Hold down the left mouse button and drag the control to the desired position. An alternative is to alter the *Location* property within the Properties window, which will allow for the accurate placement of the control – try it!

How to lock the position of controls

The ease with which controls can be positioned and resized makes the development of the graphical user interface straightforward. However, because controls are easy to move there is a risk of accidentally moving correctly positioned controls. Therefore, once controls are correctly positioned it is advisable to lock them in place.

To lock controls in position perform one of the following:

1. Choose Lock Controls from the Forms context menu.

2. Click Lock Controls from the Format menu.

These alternative methods are illustrated in Figure 2.14. Both these methods lock all of the controls on the current form. Any new controls placed on the form will not be locked until the lock option is activated again.

Lock Controls is a toggle command, therefore, to unlock the controls select **Lock Controls** again.

Figure 2.14 Locking controls.

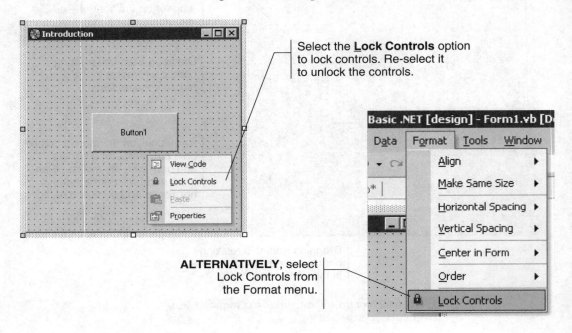

Select the **Lock Controls** option to lock controls. Re-select it to unlock the controls.

ALTERNATIVELY, select Lock Controls from the Format menu.

Anchoring controls

It is not possible to predict the screen size on which an application will execute as the user of the PC defines this. However, it is useful if controls appear in consistent positions regardless of the screen size. This can be achieved using the *Anchor* property. Anchors define to which edges of the container (e.g. a form) a certain control is bound. When a control is anchored to an edge the distance between the control's closest edge and the specified edge of the container remains constant. Figure 2.15 illustrates examples of anchoring a button.

Naming controls

All controls that are drawn on to a form are given a name by default. The first Button drawn on to a form has the default name Button1, the second is Button2, and so on. Likewise the first Label drawn on a form has the default name Label1, and the second label has the default name Label2. Figure 2.16 shows the default name of a Button as it appears in the Property window.

Figure 2.15 Examples of anchoring a button.

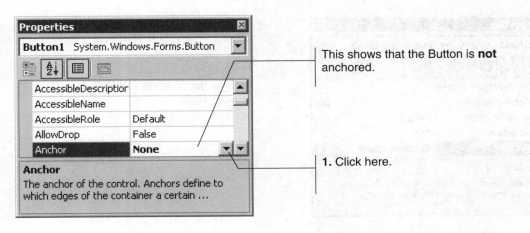

This shows that the Button is **not** anchored.

1. Click here.

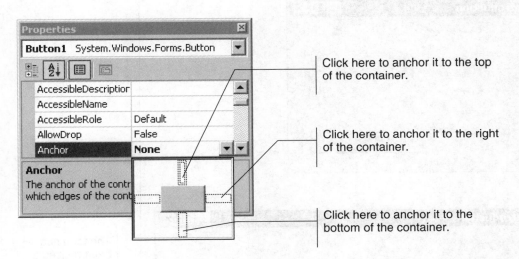

Click here to anchor it to the top of the container.

Click here to anchor it to the right of the container.

Click here to anchor it to the bottom of the container.

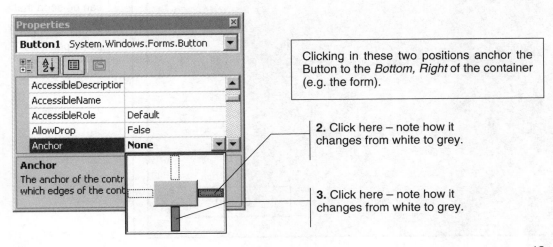

Clicking in these two positions anchor the Button to the *Bottom, Right* of the container (e.g. the form).

2. Click here – note how it changes from white to grey.

3. Click here – note how it changes from white to grey.

Figure 2.15 (cont.)

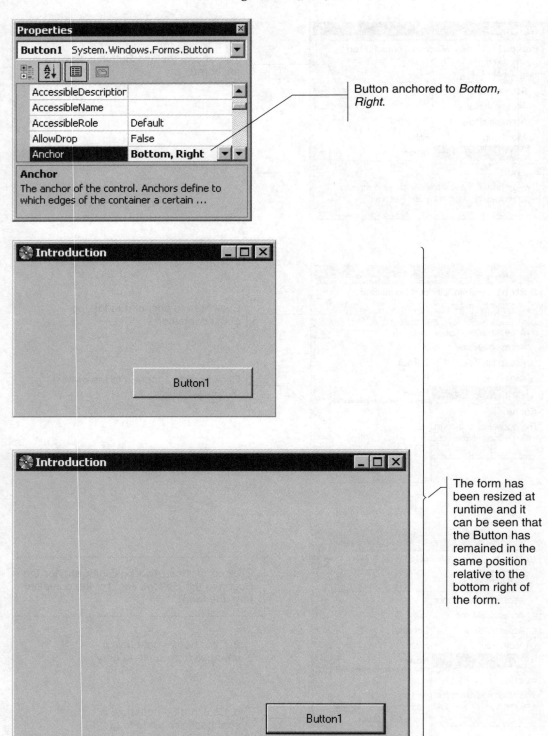

Button anchored to *Bottom, Right*.

Anchor
The anchor of the control. Anchors define to which edges of the container a certain ...

The form has been resized at runtime and it can be seen that the Button has remained in the same position relative to the bottom right of the form.

Figure 2.16 The default name of a Button.

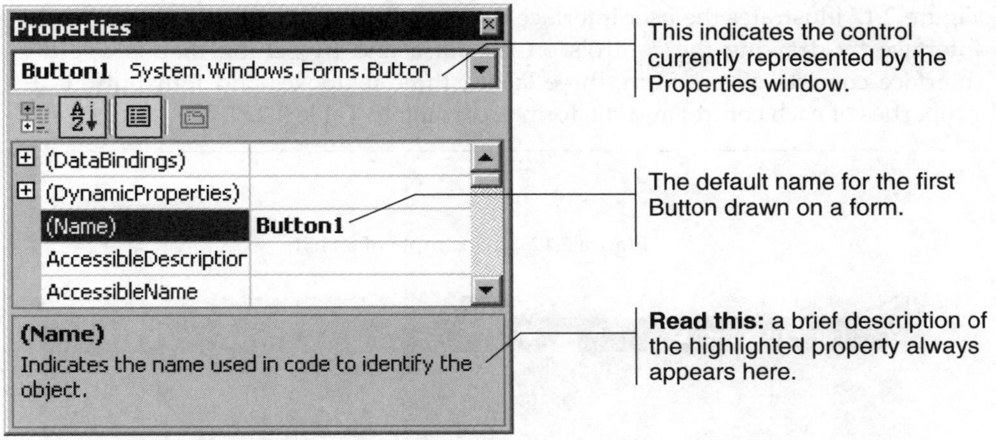

This indicates the control currently represented by the Properties window.

The default name for the first Button drawn on a form.

Read this: a brief description of the highlighted property always appears here.

The name of a control is used to identify the object (control) in the program code. However, leaving controls with their name set at the default value makes the code difficult to read, as it does not convey the purpose of the object (control).

For example, consider an application that consists of numerous controls and three happen to be Buttons. One of the Buttons is to save the data entered in a textbox; another is to activate a search and the third is to quit the application. If the name of the three Buttons were left at their default value then whenever you saw reference to them in code you would have to remember the purpose of each from their default names of Button1, Button2 and Button3. For a large software application this is a near impossible task.

Good programming practice requires that you give a Button a name that both reflects its purpose and the type of object it is. For example, a sensible name for the Button used to quit the application would be:

btnQuit

the first three lower case letters (i.e. *btn*) are used to identify the object as a Button and the remaining letters (starting with a capital) convey the purpose of the Button (i.e. quit the application).

All controls have a **recommended** three-letter prefix to be used when naming the control. The prefix for a Label is *lbl*, for a PictureBox it is *pic* and for a TextBox it is *txt*. There are many more recommend prefixes and they will be introduced throughout the book as appropriate.

QUESTION 2.1 (REVISION)

Suggest a suitable setting for the Name property of the controls described below:

1. *A Button used to activate a search.*
2. *A TextBox that displays the name of a customer.*
3. *A PictureBox used to display the logo of a company.*

PRACTICAL ACTIVITY 2.4

Figure 2.17 illustrates the user interface to an application. Your task is to reproduce the interface by drawing the controls on the form and by setting their properties. The interface consists of one form, three labels, three textboxes and four buttons. Set the properties of each control and the form according to Table 2.2.

Figure 2.17 An example of a GUI.

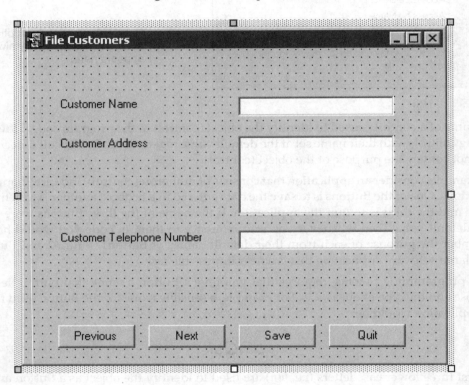

PRACTICAL ACTIVITY 2.5

Figure 2.18 illustrates the user interface to an application. Your task is to reproduce the interface by drawing the controls on the form and by setting their properties. The interface consists of one form, four labels, four textboxes and four buttons. In this activity you are not told the settings for the properties of the form and the controls. However, they should be obvious from the information conveyed by the figure. Remember to set the *Name* property of the controls!

NOTE: It is good programming practice to set the *Name* property of all controls **first** before any other properties are set.

Table 2.2 This table shows the property settings for the controls used in the application shown in Figure 2.17. All of the other properties are left at their default values. However, the *Location* and *Size* properties are set by dragging the controls, consequently, they are **not** listed.

Control	Property	Setting
Form	FormBorderStyle	Fixed3D
	Text	File Customers
	Icon	Find this in your directory
Label 1	Name	lblName
	Text	Customer Name
Label 2	Name	lblAddress
	Text	Customer Address
Label 3	Name	lblTelNum
	Text	Customer Telephone Number
TextBox1	Name	txtName
	Text	Nothing, i.e delete whatever text is there
TextBox2	Name	txtAddress
	Text	Nothing, i.e delete whatever text is there
TextBox3	Name	txtTelNum
	Text	Nothing, i.e delete whatever text is there
Button1	Name	btnPrevious
	Text	Previous
Button2	Name	btnNext
	Text	Next
Button3	Name	btnSave
	Text	Save
Button4	Name	btnQuit
	Text	Quit

Figure 2.18 An application (associated with Practical Activity 2.5)

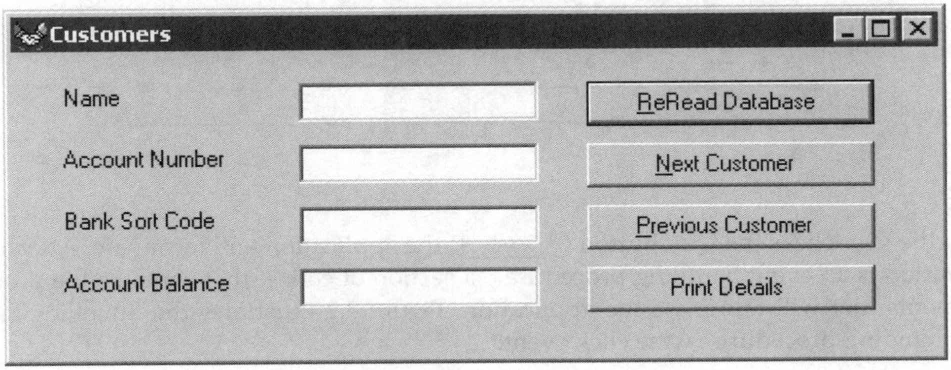

3 Coding an application

Once the Graphical User Interface has been drawn and the properties of all the controls have been set the next stage is to 'attach code' to the controls in the application.

Event handling procedures

An event handling procedure is a section of code that executes, when an event associated with the application occurs. For example, when a user clicks a button the click event handling procedure 'attached' to the button executes. Consider the graphical user interface (GUI) shown in Figure 3.1.

Figure 3.1 A typical graphical user interface (GUI).

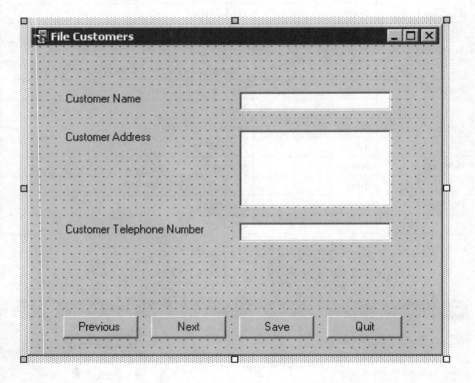

When the user clicks the Quit button (Quit) the application will terminate. Attached to this button is an event handling procedure – a section of code – that contains the program statements that will terminate the application. Figure 3.2 illustrates the 'invoking' of the event handing procedure by the click event.

Figure 3.2 Illustrating the 'invoking' of an event handling procedure.

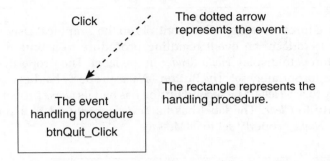

Click — The dotted arrow represents the event.

The event handling procedure btnQuit_Click — The rectangle represents the handling procedure.

The name of the event handling procedure is derived from the *Name* property setting of the object (control) and the event acting on the object. If the *Name* property for the button is set to *btnQuit* and the event acting on the button is a click event then the name of the event procedure is *btnQuit_Click(plus parameters)*. The underscore character separates the *Name* setting and the event, and the brackets appear in all procedure names. This is further illustrated in Figure 3.3.

Figure 3.3 How the name of an event handling procedure is derived.

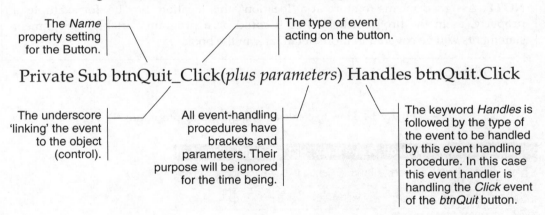

The *Name* property setting for the Button.

The type of event acting on the button.

Private Sub btnQuit_Click(*plus parameters*) Handles btnQuit.Click

The underscore 'linking' the event to the object (control).

All event-handling procedures have brackets and parameters. Their purpose will be ignored for the time being.

The keyword *Handles* is followed by the type of the event to be handled by this event handling procedure. In this case this event handler is handling the *Click* event of the *btnQuit* button.

NOTE: Unlike previous versions of Visual Basic, event handling procedures (with Visual Basic .NET) do not have to be constructed from the name of the control and the type of the event. However, this change in the language will be covered in a later chapter.

QUESTION 3.1 (REVISION)

What would be the name of the event handling procedure for both the following examples? Ignore the parameters for the time being.

1. *A Button named btnSave responding to a click event.*
2. *A PictureBox named picPrint responding to a double-click event.*

Creating an event handling procedure

Event handling procedures are 'attached' to controls on the Graphical User Interface. Figure 3.4 illustrates how to 'attach' an event handling procedure to a Button on a form. The purpose of the Button is to display *Hello Reader* in the label. The properties of the controls (objects) have been appropriately set. The Buttons' *Name* property has been set to *btnSayHello* and its *Text* property to *Say Hello*. The second Button has had its *Name* property set to *btnClear* and its *Text* property to *Clear*. The label has its *Text* property set to a zero length string (i.e. cleared) and its *Name* property set to *lblMessage*.

NOTE: A string is a list of characters that can be letters or numbers or both. Three examples of strings are: Everton; 7 Canterbury Road; and Nathan Jones. Everton is a string containing 7 characters. 7 Canterbury Road is a string containing 17 characters (the spaces between the words are also counted). A zero length string contains no characters and consequently when it is **assigned** to the *Text* property of a label the label appears to have no entry. Strings will be covered in more detail later in the book.

NOTE: Assigned means to store at a 'location', this location may be, for example, a property, as in the program below, or it could be a program variable. Assignment statements will be covered in more detail later in the book.

Figure 3.4 How to create an event handling procedure.

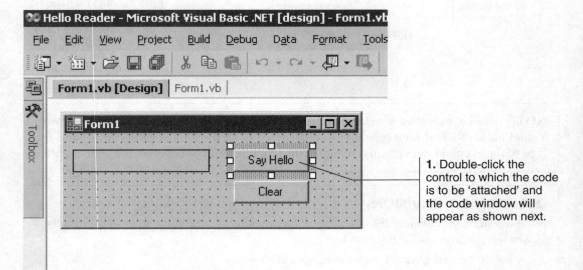

56

Figure 3.4 (cont.)

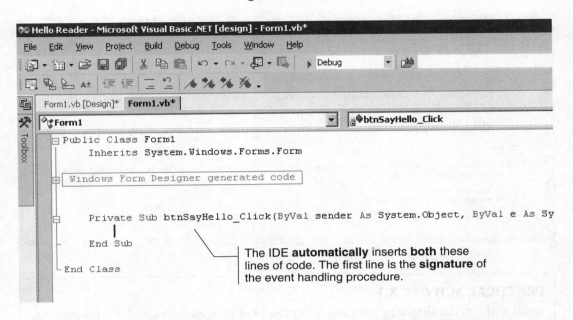

The IDE **automatically** inserts **both** these lines of code. The first line is the **signature** of the event handling procedure.

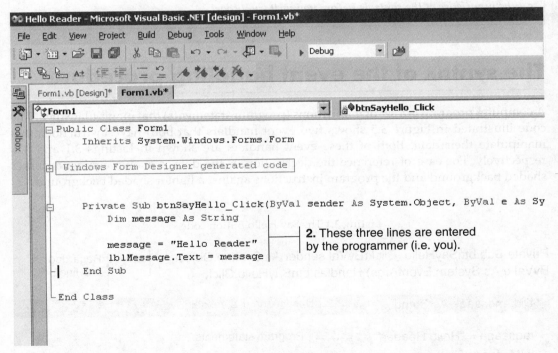

2. These three lines are entered by the programmer (i.e. you).

This process is repeated for the second button and again the developer enters code between the two lines provided by the IDE. Figure 3.5 shows the entire program for this simple application.

Figure 3.5 The code for the Hello application.

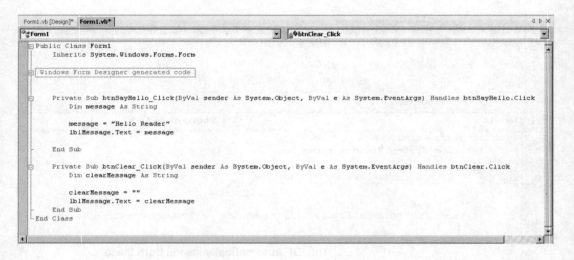

PRACTICAL ACTIVITY 3.1

Build and run the simple application as represented by Figures 3.4 and 3.5. *Remember to set the proprieties of the controls **before** you write any code!*

The syntax of the event handling procedure

A computer program is a set of instructions (program statements) that manipulate data. The code illustrated in Figure 3.5 shows two event handlers that both have instructions that manipulate their data. Both of these event handlers are shown in Listings 3.1 and 3.2, respectively. For ease of reference the declaration of the data is shown against a darker shaded background and the program instructions against a lighter shaded background.

Listing 3.1 The Say Hello Button code.

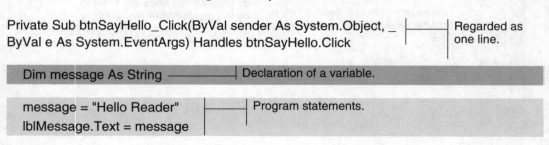

Listing 3.2 The Clear Button code.

```
Private Sub btnClear_Click(ByVal sender As System.Object, _
ByVal e As System.EventArgs) Handles btnClear.Click

    Dim clearMessage As String          ──────────┤ Declaration of a variable.

    clearMessage = ""                        ──────┤ Program statements.
    lblMessage.Text = clearMessage
End Sub
```

Declaring variables

Within the programs shown by Listings 3.1 and 3.2 data is stored in variables. These variables are declared after the **keyword** word *Dim*. The keyword *Dim* is derived from the word dimension, which in turn is derived from early versions of Basic to describe the setting aside of memory area to be used for the storing of program data.

> **NOTE**: A **keyword** is a word that has a special meaning to a compiler. It is reserved for use by the VB .NET language and it cannot be used for program variable names.

It is usual to fix the data type of the declared variable and this is achieved by using the keyword *As* and the name of the type (e.g. *String*). The declaration of a variable is illustrated by Figure 3.6.

> **NOTE**: To repeat: a variable is effectively a named area of the computer's memory used to store data.

Figure 3.6 Declaring a variable.

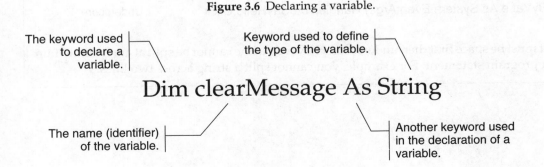

The keyword used to declare a variable.

Keyword used to define the type of the variable.

Dim clearMessage As String

The name (identifier) of the variable.

Another keyword used in the declaration of a variable.

NOTE: Variable names cannot include any spaces, cannot start with a figure and cannot be a VB .NET keyword.

NOTE: It is recommended that the names chosen for variables should adopt camel casing. This is where the first word starts with a lowercase letter and all remaining words start with a capital letter. Camel casing has been shown in Figure 3.6. i.e.

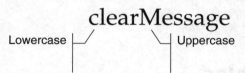

$$\text{clearMessage}$$

Lowercase   Uppercase

It is referred to as camel casing because 'there is a hump in the middle'.

IMPORTANT: The operation of the event handlers shown in Listings 3.1 and 3.2 will be described using a 'description trace'.

A description trace is a table with two columns: the first lists the Visual Basic statements in the **order they execute**; and the second describes the actions performed by each statement. Trace tables will occasionally be used throughout the book to describe the operation of Visual Basic code.

NOTE: The limitations of the table result in a statement crossing onto several lines. VB code **does not** cross over lines in this way.

NOTE: Many VB .NET program statements are very long. Sometimes they are too long to be sensibly viewed in the code window. Under these circumstances a program statement can be split across two or more lines using a space and an underscore character as shown in Listing 3.1 and repeated below for convenience.

Space

```
Private Sub btnSayHello_Click(ByVal sender As System.Object,
ByVal e As System.EventArgs) Handles btnSayHello.Click
```

Underscore

It must be space first then underscore. However, a line cannot be split at any point within a program statement. For example, you cannot split a string across two lines.

Description trace for *btnSayHello_Click*

This event handling procedure has a *String* data type variable (named *message*) that is used by the program statements.

Statement	Description
message = "Hello Reader"	This is an assignment statement that assigns the literal string *Hello Reader* to the string variable *message*. In other words, the string *Hello Reader* on the right of the assignment symbol (=) is stored in the variable *message* that is on the left hand side of the assignment symbol. A literal string always appears between quotes.
lblMessage.Text = message	A **copy** of the string stored in the string variable *message* is assigned to the *Text* property of the label (*lblMessage*). Consequently, the label displays *Hello Reader* as shown in Figure 3.7.

Figure 3.7 Displaying the string *Hello Reader* in the label.

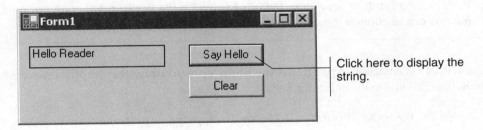

Click here to display the string.

Description trace for *btnClear_Click*

This event handling procedure has a *String* data type variable (clearMessage) that is used by the program statements.

Statement	Description
clearMessage = ""	This is an assignment statement that assigns the zero length string to the variable *clearMessage*.
lblMessage.Text = clearMessage	A copy of the string stored in the variable *clearMessage* is assigned to the *Text* property of the label (*lblMessage*). Consequently, the label displays the zero length string as shown in Figure 3.8.

Figure 3.8 Displaying the zero length string in the label.

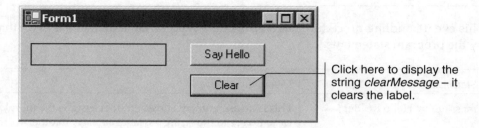

Click here to display the string *clearMessage* – it clears the label.

A simple program (Specification 3.1)

A program is developed on the following pages that meet the requirements of Specification 3.1.

SPECIFICATION 3.1

Write a program that uses three Buttons to change the background colour of a label. The Buttons are to change the colour to red, green and blue respectively.

As with all Visual Basic programs the first step is to draw the graphical user interface. A suitable GUI is shown in Figure 3.9.

Figure 3.9 A suitable GUI **before** the appropriate properties have been set.

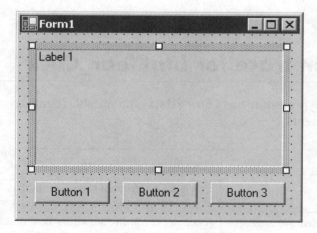

Once the GUI has been drawn, as shown in Figure 3.9, the next step is to set the properties of the form and the controls. Table 3.1 lists the controls, their properties and settings. Those properties **not** referred to in the table are left at their default setting (i.e. they are not altered).

Table 3.1 Controls and their property settings.

Control	Property	Setting
Form1	Text	Colour Demonstration
Button1	Name	btnRed
	Text	&Red (note the use of the ampersand)
Button2	Name	btnGreen
	Text	&Green (note the use of the ampersand)
Button3	Name	btnBlue
	Text	&Blue (note the use of the ampersand)
Label1	Name	lblColourDemo
	Text	Zero length string
	BorderStyle	Fixed3D

NOTE: Window applications consist of many forms and it is usual to also set the *Name* property of a form to reflect its purpose within the application. This allows for the easy identification of the form when referring to it in program code. The name property of a form should be prefixed with the three letters *frm*. For example a form responsible for obtaining customer details would have its name property, typically, set to *frmCustomerDetails*. However, as many of the programs developed in this book only use one form I have chosen to leave it at its default value of Form1. If you name a form as *frmCustomerDetails* then this also becomes the name of the class that represents the form (a form is a specific type of class).

Once the properties have been set, as indicated by Table 3.1, the GUI of Figure 3.9 will look like the GUI illustrated in Figure 3.10.

Figure 3.10 The GUI **after** its properties have been set.

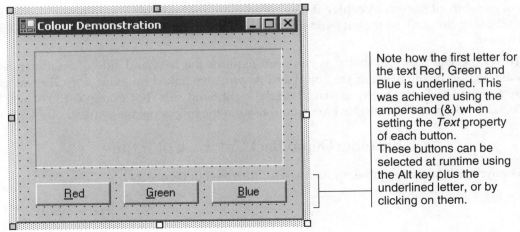

Note how the first letter for the text Red, Green and Blue is underlined. This was achieved using the ampersand (&) when setting the *Text* property of each button. These buttons can be selected at runtime using the Alt key plus the underlined letter, or by clicking on them.

NOTE: At runtime the underlines that appear on the buttons may not appear until you press the Alt key. Whether the lines appear will be dependent upon your operating system.

Having completed the GUI the next step is to 'attach' an event handling procedure to each button. The event procedures for this simple program are graphically represented by Figure 3.11.

Figure 3.11 The three event handling procedures are all invoked by their associated button being clicked or by pressing the Alt key and the single underlined letter.

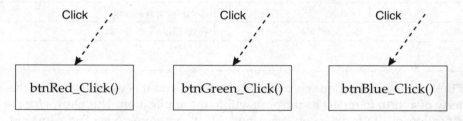

When the user clicks the Red button (Red) the label's background colour must change to red, clicking the green must change it to green and, obviously, clicking the blue must change it to blue. Therefore, code must be inserted into each of the event handling procedures to perform the desired function – change the colour of the labels background at **runtime** (the changing of the background colour at **design time** has already been shown).

Changing the settings of properties at runtime

An assignment statement **copies** the value on the right hand side of an equal sign to the variable or property on the left hand side. Assignment statements are fully covered in a later chapter.

To set the value of a property at run time requires the left-hand side of an assignment statement to be the name of the object and its property linked by a full stop. The value to be assigned to the property is placed on the right-hand side. For example, to change the *BackColor* property of a label to blue would require the following assignment:

lblColourDemo.BackColor = Color.Blue

The syntax for this assignment statement is illustrated in Figure 3.12.

Figure 3.12 Changing properties at runtime.

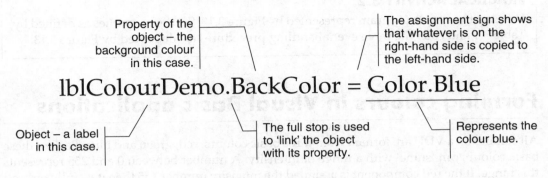

Property of the
object – the
background colour
in this case.

The assignment sign shows
that whatever is on the
right-hand side is copied to
the left-hand side.

lblColourDemo.BackColor = Color.Blue

Object – a label
in this case.

The full stop is used
to 'link' the object
with its property.

Represents the
colour blue.

NOTE: Please note that the American **and** English spellings of colour (color) are used throughout the book. When I make up names for objects I use the English spelling. However, whenever reference is made to a property that is 'part of' the VB .NET language the American spelling **has** to be used. For example, I named the label *lblColourDemo* (English spelling of Colour), whereas the background colour of a label is set by altering its *BackColor* property (American spelling).

The code that implements Specification 3.1 is shown in Figure 3.13.

Figure 3.13 Code to implement Specification 3.1.

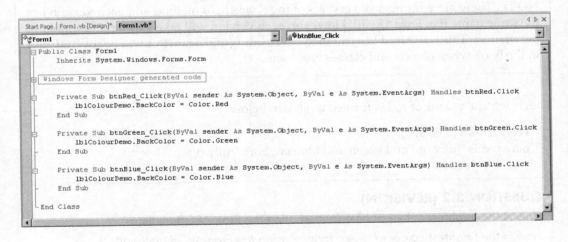

```
Public Class Form1
    Inherits System.Windows.Forms.Form

    Windows Form Designer generated code

    Private Sub btnRed_Click(ByVal sender As System.Object, ByVal e As System.EventArgs) Handles btnRed.Click
        lblColourDemo.BackColor = Color.Red
    End Sub

    Private Sub btnGreen_Click(ByVal sender As System.Object, ByVal e As System.EventArgs) Handles btnGreen.Click
        lblColourDemo.BackColor = Color.Green
    End Sub

    Private Sub btnBlue_Click(ByVal sender As System.Object, ByVal e As System.EventArgs) Handles btnBlue.Click
        lblColourDemo.BackColor = Color.Blue
    End Sub

End Class
```

PRACTICAL ACTIVITY 3.2

Develop the simple program represented by Figure 3.10. Set the properties as defined by Table 3.1 and code the three event handling procedures as illustrated by Figure 3.13.

Forming colours in Visual Basic applications

All colours on a VDU are formed from three basic colours, red, green and blue. Each of these basic colours can 'shine' with a range of intensity. A number between 0 and 255 represents this range. If the red component is assigned the intensity number 255 then it is 'fully on' and if it is assigned the number 0 then it is 'fully off' (i.e. not 'shining' at all). This number range applies in the same way to green and blue.

A **shared method** exists in Visual Basic that combines together the three basic colour components with their intensity number to produce the required colour. This is the *FromARGB* method. The format for this function is as follows:

FromARGB(Red intensity number, Green intensity number, Blue intensity number)

NOTE: A **method** is program code that performs a desired function on some data. A **shared method** is a method that is available throughout an application and it does not require an instance of a class to be created in order to use it. Methods will be covered later in the book when objects and classes are discussed.

NOTE: There are a number of versions of the *FromARGB* method and each version has the same name (i.e. *FromARGB*). However, each version will take a different number of parameters. This is referred to as method overloading and again this will be covered later in the book when objects and classes are discussed.

The 'brightest' colour of red is formed as shown below:

FromARGB (255, 0, 0)
here red is 'fully on' and green and blue are both 'fully off'.

QUESTION 3.2 (REVISION)

How is the brightest colour of blue formed using the FromARGB method?

How is the brightest colour of green formed using the FromARGB method?

NOTE: If all the colour intensity numbers in a *FromARGB* method are set to 255 then white is formed and if all these numbers are zero then black is formed.

Implementing Specification 3.1 using the *FromARGB* method

Figure 3.14 illustrates the code to implement Specification 3.1 using the *FromARGB* method.

Figure 3.14 Implementing Sspecification 3.1 using the *FromARGB* method.

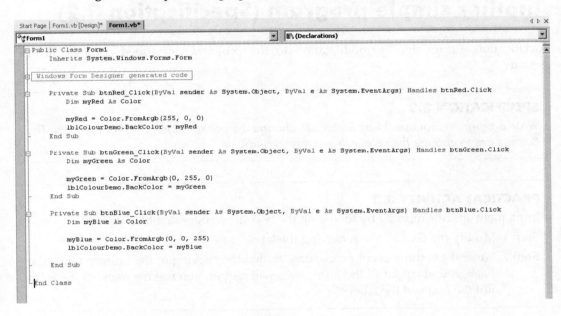

Description trace of the *btnBlue_Click* event handling procedure

A variable *myBlue* of type *Color* is declared and used in this event handler.

Statement	Description
myBlue = Color.FromARGB(0, 0, 255)	This is an assignment statement that assigns the colour formed by *FromARGB* to the variable *myBlue*.
lblColourDemo.BackColor = myBlue	The background colour of the label is set to the colour blue.

> **NOTE**: All variables have a type and VB .NET has a number of possible types most of which will be dealt with later in the book. So far you have been introduced to two types of variables, namely, *String* and *Color*. In truth, these are relatively complex variable types but for the time being just accept that they store appropriate values for the purpose they serve, e.g. the variable *myBlue* is of type *Color* and stores the colour blue.

Another simple program (Specification 3.2)

Specification 3.2 involves a modification to the program developed during Practical Activity 3.2.

> **SPECIFICATION 3.2**
> *Write a program that uses three Buttons to change the background colour of the form. The Buttons are to change the colour to red, green and blue.*

> **PRACTICAL ACTIVITY 3.3**
> Implement specification 3.2 by following the two steps suggested below:
> **Step 1**: Modify the GUI by the removing the label.
> **Step 2**: Amend the three event procedures so that the clicking of the buttons alters the background colour of the form – this will require you use the name of the form not the name of the label.

Horizontal scrollbars

A scrollbar can be used as an input device for example, to control the volume of multimedia speakers. Figure 3.15 illustrates a typical use for a scrollbar.

Figure 3.15 A typical use of a horizontal scrollbar. As the slider is moved to the right, the volume of the speakers increases.

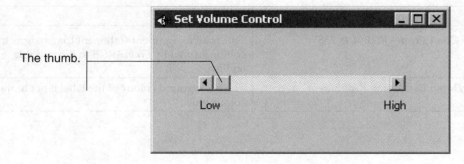

The position of the thumb is defined by the numeric value stored in the *Value* property of the scrollbar. The further the thumb is to the right the larger this numeric value. The range of values represented by a scrollbar is set by its *Min* and *Max* properties.

When a scroll bar is used as an input device its *Max* and *Min* properties are set to the appropriate range for the control. The slider can be moved in one of three ways:

1. By dragging the thumb.

2. By clicking on to the arrows at the edge of the bar – called the small change.

3. By clicking on to the space between the arrows and the thumb – referred to as the large change.

A simple program using a scrollbar

A program will be implemented to meet the following specification.

SPECIFICATION 3.3

A horizontal scrollbar controls the intensity of the colour blue displayed in a label, i.e. the background colour of the label is controlled by the position of the thumb on the horizontal scrollbar. The label also displays the Value *property of the horizontal scrollbar in the colour yellow. A Button will end the application when clicked.*

Step 1: Draw the interface as shown in Figure 3.16.

Step 2: Set the properties as listed in Table 3.2.

Step 3: Attach the event handling procedures.

Figure 3.16 The GUI **before** the properties are set.

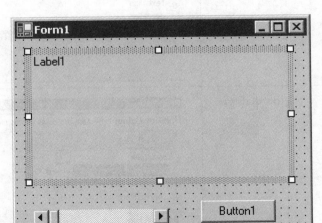

Table 3.2 The settings required for the form, label and horizontal scrollbar.

Control	Property	Setting
Form	Text	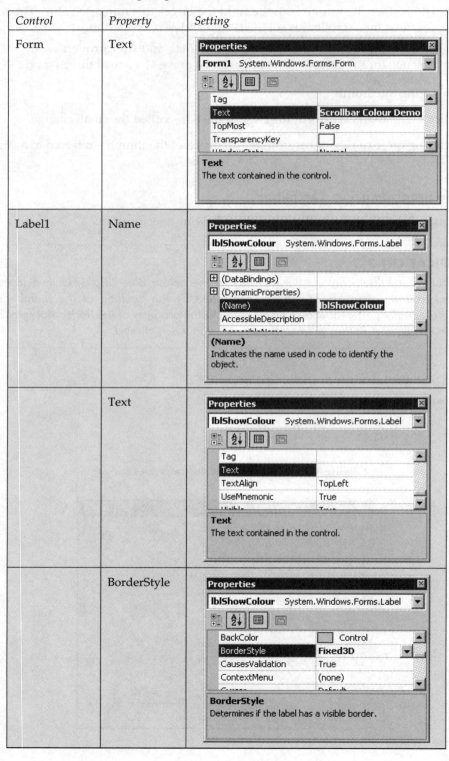
Label1	Name	
	Text	
	BorderStyle	

Table 3.2 (cont.)

Control	Property	Setting
	ForeColor	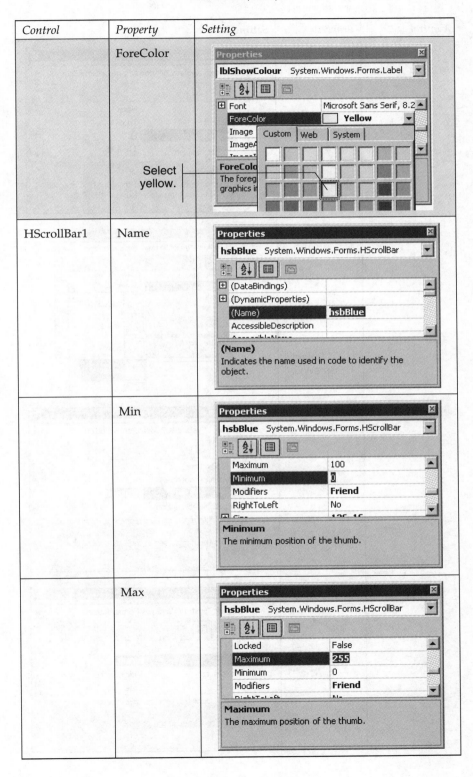 Select yellow.
HScrollBar1	Name	
	Min	
	Max	

Table 3.2 (cont.)

Control	Property	Setting
	LargeChange	
	Cursor	
Button1	Name	
	Text	

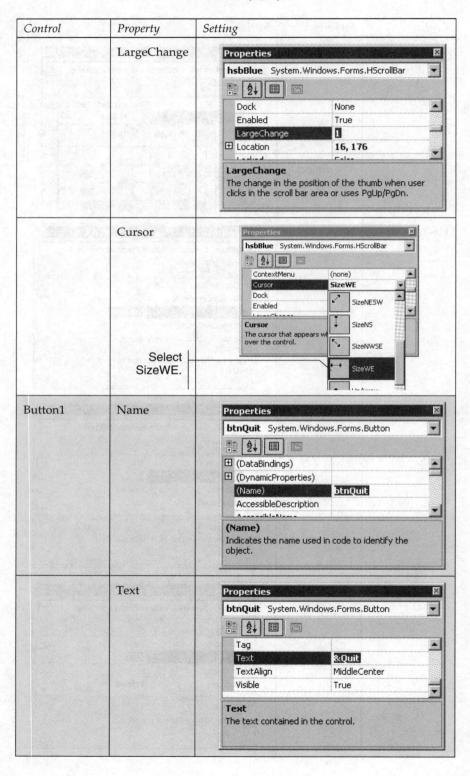

Select SizeWE.

Figure 3.17 **After** the properties are set.

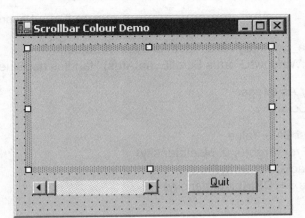

Properties of the horizontal scrollbar

As already mentioned the position of the thumb on the scrollbar is represented as a number that is supplied via the controls *Value* property. This number can reside within a range that is dictated by the *Min* and *Max* properties. Consequently, for the example under consideration the setting of the *Value* property can be between 0 and 255 (the *Min* and *Max* property settings as shown by Table 3.2). The values of the *Min* and *Max* properties were chosen to reflect the range of the colour blue that can be supplied to the *FromARGB* method.

The event handling procedure for the scrollbar of Figure 3.17 is graphically represented by Figure 3.18. The default event for a horizontal scrollbar is the *Scroll* event, which is activated when the user moves the thumb using any one of the three ways previously listed.

Figure 3.18 The *Scroll* event is handled by the *Scroll* event handling procedure for the horizontal scroll bar.

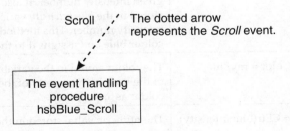

The code for the *Scroll* event handling procedure is shown in Listing 3.3.

NOTE: As a reminder: Lines of code in VB .NET are often too long to fit on to one line. Under these circumstances, a line can be 'broken across' two lines, providing a space and underscore is used – as illustrated in Listing 3.3 by the callout labels.
Space first then underscore!

Listing 3.3 The event handling procedure for the scrollbar.

Space | Underscore

```
Private Sub hsbBlue_Scroll(ByVal sender As System.Object,
ByVal e As System.Windows.Forms.ScrollEventArgs) Handles hsbBlue.Scroll

    Dim blueIntensity As Integer
    Dim myBlue As Color

    blueIntensity = hsbBlue.Value
    myBlue = Color.FromArgb(0, 0, blueIntensity)
    lblShowColour.BackColor = myBlue
    lblShowColour.Text = CStr(blueIntensity)
End Sub
```

The event handling procedure shown in Listing 3.3 has local variables *myBlue* declared as *Color* and *blueValue* declared as an *Integer* (a type used to store whole numbers). When the user scrolls the thumb the event handling procedure executes. This execution is described by the following description trace.

Statement	Description
blueIntensity = hsbBlue.Value	The number stored in the *Value* property of the Horizontal Scrollbar is assigned to the variable *blueIntensity*. This number will be between 0 and 255 depending upon the position of the thumb. As the *Value* property stores a numeric type it had to be assigned to a variable of an appropriate type, namely, an *Integer*. An *Integer* can store a whole number
myBlue = Color.FromArgb(0, 0, blueIntensity)	The method *FromARGB* takes a zero for its red and green intensity number. It also receives what is stored in the *blueIntensity* variable for its blue intensity number. This method forms an appropriate colour blue and assigns it to the variable *myBlue*.
lblShowColour.BackColor = myBlue	The colour stored in the variable *myBlue* is assigned to the *BackColor* property of the label changing its colour as appropriate.
lblShowColour.Text = CStr(blueIntensity)	The numeric value stored in the variable *blueIntensity* is converted to a string by the conversion function *CStr* and this string is then assigned to the *Text* property of the label.

As the user drags the thumb to the right the *Value* property of the horizontal scrollbar increases; increasing the intensity of the colour blue. When the slider is dragged to the left the number in the *Value* property reduces and the intensity of the colour blue decreases.

The code for the Quit button is shown in Listing 3.4.

Listing 3.4 The code for the Quit button.

```
Private Sub btnQuit_Click(ByVal sender As System.Object, _
ByVal e As System.EventArgs) Handles btnQuit.Click

    Close()
    End
End Sub
```

Again note the use of the space and underscore.

The description trace for Listing 3.4.

Statement	Description
Close()	Closes the current form.
End	Terminates execution immediately.

PRACTICAL ACTIVITY 3.4

Develop the program to meet the requirement of Specification 3.3. When the program is running move the thumb in the three ways listed below:

1. By dragging the thumb.
2. By clicking on to the arrows at the edge of the bar.
3. By clicking on to the space between the arrows and the thumb.

Carefully observe the effect of the three ways for moving the slider. Experiment with the *SmallChange* and *LargeChange* properties, i.e. set them to different values from within the property window and observe the effect when the program is run. Also observe the change in the cursor when it is moved from the form to over the horizontal scrollbar. Change the setting of the *Cursor* property and observe the effect when the program is run.

PRACTICAL ACTIVITY 3.5

Experiment with the *ForeColor* property of the label. Set it to different colours and observe the effect when the program is run. **NOTE**: it might not be visible if you set it to blue!

QUESTION 3.3 (DEVELOPMENT)

Review all of the Windows software you have used and reflect on all of the uses of a scrollbar. Make a short list of its uses: you will find it a useful resource for ideas for any future projects you may develop.

The signature of an event handling procedure

An example signature for an event handling procedure is shown in Figure 3.19. It can be seen that the event handling procedure has two parameters *sender* and *e*. These parameters are passed into the procedure when the button click event occurs. This relationship is shown in Figure 3.20.

Figure 3.19 The signature for an event handler.

```
Private Sub btnDemo_Click(ByVal sender As System.Object, ByVal e As _
System.EventArgs) Handles btnQuit.Click
```

Figure 3.20 The button click event and its parameters.

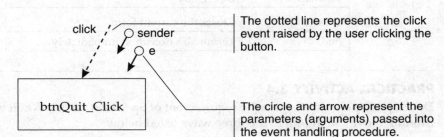

The dotted line represents the click event raised by the user clicking the button.

The circle and arrow represent the parameters (arguments) passed into the event handling procedure.

The *sender* parameter

This is an **object variable** that refers to the event source. As it is an object it will have members that can be used by the code within the *btnQuit_Click* event handler. These members convey information about the source that created the event.

An example of the information conveyed is illustrated by the code and runtime shown in Figure 3.21.

Figure 3.21 An example of using a member of the sender object variable.

```
Private Sub btnDemo_Click(ByVal sender As System.Object, _
ByVal e As System.EventArgs) Handles btnDemo.Click

    lblDisplay.Text = sender.ToString()
End Sub
```

Figure 3.21 (cont.)

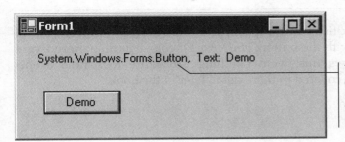

The *ToString()* member of the *sender* object assigns a string to this label. It can be seen that the object raising the event is a button that has its *Text* property set to *Demo*.

NOTE: In this example there has been no attempt to act upon this information passed to the event handler; this program has been designed to illustrate the actual passing of the information. Knowing the source of the event allows a single procedure to handle multiple events.

The e parameter

This event object encapsulates information about the event.

Figure 3.22 An example of using a member of the *e* variable (i.e. object).

```
Private Sub btnDemo_Click(ByVal sender As System.Object, ByVal e As
System.EventArgs) Handles btnDemo.Click

    lblDisplay.Text = CStr(e.GetHashCode)
End Sub
```

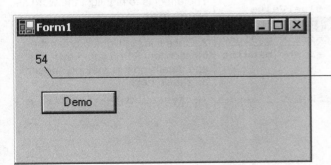

The *GetHashCode* member of the *e* parameter (i.e. object) assigns a string to this label – after conversion by the string conversion function.

NOTE: Hash codes are used to achieve efficient code execution and are outside the scope of the book. However, the *GetHashCode* member was used here to illustrate how information is passed to the event handler.

Handles btnDemo.Click

The last entry of the signature specifies that this particular event handling procedure will handle the click event associated with the button, *btnDemo*. Of course adding more 'event definitions' to the signature allows this event handling procedure to handle events generated by other controls. This is covered in more detail later in the book.

How to use the Visual Basic .NET help

The program developed to implement Specification 3.3 will be used to demonstrate how to use the Visual Basic .NET help. Figure 3.23 illustrates ways to obtain help on language features.

Figure 3.23 VB .NET help.

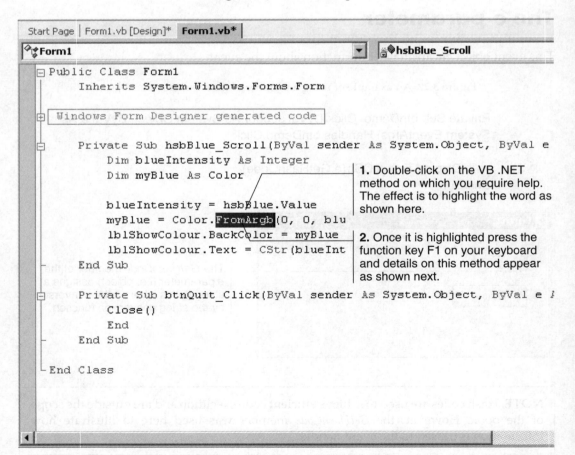

Figure 3.23 (cont.)

FromArgb Method | Form1.vb [Design]* | Form1.vb* |

▶ ▼ *.NET Framework Class Library*
Color.FromArgb Method [Visual Basic]

Creates a <u>Color</u> structure from the four 8-bit ARGB component (alpha, red, green, and blue values.

3. Click here and more details will appear as shown next.

Overload List

Creates a <u>Color</u> structure from a 32-bit ARGB value.

<u>Overloads Public Shared Function FromArgb(Integer) As Color</u>

Creates a <u>Color</u> structure from the specified **Color** structure, but with the new specified alph value. Although this method allows a 32-bit value to be passed for the alpha value, the valu limited to 8 bits.

<u>Overloads Public Shared Function FromArgb(Integer, Color) As Color</u>

Creates a <u>Color</u> structure from the specified 8-bit color values (red, green, and blue). The al value is implicitly 255 (fully opaque). Although this method allows a 32-bit value to be passe each color component, the value of each component is limited to 8 bits.

<u>Overloads Public Shared Function FromArgb(Integer, Integer, Integer) As Color</u>

Creates a <u>Color</u> structure from the four ARGB component (alpha, red, green, and blue) valu

---

FromArgb Metho..., Int32, Int32) | Form1.vb [Design]* | Form1.vb* |

▶ ▼ ▼ *.NET Framework Class Library*
Color.FromArgb Method (Int32, Int32, Int32) [Visual Basic]

Creates a <u>Color</u> structure from the specified 8-bit color values (red, green, and blue). The a value is implicitly 255 (fully opaque). Although this method allows a 32-bit value to be pass each color component, the value of each component is limited to 8 bits.

```
<Serializable>
<ComVisible(True)>
Overloads Public Shared Function FromArgb( _
    ByVal red As Integer, _
    ByVal green As Integer, _
    ByVal blue As Integer _
) As Color
```

Parameters
red
> The red component value for the new <u>Color</u> structure. Valid values are 0 through 255.

green
> The green component value for the new <u>Color</u> structure. Valid values are 0 through 255

blue
> The blue component value for the new <u>Color</u> structure. Valid values are 0 through 255.

Return Value
The <u>Color</u> structure that this method creates.

Example
The following example is designed for use with Windows Forms, and it requires PaintEventA

Figure 3.24 shows an alternative way of obtaining help.

Figure 3.24 Obtaining help.

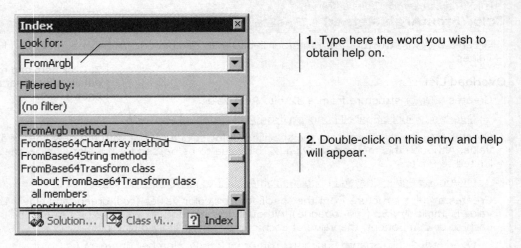

1. Type here the word you wish to obtain help on.

2. Double-click on this entry and help will appear.

4 Developing a program using event handling procedures

This chapter shows how to develop a simple program that meets the following specification **using only event handling procedures**.

SPECIFICATION 4.1

Develop a program that controls the background and foreground colours of a TextBox, i.e. allow the user to choose the colour of the text in the textbox and its background.

NOTE: A TextBox is a control that is useful for displaying information within a GUI. It is also able to act as an input mechanism for user-entered data.

Steps 1 and 2: draw the interface and set the properties

Figure 4.1 illustrates the graphical user interface designed to implement Specification 4.1. The interface has been built from one textbox, six horizontal scrollbars, thirteen labels and one button.

Figure 4.1 The graphical user interface **after** the properties have been set.

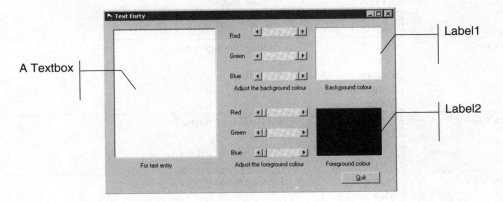

Table 4.1 lists all the controls and their property settings.

NOTE: Table 4.1 only lists the properties that have been changed; all the other properties remain set at their default values.

81

Table 4.1 Property settings for the application. All positional properties have not been included because all the controls have been dragged into position.

Control	Property	Setting
Form1	Text Icon	Text Entry Browse your computer's file system for a suitable icon.
Text1	Name Text MultiLine	txtTextArea <empty> True
Label1	Name Text BorderStyle BackColor	lblBackgroundColour <empty> Fixed3D White
Label2	Name Text BorderStyle BackColor	lblForegroundColour <empty> Fixed3D Black
Label3 through to Label13	Name Text AutoSize	Left at their default setting because they are only acting to guide the user on the GUI and there is no intention of accessing any properties of these labels with code. The setting of their *Text* property should be obvious from Figure 4.1, e.g. the label under the textbox should be set to *For text entry* True
Hscroll1	Name Max Cursor LargeChange Value	hsbRedBackground 255 SizeWE 1 255
Hscroll2	Name Max Cursor LargeChange Value	hsbGreenBackground 255 9 'Size W E 1 255
Hscroll3	Name Max Cursor LargeChange Value	hsbBlueBackground 255 SizeWE 1 255
Hscroll4	Name Max Cursor LargeChange	hsbRedForeground 255 SizeWE 1
Hscroll5	Name Max Cursor LargeChange	hsbGreenForeground 255 SizeWE 1
Hscroll6	Name Max Cursor LargeChange	hsbBlueForeground 255 SizeWE 1

> **USEFUL TIP:** It can be seen from Table 4.1 that the *LargeChange* property for all of the Scrollbars has been set at 1. A quicker method than setting each to 1 in turn would be to hold down the Ctrl key on the keyboard and at the same time click onto each scrollbar on the GUI – this highlights each scrollbar. Now set the *LargeChange* property to 1 and every highlighted scrollbar will have its *LargeChange* property set to 1.
>
> It is also possible to select more than one control on the GUI by dragging a dotted rectangle around the controls. Dragging is achieved by holding down the left mouse button while the mouse is moved.

Step 3: write the code

Once the interface is finished the next step is to attach the code to all of the possible events, i.e. write the event handling procedures.

To what events does this application respond? Events come from two main sources, the user and the system. It is usual practice to first identify the events generated by the user – and in this case it is only the user who 'fires' events, there are no system events.

> **NOTE:** An example of a user event is the clicking of a button; an example of a system event is the backing up of the hard drives at a specified time of the day.

In this application the user will alter the colour of the background and foreground using the six horizontal scrollbars. The user will also enter text in to the TextBox, however, in this simplified application there will be no attempt to process this data – the textbox is just used to display the effect of changing the colours.

There will be seven event handling procedures – one for each of the six horizontal scrollbars (each of these will be associated with the scrollbar *Scroll* event) – and a button *Click* event.

> **QUESTION 4.1 (REVISION)**
>
> *Table 4.1 lists the Name property for each of the horizontal scrollbars. Compose the name for the Scroll event handling procedures associated with each of the six scrollbars, e.g. the name property of one of the scroll bars is* hsbRedBackground, *consequently, the name of the Scroll event procedure will be:*
>
> hsbRedBackground_Scroll
>
> *You work out the name for the remaining five event procedures!*

Figure 4.2 illustrates a 'graphical description' of the calling of the event handlers, by the *Scroll* event of all six horizontal scrollbars.

Figure 4.2 Calling all the event handlers.

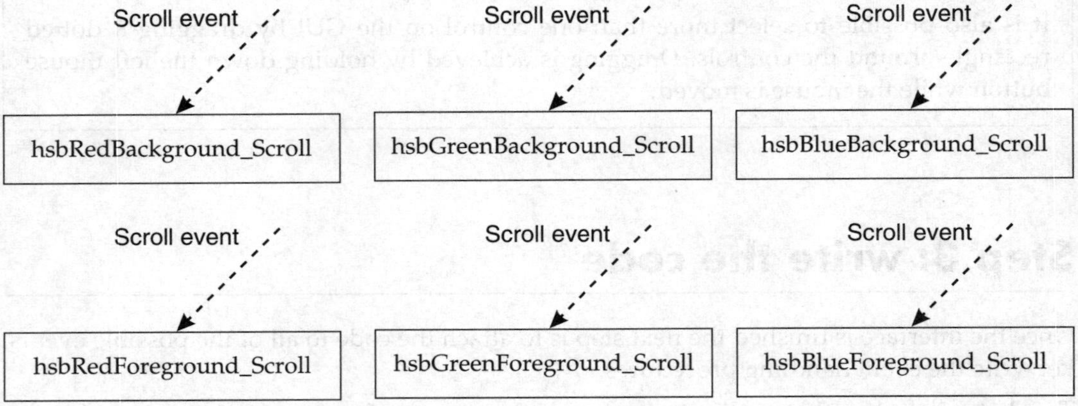

The first three event procedures, shown in Figure 4.2, are all responsible for setting the background colour of the textbox and the next three are responsible for setting the foreground colour.

The code for setting the background colour

Part of the code for setting the background colour of the textbox is shown in Listing 4.1.

Listing 4.1 Code for setting the background colour.

```
Private Sub hsbRedBackground_Scroll(ByVal sender As System.Object, _
ByVal e As System.Windows.Forms.ScrollEventArgs) Handles hsbRedBackground.Scroll
    Dim redIntensity As Integer
    Dim greenIntensity As Integer
    Dim blueIntensity As Integer
    Dim backgroundColour As Color

    redIntensity = hsbRedBackground.Value
    greenIntensity = hsbGreenBackground.Value
    blueIntensity = hsbBlueBackground.Value

    backgroundColour = Color.FromArgb(redIntensity, greenIntensity, blueIntensity)

    txtTextArea.BackColor = backgroundColour
    lblBackgroundColour.BackColor = backgroundColour
End Sub
```

Input

Process

Output

This event handling procedure has three local *Integer* variables: *redIntensity*, *greenIntensity*, and *blueIntensity*. These variables are used to store the setting of the *Value* property of the horizontal scrollbars. In the context of this procedure these variables are used as the 'intensity number' for the colour components to the *FromArgb* method. It also has one *Color* type variable called *backgroundColour*.

NOTE: Local variables have a 'lifetime' for the duration of the procedure. Once the procedure finishes executing the values in local variables are lost. The scope of these variables is also local which mean that they can only be accessed by code within the event handler in which they were declared.

The code in this event handling procedure reflects the structure of all program code. Namely, the input of data, its processing and then its output – the brackets and callout labels shown with Listing 4.1 highlight this fundamental structure.

The code shown in Listing 4.1 forms the *Scroll* event for the *hsbRedBackground* scrollbar. For this application to work the same code has to be attached to the other two horizontal scrollbars that control the background colour. Of course, the code typed in by the programmer is reused; not the template given by the IDE. Figure 4.3 shows the code to be reused in both the other scrollbars.

Figure 4.3 Code to be reused.

```
Dim redIntensity As Integer
Dim greenIntensity As Integer
Dim blueIntensity As Integer
Dim backgroundColour As Color

redIntensity = hsbRedBackground.Value
greenIntensity = hsbGreenBackground.Value
blueIntensity = hsbBlueBackground.Value

backgroundColour = Color.FromArgb(redIntensity, greenIntensity, blueIntensity)

txtTextArea.BackColor = backgroundColour
lblBackgroundColour.BackColor = backgroundColour
```

Listing 4.2 shows the handler attached to one of the other scrollbars (i.e. *hsbGreenBackground*). Compare this listing with Listing 4.1 and you will see that they are **almost** identical.

Listing 4.2 Compare this listing with Listing 4.1.

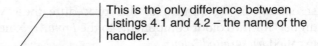

This is the only difference between Listings 4.1 and 4.2 – the name of the handler.

```
Private Sub hsbGreenBackground_Scroll(ByVal sender As System.Object, ByVal e _
As System.Windows.Forms.ScrollEventArgs) Handles hsbGreenBackground.Scroll
    Dim redIntensity As Integer
    Dim greenIntensity As Integer
    Dim blueIntensity As Integer
    Dim backgroundColour As Color

    redIntensity = hsbRedBackground.Value
    greenIntensity = hsbGreenBackground.Value
    blueIntensity = hsbBlueBackground.Value

    backgroundColour = Color.FromArgb(redIntensity, greenIntensity, blueIntensity)

    txtTextArea.BackColor = backgroundColour
    lblBackgroundColour.BackColor = backgroundColour
End Subd
```

As the code attached to the scroll event for three of the scrollbars is identical only one trace description is required.

Description trace for *hsbRedBackground_Scroll*

Statement	Description
redIntensity = hsbRedBackground.Value	The local variable *redIntensity* is assigned the setting of the *Value* property of the horizontal scrollbar *hsbRedBackground*. The value assigned to the variable *redIntensity* will depend upon the position of the thumb on the scrollbar, which is controlled by the user of the application.
greenIntensity = hsbGreenBackground.Value	The local variable *greenIntensity* is assigned the setting of the *Value* property of the horizontal scrollbar *hsbGreenBackground*. The value assigned to the variable *greenIntensity* will depend upon the position of the thumb on the scrollbar, which is controlled by the user of the application.
blueIntensity = hsbBlueBackground.Value	The local variable *blueIntensity* is assigned the setting of the *Value* property of the horizontal scrollbar *hsbBlueBackground*. The value assigned to the variable *blueIntensity* will depend upon the position of the thumb on the scrollbar, which is controlled by the user of the application.

At this point in the execution of the event handling procedure all of the data required has been **input**. The next step is to process this data.	
backgroundColour = Color.FromArgb(redIntensity, greenIntensity, blueIntensity)	The *FromArgb* method takes the values stored in the three *Integer* variables and forms a colour. It assigns this colour to the variable *backgroundColour*.
At this point in the execution of the event handling procedure the input data has been **processed**. The next step is to output this data.	
txtTextArea.BackColor = backgroundColour	The colour stored in the variable *backgroundColour* is assigned to the *BackColor* property of the textbox. Consequently, the background colour of the textbox will change.
lblBackgroundColour. BackColor = backgroundColour	The colour stored in the variable *backgroundColour* is assigned to the *BackColor* property of the label. Consequently, the background colour of the label will change.
At this point the event handling procedure stops execution and the application waits for the next event to occur.	

The code for setting the foreground colour

Part of the code for setting the foreground colour of the textbox is shown in Listing 4.3.

Listing 4.3 Setting the foreground colour.

```
Private Sub hsbRedForeground_Scroll(ByVal sender As System.Object, _
ByVal e As System.Windows.Forms.ScrollEventArgs) Handles hsbRedForeground.Scroll
    Dim redIntensity As Integer
    Dim greenIntensity As Integer
    Dim blueIntensity As Integer
    Dim foregroundColour As Color

    redIntensity = hsbRedForeground.Value
    greenIntensity = hsbGreenForeground.Value
    blueIntensity = hsbBlueForeground.Value

    foregroundColour = Color.FromArgb(redIntensity, greenIntensity, blueIntensity)

    txtTextArea.ForeColor = foregroundColour
    lblForegroundColour.BackColor = foregroundColour
End Sub
```

The code shown in Listing 4.3 must also be attached to the other two scrollbars responsible for setting the foreground colour of the textbox.

The code of Listing 4.3 is very similar to the code of Listing 4.1 so a description of all the code would be repetitive. Therefore, just one line is described.

Statement	Description
lblForegroundColour.BackColor = foregroundColour	The colour stored in the variable *foregroundColour* is assigned to the *ForeColor* property of the textbox. Consequently, the foreground colour of the textbox will change and any text typed in to this textbox will be of this colour.

PRACTICAL ACTIVITY 4.1

Implement Specification 4.1. This will involve building the GUI as shown in Figure 4.1 using the property settings given by Table 4.1. It will also require the attaching of six event handlers to the scrollbars. You 'attach' appropriate code to the Quit button (covered in Chapter 3, refer to Listing 3.4).

PRACTICAL ACTIVITY 4.2

Amend the application developed in Practical Activity 4.1 so that the foreground colour is controlled by three vertical scrollbars (the background remains controlled by the horizontal scroll bars). The three-letter prefix used for a vertical scrollbar is *vsb*.

IMPORTANT: The simple application developed here is **not** an elegant solution. It required the repeating of code in numerous places. There are better techniques when dealing with code so that this repetition does not occur. The next chapter deals with one of these techniques (methods). The rest of this chapter covers the creation of an event handling procedure that will deal with more than one object raising an event.

The use of the *Handles* keyword

Listing 4.1 is the code that handles the scroll event for the *hsbRedBackground* scrollbar. The other two scrollbars for controlling the background colour of the textbox (i.e. *hsbGreenBackground* and *hsbBlueBackground*) both have their own copies of this code – which is the same with only the signature of each of the event handling procedures being different.

Using the *Handles* keyword allows the discarding of the *hsbGreenBackground.Scroll* and *hsbBlueBackground.Scroll* event handling procedures and thus reduces the number of such procedures within the program. This is achieved by keeping the *hsbRedBackground.Scroll* event handling procedure and arranging for it to also execute when the *Scroll* event is raised by the other two horizontal scrollbars (i.e. *hsbGreenBackground* and *hsbBlueBackground*).

'Tying' events to one event handling procedure for this application is achieved by altering the signature of the *hsbRedBackground.Scroll* event handler. Figure 4.4 illustrates the changes needed to the signature of the *hsbRedBackground.Scroll* event handler. The change is shown in bold.

> **NOTE**: Of course, when you amend the solution to Specification 4.1 you will have to delete the code attached to the other two scrollbars. However, you would not normally have attached the code in the first place, because a better technique for implementing specification 4.1 exists.

Figure 4.4 Altering the event handler signature.

```
Private Sub hsbRedBackground_Scroll(ByVal sender As System.Object, ByVal e As _
System.Windows.Forms.ScrollEventArgs) Handles hsbRedBackground.Scroll, _
hsbGreenBackground.Scroll, hsbBlueBackground.Scroll
```

The keyword *Handles* follows the closing bracket of the signature, and separated by a comma are the events that the code within this event handler will service. So it can be seen that this event handling procedure will respond to three events, the *Scroll* event of all of the three scrollbars responsible for setting the background colour of the textbox. This is further highlighted by Figure 4.5.

Figure 4.5 How to use the *Handles* keyword.

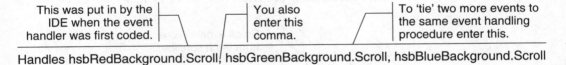

| This was put in by the IDE when the event handler was first coded. | You also enter this comma. | To 'tie' two more events to the same event handling procedure enter this. |

Handles hsbRedBackground.Scroll, hsbGreenBackground.Scroll, hsbBlueBackground.Scroll

All the code for the event handling procedure is shown in Listing 4.4 (the execution of its code has been described earlier in this chapter). Figure 4.6 illustrates the concept behind having one event handling procedure responding to more that one event.

> **NOTE**: Of course, although this works it does not follow good software engineering principles because the scroll events associated with each of the three scrollbars execute an event handler called *hsbRedBackground_Scroll*. It would be better to choose a more appropriate name for this event handling procedure. The advantage in amending the *hsbRedBackground_Scroll* event handler for the application just described was simply the fact that it was already there from a previously developed application – not a good enough reason and not good design. So assuming we are starting from scratch how do we develop an event handling procedure that executes in response to more than one event?

Listing 4.4 The event handling procedure.

```
Private Sub hsbRedBackground_Scroll(ByVal sender As System.Object, _
ByVal e As System.Windows.Forms.ScrollEventArgs) _
Handles hsbRedBackground.Scroll, hsbGreenBackground.Scroll, _
hsbBlueBackground.Scroll

    Dim redIntensity As Integer
    Dim greenIntensity As Integer
    Dim blueIntensity As Integer
    Dim backgroundColour As Color

    redIntensity = hsbRedBackground.Value
    greenIntensity = hsbGreenBackground.Value
    blueIntensity = hsbBlueBackground.Value

    backgroundColour = Color.FromArgb(redIntensity, greenIntensity, blueIntensity)

    txtTextArea.BackColor = backgroundColour
    lblBackgroundColour.BackColor = backgroundColour
End Sub
```

Figure 4.6 The concept of one event handling procedure responding to more than one event.

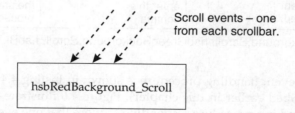

Scroll events – one
from each scrollbar.

hsbRedBackground_Scroll

Creating an events handling procedure

To create an event handling procedure that will handle **more than one event** is simply a case of creating a sensibly named procedure with the correct signature. Listing 4.5 shows the code for creating an events handling procedure (note the plural). Figure 4.7 shows the steps involved in creating the procedure.

Figure 4.7 Creating a procedure.

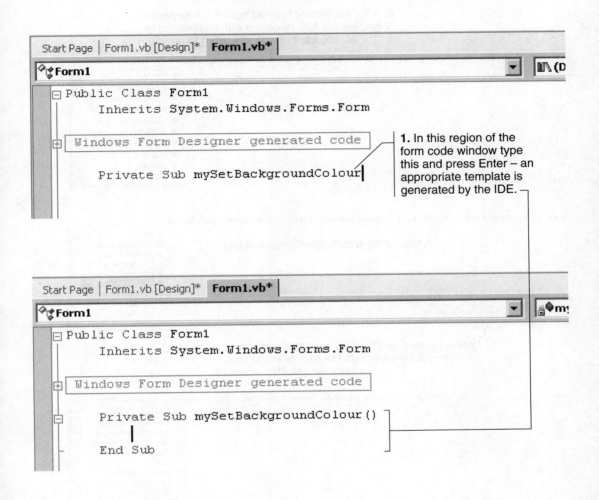

1. In this region of the form code window type this and press Enter – an appropriate template is generated by the IDE.

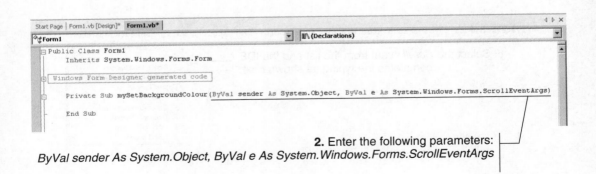

2. Enter the following parameters:
ByVal sender As System.Object, ByVal e As System.Windows.Forms.ScrollEventArgs

Figure 4.7 (cont.)

3. After the closing bracket type in the keyword
Handles; the IDE responds with intellisense to
list objects that you may wish to handle.

```
nder As System.Object, ByVal e As System.Windows.Forms.ScrollEventArgs) Handles
```

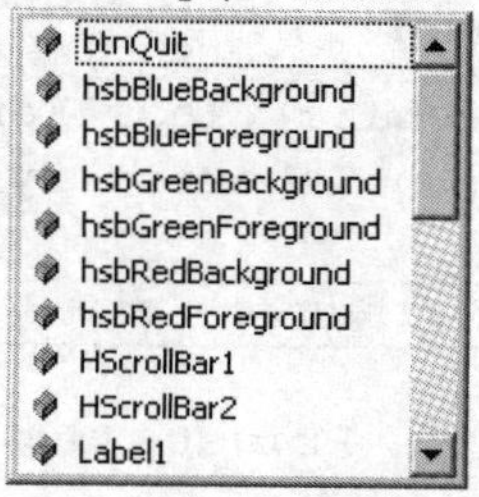

```
btnQuit
hsbBlueBackground
hsbBlueForeground
hsbGreenBackground
hsbGreenForeground
hsbRedBackground
hsbRedForeground
HScrollBar1
HScrollBar2
Label1
```

```
nder As System.Object, ByVal e As System.Windows.Forms.ScrollEventArgs) Handles |
```

4. Select the *hsbRedBackground* object.

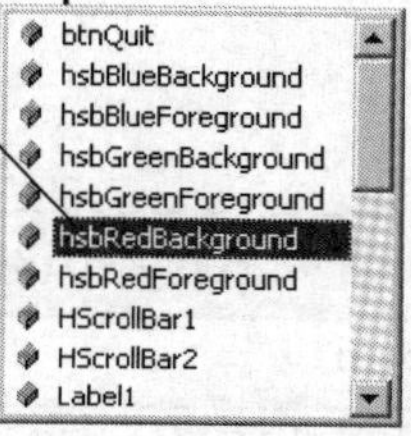

```
btnQuit
hsbBlueBackground
hsbBlueForeground
hsbGreenBackground
hsbGreenForeground
hsbRedBackground
hsbRedForeground
HScrollBar1
HScrollBar2
Label1
```

5. Type a full stop and the IDE responds again with
intellisense and lists the events associated
with the selected object.

```
:nder As System.Object, ByVal e As System.Windows.Forms.ScrollEventArgs) Handles hsbRedBackground.
```

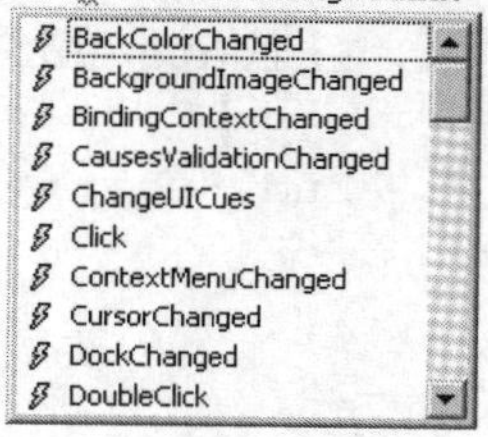

```
BackColorChanged
BackgroundImageChanged
BindingContextChanged
CausesValidationChanged
ChangeUICues
Click
ContextMenuChanged
CursorChanged
DockChanged
DoubleClick
```

```
nder As System.Object, ByVal e As System.Windows.Forms.ScrollEventArgs) Handles hsbRedBackground.
```

6. Select the *Scroll* event from the list and the IDE
completes the typing as shown next:

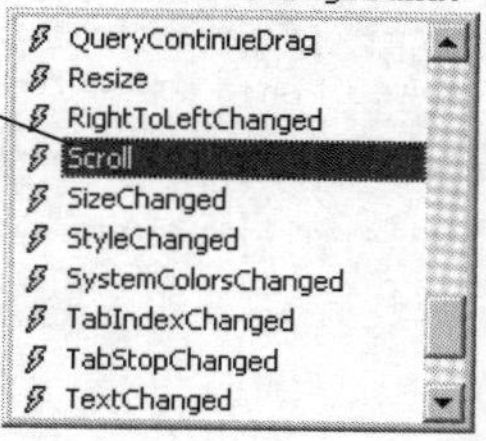

```
QueryContinueDrag
Resize
RightToLeftChanged
Scroll
SizeChanged
StyleChanged
SystemColorsChanged
TabIndexChanged
TabStopChanged
TextChanged
```

```
al sender As System.Object, ByVal e As System.Windows.Forms.ScrollEventArgs) Handles hsbRedBackground.Scroll|
```

Figure 4.7 (cont.)

7. Enter a comma and the intellisense responds again with a drop-down list, as shown.

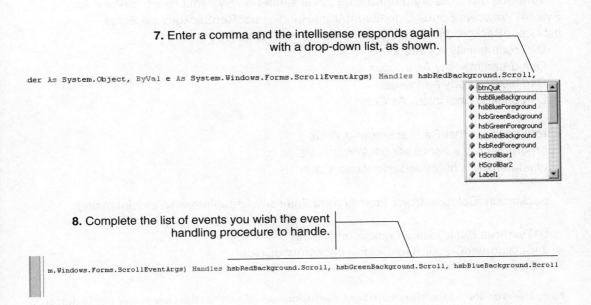

.der As System.Object, ByVal e As System.Windows.Forms.ScrollEventArgs) Handles hsbRedBackground.Scroll,

| btnQuit |
| hsbBlueBackground |
| hsbBlueForeground |
| hsbGreenBackground |
| hsbGreenForeground |
| hsbRedBackground |
| hsbRedForeground |
| HScrollBar1 |
| HScrollBar2 |
| Label1 |

8. Complete the list of events you wish the event handling procedure to handle.

m.Windows.Forms.ScrollEventArgs) Handles hsbRedBackground.Scroll, hsbGreenBackground.Scroll, hsbBlueBackground.Scroll

9. Enter the code for the event handling procedure to handle all the events.

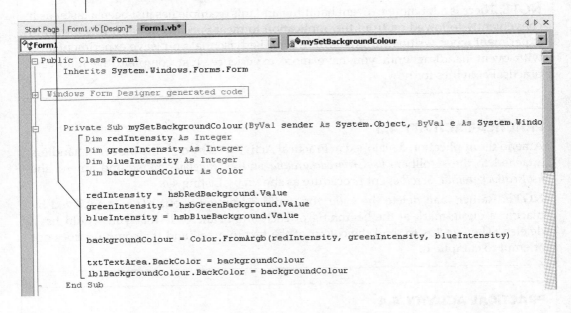

```
Start Page | Form1.vb [Design]* | Form1.vb* |

Form1                                          mySetBackgroundColour

Public Class Form1
    Inherits System.Windows.Forms.Form

    Windows Form Designer generated code

    Private Sub mySetBackgroundColour(ByVal sender As System.Object, ByVal e As System.Windo
        Dim redIntensity As Integer
        Dim greenIntensity As Integer
        Dim blueIntensity As Integer
        Dim backgroundColour As Color

        redIntensity = hsbRedBackground.Value
        greenIntensity = hsbGreenBackground.Value
        blueIntensity = hsbBlueBackground.Value

        backgroundColour = Color.FromArgb(redIntensity, greenIntensity, blueIntensity)

        txtTextArea.BackColor = backgroundColour
        lblBackgroundColour.BackColor = backgroundColour
    End Sub
```

Listing 4.5 An example of an events handling procedure.

```
Private Sub mySetBackgroundColour(ByVal sender As System.Object, ByVal e As _
System.Windows.Forms.ScrollEventArgs) Handles hsbRedBackground.Scroll, _
hsbGreenBackground.Scroll, hsbBlueBackground.Scroll
    Dim redIntensity As Integer
    Dim greenIntensity As Integer
    Dim blueIntensity As Integer
    Dim backgroundColour As Color

    redIntensity = hsbRedBackground.Value
    greenIntensity = hsbGreenBackground.Value
    blueIntensity = hsbBlueBackground.Value

    backgroundColour = Color.FromArgb(redIntensity, greenIntensity, blueIntensity)

    txtTextArea.BackColor = backgroundColour
    lblBackgroundColour.BackColor = backgroundColour
End Sub
```

Here the creation of the signature was all-important! Note that the parameter *e* was declared as *System.Windows.Forms.ScrollEventArgs*. This implies that this procedure will deal with scroll events!

NOTE: There is a lot more to event handling and this example has just been a taster as it conveniently followed on from the application to meet Specification 4.1. It is useful to experiment when writing programs, however, I advise that you leave experimentation with event handling until you have more experience. Just complete the following practical activities for now.

PRACTICAL ACTIVITY 4.3

Amend the application developed in Practical Activity 4.2 by deleting the event handlers attached to the scrollbars *hsbGreenBackground* and *hsbBlueBackground* and amend the *hsbRedBackground_Scroll* event procedure as shown by Listing 4.4.

NOTE: Rather than delete the code you could 'comment it out'. This is achieved by placing a quote mark at the beginning of each line of the code that you would have deleted. The effect is to send the colour of the text to green and the compiler does not attempt to compile it.

PRACTICAL ACTIVITY 4.4

Further amend the code so that it works with the code of Listing 4.5.

NOTE: Finally, when one event handler handles more than one event, you should note that double clicking (at design time) on one of the objects handled by this common event handler will result in the common event handler appearing in the code window – try it.

PRACTICAL ACTIVITY 4.5
Further amend the code so that the setting of the foreground colour is achieved using only one event handling procedure.

5 Using methods in a program

During Chapter 4 you developed a simple program. You will have found that there was repetition of code. This repetition can be removed using appropriate **methods**. What follows is the development of the same program but this time including methods.

Practical Activity 4.1 from Chapter 4 required the building of a program that implemented Specification 4.1. This chapter will modify this program by replacing the repeated code with a **message** that invokes an appropriate method. In fact there will be a need for two messages – one to set the background and one to set the foreground colour of the textbox.

> **NOTE**: The last chapter showed how the *Handles* keyword removed code repetition. This chapter shows an alternative way to remove code repetition.

Why have methods?

Several different event handling procedures might need the same actions performed. Consequently, rather than duplicate the code to perform the actions within these event handling procedures, the code can be put into a method. A message can then be sent to invoke this method from the event handling procedure requiring the actions it performs.

> **NOTE**: Messages and methods are a fundamental feature of object-oriented programming (OOP) but please note that their coverage in this chapter is at an introductory level.

Methods

A method, like an event handling procedure, contains program code. Unlike an event handling procedure, however, a method cannot be directly executed in response to an event. An event handling procedure must in the first instance send a message that invokes a method. However, a method can invoke another method by sending an appropriate message. Of course the method sending the message will have been invoked by the code of an event handling procedures. Please note that the code within the *Main()* method of a console can also send a message to invoke a method. It is also possible to 'tie' a fuction method to an event using the *Handles* keyword.

Figure 5.2 shows the relationship between the six event handling procedures of the program and the two methods that are invoked by appropriate messages. To make code easy to read, all methods must be given a sensible name that reflects their purpose. It can be seen from Figure 5.2 that these methods have been given the names *SetBackgroundColour()* and

Figure 5.1 This diagram illustrates the relationship between an event handling procedure, a message and a method. The dotted arrow represents an event 'invoking' an event handling procedure and the arrow represents the event handling procedure 'invoking' the method. Please note that, although similar, this is not UML notation. UML will be covered later in the book. Remember that this chapter is introductory in nature.

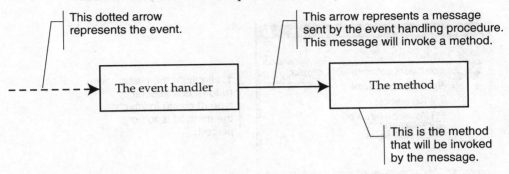

Figure 5.2 The relationship between the event handlers and the methods. Again please note that this is not UML notation – although it is similar.

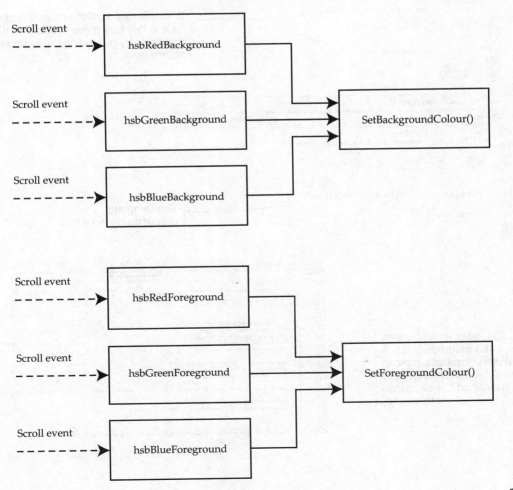

Figure 5.3 Creating a new method.

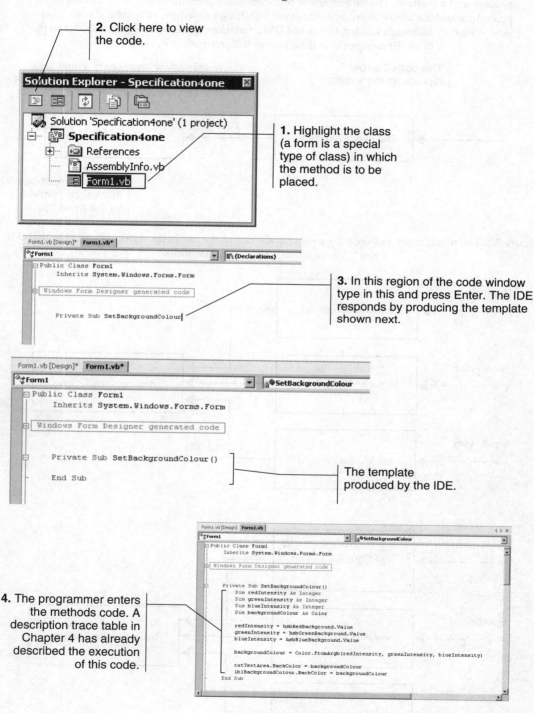

2. Click here to view the code.

1. Highlight the class (a form is a special type of class) in which the method is to be placed.

3. In this region of the code window type in this and press Enter. The IDE responds by producing the template shown next.

The template produced by the IDE.

4. The programmer enters the methods code. A description trace table in Chapter 4 has already described the execution of this code.

SetForegroundColour(). Note the capitalization of each new word in the name (identifier) of the method. This is not necessary as far as the language is concerned, but it does make it easier for programmers to read.

It can be seen from Figure 5.2 that three of the event handling procedures send a message that invokes the *SetBackgroundColour()* method and the other three event handlers send a message that invokes the *SetForegroundColour()* method.

> **NOTE**: A message and a method are synonymous. A message implies the invoking of a method, which is the execution of the program code within the method.
>
> A message can also access a property – more on this later.

Creating a method

There are a variety of ways to create a method; Figure 5.3 shows one way – you are left to research the other ways.

Sending a message to invoke a method

Three of the event handling procedures identified by Figure 5.2 send a message that invokes the *SetBackgroundColour()* method. Figure 5.4 shows the code that sends the message. It can be seen that the message is sent from each of the event handlers. Each of these messages will invoke the same method.

Figure 5.4 Invoking a method.

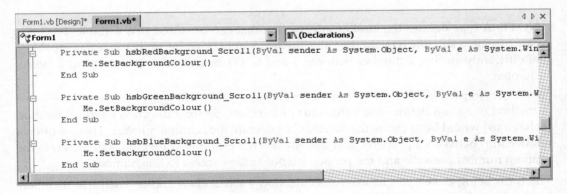

The code for the Scroll handler attached to the *hsbRedBackground* horizontal scrollbar shown in Figure 5.4 simply consists of one message that invokes the method *SetBackgroundColour()*. The other two event handlers (responsible for setting the background colour) contain the same message that invokes the same method.

The form as a class

As a form is being built, with the assistance of the IDE, code is being automatically generated 'behind the scenes'. This automatic generation of code is producing a class. When the form is saved it is saved with a **vb** extension to its file name. This extension is used for all classes in VB .NET. When the form being created is executed an instance of the class (i.e. an object) is created. All the members associated with the class are now available to the object and invoked methods execute in response to events and messages.

> **NOTE**: Those with experience of earlier version of Visual Basic should note that VB .NET saves its classes, modules and forms in a file with a **vb** extension. Earlier versions of Visual Basic use to save forms with a frm extension.

A class and objects

A class usually acts as a 'template' from which objects can be made. In fact, many objects can be made from the same class. For example, if you defined a class that performed the functionality of a die (i.e. generate any number from 1 to 6) you could create numerous dice from this class. Each die would exist in its own right, and all could be thrown independently and store a different number from 1 to 6.

Every class has members (**properties** and **methods**). A property is able to convey information about the class (such as the number generated by a die). The property (via a property procedure) accesses a class level variable (of an appropriate type) responsible for storing the value generated by the throw of the die. Of course, the class level variable, properties and methods do not 'exist' until an instance of the class is created (i.e. an object). This object then has instance variables as defined by the class level variables declared within the class.

> **NOTE**: A type defines the kind of information that can be stored in a variable. For the case of a die, a suitable type for the value thrown would be an *Integer* because it is capable of efficiently storing a number between 1 and 6. Types are covered in detail in a later chapter.

A method of a class defines the **behaviour** of the class. So for a die class a typical method (behaviour) would be to throw the die, that is, generate the random number. There is often a relationship between a property and a method – for example, a method will generate the random number for a die and the property would allow access to this number.

The form being developed to meet Specification 4.1 is a class and as such has members (methods and properties). When complete and running an instance of this class (i.e. an object) is created. This object (in this case a form) will then have methods that can be invoked and properties that can be accessed.

Messages

A program developed using OOP techniques consists of many objects that communicate with each other using messages that request a service of some kind.

For example, consider a game that uses a die to supply a number to decide how many moves a counter may make on a board. It is likely that this game would have a number of objects, and two such objects could be a board object and a die object. During execution, the board object would send a message to the die object asking it to throw itself to generate a number between 1 and 6.

The die object has the behaviour (i.e. the method) that allows for the throw of the die but it is the board that sends the message asking the die object to throw the die. **The board is asking for a service from the die using a message**.

The board would then have to send another message to the die that would access the property of the die that stored the number thrown by the die.

NOTE: A message implies that a method is available or a property can be accessed. If Object A sends a message to Object B the implication is that Object B has a member to deal with the message.

As just discussed, in object-oriented programming, there are objects in existence at the same time and these objects message each other requesting services. This can mean invoking methods or accessing properties within these objects. An object may on occasion wish to use one of its own methods. In other words, an object does not message another object to perform a service, it sends a message to itself to perform a service, e.g. it uses one of its own methods. Figure 5.5 shows code within the form class that requests the use of one of its own methods on three occasions. In other words an instance of a class, that is an object, sends a message to itself – it invokes one of its own methods.

Figure 5.5 An object invoking one of its own methods, i.e. messaging itself.

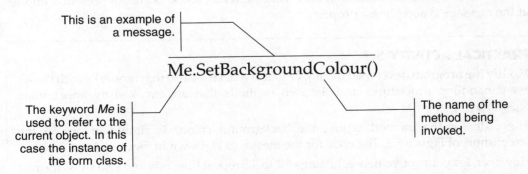

This is an example of a message.

Me.SetBackgroundColour()

The keyword *Me* is used to refer to the current object. In this case the instance of the form class.

The name of the method being invoked.

NOTE: In fact there is no need to use the keyword *Me* – you could just put the name of the method. However, the use of *Me* makes the intention of the programmer clear and is good programming practice. You can leave this keyword out if you wish, however, I will use it throughout the book. If you decide not to use the keyword *Me* then you need to know that there is an occasion when you **have** to use it. If a method within a class has a local variable of the same name as a class level variable then the keyword *Me* is used to access the class level variable – such a variable is often referred to as a shadow variable.

You can also use the keyword *Call* (without the full stop) instead of *Me*. However, I would advise against this as *Call* belongs to the 'procedural world' of Visual Basic programming, whereas *Me* is the agreed approach for object-oriented programming.

General form of a message

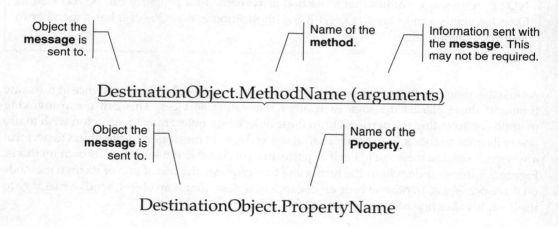

In general when the message uses brackets it implies that a method will be invoked (even when there are no arguments within the brackets). When brackets are not present it implies that the message is accessing a property.

PRACTICAL ACTIVITY 5.1

Modify the program developed during Practical Activity 4.1 so that its works with the six event handling procedures and the two methods that are invoked by appropriate messages.

The code for the method setting the background colour is shown in one of the screenshots of Figure 5.3. The code for the messages is shown in Figure 5.4.

However, for your convenience, Listings 5.1 to 5.8 repeat this code and also show the rest of the code needed to implement Specification 4.1.

Listing 5.1 The *SetBackgroundColour()* method.

```
Private Sub SetBackgroundColour()
    Dim redIntensity As Integer
    Dim greenIntensity As Integer
    Dim blueIntensity As Integer
    Dim backgroundColour As Color

    redIntensity = hsbRedBackground.Value
    greenIntensity = hsbGreenBackground.Value
    blueIntensity = hsbBlueBackground.Value

    backgroundColour = Color.FromArgb(redIntensity, greenIntensity, blueIntensity)

    txtTextArea.BackColor = backgroundColour
    lblBackgroundColour.BackColor = backgroundColour
End Sub
```

Listing 5.2

```
Private Sub hsbRedBackground_Scroll(ByVal sender As System.Object, _
ByVal e As System.Windows.Forms.ScrollEventArgs) Handles hsbRedBackground.Scroll

    Me.SetBackgroundColour()
End Sub
```

Listing 5.3

```
Private Sub hsbGreenBackground_Scroll(ByVal sender As System.Object, ByVal e _
As System.Windows.Forms.ScrollEventArgs) Handles hsbGreenBackground.Scroll

    Me.SetBackgroundColour()
End Sub
```

Listing 5.4

```
Private Sub hsbBlueBackground_Scroll(ByVal sender As System.Object, ByVal e _
As System.Windows.Forms.ScrollEventArgs) Handles hsbBlueBackground.Scroll

    Me.SetBackgroundColour()
End Sub
```

NOTE: Of course, these three event handlers could be replaced by one event handling procedure as shown in Chapter 4. This one event handler could then send a message that invoked the *SetBackgroundColour* method.

Listing 5.5 The *SetForegroundColour()* method.

```
Private Sub SetForegroundColour()
    Dim redIntensity As Integer
    Dim greenIntensity As Integer
    Dim blueIntensity As Integer
    Dim foregroundColour As Color

    redIntensity = hsbRedForeground.Value
    greenIntensity = hsbGreenForeground.Value
    blueIntensity = hsbBlueForeground.Value

    foregroundColour = Color.FromARGB(redIntensity, greenIntensity, blueIntensity)

    txtTextArea.ForeColor = foregroundColour
    lblForegroundColour.BackColor = foregroundColour
End Sub
```

Listing 5.6

```
Private Sub hsbRedForeground_Scroll(ByVal sender As System.Object, ByVal e _
As System.Windows.Forms.ScrollEventArgs) Handles hsbRedForeground.Scroll

    Me.SetForegroundColour()
End Sub
```

Listing 5.7

```
Private Sub hsbGreenForeground_Scroll(ByVal sender As System.Object, ByVal e _
As System.Windows.Forms.ScrollEventArgs) Handles hsbGreenForeground.Scroll

    Me.SetForegroundColour()
```

Listing 5.8

```
Private Sub hsbBlueForeground_Scroll(ByVal sender As System.Object, ByVal e _
As System.Windows.Forms.ScrollEventArgs) Handles hsbBlueForeground.Scroll

    Me.SetForegroundColour()
End Sub
```

A class view of the form as developed by the activities of Practical Activity 5.1

As you implemented the program for Practical Activity 5.1 you should have noticed how the IDE intellisense assisted your efforts in typing in the code and selecting the correct method for your messages. We will return to this a little later.

Lets for the moment look at the class view of the form used in implementing the program as requested by Practical Activity 5.1 Figures 5.6 and 5.7 show the Class View window for the form developed during Practical Activity 5.1.

Figure 5.6 The Class View of the form.

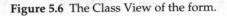

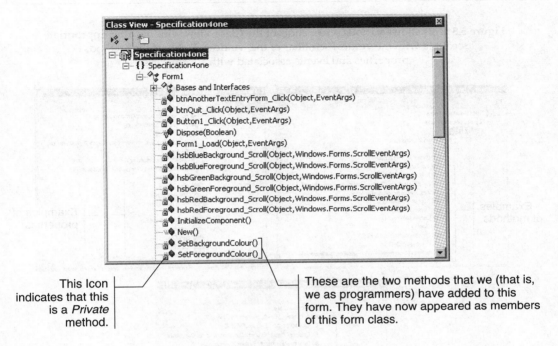

This Icon indicates that this is a *Private* method.

These are the two methods that we (that is, we as programmers) have added to this form. They have now appeared as members of this form class.

Figure 5.7 The Class View of the form.

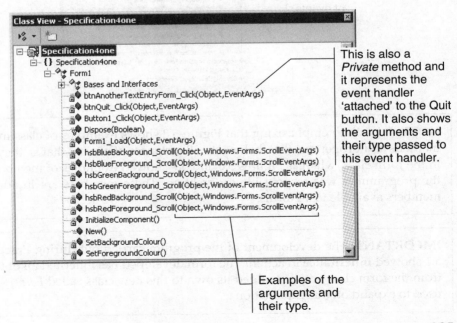

This is also a *Private* method and it represents the event handler 'attached' to the Quit button. It also shows the arguments and their type passed to this event handler.

Examples of the arguments and their type.

NOTE: The screenshots of the Class View window shown in Figures 5.6 and 5.7 have highlighted the members added to the form developed during Practical Activity 5.1. Of course, clicking on other expanding icons within the Class View window allows us to view all the members of the class. Figure 5.8 shows examples of this view.

Figure 5.8 This shows various screenshots of the Class View window after appropriate scrolling with the vertical scrollbar of the window. It shows the methods, properties and events associated with a form class.

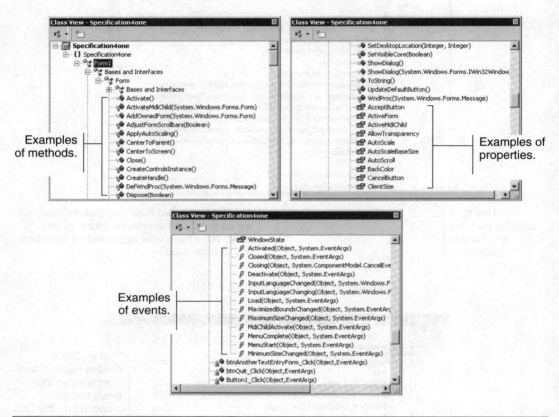

NOTE: It is worth emphasizing that Figure 5.8 shows examples of class members (e.g. methods and properties) that 'belong' to all instances of a form, that is, they are defined in the form class, whereas Figures 5.6 and 5.7 showed examples of members for which the programmer was responsible for creating. These members are in addition to the members available to all forms.

IMPORTANT: The development of the program carried out during Practical Activity 5.1 showed **inheritance** in action! The form developed has inherited all of the members from the form class and just added its own to this new class called *Form1*. Figure 5.9 is used to expand on this explanation.

Figure 5.9 Explaining Inheritance.

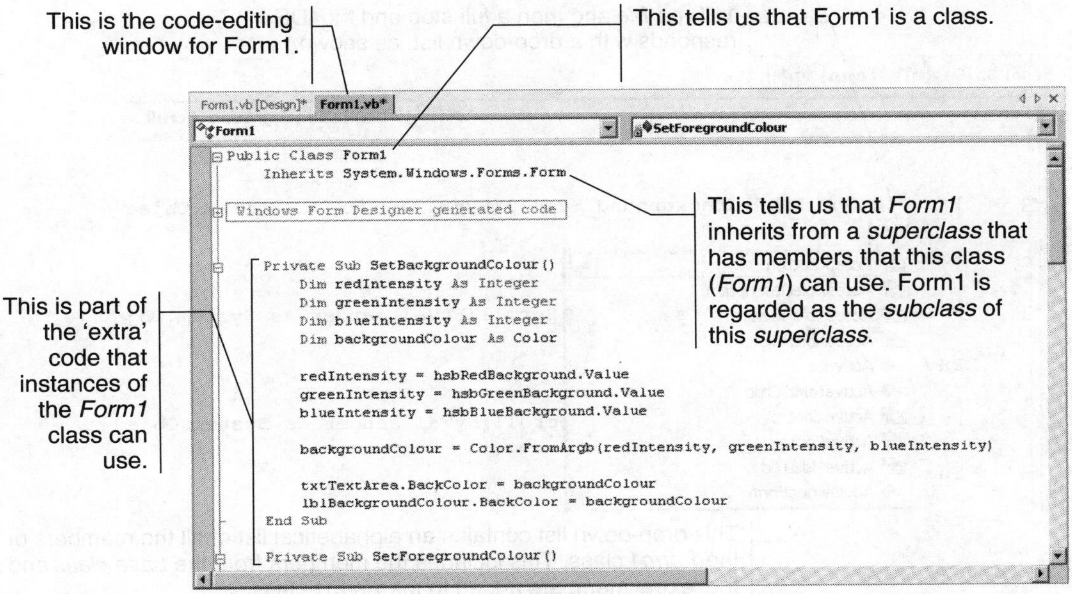

This is the code-editing window for Form1.

This tells us that Form1 is a class.

This is part of the 'extra' code that instances of the *Form1* class can use.

This tells us that *Form1* inherits from a *superclass* that has members that this class (*Form1*) can use. Form1 is regarded as the *subclass* of this *superclass*.

IMPORTANT: VB .NET uses the term **base class** for a superclass and **derived class** for a subclass.

How intellisense aids development

Lets consider the message shown in Listing 5.2: this message can be completed by intellisense. Figure 5.10 shows how intellisense aids in choosing methods for sending the message shown in Listing 5.2. **This assumes that the *SetBackground* method is already entered**.

PRACTICAL ACTIVITY 5.2

Amend the program you developed during Practical Activity 5.1 so that it uses two event handling procedures that both respond to more than one event. Have one of these event handling procedures handle the three scrollbars that set the background colour and have the other handle the scrollbars that set the foreground colour.

Have one of these event handling procedures send a message that invokes a method that sets the background colour. Have the other event handling procedure send a message that invokes a method that sets the foreground colour.

During the development of this program use intellisense whenever appropriate.

Figure 5.10 Creating a message using intellisense.

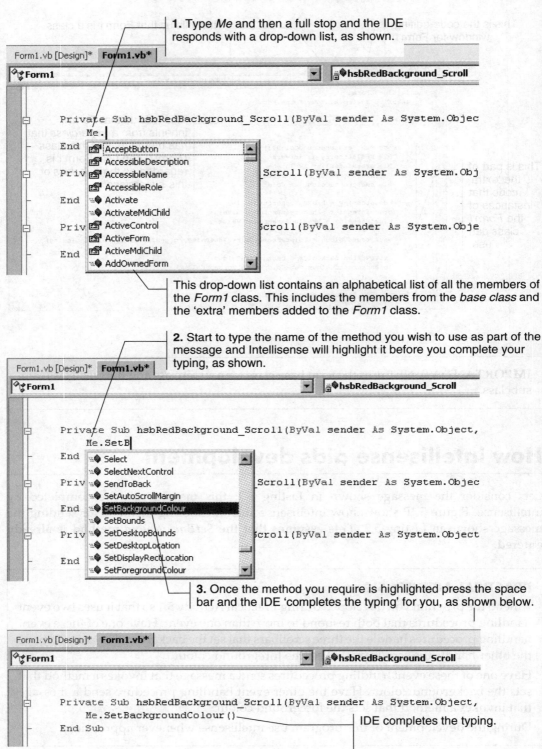

1. Type *Me* and then a full stop and the IDE responds with a drop-down list, as shown.

This drop-down list contains an alphabetical list of all the members of the *Form1* class. This includes the members from the *base class* and the 'extra' members added to the *Form1* class.

2. Start to type the name of the method you wish to use as part of the message and Intellisense will highlight it before you complete your typing, as shown.

3. Once the method you require is highlighted press the space bar and the IDE 'completes the typing' for you, as shown below.

IDE completes the typing.

Scope and lifetime of variables

Both of the methods listed in Listings 5.1 and 5.5 use local variables. These variables are only available within each of these methods. Listing 5.1 has the following variables:

```
Dim redIntensity As Integer
Dim greenIntensity As Integer
Dim blueIntensity As Integer
Dim backgroundColour As Color
```

And Listing 5.5 has the following variables:

```
Dim redIntensity As Integer
Dim greenIntensity As Integer
Dim blueIntensity As Integer
Dim foregroundColour As Color
```

At first sight it would appear that both methods have identical variables *redIntensity*, *greenIntensity* and *blueIntensity*. However, although they may share the same name (identifier) they are entirely different. Let's take *redIntensity* as an example. The *redIntensity* declared within the *SetBackgroundColour()* method is different from the *redIntensity* declared within the *SetForegroundColour()* method. They are different areas of the computer memory and consequently can store their own values. The *redIntensity* within the *SetBackgroundColour()* method stores the position of the thumb on the scrollbar responsible for setting the background colour, whereas, the other *redIntensity* stores the position of the thumb, for the scrollbar, that controls the foreground colour. However, both variables have the same **scope**. This means that only program statements from within the method (or procedure) in which they are declared can access them. They also have the same **lifetime**. This means they only exist (i.e. take up memory) during the execution time of the method in which they reside. When the event handling procedure completes its execution the values stored in these local variables are lost. Figure 5.11 illustrates the scope and lifetime of these local variables.

Class level variable of a form (sometimes known as fields)

Within the code of Listings 5.1 and 5.5 there are two **local** variables named *foregroundColour* and *backgroundColour*. The type of both these variables is *Color* and they are used to store the colour formed by the appropriate scrollbars. These colours are formed and then stored within these **local** variables and when the event handling procedure completes its execution their values are lost.

It could be useful if the colours formed were available to all the code within the *Form1* class. This can be achieved by moving these variables to a different location within the class in other words make them **class level variables**. Of course, the class declares the class level variables, but they only exist when an instance of the class is created (i.e. an object) at which

Figure 5.11 The scope and lifetime of local variables. The first figure illustrates how the local variables are associated with the program statements. There are, for example, two *redIntensity* variables one in each of the methods. A programmer may often be confused by variables that are named the same, as in this example, but the program code is not! The program statements within the *SetBackgroundColour* method only have access to its copy of the *redIntensity* variable, i.e. *redIntensity* has local scope. The second figure shows when the variables exist, and when they do not exist, i.e. their lifetime.

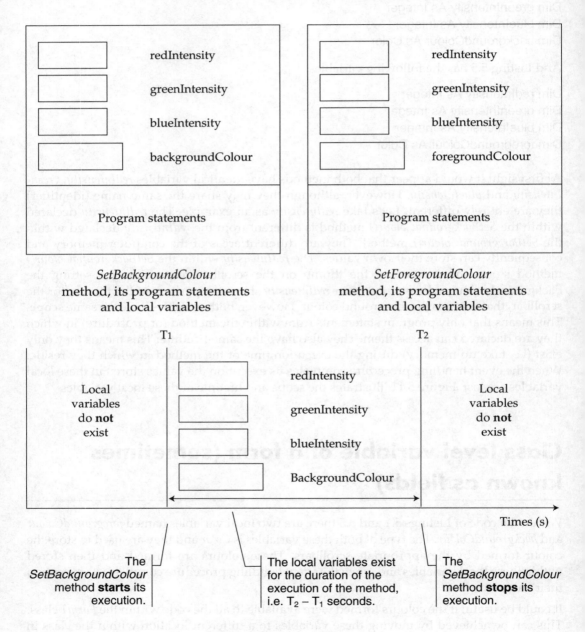

Figure 5.12 Declaring class level variables.

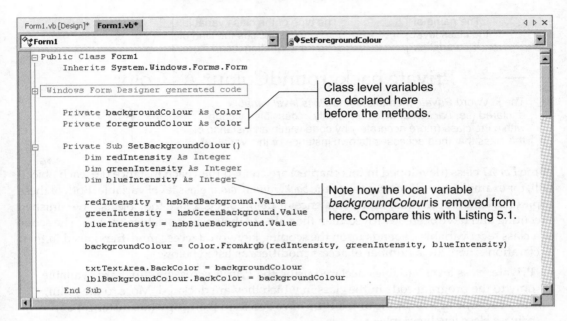

point these class level variables are referred to as instance variables. Figure 5.12 shows where to declare a **class level variable (field)**.

PRACTICAL ACTIVITY 5.3

Modify the program developed during Practical Activity 5.2 by first deleting (or 'commenting out') the local variables *backgroundColour* and *foregroundColour*. Then include *backgroundColour* and *foregroundColour* as class level variables – as shown in Figure 5.12.

Look to see where these two class level variables appear within the Class View Window!

Declaring a class level variable

Figure 5.13 shows the syntax for declaring a class level variable within a form (remember a form is just a special type of class).

Scope and lifetime of instances of class level variables

A class is a template from which objects are created. If two or more objects are created from the same class then they all have their own copy of the class level variables. If two instances

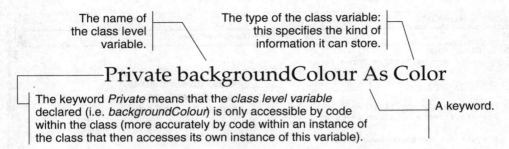

Figure 5.13 Declaring a class level variable.

of the *Form1* class (developed in this chapter) are created then each instance (i.e. each object) will, for example, have its own copy of the *backgroundColour* class level variable. Both of these copies have a lifetime equal to the existence of their objects. Once the objects have finished executing and have been destroyed then the value of their class variables are lost. The scope of a class level variable depends upon the scoping keyword (**access modifiers**) used in their declaration. There are a number of access modifiers as listed below:

- **Private**: class level variables declared using the *Private* access modifier are available only to the program code in the class in which they are declared. More to the point, only the code of the objects of the class have access to their copy (i.e. instance) of private class level variables.

- **Public**: class level variables declared using the *Public* access modifier are available to all methods and procedures in all classes. Again, any instance of the class can have their copy of class level variables accessed by any other object.

- **Protected**: class level variables declared using the *Protected* access modifier are available in the same class or a derived class (see inheritance later in the book).

NOTE: A class level variable is available to instances, that is, objects of the class and every instance has its own copy. The class level variables are referred to as instance variables with an object created from the class.

Another type of variable is the **shared** class level variable. This is a variable that 'belongs to the class' and not to objects of the class. Consequently, there is only **one** copy of a shared class level variable.

The keyword *Shared* is used when declaring a shared class level variable.

QUESTION 5.1 (DEVELOPMENT)
Use the VB .NET help to look up the meaning of the other two types of access modifiers Friend and Protected Friend with respect to class level variables.

NOTE: It is poor programming practice to declare a class level variable with the *Public* access modifier. Instances of class level variables should only be available to other objects via an appropriate method or property procedure – more on this later.

Class diagram for the *Form1* class

A class diagram can be used to show the class level variables and methods associated with a class. The class diagram shown in Figure 5.14 represents the class after Practical Activity 5.3 is complete. However, it only shows the class level variables and methods entered by the programmer (i.e. you). It does not represent the members that were automatically generated (remember a lot of work is done 'behind the scenes') by the IDE when the GUI was built, it also does not show the inherited methods.

Figure 5.14 Simplified class diagram for the form.

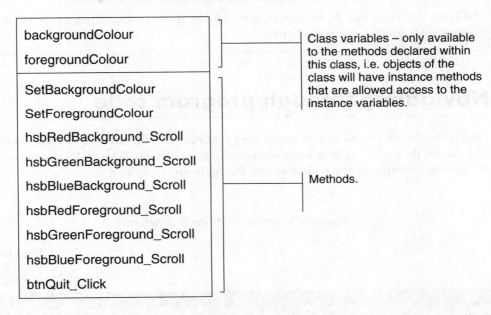

There are nine methods associated with the class; seven of the methods are event handling procedures and the other two are *Sub* methods.

QUESTION 5.2 (REVISION)

Which seven of the nine event methods listed in Figure 5.14 are event handlers?

Access modifiers and methods

Access modifiers are also used when declaring methods (as well as when declaring class level variables).

If a method is declared with a *Public* access modifier then the instance of a class in which the *Public* method resides can be sent a message from any object to invoke this *Public* instance method.

If a method is declared with a *Private* access modifier then the instance of a class in which the *Private* method resides cannot be sent a message from any object to invoke the *Private* method. *Private* methods can only be invoked from code (i.e. messages) within the instance of the class.

QUESTION 5.3 (DEVELOPMENT)

Use the VB .NET help to look up the meaning of the access modifier Protected *with respect to methods.*

NOTE: The coverage here of access modifiers is at an introductory level. A fuller treatment is given later in the book.

Navigating through program code

During the development of a program the programmer will, obviously, need to read, write and amend the code. The following sequence of screenshots (Figure 5.15) illustrates ways of navigating through an applications code during its development.

Figure 5.15 Navigating through program code.

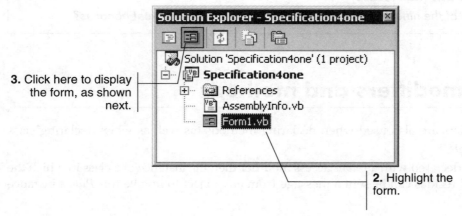

1. Click here to activate the Solution Explorer.

3. Click here to display the form, as shown next.

2. Highlight the form.

Figure 5.15 (cont.)

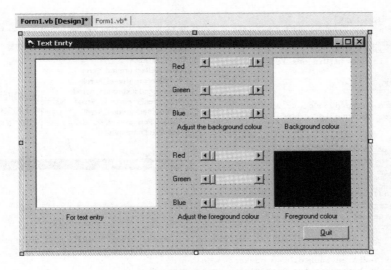

4. Click here to activate the code-editing window shown next.

5. Click here to open the drop-down list.

Figure 5.15 (cont.)

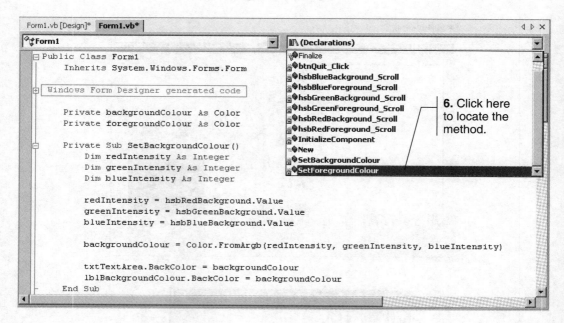

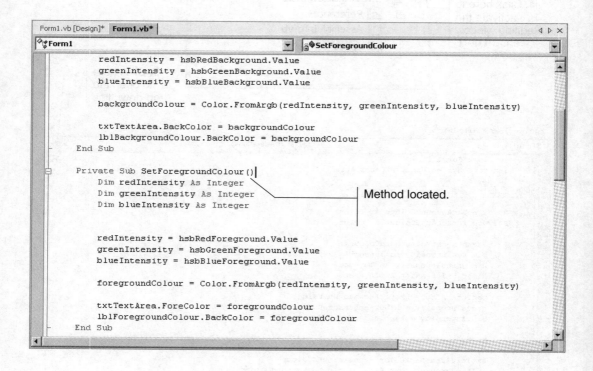

Figure 5.15 (cont.)

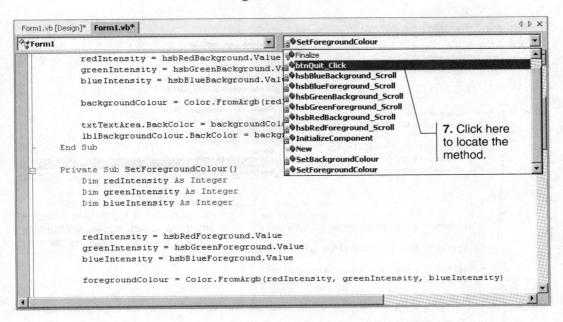

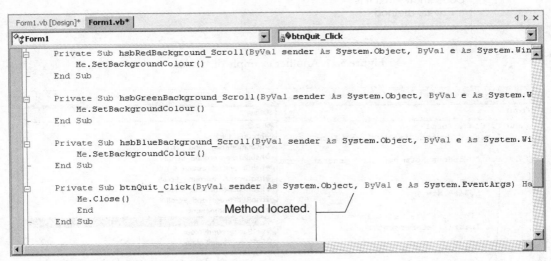

The icons used in the IDE

The IDE is a very graphical environment and it uses icons to ease the programmer's understanding of the code. Refer to the code-editing windows shown in Figures 5.16 and 5.17 for examples.

Figure 5.16 An example of an icon.

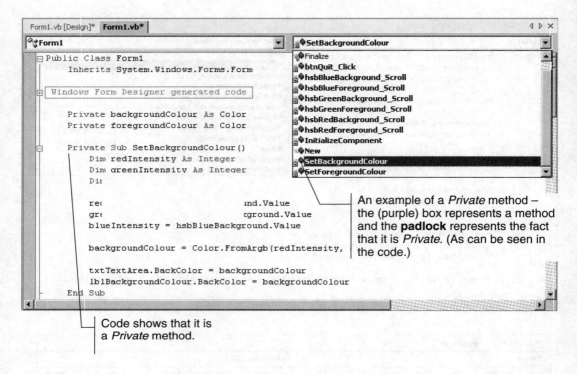

An example of a *Private* method – the (purple) box represents a method and the **padlock** represents the fact that it is *Private*. (As can be seen in the code.)

Code shows that it is a *Private* method.

Figure 5.17 Another example of an icon.

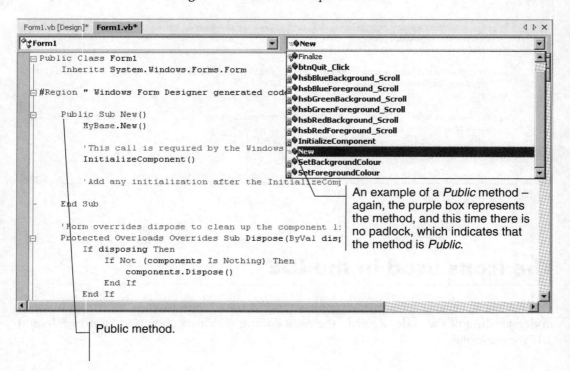

An example of a *Public* method – again, the purple box represents the method, and this time there is no padlock, which indicates that the method is *Public*.

Public method.

Figure 5.18 shows a couple of screenshots from the VB .NET help that shows some of the icons and their meaning.

Figure 5.18 Some of the icons used by the IDE.

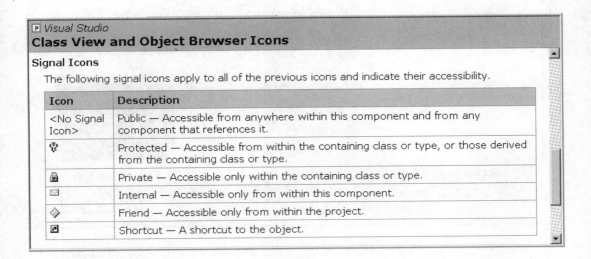

The constructor method

Constructors are special methods that allow control over the initialization of objects. They are run when an instance (an object) of a class is created. Every defined class automatically receives one default constructor. A programmer can add 'extra' constructor methods to a class using a process referred to as overloading (more on this later in the book).

Constructors can only be invoked when an object is being created (i.e. constructed). It is not possible to directly invoke a constructor using a message as in previous examples in this chapter.

NOTE: Later chapters will deal with constructors in more detail. The treatment here is meant as an introduction.

An example of a constructor in action will be demonstrated by amending the program that implemented Specification 4.1 that has been amended throughout this chapter. Figure 5.19 shows the GUI for this program with an extra button added.

Figure 5.19 The amended GUI.

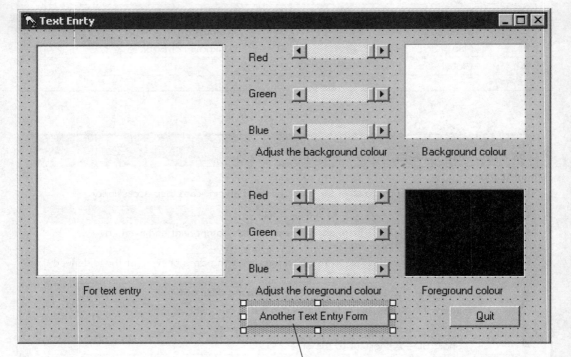

The *Text* property of the extra button is set to *Another Text Entry Form* and its *Name* property has been set to *btnAnotherTextEntryForm*.

The code for the event handling procedure 'attached' to this additional button is shown in Listing 5.9.

Listing 5.9 The additional code.

```
Private Sub btnAnotherTextEntryForm_Click(ByVal sender As System.Object, _
ByVal e As System.EventArgs) Handles btnAnotherTextEntryForm.Click

    Dim myNewForm As Form1

    myNewForm = New Form1()
    myNewForm.Show()
End Sub
```

The code for this short program is repeated in Figure 5.20 with line numbers.

Figure 5.20 The code with line numbers.

```
1.  Private Sub btnAnotherTextEntryForm_Click(ByVal sender As System.Object, _
    ByVal e As System.EventArgs) Handles btnAnotherTextEntryForm.Click

2.      Dim myNewForm As Form1

3.      myNewForm = New Form1()
4.      myNewForm.Show()
5.  End Sub
```

Line 1: This is the signature of the event handling procedure

Line 5: This marks the end of the event handling code.

Line 2: This declares a local variable with the identifier (name) *myNewForm* of the type *Form1*. This looks like a simple and straightforward declaration and it is. It looks no more complicated than declaring a variable of any type. However, the type *Form1* is in fact a class – more to the point it is the class used throughout this chapter and part of the last. It is the class that was created to produce the GUI shown in Figure 5.19 that has the code of Listings 5.1 through to 5.9 'attached'. Consequently, the variable *myNewForm* is able to store a reference to an instance of *Form1*.

Line 3: The previous line created a variable that is capable of storing a variable of type *Form1*. More precisely it can store a reference that 'points to' an instance of the *Form1* class. Line 3 creates this instance using the default constructor that is automatically supplied. This is further emphasized by Figure 5.21.

Line 4: The variable *myNewForm* holds a reference to an instance of the class *Form1*. Consequently, it has access to all of the members of this class. One of these members is the *Show()* method, which is **not** a method created by the programmer (i.e. you) during the development of the GUI shown in Figure 5.19 and the code of Listing 5.1 through to 5.9. This *Show()* method was inherited from the **base class** of *Form1* – this point is emphasized by Figure 5.22.

Figure 5.21 The creation of an object.

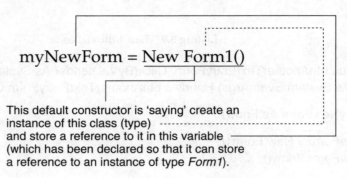

myNewForm = New Form1()

This default constructor is 'saying' create an
instance of this class (type)
and store a reference to it in this variable
(which has been declared so that it can store
a reference to an instance of type *Form1*).

Figure 5.22 The Form1 class and its base class.

This line shows
that the form
you have been
developing is
indeed a class.

This line shows that the form you have
been developing **inherits** from the
Windows Form class. Therefore this
Windows Form class is the *base* of the
Form1 class.
Instances of the *Form1* class have
rights over the members of the base
class, that is, instances of *Form1* can
use, for example, the methods of
the base class (such as *Show()*)
as well as its own methods (such
as *SetBackgroundColour()*).

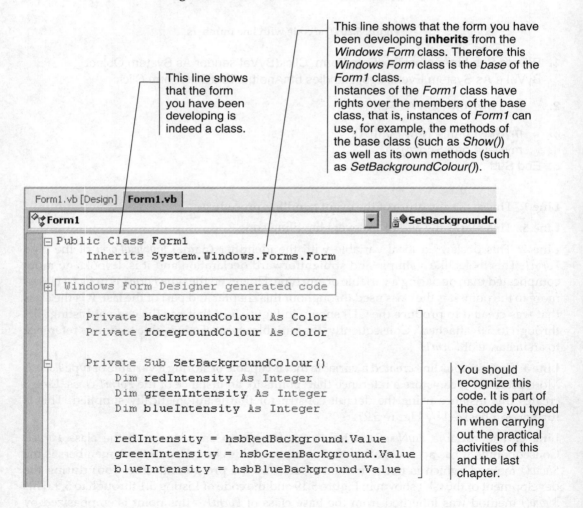

```
Form1.vb [Design]   Form1.vb

Form1                                          SetBackgroundC

Public Class Form1
     Inherits System.Windows.Forms.Form

 Windows Form Designer generated code

     Private backgroundColour As Color
     Private foregroundColour As Color

     Private Sub SetBackgroundColour()
         Dim redIntensity As Integer
         Dim greenIntensity As Integer
         Dim blueIntensity As Integer

         redIntensity = hsbRedBackground.Value
         greenIntensity = hsbGreenBackground.Value
         blueIntensity = hsbBlueBackground.Value
```

You should
recognize this
code. It is part of
the code you typed
in when carrying
out the practical
activities of this
and the last
chapter.

The effect of the execution of line 4 is the displaying of another instance of Form1. Figures 5.23 and 5.24 show typical example runtimes for this amended program.

Figure 5.23 An example runtime.

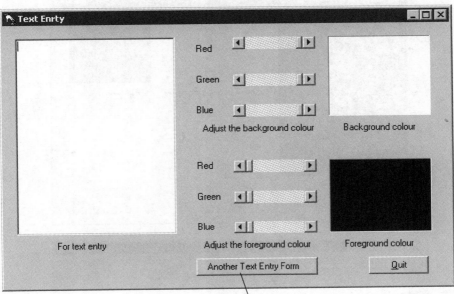

1. Click here and another instance of the form appears, as shown below.

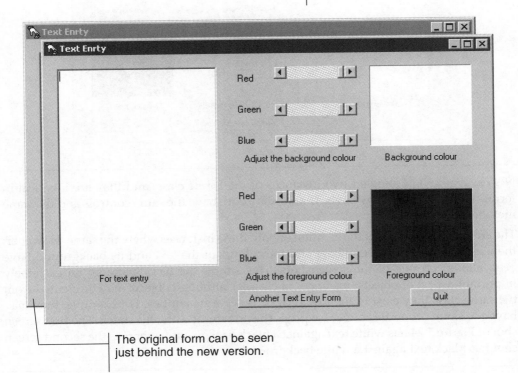

The original form can be seen just behind the new version.

Figure 5.24 An example runtime, showing that two instances of the *Form1* class are displayed. Each instance has been created from the same template (i.e. the same class) and therefore they have all the same members. (**Note**: the user has moved the scrollbars.)

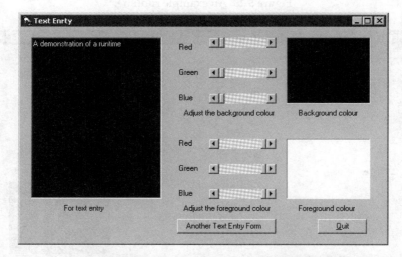

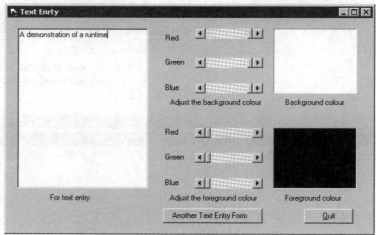

NOTE: Figure 5.24 showed two instances of the *Form1* class, and they are identical in terms of the members they have. That is, they both have the same controls and the same methods and properties.

The **state** of the controls at the creation of both these instances where the same. However, the user has moved the scrollbars and the colours of the text and its background have been altered on one of the screenshots. This simple act has illustrated an extremely important aspect of objects (instances of classes): although objects may be created from the same class they exist in their own right as separate entities. For example, they may have the same properties but these properties can be at different states. The first screen shot of Figure 5.24 has white text against a black background, whereas the second screen shot has black text against a white background.

NOTE: It is worth reflecting on what has been achieved here. The development of the original form was time consuming; it required the positioning of buttons, labels, textboxes and the attaching of event handling procedures. Figure 5.24 shows how we can easily have more than one copy of this form without having to go through the process of positioning the controls and attaching the event handling procedures. One declaration and two lines of code and you have another copy! Click the button more than once and you have more copies, as can be seen by Figure 5.25.

Figure 5.25 An example runtime.

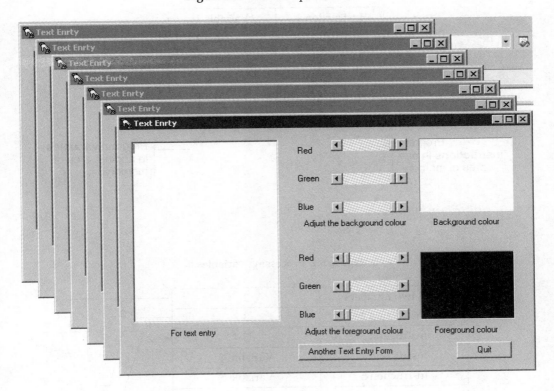

PRACTICAL ACTIVITY 5.4

Implement the amendments as suggested by Figure 5.19 and Listing 5.9. Run the program and experiment with the runtime, e.g. click the additional button more than once; change the colours on some of the forms, etc.

6 Classes and objects

Before OOP (object-oriented programming) was introduced as a way of programming, the model of a computer program could be simply represented as in Figure 6.1. Here the program instructions and data were separated with the instructions processing the data (data was kept separate in variables).

Figure 6.1 An 'old' computer program model.

Instruction 1	Variable 1
Instruction 2	Variable 2
Instruction 3	Variable 3
Instruction 4	Variable 4
Instruction 5	Variable 5
Instruction 6	Variable 6

Program **instructions** in one area of memory.

Program **variables** in another area of memory.

Figure 6.2 Processing variables.

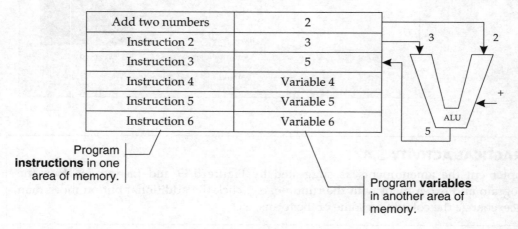

Add two numbers	2
Instruction 2	3
Instruction 3	5
Instruction 4	Variable 4
Instruction 5	Variable 5
Instruction 6	Variable 6

Program **instructions** in one area of memory.

Program **variables** in another area of memory.

Variable3 = Variable1 + Variable2 is an example of an instruction that would process data (as shown by Figure 6.2).

NOTE: This chapter relies on an understanding of variable types, which are covered in detail in a later chapter. However, for the time being it would be useful if you had a simple model of a variable type. Put simply, a variable stores data and this data may represent, for example, the number of cars leaving a production line or a person's name. A variable used to hold a number could be declared as an *Integer* type and a variable used to hold a name could be declared as a *String* type. An *Integer* variable cannot store a person's name and it usually takes up less memory than a string. You can arithmetically add numbers to a variable of type *Integer* but you cannot arithmetically add numbers to a *String* variable.

Therefore, think of variables, of different data types, as different size boxes that store different types of data that can be processed in different ways.

NOTE: OOP can and does use variables in the same way as all other kinds of programming languages. However, OOP **encapsulates methods** and **class level variables** into a class, from which objects are made. It is in this respect that OOP is different from 'older programming languages'. Class level variables and methods are no longer separate they are 'bound together' (i.e. encapsulated) within a class.

It is still possible to access a variable directly and statements like *Variable3 = Variable1 + Variable2* still exist. However, instances of class level variables should be accessed via an instance method and/or an instance property procedure.

Figures 6.3 and 6.4 illustrate suitable models for a Class in OOP.

Figure 6.3 An OOP class.

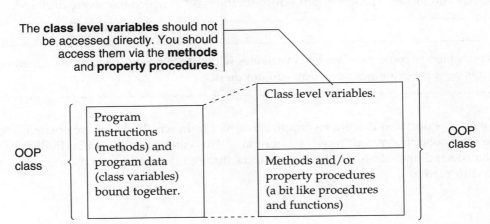

Figure 6.4 A suitable model for an object.

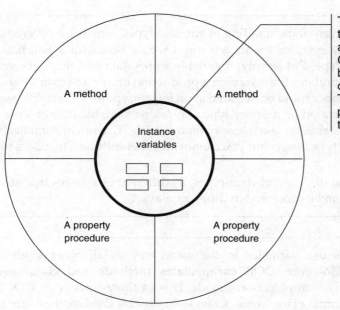

This bold circle is to indicate that the class level variables are **not** directly accessible. Class level variables can only be accessed via a method or property procedure.
Think of methods and property procedures as 'doorways' to the class level variables.

NOTE: Its methods **and/or** property procedures and class level variables define a class. Figure 6.4 illustrates that methods, property procedures and class level variables are **encapsulated** in a single entity.

Instances of the class level variables are in the middle 'surrounded' by methods and property procedures.

OOP practice recommends that class level variables are **not** directly available (i.e. not **exposed**) to all code in an application but rather they can only be accessed by the instance methods and instance property procedures of the class in which they were declared.

It is possible to expose the class level variables without the need for access via a method but it is poor programming practice – **do not do it!**

Once a class is declared it acts as a template (recipe) from which objects are created. There can be many objects created from the same class. This concept is illustrated by Figure 6.5 (and has been demonstrated in the last chapter through the creation of a form using the constructor method).

Figure 6.5 Illustrating the concept of object creation.

The recipe (class).

The loaves (objects) created from the recipe (class).

Once a useful class has been developed it can be 'stored in a library' and objects can be created from it anytime a developer requires such an object.

If a class exists that is almost what a developer requires but it does not quite have all the **behaviour** and **states** needed then a developer can use **inheritance** to achieve the desired requirements. For example, consider the recipe and loaves as represented by Figure 6.5. What if the requirement was to produce a currant loaf? Well rather than declare a completely new recipe the original recipe for the loaf could be referred to. That is, follow the recipe for the loaf but just before you finish kneading the dough add the currants. The result is a new recipe that has inherited all of the behaviour and states of the original loaf recipe. Figure 6.6 illustrates this relationship.

Figure 6.6 The relationship between two recipes (classes).

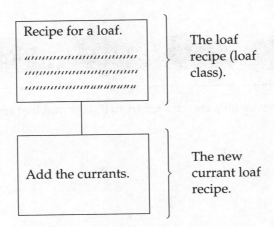

The loaf recipe (loaf class).

The new currant loaf recipe.

129

Within OOP the relationship between classes where one inherits from another is illustrated by Figure 6.7. **It is an example of a class hierarchy**.

Figure 6.7 A class hierarchy.

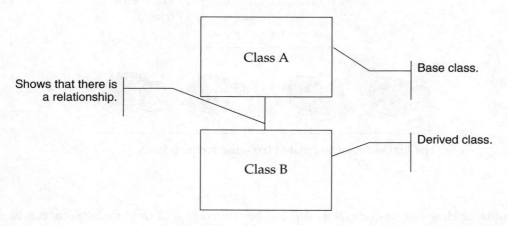

Figure 6.8 illustrates the concept of object creation from a class.

Figure 6.8 The concept of object creation.

The **currant** loaves (objects) created from the currant loaf recipe (class).

An example of a class and an object

Object-oriented design is able to represent real life objects. For example, consider a four-sided spinning top as shown in Figure 6.9.

Figure 6.9 A four-sided spinning top.

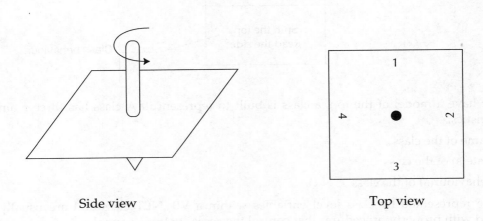

Side view   Top view

When the top stops spinning, it will come to rest on one of its four sides, which are labelled 1, 2, 3 and 4. The top could be used as a die for board games or as a 'probability tester'. If n represents the number of times the top is spun then as n gets larger (approaches infinity) the number of times it stops on any one side should be equal to $n/4$.

How is this object represented in OOD (object-oriented design)?

What can be said about the top? It is made out of plastic, it is a perfect square, it spins, it can be spun, it stops spinning, it comes to rest on one of its four sides, the spindle is threaded exactly through the centre of the square and so on. What is important, however, is what is of relevance for us to be able to model it with OOD and, ultimately, software?

Our modelling of the top (or any other object) concentrates on its relevant states and behaviour:

- A relevant **behaviour** is its ability to be spun
- A relevant **state** is the side it comes to rest on.

Figure 6.10 illustrates a model of the top (a simplified UML class diagram).

Figure 6.10 A model of the spinning top.

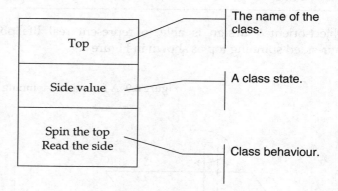

Once we have a model of the top, a class is built to represent it. A class has three main characteristics:

- the name of the class
- the state(s) of the class
- the behaviour(s) of the class.

States are represented by class level variables within a VB .NET class and are usually associated with property procedures that control the access to these variables.

Behaviours are implemented by methods within the VB .NET class and there are two kinds of methods (e.g. *Sub* methods, *Function* methods – see later).

NOTE: Methods can also be used to control access to the class level variables of a VB .NET class. Both method and property procedure access will be covered by the content of this book.

The example code shown in Figure 6.11 uses a method to access the class level variable, i.e. when an object of the class is constructed an instance method accesses an instance of the class level variable (i.e. an instance variable). The next chapter deals with property procedures.

Figure 6.11 shows the class based on the UML class diagram of Figure 6.10.

NOTE: The code shown in Figure 6.11 shows two kinds of methods: a *Function* method and a *Sub* method. When an instance of the class is created the instance of both these methods has access to the instance of the *sideValue* variable (as defined by the class level variable).

- A *Function* method can return data to the object that sent the message to invoke it.
- A *Sub* method is not used to return a value.

However, both types of methods exhibit behaviour, i.e. they can process data and therefore they offer a service on behalf of the object to which they 'belong'.

Figure 6.11 The *Top* Class.

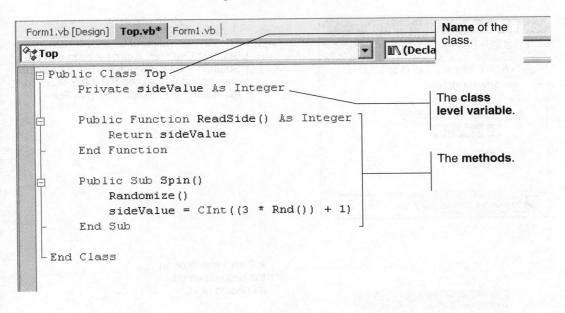

How to declare a VB .NET class

Figure 6.12 shows how to declare a class.

Figure 6.12 Declaring a class.

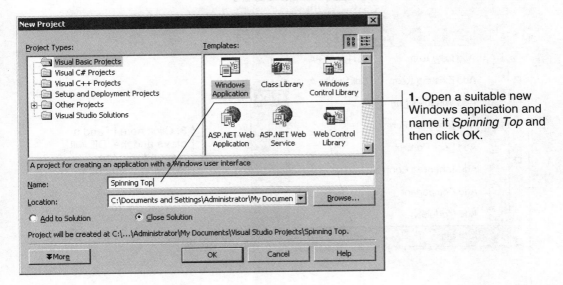

1. Open a suitable new Windows application and name it *Spinning Top* and then click OK.

Figure 6.12 (cont.)

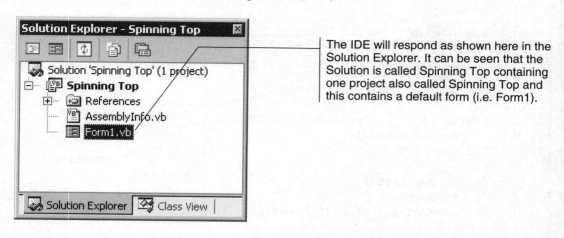

The IDE will respond as shown here in the Solution Explorer. It can be seen that the Solution is called Spinning Top containing one project also called Spinning Top and this contains a default form (i.e. Form1).

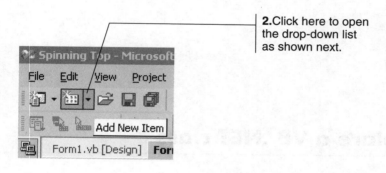

2.Click here to open the drop-down list as shown next.

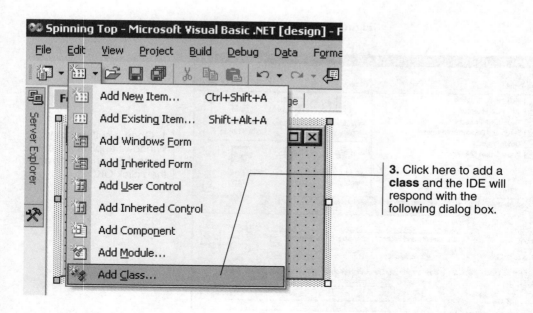

3. Click here to add a **class** and the IDE will respond with the following dialog box.

Figure 6.12 (cont.)

The IDE highlights this.

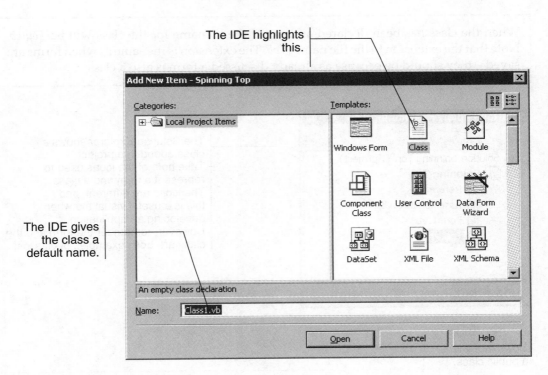

The IDE gives the class a default name.

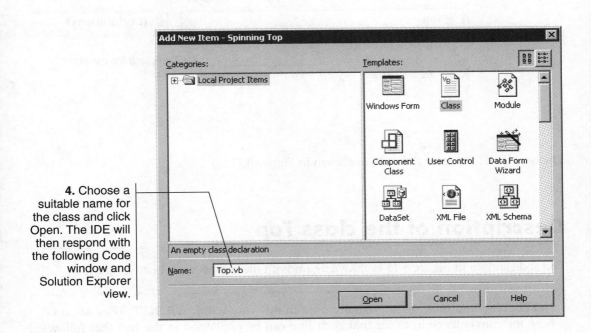

4. Choose a suitable name for the class and click Open. The IDE will then respond with the following Code window and Solution Explorer view.

Figure 6.12 (cont.)

When the class has been declared and saved the filename for the class will be *Top.vb*. Note that the extension to the file name is *vb*. The extension is the same as when forms are saved – they should be because as already discussed a form is also a class.

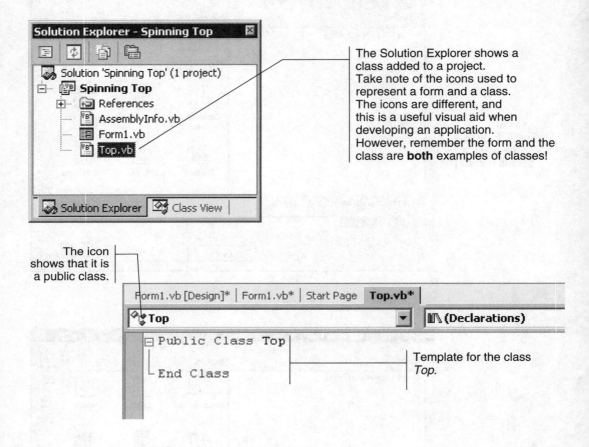

The Solution Explorer shows a class added to a project. Take note of the icons used to represent a form and a class. The icons are different, and this is a useful visual aid when developing an application. However, remember the form and the class are **both** examples of classes!

The icon shows that it is a public class.

Template for the class *Top*.

The next task is to enter the code as shown in Figure 6.11.

Description of the class *Top*

The code shown in Figure 6.11 is shown again with line numbers in Listing 6.1.

NOTE: Line numbers are not usually used in this way within VB .NET. They are used here for convenience in order that each line can be explained in the text that follows Listing 6.1.

Listing 6.1 The Top Class.

```
1.   Public Class Top
2.       Private sideValue As Integer

3.       Public Function ReadSide() As Integer
4.           Return sideValue
5.       End Function

6.       Public Sub Spin()
7.           Randomize()
8.           sideValue = CInt((3 * Rnd) + 1)
9.       End Sub
10.  End Class
```

Lines 1 and 10: These lines define the start and end of the **class** definition. Line 1 specifies that it is a *Public* class with the name *Top*.

Line 2:

Private sideValue As Integer

This line declares a class level variable named *sideValue* of type *Integer* (which means it is capable of storing a whole number) and with *Private* scope (which means it is only available to code within the class: more accurately an instance of the class level variable is available to instances of the code within an object of the class).

Lines 3 to 5: These lines declare a method that is capable of returning a value to the object invoking it (i.e. messaging it). When a method is required to return data then the keyword *Function* is used (there are other ways of returning data and they will be covered later in the book).

- **Line 3** defines a *Public* method, which means it can be invoked by other objects. It is said in OOP terminology that the object derived from this class **exposes** this method. The name of the method is *ReadSide()* and it returns an integer. All this is illustrated by Figure 6.13.

Figure 6.13 A close look at line 3.

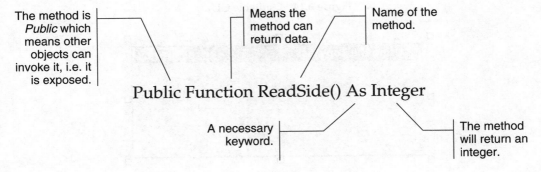

The method is *Public* which means other objects can invoke it, i.e. it is exposed.

Means the method can return data.

Name of the method.

Public Function ReadSide() As Integer

A necessary keyword.

The method will return an integer.

- **Line 4** uses the *Return* statement to return the content of the instance of the **class level variable** *sideValue* to whatever invokes the *ReadSide()* method. The class variable was declared as an integer and the function indicates that it will return an integer.

> **NOTE**: A **property procedure** is another, often preferred, mechanism for returning values of a class level variable instance – more on this later.

- **Line 5** ends the definition of the *ReadSide()* method.

Lines 6 to 9: These lines declare a method that is capable of generating a random number from 1 to 4.

- **Line 6**: This line declares a *Public* (and therefore exposed) method (which means it can be called by other objects) named *Spin()*. Note it does not use the keyword *Function* because it is not returning data to whatever invokes it instead it uses *Sub*.

- **Line 7**: Randomize() is used before *Rnd* to ensure that *Rnd* generates a different sequence of random numbers each time *Rnd* is used.

- **Line 8**: On the right-hand side of the assignment statement a random number between 1 and 4 is generated and assigned to the class level variable *sideValue* (i.e. an instance of this class level variable). *CInt* is used to convert the number generated inside the brackets to an Integer. This is necessary because *sideValue* has been declared as an *Integer* and the right-hand side generates a non-integer numeric because *Rnd* does not return a whole number.

- **Line 9**: This line ends the declaration of the method *Spin()*.

Using the class *Top*

Having defined a class to represent a spinning top the next task is to use it. This will involve creating an instance of this class (i.e. an object) and then messaging it from another object. A form object will be used to create and then use the members, of an object, of the *Top* class. A suitable GUI for this task is shown in Figure 6.14 – it consists of a label and a button. The event handling procedure attached to the button will be used to create an object of the *Top* class and then use its members. The label is used to display the number generated by the spinning top.

Figure 6.14 A suitable GUI.

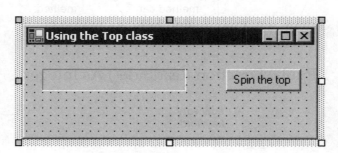

Figure 6.15 shows the code that needs to be attached to the button.

Figure 6.15 The event handling procedure.

```
Form1.vb [Design]   Form1.vb   Start Page | Top.vb                                          ◁ ▷ ×
Form1                                            ▼    btnSpin_Click                          ▼
  Public Class Form1
        Inherits System.Windows.Forms.Form

    Windows Form Designer generated code

        Private Sub btnSpin_Click(ByVal sender As System.Object, ByVal e As System.EventArgs) Ha
            Dim myTop As Top
            Dim numberGenerated As Integer

            myTop = New Top()
            myTop.Spin()
            numberGenerated = myTop.ReadSide()
            lblDisplay.Text = "The number generated is " & CStr(numberGenerated)
        End Sub
    End Class
```

Figure 6.16 shows a typical runtime.

Figure 6.16 A typical runtime.

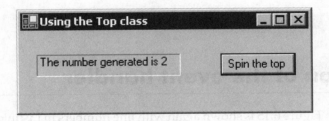

Communication between objects

The application being built has two classes (*Form1* and *Top*) and an instance of each. When run there will be two objects, one created from the *Form1* class and one created from the *Top* class. There will be communication between these objects in the form of two **messages**. The form object sends the messages to the *Top* object. This concept is shown in Figure 6.17 (**not** UML).

The *Top* class has one class variable (*sideValue*) and two methods, and Figure 6.17 shows the class variable 'surrounded by' two methods. This class variable is **not** available to outside objects and can only be accessed via its own class's methods. The *Form1* object communicates with the *myTop* object by sending it a message asking it to spin (i.e. invoke the *Spin()* method of the *myTop* object). The *Form1* object follows up this communication by sending another message that requests a copy of the data stored in the *myTop* objects copy of (i.e. instance variable) the class level variable *sideValue*. This second message results in the data being returned. This returned data is displayed in the label on the form.

Figure 6.17 The concept of communication between objects.

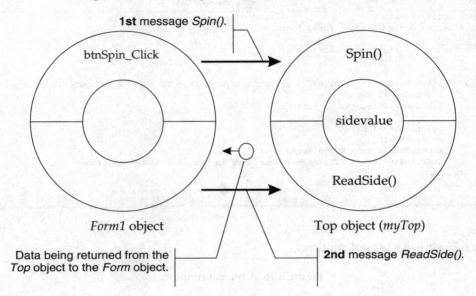

Description of the event handler

The code shown in Figure 6.15 is shown again with line numbers in Listing 6.2 – it is a button click event handling procedurer used to create and then message an instance of the *Top* class.

Listing 6.2 The event handler.

```
1.    Private Sub btnSpin_Click(ByVal sender As System.Object, ByVal e As _
      System.EventArgs) Handles btnSpin.Click

2.        Dim myTop As Top
3.        Dim numberGenerated As Integer

4.        myTop = New Top()
5.        myTop.Spin()
6.        numberGenerated = myTop.ReadSide()
7.        lblDisplay.Text = "The number generated is " & CStr(numberGenerated)
8.    End Sub
```

Lines 1 and 8: These are automatically produced by the IDE.

Line 2: This declares a **local variable** *myTop* of type *Top*. Now *Top* is a class and this means that *myTop* is able to reference an object of the class *Top*. This line does **not** create an object of class *Top*.

NOTE: A class can be, and often is, referred to as an abstract data type (ADT). Consequently, it is acceptable to refer to *myTop* as a variable of **type** *Top*.

NOTE: At this point it is worthwhile emphasizing the difference between local and class level variables. A class level variable is a variable 'scoped' to be accessed by **all** of the code within a class. For example, if a class had five methods and four property procedures (or any number of both) the program statements within **all** of these methods and property procedures would have access to an instance of a class level variable.

However, when a variable is declared inside a method then only the program statements within that method have access to it. The variable is said to be a local variable.

A class level variable instance only exists for the lifetime of an instance of the class (i.e. the lifetime of the object). A local variable only exists for the lifetime of the method execution (i.e. it is exists while the method is executing its program statements).

To ensure a distinction is made between class level and local variables, class level variables are often referred to as fields.

The diagram below uses an example of an object model (as shown in Figure 6.4) to emphasize the distinction between instances of class level and local variables. It shows an object with two class level variables and two methods.

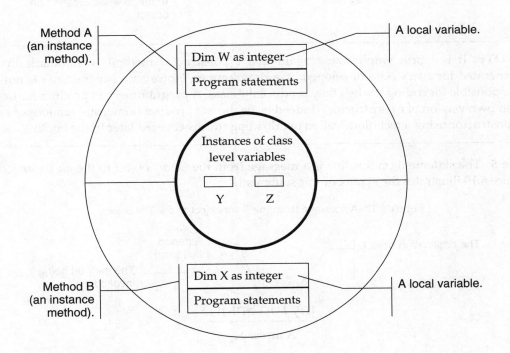

The program statements within *MethodA* can access its local variable *W*, and they can also access both of the instances of the class level variables *Y* and *Z*. However, the program statements within *MethodA* do not have access to the local variable *X*, as *X* is local to *MethodB*.

The program statements within *MethodB* can access its local variable *X*, and they can also access both of the class level variables instances *Y* and *Z*. However, the program statements within *MethodB* do not have access to the local variable *W*, as *W* is local to *MethodA*.

Line 3: This declares a local variable *numberGenerated* of type *Integer* that is used to store the number returned from messaging the instance of the *Top* class. Of course, this number is the number generated by the spinning top.

Line 4: This line is responsible for creating an object of class *Top* – this object will be known as *myTop*. The general format for creating an object of a class is shown in Figure 6.18.

Figure 6.18 How to create an object.

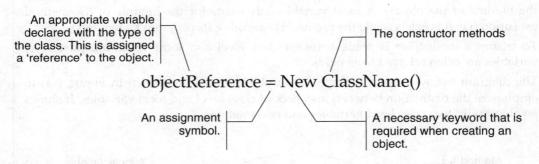

NOTE: It is worth emphasizing again that a constructor method is automatically generated for every class developed by a programmer. However a programmer is **not** responsible for coding it when they produce the class. A programmer can produce his or her own version of a constructor – indeed he or she can produce numerous versions of a constructor using a technique called overloading (this is covered later in the book).

Line 5: The statement on this line is a **message** from the *Form1* object to the *myTop* object. Figure 6.19 illustrates the syntax of this statement.

Figure 6.19 A message from the *Form* object to the *Top* object.

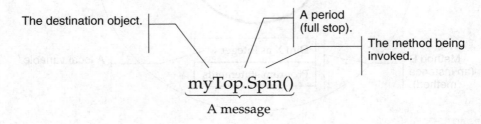

The effect of this message is to set an instance of the class level variable *sideValue* within the *myTop* object to a random number from 1 to 4. More to the point, the *Form1* instance of the object asks the *myTop* object to set its instance of the class level variable (that is, the class variable *sideValue* of the *Top* class) to a random number.

Line 6:   The statement on this line is another message from the *Form1* object to the *myTop* object. This message obtains a copy of the value stored in *sideValue* and assigns it to the local variable *numberGenerated*. Note that access to *sideValue* had to be **via** the *ReadSide()* function method – direct access was not allowed as *sideValue* was declared with the access modifier *Private*, i.e. *sideValue* was not exposed.

Line 7:   This statement converts the integer stored in *numberGenerated* to a string using *CStr*. It then concatenates this with the literal string *The number generated is* and assigns this string to the *Text* property of the label.

Icons are used to assist programmers

Figure 6.20 shows a view of a code window for the *Top* class. This view highlights the **signature** of the function method (the first line of the method) within the class and the callout labels highlight the corresponding icon. This use of icons eases the programmer's reading of the code.

Figure 6.20 The use of the graphic icons within the IDE.

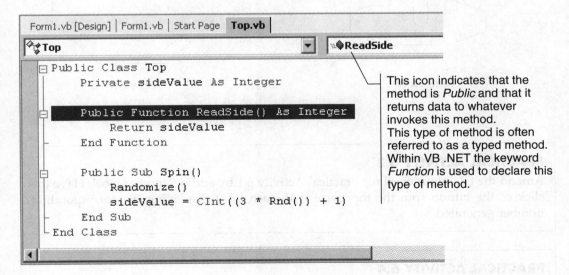

PRACTICAL ACTIVITY 6.1

Develop the *Top.vb* class and build the GUI as represented by Figure 6.14. Attach the event handling procedure to the button and run the application.

PRACTICAL ACTIVITY 6.2

For the eight-sided spinning top (object) shown in Figure 6.21 do the following:

1. Produce a UML class diagram for this object similar to the one shown in Figure 6.10.
2. Build a suitable class to represent this top and call the class *SpinningOctTop*.
3. Develop a suitable form class (i.e. GUI) that spins the top and displays the generated number in a label. In other words, develop a GUI similar to Figure 6.14 and attach a suitable event handling procedure to the button.
4. Run the application and ensure that it generates numbers from 1 to 8.

HINT: The following VB .NET statement can generate a number from 1 to 8:

sideValue = CInt((7 * Rnd) + 1)

Figure 6.21 The oct spinning top.

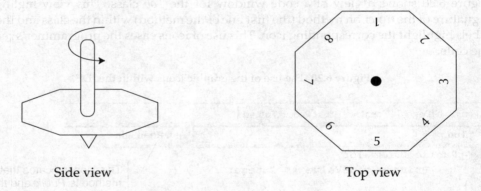

Side view   Top view

PRACTICAL ACTIVITY 6.3

Amend the GUI developed for Practical Activity 6.1 by adding another label. Have the click of the button spin the top twice with each label displaying the corresponding number generated.

PRACTICAL ACTIVITY 6.4

Using the GUI developed for Practical Activity 6.3, amend the click event handler attached to the button so that it creates two instances of the *Top* class (i.e. two spinning tops) and spins both. Have one label display the number generated by the first spinning top and have the other label display the number generated by the second spinning top.

The *Random* class

VB .NET has a very useful *Random* class that has many useful members. To use the members of this class requires the instantiating of the class, i.e., an object of this class needs to be created. The following figures and program listings show how to use some of the members of an object of the *Random* class.

> **NOTE**: In order to avoid the need to build GUIs the features of the *Random* class will be developed and discussed within a **Console application** (refer to Figure 1.40 on how to start a Console application). Consequently all of the screen shots refer to a Console application. All of the features of the *Random* class can also be used within a Windows application.

Figure 6.22 shows the declaration of a variable of type *Random*, note how the **intellisense** feature of the VB .NET IDE produces a drop-down list from which choices of classes (etc.) can be chosen.

Figure 6.22 Intellisense in action.

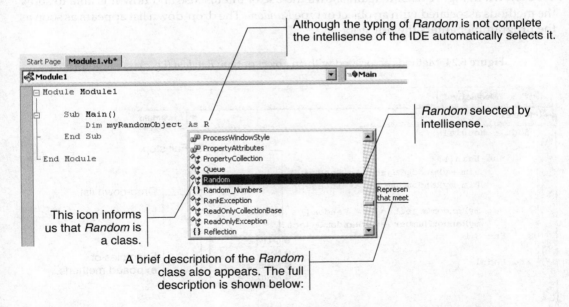

Figure 6.23 shows how to create an object of the *Random* class. Again note the intellisense feature.

Figure 6.23 Creating an object using intellisense.

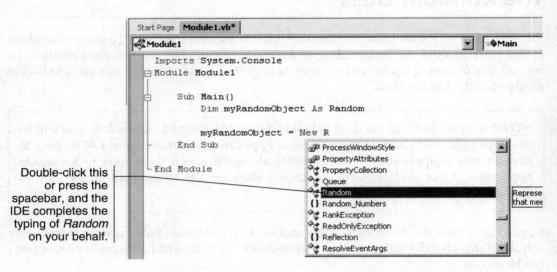

Double-click this or press the spacebar, and the IDE completes the typing of *Random* on your behalf.

Figure 6.24 shows the listing after an integer variable has been declared in addition to the code shown in Figure 6.23. It again shows the use of intellisense and how it is able to show the methods associated with an object of type *Random*. The drop-down list appears as soon as the programmer enters the full stop.

Figure 6.24 Methods associated with an object of type *Random* (i.e. class random).

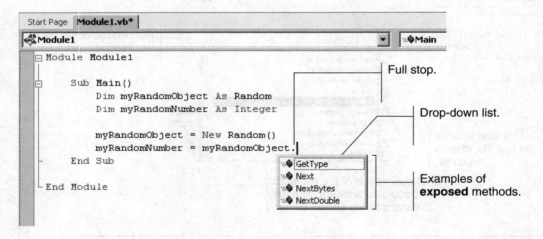

Figure 6.25 shows the code-editor window after the programmer has chosen the method *Next* and is deciding on which version of *Next* to use.

Figure 6.25 Completing the message.

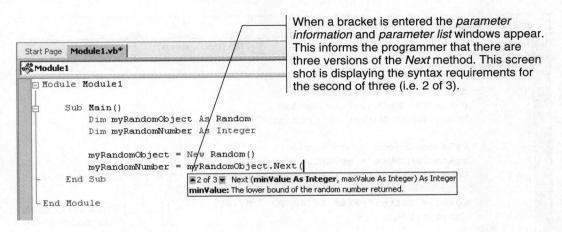

When a bracket is entered the *parameter information* and *parameter list* windows appear. This informs the programmer that there are three versions of the *Next* method. This screen shot is displaying the syntax requirements for the second of three (i.e. 2 of 3).

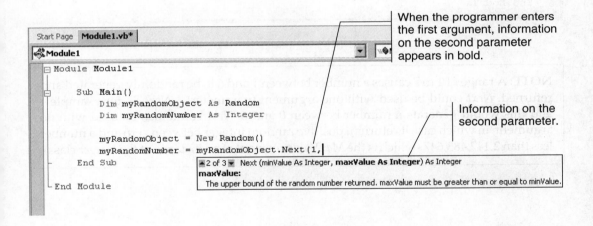

When the programmer enters the first argument, information on the second parameter appears in bold.

Information on the second parameter.

The method *Next* is an **overloaded** method that generates a random number. This means that there is more than one *Next* method; each version takes a different set of parameters.

If we required the generation of a number in the range 1 to 6 then the *Next* method needs to take two parameters that specify this range. Figure 6.26 shows the completion of the program developed during Figures 6.22 to 6.25. The number generated is output to the console using *WriteLine* as shown. The last two lines ensure that the console does not disappear from view until the user presses Enter. Obviously, this allows the user to see the output from the program.

Figure 6.26 The completed program.

```
Start Page   Module1.vb*
Module1                                    (Declarations)
 Module Module1

     Sub Main()
         Dim myRandomObject As Random
         Dim myRandomNumber As Integer

         myRandomObject = New Random()
         myRandomNumber = myRandomObject.Next(1, 7)
         Console.WriteLine("The number generated is " & CStr(myRandomNumber)

         Console.Write("PRESS ENTER TO CONTINUE ... ")        Stops the Console
         Console.Read()                                       disappearing from
     End Sub                                                  view.

 End Module
```

NOTE: A range of 1 to 7 causes a number between 1 and 6 to be randomly generated and returned. *Next* could be used with one argument (parameter) – *Next(7)*, for example – and this would generate a number between 0 and 6. *Next* could also be used with no argument, in which case it returns a positive random integer between zero and a number less than 2,147,483,647 (which is the *MaxValue* constant of an instance of the *Integer* class).

Creating an object at declaration

VB .NET is able to initialize a variable at declaration. Consequently, instead of declaring a variable and then initializing it with a program statement it can be done on one line as shown below:

Dim myVariable As Integer = 3.

Of course, a class is an example of a type, so an object can be constructed on one line, as shown in Figure 6.27.

Figure 6.27 Constructing at declaration.

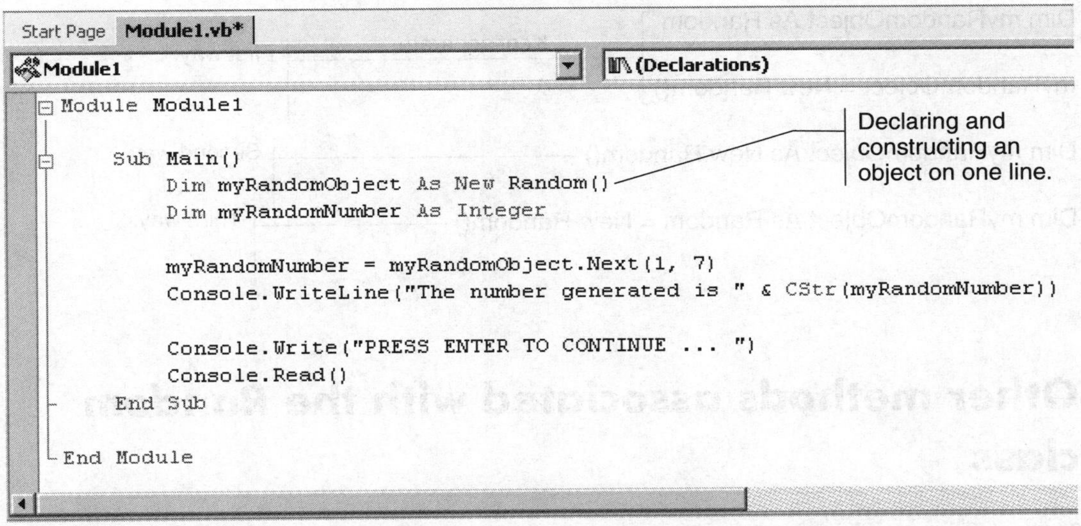

```
Start Page   Module1.vb*

Module1                                    ▼    (Declarations)

  Module Module1                                          Declaring and
                                                          constructing an
     Sub Main()                                           object on one line.
         Dim myRandomObject As New Random()
         Dim myRandomNumber As Integer

         myRandomNumber = myRandomObject.Next(1, 7)
         Console.WriteLine("The number generated is " & CStr(myRandomNumber))

         Console.Write("PRESS ENTER TO CONTINUE ... ")
         Console.Read()
     End Sub

  End Module
```

There is a third way, as shown by Figure 6.28.

Figure 6.28 The third way.

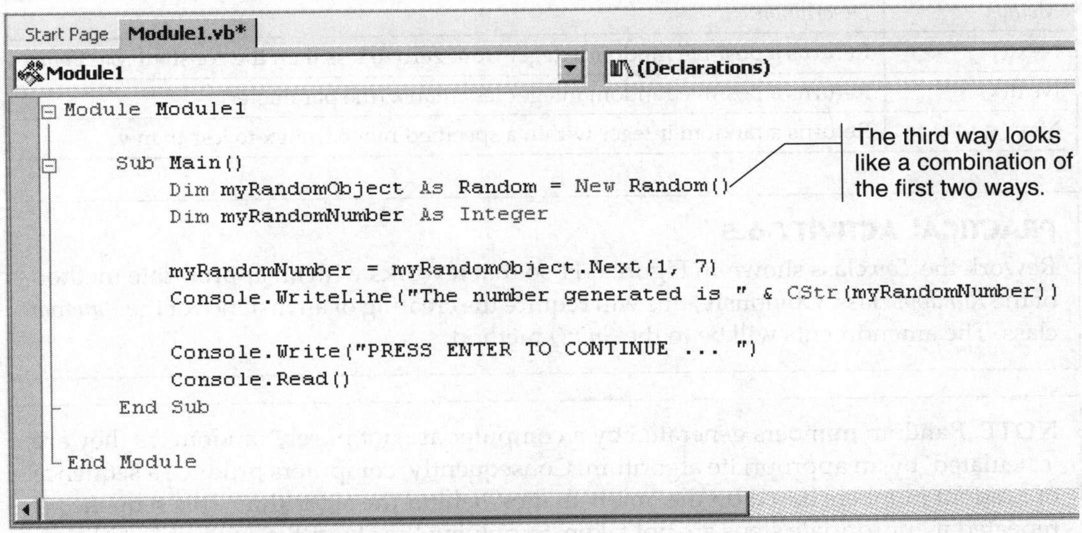

```
Start Page   Module1.vb*

Module1                                    ▼    (Declarations)

  Module Module1
                                                          The third way looks
     Sub Main()                                           like a combination of
         Dim myRandomObject As Random = New Random()      the first two ways.
         Dim myRandomNumber As Integer

         myRandomNumber = myRandomObject.Next(1, 7)
         Console.WriteLine("The number generated is " & CStr(myRandomNumber))

         Console.Write("PRESS ENTER TO CONTINUE ... ")
         Console.Read()
     End Sub

  End Module
```

Figure 6.29 lists all three ways to allow for a direct comparison. Which way you choose at this stage of your understanding is up to you. I would suggest that you keep the declaration and the construction separate.

Figure 6.29 Three ways of creating an object.

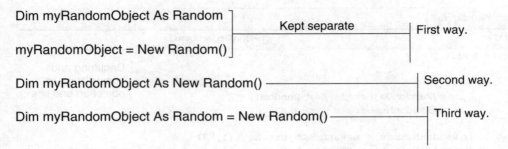

Other methods associated with the *Random* class

The intellisense of Figure 6.24 indicated the methods associated with an object of the *Random* class. A brief description of the *Next* method and its overloaded versions is shown in Table 6.1.

Table 6.1 *Next* and its overloaded versions.

Method	Description
Next()	Returns a positive random integer from zero to less than the constant *MaxValue*.
Next(x)	Returns a positive random integer less than x (the parameter)
Next(x, y)	Returns a random integer within a specified range from x to less than y.

PRACTICAL ACTIVITY 6.5

Rework the *Top* class shown in Figure 6.11 so that it works with an appropriate method of the *Random* class. Obviously, this will require the creating of an instance of the *Random* class. The amendments will be to the *Spin()* method.

NOTE: Random numbers generated by a computer are not purely random, as they are 'calculated' by an appropriate algorithm. Consequently, computers produce a sequence of random numbers based on the 'mathematics' behind the algorithm. This sequence is repeated if appropriate steps are not taken. Supplying the algorithm with an initializing number (called a **seed**) will produce a sequence associated with this seed. Ensuring that a different seed is given each time you require a random number will assist in producing a different sequence of random numbers. This seed can be derived from the system clock, which will ensure that it is different each time an instance of the *Random* class is created. Alternatively, the programmer can supply a seed during the construction of an object of the *Random* class.

There are two constructor methods associated with the *Random* class; they are listed and described in Table 6.2.

Table 6.2 The *Random* class constructor methods.

Method	Description
New()	Initializes an instance of the random number generator, using the default seed, which is based on the date and time and will therefore vary each time the object is constructed.
New(x)	Initializes an instance of the random number generator, using the specified seed passed as an argument.

PRACTICAL ACTIVITY 6.6

Experiment with the *Random* class constructor. Construct an object using the seed 3 and observe the number generated each time the Console application is executed.

Change the seed and make the same observation.

This experiment is best observed using a loop that will execute the *Next* method a number of times. Figure 6.30 illustrates a program using a loop that repeats ten times – just enter the program and observe the effect each time the application is executed (how loops work is covered in a later chapter).

Figure 6.30 Generating random numbers.

```
Start Page  Module1.vb
Module1                                           (Declarations)

Module Module1

    Sub Main()
        Dim myRandomObject As Random
        Dim myRandomNumber As Integer
        Dim i As Integer

        myRandomObject = New Random(3)
        For i = 0 To 9
            myRandomNumber = myRandomObject.Next(1, 7)
            Console.WriteLine("The number generated is " & CStr(myRandomNumber))
        Next i

        Console.Write("PRESS ENTER TO CONTINUE ... ")
        Console.Read()
    End Sub

End Module
```

Seed of three.

Using shared methods

This chapter so far has shown how to build a class (*Top*), **then** create an object of this class and **then** use its members. It then went on to show how to use an object of a class that exists within the hierarchy of VB .NET (i.e. the *Random* Class).

Both of these examples required the instantiating of the class in order to use its members, that is, an object had to be created to use the methods.

> **NOTE**: Methods that can only be invoked (messaged) when an object is created are referred to as **instance methods**.

It is possible to build a class that contains members that can be used without the need for creating an instance of the class. One such example within the VB .NET hierarchy is the *Math* class.

The program shown in Listing 6.3 uses the *Max* method of the *Math* class to find the biggest integer.

Listing 6.3   Using a shared method from the Math class.

```
Sub Main()
   Dim x As Integer

   x = Math.Max(5, 6)
   Console.WriteLine("The biggest number is " & CStr(x))

   Console.Write("PRESS ENTER TO CONTINUE ")
   Console.Read()
End Sub
```

The line containing the *Max* method (shown in bold) takes two integers (5 and 6) and returns the larger to the integer variable *x*. This method was appended to the name of the **class** (Math) after the full stop. This is emphasized by Figure 6.31. What should be noted is that it was not necessary to create an instance of the *Math* class. This particular member of the Math class is referred to as a **shared method**.

Figure 6.31 Using a *shared* method.

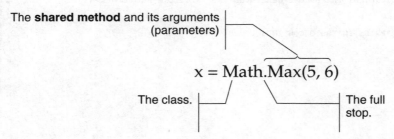

NOTE: Shared methods are sometimes referred to as class methods, as opposed to instance methods when an object is required. I recommend that you use the terms shared methods and instance methods to distinguish between these types of methods.

To create a shared method when defining a class requires the use of the keyword *Shared*.

NOTE: It is also possible to have shared class variables as opposed to instance class variables.

To create a shared class variable when defining a class also requires the use of the keyword *Shared*.

Figure 6.32 shows a screenshot of the intellisense associated with the *Math* class; it can be seen that there are numerous shared members.

Figure 6.32 Other members of the *Math* class.

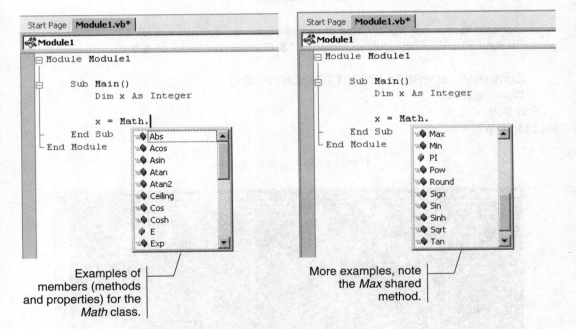

Examples of members (methods and properties) for the *Math* class.

More examples, note the *Max* shared method.

The implementation of Specification 6.1 within a console application illustrates the use of other members of the *Math* class, namely the *PI* constant and the *Round* method. Again, an object of the *Math* class was **not** required in order to use these members. Listing 6.4 shows the program that is the solution to Specification 6.1, and Figure 6.33 shows a typical runtime.

SPECIFICATION 6.1

*Write a program to read the radius of a circle and then calculate the circle's circumference.
It then displays the radius and circumference of the circle.*

Listing 6.4 Solution to Specification 6.1.

```
Module Module1

    Sub Main()
        Dim radius As Double
        Dim circumference As Double

        Console.Write("Please enter the radius of the circle in metres ")
        radius = CDbl(Console.ReadLine())

        circumference = 2 * Math.PI * radius
        circumference = Math.Round(circumference)

        Console.WriteLine("For a circle of radius equal to " & CStr(radius) & _
        "m the circumference after rounding is " & CStr(circumference) & "m")

        Console.Write("PRESS ENTER TO CONTINUE ")
        Console.Read()
    End Sub
End Module
```

Figure 6.33 A typical runtime.

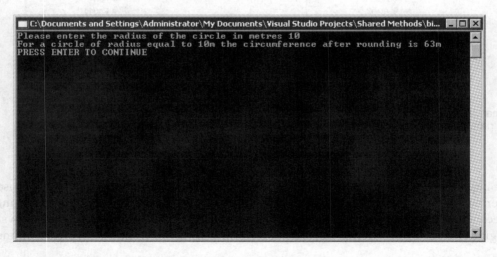

Table 6.3 lists some of the members of the *Math* class together with a brief description. To use any of these members precede them with *Math* and a full stop, e.g. *Math.PI* and *Math.Ceil(5,6)*.

Table 6.3 Members of the *Math* class

Members	Description
PI	This is a *Public* constant of the *Math* class and consequently is exposed to all code. A constant is a named value that is fixed and cannot be altered throughout the execution of a program. *Public Const PI As Double* The value of this constant is 3.14159265358979323846
E	This is *Public* constant of the *Math* class and consequently is exposed to all code. *Public Const E As Double* The value of this constant is 2.7182818284590452354
Abs	An overloaded, public and shared method that returns the absolute value of a *Decimal* type number.
Ceiling	A public and shared method that returns the smallest whole number greater than or equal to the specified number.
Floor	A public and shared method that returns the largest whole number less than or equal to the specified number.
Max	An overloaded, public and shared method that returns the larger of two numeric type variables.
Min	An overloaded, public and shared method that returns the smaller of two numeric type variables.

PRACTICAL ACTIVITY 6.7

Implement Specification 6.1 (i.e. enter and run Listing 6.4).

PRACTICAL ACTIVITY 6.8

Implement Specification 6.2.

Hint: use the shared method *Min*.

SPECIFICATION 6.2

Write a Console application to read two integers and display the smaller.

Overloaded methods

Overloading a method means defining it in multiple versions using the same name but with different **signatures**. The purpose of overloading is to define several closely related versions of a method without having to differentiate them by name.

> **NOTE:** The signature of a method is the template against which the compiler checks that the call correctly matches the declaration or definition of the method. The signature consists of the following items: the name of the method, the number, order, and data types of the arguments.

What is gained by overloading a method?

Consider the *Max* method of the *Math* class. As already observed this method finds and returns the larger of two numbers sent to it as arguments (parameters). There are various versions of the *Max* method and the intellisense associated with the IDE is able to illustrate this, as shown in Figure 6.34.

Figure 6.34 Intellisense showing overloaded methods.

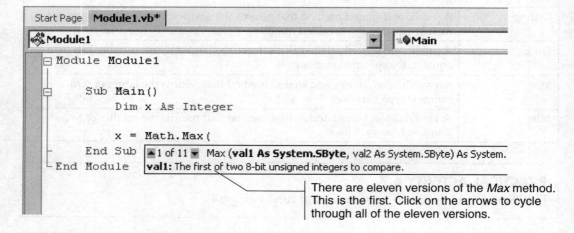

The version of the *Max* method shown in Figure 6.34 allows the arguments of the method to be of type *SByte*, and the return from this method is also of type *SByte*. Figure 6.35 shows another version of the *Max* method.

Figure 6.35 Another version of the *Max* method.

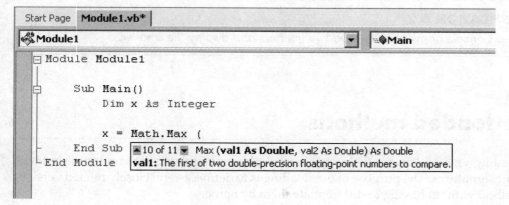

The version of *Max()* shown in Figure 6.35 is the tenth of eleven and indicates that it will take arguments of type *Double* and return the largest *Double*.

The answer to the question 'What is gained by overloading a method?' is, in this case, that the method is able to find the larger of two numbers of varying data types and it does so by using the same name of the method, that is, *Max*. The version chosen is the responsibility of the compiler and it makes the choice based upon the type and number of the parameters.

At first sight overloading may not appear to be a useful feature, but consider the following scenario. As part of a programming team you are asked to write code to locate a customer's balance from a file of customers. This has to be achieved by either using the customer's name or account number. To achieve this you could write two different methods, which you may name *FindBalanceByName* and *FindBalanceByNumber*. However, an alternative and 'cleaner' solution is to provide two methods with the same name but with different signatures. The name of the methods could simply be *FindBalance* and each would take a different argument type. One would take a string argument and the other an integer argument. Now, when you wish to find the balance of a customer, you send a message that invokes the *FindBalance* method. This message can now supply the customer's name (as a string) or account number (as an Integer) as a parameter of the message. VB .NET will then choose the appropriate version of the *FindBalance* method to locate the customer's balance from the file.

Namespaces

VB .NET has a vast collection of classes that can be used by software developers. There are so many classes that it makes sense to classify them in some way. So classes that have related behaviours are grouped together in to 'class libraries'. Each of these 'libraries' has a name referred to as *namespace*.

If a method of a particular class is to be used within an application then the 'library' to which the class belongs has to be indicated within the code. This indication is achieved using the VB .NET keyword *Imports*. One of the screenshots shown in Figure 6.36 uses a namespace (i.e. a 'library'), so that the methods *Write*, *WriteLine* and *Read* can be used without having to prefix them with *Console* and a full stop. You have seen and used these methods earlier in this chapter; however, you had to prefix them with the word *Console* and a full stop.

> **NOTE**: The *Imports* statement does not actually import anything, it just allows the code to refer to the method without having to type the full *namespace* and the *method* name. It acts as a kind of alias (more on this later).

Figure 6.36 The use of the keyword *Imports*.

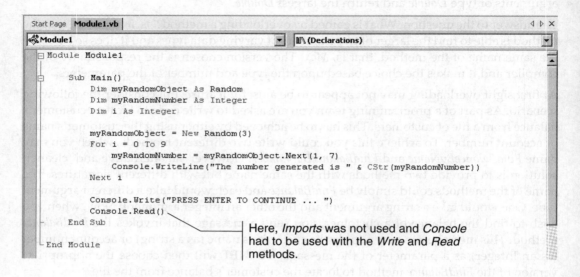

```
Start Page  Module1.vb

Module1                                              (Declarations)

Module Module1

    Sub Main()
        Dim myRandomObject As Random
        Dim myRandomNumber As Integer
        Dim i As Integer

        myRandomObject = New Random(3)
        For i = 0 To 9
            myRandomNumber = myRandomObject.Next(1, 7)
            Console.WriteLine("The number generated is " & CStr(myRandomNumber))
        Next i

        Console.Write("PRESS ENTER TO CONTINUE ... ")
        Console.Read()
    End Sub

End Module
```

Here, *Imports* was not used and *Console* had to be used with the *Write* and *Read* methods.

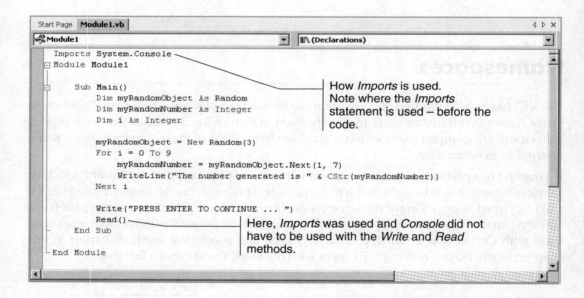

```
Start Page  Module1.vb

Module1                                              (Declarations)

  Imports System.Console
Module Module1

    Sub Main()
        Dim myRandomObject As Random
        Dim myRandomNumber As Integer
        Dim i As Integer

        myRandomObject = New Random(3)
        For i = 0 To 9
            myRandomNumber = myRandomObject.Next(1, 7)
            WriteLine("The number generated is " & CStr(myRandomNumber))
        Next i

        Write("PRESS ENTER TO CONTINUE ... ")
        Read()
    End Sub

End Module
```

How *Imports* is used.
Note where the *Imports* statement is used – before the code.

Here, *Imports* was used and *Console* did not have to be used with the *Write* and *Read* methods.

7 The Unified Modelling Language (UML)

The Unified Modelling Language (UML) is fast becoming the standard methodology for OOA (object-oriented analysis), OOD (object-oriented design) and OOP (object-oriented programming) modelling. **Some** of the many features and aspects of UML suitable for supporting OOP will be described in this chapter. UML will then be used to illustrate messaging between objects.

How to think when using objects

Object-oriented approaches to the development of code is different to traditional development where the concentration was upon data flow and the identification of functionality. The best advice I can give for developing code using objects is to consider that many objects exist within the computer (and/or computer network) at the same time. Each of these objects is able to offer services and other objects request these services using messages.

Consequently, an object-oriented program consists of many objects requesting, via messages, services from one another to perform the task of the program in question. The UML covered in this chapter shows how the communication between objects can be modelled. The best tool in my opinion for designing object-oriented programs is the collaboration diagram. This diagram highlights the messages that exist between objects in a program. As well as being a useful design tool it is also very useful in validating the responsibilities (services) allocated to objects in a program.

Therefore, the aspects of UML covered in this chapter are to support the use of the collaboration diagram. UML is much more involved than the material in this chapter suggests. However, there should be enough information within this chapter to allow for the design and coding of object-oriented programs using collaboration diagrams.

NOTE: The examples of collaboration diagram used in this book are basic but nevertheless they do highlight the messaging nature of objects.

Notes

A note is a diagram comment and has no semantic influence on other elements of a UML diagram. It is used to convey extra and supplementary information to the reader of a UML diagram. An example of a note is shown in Figure 7.1.

Figure 7.1 A note in UML.

A Comment of
some kind

A class

A rectangular box containing the class's name, as illustrated by Figure 7.2, represents a class.

Figure 7.2 How UML represents a class.

ClassA

An unnamed object (instance of a class)

A rectangular box containing the class's name underlined and preceded by a colon, as illustrated by Figure 7.3, represents an unnamed object.

Figure 7.3 How UML represents an unnamed object.

:ClassA

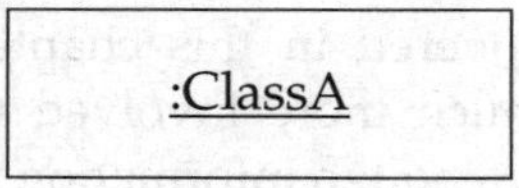

A named object (instance of a class)

A rectangular box containing the class's name underlined and preceded by a colon and an appropriate object reference, as illustrated by Figure 7.4, represents a named object.

Figure 7.4 How UML represents a named object.

Identifier:ClassA

Collaboration diagrams

Collaboration diagrams illustrate the **message** interactions between **objects**.

Links and messages

Figure 7.5 illustrates a typical format of a collaboration diagram showing a **link** and **messages**.

Figure 7.5 Collaboration diagram.

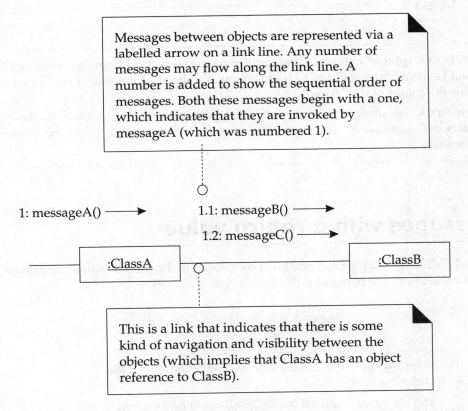

NOTE: The empty brackets indicate that the messages have no arguments (parameters).

messageA() invokes a method in the unnamed object *:ClassA*. This method (within this unnamed object) then invokes messages *messageB()* and *messageC()*, which are methods within the unnamed object *:ClassB*. The numbering of the messages indicates the order of execution.

NOTE: It is **not** usual to number the first message on a collaboration diagram. Figure 7.5 has numbered the first message in order to illustrate the use of sub-numbers.

Messages with parameters (arguments)

Figure 7.6 illustrates a typical format of a collaboration diagram showing a **message** with a **parameter**.

Figure 7.6 A message with a parameter.

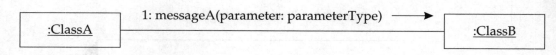

NOTE: **Examples of messages that require parameters**: The unnamed object of ClassA 'could be asking' the object of ClassB to draw it a shape. A parameter could be used to define the colour of this shape.

There could be more than one parameter; for example, in addition to the colour parameter, coordinates that define the position of the shape could be present as parameters.

Messages with a return value

Figure 7.7 illustrates a typical format of a collaboration diagram showing a **message** with a **return value**. Here the parameter and return type is also shown.

Figure 7.7 A message with a return value.

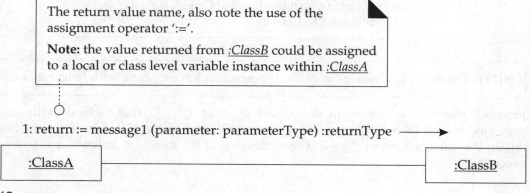

UML message syntax

NOTE: The standard syntax for a message is shown below:

return := message (parameter : parameterType) : returnType

This could also be a **parameter list**, i.e. more than one parameter

---

QUESTION 7.1 (DEVELOPMENT)

Draw a collaboration diagram to show the relationship between the objects as represented by the simple application developed in Chapter 6. The listings and GUI for this application are repeated here for convenience. Figure 7.9 shows the answer.

Listing 7.1 Repeated here for convenience.

```
Public Class Top
    Private sideValue As Integer

    Public Function ReadSide() As Integer
        Return sideValue
    End Function

    Public Sub Spin()
        Randomize()
        sideValue = CInt((3 * Rnd) + 1)
    End Sub
End Class
```

Listing 7.2 Repeated here for convenience.

```
Private Sub btnSpin_Click(ByVal sender As System.Object, ByVal e As _
System.EventArgs) Handles btnSpin.Click

    Dim myTop As Top
    Dim numberGenerated As Integer

    myTop = New Top()
    myTop.Spin()
    numberGenerated = myTop.ReadSide()
    lblDisplay.Text = "The number generated is " & CStr(numberGenerated)
End Sub
```

163

Figure 7.8 Repeated for convenience.

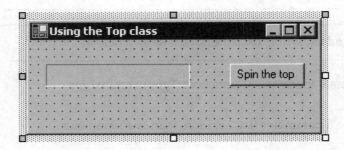

This application has two classes the *Form1* class and the *Top* class. The event handler attached to the button of the GUI creates an instance of the *Top* class and sends two messages to invoke two methods within the instance of the *Top* class. Figure 7.9 represents this relationship with a collaboration diagram.

Figure 7.9 A collaboration diagram.

This collaboration diagram shows the sequence of messages between the instances (i.e. objects) of both classes. The event handler of the *Form1* object sends two messages to the object named *myTop*. The first message 'asks' the *myTop* object to spin. This it does and it stores the number generated 'inside' the *myTop* object. Of course how the *myTop* object achieves this is of no concern to the *Form1* object. All the *Form1* object needs to know is that the *myTop* object can be sent such a message (i.e. the *myTop* object **exposes** this **instance method** *Spin()*). The second message 'asks' the *myTop* object for the value of the number it has stored, that is, the number that represents the side of the top that rests on the ground once the top has stopped spinning. This value is returned to *numberGenerated*, which is a variable 'inside' the *Form1* object (in fact it is a local variable within the button click handler).

Figure 7.10 relates the collaboration diagram to the program statements.

QUESTION 7.2 (DEVELOPMENT)

Draw a collaboration diagram to show the relationship between the objects as represented by the simple application developed in Chapter 6 during Practical Activity 6.4.

HINT: There is still only one Form1 object but there are two instances of the Top class.

Figure 7.10 Relating the diagram to code.

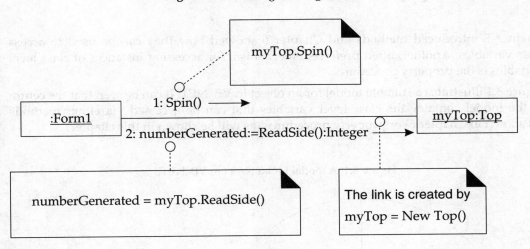

8 Property procedures

Chapter 5 introduced methods and Chapter 6 showed how they can be used to access class variables. Another, often preferred, mechanism for accessing instances of class level variables is the property procedure.

Figure 8.1 illustrates a suitable model for an object in VB .NET. It can be seen that the centre of the model contains the class level variables that can be accessed via either methods (as shown in Chapter 6) or property procedures (as will be shown in this chapter).

Figure 8.1 A model for an object in VB .NET.

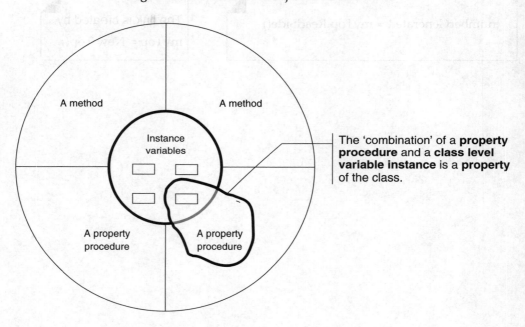

NOTE: Terminology within the programming community can be confusing. It is often the case to refer to a class as having members, and these members are attributes and methods.

During the analysis stage of software development, attributes are often referred to as states, and methods as behaviours. Another term for methods is operations and another term for attributes is properties (and sometimes fields).

I recommend that you regard VB .NET classes as having methods for behaviours and properties for states. However, class level variables can also be used to represent states if they are accessed via methods rather than property procedures.

NOTE: As just mentioned it is usual to refer to a VB .NET class as having **methods** and **properties**. However, it should be remembered that a property is indeed a 'kind of a method mechanism' that accesses a class level variable. Figure 8.1 illustrates that methods and properties are **encapsulated** into a single entity. It should be noted that a property is in fact a property procedure and a related class level variable.

OOP practice recommends that class level variables are **not** directly available to all code in an application but rather they can only be accessed by the methods or by property procedures of the class in which they reside.

Creating properties using property procedures

In Chapter 6 the four-sided spinning top shown in Figure 6.9 was implemented using methods (i.e. *Function* and *Sub*). It will be implemented again in this chapter but this time using property procedures. To distinguish between the listing a class called *Top2* will be used instead of the original *Top* class. The GUI will be almost identical and the code will be similar. The solution will be called *Spinning Top 2*.

Figure 8.2 shows the Solution Explorer and Figures 8.3, 8.4 and 8.5 show the code for the *Top2* class, the button click event handler, and the GUI, respectively.

A property procedure allows access to an instance of class level variable and usually contains the *Get* and *Set* keywords. In the context of this program, however, it is not necessary to *Set* an instance of a class level variable, the property procedure is just used to read the value of this instance variable. Consequently, it is a *ReadOnly* property procedure.

NOTE: Other examples of property procedures are covered later in this chapter.

Figure 8.2 The Solution Explorer.

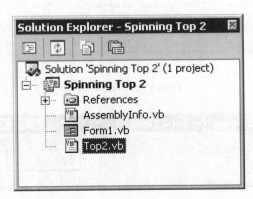

Figure 8.3 The *Top2* class code.

```
Start Page | Form1.vb [Design] | Top2.vb* | Form1.vb                              ◁ ▷ ×
⌀ Top2                                    ▼   ▥ (Declarations)                        ▼
□ Public Class Top2
      Private sideValue As Integer
□     Public ReadOnly Property TopValue() As Integer
□         Get
              Return sideValue
          End Get
      End Property
□     Public Sub Spin()
          Randomize()
          sideValue = CInt((3 * Rnd()) + 1)
      End Sub
└ End Class
```

Figure 8.4 The event handler.

```
Start Page | Form1.vb [Design]* | Top2.vb | Form1.vb*                             ◁ ▷ ×
⌀ Form1                                   ▼   ▥ (Declarations)                        ▼
□ Public Class Form1
      Inherits System.Windows.Forms.Form

  □   Windows Form Designer generated code

□     Private Sub btnSpin_Click(ByVal sender As System.Object, ByVal e As System.E
          Dim myTop As Top2
          Dim numberGenerated As Integer

          myTop = New Top2()
          myTop.Spin()
          numberGenerated = myTop.TopValue
          lblDisplay.Text = "The number generated is " & CStr(numberGenerated)
      End Sub
└ End Class
```

Figure 8.5 The GUI.

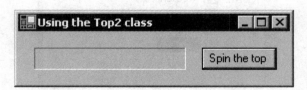

An example of a read-only property procedure is shown in **bold** within Listing 8.1 (which is the *Top2* class).

Listing 8.1 The Top2 class.

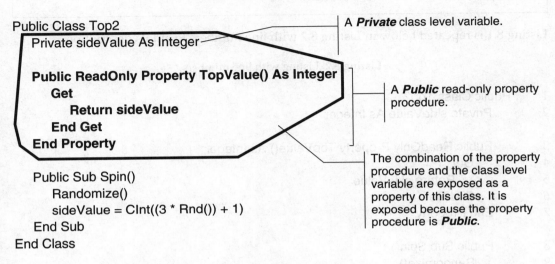

Public Class Top2
    Private sideValue As Integer

Public ReadOnly Property TopValue() As Integer
Get
Return sideValue
End Get
End Property

    Public Sub Spin()
        Randomize()
        sideValue = CInt((3 * Rnd()) + 1)
    End Sub
End Class

A *Private* class level variable.

A *Public* read-only property procedure.

The combination of the property procedure and the class level variable are exposed as a property of this class. It is exposed because the property procedure is *Public*.

Figure 8.6 shows a simplified UML class diagram that represents Listing 8.1.

Figure 8.6 A simplified UML class diagram.

The name of the class.

Top2

TopValue

A class property.

Spin

A class method.

The simplified UML diagram class of Figure 6.10 showed a class with one state and two behaviours (methods). Figure 8.6 shows a class with one property and one method. The *Read the side* behaviour is no longer required because VB .NET **exposes** the value of the side at which the top stops spinning as a property of the class – this property is called *TopValue*. It achieves this using the mechanism of a property procedure.

169

> **NOTE**: It is possible to access an instance of the *sideValue* class level variable (shown in Listing 8.1) directly by declaring it with a *Public* access modifier instead of the *Private* access modifier. However, this is against key principles of OOP and encapsulation in particular – more on this later in the text.

Listing 8.1 is repeated below in Listing 8.2 with line numbers to aid its description.

Listing 8.2 Listing with line numbers.

```
1       Public Class Top2
2           Private sideValue As Integer

3           Public ReadOnly Property TopValue() As Integer
4               Get
5                   Return sideValue
6               End Get
7           End Property

8           Public Sub Spin()
9               Randomize()
10              sideValue = CInt((3 * Rnd()) + 1)
11          End Sub
12      End Class
```

Lines 1 and 12: These lines define the start and end of the class definition. Line 1 specifies that it is a *Public* class with the name *Top2*.

Line 2: This line declares a class level variable named *sideValue* of type *Integer* and with *Private* scope that means it cannot be directly accessed by code outside instances of the class. This is an example of **data hiding** and we will return to this later in the text. The instance method *Spin()* declared within the *Top2* class has access to the instance of this variable and sets it to a random number from 1 to 4 (in exactly the same way as method described in Chapter 6). The property procedure *TopValue* also has access to an instance of this class level variable.

Lines 3 and 7: These lines define the start and end of the property procedure declaration.

Line 3 shows that the property procedure is *Public*, which exposes this as a member of the class. It is also a *ReadOnly* property procedure, which means that it is only capable of obtaining a copy of an instance of this class level variable to which it 'relates' (in this case the *sideValue* class level variable). The property procedure is named *TopValue*, which defines the name of the property it 'represents' within the class. Finally, the property procedure is capable of dealing with integers. Figure 8.7 emphasizes the features of the property procedure **signature**.

Lines 4 to 6: These lines define the mechanism that offers *TopValue* as a member (i.e. property) of the *Top2* class. The keywords *Get* and *End Get* define the start and end of the region of VB .NET statements (i.e. code) responsible for allowing the 'outside world' of code (that is other objects) access to the value represented by the *TopValue* property. It effectively

Figure 8.7 The signature of the property procedure.

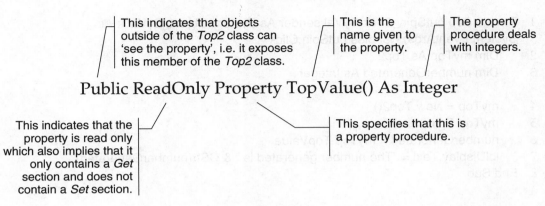

This indicates that objects outside of the *Top2* class can 'see the property', i.e. it exposes this member of the *Top2* class.

This is the name given to the property.

The property procedure deals with integers.

Public ReadOnly Property TopValue() As Integer

This indicates that the property is read only which also implies that it only contains a *Get* section and does not contain a *Set* section.

This specifies that this is a property procedure.

allows access to what is stored in this property. In this case there is only one statement between these keywords and it is responsible for returning the data stored in the instance of the integer class level variable *sideValue*. The relationship between the *TopValue* property and *sideValue* is that *sideValue* effectively stores the data for the property *TopValue*. Code (other objects) wishing to access the value that represents the side on which the *Top* stops spinning is achieved by accessing *TopValue* and not *sideValue*. Other objects have no knowledge of the existence of *sideValue* but they do know of the existence of the property *TopValue*. The class level variable *sideValue* is **hidden** within the class definition.

Lines 8 to 11: These lines declare a method that is capable of generating a random number from 1 to 4 and it operates as described in Chapter 6 (it is the same code as the *Spin()* method of Listing 6.1).

The random number generated by this method is assigned to an instance of the class level variable *sideValue*. Of course, listing 6.1 had another method (*ReadSide()*) that allowed access to this variable. However, for Listing 8.1 access to the data stored in this variable is via the property procedure *TopValue()* which is regarded as the **property** *TopValue*. Consequently, the *Spin()* method has 'effectively' stored a random number from 1 to 4 in the *TopValue* property.

The distinction between accessing these random numbers is best considered by a comparison of objects that send messages to objects of the classes *Top* and *Top2* – this will be covered later in this chapter.

Accessing the property of an object

Listing 8.3 shows the event handling procedure attached to the button of the GUI shown in Figure 8.5. The event handler uses an instance (i.e. an object) of the *Top2* class. A description of this code appears in the text after the listing.

Listing 8.3 The button event handler (numbered for ease of reference).

```
1   Private Sub butSpin_Click(ByVal sender As System.Object, ByVal e As _
    System.EventArgs) Handles butSpin.Click
2       Dim myTop As Top2
3       Dim numberGenerated As Integer

4       myTop = New Top2()
5       myTop.Spin()
6       numberGenerated = myTop.TopValue
7       lblDisplay.Text = "The number generated is " & CStr(numberGenerated)
8   End Sub
```

Line 1: This is the signature of the event handling procedure that is automatically generated by the IDE.

Line 2: This declares a **local** variable *myTop* of type *Top2* that means that *myTop* is capable of storing a reference to an instance (object) of the *Top2* class.

Line 3: This declares a **local** *Integer* variable *numberGenerated* that will be used to store the number returned from the *TopValue* property of the spinning of the top.

Line 4: This creates an instance of the *Top2* class to be 'known' by the object reference *myTop*.

Line 5: This is a message to the object *myTop* that requests a spin of the top. Of course the code in the object messaged will generate a random number from 1 to 4 and stores it, etc., etc (described earlier in the book).

> **NOTE**: Let's stop at this point. We know how the number is generated, it has already been described. What is important is that a message is sent to the object so it will perform some action. How this is achieved is of no concern to this event handler, it works, so use it. The behaviour and states are encapsulated within the object. All the event handler needs to know is what members the object exposes. This means what members (e.g. methods) of the object are available to code wishing to use the object? In this case the members consist of one method and one property. The method is *Spin()* and the property is *TopValue*. These form the **interface** of this object and 'outside code' is allowed to use to these because they were declared with the access modifier *Public*.

Line 6: The local variable *numberGenerated* within the button click event handler is assigned the value stored in the property *TopValue*. This value will be the (just generated) random number produced by sending a spin message (*Spin()*) to the object.

This line is not obviously a message to the object; rather the object has allowed us access to the value stored within its *TopValue* property. Of course in this case the access has been via a property procedure that to all intents and purposes is like a method. Consequently, I advise that you regard this type of access as a message – this will also 'fit well' with UML collaboration diagrams.

NOTE: Let's reflect on access to this property. We know that the access has been via a procedure – a property procedure. However, this mechanism is hidden and is not as explicit as the access to instances of the *sideValue* class variable shown in Listing 6.1. Listing 6.1 used a function method *ReadSide()* to access the random number. Figure 8.8 illustrates the distinction between using a method and accessing a property.

Figure 8.8 Comparison between using a method and a property procedure. Both approaches access the random number generated by the spinning top and in both cases this numbers is assigned to a local integer variable *numberGenerated*. However, the first statement taken from Listing 6.2 uses a method and the second statement taken from Listing 8.3 uses a property. **A method can be identified by the use of brackets and a property by the absence of brackets.**

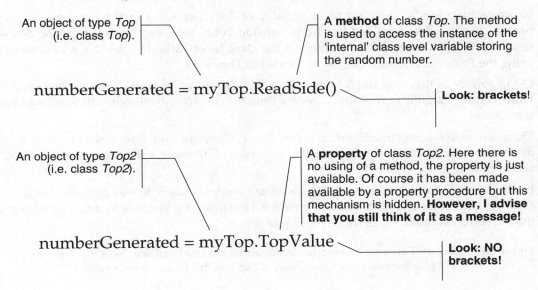

An object of type *Top*
(i.e. class *Top*).

A **method** of class *Top*. The method is used to access the instance of the 'internal' class level variable storing the random number.

numberGenerated = myTop.ReadSide()

Look: brackets!

An object of type *Top2*
(i.e. class *Top2*).

A **property** of class *Top2*. Here there is no using of a method, the property is just available. Of course it has been made available by a property procedure but this mechanism is hidden. **However, I advise that you still think of it as a message!**

numberGenerated = myTop.TopValue

Look: NO brackets!

Access modifiers used with class level variables

The classes *Top* and *Top2* have both used different mechanisms to allow access to the random number generated by a spinning top. Both are valid mechanisms and both adhere to important object oriented principles. These principles are encapsulation and data hiding.

Both classes represent the behaviour and state of a spinning top and the behaviour and state are 'tied together' (encapsulated) in a single entity.

The program statements that implement the behaviour, and the properties that represent the state are combined in one software representation (or model) of the spinning top.

The class level variable used to store the generated random number within the classes modelling the spinning top is not directly accessible (a form of data hiding) to code outside (i.e. objects of other classes) any instance of both classes. In both cases a mechanism was used

Figure 8.9 Using *Private* as an access modifier.

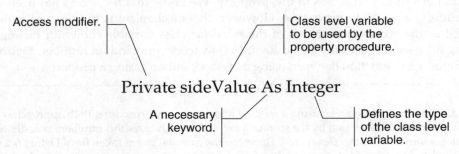

to access instances of the class level variable of the class, i.e. a method and a property procedure. The data was hidden from 'outside code' by using an appropriate **access modifier**. In both cases the declaration of the **class level variable** *sideValue* was achieved using the *Private* access modifier, as illustrated in Figure 8.9.

Using *Private* in this way hides instances of the class level variables from 'outside code'. However, the variable is available to code within the class (i.e. to all code within an object of the class).

There are other access modifiers, namely *Public*, *Protected* and *Friend*, and each will be discusses as appropriate throughout the text. What follows is a description of the *Public* access modifier.

For both the *Top* and *Top2* classes the *sideValue* class level variable was declared using the *Private* access modifier, as shown in Figure 8.9. However, it is possible to declare this using the *Public* access modifier, as shown in Figure 8.10.

Figure 8.10 Using the *Public* access modifier to declare a class level variable. Note that it is very poor OOP practice to declare a class level variable with a *Public* access modifier.

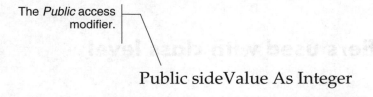

Using *Public* in this way does not hide the variable; it makes it directly available to 'outside code' (i.e. it exposes this member of the class). Consequently, if it is used there is no need for property procedures or methods. At first sight this is a saving of the extra effort needed to create methods and property procedures and is this not a good idea? The answer to this question is that it is **not** a good idea. There are numerous reasons why this would be regarded as poor object oriented programming practise. At this stage I do not wish to discuss in too much detail the reasons; instead I would rather offer you some rules for good programming practice:

1. Do **not** declare class level variables with the *Public* access modifier.

2. Always use an appropriate mechanism (e.g. property procedure) to access class variables.

Of course, rules can be an irritation, so let's give one good reason why you should not use the *Public* access modifier when declaring class level variables.

Assume a class is used to log the number of widgets produced in one day by a manufacturing company. Other objects could inform an object (of this class) of the number of widgets completed. This is illustrated in Figure 8.11.

Figure 8.11 Communication between objects involved in the manufacturing of widgets.

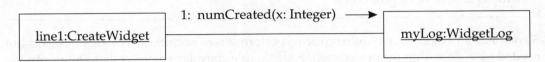

CreateWidget is a class that monitors a production line (called *line1*) and counts how many widgets are produced. At an appropriate time it sends a message (*numCreated*) to an instance (*myLog*) of class *WidgetLog*. This message sends an integer parameter (x) that contains the number of widgets produced by production *line1*.

The class *WidgetLog* will have a class level variable that stores the number of widgets created in one day. A sensible type for this variable would be an integer. The object *myLog* takes the number passed using the *numCreated* message and adds it to the value already stored in the instance of this integer variable.

An integer type is capable of storing positive and negative numbers. Of course, in the context of these objects a negative number makes no sense. For example, a production line cannot produce minus three widgets – it can only produce a positive number of widgets.

It is possible that the object *line1* might make a mistake in counting the number of widgets produced and accidentally generate a negative number. This negative number is then sent to the object *myLog* and added to the integer variable within this object thus reducing the number stored. So the mistake has spread to another object.

If you use the *Public* access modifier for declaring this class level variable there is nothing to stop this mistake spreading to the *myLog* object because it is just a storage area for an integer. However, if, for example, you declare the class level variable with a *Private* access modifier and use a method to add the integer passed to this variable you can stop the adding of a negative number. Code can be placed within the method to 'filter out' negative numbers and flag an error to the visual display unit or raise an exception.

NOTE: The *myLog* object is able to **verify** its data using a method. Simply declaring the class level variable as *Public* exposes it as a storage area for **any** integer value including negative integers – which in the context of this object is nonsensical.

Access modifiers used with methods

Access modifiers are also used with methods and the same modifiers can apply, namely *Private*, *Public*, *Protected* and *Friend*.

A *Public* method is exposed as an instance member of a class and consequently can be invoked by an appropriate message, i.e. other objects can invoke public instance methods.

> **NOTE**: Public members of a class (i.e. methods and properties) are often referred to as the **public interface** of the class, and when an object is created they become instance methods and instance properties.

Sometimes an object may require code to perform tasks not needed by other objects but needed by code within the object itself. For example consider an object that will return the price of an item after Value Added Tax (VAT) has been included. Under these circumstances the class needs to receive the item price without added VAT and return the cost with the added tax. This communication is illustrated by Figure 8.12.

Figure 8.12 Communication between objects.

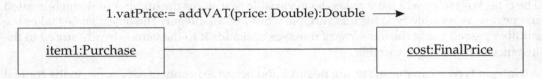

In Figure 8.12, *item* is an object of the class *Purchase* and it sends a message to the object *cost* (of class *FinalPrice*). This message invokes a method within the object *cost* that returns to *vatPrice* (an appropriate variable within the object *item*) the cost of goods purchased **after** VAT is added. The price of the item before the addition of VAT is sent with the message as a parameter (i.e. *price: Double*). The object *cost* receives the message and the parameter, which results in the execution of its exposed *AddVAT* method. This *AddVAT* method is made *Public* to ensure it can be invoked by messages from other objects.

> **NOTE**: *Double* is a VB .NET type that allows a variable of type *Double* to store a decimal fraction.

How the cost of the item after VAT is calculated is of no concern to the programmer coding the message. The programmer knows that an object of the *FinalPrice* class has a method to deal with its request because all classes make their public interface available in appropriate documentation (e.g. VB .NET on-line help). The calculation of the value added tax could be performed within the *AddVAT* method, or by another method declared within the *FinalPrice* class. If this other method were declared using the *Private* access modifier then it would only be available within objects of this class. Under these circumstances the calculation of the VAT is not part of the *FinalPrice* class public interface and objects of this class cannot be sent a message asking for the calculation of the VAT. Of course the VAT is calculated and added to the incoming price before it is returned to the variable *vatPrice* but it is done by another method inside (i.e. hidden) an object of the *FinalPrice* class.

The code shown in Listing 8.4 represents the *FinalPrice* class illustrated in the UML collaboration diagram of Figure 8.12. Figure 8.13 shows a GUI suitable for testing an object of this class.

NOTE: All of the methods declared in the following listing have formal parameters that have a name beginning with a lowercase *p*. This is not required by VB .NET but it is a useful aid to the programmer. The coding within the methods is more easily understood when parameters are quickly identified and this is helped by the inclusion of a lowercase *p*.

Listing 8.4 The *FinalPrice* class.

```
Public Class FinalPrice
    Private Function CalculateVAT(ByVal pPreVAT As Double) As Double
        Dim VAT As Double

        VAT = pPreVAT * 0.15
        Return VAT
    End Function

    Public Function AddVAT(ByVal pBeforeVAT As Double) As Double
        Dim afterVAT As Double
        Dim amountOfVAT As Double

        amountOfVAT = CalculateVAT(pBeforeVAT)
        afterVAT = pBeforeVAT + amountOfVAT
        Return afterVAT
    End Function
End Class
```

Figure 8.13 A suitable GUI to test *FinalPrice*.

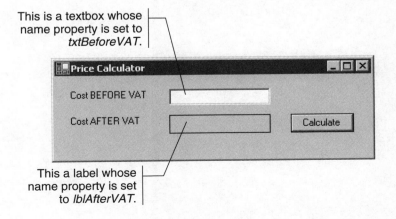

177

Listing 8.5 shows the event handling procedure attached to the Calculate button.

Listing 8.5 The event handling procedure.

```
Private Sub btnCalculate_Click(ByVal sender As System.Object, ByVal e As _
System.EventArgs) Handles btnCalculate.Click
    Dim priceBeforeVAT As Double
    Dim priceAfterVAT As Double
    Dim cost As FinalPrice

    cost = New FinalPrice()
    priceBeforeVAT = CDbl(txtBeforeVAT.Text)
    priceAfterVAT = cost.AddVAT(priceBeforeVAT)
    lblAfterVAT.Text = CStr(priceAfterVAT)
End Sub
```

The relationship between the GUI of Figure 8.13 and an instance of the *FinalPrice* class is illustrated in Figure 8.14.

Figure 8.14 The collaboration diagram.

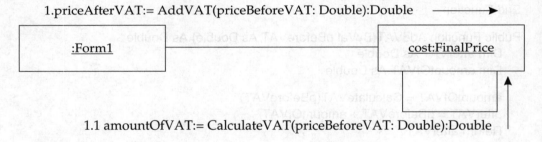

178

Description trace for execution of the GUI and the *FinalPrice* code

Statement	Description
The diagram below shows the GUI just before the user clicks the button. 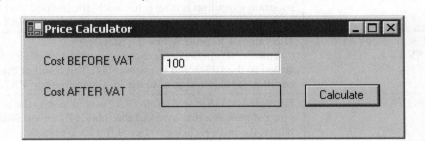	
After the user enters 100 and clicks the Calculate button the execution of the code is as follows.	
cost = New FinalPrice()	An instance of the *FinalPrice* class is created and is now known by the identifier *cost*, i.e. *cost* is the object reference.
priceBeforeVAT = CDbl(txtBeforeVAT.Text)	The contents of the textbox (i.e. 100) is converted from a string to a double and assigned to the local variable *priceBeforeVAT*.
priceAfterVAT = cost. AddVAT(priceBeforeVAT)	This is a message sent by the *form* object to the *cost* object. A copy of the value (i.e. 100) stored in the local variable *priceBeforeVAT* is sent along with the message as a parameter.

This message invokes the *AddVAT* method within the *cost* object so the next code to execute is within the *AddVAT* method of the *cost* object.

However, before the execution of this code is considered we need to understand the passing of parameters between the message and the invoked method.

The value (i.e. 100) stored in the actual parameter *priceBeforeVAT* is passed *ByVal* (this means by value) to the formal parameter *pBeforeVAT*. This means a copy of the value stored in *priceBeforeVAT* is copied into *pBeforeVAT*. Consequently, *pBeforeVAT* also stores the value 100.

Figures 8.15 illustrate the passing of a parameter between a message and the method invoked by the message.

| amountOfVAT = CalculateVAT(pBeforeVAT) | This is a message that invokes the *CalculateVAT* function method. Consequently, the next code to execute is within the method *CalculateVAT*.

NOTE: The number 100 stored in *pBeforeVAT* is passed with this message. The invoked method will calculate the VAT (which is 15 in this case) and this value is returned to the local variable *amountOfVAT*.

NOTE: This is an example of the object messaging itself. As the method *CalculateVAT* was declared with the access modifier *Private*, it in fact, can **only** be called from code within the same class (more to the point, it can **only** be called by code within the instance of this class, i.e. an object of this class). |

The 100 stored within the parameter *pBeforeVAT* is passed to the formal parameter within the function *CalculateVAT*. Consequently, *pPreVAT* also stores 100.

VAT = pPreVAT * 0.15	The local variable *VAT* is assigned the result of multiplying the 100 stored in *pPreVAT* by 0.15. Thus *VAT* stores 15, which represents the value added tax at a rate of 15%.
Return VAT	The return statement sends the 15 stored in VAT back to the code that invoked the *CalculateVAT* method in the first place. Thus the 15 is stored in *amountOfVAT*.
End Function	This signifies the end of the *CalculateVAT* method and the program execution is now returned to the method that sent message, i.e. program execution returns to the *AddVAT* method.
afterVAT = pBeforeVAT + amountOfVAT	The value of 15 returned by the message *CalculateVAT(pBeforeVAT)* and assigned to *amountOfVAT* is added to the 100 stored in *pBeforeVAT*. The result of this addition (115) is assigned to the local variable *afterVAT*.
Return afterVAT	The value of 115 stored in *afterVAT* is returned to the code that sent the message that invoked the *AddVAT* method (which was within the button click handler of the form object).
End Function	This signifies the end of the *AddVAT* method and the program execution is now returned to the method that sent the first message, i.e. program execution returns to the event handler attached to the button.
priceAfterVAT = cost. AddVAT(priceBeforeVAT)	The 115 returned is assigned to the local variable *priceAfterVAT*.
lblAfterVAT.Text = CStr(PriceAfterVAT)	The content of the variable *priceAfterVAT* is converted to a string and assigned to the *Text* property of the label. The GUI will display the 115 as shown below.

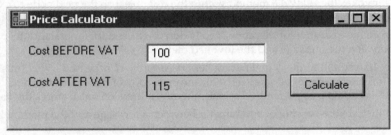

End Sub	The event handler ends its execution and the application awaits the next event.

Figure 8.15 Passing a parameter.

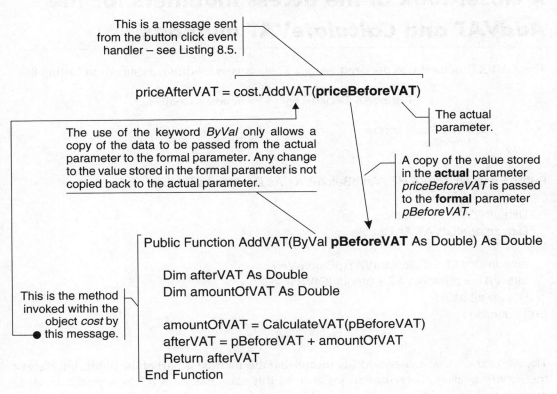

This is a message sent from the button click event handler – see Listing 8.5.

priceAfterVAT = cost.AddVAT(**priceBeforeVAT**)

The actual parameter.

The use of the keyword *ByVal* only allows a copy of the data to be passed from the actual parameter to the formal parameter. Any change to the value stored in the formal parameter is not copied back to the actual parameter.

A copy of the value stored in the **actual** parameter *priceBeforeVAT* is passed to the **formal** parameter *pBeforeVAT*.

Public Function AddVAT(ByVal **pBeforeVAT** As Double) As Double

    Dim afterVAT As Double
    Dim amountOfVAT As Double

    amountOfVAT = CalculateVAT(pBeforeVAT)
    afterVAT = pBeforeVAT + amountOfVAT
    Return afterVAT
End Function

This is the method invoked within the object *cost* by this message.

NOTE: The type of the formal and actual parameters must usually match. If you examine the code you will see that *pBeforeVAT* and *priceBeforeVAT* are both doubles. The type of the actual and the type of the formal parameters do not have to be an exact match. It is possible, for example, to pass an actual parameter of type *Integer* to a formal parameter of type *Long*. This is because they both store whole numbers and a *Long* can store a larger whole number than an *Integer*, consequently, there is no risk of losing information, in other words widening conversions are allowed (refer to Chapter 10 to read about widening conversions).

A closer look at the access modifiers for the *AddVAT* and *CalculateVAT* methods

The *AddVAT* method was declared using a *Public* access modifier, as shown in Listing 8.6.

Listing 8.6 Declared with a *Public* access modifier.

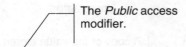

The *Public* access modifier.

```
Public Function AddVAT(ByVal pBeforeVAT As Double) As Double

    Dim afterVAT As Double
    Dim amountOfVAT As Double

    amountOfVAT = CalculateVAT(pBeforeVAT)
    afterVAT = pBeforeVAT + amountOfVAT
    Return afterVAT
End Function
```

The use of the *Public* access modifier means that this method is part of the public interface of the *FinalPrice* class. Therefore an instance of this class has *AddVAT* as a public instance method and this method can be invoked by messages from other objects.

The *CalculateVAT* method was declared using a *Private* access modifier, as shown in Listing 8.7.

Listing 8.7 Declared with a *Private* access modifier.

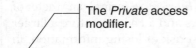

The *Private* access modifier.

```
Private Function CalculateVAT(ByVal pPreVAT As Double) As Double
    Dim VAT As Double

    VAT = pPreVAT * 0.15
    Return VAT
End Function
```

The use of the *Private* access modifier means that this method is **not** part of the public interface of the *FinalPrice* class. Therefore only code within an instance of the *FinalPrice* class can access this method.

Of course if you required the *CalculateVAT* method to be available as part of the interface of the class you would declare it as *Public*.

The general format of a property procedure

Property procedures are segments of code declared within property definitions that allow you to execute code when a property value is set or retrieved.

Visual Basic .NET has two types of property procedures: the *Get* property procedures for retrieving a property value, and the *Set* property procedures for assigning a value to a property.

The example of the property procedure shown in this chapter was one that produced a read-only property. Two other frequently used properties within VB .NET are the write-only and the read/write property.

The *Get* property procedure can be used to simple return the value of the property. The *Set* property procedure can assign a value to a property or it can assign it after it has been verified in some way. In other words property procedures are able to protect and verify their property values.

The format for the read/write property

Using both *Get* and *Set* in a pairing as illustrated below creates a read/write property:

```
Public Property PropertyName() As datatype
    Get
        Return expression ' expression is returned as property's value.
    End Get
    Set (ByVal pValue As datatype)
        value = pValue
    End Set
End Property
```

The property procedure requires an appropriate class level variable to store the data for the property, consequently, the property procedure pairing above requires access to a class level variable (shown in Figure 8.16).

Figure 8.16 Relationship between a class level variable and a property procedure. The arrowed lines show the relationship.

```
Private value as datatype

Public Property PropertyName() As datatype
    Get
        Return value
    End Get
    Set (ByVal pValue As datatype)
        value = pValue
    End Set
End Property
```

Let's consider a program that implements the following simple specification.

SPECIFICATION 8.1

Develop and test a class that allows for the setting and retrieving of the balance of a bank account.

Figure 8.17 shows a suitable GUI for testing the *Account* class used to implement Specification 8.1. The code for the *Account* class is shown in Figure 8.18 and the code attached to the GUI is shown in Figure 8.19.

Figure 8.17 A suitable GUI.

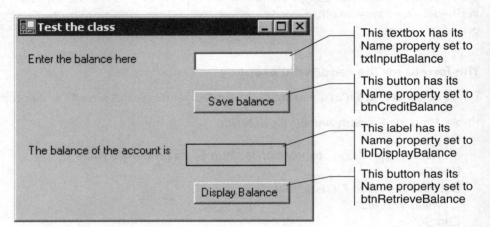

Figure 8.18 The Account class.

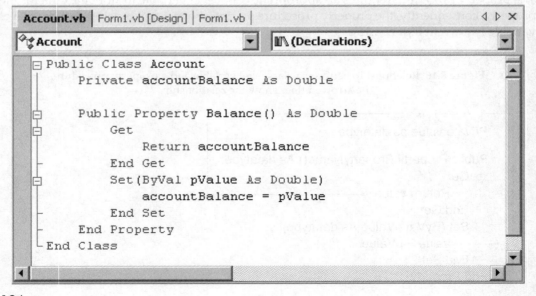

```vb
Public Class Account
    Private accountBalance As Double

    Public Property Balance() As Double
        Get
            Return accountBalance
        End Get
        Set(ByVal pValue As Double)
            accountBalance = pValue
        End Set
    End Property
End Class
```

Figure 8.19 The testing code.

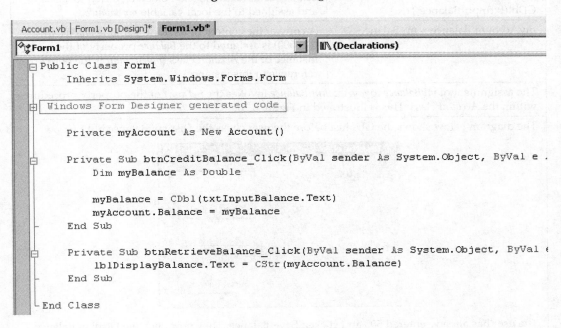

```
Account.vb | Form1.vb [Design]* | Form1.vb*

Form1                                    ▼    (Declarations)

 Public Class Form1
      Inherits System.Windows.Forms.Form

    Windows Form Designer generated code


      Private myAccount As New Account()

      Private Sub btnCreditBalance_Click(ByVal sender As System.Object, ByVal e .
          Dim myBalance As Double

          myBalance = CDbl(txtInputBalance.Text)
          myAccount.Balance = myBalance
      End Sub

      Private Sub btnRetrieveBalance_Click(ByVal sender As System.Object, ByVal e
          lblDisplayBalance.Text = CStr(myAccount.Balance)
      End Sub

  End Class
```

A typical execution of the program represented by Figures 8.17 to 8.19 is described in the following trace table.

Statement	Description
When the project is executed the code associated with the instance of the *Form1* class is executed first.	
Private myAccount As New Account()	This declaration creates an instance of the *Account* class that is available to all the code within the instance of the *Form1* class because it is declared in the declaration area of the form code window. *myAccount* is a class level variable of type *Account* and 'refers to' an *Account* object.
The diagram below shows the GUI just before the user clicks the Save Balance button.	

Test the class

Enter the balance here `500`

Save balance

The balance of the account is

Display Balance

The user enters 500 and clicks Save Balance; the execution of the code is as follows.

myBalance = CDbl(txtInputBalance.Text)	The 500 entered in the text box is converted to a *Double* and assigned to the local variable *myBalance*.
myAccount.Balance = myBalance	A copy of the content of the local variable *myBalance* (i.e. 500) is assigned to the *Balance* property of the instance of the *Account* class (*myAccount* is the object reference to this instance).

The assignment of *myBalance* to *myAccount.Balance* invokes the *Set* part of the property procedure within the *Account* class. This is illustrated in Figure 8.20.

The diagram below shows the GUI just before the user clicks the Display Balance button.

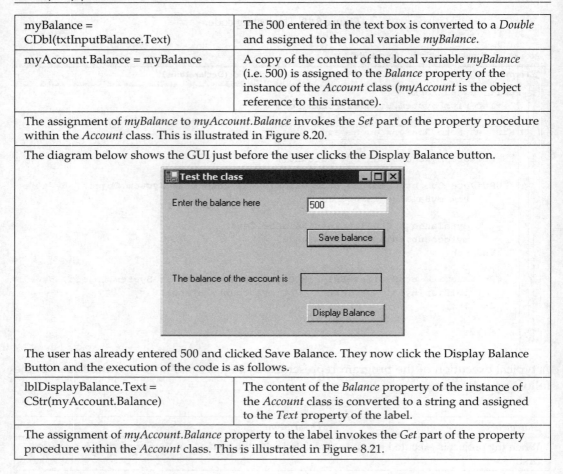

The user has already entered 500 and clicked Save Balance. They now click the Display Balance Button and the execution of the code is as follows.

lblDisplayBalance.Text = CStr(myAccount.Balance)	The content of the *Balance* property of the instance of the *Account* class is converted to a string and assigned to the *Text* property of the label.

The assignment of *myAccount.Balance* property to the label invokes the *Get* part of the property procedure within the *Account* class. This is illustrated in Figure 8.21.

Figure 8.20 Invoking the *Set* property procedure.

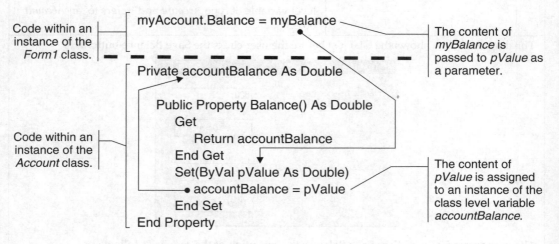

Figure 8.21 Invoking the *Get* property procedure.

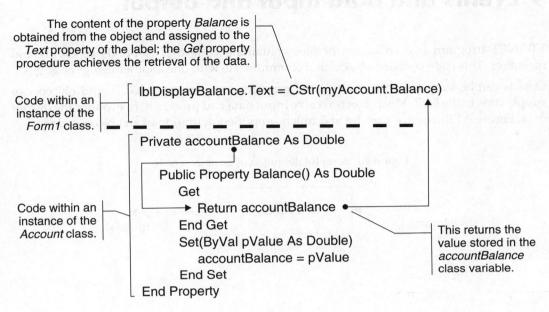

The content of the property *Balance* is obtained from the object and assigned to the *Text* property of the label; the *Get* property procedure achieves the retrieval of the data.

Code within an instance of the *Form1* class.

```
lblDisplayBalance.Text = CStr(myAccount.Balance)
```

Code within an instance of the *Account* class.

```
Private accountBalance As Double

    Public Property Balance() As Double
        Get
            Return accountBalance
        End Get
        Set(ByVal pValue As Double)
            accountBalance = pValue
        End Set
    End Property
```

This returns the value stored in the *accountBalance* class variable.

QUESTION 8.1 (DEVELOPMENT)

Use the VB .NET on-line help to discover how to create a write-only property using a property procedure.

QUESTION 8.2 (DEVELOPMENT)

Use the VB .NET on-line help to discover the difference between passing a parameter by value and passing a parameter by reference, as represented by the keywords ByVal and ByRef.

9 Events and data input and output

VB .NET program is a collection of files containing code that responds to events and messages. This code contains objects that communicate with one another using messages.

Objects can be supplied with data via the graphical user interface (GUI), and objects can supply data to the GUI. Most objects receive input data and process it, to produce the output data. Figure 9.1 illustrates a useful and much simplified definition of an objects code.

Figure 9.1 A useful definition of an objects code.

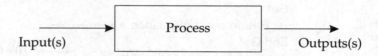

Input(s) → Process → Outputs(s)

Useful definition of program code within an object

Program code consists of high-level language statements that process input data to produce output data.

This chapter will deal with:

- The various ways data is **input** from GUIs and **output** to GUIs.
- How the user can generate **events** using various controls.
- Input and output when using a Console.

Later chapters will deal with how the data is processed.

A windows application developed using VB .NET involves designing the interface that the user will see, by drawing the controls, setting their properties and then writing the code.

Controls are used to obtain the data input, react to the events and to display the data output. Typical and frequently used controls for performing input, output and event capture, are labels, textboxes, list boxes and buttons.

Other controls in VB .NET allow a VB application to access and manipulate data from other applications, such as Microsoft Access.

All controls used in VB .NET have their own set of properties, methods and events. This chapter will look at some of the available controls used in VB .NET, starting with the button.

The button

The vast majority of VB .NET applications will contain buttons that once clicked activate actions within the application. When clicked, a button appears to be pushed in, and therefore is often referred to as a push button.

Associated with a button is a set of properties, events and methods.

NOTE: A button is derived from a *Button* class! Every button drawn on a form is an instance of this class.

Properties of a button

A button has many properties listed in its property box. It is not possible within one textbook to describe all of these properties. Instead the common and more frequently used properties will be described and you are left to discover the other properties using the comprehensive VB .NET on-line help facility.

Like all controls the most important property for a button is its *Name* property. This is used to identify the button in the program code. This name is always set by default to *Button1* for the first button drawn and *Button2* for the second and so on. However, good programming practice dictates that every control should be renamed to reflect its purpose and object type. Consequently, a button used to quit an application would have its name property set to *btnQuit*.

The *Text* property of a button is set to a string to reflect the purpose of the button. Therefore, for a button used to quit an application it would, typically, be set to *Quit* or *Quit the Application*.

The *Font* property is used to select the appearance of the text on the button. That is the type of font (System or Times New Roman), its size, whether it is bold or underlined, etc. Figure 9.2 illustrates the appearance of text on various buttons.

Figure 9.2 Display of different font settings.

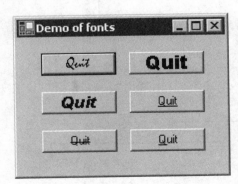

Figure 9.3 illustrates how to change the font setting for a button. Figure 9.4 illustrates an alternative way for setting fonts.

Figure 9.3 Altering a captions font.

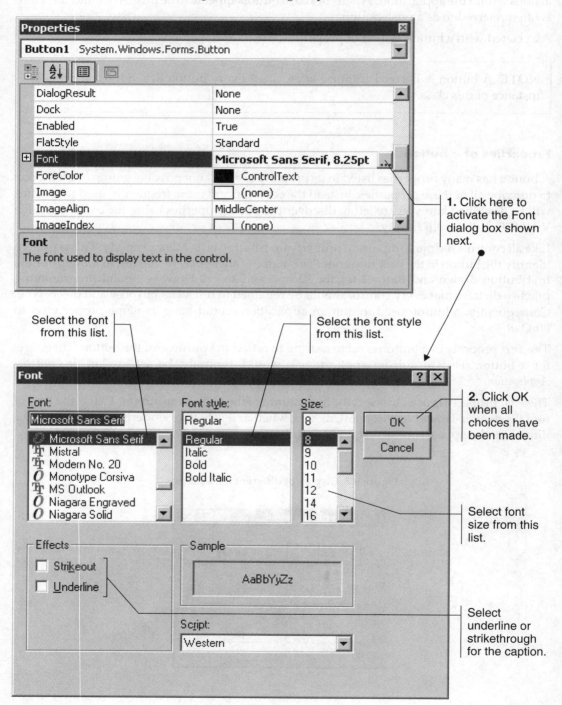

Figure 9.4 An alternative way for setting fonts.

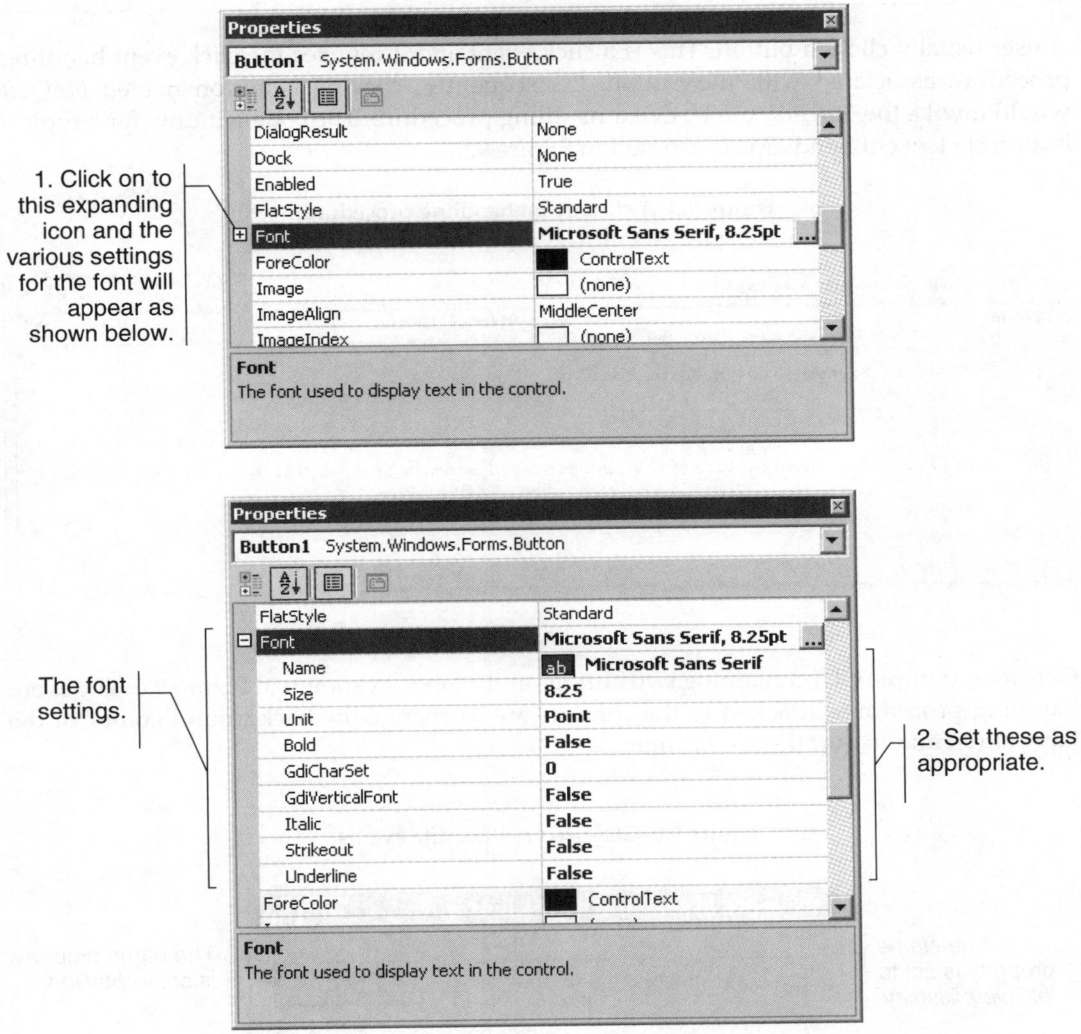

1. Click on to this expanding icon and the various settings for the font will appear as shown below.

The font settings.

2. Set these as appropriate.

PRACTICAL ACTIVITY 9.1

Draw six buttons onto a form and set all of their *Text* and *Font* properties to produce a display similar to Figure 9.2.

One of the buttons has its letter Q underlined; this is achieved by setting the *Text* property to &*Quit*. The ampersand (&) is not displayed; it is used to underline the letter Q. If the *Text* property were set to *Qui&t*, then the letter t would be underlined. The ampersand is used to set an accelerator key for the button. An accelerator key is another way of selecting the button other than clicking it. For example, if the *Text* property was set to &*Quit* then pressing the Alt key and the Q key at the same time would activate the click event handling procedure of the button.

Events associated with a button

A user usually clicks a button. This is a click event and it invokes the click event handling procedure associated with the Button. Consequently, clicking a button named *btnQuit* would invoke the *btnQuit_Click()* event handling procedure. The code window for a typical button click event handler is illustrated in Figure 9.5.

Figure 9.5 A click event handling procedure.

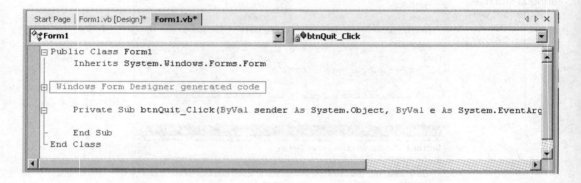

Consider a simple GUI containing two buttons and a label, as shown in Figure 9.6. The event handling procedures attached to the controls are to change the background colour of the label to red and to quit the application.

Figure 9.6 GUI used to illustrate events.

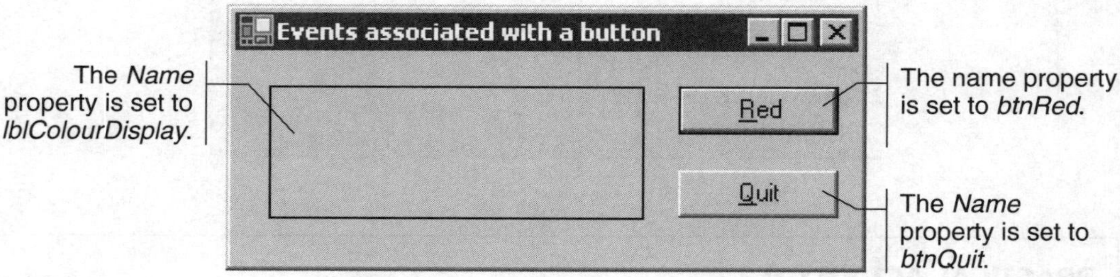

The *Name* property for each of the controls are as shown in the callout labels, the other property settings should be obvious from the look of the GUI.

Figure 9.7 shows a sequence of screenshots that illustrates the events associated with the button control.

It can be seen from Figure 9.7 that a button has many associated events. Each of the events in this list can have a related event handling procedure whose name is formed from the name of the object and the event. Consequently, the event procedure template associated with the *Enter* event of the *btnQuit* command button would appear as shown in Figure 9.8.

Figure 9.7 Events associated with a button.

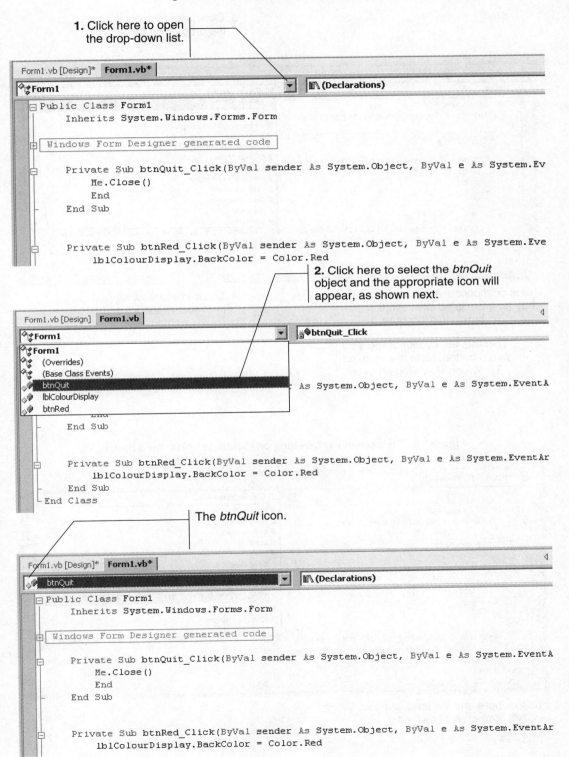

Figure 9.7 (cont.)

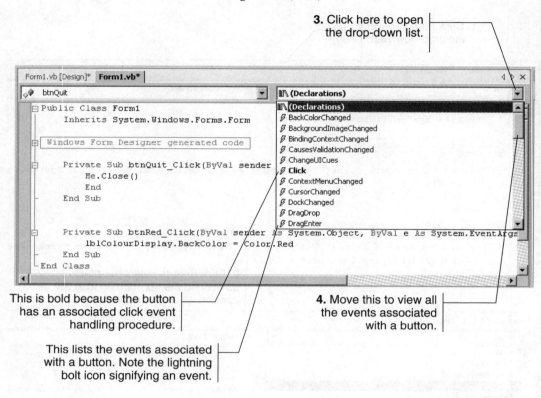

3. Click here to open the drop-down list.

This is bold because the button has an associated click event handling procedure.

4. Move this to view all the events associated with a button.

This lists the events associated with a button. Note the lightning bolt icon signifying an event.

Figure 9.8 The *Enter* event handling procedure template for a button.

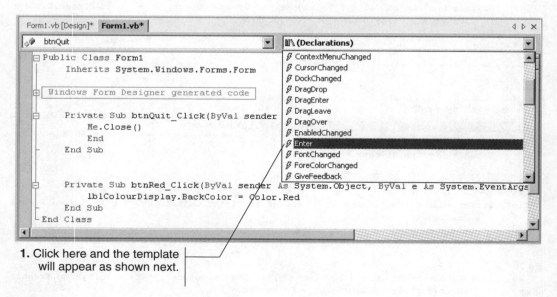

1. Click here and the template will appear as shown next.

Figure 9.8 (cont.)

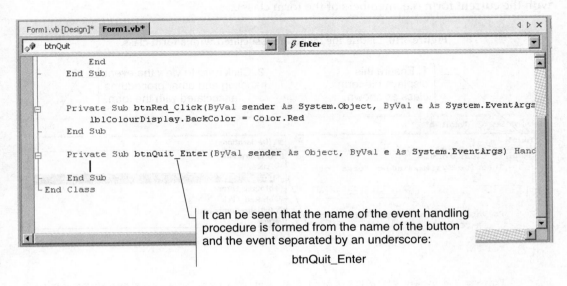

It can be seen that the name of the event handling procedure is formed from the name of the button and the event separated by an underscore:

btnQuit_Enter

Figure 9.9 shows how to list the event handlers associated with a control (a button in this case).

Figure 9.9 Event handlers.

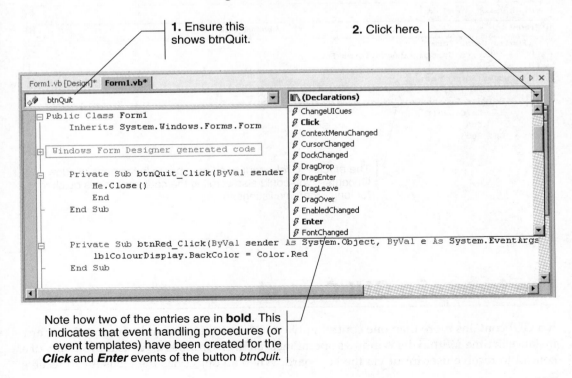

1. Ensure this shows btnQuit.

2. Click here.

Note how two of the entries are in **bold**. This indicates that event handling procedures (or event templates) have been created for the **Click** and **Enter** events of the button *btnQuit*.

195

Figure 9.10 shows how to list the members (which include the event handlers) associated with the current form (i.e. members of the form class).

Figure 9.10 Listing the members associated with a form class.

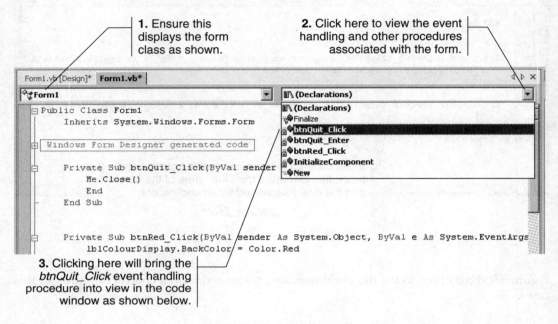

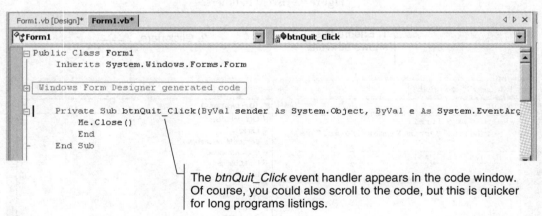

The focus of a GUI Control

If a GUI contains more than one control only one of these can respond to user input at any instance in time. Within the Windows operating system environment, **focus** is the ability of a control to receive user input via the keyboard. When an object has the focus it can receive input from the user. For example when a textbox has the focus the user can enter text into it. When a button has the focus it can be selected by pressing the space bar or Enter key on the keyboard.

Two of the events associated with a button (and many other controls) are the *Enter* and *Leave* events. The *Enter* event occurs when an object receives the focus, and the *Leave* event occurs when an object loses the focus. A *Leave* event can, for example, be used for updates (i.e. transfer the data just entered to a database) or reverse conditions that were set up by the *Enter* event.

An example of the use of the *Enter* and *Leave* events

SPECIFICATION 9.1

Develop a simple application that allows three buttons to change the background colour of a label to red, green and blue respectively. The form should also contain another three labels that inform the user what will happen to the colour of the background if they click a button and they should also indicate when a button looses and gains the focus.

Figure 9.11 illustrates the form at its launch (i.e. what it looks like when it first executes).

Figure 9.11 How the form looks at its launch.

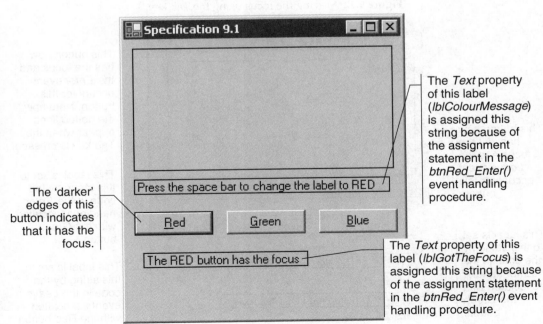

The *Text* property of this label (*lblColourMessage*) is assigned this string because of the assignment statement in the *btnRed_Enter()* event handling procedure.

The 'darker' edges of this button indicates that it has the focus.

The *Text* property of this label (*lblGotTheFocus*) is assigned this string because of the assignment statement in the *btnRed_Enter()* event handling procedure.

197

When controls are drawn onto the form at design time they have their *TabIndex* property set. The first control drawn on the GUI of Figure 9.11 was the Red button; consequently, its *TabIndex* is set to zero and the second to be drawn (i.e. the Green button) has its *TabIndex* set to one, and so on.

The focus can be changed from one control to another using the Tab key on the keyboard. The order in which the focus moves is dependent upon the *TabIndex* setting of each control. If the Red button has the focus then pressing the Tab key will result in the Green button receiving the focus because the *TabIndex* of the Red button is zero and the *TabIndex* of the Green button is one.

At the launch of the application the Red button receives the focus, which generates its *Enter* event. This event then invokes the *btnRed_Enter()* event handling procedure whose code (shown in Listing 9.1) sets the *Text* property of both labels to an appropriate string.

Listing 9.1 The *Enter* event handling procedure associated with the Red button.

```
Private Sub btnRed_Enter(ByVal sender As System.Object, ByVal e As _
System.EventArgs) Handles btnRed.Enter

    lblColourMessage.Text = "Press the space bar to change the label to RED"
    lblGotTheFocus.Text = "The RED button has the focus"
End Sub
```

Pressing the Tab key on the keyboard moves the focus to the green button, as illustrated in Figure 9.12.

Figure 9.12 Moving the focus using the Tab key.

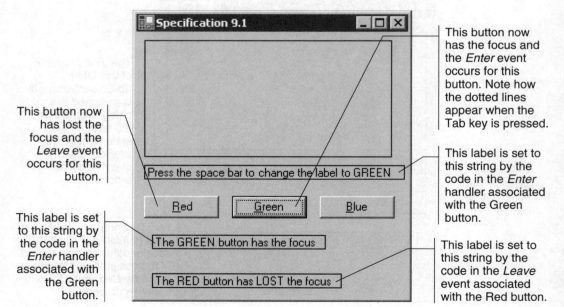

This button now has lost the focus and the *Leave* event occurs for this button.

This label is set to this string by the code in the *Enter* handler associated with the Green button.

This button now has the focus and the *Enter* event occurs for this button. Note how the dotted lines appear when the Tab key is pressed.

This label is set to this string by the code in the *Enter* handler associated with the Green button.

This label is set to this string by the code in the *Leave* event associated with the Red button.

Specification 9.1

Press the space bar to change the label to GREEN

Red   Green   Blue

The GREEN button has the focus

The RED button has LOST the focus

Listing 9.2 shows the code for the *Enter* event handling procedure associated with the Green button, and Listing 9.3 shows the code for the *Leave* event handling procedure associated with the Red button.

Listing 9.2 The *btnGreen_Enter* handler.

```
Private Sub btnGreen_Enter(ByVal sender As System.Object, ByVal e As _
System.EventArgs) Handles btnGreen.Enter

    lblColourMessage.Text = "Press the space bar to change the label to GREEN"
    lblGotTheFocus.Text = "The GREEN button has the focus"
End Sub
```

Listing 9.3 The *btnRed_Leave* handler.

```
Private Sub btnRed_Leave(ByVal sender As System.Object, ByVal e As _
System.EventArgs) Handles btnRed.Leave

    lblLostTheFocus.Text = "The RED button has LOST the focus"
End Sub
```

QUESTION 9.1 (REVISION)

1. Which control on Figure 9.12 will receive the focus when the user presses the Tab key?
2. Which control on Figure 9.12 will lose the focus when the user presses the Tab key?

Attaching code to the *Enter* event handling procedure

Figure 9.13 illustrates the sequence for attaching code to the *Enter* event handling procedure, associated with the Red command button (*btnRed*).

PRACTICAL ACTIVITY 9.2

Implement Specification 9.1. The settings for all the properties should be obvious from Figure 9.12 (with the exception of the *AutoSize* property of the label) and from the program listing shown in Listing 9.4.

The labels are to be used to display strings at runtime. How much space these strings require is unknown at design time. So rather than drag the label to the size that anticipates the amount of space, the label can automatically be resized at runtime to fit whatever size of string is assigned to its *Text* property.

To allow a label to automatically resize set its *AutoSize* property to *True*.

Figure 9.13 Coding an event procedure.

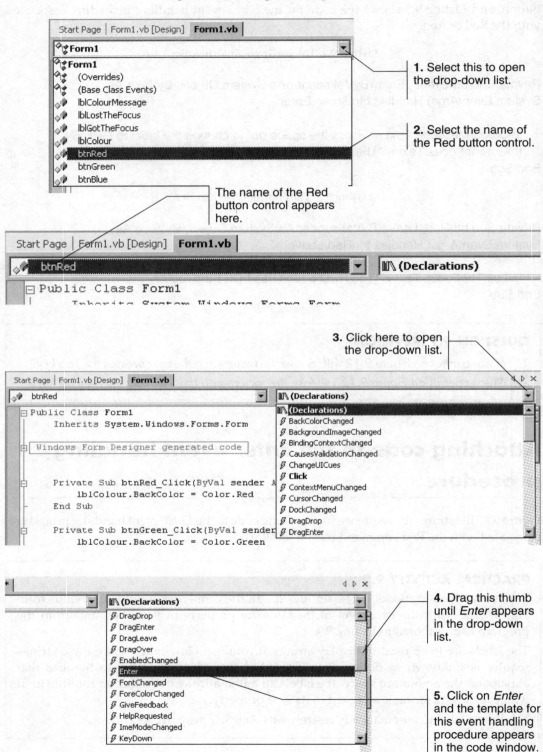

Figure 9.13 (cont.)

The template for
the *event* handling
procedure.

Note that the name of the
event handling procedure
appears here.

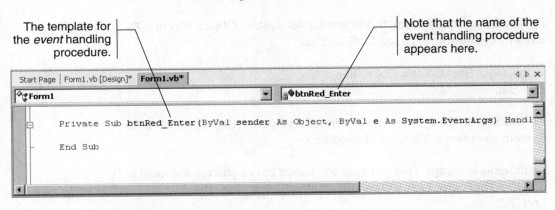

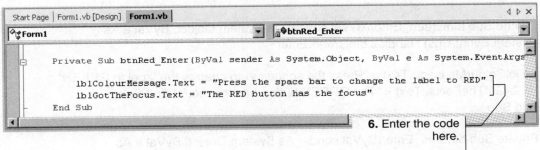

6. Enter the code
here.

NOTE: The names of the various controls placed on the form can be found from the program listings. For example, the *btnRed_Enter* handler has been derived from the setting of the *Name* property of the Red button and the event. Consequently, the *Name* of the Red button must be *btnRed*. The names for all the other controls can be found in the same way.

Remember: the rule is you must set the *Name* property of a control first before you attach code.

Listing 9.4 All the code for the event handling procedures associated with the GUI of Figure 9.12.

```
Private Sub btnRed_Click(ByVal sender As System.Object, ByVal e As _
System.EventArgs) Handles btnRed.Click

    lblColour.BackColor = Color.Red
End Sub

Private Sub btnGreen_Click(ByVal sender As System.Object, ByVal e As _
System.EventArgs) Handles btnGreen.Click

    lblColour.BackColor = Color.Green
End Sub
```

Listing 9.4 (cont.)

```
Private Sub btnBlue_Click(ByVal sender As System.Object, ByVal e As _
System.EventArgs) Handles btnBlue.Click

    lblColour.BackColor = Color.Blue
End Sub

Private Sub btnRed_Enter(ByVal sender As System.Object, ByVal e As _
System.EventArgs) Handles btnRed.Enter

    lblColourMessage.Text = "Press the space bar to change the label to RED"
    lblGotTheFocus.Text = "The RED button has the focus"
End Sub

Private Sub btnGreen_Enter(ByVal sender As System.Object, ByVal e As _
System.EventArgs) Handles btnGreen.Enter

    lblColourMessage.Text = "Press the space bar to change the label to GREEN"
    lblGotTheFocus.Text = "The GREEN button has the focus" End Sub
End Sub

Private Sub btnBlue_Enter(ByVal sender As System.Object, ByVal e As _
System.EventArgs) Handles btnBlue.Enter

    lblColourMessage.Text = "Press the space bar to change the label to BLUE"
    lblGotTheFocus.Text = "The BLUE button has the focus"
End Sub

Private Sub btnRed_Leave(ByVal sender As System.Object, ByVal e As _
System.EventArgs) Handles btnRed.Leave

    lblLostTheFocus.Text = "The RED button has LOST the focus" End Sub
End Sub

Private Sub btnGreen_Leave(ByVal sender As System.Object, ByVal e As _
System.EventArgs) Handles btnGreen.Leave

    lblLostTheFocus.Text = "The GREEN button has LOST the focus"
End Sub

Private Sub btnBlue_Leave(ByVal sender As System.Object, ByVal e As _
System.EventArgs) Handles btnBlue.Leave

    lblLostTheFocus.Text = "The BLUE button has LOST the focus"
End Sub
```

How to select a button at runtime

There are several ways to select a button at runtime: three ways are listed below and all invoke the *Click* event handling procedure.

1. Use the mouse to click the button.

2. Press an accelerator key for the button (i.e. the Alt key plus a letter).

3. Tab to the control using the Tab key and press either the space bar or Enter key on the keyboard.

NOTE: Before we move on to input and output let's reflect upon the events considered in this chapter. For each button on the GUI of Figure 9.11 we have attached three event handling procedures: a *Click* event handler, an *Enter* event handler and a *Leave* event handler.

The point I wish to emphasize is that the button control (like all controls) is able to have more than one event handling procedure 'attached'.

Also a single action by a user such as pressing the Tab key can 'fire' more than one event. For example when the focus is moved from the Red button to the Green button using the Tab key, the *Leave* event handling procedure 'attached' to the Red button is executed and then the *Enter* event handling procedure 'attached' to the Green button is executed – one user action two events.

Using TextBoxes for data input and output

TextBoxes can be used to obtain input from the GUI and to display output on the GUI.

SPECIFICATION 9.2

Write an application that allows a user to enter text in a textbox. Have a button click transfer the contents of the input textbox to an output textbox.

Figure 9.14 illustrates the GUI for the implementation of Specification 9.2.

The GUI of Figure 9.14 consists of two textboxes, two labels and one button. The properties of these controls are set as shown in Table 9.1.

Figure 9.14 GUI for Specification 9.2.

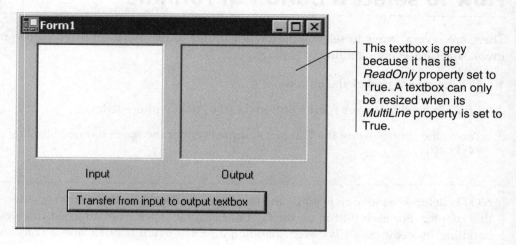

This textbox is grey because it has its *ReadOnly* property set to True. A textbox can only be resized when its *MultiLine* property is set to True.

Table 9.1 Property settings for the GUI.

Control	Property	Setting
TextBox1	Name	txtInput
	Text	Zero length string
	MultiLine	True
TextBox2	Name	txtOutput
	Text	Zero length string
	MultiLine	True
	ReadOnly	True
Label1	Name	lblInput
	AutoSize	True
	Text	Input
Label2	Name	lblOutput
	AutoSize	True
	Text	Output
Button1	Name	btnTransfer
	Text	Transfer from input to output textbox

NOTE: From Table 9.1 it can be seen that both labels have had their *Name* property set as appropriate. However, labels are often used just to guide the user of the GUI and as in this case there is no intention of ever accessing a property of these labels in code. Consequently, there is no need to set the *Name* property of these labels.

However, the advantage of naming a control, even one not accessed in any way, is that it does reflect its purpose and during the development of the program you may decide to access them (to hide them, for example).

The code attached to the button is shown in Listing 9.5.

Listing 9.5 The Button Click handler.

```
Private Sub btnTransfer_Click(ByVal sender As System.Object, ByVal e As _
System.EventArgs) Handles btnTransfer.Click

    Dim myString As String

    myString = txtInput.Text
    txtOutput.Text = myString
End Sub
```

This declares a local variable *myString* of type string.

This VB .NET program statement assigns the string entered by the user in the *txtInput* textbox to the local variable *myString*.

This VB .NET program statement assigns the string stored in the local variable *myString* to the *Text* property of the *txtOutput* textbox.

A user of this application enters text into the input textbox (*txtInput*) and clicks the button to transfer a **copy** of the text to the output textbox (*txtOutput*). This is illustrated in Figure 9.15.

Figure 9.15 The runtime **before** and **after** the button is clicked.

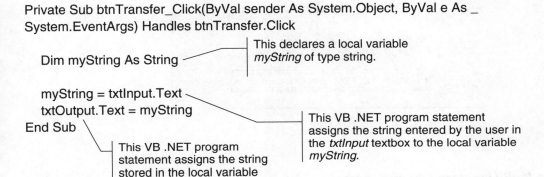

1. Enter text into the input textbox.

2. Click this button and a **copy** of the text will be transferred as shown in the next diagram.

Before

205

Figure 9.15 (cont.)

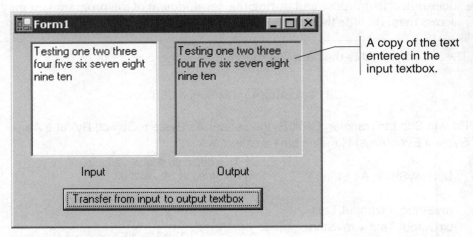

A copy of the text entered in the input textbox.

After

The *MultiLine* property of a textbox

Both of the textboxes had their *MultiLine* property set to *True*, which allows for text to continue onto the next line. When this property is set to false, the textbox ignores the carriage return and restricts data to a single line and the textbox cannot be resized.

The *ReadOnly* property of a textbox

The textbox used for the output had its *ReadOnly* property set to True. This makes the textbox, as you would expect, read only. It is possible to highlight and scroll through the text but the user cannot edit it. However, it is still possible for program code to change the contents of a *ReadOnly* text box by assigning text (i.e. a string) to its *Text* property.

PRACTICAL ACTIVITY 9.3

Implement Specification 9.2. Once the application is fully implemented, experiment with the properties of the textbox and observe the effects – for example, try the following changes:

1. Set the *ReadOnly* property of *txtOutput* to *False* and after the text has been transferred highlight the text in the output textbox and press Delete. Change the *ReadOnly* property back to *True* and attempt to delete the text.

2. Set the *MultiLine* property of the input textbox to *False* and then enter a very long sentence into the input textbox. Click the button and observe both textboxes.

Using a *MessageBox* for program output

A *MessageBox* is a predefined dialog box that displays application-related information to the user.

Listing 9.6 illustrates how to output a message using a *MessageBox*; Figure 9.16 shows the resulting output. The code is attached to the click event handler of a button.

Listing 9.6 Demonstration using the *MessageBox* class.

```
Private Sub btnDemo_Click(ByVal sender As System.Object, ByVal e As _
System.EventArgs) Handles btnDemo.Click

    Dim message As String

    message = "This is to demonstrate the use of a MessageBox"
    MessageBox.Show(message)
End Sub
```

Figure 9.16 Resulting output.

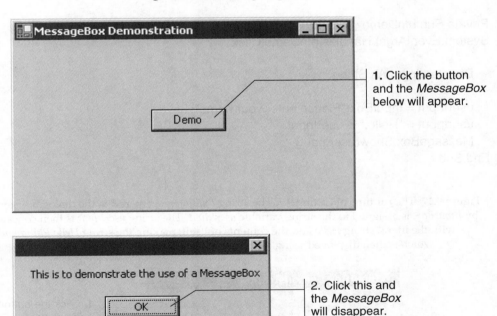

1. Click the button and the *MessageBox* below will appear.

2. Click this and the *MessageBox* will disappear.

MessageBox.Show is a message to the *MessageBox* class and *Show* is a shared method of this class, consequently there is no need for the creation of an object. The *Show* method is able to take other arguments (i.e. this method is overloaded). These will be introduced in later chapters, however.

> **NOTE:** A **shared method** does not operate on a specific instance of a class (i.e. object); it is invoked directly from the class. An instance of the class does **not** have to be created using a constructor and the keyword *New*. A shared method of a class can just be used directly.

Using an *InputBox* for program input

An **InputBox** displays a prompt in a dialog box, waits for the user to input text or click a button, and then it returns a **String** containing the content of the **InputBox**.

Listing 9.7 illustrates how to input data using an InputBox, the input is concatenated with the string *Hello* and then displayed using a **MessageBox**. Figure 9.17 shows the runtime for this code. Again, the code is attached to the click event handling procedure of a button.

Listing 9.7 Demonstration of using *InputBox*.

```
Private Sub btnDemo_Click(ByVal sender As System.Object, ByVal e As _
System.EventArgs) Handles btnDemo.Click

    Dim userInput As String

    userInput = InputBox("Please enter your name")
    userInput = "Hello " & userInput
    MessageBox.Show(userInput)
End Sub
```

Figure 9.17 The runtime of Listing 9.7. The string *Philip Jones*, entered in the dialog box generated by *InputBox*, is assigned to the string variable *userInput*. The string *userInput* is then concatenated with the literal string *Hello* and the contents of itself, making the string *Hello Philip Jones*, which is then displayed using the Shared *Show* method of the *MessageBox* class.

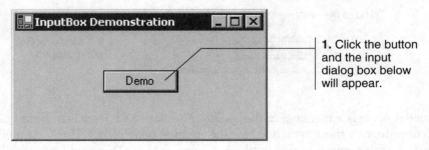

1. Click the button and the input dialog box below will appear.

Figure 9.17 (cont.)

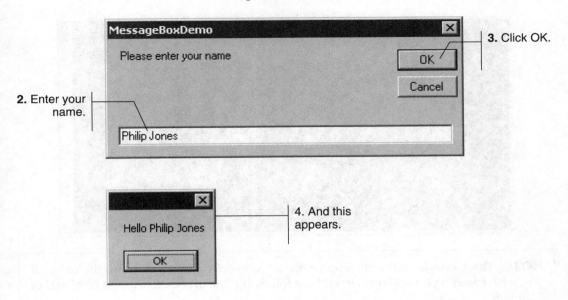

3. Click OK.

2. Enter your name.

4. And this appears.

PRACTICAL ACTIVITY 9.4

Enter and run the code shown in Listings 9.6 and 9.7.

Outputting to a Console application

Listing 9.8 shows how to output a message to a console. The string variable *myMessage* is assigned the string *"This is to demonstrate data output"* which is then output to the Console using the shared method *Write* (i.e. the *Console* class is messaged). The runtime is shown in Figure 9.18.

Listing 9.8 Output to the console.

```
Module Module1

    Sub Main()
        Dim myMessage As String

        myMessage = "This is to demonstrate data output"
        Console.Write(myMessage)
    End Sub

End Module
```

Figure 9.18 The runtime.

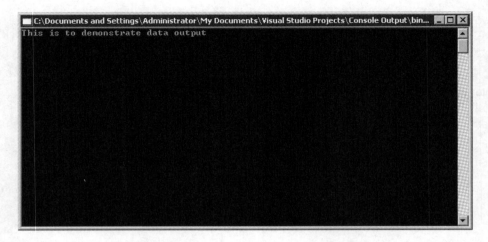

NOTE: The Console will only appear for a very brief period of time, therefore, if you wish to see it you will need to add the following line of code to the end of *Main()* of Listing 9.8:

Console.Read()

The output of the message was achieved using the *Write()* method associated with the *Console* class. *WriteLine()* is another useful method that also outputs data but puts a line feed and carriage return at the end of the output so that any further output will appear on the next line.

Inputting from a Console application

Listing 9.9 shows how to input from a Console. The string variable *userInput* is assigned the input obtained by the *ReadLine* method, which is then output using the *WriteLine* method. The last line of the code is to stop the Console disappearing before the output can be observed. The runtime is shown in Figure 9.19.

Listing 9.9 User input.

```
Module Module1
    Sub Main()
        Dim userInput As String

        userInput = Console.ReadLine()
        Console.WriteLine(userInput)
        Console.Read()
    End Sub

End Module
```

Figure 9.19 The runtime.

This appears when the Console
application is executed. It is waiting
for user input.

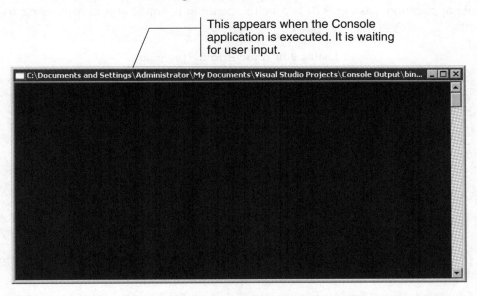

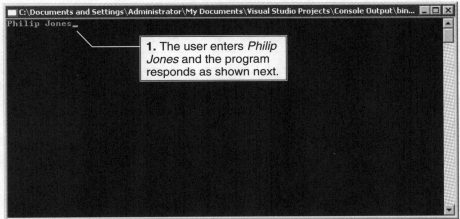

1. The user enters *Philip Jones* and the program responds as shown next.

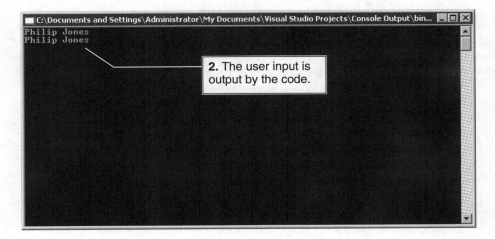

2. The user input is output by the code.

The code shown in Listing 9.9 did not give any user-friendly prompts to the user of the Console application. Listing 9.10 is a better example of input and output using friendly prompts.

Listing 9.10 A user-friendly program.

```
Module Module1

    Sub Main()
        Dim myName As String
        Dim myMessage As String

        Console.Write("Please enter your name ")
        myName = Console.ReadLine()
        myMessage = "Hello " & myName
        Console.WriteLine(myMessage)
        Console.Read()
    End Sub

End Module
```

NOTE: Listing 9.11 shows a program that behaves in exactly the same way as Listing 9.10, except that Listing 9.11 uses the *Imports* statement with the **namespace** of the **Console** class.

Listing 9.11

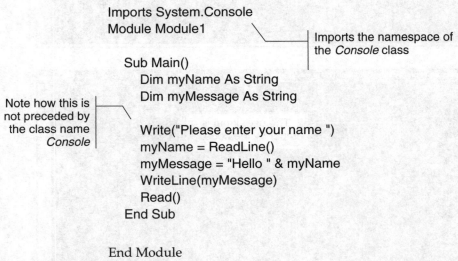

```
Imports System.Console
Module Module1                          Imports the namespace of
                                        the Console class

    Sub Main()
        Dim myName As String
        Dim myMessage As String

        Write("Please enter your name ")
        myName = ReadLine()
        myMessage = "Hello " & myName
        WriteLine(myMessage)
        Read()
    End Sub

End Module
```

Note how this is not preceded by the class name *Console*

NOTE: *Write*, *WriteLine* and *Read* are all examples of shared methods of the *Console* class.

PRACTICAL ACTIVITY 9.5

Enter and run the code shown in Listings 9.8, 9.9, 9.10 and 9.11. Type in your name and observe the output.

IMPORTANT: The latter half of this chapter has dealt with the inputting and outputting of data and in all cases this data has been in the form of text (i.e. strings). What happens if you wish to enter a number to be processed in some way, e.g. the number of hours worked by an employee or the number of pounds paid per hour? The answer is that they are still input and output as strings but they have to be converted to and from strings in order to be processed. Later chapters will deal with this in more depth – refer to Chapter 11 for more input and output techniques and refer to Chapter 13 for the tab order and verification of input data.

10 Data types and variables

The previous chapter defined program code as something that receives input data and processes this data to supply the output data. This chapter deals with program data in more depth, what it is, where it is stored when processed, the range of values program data can have, the ways in which program data can be processed, and how much memory program data uses when stored.

Input data

Data supplied as input to a VB .NET program is obtained from files. These files can be any of the following formats:

1. A text file.

2. The graphical user interface (GUI).

3. A binary file.

4. Another applications file.

5. A web page.

Output data

Output data from a VB .NET program is sent to a file. The file can be any of the following formats:

1. A text file.

2. The graphical user interface (GUI).

3. A binary file.

4. Another applications file.

5. A web page.

Text file

A text file is a sequence of binary codes (ones and zeros) that represent alphanumeric characters (letters, figures, other characters such as commas and full stops, etc.). Text files reside on magnetic or optical media, although they can temporarily reside in silicon memory (RAM) for the purpose of being processed.

The graphical user interface (GUI)

The objects (controls) of the GUI 'connect to' the keyboard, mouse, VDU and the Windows operating system. This 'connection' allows the user to enter input data via the appropriate objects (controls), while output data (processed data) is displayed via these objects (controls). An example of such controls is the *TextBox*.

Binary file

A binary file stores data in the internal representation of the computer (not codes that represent alphanumeric characters). This internal representation relates to the type of the data. Binary files also reside on magnetic and optical media, although they can temporarily reside in silicon memory (RAM) for the purpose of being processed. Access to binary files is quicker than access to text files because there is no requirement for conversion of data from one type to another.

Another applications file

Visual Basic .NET is a complete programming language that supports all the same type of data access as all other modern languages, such as C++, C# and Java. It also offers elegant ways for accessing the data of other applications. For example, it easily and directly accesses the data tables of various databases. Once the VB .NET application has access to this data it can process it. In other words, Visual Basic .NET can input the data of another application, process it and output it back to the other application or to its own files or its own GUI.

Data types

Every data item (program variable) has a data type and the type indicates:

- The range of possible values the data item can have.
- The way in which the data can be used and processed.
- The memory allocation for the data item.

Visual Basic .NET has numerous primitive data types; they are shown in Table 10.1.

Table 10.1 Visual Basic data types.

Type	Memory allocation	Range of values or brief description
The following are primitive numeric types that can store signed (i.e. positive and negative) **whole numbers**.		
Short	2 bytes	−32,768 to +32.767
Integer	4 bytes	−2 147 483 648 to +2 147 483 647
Long	8 bytes	−9 223 372 036 854 775 808 to +9 223 372 036 854 775 807
The following store binary codes.		
Byte	1 byte	0 to 255 (unsigned)
Char	2 bytes	A Unicode value (i.e. a code that represents characters on the keyboard plus others special characters). 0 to 65535 (unsigned)
The following are primitive numeric types that can store signed numbers that contain **decimal fractions**. They store **precision floating-point numbers**.		
Single	4 bytes	−3.402823E38 to +3.402823E38
Double	8 bytes	−1.79769313486231E308 to −4.940665645841247E-324 (negative numbers) 4.94065645841247E-324 to 1.79769313486231E308 (positive numbers)
Decimal	12 bytes	Large positive and negative numbers with 28 significant digits.
The following do not represent numbers.		
Date	8 bytes	A date and time variable
Boolean	1 byte	Stores either true or false
GUID	16 bytes	Represents a Globally unique identifier.
The following represents a variable used for storing text, i.e. a string.		
String (variable length)	10 bytes + (2 * string length)	0 to approximately 2 billion Unicode characters.
The following is a reference variables ('points to' an object).		
Object	4 bytes	Any type can be stored in a variable of type Object.

NOTE: *Integer* is an example of a primitive data type – in other words a variable of type *Integer* can store whole numbers. However, it is also possible to have an object that represents an integer – an integer object.

Integer type

A variable of this data type embraces all positive and negative **whole** numbers including zero. Computers cannot cope with infinitely large numbers. Consequently, there is a restriction on the range of numbers that the integer type can represent.

An integer type variable can be used to store the number of cars leaving a production line. A variable capable of storing a whole number is ideal, because you cannot have half a car.

The following operators can process an integer:

+   addition

–   subtraction

*   multiplication

\   integer division (i.e. 7 \ 3 equals 2 i.e. number 3 goes into 7 twice)

Mod   finds the remainder when numbers are divided (i.e. 7 MOD 3 equals 1 because 3 'goes into' 7 twice but the remainder is one).

Long type

This is similar to the integer type except it has a larger range, i.e. a variable of this type can represent bigger numbers. However, it takes up **more** memory storage than an integer type variable.

Short type

Again this is similar to the integer type except it has a smaller range. It also takes up **less** storage than an integer variable.

> **NOTE**: It is tempting to think that the smaller the storage size of a variable the quicker it is processed. While in general this is true it is not always the case, it depends upon the architecture of the CPU and supporting circuitry and how this manipulates 'chunks of data' on its data bus. For example, on 32-bit systems *Integer* operations are faster than either *Short* or *Long* operations.

> **NOTE**: Whenever you require a variable to store a whole number you would choose its type as a *Short*, *Integer* or *Long*. In practice you would choose the type based on the range of number you can predict it will store. If your prediction were that a variable would store a number between minus twenty to plus twenty thousand then a suitable data type for this variable would be a *Short*. Of course, you could make it an *Integer* or a *Long*, but this would just waste memory. However, if speed of access was a consideration you may decide for a 32-bit architecture computer to choose an *Integer*.

Single type

A variable of this type can store a single-precision floating-point number, i.e. all positive and negative numbers that have fractional parts. Again there is a restriction on the range of numbers the *Single* type can represent. There is also a restriction on the **precision** with which it can represent a real number. For example, the fraction two thirds is represented by the recurring decimal fraction 0.666666666666, etc. (i.e. to infinity). A computer cannot represent recurring fractions accurately. Instead it represents so many significant places.

A variable of type single can be used to store the dimensions of a building in metres because it needs to store the fractional numbers that represent the centimetres.

A single can be processed; for example, by the following operators:

+   addition

−   subtraction

*   multiplication

/   floating point division.

NOTE: There are different symbols for integer and floating point divisions. For integer division the symbol is \, while for floating point division the symbol is /. Integer division returns a whole number, floating point division returns a number with a fractional part.

Double type

A variable of this type can store a double-precision floating-point number and is similar to the single type except it takes twice the memory storage; consequently it can represent a larger range of numbers than the single data type variable.

Decimal type

Variables of this type can store the largest range of numbers with the highest precision It has the following range of numbers:

+/−79,228,162,514,264,337,593,543,950,335 with no decimal point

+/−7.9228162514264337593543950335 with 28 places to the right of the decimal

The smallest non-zero number is

+/−0.0000000000000000000000000001

Boolean type

A variable of this data type can store one of two possible values, **True** or **False**. A *Boolean* variable can be used as an indicator. For example, a *Boolean* variable may be called *Overdrawn*. If *Overdrawn* is true then a letter is sent to a customer informing them that they must bring their account up to date. However, if *Overdrawn* is false the customer is sent a letter asking if they would like a loan.

NOTE: The treatment of data types in this chapter is not exhaustive. I recommend that you read about other data types in the VB .NET help.

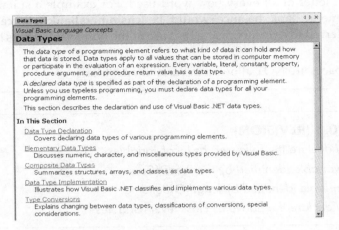

Declaration of variables

Variables are used to store values while the program statements are executed. Variables are declared as illustrated in Figure 10.1.

Figure 10.1 Declaring a variable.

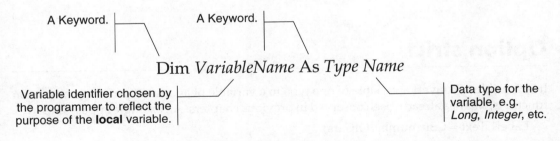

I recommend that you declare **local variables** as shown above. However, when you declare **class level variables** declare them as shown below (using *Private* instead of *Dim*).

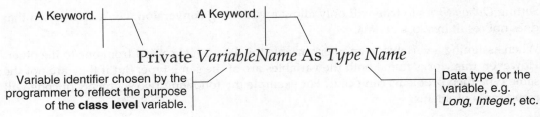

NOTE: For VB .NET code it is common practice to use camel casing for variable identifiers. This means that the first letter in the identifier is lowercase, as are all others except the first letter of all every new word used. For example a suitable identifier to store a customer's bank balance would be **customersBankBalance**. This type of identifier is referred to as camel casing because of the humps it exhibits by using capital letters.

Remember: Spaces are NOT allowed in variable identifiers.

QUESTION 10.1 (REVISION)

How would you declare the following as local variables?

1. *An Integer variable identified by numberOfCars.*
2. *A Double variable identified by lengthOfBuilding.*

How would you declare the above as class level variables?

Implicit and explicit declaration

The Visual Basic compiler, by default, requires that you declare every variable before you use it. This is refereed to as explicit declaration. You do not have to declare a variable before using it – referred to as implicit declaration. However, it is **very poor programming practice** to implicitly declare a variable because it can result in bugs that are difficult to correct.

Option strict

It is possible to convert a variable of one type to a variable of another type using conversion functions; this has already been observed in previous chapters. An example appears below:

    Label1.Text = CStr(numberOfCars)

numberOfCars is an integer variable storing a whole number and CStr is a function that converts the integer to a string so that it can be copied to the *Text* property of the Label.

Sometimes information can be lost in the conversion process. Converting a *Double* to an *Integer* will lose the decimal fraction. This is not desirable, so setting *Option Strict* to true (the default setting) will not allow any conversion that loses data.

Setting *Option Strict* to true will only allow a **widening conversion**, i.e., a conversion that does not result in a loss of data.

When assigning a variable to another variable the data is just copied from one to the other. However, this works fine if both the variables are of the same type. But if they are not the same type then problems can occur. For example the following two segments of code will result in no problems:

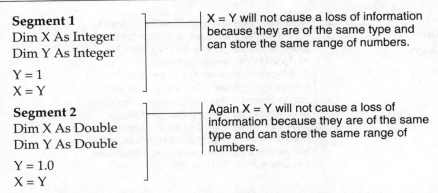

Segment 1
Dim X As Integer
Dim Y As Integer

Y = 1
X = Y

X = Y will not cause a loss of information because they are of the same type and can store the same range of numbers.

Segment 2
Dim X As Double
Dim Y As Double

Y = 1.0
X = Y

Again X = Y will not cause a loss of information because they are of the same type and can store the same range of numbers.

The following two segments can cause problems:

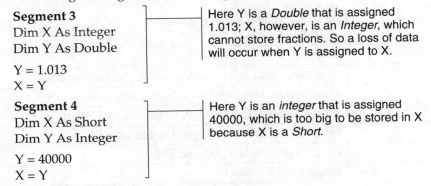

Segment 3
Dim X As Integer
Dim Y As Double

Y = 1.013
X = Y

Here Y is a *Double* that is assigned 1.013; X, however, is an *Integer*, which cannot store fractions. So a loss of data will occur when Y is assigned to X.

Segment 4
Dim X As Short
Dim Y As Integer

Y = 40000
X = Y

Here Y is an *integer* that is assigned 40000, which is too big to be stored in X because X is a *Short*.

The following segment will not cause problems:

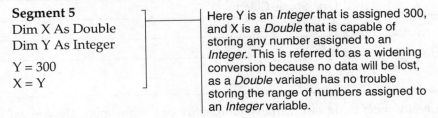

Segment 5
Dim X As Double
Dim Y As Integer

Y = 300
X = Y

Here Y is an *Integer* that is assigned 300, and X is a *Double* that is capable of storing any number assigned to an *Integer*. This is referred to as a widening conversion because no data will be lost, as a *Double* variable has no trouble storing the range of numbers assigned to an *Integer* variable.

All five segments of code have attempted **implicit conversions**. For example, Segment 5 has converted the *Integer* data stored in Y to *Double* data and stored it in the *Double* variable X. This conversion has resulted in the 300 being stored in more memory in the internal format of a *Double*.

This implicit conversion is poor programming practice because unless you are very careful data can be lost, as in the case of code segment 3.

Setting **Option Strict** to on (the default) will only allow **widening** conversions. This explicitly disallows any data type conversions in which data loss would occur.

Therefore, you should leave Option Strict set to on; you are also strongly recommended never to code for implicit conversion. Always use the conversion functions supplied with VB .NET. If you reconsider segment 5, you will remember that no data was lost – because it was a widening conversion. However, you should still not use this approach – instead it should be as shown in segment 6 below.

Segment 6
Dim X As Double
Dim Y As Integer

Y = 300
X = CDbl(Y)

Here the conversion function *CDbl* (convert to a Double) has been used to change the data stored in the *Integer* to a *Double* before it is assigned to the *Double* variable.
This happens anyway, so why use the conversion function? Well, first, it is an ideal way to comment your code, allowing the types of variable to be easily spotted, and second, and more importantly, it forces the programmer to concentrate on assignment statements to ensure that they avoid **narrowing conversion** (i.e. conversions that lose data).

Table 10.2 gives a partial list of widening conversions.

Table 10.2   Widening conversions.

Type	Widens to
Byte	Byte, Short, Integer, Long, Decimal, Single, Double, Object
Char	Char, Integer, Long, Decimal, Single, Double, String, Object
Short	Short, Integer, Long, Decimal, Single, Double, Object
Integer	Integer, Long, Decimal, Single, Double, Object
Long	Long, Single, Decimal, Double, Object
Single	Single, Double, Object
Double	Double, Object
Date	Date, String, Object
String	String, Object
Array	Object

NOTE: If you really wish to declare variables implicitly or assign implicitly you can obtain guidance from the Visual Basic help facility. However, I have no intention of guiding you because it is very poor programming practice!

Type conversion functions

These functions are compiled in-line, meaning the conversion code is part of the code that evaluates the expression. Execution is faster because there is no call to a method to accomplish the conversion. Each function forces an expression to a specific data type. Table 10.3 lists the conversion functions.

The required expression argument to the conversion functions is any string expression or numeric expression.

Table 10.3 Conversion functions.

Function	Return Type	Range for expression argument
CBool	Boolean	Any valid String or numeric expression.
CByte	Byte	0 to 255.
CChar	Char	0 to 65535.
CDate	Date	Any valid representation of a date and time.
CDbl	Double	−1.79769313486231E308 to −4.94065645841247E-324 for negative values. 4.94065645841247E-324 to 1.79769313486232E308 for positive values.
CDec	Decimal	+/−79,228,162,514,264,337,593,543,950,335 for zero-scaled numbers, i.e. numbers with no decimal places. For numbers with 28 decimal places, the range is +/−7.9228162514264337593543950335. The smallest possible non-zero number is 0.0000000000000000000000000001.
CInt	Integer	−2,147,483,648 to 2,147,483,647; fractions are rounded.
CLng	Long	−9,223,372,036,854,775,808 to 9,223,372,036,854,775,807; fractions are rounded.
CObj	Object	Any valid expression.
CShort	Short	−32,768 to 32,767; fractions are rounded.
CSng	Single	−3.402823E38 to −1.401298E-45 for negative values; 1.401298E-45 to 3.402823E38 for positive values.
CStr	String	Returns for CStr depend on the expression argument – see Table 10.4

Table 10.4 Returns for the *CStr* function.

If expression is	CStr returns
Boolean	A string containing "True" or "False".
Date	A string containing a date in the short date format of your system.
Numeric	A string representing the number.

The scope of variables

Variables declared inside an event handling procedure can only be accessed by that procedures code. The variable has a scope *local* to the handler and is often referred to as a **local variable**. Likewise variables declared within a method are local to the method and, consequently, only have a local scope.

Where and how a variable is declared fixes its scope. Some variables can have a broader scope that allows them to be accessed throughout an application or throughout a subset of the application. For example, class level variables (declared with the *Private* access modifier) can be accessed by all the code within an instance of the class.

Lifetime of variables

Local variables are usually used to store the intermediate results of calculations. Consequently, the values they store have no long-term use. Therefore, local variables are only valid during the execution of the method in which they are declared. The value they store 'disappears' when the method finishes executing. They have a lifetime equal to the duration of the method execution (a local variable within an event handling procedure has a lifetime equal to the duration that the event handling procedure executes).

Variables with a broader scope can have a lifetime equal to the duration of the **applications** execution. These variables store information that is needed by program code throughout the application and for all the time the application is running. An instance of a class level variable has a lifetime equal to the existence of an object of the class.

NOTE: As soon as the object is no longer in use it is **garbage collected**, i.e. removed from memory. At this moment of removal, the objects instance variables cease to exist along with the object.

When created objects take up computer resources (such as RAM space) and when running an object-oriented program can have many active objects. To ensure efficiency, when objects are no longer required they are automatically removed in order to release computer resources.

The removal of an object is not the responsibility of the programmer; it is automatically done by a mechanism referred to as **garbage collection**. However, a programmer can 'mark' an object for removal and when the garbage collector is active it will remove the object. However, most of the time the garbage collector decides when to remove an object.

Constants

A constant is a meaningful name that takes the place of, for example, a number that does not change throughout the program code. There are two sources for constants in Visual Basic:

1. System-defined constants.
2. User-defined constants.

System-defined constants

These are constants that are supplied by VB .NET and other applications accessed by VB .NET. For example, numbers between 1 and 7 can represent the days of the week – number one for *Sunday* and number 2 for *Monday*, and so on. However, instead of using the actual numbers in the code you can use the words *Sunday* and *Monday*, which makes programs much easier to read and understand.

NOTE: A number of intrinsic constants and enumerations to facilitate coding are provided by Visual Basic .NET.

Constants store values that remain constant throughout the execution of an application. They are meaningful names that take the place of a number or string and make code more readable.

Enumerations offer an easy way to work with sets of related constants. An enumeration is a symbolic name for a set of values *Sunday*, *Monday*, etc., are related constants and in fact 'belong to' an enumeration.

User-defined constants

Programmers can create their own constants to improve the readability of their code. An example of declaring a constant is shown in Figure 10.2.

Figure 10.2 Declaring a constant.

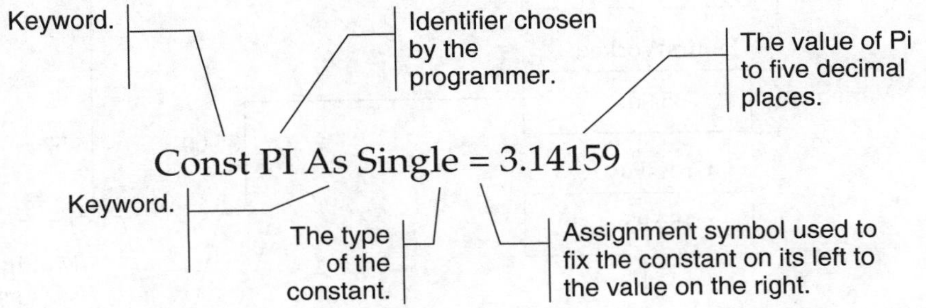

Keyword.

Identifier chosen by the programmer.

The value of Pi to five decimal places.

$$\text{Const PI As Single} = 3.14159$$

Keyword.

The type of the constant.

Assignment symbol used to fix the constant on its left to the value on the right.

To avoid confusing variables and constants when reading code you are recommended to CAPITALIZE every meaningful constant identifier (name). Constants can be assigned to variables and properties but they are **not** the same as variables. You **cannot** assign a value to a constant in program code.

NOTE: Once a constant has been declared its value remains fixed.

Scope of a constant

The scope of a constant is dependent, like a variable, upon where it is declared. The scope rules that apply to variables also apply to constants, e.g. a constant declared in a handler is local to that handler.

Performing calculations and assigning values to variables

The calculation of a worker's gross pay is achieved by the multiplication of the number of hours worked by the rate of pay per hour. VB .NET would perform this calculation using the following assignment statement:

grossPay = payRate * hoursWorked

The contents of the variables *payRate* and *hoursWorked* are multiplied together with the result being assigned (stored in) to the variable *grossPay*. This process is illustrated in Figure 10.3.

Figure 10.3 The execution of an assignment statement.

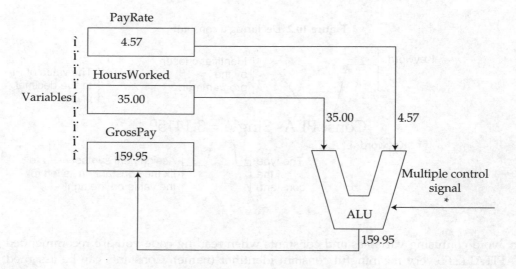

NOTE: ALU stands for arithmetic and logic unit. It is the part of the computer's central processing unit (CPU) that is responsible for adding, subtracting and other arithmetic operations; it also performs comparison (i.e. is x greater than y) and logic operations.

A closer look at an assignment statement

An assignment statement is a way of assigning a value to a variable or property. The simplest form of an assignment statement is:

Variable = expression

The assignment symbol '=' signifies the assignment of the value on the right hand side, to the variable on the left hand side.

> **NOTE**: A **definition** of an assignment statement is given below:
>
> The expression on the right hand side is evaluated (worked out) and the resulting value is copied to the variable on the left hand side.

Consequently, it is acceptable to have an assignment statement of the form:

count = count + 1

This assignment statement means take the value of the variable *count*, add one to it (i.e. evaluate the right hand side) and store the result in the variable *count* – this will overwrite the original value stored there. Figure 10.4 illustrates how the ALU is used to execute this assignment statement.

Figure 10.4 Execution of the assignment statement.

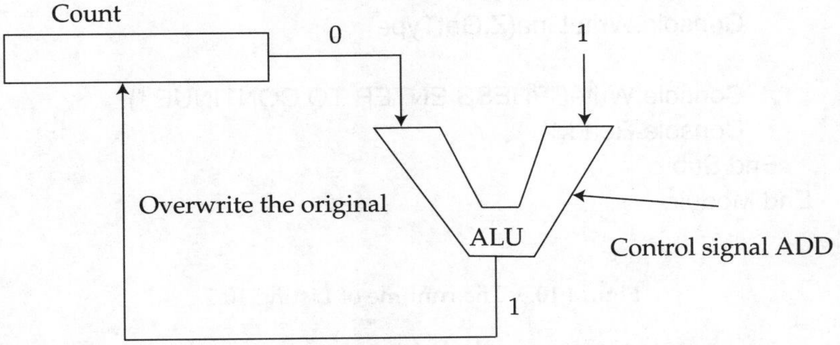

Primitive data types and objects

Integer, *Long* and *Double* are examples of primitive data types. Along with other primitive data types, they are the basic building blocks for the representation of data. For most of the time, they should be regarded as simple primitive data types and, therefore, as simple building blocks to represent data. For example, an array (see a later chapter) is a data structure that is 'built' from these primitive data types.

A closer look at these types, however, will show that they are in fact an alias for instances of classes – objects, in other words.

So within code it is possible to treat an *Integer* data type variable as a primitive type variable or as an object.

Listing 10.1   Primitive types or objects?

```
Module Module1
    Sub Main()
        Dim X As Integer
        Dim Y As Integer
        Dim Z As Integer

        X = 10
        Y = 20
        Z = X + Y

        Console.WriteLine("The value of X is " & X)
        Console.WriteLine("The value of Y is " & Y)
        Console.WriteLine("The value of Z is " & Z)

        Console.WriteLine(X.MaxValue)
        Console.WriteLine(Y.MinValue)
        Console.WriteLine(Z.GetType)

        Console.Write("PRESS ENTER TO CONTINUE ")
        Console.Read()
    End Sub
End Module
```

Figure 10.5 The runtime of Listing 10.1.

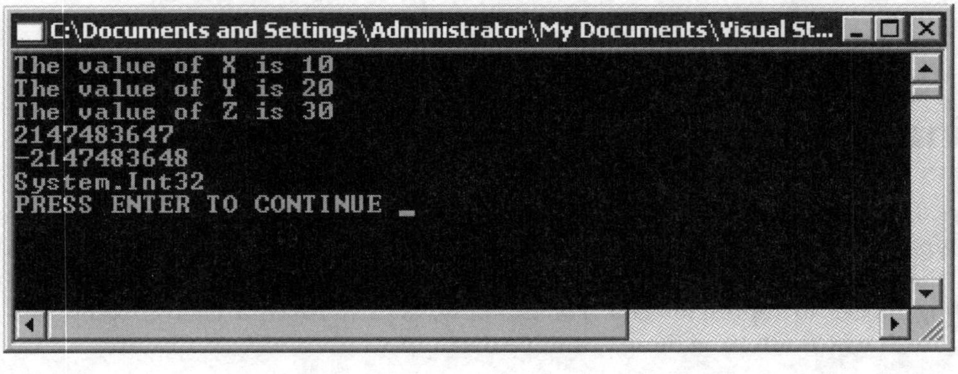

As it can be treated as an object it will have members that can be used within code. Listing 10.1 shows three primitive *Integer* variables being treated as primitive data types and also as objects. Figure 10.5 shows the runtime for Listing 10.1.

The first six program statements of Listing 10.1 treat the variables as primitive data types. The next three program statements treat the variables as objects and access members of the class. These members are *MaxValue*, *MinValue* and *GetType*. The runtime of Figure 10.5 illustrates the values stored in these properties. For example, *MaxValue* stores the maximum value that can be stored in an integer and this is displayed in the Console as 2147483647 by the program statement *Console.WriteLine(X.MaxValue)*.

QUESTION 10.2 (DEVELOPMENT)

Use the VB .NET help (or common sense) to discover the purpose of the other members of the integer class shown in Listing 10.1.

NOTE: An array, as just mentioned, is made up from primitive data types. However, an array can also be treated as an object – more on this in Chapter 20.

11 Program logic constructs and further data input and output

Program code is made up of three basic constructs that order the execution of program statements:

- Sequence
- Selection
- Repetition (iteration).

This chapter will deal with the sequential construct and following chapters will deal with selection and iteration. All of the constructs will be represented by three techniques:

- Flowcharts
- Nassi-Schneiderman charts (N-S charts)
- Structured English.

Structured English and N-S charts are examples of techniques used to express program design algorithms. Flowcharts are used to express the logic of program constructs and should **never** (except for teaching purposes) be used to express program design. A flowchart represents a 'mental picture' that programmers should carry in their mind as an aid to memorizing the logic of a program construct.

N-S charts are a graphical representation of program constructs that **ensures** the program designer uses the constructs that are available to them in the chosen high-level language (in this case, VB .NET).

Structured English is a non-graphical method that also ensures that a program designer uses the constructs that are available within the high-level language.

Both Structured English and N-S charts produce designs that do not require the use of branching statements, typically *goto* in many languages. Avoiding this statement is essential if a high-quality design is to be achieved.

Sequence

This describes a sequence of actions, as represented by program statements, which a program carries out one after another, **unconditionally**. For example, consider a program that reads in two numbers from the keyboard, multiplies them together and then displays the answer on the visual display unit (VDU).

Flowchart representation

The flowchart representation for a sequence is shown in Figure 11.1.

Figure 11.1 Flowchart representation of sequence.

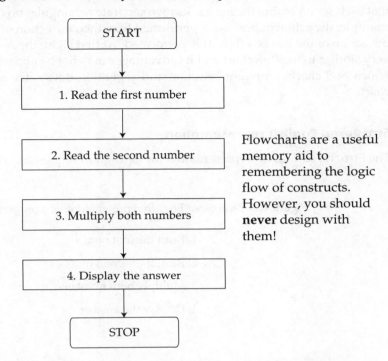

Flowcharts are a useful memory aid to remembering the logic flow of constructs. However, you should **never** design with them!

The flowchart shows the *flow* of control for the program. The first symbol is the START symbol; followed by the arrow showing the next action to be performed, which is in turn followed by another arrow showing the next action to be performed and so on until the STOP symbol is reached. Each rectangle symbol represents an action to be performed – for example, *Read the first number*. Every action shown in a sequence must be completed **before** another action is started. When one action is complete the next action is started; and no conditions have to be met before the next action can start. So for the multiplication example given, the first step (action) of the design will involve the reading of a number from the computer keyboard, the second step will involve the reading of another number from the keyboard. The third step will involve the multiplication of these numbers by the arithmetic and logic unit (ALU). The fourth and final step will be to display the product on the VDU.

N-S chart representation

Figure 11.2 shows the N-S chart representation for a program sequence.

Figure 11.2 An N-S chart representation of sequence.

1. Read the first number
2. Read the second number
3. Multiply both numbers
4. Display the answer

The N-S chart for sequence essentially lists the sequence of actions to be performed, except that each action within the list has its own separate rectangular box. So for the multiplication example, the action of box one is performed first, then the action of box two, and so on, until the action of the last box (box 4) is performed. At first sight, the N-S chart may appear to be very similar to the flowchart and its advantages may not be apparent. However, the way in which N-S charts represent selection and repetition does offer advantages over the flow chart.

Structured English representation

The Structured English representation for a program sequence is shown in Figure 11.3.

Figure 11.3 Structured English representation of a program sequence.

1. Read the first number

2. Read the second number

3. Multiply both numbers

4. Display the answer

The Structured English representation of sequence is a numbered list of actions that are performed one after another, unconditionally.

A sequential VB .NET program

SPECIFICATION 11.1

Develop a simple application that will prompt the user for two whole numbers and display the product of these numbers.

NOTE: The implementation of Specification 11.1 will be achieved using a Console application and not a Window application. This way the features of the language covered will be emphasized and the development of a GUI will not 'get in the way'.

The solution to Specification 11.1 is derived in five steps:

1. Develop an **algorithm** represented by an N-S chart (i.e. a design).

2. Produce a data table to identify the variables required.

3. Derive a simple test plan.

4. Convert the design to code and run.

5. Test the runtime against the test plan.

> **NOTE**: An algorithm is a computer programming term used to describe the steps of a solution to a defined problem (specification). It outlines the order of actions a program should undertake in order to implement the solution to the specification.

Step 1: Develop the algorithm

The N-S chart below represents the solution (i.e. design algorithm) to implement the specification.

1.	Read the first number
2.	Read the second number
3.	Multiply both numbers
4.	Display the answer

This design will process two items of data to produce a third. The input data to this program will be to variables identified as *firstNumber* and *secondNumber*, these variables will be processed (i.e. multiplied) to produce the output data (stored in a variable identified as *product*). The relationship between the input data, process and output data for this design is illustrated in Figure 11.4.

Figure 11.4 Design 'mapped' onto a program definition.

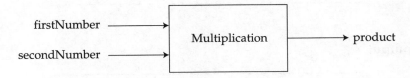

Step 2: Produce a data table

The production of a data table forces consideration of the variables (and their type) needed to implement the specification. When the specification defines a difficult problem it is often necessary to consider the structure of the variables and their type first – particularly if arrays, user defined structures and classes are required (see later). The data table for this specification and solution is shown below:

233

Identifier	Type	Description
firstNumber	Integer	Stores the number entered at the keyboard.
secondNumber	Integer	Stores the number entered at the keyboard.
product	Integer	Stores the product of *firstNumber* and *secondNumber* and has its content sent to the Console.

Step 3: Derive a simple test plan

A test plan is a table that lists the input(s) that should be supplied to the prompts of the program when it is executed and it indicates the output(s) expected for the supplied input(s).

In the case of this program the user will enter 7 and 8 in response to the prompts and the computer will process this data and produce the expected output, namely 56, the product of 7 and 8.

> **NOTE** : The development of a test plan is an 'acid test' that should not be skipped. If you can derive a test plan for the program you are about to code, then you understand the specification. Consequently, the probability of your design being correct is greatly improved!

Not every test plan will follow the following format; different format test plans will be presented throughout the text wherever necessary.

Supplied input

User-friendly message	Input data (user response)
Enter a number	7
Enter another number	8

Expected output

User-friendly message	Output data
The product of the input numbers is	56

Step 4: Convert the design to code

The code for the design is shown in Listing 11.1. The data table indicates that there is a need for three variables, *firstNumber*, *secondNumber* and *product*. These are declared as local integers in the *Main()* function.

> **NOTE**: The first program statement to execute in a Console application is the first program statement within the *Main()* function.

Figure 11.5 shows the sequence of events required to develop a Console application.

Figure 11.5 A Console application.

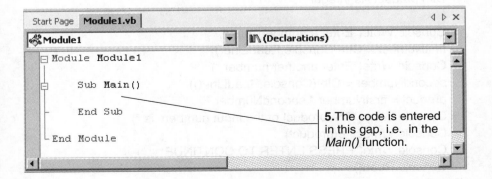

Figure 11.5 (cont.)

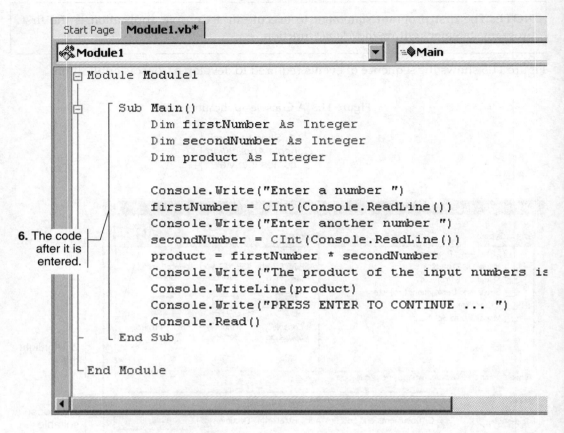

6. The code after it is entered.

Listing 11.1 Code for the design.

```
Sub Main()
    Dim firstNumber As Integer
    Dim secondNumber As Integer
    Dim product As Integer

    Console.Write("Enter a number ")
    firstNumber = CInt(Console.ReadLine())
    Console.Write("Enter another number ")
    secondNumber = CInt(Console.ReadLine())
    product = firstNumber * secondNumber
    Console.Write("The product of the input numbers is ")
    Console.WriteLine(product)
    Console.Write("PRESS ENTER TO CONTINUE ... ")
    Console.Read()
End Sub
```

When this application is run the code within the *Sub Main()* is executed first. This code contains the declaration of the three variables and the program statements.

NOTE: There are **nine** program statements whereas the NS chart design only had **four** steps. Five of the program statements are included to make the program **user-friendly**. The essence of the program still has the four steps as represented by the N-S chart design.

NOTE: A **user-friendly** program issues prompts to the user of the application informing them of the next task they should complete and it also describes the output they observe. For example, if the application required a user to enter a number a user-friendly prompt would be *Please enter a number*, or simply *Enter a number*. If the application were to output the product of input numbers then just before the output of the product a user-friendly prompt would be *The product of the input numbers is...* .

Description trace for *Sub Main()*

Statement	Description
When the application is executed the Console will appear as shown below:	

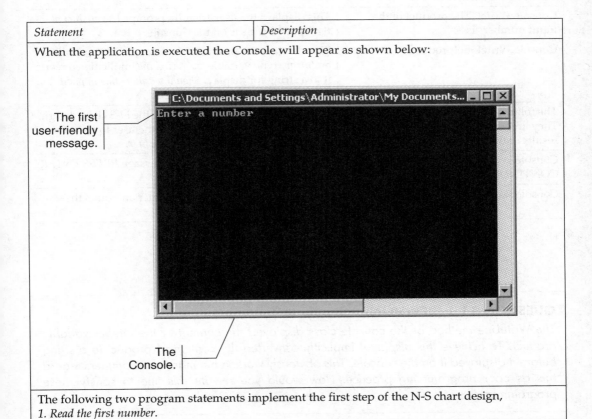

The following two program statements implement the first step of the N-S chart design, *1. Read the first number.*

| Console.Write("Enter a number ") | This statement displays the string *Enter a number* on the Console as shown above. |
| firstNumber = CInt(Console.ReadLine()) | This statement reads the 'numeric' string entered by the user, converts it to an integer using *CInt* and assigns it to the integer variable *firstNumber*. |

The following two program statements implement the second step of the N-S chart design, i.e.
2. Read the second number.

| Console.Write("Enter another number") | This statement displays the user-friendly prompt *Enter another number* on the Console. |
| secondNumber = CInt(Console.ReadLine()) | This statement reads the 'numeric' string entered by the user, converts it to an integer and assigns it to the integer variable *secondNumber*. |

The following statement implements the third step of the N-S Chart design, i.e.
3. Multiply both numbers, (find the product).

| product = firstNumber * secondNumber | A copy of the number stored in *firstNumber* and a copy of the number stored in *secondNumber* is sent to the ALU. The ALU is sent a signal to multiply its inputs. The result of this multiplication is output from the ALU and assigned to the variable *product*. |

The following two statements implement step four of the N-S chart design,
4. Display the answer.

| Console.Write("The product of the input numbers is ") | This displays the user-friendly prompt *The product of the input numbers is* on the Console. |
| Console.WriteLine(product) | This displays the product calculated. **NOTE**: *product* is an *Integer* type variable, so *WriteLine* implicitly converts it to a string for display. *Should we allow this implicit conversion? – refer to Question 11.1.* |

The following two program statements do not implement any of the steps of the N-S chart design. They are used to maintain the presence of the Console on the VDU to allow the user to view the results of the application. The console will disappear when the user presses *Enter*.

| Console.Write("PRESS ENTER TO CONTINUE ... ") | This displays the user-friendly message *PRESS ENTER TO CONTINUE ...* on the Console. |
| Console.Read() | This waits for the user to press Enter and quits the application when this occurs. |

QUESTION 11.1 (REVISION)

The WriteLine method of the console class displayed the content of the integer variable product. To achieve this display it implicitly converted the content of product to a string before it displayed it on the console. This obviously worked but many programmers regard this as poor programming practice. How would you rewrite this line to satisfy these programmers?

PRACTICAL ACTIVITY 11.1

Complete steps 4 and 5, i.e. code, run and test the program against the test plan.

Figure 11.6 illustrates the runtime for this program.

Figure 11.6 Run time sequence for the sequential program.

The first program statement issues this user-friendly prompt and waits for the user to enter 7 (as suggested by the test plan).

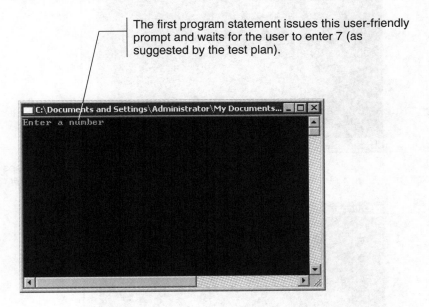

The user enters 7 and presses Enter. The second statement assigns this 7 to *firstNumber* and the next screen output occurs.

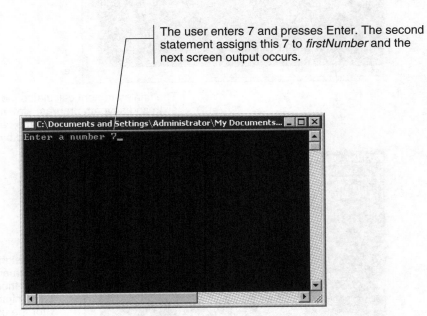

Figure 11.6 (cont.)

The third program statement issues this user-friendly message and waits for the user to enter 8 (as suggested by the test plan).

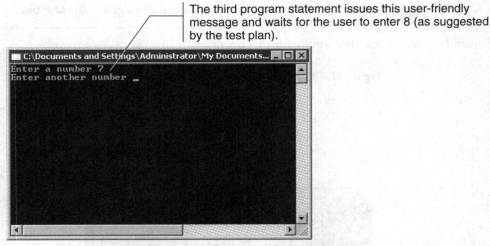

The users enters 8 and presses Enter. The fourth statement assigns this 8 to *secondNumber* and the next screen output occurs.

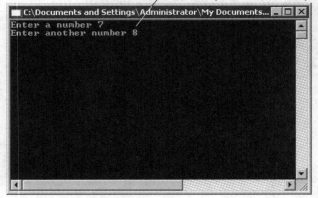

The fifth statement calculates the product and the sixth and seventh program statements issue this user-friendly message and the calculated product. The product is 56 as predicted by the test plan.

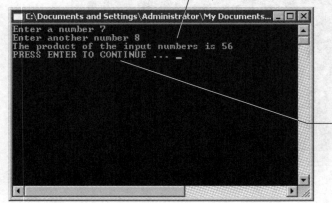

The eighth program statement issues this user-friendly message. The ninth statement waits for the user to press Enter to end the console and remove it from the VDU.

The application just discussed used a number of program statement that were not fully explained. The following pages will expand upon these program statements.

Displaying user-friendly prompts in a Console

A user friendly-prompt can be displayed in a Console using the *Write()* method and *WriteLine()* method. Both of these are **shared methods** of the *Console* class. In other words, to display a user-friendly prompt within a Console a message is sent to the *Console* class. To use a shared method an object of the class in not required. The user-friendly prompt to be displayed is passed as a parameter with this message.

Figure 11.7 A message to Console class.

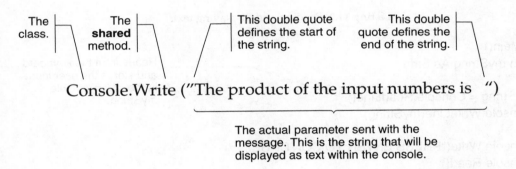

| The class. | The **shared** method. | This double quote defines the start of the string. | This double quote defines the end of the string. |

Console.Write ("The product of the input numbers is ")

The actual parameter sent with the message. This is the string that will be displayed as text within the console.

NOTE: The *WriteLine()* and *Write()* methods are similar in their functionality – they both output strings (i.e. text) to the Console. However, the *WriteLine()* method also adds a carriage return and line feed at the end of the string. This causes the cursor to move to a new line.

NOTE: If you refer to Figure 11.7 you will see that the actual parameter of the *Write()* method has a space after the letter *s* of the word *is*. This ensures that when the next program statement of Listing 11.1 outputs the value stored in the variable *product* it gives a sensible display, in other words it looks like:

The product of the input numbers is 56

rather than

The product of the input numbers is56

When using strings for text output always use appropriate gaps to ensure sensible output!

241

Obtaining data from the keyboard when using a Console application

When a user of a console application enters data at the keyboard it can be read using the *ReadLine()* and *Read()* methods. Like *Write()* and *WriteLine()* both *ReadLine()* and *Read()* are **shared methods** of the *Console* class.

To read a line of text entered in the Console window requires the use of the *ReadLine()* method. Of course, anything read from the keyboard has to be stored in an appropriate variable. The *ReadLine()* method treats all of the data entered at the keyboard as a string, consequently, the variable used to store this string needs to be declared as a *String* type variable. Listing 11.2 shows the reading of data from the keyboard and its storing in a variable of type string. The contents of this variable is then displayed using the *WriteLine()* method.

Listing 11.2 Reading and displaying text.

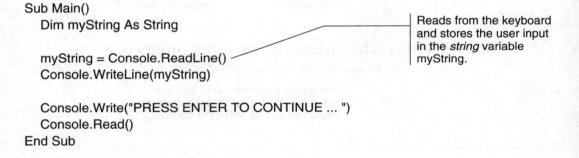

```
Sub Main()
    Dim myString As String

    myString = Console.ReadLine()          Reads from the keyboard
    Console.WriteLine(myString)            and stores the user input
                                           in the string variable
                                           myString.
    Console.Write("PRESS ENTER TO CONTINUE ... ")
    Console.Read()
End Sub
```

PRACTICAL ACTIVITY 11.2

Enter and run Listing 11.2. Please note that the program does not have any user-friendly prompts, so at launch you need to remember to type some data and then press Enter.

PRACTICAL ACTIVITY 11.3

Amend Listing 11.2 so that it does include user-friendly prompts. Run it to make sure that it works.

Listing 11.3 shows a program that does not compile (Option Strict set to true) because there are incompatible data types. The program is very similar to Listing 11.2 but the variable used to store the input data is of type *Integer* not type *String*.

Listing 11.3 A program that will **not** compile.

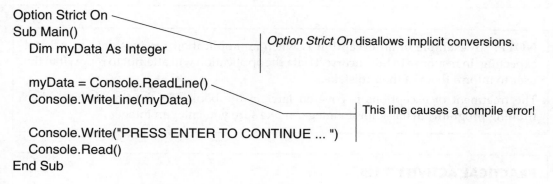

```
Option Strict On
Sub Main()
    Dim myData As Integer

    myData = Console.ReadLine()
    Console.WriteLine(myData)

    Console.Write("PRESS ENTER TO CONTINUE ... ")
    Console.Read()
End Sub
```

Option Strict On disallows implicit conversions.

This line causes a compile error!

PRACTICAL ACTIVITY 11.4

Enter and run Listing 11.3 and observe the compile error.

ReadLine() treats the data entered at the keyboard as a *String* (i.e. text) and the attempt to assign it to an *Integer* variable is not allowed. However, it is possible to use a conversion function to explicitly convert a *String* to an *Integer* as shown by the amendment to Listing 11.3 in Listing 11.4. The amendment is shown in bold.

Listing 11.4 The amendment of Listing 11.3.

```
Sub Main()
    Dim myData As Integer

    myData = CInt(Console.ReadLine())
    Console.WriteLine(myData)

    Console.Write("PRESS ENTER TO CONTINUE ... ")
    Console.Read()
End Sub
```

> **NOTE:** The conversion function *CInt* is used to convert the text entered to an *Integer*. However, this assumes that the user has the discipline to ensure that they enter an integer. For example, if they entered *1245* then this program will work at runtime. However, if they were to enter *12qwe4*, which is plainly not an integer (because it contains letters and not all figures), then the program will throw an **exception**.

> **NOTE:** An example of an **exception** is when an application receives data it was not expecting. In response to this incorrect data the application will attempt to report it to the user to inform them of their mistake.
>
> The treatment of exceptions is covered later in the book. For the time being, when running programs that ask for an integer make sure you enter an integer.

> **PRACTICAL ACTIVITY 11.5**
>
> Enter and run the program shown in Listing 11.4.
>
> Enter an integer (e.g. *1245*) and observe the effect.
>
> Enter a non-integer (e.g. 12qwe4) and observe the effect.
>
> Enter a real number (e.g. *3.142*) and observe the effect.

> **QUESTION 11.2 (DEVELOPMENT)**
>
> *As we have just discussed, the ReadLine() method treats the data entered at the keyboard as a string. Use the VB .NET on-line help to discover how the Read() method treats the data entered at the keyboard.*

Implementing Specification 11.1 as a Windows application

An **InputBox** displays a prompt in a dialog box, waits for the user to input text or click a button, and then returns a String containing the contents of the InputBox. If the user does not enter any text and just clicks the button a zero length string is returned.

A **MessageBox** is a predefined dialog box that displays application-related information to the user.

Listing 11.5 shows a program attached to the click event of a button that uses an InputBox to supply text to an application. This text is then displayed in a MessageBox. The program is another implementation of specification 11.1. Whereas Listing 11.1 implemented the specification using a Console application, Listing 11.5 implements the specification within a Windows Application attached to the click event of a button.

Figure 11.8 shows the runtime for the program shown in Listing 11.5.

Listing 11.5 Another implementation of Specification 11.1.

```
Private Sub btnSpec11one_Click(ByVal sender As System.Object, ByVal e As _
System.EventArgs) Handles btnSpec11one.Click
    Dim firstNumber As String
    Dim secondNumber As String
    Dim product As Integer
    Dim productString As String

    firstNumber = InputBox("Enter a number", "Finding the product", "0")
    secondNumber = InputBox("Enter another number", "Finding the product", "0")
    product = CInt(firstNumber) * CInt(secondNumber)
    productString = "The product is " & CStr(product)
    MessageBox.Show(productString, "Finding the product", MessageBoxButtons.OK)
End Sub
```

Figure 11.8 The runtime for Listing 11.5.

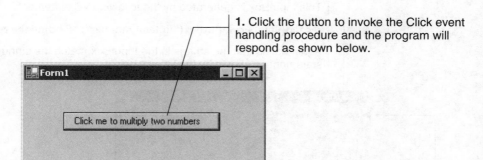

1. Click the button to invoke the Click event handling procedure and the program will respond as shown below.

245

Figure 11.8 (cont.)

This InputBox is generated by the following VB statement:

firstNumber=InputBox("Enter a number", "Finding the product", "0")

Notice that the strings in the InputBox match the strings in the statement as shown by the arrows below.

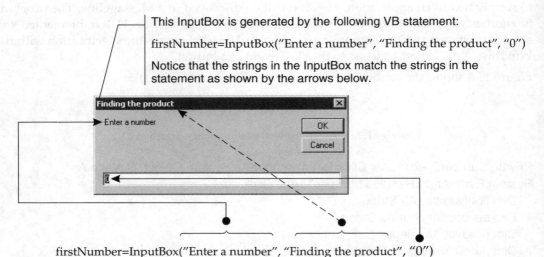

firstNumber=InputBox("Enter a number", "Finding the product", "0")

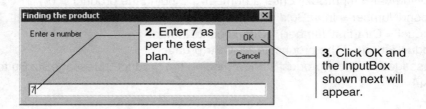

2. Enter 7 as per the test plan.

3. Click OK and the InputBox shown next will appear.

On the click of OK the string 7 is copied to the string variable *firstNumber*. The number seven will be used as a number within the program, but at the moment it is a string.

This InputBox is generated by the following VB statement:

secondNumber=InputBox("Enter a number", "Finding the product", "0")

Again notice that the strings in the InputBox match the strings in the statement as shown by the arrows below.

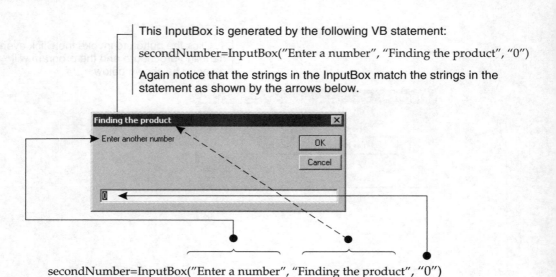

secondNumber=InputBox("Enter a number", "Finding the product", "0")

Figure 11.8 (cont.)

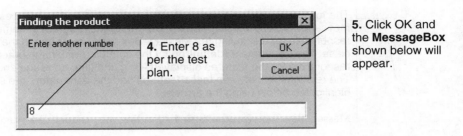

5. Click OK and the **MessageBox** shown below will appear.

On the click of OK the number 8 is copied to the string variable *secondNumber*. The following program statement is then executed:

product = CInt(firstNumber) * CInt (secondNumber)

The *String* variables *firstNumber* and *secondNumber* are converted to integers using the *CInt* function. These integer values are then multiplied together with the result (56 as predicted by the test plan) being assigned to the *Integer* variable *product*.

The value stored in the integer variable product cannot be displayed in a MessageBox in its current form. It has to be converted to a string before it can be used as a parameter to the MessageBox. The following program statement achieves this:

productString = "The product is " & CStr(product)

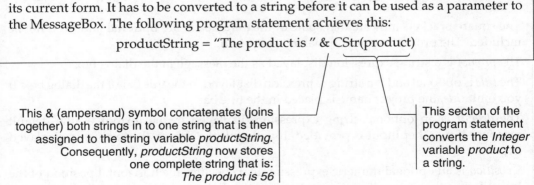

This & (ampersand) symbol concatenates (joins together) both strings in to one string that is then assigned to the string variable *productString*. Consequently, *productString* now stores one complete string that is:
The product is 56

This section of the program statement converts the *Integer* variable *product* to a string.

Figure 11.8 (cont.)

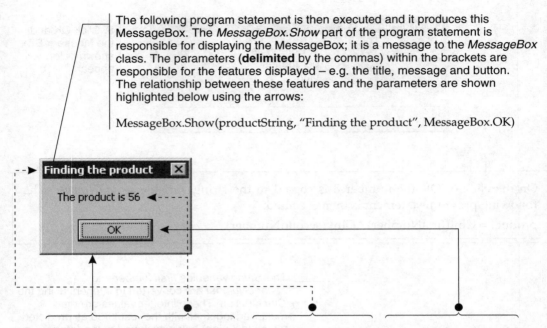

The following program statement is then executed and it produces this MessageBox. The *MessageBox.Show* part of the program statement is responsible for displaying the MessageBox; it is a message to the *MessageBox* class. The parameters (**delimited** by the commas) within the brackets are responsible for the features displayed – e.g. the title, message and button. The relationship between these features and the parameters are shown highlighted below using the arrows:

MessageBox.Show(productString, "Finding the product", MessageBox.OK)

MessageBox.Show(productString, "Finding the product", MessageBoxButtons.OK)

NOTE: The general format of the *InputBox* function is:

InputBox(prompt [,title] [,default] [,x position] [,y position])

The square brackets indicate that some of the parameters are **optional** and need not be included. The prompt is not optional: it is **required**.

The *prompt* is a string expression displayed as the message in the dialog box.

The *title* is optional and is a string expression displayed in the title bar of the dialog box. If you omit *title*, the project name is placed in the title bar.

The *default* is an optional string expression displayed in the textbox as the default response if no other input is provided. If you omit the *default*, the textbox is displayed empty.

x position is an optional numeric expression that specifies the horizontal position of the **InputBox** on the screen. If you omit *x position* the dialog box is horizontally centred.

y position is an optional numeric expression that specifies the vertical position of the *InputBox* on the screen. If you omit *y position* the dialog box is positioned approximately one-third of the way down the screen.

For Listing 11.5 the optional parameters *x position* and *y position* are not used.

NOTE: To **delimit** means, for example, to end a section of a statement; so each of the parameters within the *Show* method end with a comma.

NOTE: The strings displayed in the **InputBox** are passed as parameters to the *InputBox* function (a function is similar to a method). Commas (as highlighted by the arrows below) separate these parameters. The strings appear between the double quotes.

firstNumber = InputBox("Enter a number", "Finding the product", "0")

⬆ ⬆

NOTE: *Show* is a **shared** method of the *MessageBox* class. This means that it is **not** necessary to create an object of this class in order to use this method. Such methods in other object-oriented languages are often referred to as static methods.

PRACTICAL ACTIVITY 11.6

Implement Specification 11.1 using the *MessageBox* class and the *InputBox* function, i.e. use Listing 11.5.

a)   Attach the code to the click event of a Button.

b)   Then attach the code to the click event of a **PictureBox**.

Overloaded method

The *Show* method is declared within the *MessageBox* class as a *Public Shared* method, and consequently forms part of the public interface of the class. This means it can be invoked from any code we write. The *Show* method is also overloaded; this means that there is more than one *Show* method within the class and each method has the **same name**. The type and the number of their parameters distinguish them, however. Figure 11.9 illustrates program statements using the *Show* method and the corresponding output (it is assumed in all cases that *productString* is a string type variable storing the string *The product is 56*).

Table 11.1 lists some of the *Show* methods within the *MessageBox* class.

Figure 11.9 Examples of the shared *Show* method.

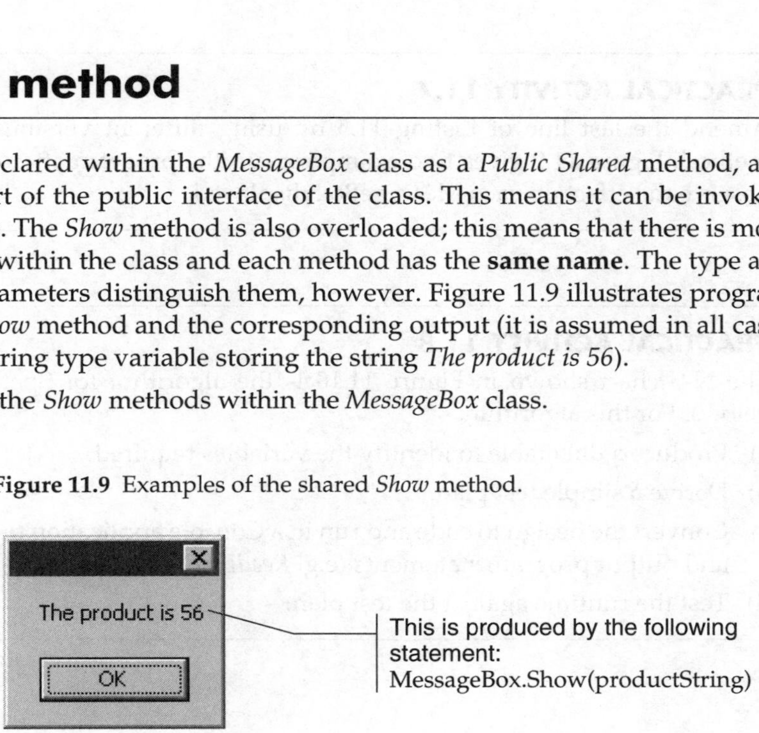

This is produced by the following statement:
MessageBox.Show(productString)

Figure 11.9 (cont.)

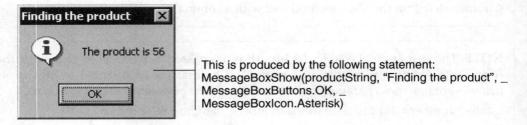

This is produced by the following statement:
MessageBoxShow(productString, "Finding the product", _
MessageBoxButtons.OK, _
MessageBoxIcon.Asterisk)

Table 11.1 Some of the *Show* methods.

The Show *methods*	Description
Overloads Public Shared Function Show(String) As DialogResult	Displays a MessageBox with specified text.
Overloads Public Shared Function Show(String, String) As DialogResult	Displays a MessageBox with specified text and caption.
Overloads Public Shared Function Show(String, String, MessageBoxButtons) As DialogResult	Displays a MessageBox with specified text, caption, and buttons.
Overloads Public Shared Function Show(String, String, MessageBoxButtons, MessageBoxIcon) As DialogResult	Displays a MessageBox with specified text, caption, buttons, and icon.

PRACTICAL ACTIVITY 11.7

Amend the last line of Listing 11.5 by using different versions of the **shared** *Show* method. Figure 11.9 gives two examples; run the program after each amendment and observe the effect on each MessageBox displayed.

PRACTICAL ACTIVITY 11.8

The N-S chart shown in Figure 11.10 is the algorithm for Specification 11.2 (shown below). For this algorithm:

a) Produce a data table to identify the variables required.

b) Derive a simple test plan.

c) Convert the design to code and run in a Console application using appropriate input and output program statements (e.g. *ReadLine*, *Write*, etc.)

d) Test the runtime against the test plan.

SPECIFICATION 11.2

Develop a simple application that will prompt the user for the height, width and depth of a box. Calculate and then display the volume of the box.

Figure 11.10 N-S chart for Specification 11.2.

1.	Enter the height
2.	Enter the width
3.	Enter the depth
4.	Calculate the volume
5.	Display the volume

PRACTICAL ACTIVITY 11.9

Implement Specification 11.2 again but this time attach the program code to the click event of a *PictureBox* and use the *InputBox* function and *MessageBox.Show* message for the inputting and outputting of data.

PRACTICAL ACTIVITY 11.10

Implement Specification 11.2 again but this time use a GUI that uses textboxes for the inputting and outputting of data.

12 Making decisions and operators

Before selection and iteration constructs are considered it is necessary to look at how computer programs make decisions.

Conditional tests

A program is able to make decisions. These decisions may result in the actions of a program, or segment of a program, being repeated. A decision may also result in one segment of a program being chosen for execution over another segment.

Conditional tests make the decisions in a VB .NET program. A conditional test (or conditional statement) can consist of comparisons between variables using relational operators. It can also consist of logical operators 'working on' variables. Also, a conditional test can consist of a combination of both logical and relational operators. Table 12.1 shows relational operators and their meaning. Table 12.2 shows logical operators and their meaning.

Table 12.1 Relational operators and their meaning.

Relational operator	Meaning
<	less than
<=	less than or equal to
>=	greater than or equal to
>	greater than
=	equal to
<>	not equal to
Like	Fuzzy string comparison

Table 12.2 Logical operators and their meaning.

Logical operator	Meaning
And	logical AND
Or	logical OR
Not	logical NOT
Xor	exclusive OR

> **IMPORTANT**: There is only one of two possible outcomes from a conditional test (conditional statement): **True** or **False**.

Examples of conditional statements (using only relational operators)

Example 12.1

firstNumber > secondNumber

This conditional test is asking whether the content of the variable *firstNumber* is greater than the content of the variable *secondNumber*.

If the *firstNumber* content is greater than the *secondNumber* content then the evaluation of this test (i.e. the result) is **True**.

If the *firstNumber* content is less than the *secondNumber* content then the result is **False**.

If the *firstNumber* content is the same as the *secondNumber* content then the result is **False** (*firstNumber* has to be greater than *secondNumber* to be true).

Example 12.2

firstNumber >= secondNumber

This conditional test is asking whether the content of the variable *firstNumber* is greater than or equal to the content of the *secondNumber*.

If the *firstNumber* content is greater than the *secondNumber* content then the result is **True**.

If the *firstNumber* content is less than the *secondNumber* content then the result is **False**.

If the *firstNumber* content is the same as the *secondNumber* content then the result is **True**.

QUESTION 12.1 (REVISION)
Decide whether each of the following conditional tests is true or false.

The value of each variable in the examples are as defined by the following three assignment statements:

firstNumber = 5 ⎤
secondNumber= 6 ⎬ The assignment statements.
thirdNumber= 6 ⎦

1. firstNumber <= secondNumber
2. firstNumber < secondNumber
3. firstNumber <> secondNumber
4. firstNumber > secondNumber
5. firstNumber >= secondNumber
6. firstNumber = secondNumber
7. secondNumber <> thirdNumber
8. secondNumber >= thirdNumber

9. secondNumber = thirdNumber
10. secondNumber > thirdNumber

The *Like* operator

The *Like* operator allows for comparisons between variables to include wildcards. Consequently, it allows for **inexact** matches. Table 12.3 lists wildcards that can be used with the *Like* operator.

Table 12.3 Wildcards and their meaning.

Wildcards	Meaning
?	Any single character
#	Any single digit
*	Zero or more characters
[set]	Any character in the set
[!set]	Any character except those in the set

Examples of the use of the *Like* operator and wildcards

Example 12.3

If the string variable *surname1* was assigned the string Smith (i.e. *surname1* = "*Smith*") and *surname2* was assigned Smyth (i.e. *Surname2* = "*Smyth*") then both the following statements would be **True**.

surname1 **Like** "Sm?th"

surname2 **Like** "Sm?th"

The statements are true because the contents of the each variable are exactly the same as the string *Sm?th* except for one character position. However, this position is represented by a wildcard which means that the variable being compared to *Sm?th* using the *Like* operator can have any value in this position.

Example 12.4

If the *Char* variable *digit* were assigned the character 6 (i.e. *digit* = "*6*") then the following statement would be **True**.

digit **Like** "[0-9]"

This statement is **True** because the character 6 belongs to (is *in*) the set of characters from 0 to 9.

QUESTION 11.2 (REVISION)

Answer each of the following:

1. A Char *variable is assigned the character* a (*i.e.* letter = "a") *therefore, is the following statement True or False?*

$$\text{letter Like "[a-z]"}$$

2. A Char *variable is assigned the character* R (*i.e.* letter = "R") *therefore is the following statement True or False?*

$$\text{letter Like "[a-z]"}$$

Logical operators

Relational operators are fairly easy to understand in that they relate to everyday ideas, such as, is this value greater than that one, etc. To understand logical operators requires the learning of their definition. The following operators will be considered in turn:

1. Logical *Or*.

2. Logical *And*.

4. Logical *Not*.

5. Logical *XOR*.

NOTE: Logical operators are defined by their truth tables.

Logical Or

result = Expression1 **Or** Expression2

The truth table for logical *Or* is shown in Table 12.4.

Table 12.4 The logical *Or* truth table.

Expression1	Expression2	Result
False	False	False
False	True	True
True	False	True
True	True	True

NOTE: For the *Or* operator the result is true if **one or more** of the expressions are true. The result is false if **all** the expressions are false.

Logical *And*

result = Expression1 *And* Expression2

The truth table for logical *And* is shown in Table 12.5.

Table 12.5 A two input *And* truth table.

Expression1	Expression2	Result
False	False	False
False	True	False
True	False	False
True	True	True

NOTE: For the *And* operator the result is true if **all** the expressions are true. The *result* is false if **one or more** expressions are false.

Logical *Not*

result = **Not** Expression

The truth table for the logical *Not* operator is shown in Table 12.6.

Table 12.6 *Not* truth table.

Expression	Result
False	True
True	False

NOTE: The result is *Not* the expression. For the *Not* operator if the expression is false then the result is true, and if the expression is true the result is false.

Logical *Xor*

result = Expression1 **Xor** Expression2

The truth table for logical *Xor* is shown in Table 12.7.

Table 12.7 A two-input *Xor* truth table.

Expression1	Expression2	Result
False	False	False
False	True	True
True	False	True
True	True	False

NOTE: For the *Xor* operator the result is true if the expressions are different.

Demonstration of logical operators

The code of a Console application illustrated in Listing 12.1 shows the results from logical operations in the console window. Logical operators used in this program are taken out of context. However, the program represents a useful teaching aid and similar programs will be used to test your understanding in revisions questions later in the chapter. Figure 12.1 shows the runtime for this listing.

Listing 12.1 Demonstrating logic operators.

```
Module Module1

    Sub Main()
        Console.WriteLine(False And False)
        Console.WriteLine(False And True)
        Console.WriteLine(True And False)
        Console.WriteLine(True And True)
        Console.WriteLine()
        Console.WriteLine(False Or False)
        Console.WriteLine(False Or True)
        Console.WriteLine(True Or False)
        Console.WriteLine(True Or True)
        Console.WriteLine()
        Console.WriteLine(Not (False Or False))
        Console.WriteLine(Not (False Or True))
        Console.WriteLine(Not (True And False))
        Console.WriteLine(Not (True And True))
        Console.Write("PRESS ENTER TO CONTINUE ... ")
        Console.Read()
    End Sub

End Module
```

This statement gives a line space as shown by the arrow.

Figure 12.1 The runtime for Listing 12.1.

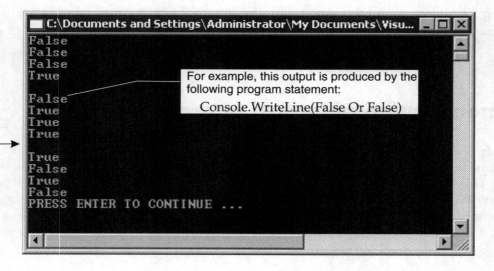

For example, this output is produced by the following program statement:

Console.WriteLine(False Or False)

Program trace for Listing 12.1

Statement	Description
Console.WriteLine(False And False)	The *Console.WriteLine* statement outputs to the Console, the result of '**Anding**' together False and False. Therefore it outputs False.
Console.WriteLine(False And True)	The *Console.WriteLine* statement outputs to the Console, the result of '**Anding**' together False and True. Therefore it outputs False.
Console.WriteLine(True And False)	The *Console.WriteLine* statement outputs to the Console, the result of '**Anding**' together True and False. Therefore it outputs False.
Console.WriteLine(True And True)	The *Console.WriteLine* statement outputs in the Console, the result of '**Anding**' together True and True. Therefore it outputs True.
Console.WriteLine()	This outputs an empty line.
Console.WriteLine(False Or False)	The *Console.WriteLine* statement outputs in the Console, the result of '**Or ing**' together False and False. Therefore it outputs False.
This program continues until the third to last statement, which is described below:	
Console.WriteLine(Not (True And True))	True And True is True. This value of True is then '**Not'ed**' to give False. Consequently, the *Console. WriteLine* statement outputs False to the Console.
Console.Write("PRESS ENTER TO CONTINUE ... ") Console.Read()	These two lines allow the user to view the console output. The operations of these two lines were discussed in a previous chapter.

QUESTION 12.3 (REVISION)

What is the output from the code shown in Listing 12.2?

Listing 12.2 Listing for Question 12.3

```
Module Module1

    Sub Main()
        Console.WriteLine(False Xor False)
        Console.WriteLine(True Xor False)
        Console.WriteLine(Not (False And False))
        Console.WriteLine(Not (False Xor True))
```

Listing 12.2 (cont.)

```
Console.WriteLine(Not (True And True))
Console.WriteLine(Not (True And False))
Console.Write("PRESS ENTER TO CONTINUE ... ")
Console.Read()
End Sub

End Module
```

Operator precedence

Logical operators

Consider the following logical operation:

Not True And False

If the **And** is performed first the result is as follows:

Not True And False

Not   False

True

That is:

Not True **And** False = **Not** False = True

However, **if** the **Not** is performed first the result is as follows:

Not True **And** False = False **And** False = False

The result obtained differed. This must **not** be allowed to happen and a computer overcomes this problem by giving different priorities to operators. The logical *Not* operator has a higher priority than the logical *And* operator. This means that the computer will always evaluate the *Not* before the *And*. Consequently, the correct result to the above operation is:

Not True **And** False = False **And** False = False

All operators in the Visual Basic .NET language have a priority.

Arithmetic operators

If you wished to obtain the average of three numbers you would add all three and divide by three. In Visual Basic .NET the correct way to obtain the average is shown below:

$$average = (x + y + z) / 3$$

The incorrect way for obtaining the average is shown below:

$$average := x + y + z / 3$$

Division has a higher priority than addition. Therefore, for this expression the division will be done before the addition. This obviously will not find the average. Whereas, for the first expression brackets are used to ensure that the addition is performed first. **Brackets have the highest priority**.

Operator categories

There are three main categories of operators:

1. Arithmetic operators (e.g. +, * and \).

2. Comparison operators (e.g. >, <> and >=).

3. Logical operators (e.g. And, Or and Xor).

When expressions contain operators from more than one category, arithmetic operators are evaluated first, comparison operators are evaluated next, and logical operators are evaluated last.

Comparison operators all have equal precedence and are evaluated in the left to right order in which they appear.

Arithmetic operators are evaluated in the order of precedence as shown in Table 12.8.

Logical operators are evaluated in the order of precedence as shown in Table 12.9.

Table 12.8 Precedence of arithmetic operators.

Operator	Priority number
Exponentiation (^)	1
Negation (-)	2
Multiplication and division (*,/)	3
Integer division (\)	4
Modulo arithmetic (Mod)	5
Addition and subtraction (+,-)	6

Table 12.9 Precedence of logical operators.

Operator	Priority number
Not	1
And	2
Or	3
Xor	4

Multiplication and division have the same priority, and when they occur together in an expression each operation is evaluated as it occurs from left to right. Likewise, when addition and subtraction occur together in an expression, each operation is evaluated in order of appearance from left to right.

> **NOTE:** The string concatenation operator (&) is not an arithmetic operator, but in precedence it does fall after all arithmetic operators and before all comparison operators. Similarly, the *Like* operator, while equal in precedence to all comparison operators, is actually a pattern-matching operator.

The highest priority of all is the bracket. You are strongly advised to make frequent use of brackets to ensure the correct evaluation of logical, arithmetic and relational operations. Careful use of brackets will overcome all difficulties associated with priorities. Indeed, armed with brackets you may never need to learn the order of priorities!

QUESTION 12.4 (REVISION)

What is the output from the program shown in Listing 12.3?

Listing 12.3 Program referred to in Question 12.4.

```
Module Module1

    Sub Main()
        Dim A As Integer
        Dim B As Integer
        Dim C As Integer
        Dim D As Integer
        A = 1
        B = 2
        C = 3
        D = 2
```

Listing 12.3 (cont.)

```
      Console.WriteLine(A <> B And C = D)
      Console.WriteLine(A = B Or B = C)
      Console.WriteLine(B = C Xor D <> A)
      Console.WriteLine(A >= C Or D >= B)
      Console.WriteLine(A <= B And C <> D)
      Console.WriteLine(A <> B And B <> C)
      Console.WriteLine(B = C Xor D <> A)
      Console.WriteLine(A < C Or D > B)
      Console.WriteLine(Not (A < C) And Not (D > B))
      Console.WriteLine(Not (A < C Or D > B))

      Console.Write("PRESS ENTER TO CONTINUE ... ")
      Console.Read()
   End Sub

End Module
```

A real example

All of the examples of operators given in this chapter to date have been taken out of context. Consider Specification 12.1.

SPECIFICATION 12.1

A bank will offer a customer a loan if they are 21 or over and have a balance of at least £250 in their current account. Write a program that will, based on a customer's age and balance, produce a decision on whether they will be offered a loan.

This program will not be produced but the conditional test that makes the decision will.

The conditional test must produce *True* if the customer is 21 or over and they have a balance of £250 or more. Any other variation must produce *False*.

For example if they are 30 but only have a balance of £100 they will not be offered a loan and the conditional test must produce *False*.

False must also be produced if they have a balance of £1000 but are only 18 years of age.

The conditional test that will meet the requirement is shown below:

$$(age >= 21) \text{ And } (balance >= 250)$$

To be convinced of the 'correctness' of this conditional test requires a number of tests. These tests are given in Table 12.10.

Table 12.10 Testing the conditional test.

Customer age	Customer balance	age >= 21	balance >= 250	(age >= 21) And (balance >= 250)
20	249	False	False	False And False = False
20	250	False	True	False And True = False
20	251	False	True	False And True = False
21	249	True	False	True And False = False
21	250	True	True	True And True = True
21	251	True	True	True And True = True
22	249	True	False	True And False = False
22	250	True	True	True And True = True
22	251	True	True	True And True = True

The numbers of tests are governed by the boundary of the relational tests. Three values of *age* are chosen: 20, 21 and 22; i.e. below 21, at 21 and above 21. Likewise three values of *balance* are chosen: 249 (below), 250 (at) and 251 (above).

13 Selection

At the end of a calendar month the customers of a bank have their accounts inspected by a computer program. If an account is overdrawn then the program issues instructions to send a letter to the customer, informing them to bring their account into credit. However, if their account is in credit the program issues instructions to send a letter that asks the customer whether they would like a loan.

Depending upon the balance of a customer's account the program will execute one of two sets of instructions. Either instructions to issue a 'warning letter', that is, *you are overdrawn and do something about it* or instructions to issue a 'friendly letter' to drum up business for the bank, that is, *as a valued customer of the bank we would like to offer you a loan facility*. The program will **select** which set of instructions to execute based upon a conditional test (i.e. if the balance is greater than or equal to zero, the customer is sent a friendly letter **else** the customer is sent a warning letter). Consequently, the program will choose one of two routes through the code, i.e. choose between two different actions.

Selection is the program construct that allows a program to choose between different actions. It allows for alternative paths to be taken through a program.

The selection constructs used in VB .NET are:

- *If .. Then*
- *If .. Then .. Else*
- *If .. Then .. ElseIf .. Else*
- *Select Case*

Figure 13.1 shows the control flow for the (a) *If .. Then* selection construct and b) the *If .. Then .. Else* selection construct.

Figure 13.1 Flowchart for (a) the *If .. Then* and (b) the *If..Then..Else* selection construct.

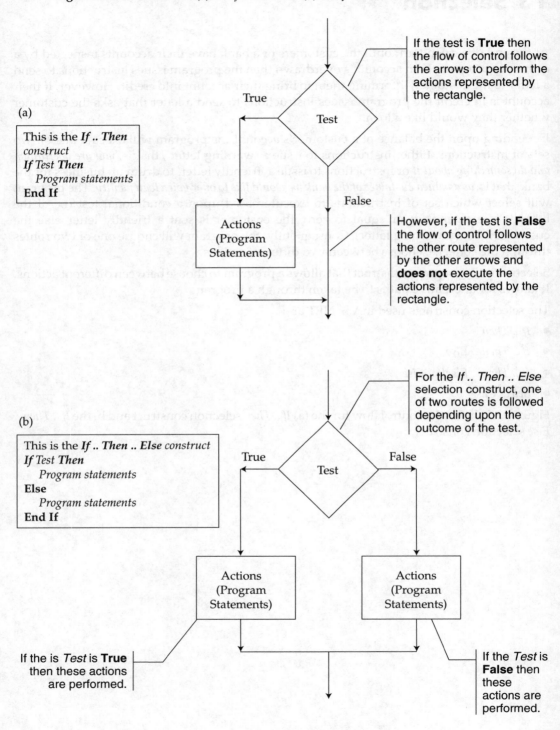

(a)

This is the **If .. Then**
construct
If *Test* **Then**
     Program statements
End If

True

Test

If the test is **True** then
the flow of control follows
the arrows to perform the
actions represented by
the rectangle.

Actions
(Program
Statements)

False

However, if the test is **False**
the flow of control follows
the other route represented
by the other arrows and
does not execute the
actions represented by the
rectangle.

(b)

This is the **If .. Then .. Else** *construct*
If *Test* **Then**
     Program statements
Else
     Program statements
End If

For the *If .. Then .. Else*
selection construct, one
of two routes is followed
depending upon the
outcome of the test.

True   Test   False

Actions
(Program
Statements)

Actions
(Program
Statements)

If the is *Test* is **True**
then these actions
are performed.

If the *Test* is
False then
these
actions are
performed.

It has been previously stated that flowcharts should never be used to express program design, however, the constructs of Figures 13.1 should remain with you as a 'mental picture' of the flow of control through selection constructs. Better methods, for use in program design, are N-S Charts and Structured English. Figures 13.2 and 13.3 show the N-S chart representation for three selection constructs.

Figure 13.2 N-S Charts for the *If .. Then* and *If .. Then .. Else* constructs.

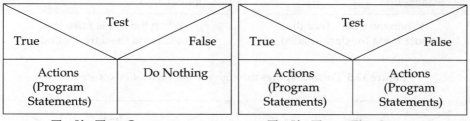

Figure 13.3 N-S Chart for the *Select Case* construct.

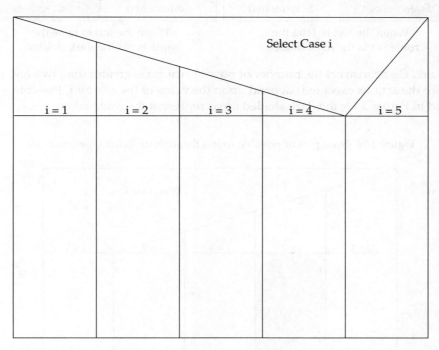

For the *If .. Then* and the *If .. Then .. Else* constructs, the state of their test can be **true** or **false**. Figures 13.4 and 13.5 show the possible routes through the designs (and hence programs) represented by these constructs.

Figure 13.4 Possible routes through the *If .. Then* construct.

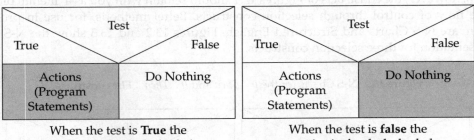

When the test is **True** the
route is via the dark shaded.

When the test is **false** the
route is via the dark shaded.

Figure 13.5 Possible routes through the *If .. Then .. Else* construct.

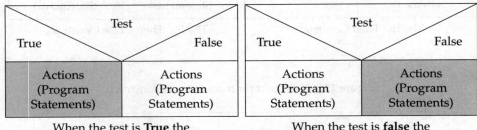

When the test is **True** the
route is via the dark shaded.

When the test is **false** the
route is via the dark shaded.

For the *Select Case* construct the number of possible routes is greater than two and the route (and hence the actions executed) depend upon the value of the *selector* **i**. Possible routes are illustrated in Figure 13.6; the dark shaded areas represent the route taken.

Figure 13.6 Examples of possible routes through the *Select Case* construct.

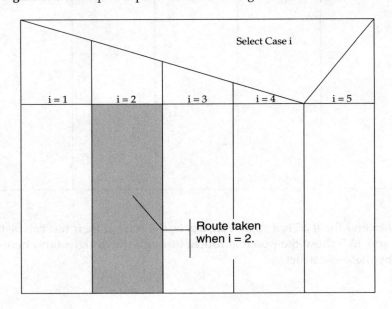

Figure 13.6 (cont.)

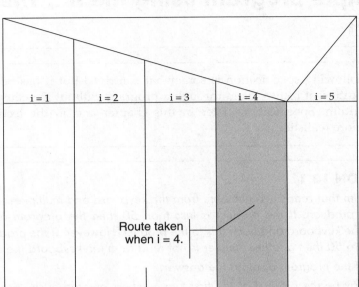

The format of the *If .. Then* construct

Figure 13.7 shows the outline of an N-S chart representing the *If .. Then* construct and its relationship to a VB .NET selection construct.

Figure 13.7 Visual Basic selection construct (The *If .. Then* construct).

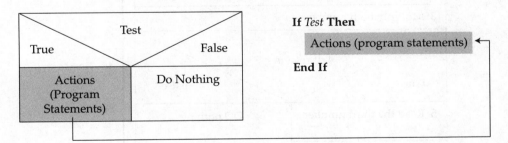

If the outcome of the test is **True** then the actions represented by the shaded area between the keywords words *If* and *End If* are executed. If the condition is **False** then the statements (represented by the shaded area) are **not** executed.

An example program using the *If .. Then* construct

NOTE: The following specification is somewhat contrived but it has been chosen to highlight the different routes taken through a program without the complication of a difficult algorithm. Specifications later in this chapter and in the lecturer support material are more realistic.

SPECIFICATION 13.1

Write a program that reads two numbers from the keyboard and multiplies them together (i.e. finds the product). If the product is less than 50 then the program reads another number from the keyboard and adds this to the product. However, if the product is greater than or equal to 50 then another number is not read from the keyboard (i.e. do nothing).

The last line of the program displays the answer.

The answer may be the product of the first two numbers entered or the product with the addition of a third number.

The design for Specification 13.1 is shown in Figure 13.8.

Figure 13.8 A design involving selection that implements Specification 13.1.

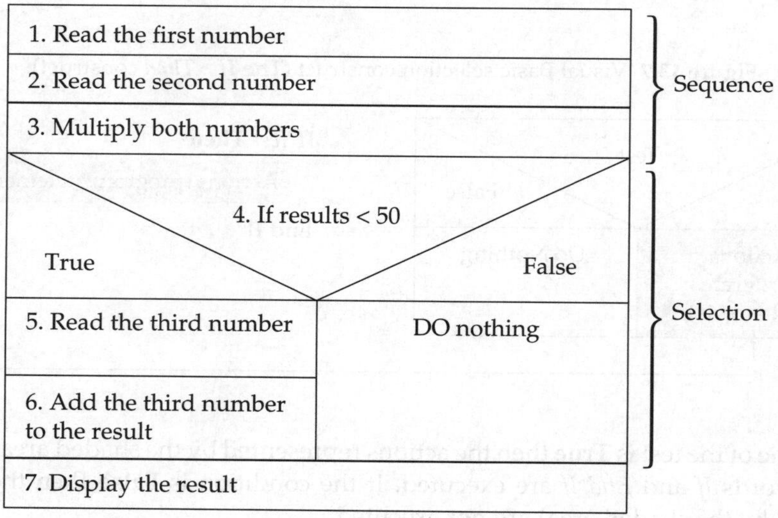

Possible routes through this design (program)

There are two possible routes through this program.

If the result at step 3 is less than 50 then the route through the design is defined by the execution of the following steps: 1, 2, 3, 4, 5, 6 and 7.

However, if the result at step 3 is greater than or equal to 50 then the following steps are followed 1, 2, 3, 4 and 7, i.e. steps 5 and 6 are **not** executed.

In other words steps 5 and 6 are executed when the evaluation of step 4 (the test *If result < 50*) is **True**. When the test of step 4 is **False** then steps 5 and 6 are not executed.

The design of Figure 13.8 is represented in Figure 13.9 by Structured English.

Figure 13.9 Structured English design.

```
1. Read the first number
2. Read the second number
3. Multiply the two numbers
4. If result < 50 Then
       5. Read a third number
       6. Add third number to the result
   End If
7. Display the result
END
```

The flow of control represented by the Structured English design, shown in Figure 13.9, is obviously the same as that for the Nassi-Schneiderman design shown in Figure 13.8. When the outcome of step 4 (*If result < 50*) is true then steps 5 and 6 are executed. The selection construct is represented by the words **If, Then** and **End If**. Whenever the outcome of the condition is true, then the steps embraced by the words **Then** and **End If** are executed and for the design shown in Figure 13.9 these are steps 5 and 6. The final **END** defines the end of the design and has nothing to do with the selection construct. Notice how the steps within the selection construct are indented, this improves the visual appeal of the design.

The design of Figure 13.8 will be coded and as per previous examples the following steps will be followed (step 1, the design, is already completed).

2. Produce a data table.

3. Derive a simple test plan.

4. Convert the design to code and run.

5. Test the runtime against the test plan.

Step 2: Produce a data table

Identifier	Type	Description
firstNumber	Integer	Stores the number entered at the keyboard.
secondNumber	Integer	Stores the number entered at the keyboard.
thirdNumber	Integer	Stores the number entered at the keyboard.
result	Integer	Stores the evaluation of the processing of the program, and has its content copied to the visual display unit. The evaluation stored in this variable may be the product or the product plus the third number. It all depends upon the path selected by the program and this selection depends upon the value of the product derived from the first two numbers input by the user.

Step 3: Derive a simple test plan

The test plan must test the outcome of all the possible execution paths through the program. Consequently, the input numbers supplied must be chosen so that the product of the first two numbers are less than 50, for one test, and more than 50 (or equal to 50) for the second test.

Test 1

Supplied input

User-friendly prompt	Input data (user response)
Enter the first number	8
Enter the second number	9

Expected output

User-friendly prompt	Output data (user response)
The answer is	72

Test 2

Supplied input

User-friendly prompt	Input data (user response)
Enter the first number	8
Enter the second number	2
Enter the third number	5

Expected output

User-friendly prompt	Output data (user response)
The answer is	21

For Test 1 the product of the first two numbers is greater than 50 so the program will **not** ask for a third number and the result is therefore the product of the supplied input (8 times 9). Whereas, for Test 2 the product of the first two numbers is less than 50, consequently, the program **does** ask for a third number. The output of Test 2 is therefore 8 times 2 plus 5, i.e. 21.

Step 4: Convert the design to code and run

The code for the design is shown in Listing 13.1.

> **NOTE**: Listing 13.1 shows the program implemented as a Console application **not** a Windows application.

Listing 13.1 A Console application implementing the design of Figure 13.8.

```
Option Strict On
Option Explicit On
Module Module1

    Sub Main()
        Dim firstNumber As Integer
        Dim secondNumber As Integer
        Dim thirdNumber As Integer
        Dim result As Integer

        Console.Write("Enter the first number ")
        firstNumber = CInt(Console.ReadLine())
        Console.Write("Enter the second number ")
        secondNumber = CInt(Console.ReadLine())
        result = firstNumber * secondNumber
        If result < 50 Then
            Console.Write("Enter the third number ")
            thirdNumber = CInt(Console.ReadLine())
            result = result + thirdNumber
        End If
        Console.WriteLine("The answer is " & result)
        Console.Write("PRESS ENTER TO CONTINUE ... ")
        Console.Read()
    End Sub

End Module
```

PRACTICAL ACTIVITY 13.1

Enter and run the program of Listing 13.1 and test it against tests 1 and 2. **Remember that it runs within a Console application!!**

Routes through the program

There are two possible routes through the program of Listing 13.1. When run against Test 1, the route through the program is represented by Figure 13.10. The statements that execute are highlighted in bold.

Figure 13.10 One possible route through the 'selection' program when run against Test 1. The numbers input to the program are 8 and 9 and their product is 72. The *If .. Then* constructs conditional test is therefore false, consequently, the statements inside this construct are not executed, i.e. they are 'skipped over'.

```
Option Strict On
Option Explicit On
Module Module1

    Sub Main()
        Dim firstNumber As Integer
        Dim secondNumber As Integer
        Dim thirdNumber As Integer
        Dim result As Integer

        Console.Write("Enter the first number ")
        firstNumber = CInt(Console.ReadLine())
        Console.Write("Enter the second number ")
        secondNumber = CInt(Console.ReadLine())
        result = firstNumber * secondNumber
        If result < 50 Then
            Console.Write("Enter the third number ")
            thirdNumber = CInt(Console.ReadLine())
            result = result + thirdNumber
        End If
        Console.WriteLine("The answer is " & result)
        Console.Write("PRESS ENTER TO CONTINUE ... ")
        Console.Read()
    End Sub

End Module
```

When run against Test 2, the route through the program is represented by Figure 13.11, again the statements that execute are highlighted in bold and larger font.

Figure 13.11 Another route through the program. This time the program is run against Test 2. The first two numbers entered are 8 and 2; their product is 16, consequently, the conditional test of the *If .. Then* construct is true and the statements 'inside' this construct are executed. The third number entered is 5 and therefore the output from the program is 21 (16 + 5).

```
Option Strict On
Option Explicit On
Module Module1

    Sub Main()
        Dim firstNumber As Integer
        Dim secondNumber As Integer
        Dim thirdNumber As Integer
        Dim result As Integer

        Console.Write("Enter the first number ")
        firstNumber = CInt(Console.ReadLine())
        Console.Write("Enter the second number ")
        secondNumber = CInt(Console.ReadLine())
        result = firstNumber * secondNumber
        If result < 50 Then
            Console.Write("Enter the third number ")
            thirdNumber = CInt(Console.ReadLine())
            result = result + thirdNumber
        End If
        Console.WriteLine("The answer is " & result)
        Console.Write("PRESS ENTER TO CONTINUE ... ")
        Console.Read()
    End Sub

End Module
```

Description trace when run against Test 1

Statements	Description
The following two program statements implement step 1 of the N-S chart shown in Figure 13.8.	
Console.Write("Enter the first number ")	The Console displays the user-friendly prompt *Enter the first number*.
firstNumber = CInt(Console.ReadLine())	The user enters the number 8 at the keyboard and this is read by the *ReadLine* method. This number eight will be treated as a string that needs to be converted by *CInt* to an *Integer* variable before it is assigned to the *Integer* variable *firstNumber*.

The following two program statements implement step 2 of the N-S chart shown in Figure 13.8.	
Console.Write("Enter the second number ")	The Console displays the user-friendly prompt *Enter the second number.*
secondNumber = CInt(Console.ReadLine())	The user enters 9 and this is assigned to the variable *secondNumber.* Again *CInt* is used.
The following program statement implements step 3 of the N-S chart shown in Figure 13.8.	
result = firstNumber * secondNumber	The value stored in the variable *firstNumber* is multiplied by the value stored in the variable *secondNumber.* The evaluation of this multiplication, which is 72, is assigned (i.e. stored) in the variable *result.* Consequently, the integer variable *result* contains the integer 72.
The following represents step 4 of the N-S chart shown in Figure 13.8.	
If result < 50 Then	This conditional test asks if the content of the variable result is less than 50 (i.e. 72 < 50). It is **not** so **False** is the outcome. Consequently, the statements 'inside' the *If.. Then* construct are **not** executed i.e. they are 'skipped over'.
The following program statement represents step 7 of the N-S chart shown in Figure 13.8. Of course, when run against test 1 steps 5 and 6 are NOT executed.	
Console.WriteLine("The answer is " & result)	The Console displays the literal string *The answer is* and a copy of the content of the variable *result.* The ampersand sign (&) is always used to 'join together' strings with variables in this way. Of course the variable *result* is an *Integer* type variable, however, the *WriteLine* method **implicitly** converts its content to a string before it joins it together with the first string.
The following two lines are not part of the design.	
Console.Write ("PRESS ENTER TO CONTINUE ... ") Console.Read()	These lines have been described before – they allow the console to be observed before it disappears from view.

Description trace when run against Test 2

Statements	*Description*
The following two program statements implement step 1 of the N-S chart shown in Figure 13.8.	
Console.Write("Enter the first number ")	The Console displays the user-friendly prompt *Enter the first number.*
firstNumber = CInt(Console.ReadLine())	The user enters 8 and this assigned to the variable *firstNumber* – again *CInt* is used.

The following two program statements implement step 2 of the N-S chart shown in Figure 13.8.	
Console.Write("Enter the second number ")	The Console displays the user-friendly prompt *Enter the second number*
secondNumber = CInt(Console.ReadLine())	The user enters 2 and this assigned to the variable *secondNumber* – again *CInt* is used.

The following program statement implements step 3 of the N-S chart shown in Figure 13.8.	
result = firstNumber * secondNumber	The value stored in the variable *firstNumber* is multiplied by the value stored in the variable secondNumber. The result of the multiplication, which is 16, is assigned (i.e. stored) in the variable result. Consequently, integer variable result contains the integer 16.

The following represents step 4 of the N-S chart shown in Figure 13.8.	
If result < 50 Then	This conditional test asks if the content of the variable *result* is less than 50 (i.e. 16 < 50). It is consequently **True** is the outcome. Therefore, the statements 'inside' the *If .. Then* construct **ARE** executed.

The following program statements implements step 5 of the N-S chart shown in Figure 13.8.	
Console.Write("Enter the third number ")	The console displays the user-friendly prompt *Enter the third number*
thirdNumber = CInt(Console.ReadLine())	The user enters the number 5 at the keyboard and this is read by the *ReadLine* method. This number five will be treated as a string, which needs to be converted by *CInt* before it is assigned to the *Integer* variable *thirdNumber*.

The following program statement implements step 6 of the N-S chart shown in Figure 13.8.	
result = result + thirdNumber	The content of the variable result (i.e. 16) is added to the contents of the variable *thirdNumber* (i.e. 5). The result of the addition (i.e. 21) is assigned to the variable *result*. Consequently, the integer variable *result* stores the integer 21.

The following program statement represents step 7 of the N-S chart shown in Figure 13.8.	
Console.WriteLine("The result is " & result)	The console displays the string *The answer is* and a copy of the content of the variable *result*.

The following two lines are **not** part of the design.	
Console.Write ("PRESS ENTER TO CONTINUE ... ") Console.Read()	These lines have been described before – they allow the console to be viewed.

Implementing Specification 13.1 within a Windows application

Listing 13.2 shows code attached to the *Form_Click* event handling procedure, i.e. the code is executed when the user clicks the form.

Listing 13.2 Implementing Specification 13.1 within a Window application.

```
Private Sub Form1_Click(ByVal sender As Object, ByVal e As System.EventArgs)
Handles MyBase.Click
    Dim firstNumber As Integer
    Dim secondNumber As Integer
    Dim thirdNumber As Integer
    Dim result As Integer
    Dim resultString As String

    firstNumber = CInt _
    (InputBox("Enter the first number", "A Selection example", "0"))

    secondNumber = CInt _
    (InputBox("Enter the second number", "A Selection example", "0"))

    result = firstNumber * secondNumber
    resultString = "The result is " & CStr(result)
    If result < 50 Then
        thirdNumber = CInt _
        (InputBox("Enter the third number", "A Selection example", "0"))
        result = result + thirdNumber
        resultString = "The result is " & CStr(result)
    End If
    MessageBox.Show(resultString, "A Selection example", MessageBoxButtons.OK)
End Sub
```

PRACTICAL ACTIVITY 13.2

Enter and run the program of Listing 13.2 and test it against Tests 1 and 2. Remember that it runs within a Windows Application! The sequence of screen shots below shows how to create a form click event.

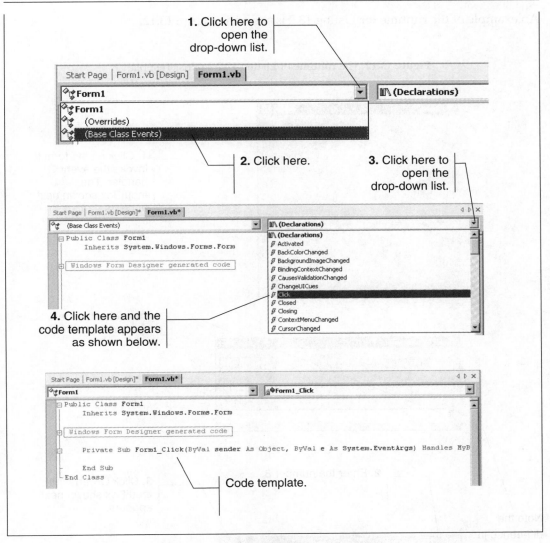

1. Click here to open the drop-down list.

2. Click here.

3. Click here to open the drop-down list.

4. Click here and the code template appears as shown below.

Code template.

QUESTION 13.1 (REVISION)

Produce a description trace for the program shown in Listing 13.2 for Tests 1 and 2.

NOTE: *MessageBox.Show* is a message that invokes one of the overloaded shared *Show* methods associated with the MessageBox class. The method used required the first two of its actual parameters to be strings. Consequently, the following program statement generated the appropriate string.

resultString = "The result is " & CStr(result)

The content of the integer variable *result* had to be converted to a string before it was concatenated with the literal string *"The Result is "*.

An example of the runtime for Listing 13.2 is shown in Figure 13.12.

Figure 13.12 The runtime of Listing 13.2 against Test plan 1.

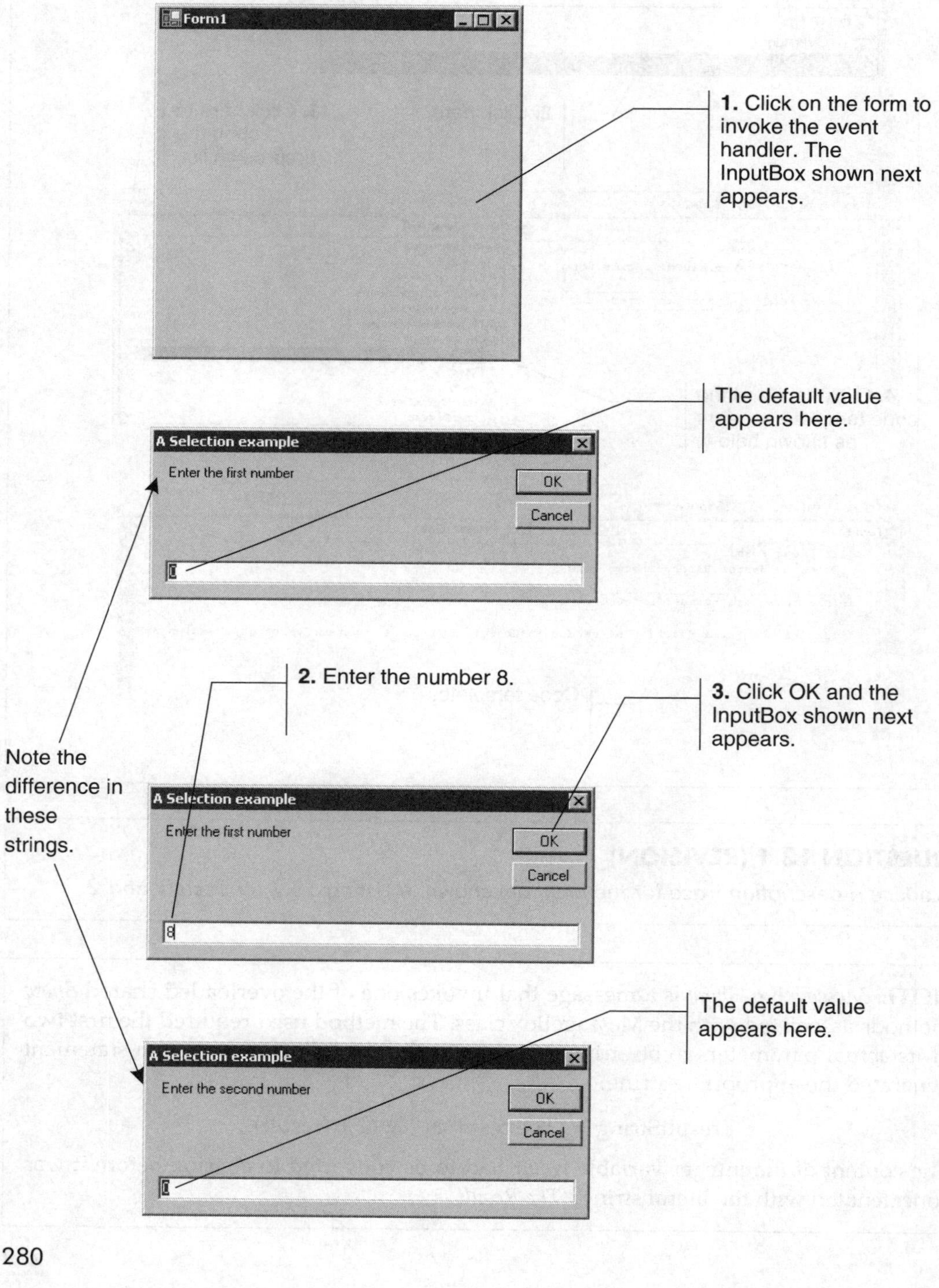
Form1
1. Click on the form to invoke the event handler. The InputBox shown next appears.
The default value appears here.
A Selection example
Enter the first number
OK
Cancel
2. Enter the number 8.
3. Click OK and the InputBox shown next appears.
Note the difference in these strings.
A Selection example
Enter the first number
OK
Cancel
8
The default value appears here.
A Selection example
Enter the second number
OK
Cancel

Figure 13.12 (cont.)

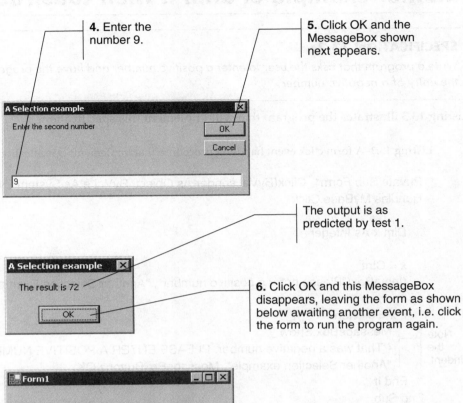

4. Enter the number 9.

5. Click OK and the MessageBox shown next appears.

The output is as predicted by test 1.

6. Click OK and this MessageBox disappears, leaving the form as shown below awaiting another event, i.e. click the form to run the program again.

PLEASE NOTE: If you select the Cancel button when running the program represented by Listing 13.2 it will throw an exception. An exception in this case is an error resulting from the attempt to convert a non-numeric string to an integer (pressing Cancel returns an empty string). For the time being, ignore this exception and do not press Cancel when running the program. Exceptions and how to handle them are covered in a later chapter.

Another example of an *If .. Then* construct

SPECIFICATION 13.2

Write a program that asks the user to enter a positive number and have the program report the entry of a negative number.

Listing 13.3 illustrates the program that will implement this specification.

Listing 13.3 A form click event handling procedure that implements Specification 13.2.

```
Private Sub Form1_Click(ByVal sender As Object, ByVal e As System.EventArgs) _
Handles MyBase.Click

    Dim x As Integer

    x = CInt _
    (InputBox("Please enter a positive number", "Another Selection Example", "0"))

        If x < 0 Then
            MessageBox.Show _
            ("That was a negative number. PLEASE ENTER A POSITIVE NUMBER", _
            "Another Selection example", MessageBoxButtons.OK)
        End If
End Sub
```

Note the indent.

NOTE: Listing 13.3 adopts the block structure for the *If .. Then* construct, which is good programming practice. This means that the code within the *If .. Then* construct is given an extra indent. This makes the code easier to read and debug.

PRACTICAL ACTIVITY 13.3

Enter and run the program of Listing 13.3 and test it against an appropriate test plan.

PRACTICAL ACTIVITY 13.4

Write a program within a Console Application that will offer the same functionality as Listing 13.3, i.e. implement Specification 13.2 within a Console application.

The format of the *If .. Then .. Else* construct

> **NOTE**: The *If .. Then* construct selects between either executing a section of code or not executing it. Whereas the *If .. Then .. Else* construct selects between executing one section of code or another section of code.

Figure 13.13 shows the outline of an N-S chart representing the *If .. Then .. Else* construct and its relationship to the VB .NET selection construct.

Figure 13.13 VB .NET selection construct (the *If .. Then .. Else* construct).

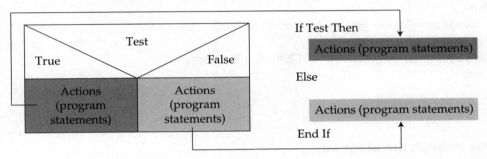

For the VB .NET construct shown in Figure 13.13 if the outcome of the condition is *True* then the program statements (represented by the dark shaded area) after the keyword *Then* and before the keyword *Else* are executed.

For the VB .NET construct shown in Figure 13.13 if the outcome of the condition is *False* then the program statements (represented by the light shaded area) after the keyword word *Else* and before the keywords *End If* are executed.

An example use of an *If .. Then .. Else* construct

SPECIFICATION 13.3

Write a program that asks users to enter their age. If they are old enough to vote the program reports back their age and asks them to collect their polling card; however, if they are not old enough to vote the program again reports back their age but this time tells them that they are too young to vote.

Listing 13.4 illustrates the program that will implement Specification 13.3.

Listing 13.4 An example use of the *If .. Then .. Else* construct that implements Specification 13.3.

```
Private Sub btnPollingCard_Click(ByVal sender As System.Object, ByVal e As _
System.EventArgs) Handles btnPollingCard.Click
    Dim age As Integer
    Dim message As String

    age = CInt(InputBox("Please enter your age"))
    If age >= 18 Then
        message = " collect your polling card"
    Else
        message = " sorry you are too young to vote"
    End If
    MessageBox.Show("You are " & CStr(age) & message)
End Sub
```

Routes through the program

There are two possible routes through the program of Listing 13.4.

When the user enters their age as 18 or over, the route through the program is illustrated by Figure 13.14. If the user enters their age as 17 or under, the route through the program is illustrated by Figure 13.15. In both figures, the statements that execute are highlighted in bold font.

Figure 13.14 The route through the program when the user enters their age as 18 or over.

```
Private Sub btnPollingCard_Click(ByVal sender As System.Object, ByVal e As_
System.EventArgs) Handles btnPollingCard.Click
    Dim age As Integer
    Dim message As String

    age = CInt(InputBox("Please enter your age"))
    If age >= 18 Then
        message = " collect your polling card"
    Else
        message = " sorry you are too young to vote"
    End If
    MessageBox.Show("You are " & CStr(age) & message)
End Sub
```

Figure 13.15 The route through the program when the user enters their age as 17 or under.

```
Private Sub btnPollingCard_Click(ByVal sender As System.Object, ByVal e As_
System.EventArgs) Handles btnPollingCard.Click
    Dim age As Integer
    Dim message As String

    age = CInt(InputBox("Please enter your age"))
    If age >= 18 Then
        message = " collect your polling card"
    Else
        message = " sorry you are too young to vote"
    End If
    MessageBox.Show("You are " & CStr(age) & message)
End Sub
```

Description trace when the user enters 18 or over

Statement	Description
age = CInt(InputBox("Please enter your age"))	The user enters 18 (or over), which is converted to an integer using the *CInt* function and assigned to the *Integer* variable age.
If age >= 18 Then	The content of *age* is compared with 18 using the relational operator >= and *True* is evaluated. Consequently, the statement **after** the keyword *Then* and **before** the keyword *Else* is executed.
message = " collect your polling card"	The *String* variable *message* is assigned the string *collect your polling card*.
MessageBox.Show("You are " & CStr(age) & message)	The string *You are*, the content of the integer variable *age* and the content of the string variable *message* are displayed in a message box.
	Note how content of the *age* variable is converted to a string using the *CStr* function.
	Also note the how the ampersand is used to concatenate ('join together') the separate strings.

Figure 13.16 illustrates the runtime when the user enters their age as 18.

Figure 13.16 Runtime when the user enters their age as 18.

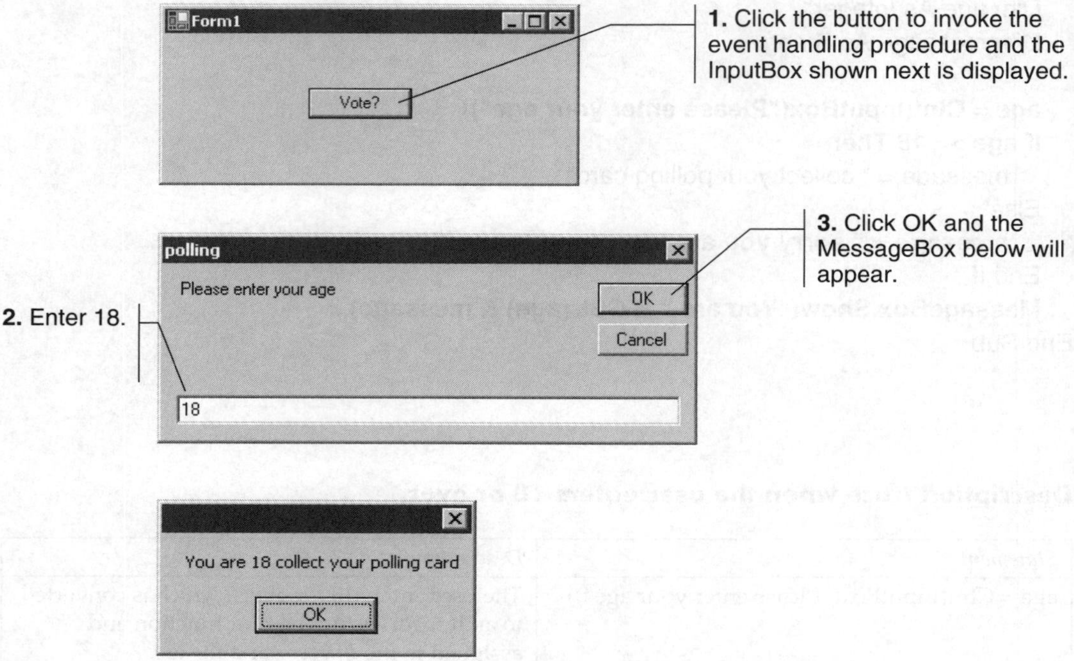
Form1
Vote?
1. Click the button to invoke the event handling procedure and the InputBox shown next is displayed.
polling
Please enter your age
OK
Cancel
18
2. Enter 18.
3. Click OK and the MessageBox below will appear.
You are 18 collect your polling card
OK

Description trace when the user enters 17 or under

Statement	*Description*
age = CInt(InputBox("Please enter your age"))	The user enters 17 (or under), which is converted to an integer by *CInt* and assigned to the *Integer* variable *age*.
If Age >= 18 Then	The content of *age* is compared with 18 using the relational operator >= and *False* is evaluated because 17 is not greater than or equal to 18. Consequently, the statement **after** the keyword *Else* and **before** the keywords *End If* are executed.
message = " sorry you are too young to vote"	The string variable *message* is assigned the string *sorry you are too young to vote*
MessageBox.Show("You are " & CStr(age) & message)	The string *You are*, the content of the integer variable *age* and the content of the string variable *message* are displayed in a MessageBox. Again note the use of the *CStr* function and ampersand operator (&).

Figure 13.17 illustrates the runtime when the user enters their age as 17.

Figure 13.17 Runtime when the user enters their age as 17.

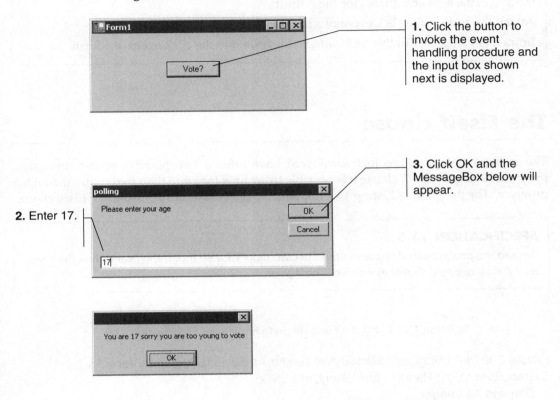

1. Click the button to invoke the event handling procedure and the input box shown next is displayed.

3. Click OK and the MessageBox below will appear.

2. Enter 17.

PRACTICAL ACTIVITY 13.5

Enter and run the program of Listing 13.4 and test it against an appropriate test plan.

PRACTICAL ACTIVITY 13.6

Amend and then run Listing 13.4 so that the InputBox and MessageBox display a title. Also arrange for the InputBox to display a default of zero.

PRACTICAL ACTIVITY 13.7

Write a program within a Console application that will offer the same functionality as Listing 13.4, i.e. implement Specification 13.3 within a Console application.

PRACTICAL ACTIVITY 13.8

Implement Specification 13.4 within a Windows application that uses a textbox for user input (i.e. the age) and a label for the output.

Attach the code to the click event of a button.

Implement it again, but this time 'attach' the code it to the click event of a form.

The *ElseIf* clause

The examples of selections just considered have offered two possible routes through a program. Using the *ElseIf* clause it is possible to arrange for more than two routes through a program. The program of Listing 13.5 implements Specification 13.5 using the *ElseIf* clause.

SPECIFICATION 13.5

Amend the program that implemented Specification 13.4 so that if the user enters their age as 17 they are told that they can vote next year.

Listing 13.5 Using the *ElseIf* clause to implement Specification 13.5.

```
Private Sub btnPollingCard_Click(ByVal sender As System.Object, ByVal e As _
System.EventArgs) Handles btnPollingCard.Click
    Dim age As Integer
    Dim message As String

    age = CInt(InputBox("Please enter your age"))
    If age >= 18 Then
        message = " collect your polling card"
    ElseIf age = 17 Then
        message = " you can vote next year"
    Else
        message = " sorry you are too young to vote"
    End If
    MessageBox.Show("You are " & CStr(age) & message)
End Sub
```

Figure 13.18 shows the route through the program if the user enters their age as 17, again the bold and larger text highlight the program statements that execute.

Figure 13.18 This shows the route through the program when the user enters their age as 17. Only one of the three possible routes is taken.

```
Private Sub btnPollingCard_Click(ByVal sender As System.Object, ByVal e As_
System.EventArgs) Handles btnPollingCard.Click
    Dim age As Integer
    Dim message As String

    age = CInt(InputBox("Please enter your age"))
    If age >= 18 Then
        message = " collect your polling card"
    ElseIf age = 17 Then
        message = " you can vote next year"
    Else
        message = " sorry you are too young to vote"
    End If
    MessageBox.Show("You are " & CStr(age) & message)
End Sub
```

Figure 13.19 shows the output from the program when the user enters their age as 17.

Figure 13.19 The output when the user enters 17.

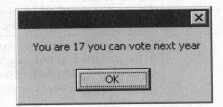

NOTE: The *Else* and *ElseIf* clauses are both optional. You can have as many *ElseIf* clauses as you want in an *If* construct, but none can appear after an *Else* clause. *If* selection constructs can be nested, i.e. contained within one another to achieve multiple paths through a program.

The *Select Case* construct

Another method for implementing selection is to use the ***Select Case*** construct. This can implement more than two routes through a program and is often preferred to using the *ElseIf* clause and **nested** *If .. Then .. Else* constructs. Listing 13.6 shows how Specification 13.5 can be implemented using a *Select Case* construct.

Listing 13.6 Implementing Specification 13.4 with a *Select Case* construct.

```
Private Sub btnPollingCard_Click(ByVal sender As System.Object, ByVal e As
System.EventArgs) Handles btnPollingCard.Click
    Dim age As Integer
    Dim message As String

    age = CInt(InputBox("Please enter your age"))
    Select Case age
        Case Is >= 18
            message = " collect your polling card"
        Case Is = 17
            message = " you can vote next year"
        Case Is < 17
            message = " sorry you are too young to vote"
    End Select
    MessageBox.Show("You are " & CStr(age) & message)
End Sub
```

Description trace when the user enters 17

Statement	Description
age = CInt(InputBox("Please enter your age"))	The user enters 17, which is converted to an integer and assigned to the integer variable *age*.
Select Case age Case Is = 18	The keyword *Is* implicitly represents the variable *age* in the construct. In this case the comparison is asking whether 17 >= 18 which of course is *false*. Consequently, the statement *message = " collect your polling card* is **not** executed.
Case Is = 17	In this case the comparison is asking whether 17 = 17 which of course is *true*. Consequently, the following statement is executed.
message = " you can vote next year"	The string *you can vote next year* is assigned to the string variable *message*.
Case Is < 17	This comparison is not made because only one path through a *Select Case* construct is ever executed and that has just happened.
MessageBox.Show("You are " & CStr(age) & message)	The MessageBox displays the output from the program.

The route through the program when the user enters their age as 17 is illustrated in Figure 13.20. Again the executed statements are shown in bold text.

Figure 13.20 Route through the program when the user enters 17.

```
Private Sub btnPollingCard_Click(ByVal sender As System.Object, ByVal e As_
System.EventArgs) Handles btnPollingCard.Click
    Dim age As Integer
    Dim message As String

    age = CInt(InputBox("Please enter your age"))
    SelectCase age
        Case is >= 18
            message = " collect your polling card"
        Case is = 17
            message = " you can vote next year"
        Case is <17
            message = " sorry you are too young to vote"
    End Select
    MessageBox.Show("You are " & CStr(age) & message)
End Sub
```

PRACTICAL ACTIVITY 13.9

Enter and run the program shown in Listing 13.6.

Amend the program so that the InputBoxes and MessageBox show a title and all InputBoxes have a default value.

Test the program with ages entered as 16, 17 and 18.

PRACTICAL ACTIVITY 13.10

Implement each of the N-S chart designs shown in Figures 13.21, 13.22 and 13.23 as a *Form_Click* event procedure within a Windows application. Follow the recommended steps as below (use *MessageBox.Show* and *InputBox* as shown in the previous program listings):

1. Produce a data table.
2. Derive a simple test plan.
3. Convert the design to code and compile.
4. Test the runtime against the test plan.

Figure 13.21 An N-S chart design.

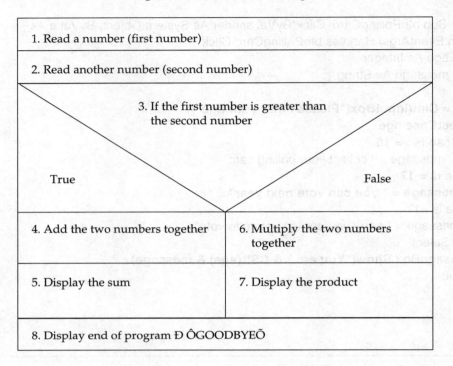

Figure 13.22 An N-S chart design.

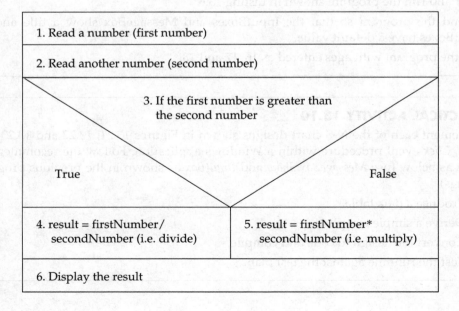

Figure 13.23 An N-S chart design.

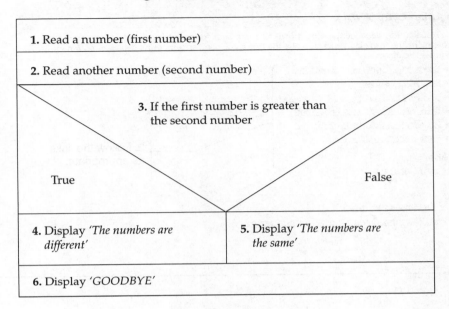

1. Read a number (first number)

2. Read another number (second number)

3. If the first number is greater than the second number

True

False

4. Display *'The numbers are different'*

5. Display *'The numbers are the same'*

6. Display *'GOODBYE'*

PRACTICAL ACTIVITY 13.11

Again implement each of the N-S chart designs shown in Figures 13.21, 13.22 and 13.23, but this time within a Console application.

QUESTION 13.2 (DEVELOPMENT)

Produce a description trace for the program shown in Listing 13.7. Confirm your trace table by single stepping through the program. Use the VB .NET help to learn how to single step through a program. Type execution control into the help index and press Enter and help will appear. This is illustrated below:

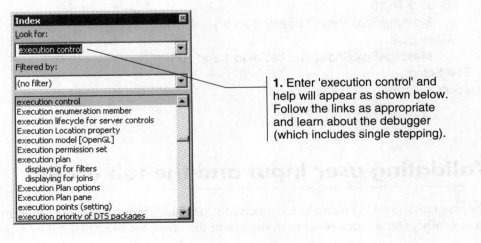

1. Enter 'execution control' and help will appear as shown below. Follow the links as appropriate and learn about the debugger (which includes single stepping).

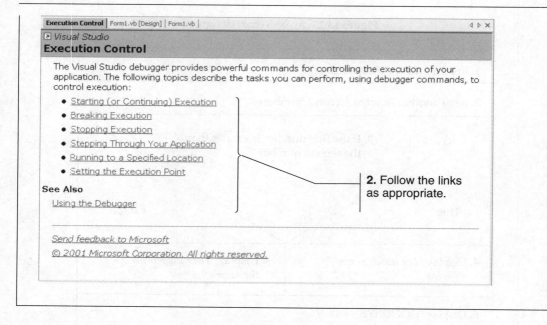

Listing 13.7 Listing for Question 13.2.

```
Private Sub Form1_Click(ByVal sender As Object, ByVal e As System.EventArgs) _
Handles MyBase.Click

    Dim Number As Integer = 9

    Select Case Number
        Case 1 To 5
            MessageBox.Show("Between 1 and 5")
        Case 6, 7, 8
            MessageBox.Show("Between 6 and 8")
        Case 9 To 10
            MessageBox.Show("Greater than 8")
        Case Else
            MessageBox.Show("Not between 1 and 10")
    End Select
End Sub
```

Validating user input and the tab order

The program shown in Listing 13.6 is inherently 'unstable'. If the user of the program were to accidentally enter a value other than the age of the voter, for example, it they typed in *2w* instead of 22 then the program would fail. This is because the conversion function *CInt* would not be able to perform the conversion – the program would **throw an exception**.

The following simple application will be used to demonstrate how to validate user input. It will also discuss the tab order and the related properties *TabIndex* and *TabStop*.

SPECIFICATION 13.5

Develop a Windows Application that receives two integers from the user via textboxes. These numbers can be added, subtracted, divided or multiplied by the clicking on an appropriate button. The result of the integer arithmetic operation is to be displayed in a textbox.

Figure 13.24 illustrates the GUI for this specification.

Figure 13.24 GUI for specification 13.5 consists of three textboxes, three labels and four buttons.

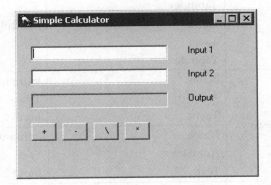

The properties for the GUI are set as represented by Table 13.1.

Table 13.1 The property settings for the GUI of Figure 13.24.

Control	Property	Setting
Form	Text	Simple Calculator
	Icon	~icons\computer\Key04
TextBox1	Name	txtInput1
	TabIndex	0
	Text	<empty> i.e. zero length string
TextBox2	Name	txtInput2
	TabIndex	1
	Text	<empty>

Table 13.1 (cont.)

Control	Property	Setting
TextBox3 *Note these settings* {	Name TabIndex ReadOnly TabStop	txtOutput 2 True False
Button1	Name Text TabIndex	btnAddition + 3
Button2	Name Text TabIndex	btnSubtraction - 4
Button3	Name Text TabIndex	btnDivision \ 5
Button4	Name Text TabIndex	btnMultiplication * 6
Label1	Name AutoSize Text	lblInput1 True Input 1
Label1	Name AutoSize Text	lblInput2 True Input 2
Label1	Name AutoSize Text	lblOutput True Output

The tab order

Most controls have a *TabIndex* property, which is a unique number that identifies each control on a form. At runtime a controls *TabIndex* determines the order in which the control will receive the focus when the user presses the Tab key on the keyboard. Pressing the Tab key cycles through the controls on a form in a sequence defined by the *TabIndex* of each control. Pressing the Shift and Tab keys together cycles through the controls in the opposite direction.

When the 'Simple Calculator' application is run the textbox used for Input 1 receives the focus because its *TabIndex* property is set to 0. When the user presses the Tab key, the focus moves to the textbox used for Input 2 because its *TabIndex* is set at 1. Another press of the Tab key moves the focus to the button responsible for adding the two input numbers even though its *TabIndex* is set to 3. This is because the *TabStop* property of the third textbox (whose *TabIndex* is 2) is set to false. Setting the *TabStop* index of a control to false removes it from the tab order. Figure 13.25 shows the GUI for the 'Simple Calculator' with the add button highlighted by a dotted rectangle (because it has the focus), it also shows the condition of the GUI when the user presses the Tab key again.

Figure 13.25 Effect of pressing the Tab key at runtime.

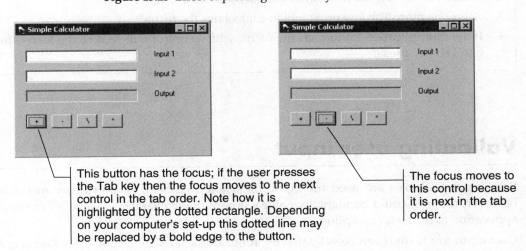

This button has the focus; if the user presses the Tab key then the focus moves to the next control in the tab order. Note how it is highlighted by the dotted rectangle. Depending on your computer's set-up this dotted line may be replaced by a bold edge to the button.

The focus moves to this control because it is next in the tab order.

The *TabStop* property

This property enables you to add or remove a control from the tab order on a form. For example, there is no requirement for the calculators output textbox to receive the focus. Consequently, it is removed from the tab order by setting its *TabStop* property to *False*. This property is *True* by default designating the control as a tab stop (i.e. by default it is part of the tab order).

When the *TabStop* is set to false the object is bypassed when the user is tabbing, although the object still holds its place in the actual tab order, as determined by the *TabIndex* property.

For the 'Simple Calculator' application the *TabIndex* property for the three textboxes and the four buttons were set at 0 through to 6 (refer to table 13.1) and the *TabStop* property for the output textbox was set to false, thus removing it from the tab order, but leaving its *TabIndex* as 2.

By default the *TabIndex* property for a control is set to a number that reflects the order in which it was drawn on to the form. If an empty form has three buttons drawn, the *TabIndex* property for the first drawn button will be 0 and for the third drawn it will be 2. If you carefully design the GUI then the tab order can be set to suit the application, however, if the controls are drawn in the wrong sequence it is easy to reset the *TabIndex* property to suit the application using the properties window.

PRACTICAL ACTIVITY 13.12

Develop and run the GUI as represented by Figure 13.24 and Table 13.1. Experiment with the GUI to enable you to answer the following questions.

1. Immediately after launching the application which control has the focus?
2. Which control has the focus after the user presses the Tab key twice?
3. After one more Tab key press which control has the focus?
4. If the multiplication button has the focus, which control will receive the focus after one Tab key press?

Validating user input

Both input textboxes are used for inputting whole numbers; as previously mentioned, however, the user could accidentally enter a non-numeric character, which will cause the application to throw an exception.

User input to a textbox can be validated by, for example, attaching code to its *KeyUp* event. This code can be written to only allow numeric characters entry (i.e. 0 through to 9), any accidental entry of non-numeric characters can be 'trapped' and code can be used to clear the textbox.

Keyboard events

There are three keyboard events:

- *KeyDown*
- *KeyUp*
- *KeyPress*

When a textbox has the focus and the user presses a key on the keyboard, it triggers the *KeyDown* event for that textbox; when they release the key it triggers the *KeyUp* event. A *KeyPress* event is triggered when the key goes down and up.

All of the event handling procedures associated with keyboard events are supplied with parameters that carry information about, for example, which key was pressed. The supply of information (parameters) to the *KeyUp* event handler is illustrated in Figure 13.26.

Figure 13.26 *KeyUp* parameters (arguments). The dotted arrow represents the *KeyUp* event. The circles and arrows represent the parameters passed to the event handling procedure – these carry information about what key was pressed, etc.

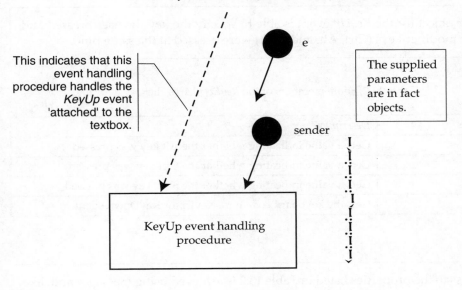

The signature of the *KeyUp* event handler is shown in Figure 13.27. It is created from the name of the object and the event. It has parameters embraced by brackets.

Figure 13.27 The signature for the *KeyUp* event handler.

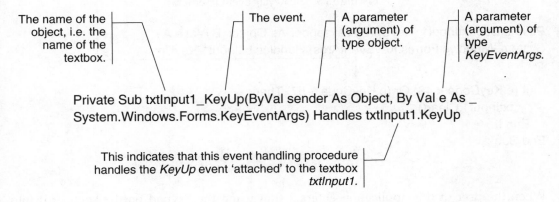

The event handling procedure for validating the text entry to the *txtInput1* textbox is illustrated in Listing 13.8. Figures 13.26 and 13.27 have both shown that the event handling procedure is automatically supplied with two parameters **sender** and *e*. For this example the program statements within the event handling procedure have not used the information supplied by *sender*. It has however used the information supplied by the parameter *e*.

The parameter *e* is a reference to an object of the *KeyEventArgs* class. Consequently, it has members that can be used. A list of some of its members (properties in this case) and a brief description is given in Table 13.2. It has methods but they are not listed in this table – use the VB .NET online help to view other members.

NOTE: The *e* object for the *KeyUp* event is able to specify the key the user pressed and whether any modifier keys (Ctrl, Alt, and Shift) were pressed at the same time.

Table 13.2 Some members of the *KeyEventArgs* class.

Public properties	Description
Alt	Gets a value indicating whether the Alt key was pressed
Control	Gets a value indicating whether the Ctrl key was pressed
Shift	Gets a value indicating whether the Shift key was pressed
KeyCode	Gets the keyboard code for a KeyUp or KeyDown event.

NOTE: Access to the properties listed in Table 13.2 is achieved using messages and, like most messages, this requires an object reference, a full stop and a member of the class (a property in this case). An example is shown in Listing 13.8.

Listing 13.8 The *KeyUp* event handler.

```
Private Sub txtInput1_KeyUp(ByVal sender As Object, ByVal e As _
System.Windows.Forms.KeyEventArgs) Handles txtInput1.KeyUp


  If (e.KeyCode < 48) Or (e.KeyCode > 57) Then
      txtInput1.Clear()
  End If
End Sub
```

When the user of this application enters 7 (**not** using the keypad on the keyboard) into *txtInput1* it is allowed entry into the textbox. The *KeyCode* for Key 7 is 55. This information is supplied to the *KeyUp* event handling procedure by *e.KeyCode*. This is then used in the conditional test of the *If .. Then* selection construct and it proves to be **False**. Consequently, the statement within the selection construct is **not** executed. If the user enters *A* by mistake, the conditional test works out to be **True** and the statement within the selection construct is executed. This statement is the message *txtInput1.Clear()* and *Clear()* is a method that clears the textbox of its entire content. As non-numeric values are not allowed entry it is not possible to attempt to add, subtract, divide or multiply them. Consequently, the program will not throw an exception for the entry of non-numeric values, as they cannot be entered.

NOTE: The numbers 48 and 57 where used in Listing 13.8 because they represent the 'number codes' for the figures 0 and 9.

NOTE: The application is still far from stable, however, making the textbox validate its own input is a start.

Developing the application further

There needs to be more code attached to the GUI of Figure 13.24. It should be obvious from the GUI that there needs to be an event handling procedure attached to each button. There also needs to be a *KeyUp* event handling procedure attached to the second textbox (*txtInput2*) so it can also validate user input. In total, therefore, there are six event handling procedures.

At its launch the GUI is an instance of a class and it is highly likely that this class will require class level variables. This case is no different: there needs to be three class level variables and at the launch of the GUI the instances of two of these variables will be used to store the data input via the textboxes and the instance of the third variable will be used to store the result of the arithmetic operations. These class level variables will be made private which adopts the rule of data hiding ('outside code' does not need direct access).

The class diagram for the Window application as represented by the GUI of Figure 13.24 is shown in Figure 13.28.

Figure 13.28 A class diagram.

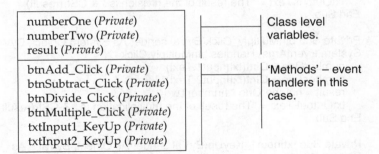

NOTE: You will note that the class diagram indicates that the methods are *Private*. The IDE assigns *Private* to event handling procedures by **default**.

Listing 13.9 shows the code 'attached' to the GUI of Figure 13.25. It can be seen that the Button event handling procedures are very similar; they all obtain data from the input textboxes, convert them to integers and assign them to the instance variables (*numberOne* and *numberTwo*). These instance variables are then processed with the result being stored in the instance variable *result*. The variable *result* is then converted to a string and assigned to the *Text* property of the output textbox.

Listing 13.9 Listing for Specification 13.5

```
Private numberOne As Integer
Private numberTwo As Integer
Private result As Integer

Private Sub btnAdd_Click(ByVal sender As System.Object, ByVal e As _
System.EventArgs) Handles btnAdd.Click
    numberOne = CInt(txtInput1.Text)
    numberTwo = CInt(txtInput2.Text)
    result = numberOne + numberTwo
    txtOutput.Text = "The result of the addition is " & CStr(result)
End Sub

Private Sub btnSubtract_Click(ByVal sender As System.Object, ByVal e As _
System.EventArgs) Handles btnSubtract.Click
    numberOne = CInt(txtInput1.Text)
    numberTwo = CInt(txtInput2.Text)
    result = numberOne – numberTwo
    txtOutput.Text = "The result of the subtraction is " & CStr(result)
End Sub

Private Sub btnDivide_Click(ByVal sender As System.Object, ByVal e As _
System.EventArgs) Handles btnDivide.Click
    numberOne = CInt(txtInput1.Text)
    numberTwo = CInt(txtInput2.Text)
    If numberTwo <> 0 Then
        result = numberOne \ numberTwo
        txtOutput.Text = "The result of the division is " & CStr(result)
    Else
        txtOutput.Clear()
        MessageBox.Show("You should not divide by ZERO")
    End If
    txtOutput.Text = "The result of the division is " & CStr(result)
End Sub

Private Sub btnMultiply_Click(ByVal sender As System.Object, ByVal e As _
System.EventArgs) Handles btnMultiply.Click
    numberOne = CInt(txtInput1.Text)
    numberTwo = CInt(txtInput2.Text)
    result = numberOne * numberTwo
    txtOutput.Text = "The result of the multiplication is " & CStr(result)
End Sub

Private Sub txtInput1_KeyUp(ByVal sender As Object, ByVal e As _
System.Windows.Forms.KeyEventArgs) Handles txtInput1.KeyUp
    If (e.KeyCode < 48) Or (e.KeyCode > 57) Then
        txtInput1.Clear()
    End If
End Sub

Private Sub txtInput2_KeyUp(ByVal sender As Object, ByVal e As
System.Windows.Forms.KeyEventArgs) Handles txtInput2.KeyUp
    If (e.KeyCode < 48) Or (e.KeyCode > 57) Then
        txtInput2.Clear()
    End If
End Sub
```

However, the event handling procedure attached to the *btnDivide* object is more involved. It includes an *If .. Then .. Else* construct which is used to 'trap' an attempt to divide by zero. If a zero is entered in the second input textbox and the divide button is clicked the user is given a message indicating that they tried to divide by zero (anything divided by zero is infinity) and the textbox is cleared. Any other input (providing it is within the range of an integer) is accepted and the calculation is performed.

PRACTICAL ACTIVITY 13.5

Attach the code of Listing 13.9 to the GUI you developed during Practical Activity 13.4, and run and test the application.

PRACTICAL ACTIVITY 13.6 (DEVELOPMENT)

Clicking any of the calculation buttons when the GUI does not have any value entered in either of its input textboxes will cause an exception. Consequently, the program is far from stable. See if you can fix this problem with appropriate code.

---

14 Repetition (iteration)

To decide whether a customer has the appropriate funds to secure a loan a computer program 'asks' a sequence of questions. Once these questions are answered the customer is given a rating that defines their suitability for the loan. These questions will be the same for all customers and a suitable Structured English design for this program is represented by Figure 14.1.

Figure 14.1 Structured English design for calculating a suitability rating.

1. Obtain customer's net monthly income

2. Obtain customer's monthly outgoings

3. Obtain the length of time the customer has been in their current employment

4. Calculate the rating from the information supplied

The bank that uses this program will obviously have more than one customer. Therefore, these program steps need to be repeated. Once step 4 has executed the program moves the flow of control back to step 1.

Some of the numerous program constructs in Visual Basic .NET that allow a program segment to be repeated are listed below:

- *Do .. Loop Until*
- *Do .. Loop While*
- *Do While .. Loop*
- *Do Until .. Loop*
- *For .. Next*

We will start the coverage of repetition by describing the *Do .. Loop Until* construct.

The *Do .. Loop Until* construct

The flow of control for this construct is illustrated by the flow chart of Figure 14.2. The actions within the loop are executed at least once. Further executions within the loop are dependent upon the outcome of the conditional test. If the test is *false* then the actions are repeated. However, if the conditional test is *true* then the actions are not repeated and the loop is exited.

Figure 14.2 *Do .. Loop Until.*

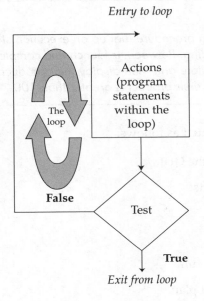

Entry to loop

This is an example of a **post-conditioned** loop, i.e. the test appears at the **end** of the loop.

It is also an example of a **non-deterministic** loop. The number of times the loop is executed is not determined on entry to the loop.

How often the loop executes is dependent on how the values within the loop (that are also used in the test) change during the execution of the program statements within the loop.

Exit from loop

N-S chart and VB .NET representation of the *Do .. Loop Until* construct

The N-S chart and program layout for the *Do .. Loop Until* construct is illustrated in Figure 14.3.

Figure 14.3 *Do .. Loop Until* construct.

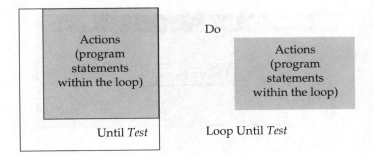

The program statements represented by the shaded area are repeated until the test is *true*. In other words the actions are repeated when the test is *false*.

The keywords *Do* and *Loop* 'bracket' the program statements to be executed. The keyword *Do* comes before the first program statement within the loop and the keyword *Loop* is immediately after the last program statement inside the loop.

305

An example using the *Do .. Loop Until* construct

SPECIFICATION 14.1

Write a button click event handling procedure that up on execution states its purpose and upon completion indicates it is ending. Between its launch and completion it is to read two numbers from the keyboard, calculate and then display their product. It continues to find the product of input numbers until their product is greater than 100.

This specification will be implemented as follows:

1. Build and set the properties of the GUI.

2. Design the code using N-S charts.

3. Produce a data table.

4. Derive a simple test plan.

5. Convert the design to code and run.

6. Test the runtime against the test plan.

Step 1: Build and set the properties of the GUI

The specification has been designed, for 'educational reasons', to highlight the operation of the *Do .. Loop Until* construct; consequently, there no need for a proper GUI; it just is a button on a form (shown in Figure 14.4).

Figure 14.4 Simple GUI for Specification 14.1.

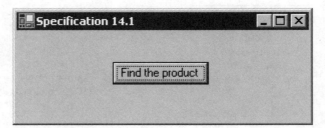

Step 2: Design the code using N-S charts

The design algorithm for Specification 14.1 is shown in Figure 14.5. The 'flow through the design' successfully implements Specification 14.1. Step 1 of the design displays a string introducing the purpose of the program. Then steps 2, 3, 4 and 5 are executed (i.e. the instructions inside the loop). After step 5 the conditional test of step 6 is executed and if the product (calculated in step 4) is greater than 100 (i.e. the conditional test is *True*) then step 7 is executed and a string is displayed to indicate the end of the program. However, if the conditional test is *False* then steps 2, 3, 4 and 5 are executed again, i.e. they are repeated.

Figure 14.5 The design for Specification 14.1.

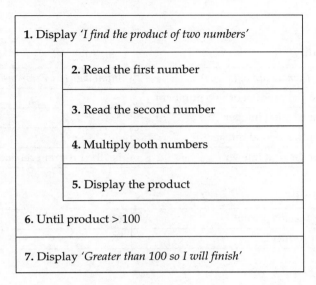

1. Display *'I find the product of two numbers'*

2. Read the first number

3. Read the second number

4. Multiply both numbers

5. Display the product

6. Until product > 100

7. Display *'Greater than 100 so I will finish'*

Step 3: Produce a data table

Identifier	Type	Description
firstNumber	Integer	Stores the number entered at the keyboard.
secondNumber	Integer	Stores the number entered at the keyboard.
product	Integer	Stores the product of the values of the variables *firstNumber* and *secondNumber* and has its content displayed on the VDU. Its value is also used in the test to decide on whether the loop is repeated or not.

Step 4: Derive a simple test plan

When developing a test plan it is important that every conditional test appearing within the constructs of the program are fully considered. For this design (and program) there is only one conditional test that asks whether the content of a variable is greater than 100. Therefore, there is a need for three tests, which must test the **boundary** of the conditional test. This means that the numbers input must produce a product that is below, above and at the boundary of the conditional test. The input numbers should therefore produce a product of 99, 100 and 101; which are a set of numbers that are below, above and at the boundary. The number 99 is just below the boundary of the conditional test, the number 100 is at the boundary and 101 is just above the boundary.

The three tests used to test the boundary of the conditional test are shown below.

Test 1

Supplied input

User-friendly prompt	Input data (user response)
I find the product of two numbers	
Enter the first integer	33
Enter the second integer	3
Enter the first integer	i.e. the program repeats.

Expected output

User-friendly prompt	Ouput data
The product is	99

Test 2

Supplied input

User-friendly prompt	Input data (user response)
I find the product of two numbers	
Enter the first integer	50
Enter the second integer	2
Enter the first integer	i.e. the program repeats.

Expected output

User-friendly prompt	Ouput data
The product is	100

Test 3

Supplied input

User-friendly prompt	Input data (user response)
I find the product of two numbers	
Enter the first integer	101
Enter the second integer	1

Expected output

User-friendly prompt	Ouput data
The product is	101
Greater than 100 so I will finish	i.e. the loop in exited.

Step 5: Convert the design to code and compile

The program illustrated in Listing 14.1 implements the design of Figure 14.5.

Listing 14.1 The code for the design illustrated in Figure 14.5.

```
Private Sub btnProduct_Click(ByVal sender As System.Object, ByVal e As _
System.EventArgs) Handles btnProduct.Click
    Dim firstNumber As Integer
    Dim secondNumber As Integer
    Dim product As Integer

    MessageBox.Show("I find the product of two numbers")
    Do
        firstNumber = CInt(InputBox("Enter the first integer", "Read Number", "0"))
        secondNumber = CInt (InputBox("Enter the second integer", "Read Number", "0"))
        product = firstNumber * secondNumber
        MessageBox.Show("The product is " & CStr(product))
    Loop Until product 100
    MessageBox.Show("Greater than 100 so I will finish")
End Sub
```

PRACTICAL ACTIVITY 14.1

Complete step 6, i.e. test the runtime against the test plan.

The output from the program when tested against test 1 is illustrated in Figure 14.6.

Figure 14.6 Output when tested against test 1.

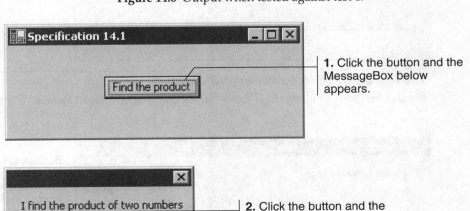

1. Click the button and the MessageBox below appears.

2. Click the button and the InputBox below appears.

This was 'generated' by the following VB statement:
MessageBox.Show("I find the product of two numbers")

Figure 14.6 (cont.)

Title

Prompt

Default

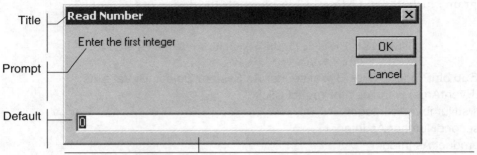

This was 'generated' by the following VB statement:

firstNumber = CInt(InputBox("Enter the first integer", "Read Number", "0"))

3. Enter 33.

4. Click OK and the 33 is converted to an integer and assigned to integer variable *firstNumber*.

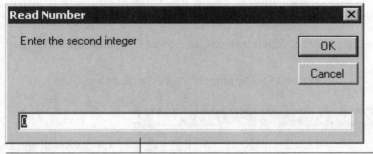

This was 'generated' by the following VB statement:

secondNumber = Cint(InputBox("Enter the second integer", "Read Number", "0"))

5. Enter 3.

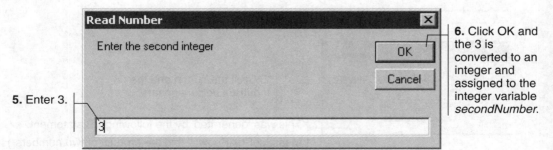

6. Click OK and the 3 is converted to an integer and assigned to the integer variable *secondNumber*.

Figure 14.6 (cont.)

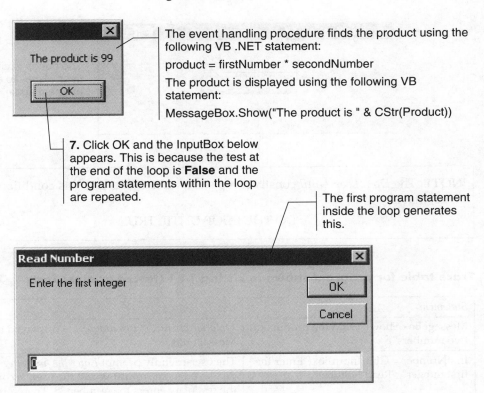

The event handling procedure finds the product using the following VB .NET statement:

product = firstNumber * secondNumber

The product is displayed using the following VB statement:

MessageBox.Show("The product is " & CStr(Product))

7. Click OK and the InputBox below appears. This is because the test at the end of the loop is **False** and the program statements within the loop are repeated.

The first program statement inside the loop generates this.

The output when tested against test 3 is almost the same as shown in Figure 14.6 until after the product is displayed. The difference is shown in Figure 14.7.

Figure 14.7 The output from the procedure when tested against test 3.

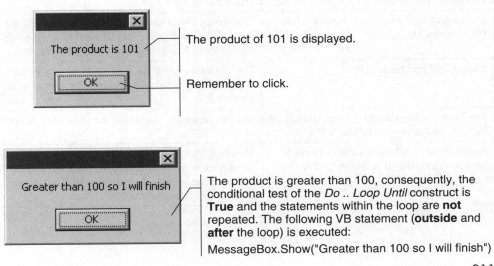

The product of 101 is displayed.

Remember to click.

The product is greater than 100, consequently, the conditional test of the *Do .. Loop Until* construct is **True** and the statements within the loop are **not** repeated. The following VB statement (**outside** and **after** the loop) is executed:

MessageBox.Show("Greater than 100 so I will finish")

Figure 14.7 (cont.)

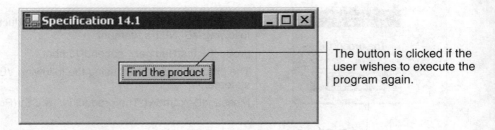

NOTE: The *Do .. Loop Until* construct repeats its statements **until** its conditional test is **True**, that is:

DO THE LOOP UNTIL TRUE.

Trace table for program shown in Listing 14.1 (tested against Tests 1, 2 and 3)

Statement	*Description*
MessageBox.Show("I find the product of two numbers")	*I find the product of two numbers* is displayed in a MessageBox.
firstNumber = CInt(InputBox("Enter the first integer", "Read Number", "0"))	The user-friendly prompt *Enter the first integer* is displayed in an **InputBox** and the user, according to the test plan, enters the number 33. Therefore, *firstNumber* is assigned 33. *CInt* converts the string to an integer.
secondNumber = CInt(InputBox("Enter the second integer", "Read Number", "0"))	The user-friendly prompt *Enter the second integer* is displayed in an **InputBox** and the user enters the number 3. Therefore, *secondNumber* is assigned 3. *CInt* converts the string to an integer.
product = firstNumber * secondNumber	*product* is assigned 99 (i.e. 33 * 3)
MessageBox.Show("The product is " & CStr(product))	The string *The product is* and the contents of the variable *product* (after it is converted to a string) are concatenated and displayed in a **MessageBox**.
Loop Until product > 100	The variable *product* is storing 99 therefore the test *product > 100* is False, consequently, the loop is repeated.
The loop is entered again immediately after the keyword *Do*, consequently, the next statement to be executed is shown below	
firstNumber = CInt(InputBox("Enter the first integer", "Read Number", "0"))	The user-friendly message *Enter the first integer* is displayed in an **InputBox** and the user, according to the test plan, enters the number 50. Therefore, *firstNumber* is assigned 50.

secondNumber = CInt(InputBox("Enter the second integer", "Read Number", "0"))	The user-friendly message *Enter the second integer* is displayed in an **InputBox** and the number 2 is entered by the user. Therefore, *secondNumber* is assigned 2.
product = firstNumber * secondNumber	*product* is assigned 100 (i.e. 50 * 2).
MessageBox.Show("The product is " & CStr(Product))	The string *The product is* and the contents of the variable *product* (after it is converted to a string) are concatenated and displayed in a **MessageBox**.
Loop Until product >100	This test is **False** therefore the loop **is** repeated, i.e. 100 is not greater than 100.
firstNumber = CInt(InputBox("Enter the first integer", "Read Number", "0"))	The user-friendly message *Enter the first integer* is displayed in an **InputBox** and the user – according to the test plan, enters the number 101. Therefore, *firstNumber* is assigned 101.
secondNumber = CInt(InputBox("Enter the second integer", "Read Number", "0"))	The user-friendly message *Enter the second integer* is displayed in an **InputBox** and the number 1 is entered by the user. Therefore, *secondNumber* is assigned 1.
product = firstNumber * secondNumber	*product* is assigned 101 (i.e. 101 * 1).
MessageBox.Show("The product is " & CStr(Product))	The string *The product is* and the contents of the variable *product* (after it is converted to a string) are concatenated and displayed in a **MessageBox**.
Loop Until product >100	This test is **True** therefore the loop is **not** repeated, i.e. 101 is greater than 100
MessageBox.Show("Greater than 100 so I will finish")	Displays the string *Greater than 100 so I will finish* in a **MessageBox**. This statement is outside the loop immediately after the keywords *Loop Until*.

PRACTICAL ACTIVITY 14.2

Implement the two N-S chart designs shown in Figure 14.8 as a button click event handler. Follow the recommended development sequence as below:

1. Produce a data table.
2. Derive a simple test plan.
3. Convert the design to code and run.
4. Test the runtime against the test plan.

Use a MessageBox and an InputBox to interact with the user for both designs.

Figure 14.8 Design for Practical Activity 14.2.

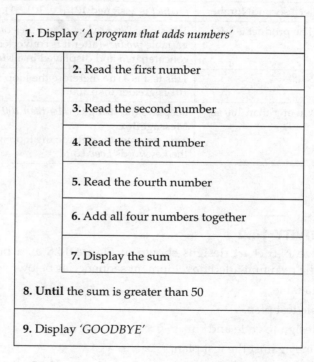

1. Read the first number
2. Read the second number
3. Read the third number
4. Add all three numbers together
5. Display the sum

6. Until the sum is greater than 100

1. Display *'A program that adds numbers'*
2. Read the first number
3. Read the second number
4. Read the third number
5. Read the fourth number
6. Add all four numbers together
7. Display the sum

8. Until the sum is greater than 50

9. Display *'GOODBYE'*

The *Do .. Loop While* construct

This loop is very similar to the *Do .. Loop Until* construct. The main difference is that the *Do .. Loop Until* loop leaves the loop when the test is **true** and the *Do .. Loop While* loop leaves the loop when the test is **false**. The flow of control for this construct is illustrated by the flow chart of Figure 14.9. The actions within the loop are executed **at least once**. Further executions within the loop are dependant upon the outcome of the conditional test. If the test is **true** then the actions are repeated. However, if the conditional test is **false** then the actions are **not** repeated and the loop is exited.

Figure 14.9 *Do .. Loop While* iteration.

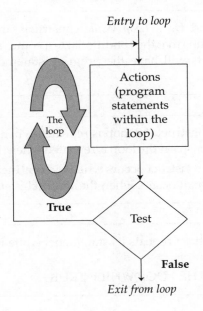

Entry to loop

A **post-conditioned** and a **non-deterministic** loop.

This shows the loop being repeated when the test is true, whereas Figure 14.2 shows the loop being repeated when the test is false.

N-S chart and VB .NET representation of the *Do .. Loop While* construct

The N-S chart and program layout for the *Do .. Loop While* construct is illustrated in Figure 14.10.

Figure 14.10 *Do .. Loop While* construct.

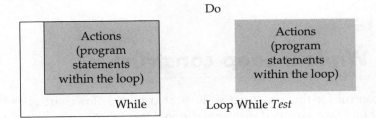

The actions represented by the shaded area are repeated while the condition test is **True**. The keywords *Do* and *Loop* 'bracket' the actions to be repeated.

NOTE: The *Do .. Loop Until* and *Do .. Loop While* constructs are both examples of **non-deterministic loops**, which mean the number of iterations around the loop is **not known** on entry to the loop. The exit from the loop is dependent upon the data used in the conditional test at the end of the loop (often referred to as **sentinel**). Of course, the value of this data is calculated within the loop and there is no telling when it will achieve the value that will result in the exit from the loop.

NOTE: The *Do .. Loop Until* and *Do .. Loop While* constructs are both examples of **post-conditioned loops**. This means that the conditional test comes at the end of the loop and consequently both constructs will have the program statements within the loop executed **at least once**.

NOTE: For the *Do .. Loop Until* construct the loop is repeated when the **sentinel** is *false*, whereas for the *Do .. Loop While* construct the loop is repeated when the **sentinel** is *true*.

The exit from the *Do .. Loop Until* construct occurs when the **sentinel** is *true*, whereas for the *Do .. Loop While* construct the exit occurs when the **sentinel** is *false*.

NOTE: The *Do .. Loop While* construct repeats its statements while its conditional test is **True**, that is:

DO THE LOOP WHILE TRUE

PRACTICAL ACTIVITY 14.3

Rewrite the event handling procedure shown in Listing 14.1 so that it performs in the same way but using the *Do .. Loop While* construct instead of the *Do .. Loop Until* construct. Enter and run your solution.

HINT: While **Not** (*conditional test*).

The *Do While .. Loop* construct

The flow of control for this construct is illustrated by the flowchart of Figure 14.11. The actions of this loop are executed if the conditional test is **true** and are **not** executed if the conditional test is **false**. As the conditional test appears **before** the actions within the loop then it is possible that they may *never* be executed.

Upon the completion of the actions the flow of control returns to the conditional test, where an outcome of **true** results in the actions being repeated. However, if the outcome of the conditional test is **false** the loop is exited.

Therefore, as the conditional test appears **before** the actions of the *Do While .. Loop* the variables used within the conditional test must have valid values **before** (or **within**) the conditional test **as well as inside** the loop.

Figure 14.11 *Do While .. Loop* iteration.

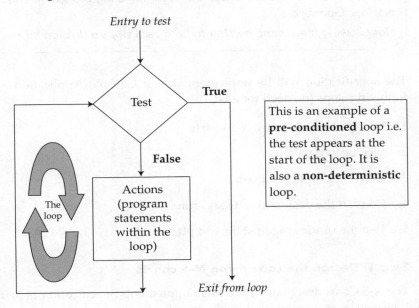

Entry to test

Test

True

False

The loop

Actions (program statements within the loop)

Exit from loop

This is an example of a **pre-conditioned** loop i.e. the test appears at the start of the loop. It is also a **non-deterministic** loop.

N–S chart and VB .NET representation for the *Do While .. Loop* construct

The N–S chart and program layout for the *Do While .. Loop* construct is illustrated in Figure 14.12.

Figure 14.12 *The Do While .. Loop.*

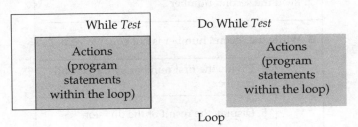

While *Test*

Actions (program statements within the loop)

Do While *Test*

Actions (program statements within the loop)

Loop

The actions represented by the shaded area are executed if the conditional test is true. The exit from the loop occurs when the conditional test is false. The program statements inside the loop are 'bracketed' by the keywords *Do While* and *Loop*.

An example using the *Do While .. Loop* construct

SPECIFICATION 14.2

Write code within the Main() of a console application that uses a Do While .. Loop to read two numbers. It then divides the first number entered by the second number. However, if the second number entered is a zero the event handling procedure ends with a message that displays Goodbye.

Not allowing the second number to be a zero stops a division by zero.

The specification will be implemented as a Console Application – this will involve the following steps (no need for a GUI):

1. Design the code using N-S charts.

2. Produce a data table.

3. Derive a simple test plan.

4. Convert the design to code and run.

5. Test the runtime against the test plan.

Step 1: Design the code using N-S charts

The N-S Chart design of Figure 14.13 implements Specification 14.2; it includes a *Do While .. Loop* construct, as requested by the specification.

Figure 14.13 A design using a *Do While .. Loop*.

1. Read the first number
2. Read the second number
3. While the second number is not equal to zero
4. Divide the first number by the second number
5. Display the result of the division
6. Read the first number
7. Read the second number
8. Display *'GOODBYE'*

For the design of Figure 14.13, actions 1 and 2 are executed in sequence. If the result of the conditional test is true then actions 4, 5, 6 and 7 are executed. Upon completion of action 7 the conditional test of action 3 is executed again. This is repeated until the conditional test is false. Upon false action 8 is executed and the program ends.

Step 2: Produce a data table

Identifier	Type	Description
firstNumber	Integer	Stores the number entered at the keyboard. Used twice in the program before the loop and within the loop.
secondNumber	Integer	Stores the number entered at the keyboard. Used three times in the program once before the loop, once within the loop and it is also used in the conditional test. If the *secondNumber* is zero then the loop is not entered. This avoids the possibility of a division by zero.
result	Integer	Stores the result of the integer division of the *firstNumber* by the *secondNumber* and has its content displayed on the VDU.

Step 3: Derive a simple test plan

There is a need for two tests. The first test will check what happens when the loop is not entered. This happens when the value of the *secondNumber* is zero. The second test plan will check what happens when the loop is entered. This occurs when the *secondNumber* is not zero (non-zero).

Test 1

Supplied input

User-friendly prompt	Input data (user response)
Enter the first number	4
Enter the second number	0

Expected output

User-friendly prompt	Output data
GOODBYE	

Test 2

Supplied input

User-friendly prompt	Input data (user response)
Enter the first number	4
Enter the second number	2
Enter the first number	19
Enter the second number	4
Enter the first number	0
Enter the second number	10
Enter the first number	98
Enter the second number	0

319

Expected output

User-friendly prompt	Output data
The result of the integer division is	2
The result of the integer division is	4 (remember it is integer division)
The result of the integer division is	0
GOODBYE	

Step 4: Convert the design to code and compile

Listing 14.2 illustrates the program for the design of Figure 14.13.

Listing 14.2 The code that implements the design of Figure 14.13.

```
Sub Main()
    Dim firstNumber As Integer
    Dim secondNumber As Integer
    Dim result As Integer

    Console.Write("Enter the first number ")
    firstNumber = CInt(Console.ReadLine())
    Console.Write("Enter the second number ")
    secondNumber = CInt(Console.ReadLine())
    Do While secondNumber <> 0
        result = firstNumber \ secondNumber
        Console.Write("The result of the integer division is ")
        Console.WriteLine(result)
        Console.Write("Enter the first number ")
        firstNumber = CInt(Console.ReadLine())
        Console.Write("Enter the second number ")
        secondNumber = CInt(Console.ReadLine())
    Loop
    Console.WriteLine("GOODBYE")
    Console.Write("PRESS ENTER TO CONTINUE ... ")
    Console.Read()
End Sub
```

PRACTICAL ACTIVITY 14.4

You complete step 5, that is, test the runtime against the test plan.

Description trace when tested against Test 1

Statement	Description
Console.Write("Enter the first number ")	The Console displays the user-friendly prompt *Enter the first number.*
firstNumber = CInt(Console.ReadLine())	In response to the prompt the user enters 4, which is converted to an integer and assigned to the integer variable *firstNumber.*
Console.Write("Enter the second number ")	The Console displays the user-friendly prompt *Enter the second number.*
secondNumber = CInt(Console.ReadLine())	In response to the prompt the user enters 0 that is converted to an integer and assigned to the variable *secondNumber.*
Do While secondNumber <> 0	The outcome of the conditional test is **False** because the content of *secondNumber* is equal to zero. Consequently, the *Do While .. Loop* is **not entered**.
Console.WriteLine("GOODBYE")	The string *GOODBYE* is displayed in the Console.
Console.Write("PRESS ENTER TO CONTINUE ... ") Console.Read()	These two lines have been described before.

The runtime of Listing 14.2 when run against test 1 is shown in Figure 14.14.

Figure 14.14 Runtime of Listing 14.2 when run against test 1.

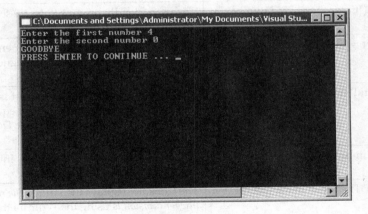

Description trace when tested against Test 2

Statement	Description
Console.Write("Enter the first number ")	The Console displays the user-friendly prompt *Enter the first number.*
firstNumber = CInt(Console.ReadLine())	In response to the prompt the user enters 4, which is converted to an integer and assigned to the variable *firstNumber.*

Console.Write("Enter the second number ")	The user-friendly prompt *Enter the second number* is displayed in the Console.
secondNumber = CInt(Console.ReadLine())	In response to the prompt the user enters 2, which is converted to an integer and assigned to the variable *secondNumber*.
Do While secondNumber <> 0	The outcome of the conditional test is **True** because the content of *secondNumber* is not equal to zero. Consequently, the *Do While .. loop* **is** entered.
result = firstNumber \ secondNumber	*result* is assigned 2 because 2 'goes into' 4 twice.
Console.Write("The result of the integer division is ")	The Console displays the string, *The result of the integer division is . . .* The string has a space after the letter s of the word *is*, and a *Write* method is used so the cursor is left at the end of this line.
Console.WriteLine(result)	The content of the variable *result* (i.e. 2) is displayed in the Console on the same line as the output of the string *The result of the integer division is*. Of course, the variable *result* is of type integer and this has been implicitly converted by the *WriteLine* method to a string.
Console.Write("Enter the first number ")	The Console displays the user-friendly prompt *Enter the first number*.
firstNumber = CInt(Console.ReadLine())	In response to the prompt the user enters 19, which is converted to an integer and assigned to the variable *firstNumber*.
Console.Write("Enter the second number ")	The user-friendly prompt *Enter the second number* is displayed in the Console.
secondNumber = CInt(Console.ReadLine())	In response to the prompt the user enters 4, which is converted to an integer and assigned to the variable *secondNumber*.
Do While secondNumber <> 0	The outcome of the conditional test is **True** because the content of *secondNumber* is not equal to zero (i.e. it is 4 this time). Consequently, the *Do While .. loop* **is** entered again.
result = firstNumber \ secondNumber	*result* is assigned 4 because 4 'goes into' 19 four times (with a remainder of three).
Console.Write("The result of the integer division is ")	The Console displays the string, *The result of the integer division is* using the *Write* method, and consequently, the cursor is left at the end of the line. Note that the string has a space after the letter s of the word *is*.
Console.WriteLine(result)	The content of the variable *result* (i.e. 4) is displayed in the Console on the same line as the output of the string *The result of the integer division is*. Of course, the variable *result* is of type integer and this has been implicitly converted by the *WriteLine* method to a string.

Console.Write("Enter the first number ")	The Console displays the user-friendly prompt *Enter the first number.*
firstNumber = CInt(Console.ReadLine())	In response to the prompt the user enters 0, which is converted to an integer and assigned to the variable *firstNumber.*
Console.Write("Enter the second number ")	The user-friendly prompt *Enter the second number* is displayed in the Console.
secondNumber = CInt(Console.ReadLine())	In response to the prompt the user enters 10, which is converted to an integer and assigned to the variable *secondNumber.*
Do While secondNumber <> 0	The outcome of the conditional test is **True** because the content of *secondNumber* is not equal to zero (i.e. it is 10 time). Consequently, the *Do While .. loop* **is** entered again.
result = firstNumber \ secondNumber	*result* is assigned 0 because 10 'goes into' 0 zero times.
Console.Write("The result of the integer division is ")	The Console displays the string, *The result of the integer division is.*
Console.WriteLine(result)	The content of the variable *result* (i.e. 0) is displayed in the Console on the same line as the output of the string *The result of the integer division is.* Of course, the variable *result* is of type integer and this has been implicitly converted by the *WriteLine* method to a string.
Console.Write("Enter the first number ")	The Console displays the user-friendly prompt *Enter the first number.*
firstNumber = CInt(Console.ReadLine())	In response to the prompt the user enters 98, which is converted to an integer and assigned to the variable *firstNumber.*
Console.Write("Enter the second number ")	The user-friendly prompt *Enter the second number* is displayed in the Console.
secondNumber = CInt(Console.ReadLine())	In response to the prompt the user enters 0 that is converted to an integer and assigned to the variable *secondNumber.*
Do While secondNumber <> 0	The outcome of the conditional test is **False** because the content of *secondNumber* is equal to zero (i.e. it is 0 this time). Consequently, the *Do While .. loop* is **not** re-entered.
Console.Write("GOODBYE ")	The string GOODBYE is displayed in the Console.
Console.Write("PRESS ENTER TO CONTINUE ... ") Console.Read()	These two lines have been described before.

The runtime of Listing 14.2 when run against test 2 is shown in Figure 14.15.

Figure 14.15 Runtime of Listing 14.2 when run against test 2.

```
C:\Documents and Settings\Administrator\My Documents\Visual...
Enter the first number 4
Enter the second number 2
The result of the integer division is 2
Enter the first number 19
Enter the second number 4
The result of the integer division is 4
Enter the first number 0
Enter the second number 10
The result of the integer division is 0
Enter the first number 98
Enter the second number 0
GOODBYE
PRESS ENTER TO CONTINUE ...
```

NOTE: The *Do .. Loop While* and the *Do While .. Loop* constructs are both examples of non-deterministic loops, which mean the number of iterations around the loop is not known on entry to the loop. When the loop is left is dependent upon the data used in their conditional test (often referred to as sentinel). Of course, the value of this data is calculated or assigned within the loop and there is no telling when it will achieve the value that will result in the exit from the loop.

NOTE: The *Do .. Loop While* loop is an example of a post-conditioned loop which means that the conditional test comes at the **end** of the loop and the loop will be entered and consequently executed **at least once**.

Whereas, the *Do While .. Loop* is an example of a pre-conditioned loop, which means that the conditional test comes at the beginning of the loop and consequently the loop may never be entered.

NOTE: For both the *Do .. Loop While* and *Do While .. Loop* constructs the loop is entered (repeated) when the sentinel is true and the loop is exited (not entered) when the sentinel is false.

QUESTION 14.1 (Revision)

Listing 14.2 allowed a WriteLine method to implicitly convert the value stored in the integer variable result to a string. Is this good programming practice?

PRACTICAL ACTIVITY 14.5

Implement the N-S chart design shown in Figure 14.16 as a button click event within a Windows application and as a Console application. Follow the recommended steps as below:

1. Produce a data table.
2. Derive a simple test plan.
3. Convert the design to code and compile.
4. Test the runtime against the test plan.

Figure 14.16 N-S chart design for Practical Activity 14.5. This design represents a program that adds together two numbers and displays the sum. It will continue to add until the user enters two consecutive zeros.

1. Read the first number
2. Read the second number
3. While the first and second numbers are not equal to zero

	4. Add the numbers
	5. Display the sum
	6. Read the first number
	7. Read the second number

8. Display *'GOODBYE'*

The *Do Until .. Loop* construct

The flow of control for this construct is illustrated by the flowchart of Figure 14.17. The actions of this loop are executed if the conditional test is **False** and are **not** executed if the conditional test is **True**. As the conditional test appears before the actions then it is possible that the actions within the loop may *never* be executed.

Upon the completion of the actions the flow of control returns to the conditional test, where a further **False** outcome will result in the actions being repeated. However, if the outcome is **True** the loop is exited. As the conditional test appears before the actions of the loop the variables used within the conditional test must have valid values **before** (or **within**) the conditional test **as well as inside** the loop.

Figure 14.17 The flowchart for a *Do Until .. Loop*.

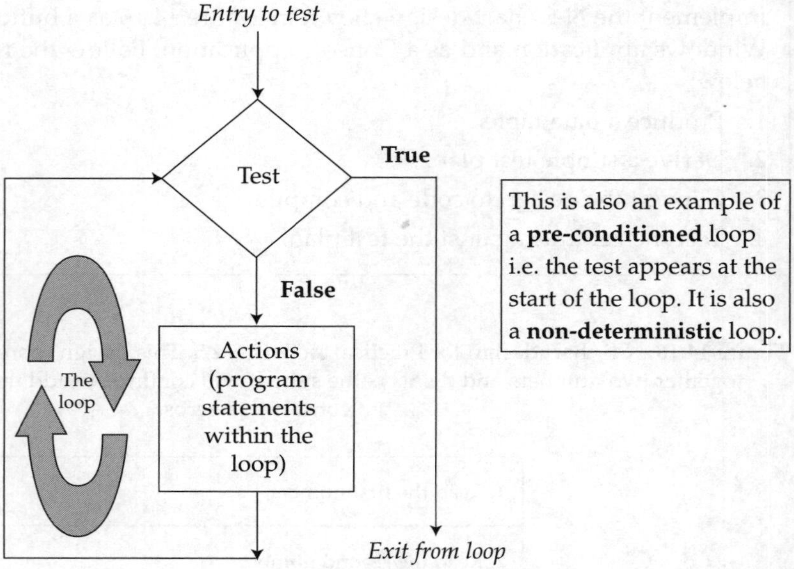

Entry to test

Test

True

This is also an example of a **pre-conditioned** loop i.e. the test appears at the start of the loop. It is also a **non-deterministic** loop.

False

The loop

Actions (program statements within the loop)

Exit from loop

N-S chart and VB .NET representation of the *Do Until .. Loop* construct

The N-S chart and program layout for the *Do Until .. Loop* construct is illustrated in Figure 14.18.

Figure 14.18 The *Do Until .. Loop* construct.

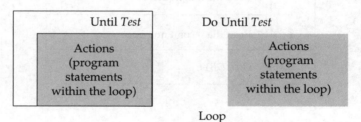

Until *Test*

Actions (program statements within the loop)

Do Until *Test*

Actions (program statements within the loop)

Loop

The actions represented by the shaded area are executed if the conditional test is **False**. When the conditional test is **True** the loop is exited. The program statements inside the loop are 'bracketed' by the reserved words *Do Until* and *Loop*.

QUESTION 14.2 (DEVELOPMENT)
Compare the Do Until .. Loop with the Do While .. Loop.

PRACTICAL ACTIVITY 14.6

Rewrite the code shown in Listing 14.2 so that it performs in the same way except it uses the *Do Until .. Loop* construct instead of the *Do While .. Loop* construct.

Enter and run your solution.

HINT: Consider the *Not* operator.

The *For .. Next* construct

The *Do .. Loop Until, Do .. Loop While, Do While .. Loop* and *Do Until .. Loop* constructs are all examples of **non-deterministic loops**. This means that the number of times around the loop is **unknown** on entry to the loop. What dictates the execution or otherwise of the statements within the loop is the conditional test. The outcome of the conditional test is dependent upon data that is either input or processed inside the loop.

For example the first program in this chapter contains a loop that repeats when the product of two numbers is less than or equal to one hundred. When will the product be greater than one hundred? The answer is when the numbers entered by the user result in a product greater than one hundred. There is no way of knowing when the user will enter numbers that take the product over one hundred, it could be on the first or the thousandth time through the loop.

The number of times around a *For .. Next* loop is **fixed** and the entering and leaving of the loop is **not** dependent upon a conditional test. A *For .. Next* loop is an example of a **deterministic loop**, i.e. the number of times around the loop is determined on entry to the loop.

N-S chart and VB .NET representation of the *For .. Next* construct

The N-S chart and program layout for the *For .. Next* construct is illustrated in Figure 14.19.

Figure 14.19 The *For..Next* loop.

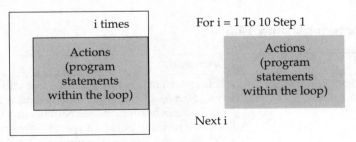

The number of times around the loop is from 1 to 10 in steps of 1. Each time through the loop the value of the integer variable *i* is incremented. The first time through the loop the variable *i* has the value 1 and the second time it has the value 2 and so on until the tenth and last time through the loop the variable *i* has the value 10. The range assigned to *i* and the size of the step can fix the number of times through the loop. The identifier (name) of the variable incremented was chosen as *i*, which is common practice among programmers. Of course this variable can be any sensible identifier, such as, *count*, which reflects a common use of the *For .. Next* construct i.e. to count the times through a loop – which can act as a measure of the number of times an action has been performed.

A *For .. Next* construct is frequently used to access structured data types such as arrays (covered in a later chapter).

An example use of the *For .. Next* construct

SPECIFICATION 14.3

Write a Console application to output the ANSI characters A, B, C, D, E and F together with their ordinal number.

The solution to Specification 14.3 is shown in Listing 14.3.

Listing 14.3 Solution to Specification 14.3.

```
Module Module1

    Sub Main()
        Dim i As Integer
        Console.WriteLine("Number" & Space(4) & "Character")
        For i = 65 To 70 Step 1
            Console.WriteLine(Space(2) & CStr(i) & Space(10) & Chr(i))
        Next i
        Console.Write("PRESS ENTER TO CONTINUE ... ")
        Console.Read()
    End Sub
End Module
```

Description trace for Listing 14.3

Statement	Description
Console.WriteLine("Number" & Space(4) & "Character")	This statement is before and therefore outside the *For .. Next* loop and is only executed once. It creates a two-column header labelled Number and Character. The *Space(4)* function puts four spaces between the strings *Number* and *Character*. The output is achieved by using the message *Console.WriteLine*.
For i = 65 To 70 Step 1	On the first pass through the loop the variable *i* is assigned the value 65.

Console.WriteLine(Space(2) & CStr(i) & Space(10) & Chr(i))	This statement outputs two spaces as defined by *Space(2)*, the value of the integer variable *i* after it is converted to a string using *CStr*. Ten more spaces as defined by *Space(10)* and the character that represents the value of *i* as produced by the function *Chr(i)* – which in this case is *A* (CAPITAL) All of these 'separate parts' of the *WriteLine* parameter are concatenated together using the & (ampersand) operator.
Next i	This causes the flow of control to return into the loop again. However, this time the variable *i* has been incremented by 1 to the value of 66.
Console.WriteLine(Space(2) & CStr(i) & Space(10) & Chr(i))	66 and B is output.
Next i	This causes the flow of control to return into the loop again. However, this time the variable *i* has been incremented by 1 to the value of 67.
Console.WriteLine(Space(2) & CStr(i) & Space(10) & Chr(i))	67 and C is output.
The loop is repeated until the value of *i* reaches 70 then the flow is as follows.	
Console.WriteLine(Space(2) & CStr(i) & Space(10) & Chr(i))	This statement outputs two spaces as defined by *Space(2)*, the value of the integer variable *i* after it is converted to a string using *CStr*. Ten more spaces as defined by *Space(10)* and the character that represents the value of *i* as produced by the function *Chr(i)* – which in this case is *F* (CAPITAL) All of these 'separate parts' of the *WriteLine* parameter are concatenated together using the & (ampersand) operator.
The looping ends because *i* is at 70.	
Console.Write("PRESS ENTER TO CONTINUE ... ") Console.Read()	These two lines have been described before.

The output from the program of Listing 14.3 is shown in Figure 14.20.

Figure 14.20 Output from the program shown in Listing 14.3.

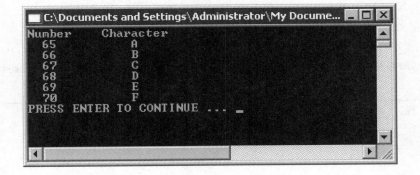

329

NOTE: The *Space* function is used to achieve sensible positions of the column headings and the corresponding outputs. Observe Figure 14.20 to see how the outputs line up under the headings.

PRACTICAL ACTIVITY 14.7

Amend the Listing 14.3 so that it outputs the character set for

a) The ordinal number range 48 to 57.

b) The ordinal number range 33 to 47.

c) The ordinal number range 180 to 190.

Run each example and observe the output.

PRACTICAL ACTIVITY 14.8

Observe the effect of changing the parameter within the *Space* function of Listing 14.3, i.e. amend then run the program

---

PRACTICAL ACTIVITY 14.9 (REVISION)

How would the code shown in Listing 14.3 be altered if the namespace *System.Console* were placed as shown below

The namespace is put here using the keyword
Imports before the module code.

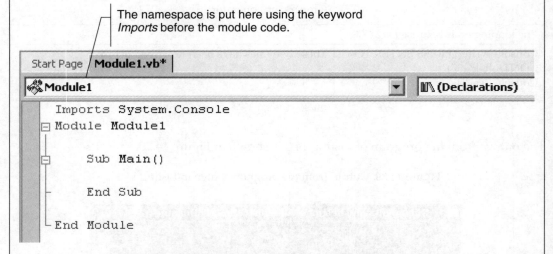

```
Imports System.Console
Module Module1

    Sub Main()

    End Sub

End Module
```

The answer is shown below. If you compare Listings 14.3 and 14.4 the answer should be obvious.

Listing 14.4 The use of a namespace.

```
Imports System.Console
Module Module1
    Sub Main()
        Dim i As Integer

        WriteLine("Number" & Space(4) & "Character")
        For i = 65 To 70 Step 1
            WriteLine(Space(2) & CStr(i) & Space(10) & Chr(i))
        Next i
        Write("PRESS ENTER TO CONTINUE ... ")
        Read()
    End Sub
End Module
```

15 Nested constructs

The last three chapters dealt with the programming constructs, sequence, selection and repetition (iteration). This chapter shows how these constructs can be nested inside one another. This nesting will be demonstrated by implementing Specification 15.1.

SPECIFICATION 15.1

Write a program that will find all the prime numbers from 2 to 100.

The solution to Specification 15.1 will be shown as N-S charts. You should study these charts to see how it is a solution to the specification. The chapter will concentrate on converting the design to a program and in the process nested structures will be highlighted.

Figures 15.1 and 15.2 are the N-S charts that are the solution to Specification 15.1. There are two charts, because presenting the design as one chart would be too cluttered.

These charts also illustrate **stepwise refinement**. Step 2 of the first chart simply specifies *Test to see if the potential prime is prime*; there is no indication of how this is achieved. The designer (often the programmer but not always) has identified what needs to be done at step 2 but the solution of how it is achieved is refined (solved) later. The second chart shows this refinement – which is the solution to step 2 of the first chart.

Stepwise refinement involves a 'broad brush' design in the first instance that identifies the main steps of the solution. These steps are then refined to include more detail. This process is iterative with many attempts until the design is complete.

Once the design is complete the programmer develops a test plan, a data table and converts the design to code. This process of converting the design code will be outlined in this chapter (you are left to consider the test plan and data table).

Figure 15.1 The top-level N-S chart.

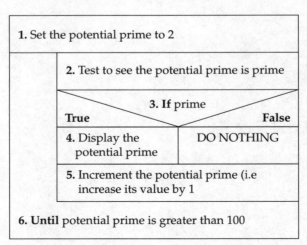

Step 1 of this design starts with number two and at this point regards it as a potential prime; this means it may be a prime number so lets test it to see if it is a prime number.

Step 2 performs the test to see if it is a prime number. There is no attempt at this stage to show how this is achieved.

Step 3 has assumed that **step 2** has found whether it is prime or not. If it is prime then **step 4** is executed, and this displays the potential prime (which has just been proved to be a prime number). However, if it is not a prime number it is not displayed (i.e. step four is not executed). After the selection construct **step 5** takes the current potential prime and increases it by one, this is now the new potential prime and this will be tested again by **step 2**. The design takes us back to **step 2** because **step 6** is the conditional test of a *Do .. Loop Until* construct and **steps 2, 3, 4** and **5** are **inside this loop** (step 1 is before this loop). The conditional test of the loop will allow for all numbers from 2 to 100 to be tested to see if they are a prime number.

NOTE: Steps 3 and 4 form the selection construct and this selection construct is regarded as being **nested** inside the *Do .. Loop Until* construct, i.e. a selection construct is **nested** inside a loop construct.

Figure 15.2 The refinement of step 2.

2.1. Set the divider to half of the potential prime		
2.2. Set the remainder 1		
2.3. While (the divider is greater than 1) **And** (the remainder is not equal to zero)		
	2.4. Find the remainder when the divider divides the potential prime	
	2.5. Decrement the divider by 1 (i.e. reduce its value by 1)	
	2.6. If the remainder is zero	
True		**False**
2.7. Set prime to **false**		**2.8.** Set prime to **true**

This design is the refinement of step 2 and consequently its steps are numbered accordingly, i.e. 2.1, 2.2, etc.

You are left to study the workings of this design.

The design shows a sequence (steps 2.1 and 2.2), followed by a loop (steps 2.3, 2.4 and 2.5), which in turn is followed by a selection (steps 2.6, 2.7 and 2.8). The important point is that all of these steps are nested inside the loop shown in the first top level N-S chart (Figure 15.1).

A Console application will be used to implement this solution, as it will allow concentration on the language and not the GUI.

The program that implements this is shown in Listing 15.1 and the program runtime is shown in Figure 15.3. A data table would show that this program requires four variables. They are as follows:

- An integer variable to hold the potential prime.
- An integer variable to hold the divider.
- An integer variable to hold the remainder.
- A Boolean variable to flag whether the potential prime is prime or not prime.

Listing 15.1 Implementing the design.

```
Module Module 1
    Sub Main ()
        Dim potentialPrime As Integer
        Dim divider As Integer
        Dim remainder As Integer
        Dim prime As Boolean

        potentialPrime = 2
        Do
            divider = potentialPrime \2
            remainder = 1
            Do While (divider > 1) And (remainder <> 0)
                remainder = potentialPrime Mod divider
                divider = divider - 1
            Loop
            If remainder = 0 Then
            prime = False
            Else
            prime = True
            End If
            If prime Then
                Console.WriteLine ("A prime number is " & CStr (potentialPrime))
            End If
            potential Prime = potentialPrime + 1
        Loop Until potentialPrime > 100

        Console.Write ("PRESS ENTER TO CONTINUE")
        Console.Read ()
    End Sub
End Module
```

Figure 15.3 The runtime.

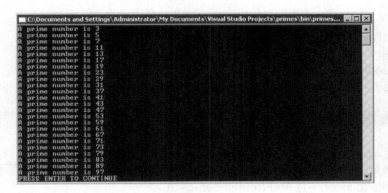

Figures 15.4 and 15.5 relate the listing to the steps of the N-S charts.

NOTE: Note how the code is indented; this improves the visual appeal of the program and makes it easier to read. It also emphasizes the program constructs.

Figure 15.4 Relating the code to the first N-S chart shown in Figure 15.1.

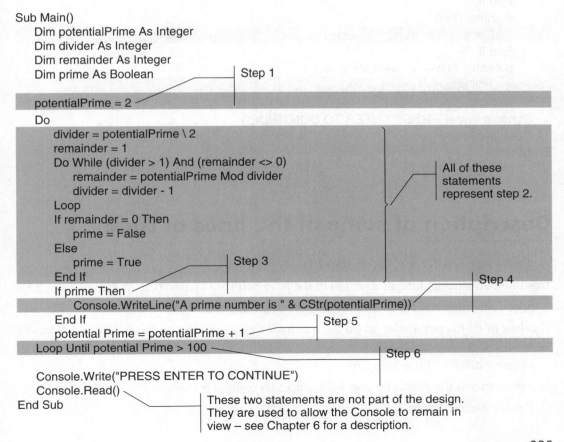

```
Sub Main()
    Dim potentialPrime As Integer
    Dim divider As Integer
    Dim remainder As Integer
    Dim prime As Boolean                    | Step 1

    potentialPrime = 2
    Do
        divider = potentialPrime \ 2
        remainder = 1
        Do While (divider > 1) And (remainder <> 0)
            remainder = potentialPrime Mod divider           All of these
            divider = divider - 1                            statements
        Loop                                                 represent step 2.
        If remainder = 0 Then
            prime = False
        Else
            prime = True                    | Step 3
        End If                                                          | Step 4
        If prime Then
            Console.WriteLine("A prime number is " & CStr(potentialPrime))
        End If                              | Step 5
        potential Prime = potentialPrime + 1
    Loop Until potential Prime > 100                         | Step 6

    Console.Write("PRESS ENTER TO CONTINUE")
    Console.Read()                          These two statements are not part of the design.
End Sub                                     They are used to allow the Console to remain in
                                            view – see Chapter 6 for a description.
```

Figure 15.5 Relating the code to the second N-S chart shown in Figure 15.2.

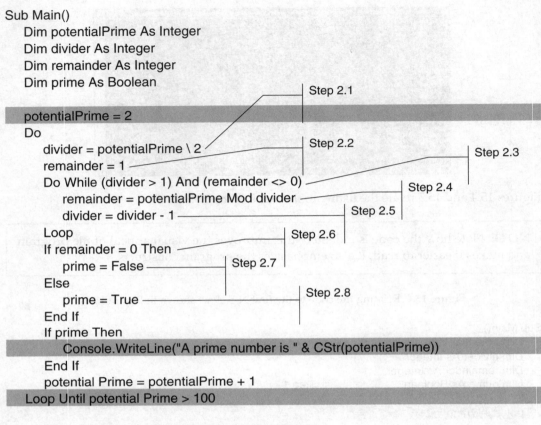

```
Sub Main()
    Dim potentialPrime As Integer
    Dim divider As Integer
    Dim remainder As Integer
    Dim prime As Boolean
                                                          Step 2.1
    potentialPrime = 2
    Do
        divider = potentialPrime \ 2                       Step 2.2
        remainder = 1                                                        Step 2.3
        Do While (divider > 1) And (remainder <> 0)
            remainder = potentialPrime Mod divider             Step 2.4
            divider = divider - 1                      Step 2.5
        Loop
        If remainder = 0 Then                 Step 2.6
            prime = False                  Step 2.7
        Else
            prime = True                      Step 2.8
        End If
        If prime Then
            Console.WriteLine("A prime number is " & CStr(potentialPrime))
        End If
        potential Prime = potentialPrime + 1
    Loop Until potential Prime > 100

    Console.Write("PRESS ENTER TO CONTINUE")
    Console.Read()
End Sub
```

Description of some of the lines of code

divider = potentialPrime \ 2 (i.e. step 2.1)

This line performs an integer division of the *potentialPrime* by two (e.g. 7\2 gives 3 not 3.5).

remainder = potentialPrime Mod divider (i.e. step 2.4)

This line finds the remainder when the *potentialPrime* is divided by the *divider* (e.g. 7 Mod 2 gives 1).

divider = divider - 1 (i.e. step 2.5)

This decrements the *divider* by one, i.e. reduces its content by one.

If prime Then (i.e. step 3)

It is usual for an *If* conditional test to have a relational operator, such as, *If prime = True*. However, *prime* is a *Boolean* type and is either already True or False so it is allowed to be the conditional test in this way.

QUESTION 15.1 (REVISION)

What would happen if you altered the following line of the program shown in Listing 15.1 in the way indicated below?

    divider = potentialPrime \ 2

changed to:

    divider = potentialPrime / 2

PRACTICAL ACTIVITY 15.1

Enter and run the program as shown in Listing 15.1.

The implementation of Specification 15.1 is repeated on the following pages using a different programming technique that involves objects. Step 2 of the design is implemented by messaging an object that is capable of indicating whether an integer is or is not prime. Listing 15.2 contains this message and Listing 15.3 shows the class containing the code for the method that is invoked (of course there will be an instance of this class that is messaged). The UML collaboration diagram of Figure 15.6 shows the messaging.

Listing 15.2 The Console application code.

```
Module Module1

    Sub Main()
        Dim potentialPrime As Integer
        Dim prime As Boolean
        Dim primeFinder As FindIfPrime

        primeFinder = New FindIfPrime()
        potentialPrime = 2
        Do
            prime = primeFinder.IsItPrime(potentialPrime)
            If prime Then
                Console.WriteLine("A prime number is " & CStr(potentialPrime))
            End If
            potentialPrime = potentialPrime + 1
        Loop Until potentialPrime > 100
```

Declares a variable capable of referencing an instance of the *FindIfPrime* class.

Creates an object of the *FindIfPrime* class.

This is a **message** to the instance of the *FindIfPrime* class that returns true or false to the local variable *prime*.
This message invokes the *IsItPrime* instance method of an instance of the *FindIfPrime* class.

337

Listing 15.2 (cont.)

```
      Console.Write("PRESS ENTER TO CONTINUE")
      Console.Read()
   End Sub

End Module
```

The message takes the potential prime as an actual parameter. *True* is returned if the potential prime is a prime number. However, if the potential prime is not a prime number *False* is returned.

Listing 15.3 The *FindIfPrime* class code.

```
Public Class FindIfPrime

   Public Function IsItPrime(ByVal pPotentialPrime As Integer) As Boolean
      Dim divider As Integer
      Dim remainder As Integer

      divider = pPotentialPrime \ 2
      remainder = 1
      Do While (divider > 1) And (remainder <> 0)
         remainder = pPotentialPrime Mod divider
         divider = divider - 1
      Loop
      If remainder = 0 Then
         Return False
      Else
         Return True
      End If
   End Function

End Class
```

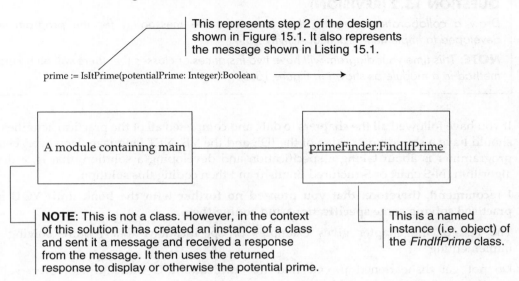

Figure 15.6 The UML Collaboration Diagram.

This represents step 2 of the design shown in Figure 15.1. It also represents the message shown in Listing 15.1.

prime := IsItPrime(potentialPrime: Integer):Boolean

A module containing main

primeFinder:FindIfPrime

NOTE: This is not a class. However, in the context of this solution it has created an instance of a class and sent it a message and received a response from the message. It then uses the returned response to display or otherwise the potential prime.

This is a named instance (i.e. object) of the *FindIfPrime* class.

NOTE: The class shown in Listing 15.3 only has one method and no properties. It would normally be very unusual to have a class of this nature. It has simply been used here to illustrate another example of messaging in the context of a slightly more complex algorithm than that previously covered and also as revision for showing the messaging syntax associated with collaboration diagrams.

PRACTICAL ACTIVITY 15.2

Enter and run the program as represented by Listings 15.2 and 15.3. You may wish to read Chapter 16 before you attempt this.

PRACTICAL ACTIVITY 15.3

Create a Windows application that will display all the prime numbers from 2 to 100 in a textbox. Attach the code to the click event of a button.

PRACTICAL ACTIVITY 15.4

Create another Windows application that will display all the prime numbers from 2 to 100 in a textbox. However, this time have your Windows application use the class as defined by Listing 15.2. Again attach the code to the click event of a button – this event handling procedure will need to create an instance of the class of Listing 15.2 and send it a message.

339

QUESTION 15.2 (REVISION)

Draw a collaboration diagram that represents the messaging for the program you developed to implement Practical Activity 15.4.

NOTE: *This time your diagram will have two instances of classes (i.e. there will be no main method in a module as shown in Figure 15.6).*

If you have followed all the chapters to date and completed all of the practical activities you should have a sound knowledge of the IDE and the VB .NET language. However, being a programmer is about taking a specification and developing a solution, that is, a design algorithm (N-S chart or Structured English) and then coding this solution.

I recommend, therefore, that you proceed no further with the book until YOU have practised solving some specifications and coding them.

The rest of the chapter gives examples of specifications that require solving and implementing.

Do not get disheartened if you find this difficult, it is difficult. However, solving specifications will very quickly improve your ability as a programmer and, as they say, practice makes . . .

PRACTICAL ACTIVITY 15.5

For each of the following specifications produce:

- An algorithm expressed as an N-S chart or Structured English design.
- A data table.
- A test plan (with full boundary testing)
- The program.

SPECIFICATION 15.2

Write a Console application that converts Pounds to Dollars. The current exchange rate is part of the program input.

SPECIFICATION 15.3

Write a Windows application that converts Pounds to Dollars. Again the current exchange rate is part of the program input. All inputs must be via textboxes and the output must be to a label. The program is to be attached to the click event of a button.

SPECIFICATION 15.4

The powers of three are 1, 9, 27, 81, 243 and so on. To get the next power of 3, you multiply the previous one by 3. Write a Console application that will output the first power of 3 that exceeds 1000.

SPECIFICATION 15.5

The powers of four are 1, 16, 64, 256 and so on. To get the next power of 4, you multiply the previous one by 4. Write a Windows application that will output to a label the first power of 4 that exceeds 1000. The program is to be attached to the click event of a button.

SPECIFICATION 15.6

Write a Console application in which the user is asked repeatedly to input integers from 1 to 7 (integers over 7 and under 1 should not be allowed entry). The program should inform the user when they enter an integer that puts the sum of the input integers over 21. In addition to printing the message OVER 21, the computer should print the sum and the last integer entered.

SPECIFICATION 15.7

Shirts are on sale for £20 each if more than four are purchased and £24 each otherwise. Write a Windows application that will read in the number of shirts purchased and print out the total cost. Attach the program to the click event of a picture box that displays a suitable picture. The choice of input is left up to you.

SPECIFICATION 15.8

Write a Console application that received two integers as input and prints the message opposite signs if one integer is negative and the other is positive, otherwise the message should be the same signs.

SPECIFICATION 15.9

An employee receives basic pay for the first 35 hours worked and is paid at 2 times the basic pay for each hour worked over 35 hours. Write a Console application that will calculate and display on the VDU the employees wage based on the basic pay and hours worked both of which are entered by the user.

SPECIFICATION 15.10

Write a Console application that will calculate and display the cost of postage based on the weight of a letter. The weight is entered and the cost of postage is calculated according to the following:

● The first 20 grams cost £0.60.

● Each gram over 20 grams costs an extra £0.05.

SPECIFICATION 15.11

Write a Console application that will receive two different positive integers and display the difference between the larger and the smaller. Make sure that 2 is output when both 9 then 11 and 11 then 9 is input.

SPECIFICATION 15.12

A repeat until loop is often used to edit input. Produce a Console application that asks the user to enter a non zero integer and then print its reciprocal. Use a repeat until loop to force the user to re-enter the value if a 0 is entered by mistake.

SPECIFICATION 15.13

Write a Console application in which the user is asked to input ten odd integers to be summed. Construct your program so that it will not fail if the user enters some even integers. Inform the user when they accidentally enter an even number. The program should exit the loop and print the sum after ten odd integers have been entered.

SPECIFICATION 15.14

5! (read 5 factorial) is equal to the product 5 times 4 times 3 times 2 times 1. Produce a button click event handling procedure that will calculate the factorial of an inputted positive integer. When this program is run with the user inputting 5, the output (to be displayed in a label) should be

5 factorial is 120

What happens if a large positive integer is entered into this program and why?

SPECIFICATION 15.15

Develop the GUI shown in Figure 15.8 and make it perform the following:

*The three buttons in the **top** left of the GUI when clicked change the background colour of the PictureBox to red, green and blue as specified by the button.*

*The three buttons in the **bottom** left of the GUI when clicked change the background colour of the form to red, green and blue as specified by the button.*

The four buttons in the middle will move the PictureBox around the form in the direction specified by the button.

The Off button will disable all of the buttons apart from the On button.

The On button is used to enable all of the buttons disabled by the Off button.

The Quit button unloads the form and quits the application.

Hint: you will need to modify members of the controls. These members will be the BackColor for the PictureBox and Form when changing colours; the Top and Left properties of the PictureBox when moving it. The Enabled property of the buttons will need modifying when enabling and disabling the buttons.

Figure 15.7 For Specification 15.15.

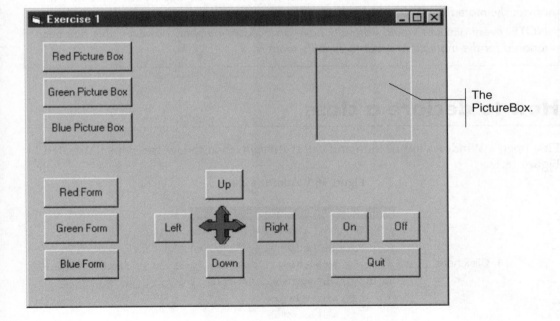

The PictureBox.

16 Building a class

This chapter will show you how to build a class, create an object of this class and test it with a 'testing class'. All of this process will be covered through the implementation of the following specification.

SPECIFICATION 16.1

Every bank customer has an account balance, a name and a credit rating (from 0 to 5). Build a class that allows for all of the following:

- *The reading (getting) and setting (writing) of the customers' name.*
- *The ability to change the customers' name.*
- *The reading of the balance.*
- *Credit the balance.*
- *Debit the balance.*

A customer credit rating is based on their balance; a score of one is awarded for every £200 of their balance up to a maximum of 5. Therefore, a balance of £199 would attract a rating of zero, whereas a balance of £210 would have a rating of one. A balance of £1000 and £1010 both would attract a rating of five.

Whenever a new account is created at least £100 has to be deposited. Although, and obviously, more than £100 will be accepted when a new account is created.

NOTE: every account would normally have an account number, however, this has been ignored for the moment in order to simplify matters.

How to declare a class

First open a Windows application and call it *Account*, then follow the steps illustrated by Figure 16.1.

Figure 16.1 Adding a class.

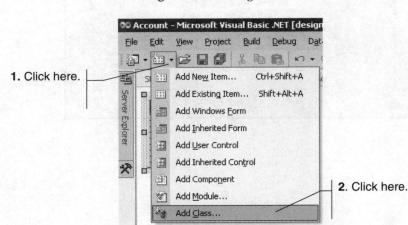

Figure 16.1 (cont.)

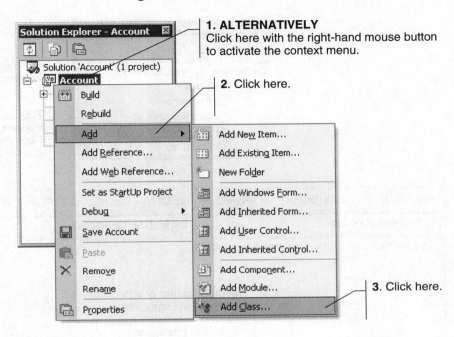

1. ALTERNATIVELY
Click here with the right-hand mouse button to activate the context menu.

2. Click here.

3. Click here.

4. Select this.

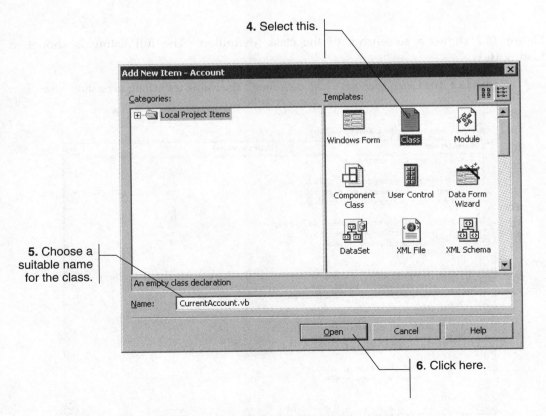

5. Choose a suitable name for the class.

6. Click here.

Figure 16.1 (cont.)

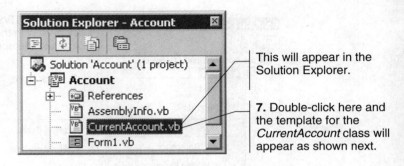

This will appear in the Solution Explorer.

7. Double-click here and the template for the *CurrentAccount* class will appear as shown next.

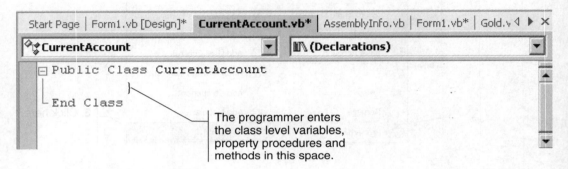

The programmer enters the class level variables, property procedures and methods in this space.

Figure 16.2 shows a screenshot of the class 'definition'. The full listing is shown in Listing 16.1.

Figure 16.2 The *CurrentAccount* Class 'definition'. The listing is too long to be shown on one screenshot.

Figure 16.2 (cont.)

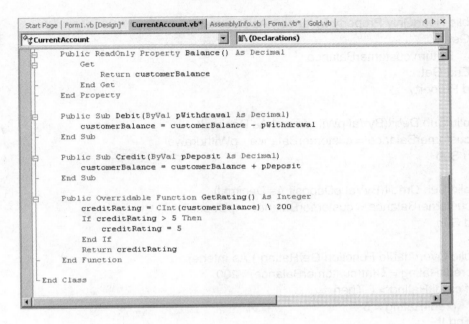

Listing 16.1 The *CurrentAccount* class.

Public Class CurrentAccount

    Private customerName As String
    Private customerBalance As Decimal
    Private creditRating As Integer

    Public Sub New(ByVal pName As String)
       customerName = pName
       customerBalance = 100
    End Sub

    Public Sub New(ByVal pName As String, ByVal pInitialDeposit As Decimal)
       customerName = pName
       customerBalance = pInitialDeposit
    End Sub

    Public Property Name() As String
       Get
          Return customerName
       End Get
       Set(ByVal pValue As String)
          customerName = pValue
       End Set
    End Property

Listing 16.1 (cont.)

```
Public ReadOnly Property Balance() As Decimal
    Get
        Return customerBalance
    End Get
End Property

Public Sub Debit(ByVal pWithdrawal As Decimal)
    customerBalance = customerBalance - pWithdrawal
End Sub

Public Sub Credit(ByVal pDeposit As Decimal)
    customerBalance = customerBalance + pDeposit
End Sub

Public Overridable Function GetRating() As Integer
    creditRating = CInt(customerBalance) \ 200
    If creditRating > 5 Then
        creditRating = 5
    End If
    Return creditRating
End Function

End Class
```

NOTE: The description of Listing 16.1 follows; rather than number a relatively long listing each part of the description will be associated with a repeat of the code being described and this code will appear in a box.

```
Private customerName As String
Private customerBalance As Decimal
Private creditRating As Integer
```

These three lines are the class level variables (often referred to as fields). Their purpose should be obvious from their names, e.g. the *String* variable *customerName* is used to store the name of the customer who holds an account. All three class level variables are declared with the *Private* modifier; consequently, the *CurrentAccount* class does NOT expose these class level variables. The class variables are 'associated' with the methods and the property procedures of the *CurrentAccount* class.

```
Public Sub New(ByVal pName As String)
    customerName = pName
    customerBalance = 100
End Sub
```

Every class is automatically supplied with a constructor method called *New*, by default. However, the default method, although useful in that it creates an instance of the class, does nothing else. For example, it does not set any instances of class level variables or take any parameters that could be used to set instance variables. If you wished to create an instance of a class and at the same time set instance variables of the object then you have to declare another version of the *New* constructor method. The code above is such an example of a constructor method. It takes a parameter, which is the name of the customer (*pName*). It is a *ByVal* parameter declared as *String* type.

ByVal means that a **copy** of the value of the actual parameter in the constructor message is passed to the formal parameter *pName* – it is an example of an input parameter, that is, data is passed with the message to the method. Any change in the formal parameter *pName* will **not** be reflected back to the actual parameter passed with the message.

The two program statements within this method are used to access two variables. The first line takes the value of the parameter 'passed in' and assigns it to the *customerName* variable of the created object. Note how the type of the parameter and the variable are the same (both strings). The second statement assigns 100 to the *customerBalance* variable (an account must have at least an initial balance of £100 – part of the specification).

This constructor method is declared with a *Public* access modifier so that it is exposed to other objects, i.e. it is part of the **public interface**.

NOTE: When using *ByVal*, whatever happens to the value of the formal parameter *pName* within the mechanics of the method will have no effect upon the value of the actual parameter. The actual parameter will have the same value before, during and after the execution of the method. The program statements within the method however can change the value of the formal parameter (which received a copy of the actual parameter).

NOTE: Another way of declaring a formal parameter is to use the keyword *ByRef*. If *ByRef* is used for a non-reference type variable (e.g. an integer) then the method can modify the actual parameter i.e. the parameter can act as an output parameter.

NOTE: The advantage of passing *ByRef* is that the method can return a value to the invoking message through that argument. The advantage of passing *ByVal* is that it protects a variable from being changed by the method.

For a parameter, Table 16.1 summarizes the interaction between the parameter's data type and the passing mechanism.

Table 16.1 *ByVal* and *ByRef*.

Parameter type	*Passed* ByVal	*Passed* ByRef
Value type that contains a value, e.g. an integer variable.	The method cannot change the variable or any of its members.	The method can change the variable and its members.
Reference type, e.g. an object reference.	The method cannot change the variable but can change members of the instance to which it points.	The method can change the variable and members of the instance to which it points.

```
Public Sub New(ByVal pName As String, _
ByVal pInitialDeposit As Decimal)

    customerName = pName
    customerBalance = pInitialDeposit
End Sub
```

This shows another example of a *New* constructor method. It is also declared with *Public*, for the same reasons as outlined for the *New* constructor just described. This constructor only differs from the last by the number of parameters it takes and by the second program statement. This constructor takes two parameters: the customers name (*pName*) and the initial deposit (*pInitialDeposit*). It takes another parameter because the specification indicated that the minimum initial deposit was £100; however, more than £100 is allowed.

When this class is used, and more to the point, when an instance of this class is created, which of these constructors are to be used? The answer is that you would create the account with the first constructor unless you wished the initial deposit to be more than £100, in which case you would use the second constructor.

NOTE: What happens if less than £100 was offered as an initial deposit is not considered – this is just to keep things simple at this stage. Obviously a more robust program would have to consider this!

NOTE: If one or more programmer constructors are declared within a class then VB .NET will **not** create a default – no argument (i.e. no parameters) – constructor for you.

```
Public Property Name() As String
    Get
        Return customerName
    End Get
    Set(ByVal pValue As String)
        customerName = pValue
    End Set
End Property
```

Part of the specification required that the name of the customer be available as part of the public interface (i.e. exposed). The specification also required the possibility for changing the name of a customer. Both of these requirements have been achieved using the property procedure shown here. Outside code can access the instance variable *customerName* via the property *Name* (i.e. via the property procedure *Name*).

```
Public ReadOnly Property Balance() As Decimal
    Get
        Return customerBalance
    End Get
End Property
```

Another requirement was for the balance to be available but not directly alterable. The *customerBalance* variable can be altered by a withdrawal or deposit but it cannot be set to a new value. A *ReadOnly* property procedure is the mechanism used to achieve this. Note how there is no *Set* part of a *ReadOnly* property procedure.

```
Public Sub Debit(ByVal pWithdrawal As Decimal)
    customerBalance = customerBalance – pWithdrawal
End Sub
```

This *Public* method uses the value of the actual parameter supplied with the message to reduce variable *customerBalance*. The content of the actual parameter is passed by value (*ByVal*) to the formal parameter *pWithDrawal* and this is then subtracted from the *customerBalance* as can be seen by the one and only program statement within this method.

```
Public Sub Credit(ByVal pDeposit As Decimal)
    customerBalance = customerBalance + pDeposit
End Sub
```

This is very similar to the previous method except this time the content passed from the actual parameter of the invoking message to the formal parameter (*pDeposit*) is added to the *customerBalance* variable.

```
Public Overridable Function GetRating() As Integer
    creditRating = CInt(customerBalance) \ 200
    If creditRating > 5 Then
        creditRating = 5
    End If
    Return creditRating
End Function
```

The credit rating is from 0 to 5 and the code within this **Function** method uses the *customerBalance* variable to calculate the rating. It uses **integer division** and divides the balance by 200. The result of the integer division gives the rating. For example 250 divided by 200 gives 1 and this is the credit rating for the customer. One thousand and twenty (1020) divided by 200 gives a credit rating of 5. However, 30000 divided by 200 gives 150 which is obviously outside the range of allowed credit ratings. The *If Then* construct ensures that the rating is never greater than 5.

The use of a *Function* method allows for the returning of the rating to the object sending the invoking message. It can be seen that it returns an *Integer* type and the *Return* program statement 'performs the honours'. This is illustrated by Figure 16.3.

Figure 16.3 Returning a credit rating.

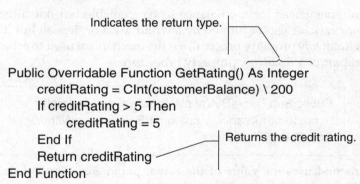

Indicates the return type.

```
Public Overridable Function GetRating() As Integer
    creditRating = CInt(customerBalance) \ 200
    If creditRating > 5 Then
        creditRating = 5
    End If
    Return creditRating
End Function
```

Returns the credit rating.

NOTE: The keyword *Overridable* is used in Figure 16.3. In the context of this example it can be omitted and the code will still work. However, it is include here because in the next chapter another *GetRating* method will override this version (this is not the same as overloading). A fuller description of the use of *Overridable* (a type of **Polymorphism**) is given in the next chapter and further coverage appears in Chapter 19.

Testing the *CurrentAccount* class

Creating an instance of the *CurrentAccount* class from within an instance of a form class and then accessing its members with appropriate messages and then displaying the results of these messages on a GUI can achieve the testing of this class.

> **NOTE**: A full and true test of the class is not attempted here. The emphasis is on showing how the members of an object of the *CurrentAccount* class can be used and accessed.

A suitable (but rather crude) GUI for testing this class is shown in Figure 16.4.

Figure 16.4 A suitable GUI.

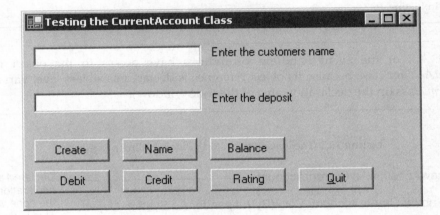

How an instance of the *CurrentAccount* class is created and then messaged to access and alter its members is illustrated by the following sequence of figures, starting with Figure 16.5.

> **NOTE**: The figures assume that the tasks are performed in the sequence shown. If you choose a different sequence when you run the program then it will respond differently to that shown here.

Figure 16.5 Creating an instance of *CurrentAccount*.

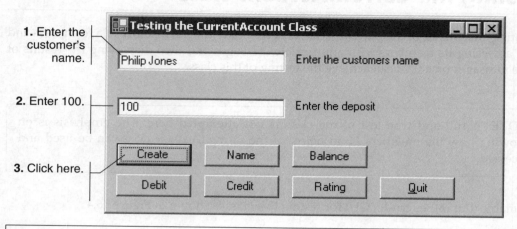

1. Enter the customer's name.

2. Enter 100.

3. Click here.

Once the Create button is clicked its event handling procedure is executed. The code for this is shown in Listing 16.2.

NOTE: All of the event handling procedures have access to the object of the *CurrentAccount* class because its object reference is declared as a class level variable of the *Form* class (in the declaration area of the code window).

Listing 16.2 The *btnCreateAccount_Click* handling procedure.

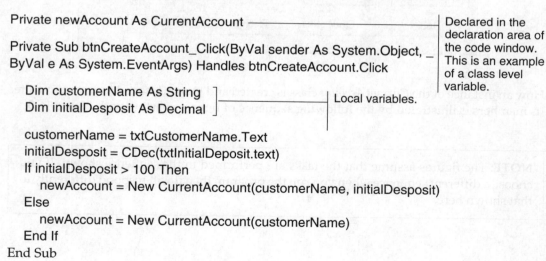

```
Private newAccount As CurrentAccount

Private Sub btnCreateAccount_Click(ByVal sender As System.Object, _
ByVal e As System.EventArgs) Handles btnCreateAccount.Click

    Dim customerName As String
    Dim initialDesposit As Decimal

    customerName = txtCustomerName.Text
    initialDesposit = CDec(txtInitialDeposit.text)
    If initialDesposit > 100 Then
        newAccount = New CurrentAccount(customerName, initialDesposit)
    Else
        newAccount = New CurrentAccount(customerName)
    End If
End Sub
```

Declared in the declaration area of the code window. This is an example of a class level variable.

Local variables.

The first two program statements of the event handling procedure shown in Listing 16.2 assign the content of the textboxes to the local variables *customerName* and *initialDesposit*. In the case of the *initialDesposit* variable its assigned value is converted to a *Decimal* from the *String* value entered in the textbox using the *CDec* function.

354

As the *initialDeposit* (as shown in Figure 16.5) is **not** greater than 100 the constructor in the *Else* part of the selection construct is executed. This constructor has the local variable *customerName* as its actual parameter. This is passed by value (*ByVal*) to the formal parameter *pName*. This is illustrated in Figure 16.6.

Figure 16.6 Passing a parameter.

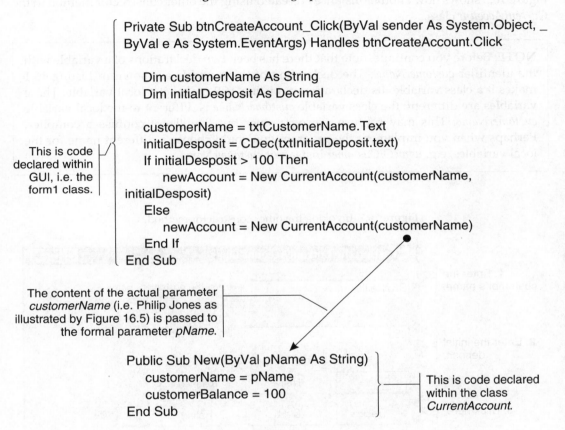

The content of the formal parameter *pName* (i.e. *Philip Jones*) is assigned to the variable *customerName* within the instance of the *CurrentAccount* class. Note the class level variable *customerName* is a different variable to the local variable *customerName*. Just because they share the same name does **not** mean they are the same variable!

Once this constructor has executed the instance variables of this particular instance of the *CurrentAccount* class will be set as shown below.

customerName will be storing *Philip Jones* because of the following statement:

customerName = pName

> customerBalance will be storing 100 because of the following statement:
>
> customerBalance = 100

Figure 16.7 shows how another instance is created using the other constructor method in the *CurrentAccount* class.

NOTE: Before you continue, note that there has been two declarations of a variable with the identifier *customerName*. The declaration of this variable as shown in Listing 16.1 makes it a class variable. Its declaration in Listing 16.2 makes it a local variable. These variables are different: the class variable *customerName* is different to the local variable *customerName*. This may confuse a programmer but it will not confuse a compiler. Perhaps when you implement the program you could choose a different name for the local variables, e.g. *nameOfCustomer* instead of *customerName*.

Figure 16.7 Invoking the other constructor method.

1. Enter the customer's name.

2. Enter the initial deposit.

3. Click here.

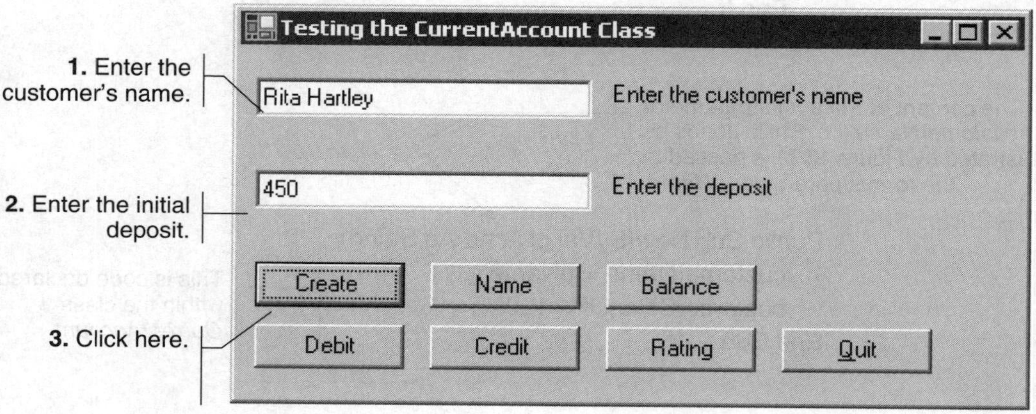

In the case represented by Figure 16.7 the value of the *initialDeposit* is £450; consequently, the constructor in the *If part* of the selection (within the *btnCreateAccount_Click* event handling procedure) is executed. The passing of the parameters is illustrated by Figure 16.8.

Figure 16.8 Passing parameters.

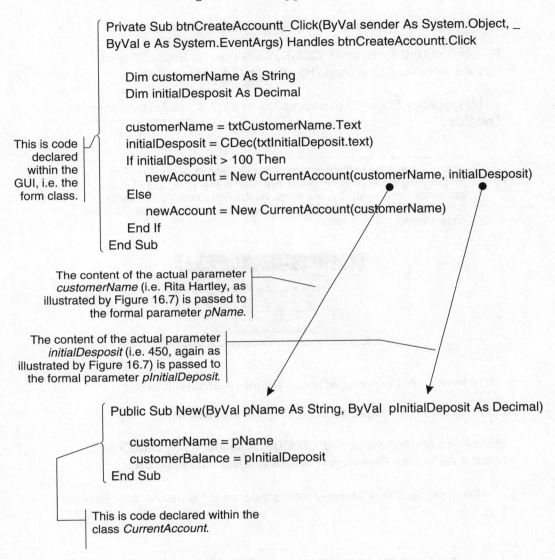

This is code declared within the GUI, i.e. the form class.

```
Private Sub btnCreateAccountt_Click(ByVal sender As System.Object, _
ByVal e As System.EventArgs) Handles btnCreateAccountt.Click

    Dim customerName As String
    Dim initialDesposit As Decimal

    customerName = txtCustomerName.Text
    initialDesposit = CDec(txtInitialDeposit.text)
    If initialDesposit > 100 Then
        newAccount = New CurrentAccount(customerName, initialDesposit)
    Else
        newAccount = New CurrentAccount(customerName)
    End If
End Sub
```

The content of the actual parameter *customerName* (i.e. Rita Hartley, as illustrated by Figure 16.7) is passed to the formal parameter *pName*.

The content of the actual parameter *initialDesposit* (i.e. 450, again as illustrated by Figure 16.7) is passed to the formal parameter *pInitialDeposit*.

```
Public Sub New(ByVal pName As String, ByVal  pInitialDeposit As Decimal)

    customerName = pName
    customerBalance = pInitialDeposit
End Sub
```

This is code declared within the class *CurrentAccount*.

Once this constructor has executed the variables of this particular instance of the *CurrentAccount* class will be set as shown below.

customerName will be storing *Rita Hartley* because of the following statement: customerName = pName   and of course because *pName* has just been passed *Rita Hartley*
customerBalance will be storing 450 because of the following statement: customerBalance = pInitialDeposit   and of course because *pInitialDeposit* has just been passed 450.

Figure 16.9 shows what happens when the Name button is clicked.

Figure 16.9 Clicking the Name button.

```
Private Sub btnDisplayName_Click(ByVal sender As System.Object, _
ByVal e As System.EventArgs) Handles btnDisplayName.Click

    MessageBox.Show("The customer's name is " & newAccount.Name)
End Sub
```

This is a message to the instance of the *CurrentAccount* class. This message uses the property procedure *Name*. The value stored in the *customerName* variable is accesses via the *Get part* of this property procedure. The effect is to display the returned name in the MessageBox shown below.

Figure 16.10 shows what happens when the Balance button is clicked.

Figure 16.10 Clicking the Balance button.

```
Private Sub btnDisplayBalance_Click(ByVal sender As System.Object, _
ByVal e As System.EventArgs) Handles btnDisplayBalance.Click

    MessageBox.Show("The customer's balance is " & newAccount.Balance)
End Sub
```

This is a message to the instance of the *CurrentAccount* class. This message uses the property procedure *Balance*. The value stored in the *customerBalance* variable is accessed via the *Get part* of this property procedure (as it is a *ReadOnly* property procedure there is in fact only a *Get* part). The effect is to display the balance in the MessageBox shown below.

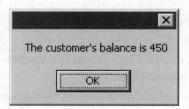

Figure 16.11 shows what happens when the Rating button is clicked.

Figure 16.11 Clicking the Rating button.

```
Private Sub btnDisplayRating_Click(ByVal sender As System.Object, _
ByVal e As System.EventArgs) Handles btnDisplayRating.Click

    MessageBox.Show("The credit rating is " & newAccount.GetRating())
End Sub
```

This is a message to the instance of the *CurrentAccount* class. This message uses the *Function* method *GetRating()*. This method returns the credit rating based on the value stored in the instance variable *customerBalance*, which is £450. Consequently, it returns a credit rating of 2. This is displayed in the MessageBox shown below.

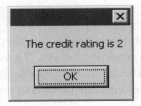

Figure 16.12 shows what happens when the Debit button is clicked.

Figure 16.12 Clicking the Debit button.

```
Private Sub btnDebitAccount_Click(ByVal sender As System.Object, _
ByVal e As System.EventArgs) Handles btnDebitAccount.Click

    Dim withdrawal As Decimal

    withdrawal = CDec(InputBox("How much is being withdrawn? "))
    newAccount.Debit(withdrawal)
End Sub
```

The first line of this event handling procedure displays the Inputbox shown below.

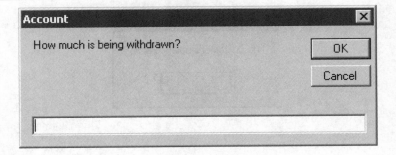

Figure 16.12 (cont.)

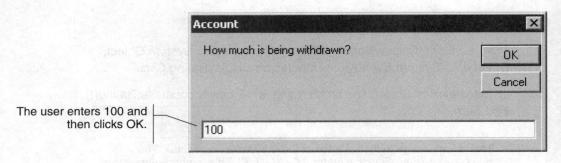

The user enters 100 and
then clicks OK.

The value of 100 is assigned to the local variable *withdrawal* (note how it first converted to type decimal by *CDec*).

The next program statement (repeated below for convenience) is a message to the instance of the *CurrentAccount* class. The value of 100 is passed with the message as shown. This is then subtracted from the *customerBalance* class (i.e. instance variable) variable (450–100) giving 350.

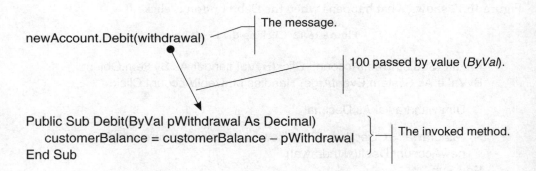

The message.

newAccount.Debit(withdrawal)

100 passed by value (*ByVal*).

Public Sub Debit(ByVal pWithdrawal As Decimal)
    customerBalance = customerBalance – pWithdrawal
End Sub

The invoked method.

To ensure that the balance is as predicted, clicking the Balance button should give the following display.

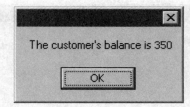

The customer's balance is 350

OK

Figure 16.13 shows what happens when the Credit button is clicked.

Figure 16.13 Clicking the Credit button.

```
Private Sub btnCreditBalance_Click(ByVal sender As System.Object, _
ByVal e As System.EventArgs) Handles btnCreditBalance.Click
    Dim deposit As Decimal

    deposit = CDec(InputBox("How much is being deposited? "))
    newAccount.Credit(deposit)
End Sub
```

The first line of this event handling procedure displays the InputBox as shown below.

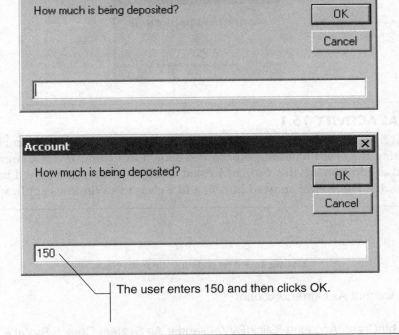

The user enters 150 and then clicks OK.

The value of 150 is assigned to the local variable *deposit* (note how it is first converted to type decimal by *CDec*).

The next program statement (repeated below for convenience) is a message to the instance of the *CurrentAccount* class. The value of 150 is passed with the message as shown. This then added to the *customerBalance* class (i.e. instance variable) variable (350 + 150), giving 500.

Figure 16.13 (cont.)

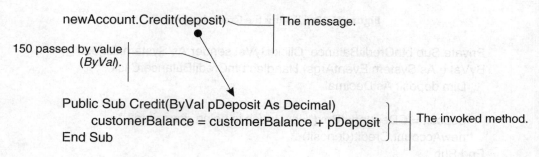

newAccount.Credit(deposit) — The message.

150 passed by value (*ByVal*).

```
Public Sub Credit(ByVal pDeposit As Decimal)
    customerBalance = customerBalance + pDeposit
End Sub
```
— The invoked method.

To ensure that the balance is as predicted, clicking the Balance button should give the following display.

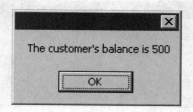

The customer's balance is 500

OK

PRACTICAL ACTIVITY 16.1

Implement Specification 16.1. This involves building the GUI as shown in Figure 16.4 and attaching the event handling procedures shown in Listing 16.3. Of course, it also requires the addition of the *CurrentAccount* class as represented by Listing 16.1. Remember that Figure 16.1 showed how to add a class to a Windows application.

Listing 16.3 The code for the form class.

```
Private newAccount As CurrentAccount

Private Sub btnCreateAccountt_Click(ByVal sender As System.Object, ByVal e _
As System.EventArgs) Handles btnCreateAccountt.Click
    Dim customerName As String
    Dim initialDesposit As Decimal

    customerName = txtCustomerName.Text
    initialDesposit = CDec(txtInitialDeposit.text)
```

Listing 16.3 (cont.)

```
    If initialDesposit > 100 Then
        newAccount = New CurrentAccount(customerName, initialDesposit)
    Else
        newAccount = New CurrentAccount(customerName)
    End If
End Sub

Private Sub btnDisplayName_Click(ByVal sender As System.Object, ByVal e _
As System.EventArgs) Handles btnDisplayName.Click
    MessageBox.Show("The customer's name is " & newAccount.Name)
End Sub

Private Sub btnDisplayBalance_Click(ByVal sender As System.Object, ByVal e _
As System.EventArgs) Handles btnDisplayBalance.Click
    MessageBox.Show("The customer's balance is " & newAccount.Balance)
End Sub

Private Sub btnDebitAccount_Click(ByVal sender As System.Object, ByVal e _
As System.EventArgs) Handles btnDebitAccount.Click
    Dim withdrawal As Decimal
    withdrawal = CDec(InputBox("How much is being withdrawn? "))
    newAccount.Debit(withdrawal)
End Sub

Private Sub btnCreditBalance_Click(ByVal sender As System.Object, ByVal e _
As System.EventArgs) Handles btnCreditBalance.Click
    Dim deposit As Decimal
    deposit = CDec(InputBox("How much is being deposited? "))
    newAccount.Credit(deposit)
End Sub

Private Sub btnDisplayRating_Click(ByVal sender As System.Object, ByVal e _
As System.EventArgs) Handles btnDisplayRating.Click
    MessageBox.Show("The credit rating is " & newAccount.GetRating())
End Sub

Private Sub btnQuit_Click(ByVal sender As System.Object, ByVal e As _
System.EventArgs) Handles btnQuit.Click
    Me.Close()
    End
End Sub
```

PRACTICAL ACTIVITY 16.2

Amend the testing class so that it outputs a messagebox that displays a £ symbol when displaying the balance as shown below.

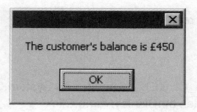

PRACTICAL ACTIVITY 16.3

The GUI and associated code did not test the ability to change the customer's name once it was created. Amend the GUI and attach suitable code to test this feature of the *CurrentAccount* class.

PRACTICAL ACTIVITY 16.4

Implement Specification 16.1 again, but this time create an instance of the class from within a Console application and test it as appropriate.

A Class View

VB .NET has a Class View window in addition to the Solution Explorer. Whereas the Solution Explorer gives a view of all of the files within a project; the Class View window gives an overview of the classes within the project and the members of each class. Figure 16.14 shows how to activate the Class View window, and Figures 16.15 to 16.21 show various views and describes what they indicate. The window display is for the *Account* solution developed in this chapter.

Figure 16.14 How to activate the Class View window.

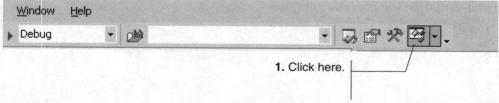

Figure 16.14 (cont.)

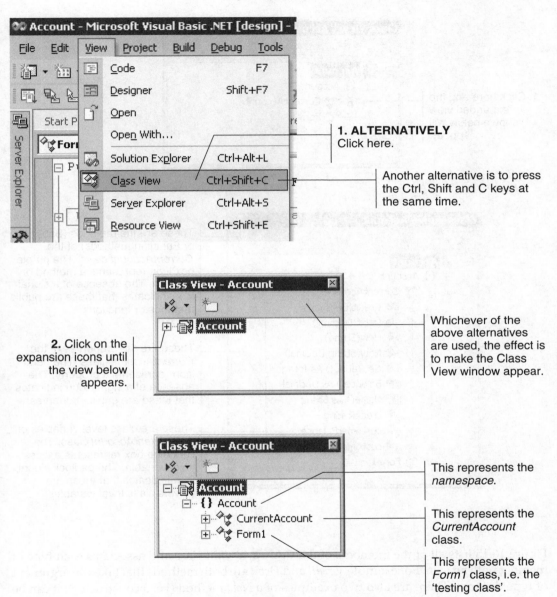

1. ALTERNATIVELY
Click here.

Another alternative is to press
the Ctrl, Shift and C keys at
the same time.

2. Click on the
expansion icons until
the view below
appears.

Whichever of the
above alternatives
are used, the effect is
to make the Class
View window appear.

This represents the
namespace.

This represents the
CurrentAccount
class.

This represents the
Form1 class, i.e. the
'testing class'.

Both of the classes shown in the Class View window have an associated expanding button.
This section will discuss only the *CurrentAccount* class in detail; you are left to discover the
members of the *Form1* class yourself.

Figure 16.15 The view of the *CurrentAccount* class.

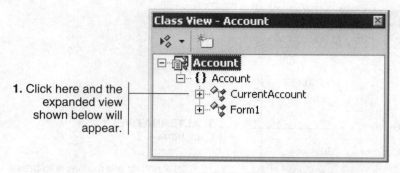

1. Click here and the expanded view shown below will appear.

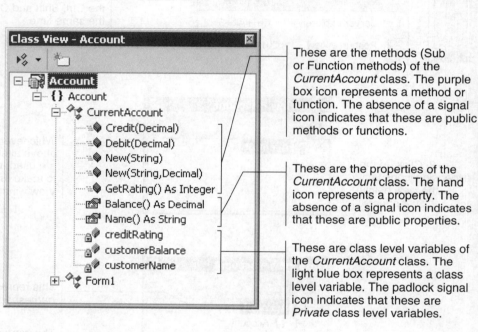

These are the methods (Sub or Function methods) of the *CurrentAccount* class. The purple box icon represents a method or function. The absence of a signal icon indicates that these are public methods or functions.

These are the properties of the *CurrentAccount* class. The hand icon represents a property. The absence of a signal icon indicates that these are public properties.

These are class level variables of the *CurrentAccount* class. The light blue box represents a class level variable. The padlock signal icon indicates that these are *Private* class level variables.

Figure 16.15 lists all of the members of the *CurrentAccount* class and associates each type of member with an icon. For example, *Credit* and *Debit* are both methods that takes an argument of type decimal. There are also two examples of a *New* method (i.e. a constructor): it can be seen that one takes a string argument, whereas the other takes a string and a decimal argument.

Balance and *Name* are both examples of properties (implemented by property procedures). The types associated with these properties are also clear from the Class View.

The icon associated with *creditRating* indicates that it is a private (indicated by the padlock) class level variable. The same icon is associated with *customerBalance* and *customerName* and of course they are both examples of class level variables.

GetRating() is an example of a *Function* method that returns an integer.

NOTE: If you have implemented Specification 16.1 then the view shown by Figure 16.15 should be very familiar. They all relate to the code, indeed if you double-click on any of the members within the Class View then the code window will appear and the cursor will be alongside the code for the member you clicked – try it!

The view shown by Figure 16.15 was **sorted** by type; Figure 16.16 shows a view **grouped** by type.

Figure 16.16 View grouped by type.

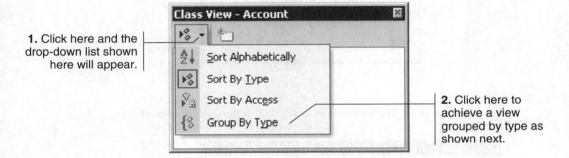

1. Click here and the drop-down list shown here will appear.

2. Click here to achieve a view grouped by type as shown next.

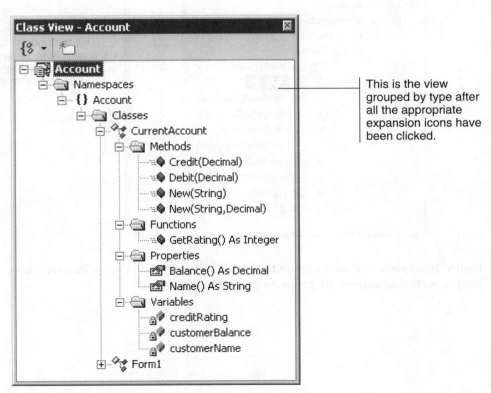

This is the view grouped by type after all the appropriate expansion icons have been clicked.

Figure 16.16 (cont.)

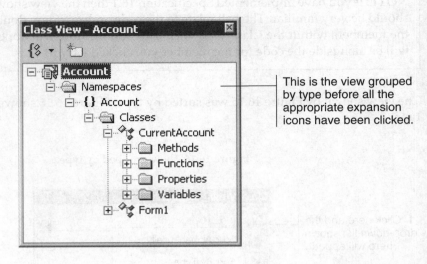

This is the view grouped by type before all the appropriate expansion icons have been clicked.

Figure 16.17 The methods associated with the *CurrentAccount* class.

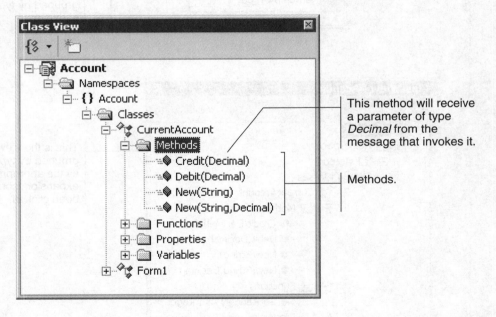

This method will receive a parameter of type *Decimal* from the message that invokes it.

Methods.

Figure 16.18 shows all of the properties associated with the *CurrentAccount* class. These are the properties as defined by property procedures.

Figure 16.18 The properties associated with the *CurrentAccount* class.

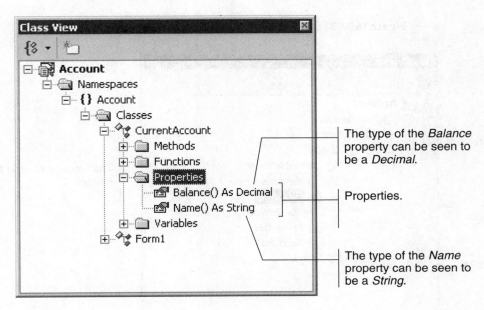

The type of the *Balance* property can be seen to be a *Decimal*.

Properties.

The type of the *Name* property can be seen to be a *String*.

Figure 16.19 shows all of the class level variables associated with the *CurrentAccount* class.

Figure 16.19 The class level variables associated with the *CurrentAccount* class.

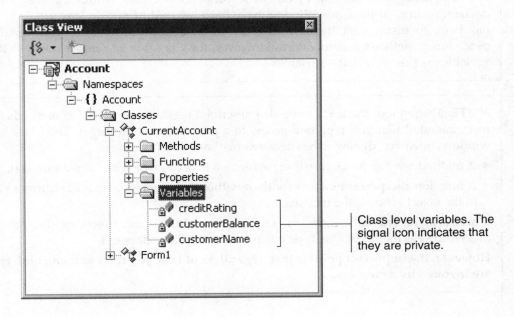

Class level variables. The signal icon indicates that they are private.

Figure 16.20 shows the function associated with the *CurrentAccount* class.

Figure 16.20 The function associated with the *CurrentAccount* class.

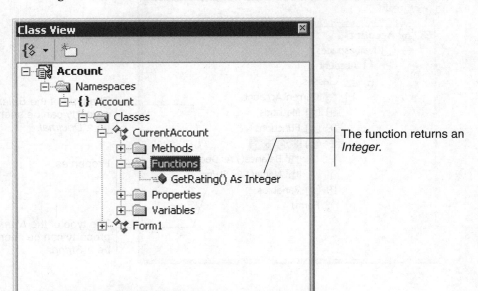

The function returns an *Integer*.

NOTE: Throughout the text to date, the variables declared within the class in the declaration area of the Code Window have been referred to as *class level variables*. This has been to distinguish them from local variable declared within event handling procedures, methods and functions. However, the Class View window refers to these variables as precisely that – variables.

NOTE: Throughout the text I have also described messages as invoking methods (and recommended that you regarded access to a property as a message). The Class View window, however, distinguishes between methods and functions:

- A method is a *Sub* procedure that performs a task (with or without parameters).
- A function also performs a task (with or without parameters), but also returns a value to the object sending the message.

I prefer to regard both methods (i.e. *Sub* procedures) and functions (i.e. *Function* procedures) as methods. One type returns data, the other does not.

However, the important point is that, regardless of how you refer to them, both types are invoked by a message.

PRACTICAL ACTIVITY 16.5

Experiment with the Class View window, selecting members and interpreting the information it conveys.

Double-click on members and observe how this takes you to the associated code. An example of this is illustrated in Figure 16.21.

Also experiment with the context menu of the Class View window.

Figure 16.21 Double-clicking on members.

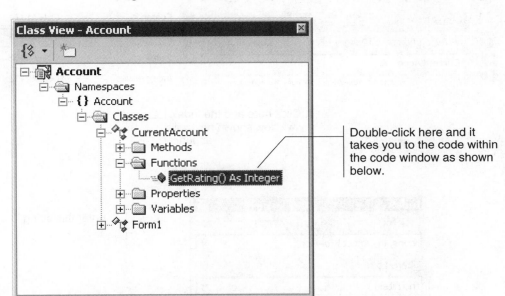

Double-click here and it takes you to the code within the code window as shown below.

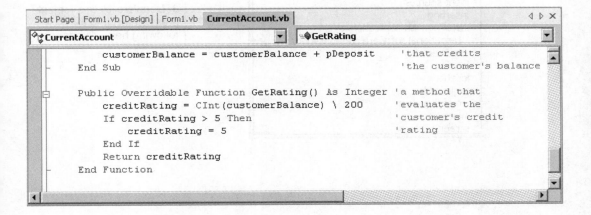

PRACTICAL ACTIVITY 16.6

Use the VB .NET help to observe and learn the meaning of the icons associated with the Class View window. Figure 16.22 illustrates how to achieve this.

Figure 16.22 Using the help.

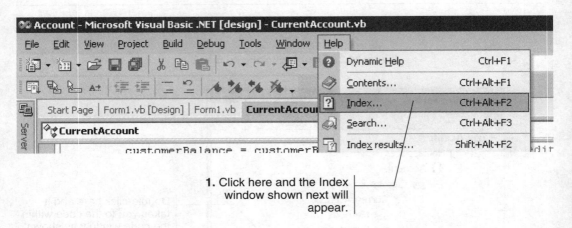

1. Click here and the Index window shown next will appear.

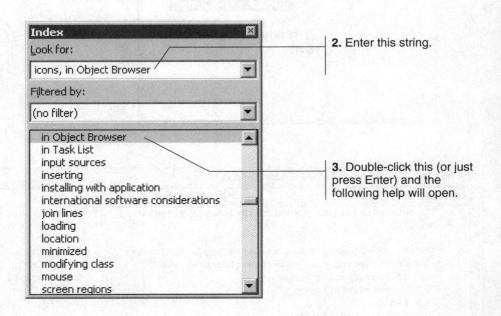

2. Enter this string.

3. Double-click this (or just press Enter) and the following help will open.

Figure 16.22 (cont.)

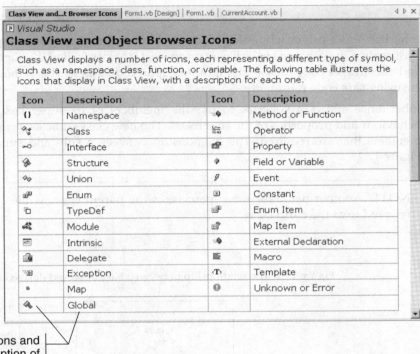

This shows the icons and gives a brief description of what they mean.

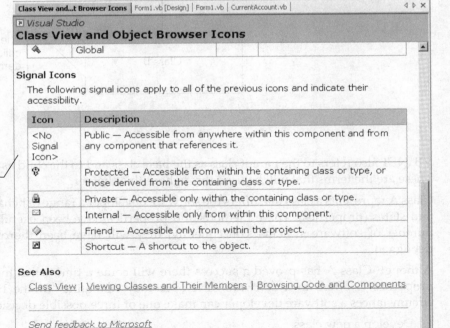

Scroll down the page to find this information on the signal icons and a brief description of what they mean.

17 Inheritance

Inheritance is a primary building block of object-oriented programming that allows a new class (called the subclass) to be based on an existing class (called the superclass). It facilitates and encourages code reusability. It builds upon code that has been thoroughly tested, thus ensuring **safe** code reusability.

Inheritance allows a subclass to use the members of its superclass, i.e. it inherits the behaviour and properties of the superclass. The new class (subclass) can then add any new members that are required. The relationship between a sub- and superclass is shown in Figure 17.1.

NOTE: Another name for the superclass is the **parent** class, while a subclass is often referred to as the **child** class.

Figure 17.1 The relationship between a base class and derived class.

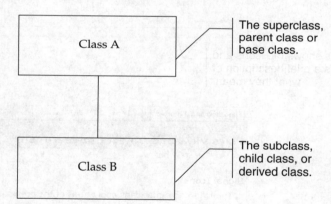

VB .NET also refers to the parent class as the **base** class and to the child as the **derived** class. These are the terms that will be used throughout this chapter.

Class A represents a class that offers the software developer a range of behaviours (methods) and states (properties). These methods and properties have been usefully employed in a number of software systems; consequently, they will have been thoroughly tested and debugged.

Although Class A has proved a success there will come a time when the behaviours and properties it offers to a software developer may not quite 'fit the bill'. Under these circumstances a software developer can make one of three possible decisions:

1. Develop a new class.

2. Amend Class A.

3. Inherit the functionality of Class A within a new class, and add the extra behaviour and states to the new class.

> **NOTE**: As well as adding new behaviours the derived class is able to modify behaviour using a technique called overriding – more on this later.

A decision to develop a new class is inefficient in terms of resources. Asking a programmer to develop a new class when one class already exists that almost 'fits the bill' is expensive. Why not reuse a class that already exists using inheritance and add the extras required?

Amending a class that already exists is dangerous. This class will have been thoroughly tested and released by the software developers to be used within various software projects. Allowing a programmer to amend this class risks its corruption, i.e. a programmer might inadvertently alter the class's current behaviour and properties.

Allowing a class to inherit from an exiting class means that all the base class data structures and algorithms are immediately available to the derived class without the need for any extra work. A software developer can then add new behaviours and states and just test and debug the new additions. This is a much more efficient approach to the development of software.

> **NOTE**: Inheritance achieves software reuse directly – a key and fundamental aim of good software engineering practice.

The members of a derived class are always an extension of the base class. The declaration of a derived class just adds the new members it requires, consequently, it has a larger set of members. A derived class can also **override** the inherited behaviour of the base class. It achieves this by the addition of a method that has the same **signature** (i.e. same name and parameters) as a method in the base class but that has **different behaviour** (i.e. different program statements within the body of the method).

For example, the implementation of Specification 16.1 has a method that calculated a credit rating based on the balance of a current account. The *CurrentAccount* class, in which this method resides, is a useful class that could be extended to support the definition of a new type of account called a *Gold* account. A credit rating is also calculated from the balance of a *Gold* account. However, the way in which the rating is derived is different. So the new derived class would override this method of the base class and replace it with its own version. Other methods of the base (such as the *Debit* and *Credit* method) are useful for the new class and this new class simple inherits them, i.e. there is no attempt to override them.

> **NOTE**: A previous chapter dealt with a technique called **overloading**. This chapter has introduced, and will further cover, the technique of **overriding**. Please note that these are different techniques used for different purposes, so do not 'mix them up'.

Inheritance is transitive in nature, which means that a derived class inherits directly from its parent and from all of the base classes above the parent class. A class hierarchy diagram represents this transitive nature, and one such example is shown in Figure 17.2.

Figure 17.2 An example of a class hierarchy.

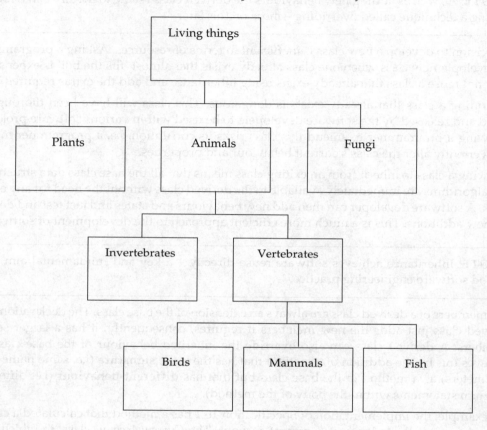

Mammals are a classification of living things to which we as humans belong. We, like all mammals, breathe oxygen and have a backbone. Of course, we also share both of these characteristics with eagles, which belong to the classification of Birds.

The characteristic (class member) for requiring oxygen is defined right at the top of the class hierarchy, and plants and animals 'inherit' this because they are the subclass (derived class) to the 'Living things' superclass (base class).

Humans and eagles inherit the need for oxygen from the top of the hierarchy, from the superclass of the superclass of the superclass of the superclass, and both have inherited a backbone from the superclass of the superclass.

Of course, eagles and other birds can fly, so this behaviour will belong to the Birds class and consequently is inherited by all birds.

Most mammals do not fly; consequently this behaviour will not be part of the Mammals class.

Bats are mammals, however, and they do fly. In this case, the Bat class will still inherit from the Mammals class and add the ability to fly as one of its behaviours.

As the ostrich shows, not all birds fly. In this case, the ostrich will still inherit from the Bird class but within the Ostrich class the fly behaviour will be overridden and replaced with the ability to run very fast.

This chapter will deal with two types of inheritance:

1. Inheritance.
2. Visual inheritance (nothing more than a particular type of inheritance).

Implementing inheritance with VB .NET

The implementation of Specification 16.1 was achieved by the development of the *CurrentAccount* class. Assume that this class has been tested thoroughly.

The bank for which you are developing the software system (of which Specification 16.1 plays a small part), also offer another type of account referred to as the Gold account. This new account offers interest on account balances and has a different way for calculating credit ratings. However, in all other respects the *Gold* account is the same as the current account they offer their customers.

By referring to the class hierarchy (and the members of each class in this hierarchy) of the software system the development team of programmers would recognize that the *CurrentAccount* class had most of the behaviours and states required for the new Gold account. Consequently, they would develop a new class that inherits from this class and add the necessary extra members – they would produce a **derived class** from the *CurrentAccount* class, which would now be regarded as the **base class**. Specification 17.1 formalizes the requirements of the Gold Account.

SPECIFICATION 17.1

The Gold account must have all the same behaviours and states as the current account, except for the way in which the credit rating is calculated. Plus it must also offer interest of 3% on the balance at the end of a calendar month and this amount is automatically added to the balance.

The credit rating is again within the same range of 0 to 5. However, a score of one is allocated for every multiple of £100 (not £200 as for specification 16.1).

To implement Specification 17.1, a new class will be added to the *Account* solution developed in Chapter 16. The sequence of actions required to add this new class is shown in Figure 17.3.

Figure 17.3 Adding a new class to the *Account* solution.

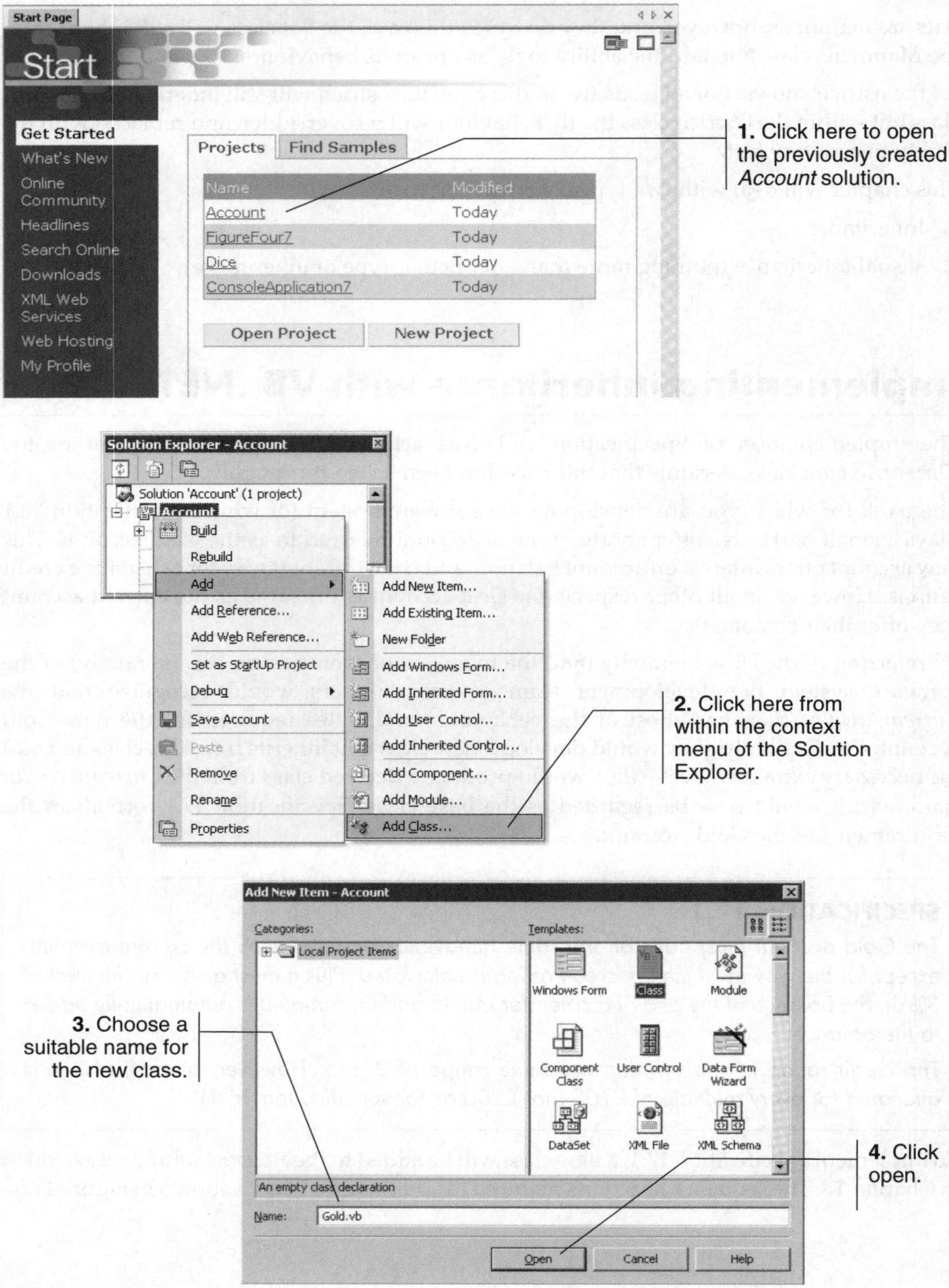

1. Click here to open the previously created *Account* solution.

2. Click here from within the context menu of the Solution Explorer.

3. Choose a suitable name for the new class.

4. Click open.

Figure 17.3 (cont.)

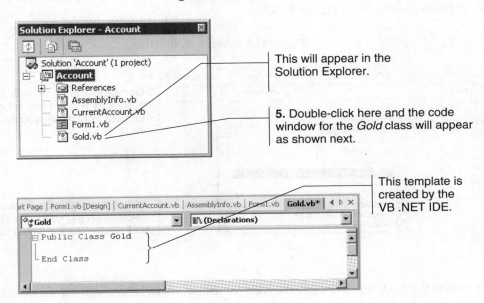

This will appear in the Solution Explorer.

5. Double-click here and the code window for the *Gold* class will appear as shown next.

This template is created by the VB .NET IDE.

Once the template is in place as shown by the last screenshot of Figure 17.3, then the code for the new class is entered. The first step is to indicate that this new *Gold* class will inherit from the *CurrentAccount* class. This is achieved by entering the words shown below immediately after the first line of the template, i.e.:

Inherits CurrentAccount

Figure 17.4 shows the template after this is entered.

NOTE: It would be normal to register the *Account* class and import its namespace if you wished to extend it. However, Figure 17.3 shows a simpler approach that allows for the emphasis to remain on the fundamentals of inheritance.

The *Gold* class is able to inherit from the *CurrentAccount* class because it is in the same solution.

Figure 17.4 The first step in using inheritance.

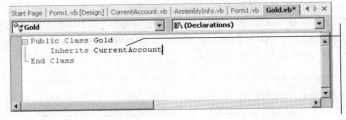

Enter the word *Inherits* and the name of the class from which the inheritance is to occur – in this case the *CurrentAccount* class. *CurrentAccount* is now the base class for the *Gold* class, and the *Gold* class is the derived class.

The intellisense feature of VB .NET assists in the typing (and choice) of the base class you wish to use, as shown in Figure 17.5.

Figure 17.5 Intellisense in action.

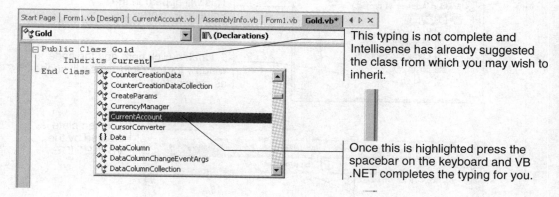

Of course the next step is to enter the code for the new class. However, before we do this let's reflect on what has already been achieved. Figure 17.6 shows the Class View window for the Account solution. It can be seen that the Account solution now has three classes: the *CurrentAccount* class, the *Form1* class and the *Gold* class.

Figure 17.6 The Class View window for the Account solution before any code is entered into the *Gold* class.

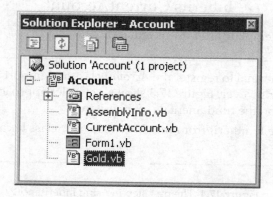

Clicking onto the expansion icon next to the *Gold* class offers the view as shown by Figure 17.7. Indented after the *Gold* class is another expansion icon followed by the words **Bases and Interfaces**. Expanding more icons will inform us about any base class from which the *Gold* class is derived – this view is shown in Figure 17.8.

NOTE: Interfaces are covered in a later chapter.

Figure 17.7 The view after expanding the icon.

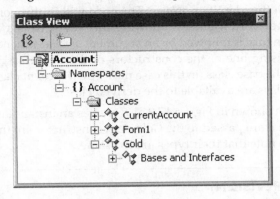

Figure 17.8 The view after further expanding the icons.

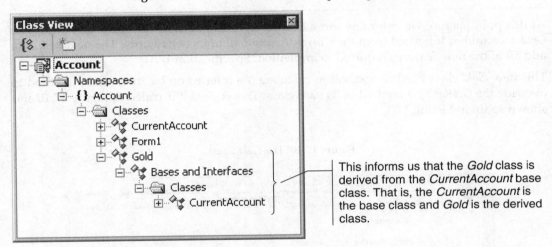

This informs us that the *Gold* class is derived from the *CurrentAccount* base class. That is, the *CurrentAccount* is the base class and *Gold* is the derived class.

In order for the *Gold* class to inherit from the *CurrentAccount* class we need to code the *Gold* class constructors. These constructors have to message the constructors of its base class. The code that achieves this is shown in Figure 17.9.

Figure 17.9 Coding the constructors of the *Gold* class.

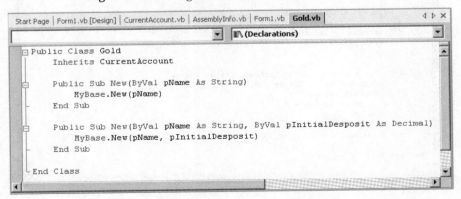

```
Public Class Gold
    Inherits CurrentAccount

    Public Sub New(ByVal pName As String)
        MyBase.New(pName)
    End Sub

    Public Sub New(ByVal pName As String, ByVal pInitialDesposit As Decimal)
        MyBase.New(pName, pInitialDesposit)
    End Sub

End Class
```

The first constructor shown in Figure 17.9 has a signature that contains a pass by value formal parameter with the identifier *pName*. The code within this constructor refers to the base class using the Keyword *MyBase*. Following this keyword is a full stop and another keyword *New*, which in turn is followed by an argument *pName*. Whenever an instance of the *Gold* class is created using one of the constructors of the *Gold* class, this constructor then creates an instance of the base class (in this case the *CurrentAccount* class). This way all of the members of the base class are available to the derived class.

The second constructor shown in Figure 17.9 also creates an instance of the base class. Note how the parameters that are passed to the *Gold* class constructor are then passed to the base class constructor. Also note that their types are the same.

QUESTION 17.1 (REVISION)

Do the parameters of the Gold constructor have to be identical to the parameters, of the constructor, of CurrentAccount class?

At this point, before we enter any more code, let's reflect on what has been achieved. The *Gold* account has inherited from the *CurrentAccount* all of its behaviours. The next task is to add all of the new features required to implement Specification 17.1.

This new *Gold* class needs a method to calculate 3% interest on balances and a method to override the *GetRating()* method of its base class. This code is illustrated in Figure 17.10 and shown again in Listing 17.1

Figure 17.10 The *Gold* Class.

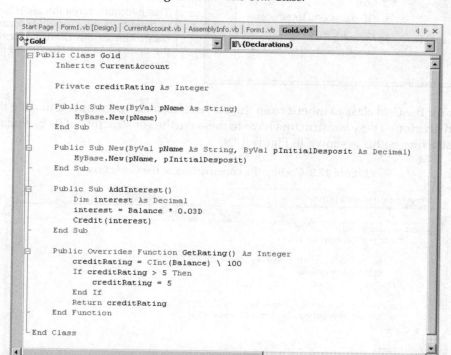

```vb
Start Page | Form1.vb [Design] | CurrentAccount.vb | AssemblyInfo.vb | Form1.vb   Gold.vb*
Gold                                        (Declarations)

Public Class Gold
        Inherits CurrentAccount

        Private creditRating As Integer

        Public Sub New(ByVal pName As String)
            MyBase.New(pName)
        End Sub

        Public Sub New(ByVal pName As String, ByVal pInitialDesposit As Decimal)
            MyBase.New(pName, pInitialDesposit)
        End Sub

        Public Sub AddInterest()
            Dim interest As Decimal
            interest = Balance * 0.03D
            Credit(interest)
        End Sub

        Public Overrides Function GetRating() As Integer
            creditRating = CInt(Balance) \ 100
            If creditRating > 5 Then
                creditRating = 5
            End If
            Return creditRating
        End Function

End Class
```

Listing 17.1 The *Gold* Class.

```
Public Class Gold
    Inherits CurrentAccount

    Private creditRating As Integer

    Public Sub New(ByVal pName As String)
        MyBase.New(pName)
    End Sub

    Public Sub New(ByVal pName As String, ByVal pInitialDesposit As Decimal)
        MyBase.New(pName, pInitialDesposit)
    End Sub

    Public Sub AddInterest()
        Dim interest As Decimal
        interest = Balance * 0.03D
        Credit(interest)
    End Sub

    Public Overrides Function GetRating() As Integer
        creditRating = CInt(Balance) \ 100
        If creditRating question 5 Then
            creditRating = 5
        End If
        Return creditRating
    End Function

End Class
```

The first two methods shown in Listing 17.1 are constructors. These constructors all invoke their 'equivalents' within the base class (i.e. *CurrentAccount*) and this is achieved using the keyword *MyBase* followed by the name of the method, as illustrated by Figure 17.11.

Figure 17.11 Invoking a method in the base class.

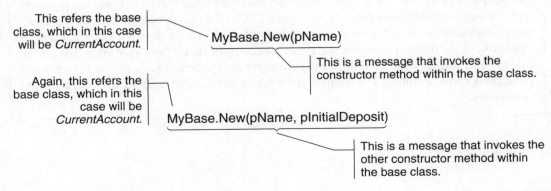

This refers the base class, which in this case will be *CurrentAccount*.

MyBase.New(pName)

This is a message that invokes the constructor method within the base class.

Again, this refers the base class, which in this case will be *CurrentAccount*.

MyBase.New(pName, pInitialDeposit)

This is a message that invokes the other constructor method within the base class.

```
Public Sub AddInterest()
    Dim interest As Decimal
    interest = Balance * 0.03D
    Credit(interest)
End Sub
```

This method from Listing 17.1 calculates the interest on the *Balance* and then credits this *interest* to the *Balance* using the *Credit* method. The following trace table describes each of the program statements in detail.

Description Trace for the *AddInterest* method

Statement	Description
interest = Balance * 0.03D	The local variable *interest* is assigned three per cent of the value of the property *Balance*.
	This is simply achieved by multiplying the value of the *Balance* by the decimal fraction *0.03*. As *interest* is of type *Decimal* then the *0.03* is followed by a capital *D* to ensure a *Decimal* is evaluated. This could have been done differently using conversion functions but in this context this is easier.
	This *AddInterest* method is the 'extra method' of the *Gold* class. It can be seen that it used the property *Balance* as declared in the base class *CurrentAccount*. It was able to gain access to this property because the property procedure declared in the *CurrentAccount* class was exposed with the *Public* access modifier.
Credit(interest)	The interest just calculated is added to the balance using the method *Credit* inherited from the base class.

NOTE: Code is far easier to read when as much information as possible is conveyed to the programmer. The program statements within the *AddInterest* method use a method and property of its base class. More information is conveyed if both of these are prefixed with the keyword *MyBase* as shown by Figure 17.12 – the keyword is highlighted in bold. Some software houses will expect you to adopt this style. I have decided against it within this textbook, as there are times when it can overcomplicate matters – see later. To convey this type of information to fellow programmers and yourself (when you forget what your own code is doing) I recommend that you write brief and to the point in-line comments.

Figure 17.12 Using the keyword *MyBase*.

```
Public Sub AddInterest()
    Dim interest As Decimal

    interest = MyBase. Balance * 0.03D
    MyBase.Credit(interest)
End Sub
```

Using *MyBase* to access base class methods

MyBase refers to the base class and its inherited members. It can be used to access *Public* members defined in the base class but it **cannot** be used to access *Private* members in the base class.

The method that *MyBase* qualifies does not need to be defined in the immediate base class – instead it may be defined in an indirectly inherited base class. In order for a *MyBase*-qualified reference to compile correctly, a base class in the inheritance chain must contain a method matching the name and types of parameters appearing in the message.

MyBase is a keyword and cannot be assigned to a variable, passed to procedures, or used in an *Is* comparison, i.e. *MyBase* is not a real object.

NOTE: The *MyBase* keyword 'behaves like' an object variable referring to the base class of the current instance of a class.

MyBase is commonly used to access base class members that are overridden in a derived class. In particular, *MyBase.New* is used to explicitly invoke a base class constructor from a derived class constructor.

It is invalid to use *MyBase* to call *MustOverride* base methods.

I therefore recommend that you only use *MyBase* to access base class members that are overridden in a derived class, i.e. do not use it to comment your code!

Of course, it has to be used in constructors, as just shown.

```
Public Overrides Function GetRating() As Integer
    creditRating = CInt(Balance) \ 100
    If creditRating > 5 Then
        creditRating = 5
    End If
    Return creditRating
End Function
```

This method from Listing 17.1 calculates the customer's credit rating and overrides the method used to perform the same task in the base class. Consequently, the behaviour of any instance of the *Gold* class is different when it comes to calculate the customer's credit rating – which was a requirement of Specification 17.1. The only change to the mechanics of this method, over the one appearing in the base class, is in the first statement, which divides the balance by 100 instead of 200 (although many changes are allowed!).

The mechanism that achieves overriding is illustrated in Figure 17.13, which shows the signature of the original method in the *CurrentAccount* class and the method in the *Gold* class.

Figure 17.13 The signatures showing how overriding is achieved.

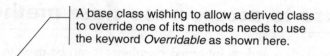

A base class wishing to allow a derived class to override one of its methods needs to use the keyword *Overridable* as shown here.

Public Overridable Function GetRating() As Integer

A method within a derived class wishing to override a method of its base class needs to use the keyword *Overrides* as shown here. In all other respects the signatures are identical! The example discussed in this chapter only shows a change in one program statement. However, there could many changes to the program statements.

Public Overrides Function GetRating() As Integer

NOTE: For this 'overriding' method to work the derived class needed a class level variable to store the credit rating. The derived class **cannot** (in this case) use the instance variable of the base class because it was declared as *Private*. Consequently, the third line of the *Gold* class (Listing 17.1) declares its own version of an appropriate class level variable.

If a base class wished to allow a derived class instance direct access to one of it class level variables it could declare the class level variable as *Protected* – a later practical activity will ask you to experiment with this 'mechanism'.

Testing the *Gold* class

Amending the instance of the form class used to test the *CurrentAccount* class will be used to test* the *Gold* class. Figure 17.14 shows the amended form.

*****NOTE**: A full and true test of the class is not attempted here. The emphasis is on showing the messaging to members of an object of the *Gold* class.

Figure 17.14 The amended form.

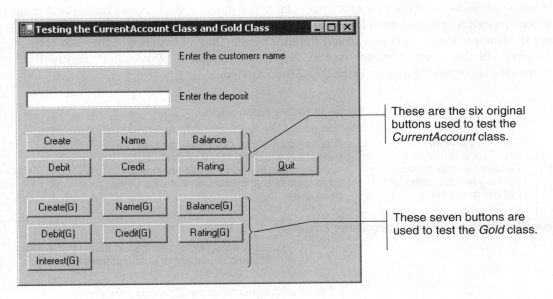

NOTE: All of the event handling procedures have access to the object of the *Gold* class because its object reference is declared as a class level variable (often known as a form level variable) of the *Form1* class (in the declaration area of the code window).

The code attached to the Create(G) button that creates an instance of the *Gold* class is shown in Listing 17.2.

Listing 17.2 Creating an instance of the *Gold* class.

Declared in the declaration area of the code window. This way there is access to this class variable throughout the instance of the form.

```
Private newGoldAccount As Gold

Private Sub btnCreateGoldAccountt_Click(ByVal sender As System.Object, _
ByVal e As System.EventArgs) Handles btnCreateGoldAccountt.Click
    Dim customerName As String
    Dim initialDesposit As Decimal
    customerName = txtCustomerName.Text
    initialDesposit = CDec(txtInitialDeposit.Text)
    If initialDesposit > 100 Then
        newGoldAccount = New Gold(customerName, initialDesposit)
    Else
        newGoldAccount = New Gold(customerName)
    End If
End Sub
```

The code shown in Listing 17.2 is virtually identical to the code described in Chapter 16 for creating an instance of the *CurrentAccount* class. The name of the account holder and their initial deposit is obtained from the same textboxes and the same selection construct is used, for the same reasons. Of course, the difference here is that an instance of the *Gold* class is created and the object reference is *newGoldAccount* instead of *newAccount*. Figure 17.15 shows the constructors used in Listing 17.2 in more detail.

Figure 17.15 The constructors.

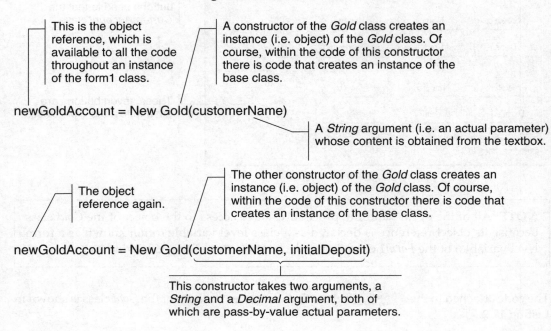

The code attached to the Name(G) button that displays the name of the Gold account customer is shown in Listing 17.3. Figure 17.16 shows one of the messages used in Listing 17.3 in more detail.

NOTE: *MessageBox.Show (...)* is also a message, but this was discussed earlier in the book.

Listing 17.3 Displaying the name of the Gold account customer.

```
Private Sub btnDisplayGoldName_Click(ByVal sender As System.Object, _
ByVal e As System.EventArgs) Handles btnDisplayGoldName.Click

    MessageBox.Show("The customer's name is " & newGoldAccount.Name)
End Sub
```

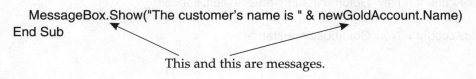

This and this are messages.

Figure 17.16 A closer look at a message from Listing 17.3.

The code attached to the `Balance(G)` button that displays the balance of the Gold account customer is shown in Listing 17.4. Figure 17.17 shows the message used in Listing 17.4 in more detail.

Listing 17.4 Displaying the balance of the Gold account customer.

```
Private Sub btnDisplayGoldBalance_Click(ByVal sender As System.Object, _
ByVal e As System.EventArgs) Handles btnDisplayGoldBalance.Click

    MessageBox.Show("The customer's balance is £" & newGoldAccount.Balance)
End Sub
```

Figure 17.17 A closer look at a message from Listing 17.4.

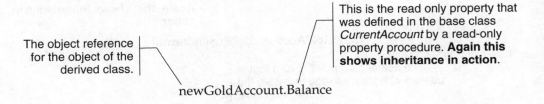

The code attached to the `Debit(G)` button that debits the balance of the Gold account customer is shown in Listing 17.5. Figure 17.18 shows the runtime when the user debits £100 and Figure 17.19 describes the message used in Listing 17.5 in more detail.

Listing 17.5 Debiting the Gold account balance.

```
Private Sub btnDebitGoldAccount_Click(ByVal sender As System.Object, _
ByVal e As System.EventArgs) Handles btnDebitGoldAccount.Click

    Dim withdrawal As Decimal

    withdrawal = CDec(InputBox("How much is being withdrawn? "))
    newGoldAccount.Debit(withdrawal)
End Sub
```

389

Figure 17.18 The runtime when debiting the balance.

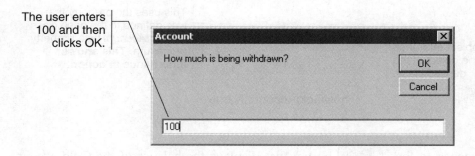

The user enters 100 and then clicks OK.

> This 100 is assigned to the local variable *withdrawal*, which then acts as the actual parameter of the message shown in Listing 17.5 and detailed in Figure 17.19. The effect is to debit the balance by £100 and this was achieved using the *Debit* method.

Figure 17.19 The message.

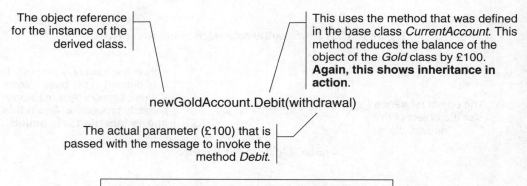

The object reference for the instance of the derived class.

This uses the method that was defined in the base class *CurrentAccount*. This method reduces the balance of the object of the *Gold* class by £100. **Again, this shows inheritance in action**.

newGoldAccount.Debit(withdrawal)

The actual parameter (£100) that is passed with the message to invoke the method *Debit*.

> It is worth emphasizing that, although *Debit* is a method of the base class, it is used by an instance of the derived class to reduce the balance, of this instance, of the derived class.

The code attached to the Credit(G) button that credits balance of the Gold account customer is shown in Listing 17.6. Figure 17.20 shows the runtime when the user credits £200 and Figure 17.21 shows the message used in Listing 17.6 and describes it in more detail.

Listing 17.6 Crediting the balance.

```
Private Sub btnCreditGoldBalance_Click(ByVal sender As System.Object, _
ByVal e As System.EventArgs) Handles btnCreditGoldBalance.Click

    Dim deposit As Decimal

    deposit = CDec(InputBox("How much is being deposited? "))
    newGoldAccount.Credit(deposit)
End Sub
```

Figure 17.20 The runtime when crediting the balance.

The user enters 200 and then clicks OK.

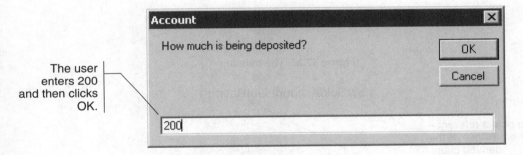

This 200 is assigned to the local variable *deposit*, which then acts as the actual parameter of the message shown in Listing 17.6 and detailed in Figure 17.21. The effect is to credit the balance by £200 and this was achieved using the *Credit* method.

Figure 17.21 The message.

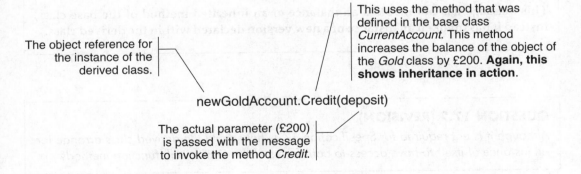

This uses the method that was defined in the base class *CurrentAccount*. This method increases the balance of the object of the *Gold* class by £200. **Again, this shows inheritance in action**.

The object reference for the instance of the derived class.

newGoldAccount.Credit(deposit)

The actual parameter (£200) is passed with the message to invoke the method *Credit*.

Again it is worth emphasizing that, although *Credit* is a method of the base class, it is used by an instance of the derived class to increase the balance, of this instance, of the derived class.

The code attached to the [Rating(G)] button calculates and displays the credit rating for the Gold account customer and it is shown in Listing 17.7. Figure 17.22 shows the message used in Listing 17.6 and describes it in more detail.

Listing 17.7 Calculating and displaying the credit rating.

```
Private Sub btnDisplayGoldRating_Click(ByVal sender As System.Object, _
ByVal e As System.EventArgs) Handles btnDisplayGoldRating.Click

    MessageBox.Show("The credit rating is " & newGoldAccount.GetRating())
End Sub
```

Figure 17.22 The message.

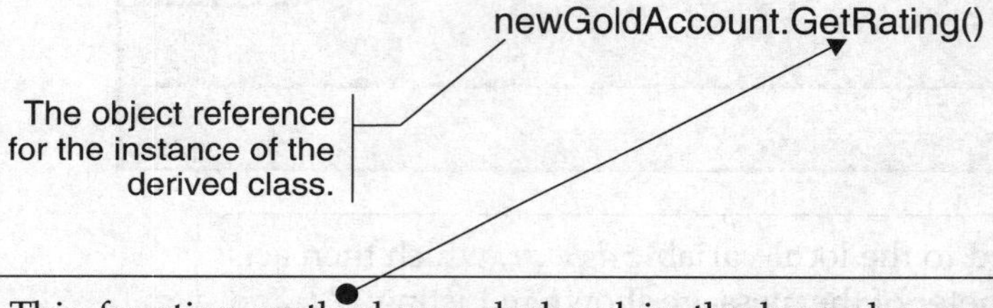

newGoldAccount.GetRating()

The object reference for the instance of the derived class.

This function method was declared in the base class **and** in the derived class. This message uses the method declared in the derived class. This is because the method in the base class was 'marked' as *Overridable* and the method in the derived class was 'marked' as *Overrides*. The effect is to alter the behaviour of any instance of the derived class when compared to any instance of the base class.

The program statements within the function method of the derived class calculate the credit rating using different rules to the base class.

This message has not invoked an instance of an inherited method of the base class, instead it has invoked an instance of a new version declared within the derived class.

QUESTION 17.2 (REVISION)
Although it is not required for Specification 17.1, how could the derived class arrange for an instance of itself to have access to both forms of the GetRating() function method?

Figure 17.23 illustrates a runtime that highlights the different effect of creating and then displaying the credit rating for both types of customer (i.e. a current account and gold account customer).

Figure 17.23 Illustrating overriding in action.

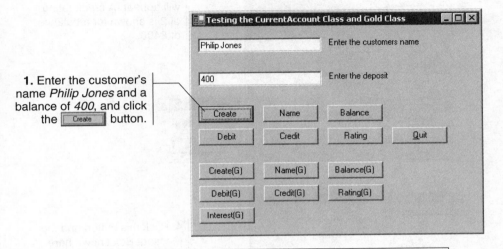

1. Enter the customer's name *Philip Jones* and a balance of *400*, and click the [Create] button.

Once the Create button has been clicked an instance of the *CurrentAccount* class is created.

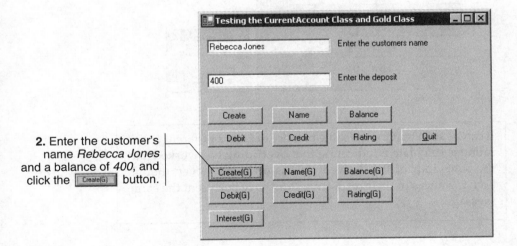

2. Enter the customer's name *Rebecca Jones* and a balance of *400*, and click the [Create(G)] button.

Once the Create(G) button has been clicked an instance of the *Gold* class is created.

At this moment in time the application has **two** objects in existance. These two objects are an object of the *CurrentAccount* class and an object of the *Gold* class.

These objects exist in their own right and are totally independent of each other. Of course, they share many common behaviours and properties. However, the behaviours are 'their own' and their properties can be set to different values.

Figure 17.23 (cont.)

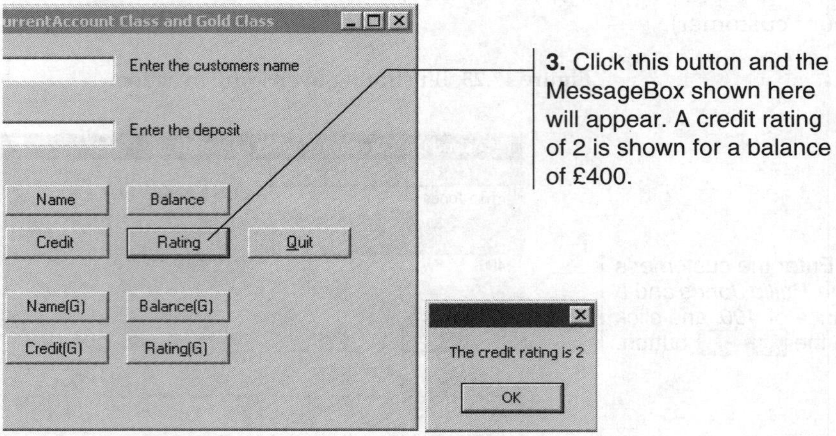

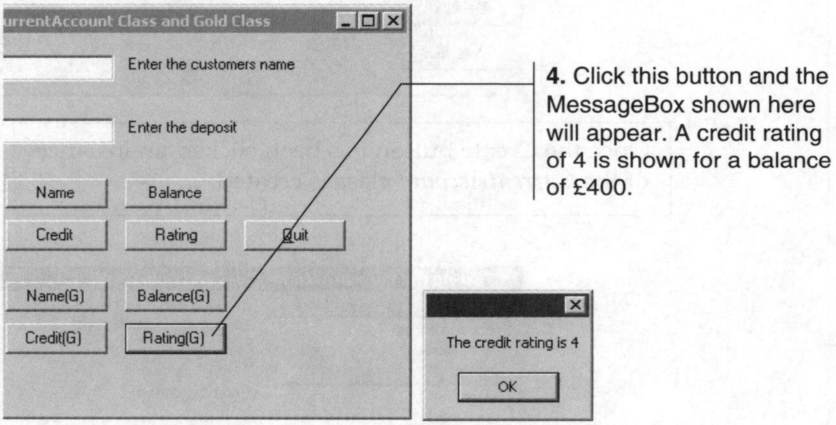

3. Click this button and the MessageBox shown here will appear. A credit rating of 2 is shown for a balance of £400.

4. Click this button and the MessageBox shown here will appear. A credit rating of 4 is shown for a balance of £400.

It can be seen that for the same balance of £400 a different credit rating is calculated, indicating that overriding has worked and the behaviour of the derived class is different – even though both instances of their respective class have been sent the **same message**.

Polymorphism

The sending of a message to an object and being serviced by this object is fundamental to object-oriented programming. Figure 17.23 has illustrated the sending of messages to an instance of the *CurrentAccount* class and to an instance of the *Gold* class. It can be seen that these messages are identical but they result in different behaviour. They both return a credit rating but this rating is calculated in different ways. The ability to send the same message and invoke different behaviour is an example of polymorphism. What is useful is that the object receiving the message makes the decision as to which behaviour is invoked. The part UML collaboration diagram shown in Figure 17.24 illustrates this.

Figure 17.24 A collaboration diagram illustrating polymorphism as implemented by overriding.

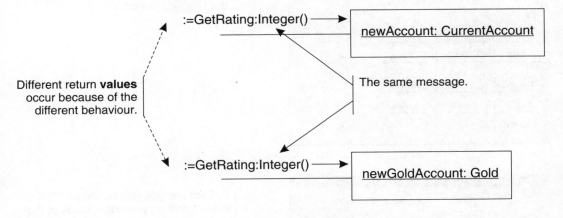

NOTE: Polymorphism will allow different kinds of objects, that are all able to process a common set of messages, to be used interchangeably, and to process those messages in their own way.

It is possible to use an object created from a derived class in any situation where an object created from the base class is expected. This allows you, for example, to write client-side code in terms of a generic base class and substitute objects created from any class down the inheritance hierarchy. This is often referred to as implicit compatibility between a derived class and its base class.

Polymorphism is also available when you use interfaces – more on this later.

The code attached to the `Interest(G)` button calculates interest on the account balance and then adds this interest to the balance. It shows the balance before and after the interest is added. The code that performs this is shown in Listing 17.8. An example runtime for the code of Listing 17.8 is shown in Figure 17.25. Figure 17.26 describes the execution of the message used in Listing 17.8 in more detail.

Listing 17.8 Calculating interest and adding it to the account balance.

```
Private Sub btnAddInterest_Click(ByVal sender As System.Object, ByVal e As _
System.EventArgs) Handles btnAddInterest.Click
    MessageBox.Show("The balance BEFORE interest is " & newGoldAccount.Balance)
    newGoldAccount.AddInterest()
    MessageBox.Show("The balance AFTER interest is " & newGoldAccount.Balance)
End Sub
```

Figure 17.25 An example runtime.

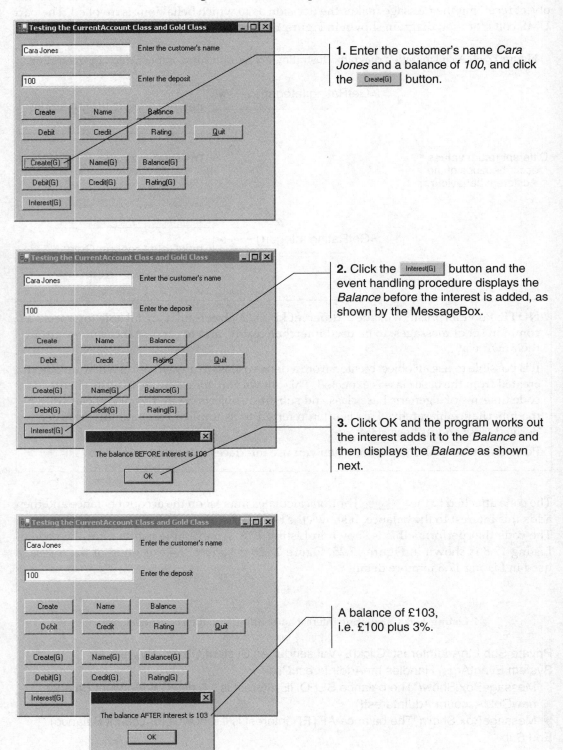

1. Enter the customer's name *Cara Jones* and a balance of *100*, and click the Create(G) button.

2. Click the Interest(G) button and the event handling procedure displays the *Balance* before the interest is added, as shown by the MessageBox.

The balance BEFORE interest is 100

3. Click OK and the program works out the interest adds it to the *Balance* and then displays the *Balance* as shown next.

A balance of £103, i.e. £100 plus 3%.

The balance AFTER interest is 103

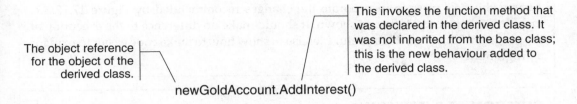

Figure 17.26 The message used in Listing 17.8.

This invokes the function method that was declared in the derived class. It was not inherited from the base class; this is the new behaviour added to the derived class.

The object reference for the object of the derived class.

newGoldAccount.AddInterest()

Let's emphasize what happened here. A class called *CurrrentAccount* was already developed and shown to be working. However, it did not offer all the behaviours required: it could not add interest based on the balance.

So a new class was developed, called the *Gold* class, that inherited the behaviours from the *CurrentAccount* class. It then added the extra behaviours to the *Gold* class.

NOTE: Let's ask another question. Why not add the extra behaviour required to the *CurrentAccount* class? Well in fact you could if you wanted to. However, the classes in this chapter are not in truth that useful, they are just used for teaching purposes. However, the question is still valid. Why have a derived class, why not add the extra behaviour to the base class?

A Development team of programmers build classes and then **thoroughly** test them. Adding extra behaviours to a class that has been tested is dangerous because you might inadvertently add errors. Consequently, if you did alter the base class you would have to test it **ALL** again.

Adding the extra behaviour to a derived class will only require the testing of these extras.

In the public domain and within VB .NET there are numerous useful classes that can be used to service the requirement of your program. You do not have access to program code for these classes, however. So if you wished to add behaviours to these classes to suit your purposes you would not be able to. However, you can inherit from these classes and produce a derived class and give this derived class the extra behaviours required.

PRACTICAL ACTIVITY 17.1

Implement Specification 17.1. This involves amending the *Account* solution developed in Chapter 16. The amendments require changes to the GUI as represented by Figure 17.14 and the attaching of the event handling procedures as shown by Listings 17.2 through to 17.8. You will also have to add the *Gold* class as represented by Listing 17.1.

PRACTICAL ACTIVITY 17.2

Amend the *Gold* class to incorporate the changes recommended by Figure 17.12, i.e. include the keyword *MyBase* as shown. It should make no difference to the execution of the program! However, it is a useful exercise to show how to make code easier to read for a programmer.

QUESTION 17.3 (REVISION)

Is it a good idea to use the keyword MyBase in the way suggested by Practical Activity 17.2?

Access modifiers and inheritance

The listings from Chapters 16 and 17 have shown that either the *Public* or *Private* modifiers have been used when declaring class level variables, property procedures and methods of classes.

VB .NET has a number of modifiers; three are described in Table 17.1.

Table 17.1 Access modifiers used for inheritance.

Access modifier	Description when using inheritance
Private	Only objects of the class in which the modifier *Private* is used for members can have access to those members.
Public	All code (that can access an object of a class, i.e. they have an appropriate object reference to the instance of the class) can access members declared as *Public*.
Protected	Access is limited to objects of the base class and any objects of classes that are descendents (i.e. derived) of the base class.

Consider the following three class level variables of the *CurrentAccount* class (taken from Listing 16.1)

Public Class CurrentAccount

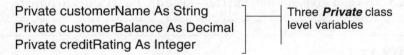

    Private customerName As String   Three *Private* class
    Private customerBalance As Decimal   level variables
    Private creditRating As Integer

These instance variables are available to all the code of any object created from the *CurrentAccount* class. In other words, instances of all of the methods, function methods and property procedures declared within the *CurrentAccount* class can access instances of these three class variables.

Any of the code within an object of the *Gold* class **cannot** access these three class variables, even though *Gold* inherits from the *CurrentAccount* class. Any object of the *Gold* class 'cannot see' the private variables of its base (parent) class.

However, instances of the *Gold* class have methods that do access the values of instances of these class level variables. For example, the *customerName* and *customeBalance* instance variables are accessed. But this access was not direct access! Objects of the *Gold* class had access via methods and property procedures that were declared as *Public* within the *CurrentAccount* class. An example of this is shown in Figure 17.27. *AddInterest* is a method of the *Gold* class that accesses the *Private customerBalance* instance variable using the *Public* property procedure *Balance* as shown by the callout label.

Figure 17.27 'Indirectly' accessing class variables of a base class.

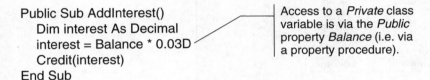

```
Public Sub AddInterest()
    Dim interest As Decimal
    interest = Balance * 0.03D
    Credit(interest)
End Sub
```

Access to a *Private* class variable is via the *Public* property *Balance* (i.e. via a property procedure).

Another 'indirect access' to an instance of a *Private* class level variable is shown in Figure 17.28 (which was taken from Listing 17.1). Here the constructor invokes its parent's constructor sending it an actual parameter *pName* and the parent constructor assigns the content of the actual parameter to the privately declared *customerName* instance variable. Of course the constructor shown in Figure 17.28 had access to the constructor in its parent's class because it was declared as *Public*.

Figure 17.28 Another access to an instance of a Private class level variable.

```
Public Sub New(ByVal pName As String)
    MyBase.New(pName)
End Sub
```

This invokes the base constructor, which has access to its own instance of its *Private* class level variable *customerName*, and the value of *pName* is therefore passed to this instance of the *Private* class level variable.

This process of passing parameters through the various constructors is illustrated by Figure 17.29.

Figure 17.29 Passing parameters from an instance of a derived class to an instance of a *Private* class level variable of a base class.

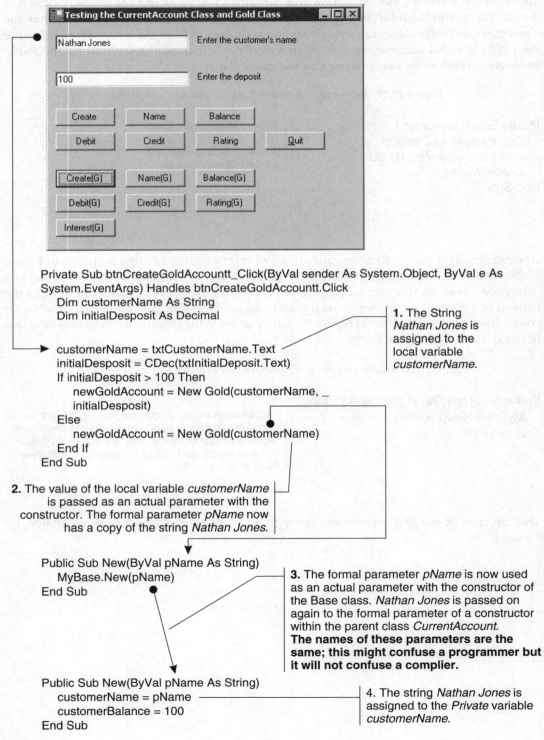

```
Private Sub btnCreateGoldAccountt_Click(ByVal sender As System.Object, ByVal e As
System.EventArgs) Handles btnCreateGoldAccountt.Click
    Dim customerName As String
    Dim initialDesposit As Decimal

    customerName = txtCustomerName.Text
    initialDesposit = CDec(txtInitialDeposit.Text)
    If initialDesposit > 100 Then
        newGoldAccount = New Gold(customerName, _
        initialDesposit)
    Else
        newGoldAccount = New Gold(customerName)
    End If
End Sub
```

1. The String *Nathan Jones* is assigned to the local variable *customerName*.

2. The value of the local variable *customerName* is passed as an actual parameter with the constructor. The formal parameter *pName* now has a copy of the string *Nathan Jones*.

```
Public Sub New(ByVal pName As String)
    MyBase.New(pName)
End Sub
```

3. The formal parameter *pName* is now used as an actual parameter with the constructor of the Base class. *Nathan Jones* is passed on again to the formal parameter of a constructor within the parent class *CurrentAccount*. **The names of these parameters are the same; this might confuse a programmer but it will not confuse a complier.**

```
Public Sub New(ByVal pName As String)
    customerName = pName
    customerBalance = 100
End Sub
```

4. The string *Nathan Jones* is assigned to the *Private* variable *customerName*.

If, during the design of the *CurrentAccount* class, a decision was made to make the class level variables *customerName*, *customerBalance* and *creditRating* as *Protected* instead of *Private* then these class level variables would be directly accessible by all instances of the *Gold* class. Under these circumstances, the *AddInterest* method could be written without the need to use the *Balance* property procedure and the *Credit* method. Listing 17.9 shows the original *AddInterest* method and Listing 17.10 shows what this method could be like if the *CurrentAccount* class was redesigned using the *Protected* access modifier instead of the *Private* access modifier.

Listing 17.9 The 'original' *AddInterest* method.

```
Public Sub AddInterest()
    Dim interest As Decimal
    interest = Balance * 0.03D
    Credit(interest)
End Sub
```

Access to the *Private* variable *customerBalance* is via the *Public* property procedure *Balance*.

Listing 17.10 The 'new' *AddInterest* method.

```
Public Sub AddInterest()
    Dim interest As Decimal
    interest = customerBalance * 0.03D
    customerBalance = customerBalance + interest
End Sub
```

The *customerBalance* variable declared in *CurrentAccount* class is directly accessible to the code within an instance of the *Gold* class because it was declared as *Protected* in the *CurrentAccount* class and *Gold* is a derived class of *CurrentAccount* (which is the base class).

As the *customerBalance* variable is directly accessible there is no need to use the *Credit* method

Listings 17.9 and 17.10 have been developed to show the difference between a *Private* and *Protected* class variable.

NOTE: Please remember that *Protected* members are accessible by objects of the base class and by objects of classes derived from the base class and any objects of classes that are derived from the derived class and so on – in other words objects of classes within the same inheritance chain have access to *Protected* members.

Objects of other classes that do not belong to the inheritance chain do not have direct access and they would have to gain access via *Public* methods and property procedures (if they exist within the class).

QUESTION 17.4 (REVISION)

If the creditRating *class level variable declared within the* CurrentAccount *class was made* Protected *would it be necessary to keep the* creditRating *class variable declared in the* Gold *class?*

PRACTICAL ACTIVITY 17.3

Amend the *Account* solution in the following ways:

● Make the three class level variables of the *CurrentAccount* class *Protected* instead of *Private*.

● Change the *AddInterest* method to the one shown in Listing 17.10.

You should decide what needs to be done with the class level variable declared in the *Gold* class (refer to Question 17.4).

If you have made all the appropriate changes run the application and make sure that it still works.

NOTE: Practical Activity 17.3 was designed to show how the difference between *Private* and *Protected* access modifiers. There is no recommendation to use *Protected* instead of *Private*. Which access modifier should be used is a design decision based on how you wish the class hierarchy chain to be used.

As a rule of thumb, you should make class level variables *Private* and only allow access via methods, function methods or property procedures.

Visual inheritance

Visual inheritance is nothing more than inheritance that involves a form inheriting from another form that has already been developed. Consider a form that contains a logo as a background image and a Quit button. The idea is that this form will act as the base form for all forms used in an application. Figure 17.30 shows how to implement visual inheritance.

Figure 17.30 Visual Inheritance.

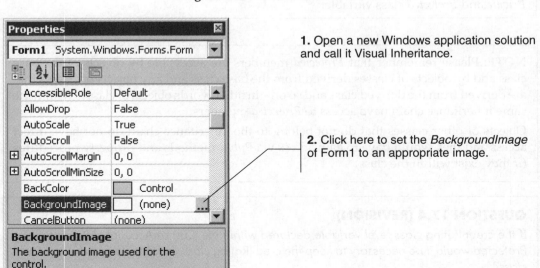

1. Open a new Windows application solution and call it Visual Inheritance.

2. Click here to set the *BackgroundImage* of Form1 to an appropriate image.

Figure 17.30 (cont.)

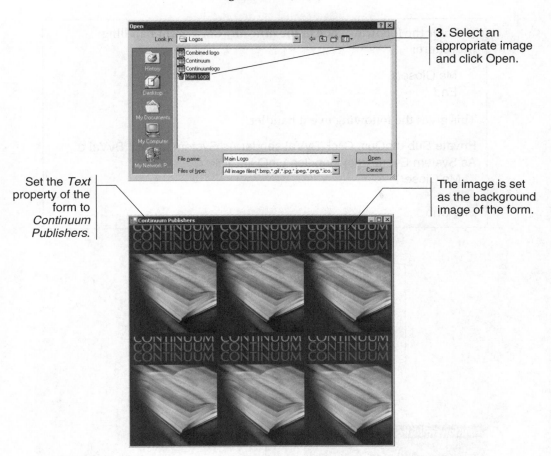

3. Select an appropriate image and click Open.

Set the *Text* property of the form to *Continuum Publishers*.

The image is set as the background image of the form.

4. Draw a button on the form. Set its *Name* property to *btnQuit* and its *Text* property to *&Quit*. The form will now look as shown below.

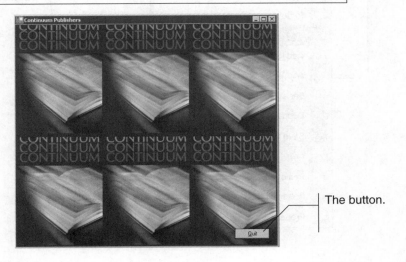

The button.

403

Figure 17.30 (cont.)

---

5. Enter the following code in the *btnQuit_Click* event handling procedure:

```
Me.Close()
End
```

This gives the following event handler:

```
Private Sub btnQuit_Click(ByVal sender As System.Object, ByVal e _
As System.EventArgs) Handles btnQuit.Click
    Me.Close()
    End
End Sub
```

This form will now act as the base form of an application developed for Continuum Publishers.

Let's add another form to the Visual Inheritance solution.

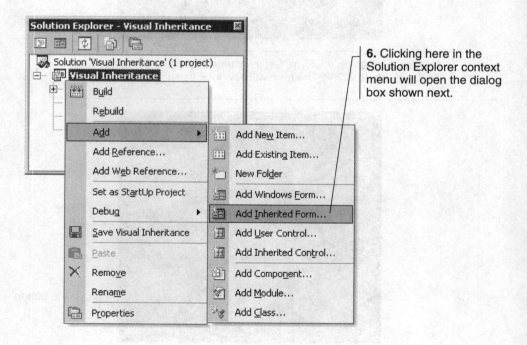

6. Clicking here in the Solution Explorer context menu will open the dialog box shown next.

Figure 17.30 (cont.)

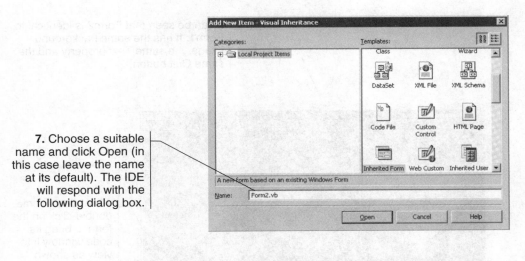

7. Choose a suitable name and click Open (in this case leave the name at its default). The IDE will respond with the following dialog box.

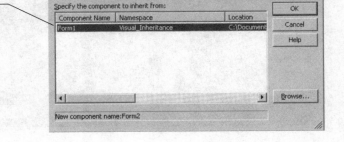

8. In this case select *Form1*, which is the form within the Visual Inheritance solution, and click OK.

Note that clicking the Browse button would allow another form to be located.

After *Form1* has been chosen as the base class for the derived class *Form2*, the Solution explorer looks as shown below.

9. Double-click on this and Form2 will open as shown next.

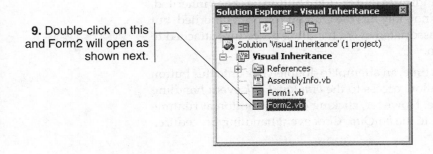

Figure 17.30 (cont.)

It can be seen that Form2 is identical to Form1. It has the same background image, the same Text property and the same Quit button.

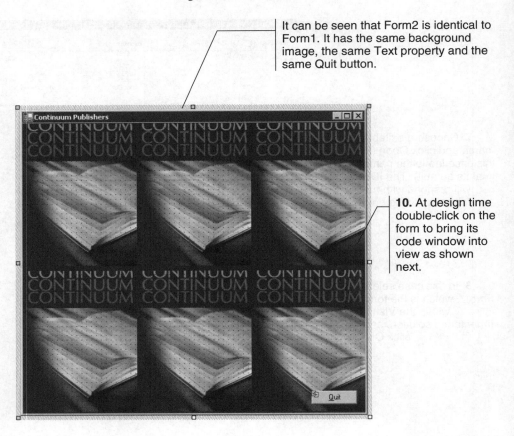

10. At design time double-click on the form to bring its code window into view as shown next.

A closer look at the Quit button shows that it has an icon in its top left corner. This is shown magnified:

The icon.

The icon indicates that the Quit button has been inherited. Note that not only has the Quit button been inherited, but also any associated event handling procedure attached to the button.

At design time, an attempt to double-click onto this button will **not** allow access to the *btnQuit_Click* event handling procedure. However, clicking onto the button at runtime will execute the *btnQuit_Click* event handling procedure.

Figure 17.30 (cont.)

It can be seen that the IDE has named the class Form2.

The IDE has also included the namespace.

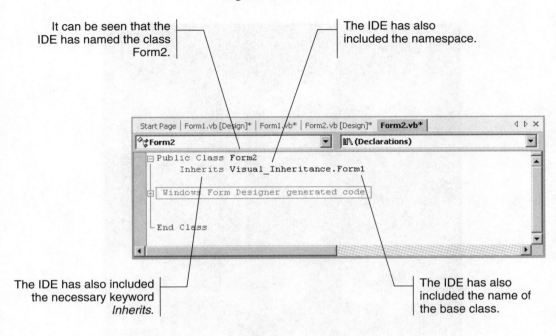

The IDE has also included the necessary keyword *Inherits*.

The IDE has also included the name of the base class.

You should also note that the code window does not show the event handling procedure attached to the Quit button. This is because it does not have access to it at design time but it is available at runtime, that is, it can be executed from Form2.

Of course, other controls can now be drawn onto Form2 and appropriate event handling procedures added.

11. Add a label and a button onto Form2 and have the button move the label vertically up the form.

Figure 17.30 (cont.)

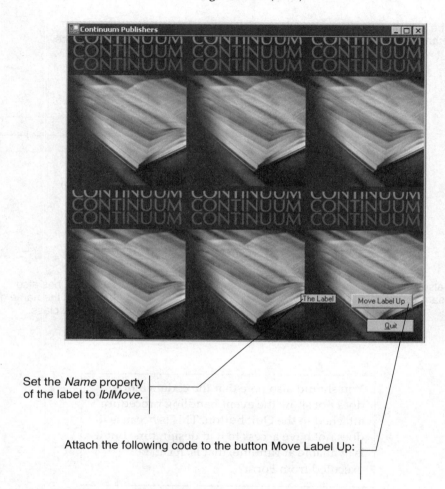

Set the *Name* property
of the label to *lblMove*.

Attach the following code to the button Move Label Up:

```
Private Sub btnMoveLabelUp_Click(ByVal sender As System.Object, _
ByVal e As System.EventArgs) Handles btnMoveLabelUp.Click
    lblMove.Top = lblMove.Top - 100
End Sub
```

We now need to run the program and observe the
runtime of Form2. There are a number of ways to
activate the execution of Form2. The method shown
next involves setting properties using the Property
Page of the Visual Inheritance project.

Figure 17.30 (cont.)

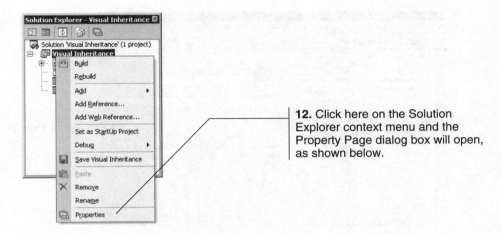

12. Click here on the Solution Explorer context menu and the Property Page dialog box will open, as shown below.

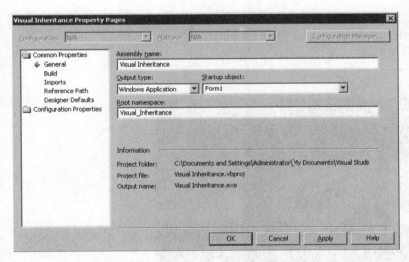

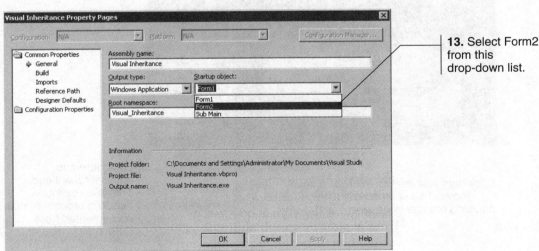

13. Select Form2 from this drop-down list.

Figure 17.30 (cont.)

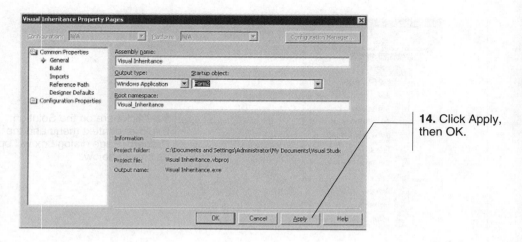

14. Click Apply, then OK.

15. Now run the application and the following form executes (i.e. Form2).

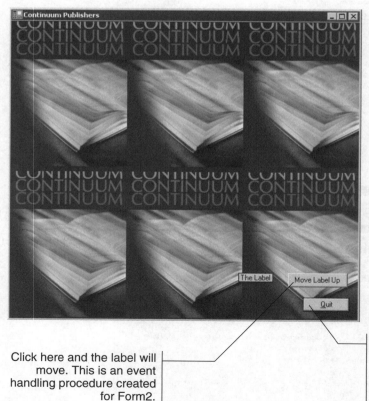

Click here and the label will move. This is an event handling procedure created for Form2.

Click here and application will end. This is an event handling procedure that was inherited from Form1.

NOTE: During Figure 17.30, an inheritance picker was used to select the form that would act as the base class for the derived class.

This is a convenient mechanism; however, you do not have to use it to achieve inheritance. Instead you could have just typed in the keyword *Inherits*, the namespace and the name of the form from which you wished to inherit – try it!

PRACTICAL ACTIVITY 17.4
Develop and run the simple program represented by Figure 17.30.

18 Abstract classes and interfaces

Abstract classes

Many software applications are now large software systems with a huge number of program statements. It is no longer possible for an individual to develop any meaningful system to challenge the systems developed by software houses. Teams of people, all of whom have specialized roles, develop software systems, starting typically with analysts who gather the requirements for a system; they concentrate on **what** a system is supposed to do. There are also designers who take the requirements and produce a design that is partitioned into numerous tasks, which are then allocated to programmers. Designers decide on **how** a system is to be built.

In the case of object-oriented design, these tasks are definitions of classes and a designer will decide upon the responsibilities for numerous classes. This is a nontrivial task and how this is achieved is outside the scope of this book. However, what this chapter considers is how a designer can ensure a programmer implements their design.

A designer of a software system, in the first instance, does not deal with the details of how program code will implement an algorithm or whether *ByVal* or *ByRef* is used when passing parameters. They concentrate on an overview of the system in terms of objects and how they communicate with one and another. To achieve this view they use a technique called abstraction, which describes a system in general terms. They concentrate on describing what a class is responsible for doing, that is, what are its behaviours.

> **NOTE**: During the design process a designer will use a technique called **factoring** to push common code back as far as possible into a base class. This base class then acts as the start of an inheritance chain.
>
> In VB .NET an abstract class can be used to define a base class resulting from a factoring process.

Once a designer has confirmed the behaviours and states of a proposed class the definition of a class is passed to a programmer who then implements the class in code.

So to repeat: an abstract class in VB .NET is a definition of a class that has come from the careful and detailed study of the proposed software system, part of this involves a technique called factoring.

What needs to be understood by a programmer is that an abstract class is a class from which objects **cannot** be created. However, it is possible to create a derived class from an abstract class and it is then possible to create objects of this derived class. An abstract class is able to impose appropriate behaviour on its subclasses. Consequently, it is useful tool for a designer to ensure that important behaviours are implemented down a hierarchy chain. Abstract classes are always near the top of the hierarchy chain, and derived, and therefore 'concrete' classes are further down the chain.

Having briefly discussed the reasons for abstract classes, the rest of this chapter will show how to implement and use such classes.

Building an abstract class

An abstract class must have at least one member method marked with the keyword *MustOverride* and the class itself must be marked with the keyword *MustInherit*.

> **NOTE**: To keep things simple, a base class will be derived for a bank account, thus the work will be similar to the specification with which you will be familiar from Chapters 16 and 17.

Start a Windows application solution called *Bank Account* and add a class called *Account*. At this point the Solution Explorer and code window should look as shown in Figure 18.1.

Figure 18.1 The Solution Explorer and *Account* class.

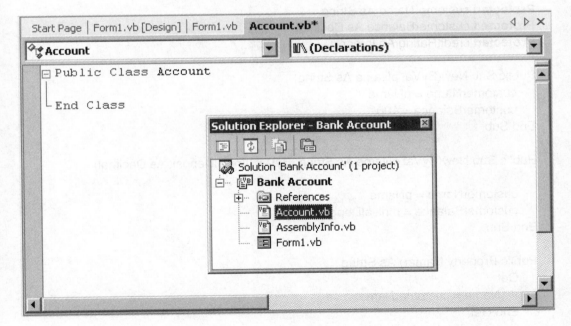

As the intention is to build an abstract base class, the keyword *MustInherit* must be added, as shown in Figure 18.2.

Figure 18.2 Adding the keyword *MustInherit*.

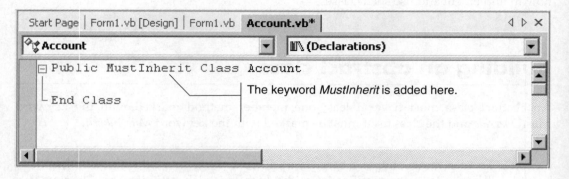

Listing 18.1 shows an abstract class for a bank account. The listing is almost identical to Listing 16.1 – the differences are shown in bold.

Listing 18.1 An abstract class for a bank account.

```
Public MustInherit Class Account
    Protected customerName As String
    Protected customerBalance As Decimal
    Protected creditRating As Integer

    Public Sub New(ByVal pName As String)
        customerName = pName
        customerBalance = 100
    End Sub

    Public Sub New(ByVal pName As String, ByVal pInitialDeposit As Decimal)

        customerName = pName
        customerBalance = pInitialDeposit
    End Sub

    Public Property Name() As String
        Get
            Name = customerName
        End Get
        Set(ByVal Value As String)
            customerName = Name
        End Set
    End Property
```

Listing 18.1 (cont.)

```
Public ReadOnly Property Balance() As Decimal
    Get
        Balance = customerBalance
    End Get
End Property

Public Sub Debit(ByVal pWithdrawal As Decimal)
    customerBalance = customerBalance - pWithdrawal
End Sub

Public Sub Credit(ByVal pDeposit As Decimal)
    customerBalance = customerBalance + pDeposit
End Sub

Public MustOverride Function GetRating() As Integer

End Class
```

The differences are extracted from Listing 18.1 and shown again in Figure 18.3.

Figure 18.3 The differences between Listings 16.1 and 18.1.

```
Public MustInherit Class Account
```

The keyword *MustInherit* is put here; this is essential when building an abstract class.

```
Protected customerName As String
Protected customerBalance As Decimal
Protected creditRating As Integer
```

These three class level variables have been made *Protected* and thus are available to instances of derived classes.

```
Public MustOverride Function GetRating() As Integer
```

This line is the signature of the *GetRating* function method with the addition of the keyword *MustOverride*. The other difference is that there is not any body to this method, i.e. there are not any program statements or declaration of local variables.

The designers of this base abstract class have chosen to declare three *Protected* class variables and **fully** declare (i.e. include a body, program statements and local variables) all but one method.

It is not possible to create an instance of this abstract class. Figure 18.4 shows an unsuccessful attempt to create an instance of the *Account* class and highlights the response from VB .NET.

Figure 18.4 A **failed** attempt to create an instance of an abstract class.

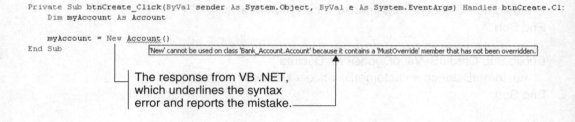

```
Private Sub btnCreate_Click(ByVal sender As System.Object, ByVal e As System.EventArgs) Handles btnCreate.Cl:
    Dim myAccount As Account

    myAccount = New Account()
End Sub
```

'New' cannot be used on class 'Bank_Account.Account' because it contains a 'MustOverride' member that has not been overridden.

The response from VB .NET,
which underlines the syntax
error and reports the mistake.

Using an abstract class

To demonstrate the use of this abstract class another class called *ChequeAccount* is added to the *Bank Account* solution as shown by Figure 18.5.

Figure 18.5 Adding another class.

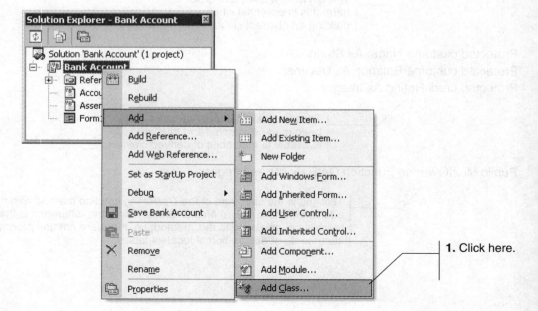

1. Click here.

Figure 18.5 (cont.)

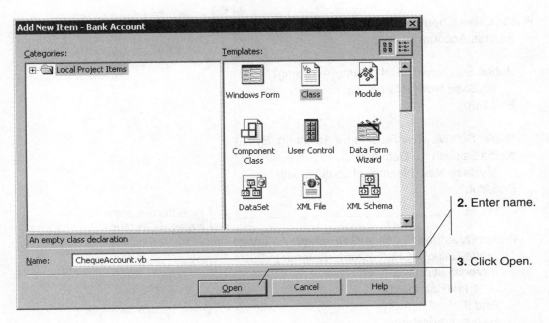

2. Enter name.

3. Click Open.

Figure 18.6 shows the class when complete and Listing 18.2 shows the complete listing for the *ChequeAccount* class.

Figure 18.6 The *ChequeAccount* class.

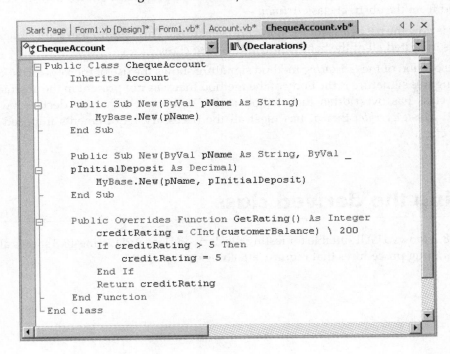

417

Listing 18.2 The *ChequeAccount* class.

```
Public Class ChequeAccount
    Inherits Account

    Public Sub New(ByVal pName As String)
        MyBase.New(pName)
    End Sub

    Public Sub New(ByVal pName As String, ByVal _
    pInitialDeposit As Decimal)
        MyBase.New(pName, pInitialDeposit)
    End Sub

    Public Overrides Function GetRating() As Integer
        creditRating = CInt(customerBalance) \ 200
        If creditRating > 5 Then
            creditRating = 5
        End If
        Return creditRating
    End Function
End Class
```

Note the use of the keyword *Overrides*.

The second line of the *ChequeAccount* class (i.e. *Inherits Account*) shows that this class has inherited from the abstract class *Account*.

Account is now the base class for the *ChequeAccount* class. This implies that the *ChequeAccount* class has inherited all of the behaviours of this base class.

Close inspection of the *GetRating* method signature shows the use of the keyword *Overrides*. Following this signature is the body of the method that was **not** present in the abstract class. As this class has overridden the method in the base class (that was declared with the keyword *MustOverride*) then it has meet all the necessary requirements imposed by the abstract class.

Testing the derived class

Figure 18.7 shows a GUI suitable for testing the derived class and Listing 18.3 shows all of the event handling procedures that require 'attaching' to this GUI.

NOTE: The names of the controls used on the GUI should be obvious from the names of the event handling procedures. Remember the name property of controls must always be set first. The name of the first event handling procedures in Listing 18.3 is *btnCreate_Click*. Consequently, the name property of the [Create] button must be set to *btnCreate* to ensuring consistency with Listing 18.3.

Figure 18.7 Shows a GUI suitable for testing the *ChequeAccount* class.

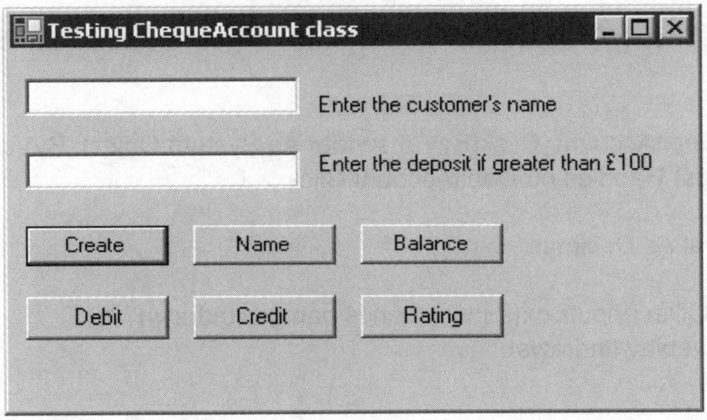

Listing 18.3 lists the event handling procedures attached to each of the buttons and the declaration of a variable of type *ChequeAccount* (i.e. the Class *ChequeAccount*).

Listing 18.3 The 'testing class'.

```
Private newAccount As ChequeAccount.

Private Sub btnCreate_Click(ByVal sender As System.Object, ByVal e As _
System.EventArgs) Handles btnCreate.Click

    Dim customerName As String
    Dim initialDesposit As Decimal

    customerName = txtCustomerName.Text
    initialDesposit = CDec(txtInitialDeposit.text)
    If initialDesposit > 100 Then
        newAccount = New ChequeAccount(customerName, initialDesposit)
    Else
        newAccount = New ChequeAccount(customerName)
    End If
End Sub
```

419

Listing 18.3 (cont.)

```
Private Sub btnDisplayName_Click(ByVal sender As System.Object, ByVal e As _
System.EventArgs) Handles btnDisplayName.Click

    MessageBox.Show("The customer's name is " & newAccount.Name)
End Sub

Private Sub btnDisplayBalance_Click(ByVal sender As System.Object, ByVal e As _
System.EventArgs) Handles btnDisplayBalance.Click

    MessageBox.Show("The customer's balance is " & newAccount.Balance)
End Sub

Private Sub btnDebitAccount_Click(ByVal sender As System.Object, ByVal e As _
System.EventArgs) Handles btnDebitAccount.Click

    Dim withdrawal As Decimal

    withdrawal = CDec(InputBox("How much is being withdrawn? "))
    newAccount.Debit(withdrawal)
End Sub

Private Sub btnCreditBalance_Click(ByVal sender As System.Object, ByVal e As _
System.EventArgs) Handles btnCreditBalance.Click
    Dim deposit As Decimal

    deposit = CDec(InputBox("How much is being deposited? "))
    newAccount.Credit(deposit)
End Sub

Private Sub btnDisplayRating_Click(ByVal sender As System.Object, ByVal e As _
System.EventArgs) Handles btnDisplayRating.Click

    MessageBox.Show("The credit rating is " & newAccount.GetRating())
End Sub
```

PRACTICAL ACTIVITY 18.1

Implement the *BankAccount* solution as represented by Listing 18.3 and the GUI shown in Figure 18.7. Remember that all of the necessary classes have to be present in the solution.

NOTE: The example of the abstract class discussed in this chapter has only marked one method as *MustOverride*. There can be as many methods marked with the keyword *MustOverride* as the designer desires, but there always has to be **at least one**.

PRACTICAL ACTIVITY 18.2

Any class derived from an abstract class does not just have to use and override the methods supplied by the base class: it can also add its own members. Add a method to the *ChequeAccount* class that allows for interest of 5% to be added to the account's balance. Test the newly amended class as appropriate.

Interfaces

Abstract classes allow a designer to start an inheritance chain by collecting together (by a process of factoring) common behaviour for the hierarchy.

Inheritance in VB .NET is implemented using single inheritance; multiple inheritance is not possible.

Multiple inheritance is where a class is able to inherit from more than one base classes. Figure 18.8 shows the concept of single inheritance, while Figure 18.9 shows the concept of multiple inheritance.

Figure 18.8 The concept of single inheritance.

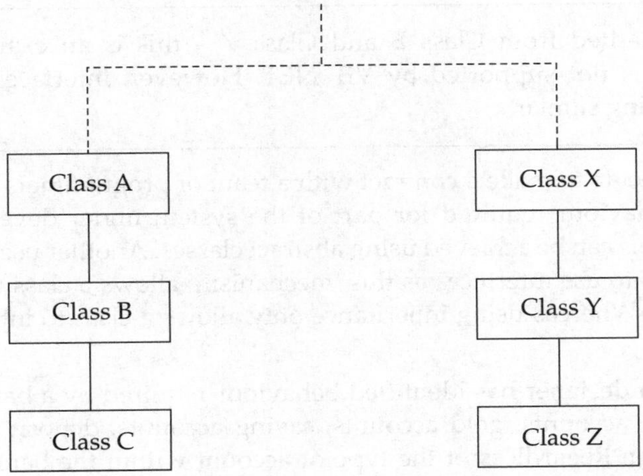

Here there are two distinct inheritance chains, classes A, B and C form one chain and Classes X, Y and Z form another chain. The dotted line represents the hierarchy above Class A and X.

It is worth noting that all objects ultimately inherit from the class at the top of the hierarchy – which is the *Object* class.

Class Y inherits from Class X and Class B inherits from Class A. It is not possible for Class Y to also inherit from Class A. Likewise it is not possible for Class B to inherit from Class Y.

Figure 18.9 The concept of multiple inheritance.

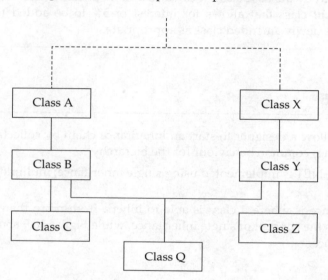

Class Q has inherited from Class B and Class Y – this is an example of multiple inheritance and is **not** supported by VB .NET. However, interfaces can be used to perform 'something similar'.

A designer may decide to make a contract with a team of programmers to ensure that they implement the behaviour required for part of the system under development. We have already seen that this can be achieved using abstract classes. Another useful and often better choice, however, is to use interfaces as this 'mechanism' allows a class to implement more than one interface. Whereas using inheritance only allows a class to inherit from one base class.

Let's assume that a designer has identified behaviour required by a banking system. This system has current accounts, gold accounts, saving accounts, deposit accounts, business accounts, and so on. Regardless of the type of account within the banking system it will always be necessary to:

- Log details on customers, such as their name, address, gender, etc.
- Process a customer's account, such as debit the account, credit the account, add interest, and so on.

These distinctly different types of behaviour could be put into an appropriately named abstract class. Classes associated with the various types of bank account could then be derived from this abstract class.

The insurance branch of the banking system also requires the logging of customer details and this is not associated with accounts. However, it is still possible to use the abstract base class just referred to in the last paragraph to implement a derived class suitable for the logging of customer details for insurance. However, any instance of this derived class would also have members not associated with the logging of customer details for insurance purposes, it would also have members associated with the processing of the customer's account. Although this is not a disaster (because the object need not use these extra members), it is not a logical relationship and is best avoided.

One solution would be to create another abstract class that has behaviour associated with the insurance business, and within this class repeat the behaviour for logging customer details. The designer could then create an appropriate derived class from this abstract class.

> **NOTE**: If a designer decided to have an abstract class for each of the behaviours identified by the bullet points above, it would not be possible to derive a class that contained both sets of behaviour, because VB .NET does not support multiple inheritance.

Another solution would be to represent the behaviours identified by the above bullet points by a mechanism referred to as an interface. It is then possible for a class to **implement** these two interfaces and thus have the combined behaviour of both.

> **NOTE**: Alternatively, build an abstract class for the account aspects of the system and build another abstract class for the insurance aspects of the system. In both cases the behaviour of these classes would be minus the ability to log details of customers. The logging of customer details could then be given to an interface.
>
> A derived class suitable for customer accounts could inherit from the abstract accounts class and implement the interface for logging customer details.
>
> Similarly, a derived class suitable for customer insurance could inherit from the abstract insurance class and implement the interface for logging customer details.

An interface does **not** contain any program statements within the definition of its methods. An interface contains only the signatures of the methods.

> **NOTE**: An interface imposes structure on any class that decides to implement the interface. It informs the class that it must supply the methods it specifies, i.e. the interface effectively lists the methods that the class has to supply the code for. **A class enters into a contract with any interface it implements**.

A class can implement more than one interface. Consequently, if it enters into a contract with more than one interface it has to supply the code for the methods that these interfaces 'list'.

Before we look at how to code and use an interface let's consider when to choose inheritance and when to chose interfaces when developing a software system. Maybe you would prefer to skip this section and then return to it when you have developed code that uses an interface.

Guidelines on when to use inheritance

It takes careful planning and a clear vision of how the hierarchy will be used to design a useful inheritance hierarchy. It is a task to be performed by an accomplished designer who is creating a framework that will be used by programmers building a variety of applications. It is not just a strategy to use when you are simply building a particular application.

From a design standpoint, think of inheritance as expressing a specialization hierarchy. If *GoldAccount* **'is a'** special kind of *Account*, you should consider making it a derived class.

However, do not use inheritance when the specialization that distinguishes a derived class from a base class is a feature that other classes will also need to support. To add theses kinds of features to a class implementing interfaces will give you much greater flexibility.

> **NOTE**: You should be cautious about creating your own base classes. It is important to express a clear specialization hierarchy that has been factored out to supply behaviours that you expect programmers to be able to use and override.

You should choose to use Inheritance when:

1. The inheritance hierarchy represents an **'is a'** relationship.

2. Code in the base class can be reused.

3. The class hierarchy is reasonably shallow and other developers are unlikely to add many more levels.

4. You wish to make global changes to derived classes by changing a base class.

These four points are discussed in order below.

Inheritance and 'is-a' relationship

An 'is-a' relationship is when the derived class is clearly a kind of the base class. For example, a class named *PlatinumBankAccount* represents an 'is-a' relationship with a base class named *BankAccount* because a Platinum account is a bank account.

Therefore classes in an inheritance hierarchy should have an 'is-a' relationship with their base class because they inherit the class level variables, properties, methods, and events defined in the base class.

NOTE: Another type of relationship between objects is a 'has a' relationship. For example a bank statement 'has a' relationship with a bank account but it is not an 'is a' relationship because the bank statement is not a type of account. A 'has a' relationship is not implemented as a class hierarchy.

Base classes and code reuse

Use inheritance to take advantage of code reuse. Classes that are well designed can be debugged once and used over and over as a basis for new classes.

Shallow class hierarchies

It is difficult to develop a deep and complex hierarchy. Consequently, use inheritance for a relatively shallow class hierarchy. A general rule is to limit hierarchies to six levels or fewer. However, the maximum depth for any particular class hierarchy depends on a number of factors that include the amount of complexity at each level.

Global changes to derived classes through the base class

A powerful feature of inheritance is the ability to make changes in a base class that propagate to derived classes. If this is used carefully a single method can be updated and many derived classes can then use this update.

NOTE: In wrong hands this can be a dangerous practice because such changes may cause problems with inherited classes designed by other people. It is important to ensure that the new base class is compatible with classes that use the original. It is also advisable to avoid changing the name or type of base class members.

When to use interfaces

Interfaces are similar to classes in that they define a set of members. Unlike classes, however, they do not provide the implementation. A class that implements an interface must implement every aspect of that interface exactly as it is defined. It is often said that the class enters into a contract with the interface.

NOTE: The most important distinction between creating a derived class and implementing an interface is that a derived class can only inherit from one base class, but a class can implement any number of interfaces.

You should choose to use interfaces when:

1. You wish to achieve safe changes to code.

2. Require flexibility in implementation.

3. There is a 'has a' relationship.

Safe changes to code

When using classes there is always a risk of later changes breaking the code. If the original assumptions for the class inheritance hierarchy turn out to be incorrect it is not always possible to safely change code in later versions. Consider an example where a base class contains a method that has defined one of its parameters as a *Boolean*. It later transpires that the parameter should have been of type *Integer*. What should you do? The obvious answer is to change the original definition of the parameter from a *Boolean* to an *Integer*. Unfortunately, classes derived from the original may now not compile correctly; they may, for example, have a method that obtains a *Boolean* from a file and then pass this *Boolean* to the method that is now expecting an *Integer*. This problem can be magnified because a single base class can affect many of its derived classes.

Interfaces solve this problem by allowing you to publish an updated interface that accepts the new data type.

Flexibility in implementation

Interfaces are:

- better suited to situations in which your applications includes many logically unrelated object types and these objects need a certain subset of common functionality;

- more flexible than base classes because you can define a single implementation that can implement multiple interfaces;

- better in situations in which you do not need to inherit from a base class;

- useful in cases where you cannot use class inheritance. For example, structures (not covered in this book) cannot inherit from classes, but they can implement interfaces.

Interfaces and 'has a' relationship

An interface is a useful mechanism for representing a 'has a' relationship. Although it is not the only mechanism, unrelated communicating objects can also represent such relationships.

How to declare and use an interface

Let's reconsider the requirements of Specification 16.1 as listed below:

- The reading (getting) and setting (writing) of the customer's name.
- The reading of the balance.
- Credit the balance.
- Debit the balance.

- Get the customer credit rating.

Of course, Chapter 16 showed how to create a class for this specification and Chapter 17 showed how to create a derived class and override the method that obtained the credit rating.

Figures 18.10, 18.11 and 18.12 shows how to create and use an Interface to meet the requirements listed above.

Figure 18.10 Creating an interface.

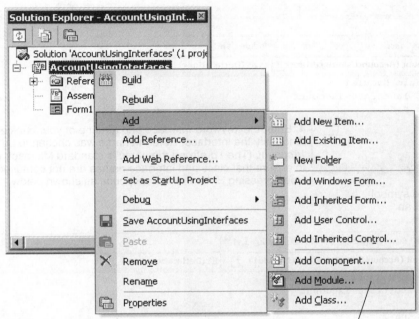

1. Open a solution and call it *AccountUsingInterfaces*.
2. Add a module to this solution using the Solution Explorer context menu, i.e. right-click with the mouse as shown above. For the purpose of this demonstration leave it at its default name of *Module1*.

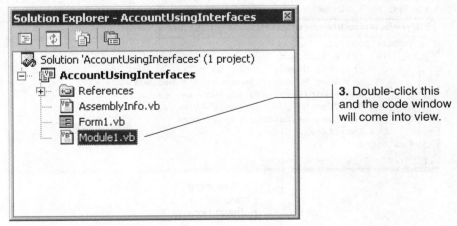

3. Double-click this and the code window will come into view.

Figure 18.10 (cont.)

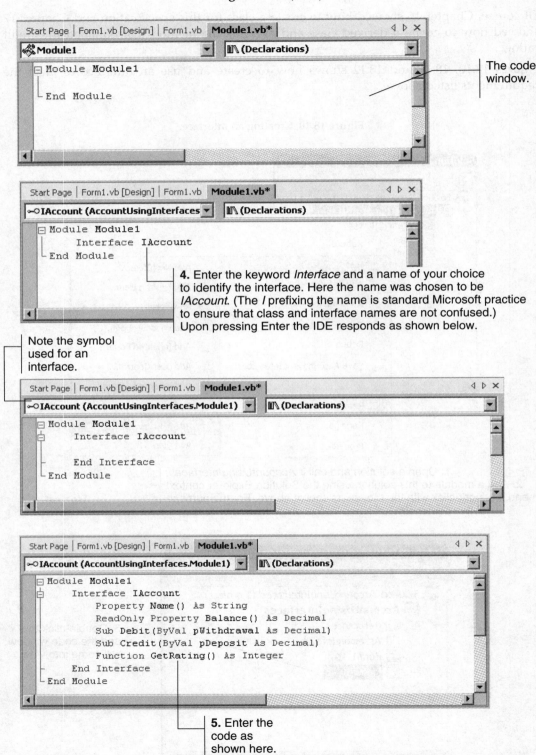

The code window.

4. Enter the keyword *Interface* and a name of your choice to identify the interface. Here the name was chosen to be *IAccount*. (The *I* prefixing the name is standard Microsoft practice to ensure that class and interface names are not confused.) Upon pressing Enter the IDE responds as shown below.

Note the symbol used for an interface.

5. Enter the code as shown here.

NOTE: Once the steps illustrated by Figure 18.10 are complete the interface is defined. Any class wishing to implement this interface would have to supply the program statements for the property procedures, methods and function methods 'listed' between the keywords *Interface* and *End Interface*. This is shown by Figure 18.11.

Figure 18.11 How a class implements an interface.

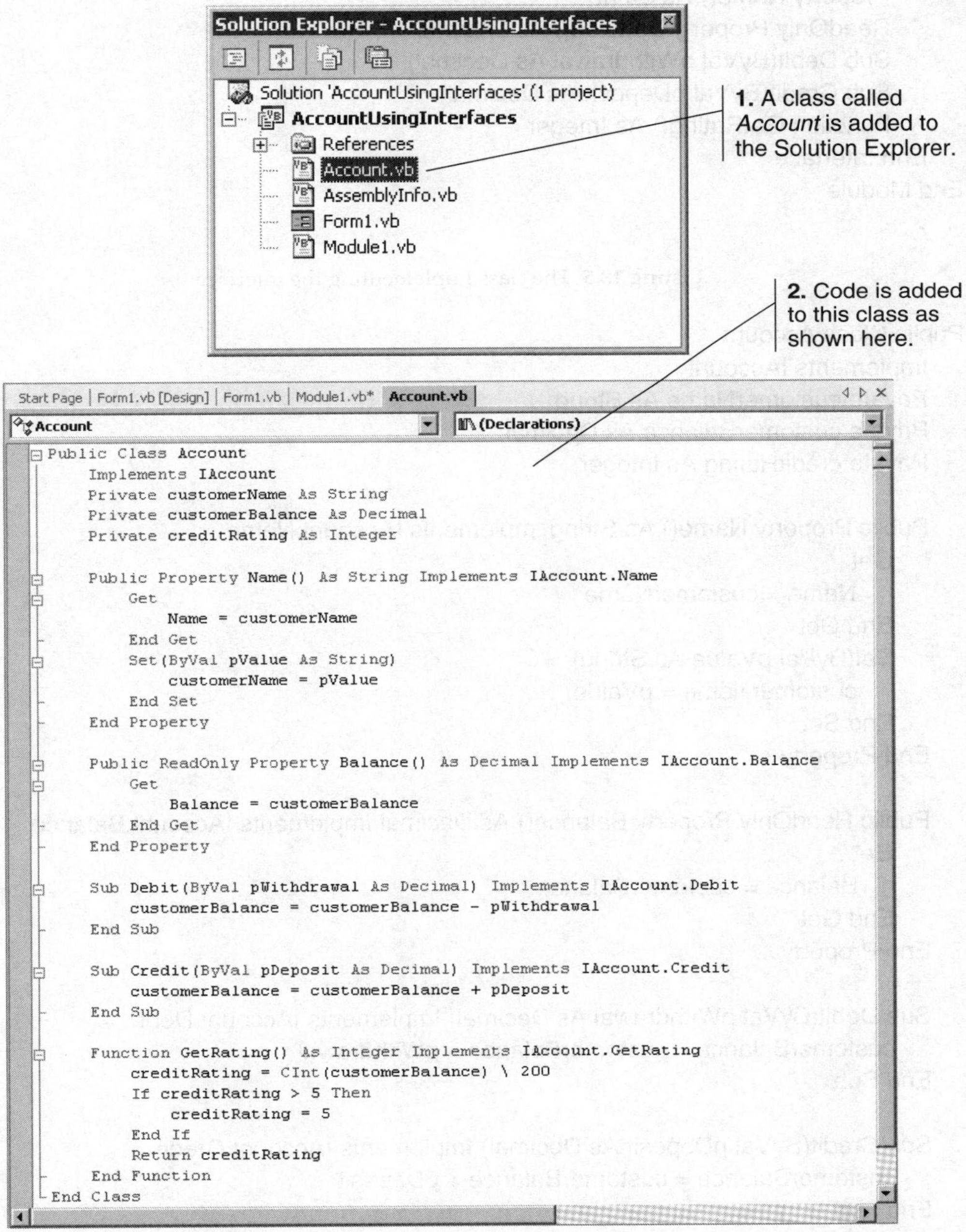
Solution Explorer - AccountUsingInterfaces
Solution 'AccountUsingInterfaces' (1 project)
AccountUsingInterfaces
References
Account.vb
AssemblyInfo.vb
Form1.vb
Module1.vb
1. A class called Account is added to the Solution Explorer.
2. Code is added to this class as shown here.
Start Page | Form1.vb [Design] | Form1.vb | Module1.vb* | Account.vb
Account
(Declarations)
Public Class Account
Implements IAccount
Private customerName As String
Private customerBalance As Decimal
Private creditRating As Integer
Public Property Name() As String Implements IAccount.Name
Get
Name = customerName
End Get
Set(ByVal pValue As String)
customerName = pValue
End Set
End Property
Public ReadOnly Property Balance() As Decimal Implements IAccount.Balance
Get
Balance = customerBalance
End Get
End Property
Sub Debit(ByVal pWithdrawal As Decimal) Implements IAccount.Debit
customerBalance = customerBalance - pWithdrawal
End Sub
Sub Credit(ByVal pDeposit As Decimal) Implements IAccount.Credit
customerBalance = customerBalance + pDeposit
End Sub
Function GetRating() As Integer Implements IAccount.GetRating
creditRating = CInt(customerBalance) \ 200
If creditRating > 5 Then
creditRating = 5
End If
Return creditRating
End Function
End Class

Listing 18.4 shows the code for the interface and Listing 18.5 shows the code for the class that uses the interface.

Listing 18.4 The interface.

```
Module Module1
    Interface IAccount
        Property Name() As String
        ReadOnly Property Balance() As Decimal
        Sub Debit(ByVal pWithdrawal As Decimal)
        Sub Credit(ByVal pDeposit As Decimal)
        Function GetRating() As Integer
    End Interface
End Module
```

Listing 18.5 The class implementing the interface.

```
Public Class Account
    Implements IAccount
    Private customerName As String
    Private customerBalance As Decimal
    Private creditRating As Integer

    Public Property Name() As String Implements IAccount.Name
        Get
            Name = customerName
        End Get
        Set(ByVal pValue As String)
            customerName = pValue
        End Set
    End Property

    Public ReadOnly Property Balance() As Decimal Implements IAccount.Balance
        Get
            Balance = customerBalance
        End Get
    End Property

    Sub Debit(ByVal pWithdrawal As Decimal) Implements IAccount.Debit
        customerBalance = customerBalance – pWithdrawal
    End Sub

    Sub Credit(ByVal pDeposit As Decimal) Implements IAccount.Credit
        customerBalance = customerBalance + pDeposit
    End Sub
```

Listing 18.5 (cont.)

```
Function GetRating() As Integer Implements IAccount.GetRating
    creditRating = CInt(customerBalance) \ 200
    If creditRating > 5 Then
        creditRating = 5
    End If
    Return creditRating
End Function
End Class
```

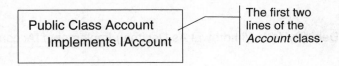

Public Class Account
Implements IAccount

The first two lines of the *Account* class.

The first two lines of the class define the name of the class as *Account* and show that this class intends to implement the behaviours of the Interface *IAccount*. The second line indicates that the class *Account* implements the interface *IAccount*. The class has **not** inherited from the Interface, what has happened is that the *Account* class has entered into a **contract** with the *IAccount* interface. This contract requires that the class supply the program statements for each of the 'method types' listed by the Interface *IAccount*.

We will look at how one aspect of this contract is implemented, namely the function *GetRating*. The code for this function is listed below using line numbers.

```
1.  Function GetRating() As Integer Implements IAccount.GetRating

2.      creditRating = CInt(customerBalance) \ 200
3.      If creditRating > 5 Then
4.          creditRating = 5
5.      End If
6.      Return creditRating
7.  End Function
```

Line 1: This is the signature of the function that corresponds to the last line defined in the interface as shown by the double-headed arrow. At the end of the signature is the keyword *Implements* followed by *IAccount.GetRating*. This specifies the link between the implementation of the function method in the class and its 'listing' in the interface.

```
Interface IAccount
    Property Name() As String
    ReadOnly Property Balance() As Decimal
    Sub Debit(ByVal pWithdrawal As Decimal)
    Sub Credit(ByVal pDeposit As Decimal)
    Function GetRating() As Integer
End Interface
```

431

Lines 2 to 6: These are the program statements that implement the function. You have seen these actual lines of code in a different context in Chapter 16, therefore they will not be described again here.

Line 7: This ends the Function Method definition.

NOTE: Every definition of a 'function type' declared in the class *Account* has at the end its first line the keyword *Implements*, the name of the Interface, and the member being implemented. Shown below is another such relationship as indicated by the double-headed arrow line.

```
Sub Debit(ByVal pWithdrawal As Decimal) Implements IAccount.Debit

      customerBalance = customerBalance – pWithdrawal
      End Sub
    Interface IAccount
      Property Name() As String
      ReadOnly Property Balance() As Decimal
      Sub Debit(ByVal pWithdrawal As Decimal)
      Sub Credit(ByVal pDeposit As Decimal)
      Function GetRating() As Integer
    End Interface
```

This 'describes' what part of the interface is being implemented.

NOTE: Before you move on, inspect Listing 18.5 to ensure that you identify all of the other relationships between the class members and the interface members shown in Listing 18.4.

You should also take note of the three class level variables declared within the class – these were necessary in order for the class to implement its behaviours.

NOTE: Of course, now we have a class that implements an interface we need to test the class. This will involve creating an instance of the class and using all of the members it has.

Testing the *Account* class (and hence the interface *IAccount*)

A simple test is used that invokes each of the methods of the *Account* class – again it is more of a demonstration of the functionality of the code rather than a proper test harness.

To perform the tests attach the code of Listing 18.6 to a button on a Windows form.

Listing 18.6 Testing the *Account* class and *IAccount* interface.

```
Protected Sub Button1_Click(ByVal sender As Object, ByVal e As System.EventArgs)

    Dim myAccount As Account

    myAccount = New Account()
    myAccount.Name = "Cara Jones"
    myAccount.Credit(700D)
    myAccount.Debit(300D)
    MessageBox.Show(myAccount.Name & " has a balance of " & _
    CStr(myAccount.Balance) & " and a credit rating of " & _
    CStr(myAccount.GetRating()))
End Sub
```

Listing 18.6 creates an instance of the *Account* class using the following line of code:

$$myAccount = New Account()$$

It then assigns the string "Cara Jones" to the name property of the object:

$$myAccount.Name = "Cara Jones"$$

It then adds £700 to the balance of the object using the *Credit* method:

$$myAccount.Credit(700D)$$

It then reduces the balance of the object by £300 (to £400) using the *Debit* method:

$$myAccount.Debit(300D)$$

From the definition of the interface it can be seen that a balance of £400 gives a credit rating of 2. Clicking on the button to run this code gives the messagebox shown in Figure 18.12.

Figure 18.12 The output from the 'test' program.

```
MessageBox.Show (myAccount.Name & " has a balance of " & _
CStr (myAccount.Balance) & " and a credit rataing of " &
CStr (myAccount.GetRating ( ) ) )
```

Cara Jones has a balance of 400 and a credit rating of 2

OK

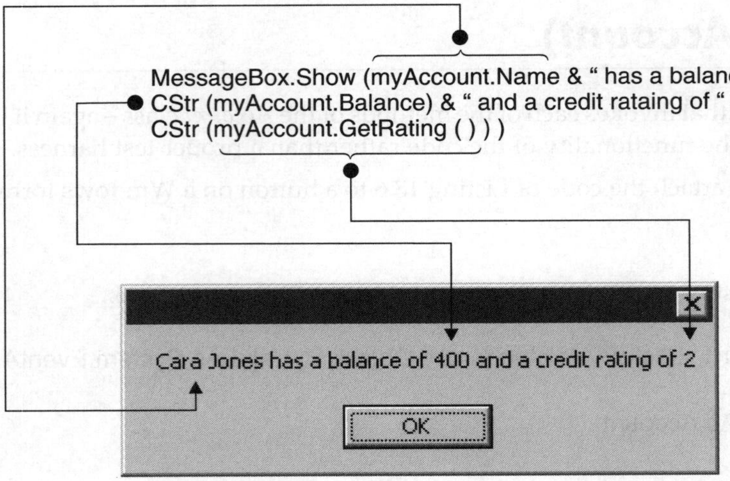

PRACTICAL ACTIVITY 18.3

Implement the program as represented by Listings 18.4, 18.5 and 18.6. Ensure that the output is the same as shown by Figure 18.12.

PRACTICAL ACTIVITY 18.4

Listing 18.5 showed how a class implemented the *IAccount* interface. Create another implementation of the same *IAccount* interface using a different class called *RipOffAccount*.

This class will implement the following changes to the methods used in the *Account* class. Every debit and credit made is subject to a £10 charge. A credit rating of one is given for every £100 (as compared to £200 for the Account class) of the balance up to a maximum of 5.

The solution and appropriate test program is shown by Listings 18.7 and 18.8.

The expected output from the test program is shown in Figure 18.13.

Listing 18.7 The *RipoffAccount*.

```
Public Class RipOffAccount
    Implements IAccount
    Private customerName As String
    Private customerBalance As Decimal
    Private creditRating As Integer
```

Listing 18.7 (cont.)

```
Public Property Name() As String Implements IAccount.Name
    Get
        Name = customerName
    End Get
    Set(ByVal Value As String)
        customerName = Value
    End Set
End Property

Public ReadOnly Property Balance() As Decimal Implements IAccount.Balance
    Get
        Balance = customerBalance
    End Get
End Property

Sub Debit(ByVal pWithdrawal As Decimal) Implements IAccount.Debit
    customerBalance = customerBalance – pWithdrawal – 10
End Sub

Sub Credit(ByVal pDeposit As Decimal) Implements IAccount.Credit
    customerBalance = customerBalance + pDeposit – 10
End Sub

Function GetRating() As Integer Implements IAccount.GetRating
    creditRating = CInt(customerBalance) \ 100
    If creditRating > 5 Then
        creditRating = 5
    End If
    Return creditRating
End Function
End Class
```

Listing 18.8 The 'testing' program.

```
Private Sub Button2_Click(ByVal sender As System.Object, ByVal e As
System.EventArgs) Handles Button2.Click
    Dim myAccount As RipOffAccount
```

435

Listing 18.8 (cont.)

```
myAccount = New RipOffAccount()
myAccount.Name = "Cara Jones"
myAccount.Credit(700D)
myAccount.Debit(300D)
MessageBox.Show(myAccount.Name & " has a balance of " & _
CStr(myAccount.Balance) & " and a credit rating of " & _
CStr(myAccount.GetRating()))
End Sub
```

Figure 18.13 The output from the 'test' program.

Cara Jones has a balance of 380 and a credit rating of 3

OK

The test program of Listing 18.8 (that tests the *RipOffAccount* class) performs exactly the same tasks and in the same order and with the same data as the program that tested the *Account* class. However, the outputs shown by Figures 18.12 and 18.13 are different because the classes have implemented the interface in different ways.

The *Credit* and *Debit* methods of the *RipOffAccount* class both subtract £10 from the balance of the account as well as perform the crediting and debiting of the account balance. This is highlighted below:

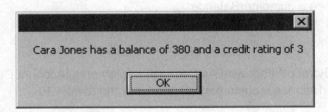

$$customerBalance = customerBalance + pDeposit - 10$$

> Reduce balance by £10 – the charge levied by the bank for every debit and credit

$$customerBalance = customerBalance - pWithdrawal - 10$$

The code used within the *GetRating* method for the *Account* and *RipoffAccount* are shown in Figure 18.14 to allow for direct comparison. You should observe that the credit rating for the *Account* class is based on every £200 in the account, whereas for the *RipoffAccount* it is based on every £100 of the balance.

Figure 18.14 Comparison of the *GetRating* method as they appear in the different classes.

```
Function GetRating() As Integer Implements IAccount.GetRating

    creditRating = CInt(customerBalance) \ 200
    If creditRating > 5 Then
        creditRating = 5
    End If
    Return creditRating
End Function
```

```
Function GetRating() As Integer Implements IAccount.GetRating

    creditRating = CInt(customerBalance) \ 100
    If creditRating > 5 Then
        creditRating = 5
    End If
    Return creditRating
End Function
```

PRACTICAL ACTIVITY 18.5

Add another class to the solution that implements the *IAccount* interface so that every credit is not charged, but every debit is charged £20.

Also base the credit rating on multiples of £400 and have a credit rating from 0 to 9.

Call the class *SilverAccount* and test it by adding another button and associated event handling procedure.

PRACTICAL ACTIVITY 18.6

Create another interface that defines the getting and setting of a customer's name and a customer's address.

Build a class that implements this interface and the *IAccount* interface. Test this class as appropriate.

Object composition

Inheritance and Interfaces are not the only option open to a designer and programmer. You can instead use a technique called **aggregation**. For example, to create a *PlatinumBankAccount* class that allows its instance (i.e. objects) to use all the code in the *BankAccount* class you declare and create an instance of a *BankAccount* object in your

PlatinumBankAccount class. You can publicly expose the internal *BankAccount* or you can keep it private. Extra members are added to the *PlatinumBankAccount* class as normal.

If *BankAccount* has a *Credit* method, your *PlatinumBankAccount* can also have a *Credit* method that simply invokes the Credit method of the private *BankAccount* instance. This technique of passing along method calls (or property calls) to an internal object is often called **delegation**.

Combining composition with interface implementation

The use of object composition and delegation does not automatically provide the polymorphism achieved with derived classes. If your *PlatinumBankAccount* object simply contains a *BankAccount* object rather than being derived from one then it is not possible to pass a *PlatinumBankAccount* object to a method that has a parameter of type *BankAccount*.

It is possible to get code reuse and polymorphism without the design headaches of inheritance and this is achieved by combining object composition and delegation with interface implementation. For example, create an *IBankAccount* interface that your *PlatinumBankAccount* implements. This gives the option of delegating to the methods and properties of the contained *BankAccount* object. Or as required the *PlatinumBankAccount* can independently implement some of the methods and properties in the *IBankAccount* interface instead of delegating to the *BankAccount* object – which is similar to overriding in derived classes.

> **NOTE:** The combination of object composition and delegation with interface implementation is often the first choice of many designers and programmers when there is a need to extend or specialize the functionality of classes.

19 Polymorphism

Polymorphism, from the Greek meaning many forms, refers to the ability to define multiple classes with functionally different, yet identically named methods that can be used interchangeably by code at runtime.

> **NOTE**: Some of the mechanics for implementing polymorphism have been covered in earlier chapters but the term polymorphism and its description was not particularly emphasized. This was deliberate in order to dedicate this chapter to the description of this important technique.

Polymorphic behaviour can take two forms:

- Method overloading
- Method overriding.

Method overloading enables programmers to specify different types of parameters in the message being sent to an object.

Method overriding enables programmers to allow a derived class to alter behaviour that it inherited from its base class.

Polymorphic methods are designed to suit the needs of individual objects. A polymorphic message is a generic message that can be understood by a number of related classes. The name of the message sent to an instance of each class is the same, but the way it is implemented depends on the object it is messaging and on the parameters included in the message.

Two other ways for accomplishing polymorphism are through the mechanism of:

- Inheritance-based polymorphism
- Interface-based polymorphism.

> **NOTE**: Each will be dealt with in turn but before we look at how VB .NET implements polymorphism let's first look at the nature of polymorphism and why it is a useful mechanism.

In non-object-oriented languages (such as C) programmers need to create two separate functions with different names to perform the same task on two different entities. This approach results in complex and redundant code. The use of polymorphism allows a programmer to avoid this problem. Polymorphism allows a programmer to define a generic message that is implemented by a number of related classes.

Consider the case of a software system that simulates the behaviour of animals. Every animal within the system can receive a message that informs them that that they have to move. Of course the way in which an animal moves will be dependent upon the type of animal and upon the type of message.

Using inheritance programmers can define a class hierarchy chain so that all objects in the chain have the same fundamental members. Consider the hierarchy shown in Figure 19.1. All objects in this hierarchy are able to move but each animal will move in a different way. For example the bird flies, the dog walks and the fish swims. Regardless of the way each animal moves they all respond to a generic message *Move* (i.e. they all have a method that is invoked by the *Move* message). *Move* is referred to as a polymorphic message, and objects of these different classes will respond to this *Move* message in different ways.

Figure 19.1 An animal hierarchy.

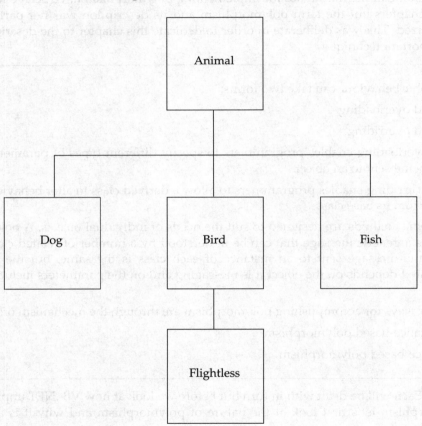

Object-oriented programs consist of communicating objects and these objects communicate using messages. Consider the case of a message that asks the bird to move. The bird could be asked to move a prescribed distance in a certain direction. This would be achieved by sending a move message with two parameters as illustrated by the part collaboration diagram of Figure 19.2.

Figure 19.2 Moving a robin.

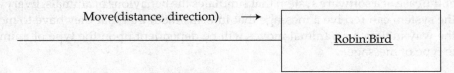

Figure 19.3 shows another part collaboration diagram showing a *Move* message to a robin, this time the parameter is a *Cat* object. Under these conditions the robin would fly away.

Figure 19.3 Moving a robin when a cat is about.

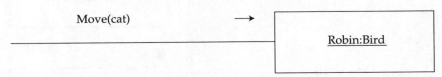

Figure 19.4 shows another part collaboration diagram showing a *Move* message to a robin, this time the parameter is a *Seeds* object. Under these conditions the robin would move towards the seeds to eat them.

Figure 19.4 Feeding a robin.

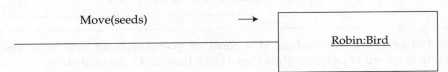

In all of the three cases shown by Figures 19.2, 19.3 and 19.4 the **same** message *Move* resulted in different object behaviour dependent upon the parameters included with the message.

This form of polymorphism is achieved using **overloading**, described in previous chapters (refer to Chapter 17).

> **NOTE**: To overload a method programmers declare another version with the same name but different parameters and the inclusion of the keyword overloads (again refer to Chapter 17).
>
> Of course this type of polymorphism was created within the class *Bird*. Here there is a method of the same name (but with different parameters) for every kind of bird movement. Which of the moves is implemented is dependent upon the parameters sent with the message.

Consider the scenario where a derived class of *Bird* is defined for flightless birds (as shown by Figure 19.1). Sending a flightless bird a *Move* message with cat as a parameter will not make it fly!

However, there will be much in common between the *Flightless* class and the *Bird* class. The *Flightless* derived class would naturally like to inherit from the *Bird* class and does; however, the method within the *Bird* class responsible for causing the bird to fly when a cat is around is **overridden** in the *Flightless* class.

Figure 19.5 shows part collaboration diagrams that illustrate *Move* methods to objects of different classes within the same hierarchy. Although they receive the identical message in terms of name and parameter they respond in different ways, the robin will fly away and the chicken will presumably run like hell!

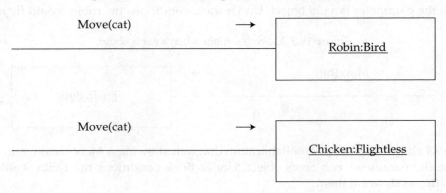

Figure 19.5 How birds respond when a cat is around.

Move(cat) ⟶ | Robin:Bird |

Move(cat) ⟶ | Chicken:Flightless |

NOTE: Examples of overriding have been covered in Chapter 17.

NOTE: Put crudely, overloading is a form of polymorphism within a class and overriding is a form of polymorphism between a base and a derived class.

QUESTION 19.1 (REVISION)
What would happen if the robin and chicken were thrown seeds?

Inheritance-based polymorphism

This form of polymorphism is achieved using **overriding** and there have been examples of this in earlier chapters.

Important keywords when using inheritance

Table 19.1 lists and describes inheritance modifiers that support inheritance (and polymorphism).

Table 19.1 Inheritance modifiers.

Keyword	Description
Inherits	Specifies the base class
NotInheritable	Prevents programmers from using the class as a base class
MustInherit	This specifies that the class is intended to be used as an abstract class (base class) only. It is **not** possible to create an instance of a *MustInherit* class directly.

Table 19.2 lists and describes keywords used when overriding function methods.

Table 19.2 Keywords for overriding when using function methods.

Keyword	Description
Overridable	Indicates that the function method can be overridden by an identically named method in a derived class.
Overrides	Indicates that this function method overrides an identically named method in a base class. The number and data types of the arguments, and the data type of the return value, must match those of the base class method.
NotOverridable	Indicates that this function method cannot be overridden in a derived class.
MustOverride	Indicates that this function method is not implemented in this class, and must be implemented in a derived class for that class to be creatable.

Table 19.3 lists and describes keywords used when overriding property procedures.

Table 19.3 Keywords for overriding when using property procedures.

Keyword	Description
Overridable	Indicates that this property can be overridden by an identically named property in a derived class
Overrides	Indicates that this property overrides an identically named property in a base class.
NotOverridable	Indicates that this property cannot be overridden in a derived class.
MustOverride	Indicates that this property is not implemented in this class, and must be implemented in a derived class for that class to be creatable.

Table 19.4 lists and describes keywords used when overriding methods (i.e. **Sub** procedures).

Table 19.4 Keywords for overriding when using Sub methods.

Keyword	Description
Overridable	Indicates that this method (Sub procedure) can be overridden by an identically named method in a derived class.
Overrides	Indicates that this method overrides an identically named method in a base class. The number and data types of the arguments must match those of the base class method.
NotOverridable	Indicates that this method cannot be overridden in a derived class.
MustOverride	Indicates that this method is not implemented in this class and must be implemented in a derived class for that class to be creatable.

Table 19.5 describes the keyword *MyBase*.

Table 19.5 *MyBase*.

Keyword	Description
MyBase	The *MyBase* keyword 'behaves like' an object reference variable by referring to the base class of the current instance of a class.
	MyBase is commonly used to access base class members that are overridden in a derived class. In particular, *MyBase.New* is used to explicitly call a **base** class constructor from a **derived** class constructor.
	Note: It is invalid to use *MyBase* to call *MustOverride* base methods.
	The code segment in Listing 19.1 illustrates a typical use of the keyword *MyBase*.

Listing 19.1 A typical use of the keyword *MyBase*.

```
Public Class TheDerivedClassName
    Inherits TheBaseClassName

    Public Overrides Function myFunction(ByVal pX as Integer) As Integer
        Return MyBase.myFunction(pX) * 4
    End Function
End Class
```

The function method *myFunction* in the base class takes an integer as an input parameter and processes it in some way and returns an integer value. The *myFunction* shown in Listing 19.1 overrides the original in the base class. Here the mechanics of this overriding function invokes the overridden function *myFunction* in the base class and multiples its return value by four before it then returns it to the object invoking the overriding function shown in Listing 19.1.

Interchange ability of objects

Interchangeable objects are another important form of polymorphism supported by inheritance. An object reference of a base class can be assigned an object of one of its derived classes and therefore take on the behaviour of the derived class. Consequently, the behaviour of the base class object is able to change its behaviour to any of its derived classes.

Consider a computer game consisting of wizards that have various magical abilities. All wizards are able to fly away from trouble, make themselves invisible and repel their enemies. 'Proud wizards' can also fly and make themselves invisible but they are able to capture their enemies. 'High wizards' can also fly and become invisible, however, they are able to transport their enemies to a dungeon to await trial. The hierarchy diagram of Figure 19.6 shows the relationship between these wizards.

Figure 19.6 Hierarchy diagram for wizards.

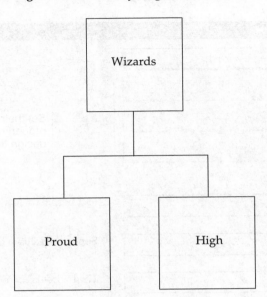

It can be seen from the hierarchy diagram of Figure 19.6 that a *Proud* and *High* wizard inherit from the *Wizard* class. These derived classes will obviously inherit from the *Wizard* class. They are able to add behaviour over and above the *Wizard* class as well as override behaviours of the *Wizard* class (this type of relationship has been covered in previous chapters). However, another relationship exists between these classes that allows for another form of polymorphism.

An instance (i.e. object reference) of the *Wizard* class can be assigned an instance (i.e. object reference) of any of its derived classes. After the assignment it takes on the behaviour of its derived class. So an instance of the *Wizard* class can exhibit the behaviour of a wizard and then the behaviour of a Proud wizard and then the behaviour of a High wizard. It can then return to exhibit the behaviour of the wizard again.

> **NOTE**: This ability of an object to change behaviour illustrates another example of polymorphism and this time this interchange of objects and hence change in behaviour in response to a message occurs at runtime.

The GUI of Figure 19.7 and Listings 19.2 to 19.5 illustrate the polymorphic relationship between the classes shown in Figure 19.6.

Clicking onto the Create Wizards button creates an instance of each type of wizard. Following this click, by a click on the Attack button displays the action carried out by each wizard in the three labels.

Figure 19.8 illustrates the GUI after the Create Wizards button and the Attack button have been clicked. The first wizard is an instance of the *Wizard* class; the second wizard is an instance of the *Proud* class and finally the third wizard is an instance of the *High* class. Figure 19.9 shows the Solution Explorer for the implementation of the wizards program.

445

Figure 19.7 The GUI used to illustrate the polymorphic relationship between the wizards.

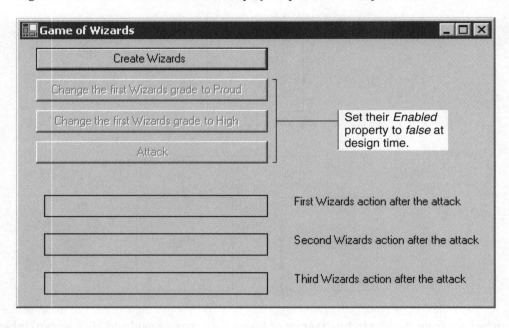

Figure 19.8 The state of the GUI after all three wizards have attacked their enemy.

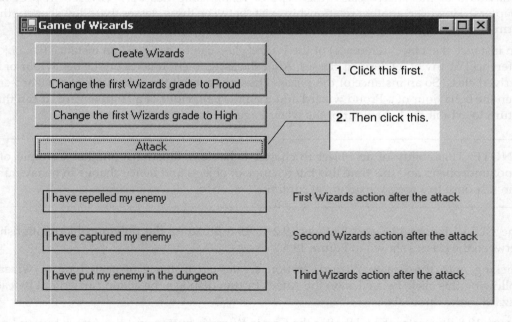

Let's consider the code responsible for performing the actions illustrated by Figure 19.8.

Figure 19.9 shows the Solution Explorer for this demonstration of object Interchange.

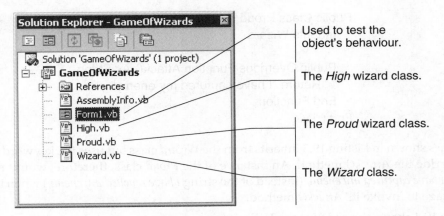

Used to test the object's behaviour.

The *High* wizard class.

The *Proud* wizard class.

The *Wizard* class.

The code for the *Wizard* class is shown in Listing 19.2.

Listing 19.2 The *Wizard* class.

```
Public Class Wizard
    Public Sub Fly()
        'appropriate code in here
    End Sub

    Public Sub Invisible()
        'appropriate code in here
    End Sub

    Public Overridable Function Attack() As String
        Return "I have repelled my enemy"
    End Function
End Class
```

Listing 19.2 has three methods: *Fly()*, *Invisible()* and *Attack()*. The first two methods do not contain code just comments indicating where appropriate code should be placed (this will not affect the demonstration of the interchangeable ability of objects).

It can be seen from Listing 19.2 that the *Attack()* method returns a string that indicates what has happened to the enemy (i.e. *I have repelled my enemy*). As usual this method will be invoked by an appropriate message. It can also be seen that this method has been 'marked' as *Overridable*. Which means that any derived class can override this method and offer different behaviour.

Listing 19.3 shows the code for the *Proud* class.

Listing 19.3 The *Proud* class.

```
Public Class Proud
    Inherits Wizard

    Public Overrides Function Attack() As String
        Return "I have captured my enemy"
    End Function
End Class
```

The class shown in Listing 19.3 inherits from the *Wizard* class but uses the keyword *Overrides* to override the *Attack()* method. An instance of the *Proud* class, therefore, would return the string *I have captured my enemy* (instead of the string *I have repelled my enemy*) when it receives a message to invoke its *Attack()* method.

Listing 19.4 shows the code for the *High* class.

Listing 19.4 The *High* class.

```
Public Class High
    Inherits Wizard

    Public Overrides Function Attack() As String
        Return "I have put my enemy in the dungeon"
    End Function
End Class
```

The *High* class also inherits from the *Wizard* class and overrides the *Attack()* method. Consequently, an instance of the *High* class would return the string *I have put my enemy in the dungeon* (instead of the string *I have repelled my enemy*) when it receives a message to invoke its *Attack()* method.

Listing 19.5 shows the code for the *Form1* class used to demonstrate the interchange ability of objects.

Listing 19.5 The code for the *Form* class.

```
Private firstWizard As Wizard
Private secondWizard As Proud
Private thirdWizard As High

Private Sub btnCreateWizards_Click(ByVal sender As System.Object, ByVal e As _
System.EventArgs) Handles btnCreateWizards.Click

    firstWizard = New Wizard()
    secondWizard = New Proud()
    thirdWizard = New High()
```

Listing 19.5 (cont.)

```
        btnChangeToProud.Enabled = True
        btnChangeToHigh.Enabled = True
        btnAttack.Enabled = True
End Sub

Private Sub btnChangeToProud_Click(ByVal sender As System.Object, ByVal e As _
System.EventArgs) Handles btnChangeToProud.Click

        firstWizard = secondWizard
End Sub

Private Sub btnChangeToHigh_Click(ByVal sender As System.Object, ByVal e As _
System.EventArgs) Handles btnChangeToHigh.Click

        firstWizard = thirdWizard
End Sub

Private Sub btnAttack_Click(ByVal sender As System.Object, ByVal e As _
System.EventArgs) Handles btnAttack.Click

        lblFirst.Text = firstWizard.Attack
        lblSecond.Text = secondWizard.Attack
        lblThird.Text = thirdWizard.Attack
End Sub
```

The listing appears again with line numbers in Figure 19.10 and is followed by a description of the code.

Figure 19.10 The listing with line numbers.

```
1.   Private firstWizard As Wizard
2.   Private secondWizard As Proud
3.   Private thirdWizard As High
4.   Private Sub btnCreateWizards_Click(ByVal sender As System.Object, ByVal e As _
     System.EventArgs) Handles btnCreateWizards.Click

5.       firstWizard = New Wizard()
6.       secondWizard = New Proud()
7.       thirdWizard = New High()
8.       btnChangeToProud.Enabled = True
9.       btnChangeToHigh.Enabled = True
10.      btnAttack.Enabled = True
11.  End Sub
```

Figure 19.10 (cont.)

12. Private Sub btnChangeToProud_Click(ByVal sender As System.Object, ByVal e As _
    System.EventArgs) Handles btnChangeToProud.Click

13.   firstWizard = secondWizard
14. End Sub

15. Private Sub btnChangeToHigh_Click(ByVal sender As System.Object, ByVal e As _
    System.EventArgs) Handles btnChangeToHigh.Click

16.   firstWizard = thirdWizard
17. End Sub

18. Private Sub btnAttack_Click(ByVal sender As System.Object, ByVal e As _
    System.EventArgs) Handles btnAttack.Click

19.   lblFirst.Text = firstWizard.Attack
20.   lblSecond.Text = secondWizard.Attack
21.   lblThird.Text = thirdWizard.Attack
22. End Sub

Lines 1 to 3: These lines declare object references to each type of Wizard and they are placed in the declaration area of the code window for the form. As they are declared within the declaration area they can be accessed by all code within an instance of the *Form1* class.

Lines 4 to 11: These lines form the event handling procedure attached to the Create Wizards button.

- **Line 5** creates an instance of the *Wizard* class.
- **Line 6** creates an instance of the *Proud* class.
- **Line 7** creates an instance of the *High* class.
- **Lines 8 to 10** enable all the other buttons (their *Enable* property was set to false at design time – why is this the case?).

Lines 12 to 14: These lines form the event handling procedure attached to the **Change the first wizards grade to Proud** button.

- **Line 13** assigns the object reference for the instance of the *Proud* class to the object reference of the instance of the *Wizard* class. After this assignment there are **two** object references to the **same** instance of the *Proud* class. The *firstWizard* now has the behaviour of the *secondWizard*.

Lines 15 to 17: These lines form the event handling procedure attached to the **Change the first wizards grade to High** button.

- **Line 16** assigns the object reference for the instance of the *High* class to the object reference of the instance of the *Wizard* class. After this assignment there are **two** object references to the **same** instance of the *High* class. The *firstWizard* now has the behaviour of the *thirdWizard*.

Lines 18 to 22: These lines form the event handler attached to Attack button.

- **Line 19** sends the message *Attack()* to the object it references and a string is returned to be displayed in a label. Of course to which object the message is sent depends on which object *firstWizard* refers to. We have just seen that clicking on to a couple of the buttons can change this object reference.

- **Line 20** sends the message *Attack()* to the instance of the *Proud* class and the string *I have captured my enemy* is returned to be displayed in a label.

- **Line 21** sends the message *Attack()* to the instance of the *High* class and the string *I have put my enemy in the dungeon* is returned to be displayed in a label.

> **NOTE**: Line 19 illustrates polymorphism in action. This line will return a string to be displayed in a label. Of course, which string is returned will depend upon which object the reference *firstWizard* 'is pointing to' at the time. It can be pointing to an instance of the class *Wizard*, an instance of the class *Proud* or an instance of the class *High*. The main point is that the **different** response obtained will result from the **same message**, namely, *firstWizard.Attack()*.

Figure 19.8 showed the GUI when the Create Wizards button was clicked followed by the Attack button.

Figure 19.11 shows the GUI when the Create Wizards button is clicked, then the Change the first Wizards grade to Proud button followed by the Attack button.

Figure 19.12 shows the GUI when the Create Wizards button is clicked, then the Change the first Wizards grade to High button followed by the Attack button.

Figure 19.11 An example runtime.

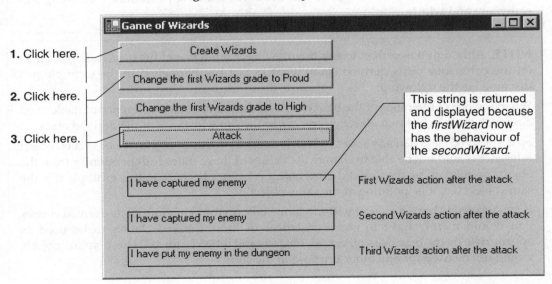

Figure 19.12 Another example runtime.

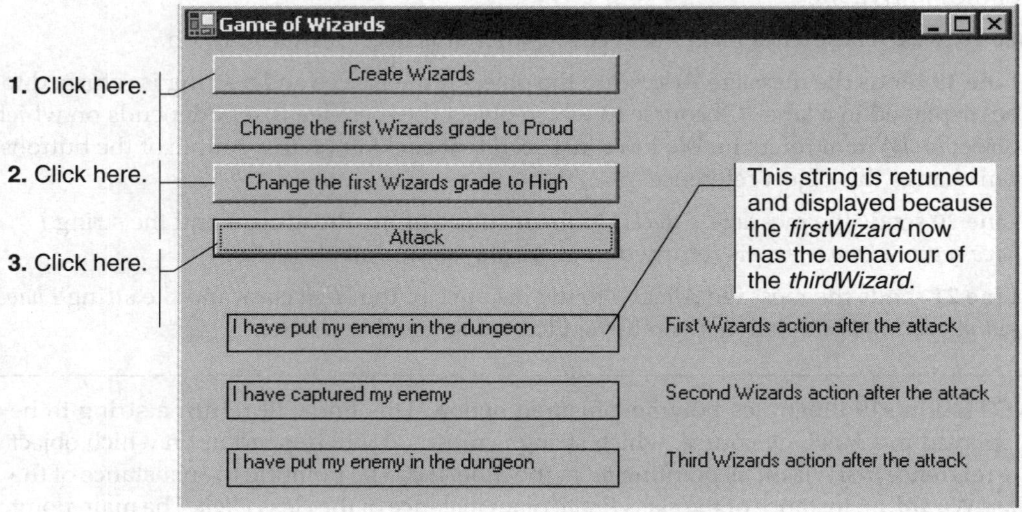

PRACTICAL ACTIVITY 19.1

Implement the program as represented by the GUI of Figure 19.7 and Listings 19.2 to 19.5. Test the working of the program as represented by the sequence of button clicks represented by Figures 19.8, 19.11 and 19.12.

PRACTICAL ACTIVITY 19.2 (DEVELOPMENT)

Add another button to the form developed for Practical Activity 19.1 and attach the following assignment statement to this button.

    secondWizard = thirdWizard

What happens when you attempt to run the event handing procedure containing this statement and why?

NOTE: Although it is correct to say that the object reference of the base class has taken on the behaviour of its derived class, what in fact has happened in the example just discussed is the following:

When the object reference of the base class is assigned the object reference of its derived classes there is in fact two object references to the same instance of the derived class.

So if a derived class had any states (which it does not in this example) the base class object reference would not be able to change the values of these states **independently** from the object 'pointed at' by the derived class object reference because in this example it is the same object (i.e. it is 'pointing at the same object').

If you wished to have a wizard within a game take on the behaviour of its derived classes you would merely have to create instances of these derived classes to be used as appropriate by the base class object reference as and when required. These 'spare' objects would not be used for any other purpose in the code.

Another example of inheritance-based polymorphism

Consider a program that is used to calculate purchase tax, which consists of a government tax and a local tax. Some goods are only charged a government tax but others are charged an additional local tax, i.e. a government tax plus a local tax.

The GUI for this program is shown in Figure 19.13 and the Solution Explorer is shown in Figure 19.14. The program listings are shown in Listings 19.6 and 19.7.

The code of Module1.vb, which contains the definition of three classes, is shown in Listing 19.6. The code attached to the Calculate Tax button is shown in Listing 19.7.

Figure 19.13 A GUI for calculating tax.

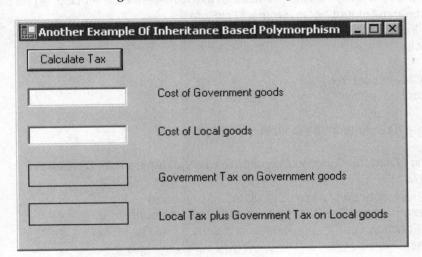

Figure 19.14 The Solution Explorer.

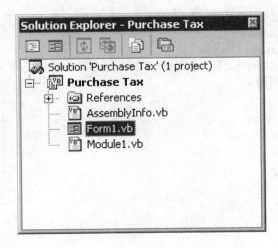

NOTE: A module is a handy way in which to declare more than one class. Of course each class could have been declared in its own file (the declaration of the constants would then have to be **shared** by a class).

Listing 19.6 The declaration of the three classes are highlighted by the shaded areas.

```
Module Module1
    Const cGovernmentTaxRate As Double = 0.1
    Const cLocalTaxRate As Double = 0.05

    Public Class BasicTax

        Public Overridable Function CalculateTax(ByVal pAmount As Double) As Double
            Return pAmount * cGovernmentTaxRate
        End Function
    End Class

    Public Class LocalTax
        Inherits BasicTax

        Private basicAmount As Double

        Public Overrides Function CalculateTax(ByVal pAmount As Double) As _
        Double
            basicAmount = MyBase.CalculateTax(pAmount)
            Return (cLocalTaxRate * pAmount) + basicAmount
        End Function
    End Class

    Public Class ObtainTax

        Public Function GetTax(ByVal pItem As BasicTax, ByVal pTotalCost As _
        Double) As Double
            Dim TotalTax As Double
            TotalTax = pItem.CalculateTax(pTotalCost)
            Return TotalTax
        End Function
    End Class
End Module
```

Note the parameter *pItem* is of type *BasicTax*, which is a class. In fact, it is the base class of the derived class *LocalTax*.

Listing 19.7 The button event handling procedure.

```
Private Sub btnCalculateTax_Click(ByVal sender As System.Object, ByVal e As _
System.EventArgs) Handles btnCalculateTax.Click
    Dim governmentItem As BasicTax
    Dim localItem As LocalTax
    Dim calcTheTax As ObtainTax
    Dim governmentCost As Double
    Dim localCost As Double

    governmentItem = New BasicTax()
    localItem = New LocalTax()
    calcTheTax = New ObtainTax()

    governmentCost = CDbl(txtGovernment.Text)
    localCost = CDbl(txtLocal.Text)

    lblGovernment.Text = "£" & CStr(calcTheTax.GetTax(governmentItem, _
    governmentCost))

    lblLocal.Text = "£" & CStr(calcTheTax.GetTax(localItem, localCost))
End Sub
```

Annotations on listing:
- Three object references to different classes. (Dim governmentItem As BasicTax / Dim localItem As LocalTax / Dim calcTheTax As ObtainTax)
- Creates three objects. (governmentItem = New BasicTax() / localItem = New LocalTax() / calcTheTax = New ObtainTax())

A typical runtime for this program is shown in Figure 19.15.

Figure 19.15 A typical runtime.

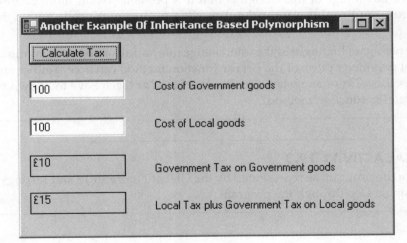

Another Example Of Inheritance Based Polymorphism

Calculate Tax

100 — Cost of Government goods

100 — Cost of Local goods

£10 — Government Tax on Government goods

£15 — Local Tax plus Government Tax on Local goods

NOTE: You are left to discover the workings of the program as suggested by Practical Activity 19.3. However, the section of the code exhibiting polymorphism is described next.

The last two program statements of Listing 19.7 both contain a message sent to the instance of the *ObtainTax* class (as represented by the object reference *calcTheTax*). Both of these messages are repeated below:

    calcTheTax.GetTax(governmentItem, governmentCost)

    calcTheTax.GetTax(localItem, localCost)

These messages invoke the *GetTax* function method, also repeated below:

```
Public Function GetTax(ByVal pItem As BasicTax, ByVal pTotalCost As Double) _
As Double

    Dim totalTax As Double

    totalTax = pItem.CalculateTax(pTotalCost)
    Return totalTax
End Function
```

The first **formal** parameter of this method is *pItem* declared *ByVal* and it is of type *BasicTax*.

BasicTax is a **base** class and *LocalTax* is a class **derived** from *BasicTax* (i.e. it inherits from *BasicTax* – refer to Listing 19.6) Consequently, the **formal** parameter *pItem* is able to accept any **actual** parameter that is an object of the class *BasicTax* or any object of the classes derived from *BasicTax*. This is precisely what it does because the **actual** parameter *governmentItem* is an instance of the *BasicTax* class and the **actual** parameter *localItem* is an instance of the *LocalTax* class (which, remember, is derived from *BasicTax*).

> **NOTE**: The advantage of this design is that it is possible to add more classes that are derived from the *BasicTax* class without needing to change the code within the *GetTax* method.
>
> This code has again highlighted the interchangeable nature of objects at runtime because the formal parameter *pItem* of the *GetTax* function method can accept either an instance of the Class *BasicTax* or an instance of the class *LocalTax* (each have their own version of the *CalculateTax* function method).

PRACTICAL ACTIVITY 19.3

Implement the program as represented by the GUI of Figure 19.15 and Listings 19.6 and 19.7 and single step through the program.

PRACTICAL ACTIVITY 19.4

Redo the program developed during Practical Activity 19.3. This time, however, do not use a module to 'group' all of the classes in one file, instead put each class in its own file.

Interface-based polymorphism

Polymorphism is achieved with interfaces by creating an interface and implementing it in different ways in several classes. It is then possible to invoke a method within these classes using the same message; consequently, there is a different response to the same message.

Again consider a program that is used to calculate purchase tax, which again consists of a government tax and a local tax. Some goods are only charged a government tax (10%) but others are charged only a local tax (15%).

The GUI for this program is shown in Figure 19.16 and the Solution Explorer is shown in Figure 19.17. The program listings are shown in Listings 19.8 and 19.9.

Figure 19.16 A GUI for calculating the tax.

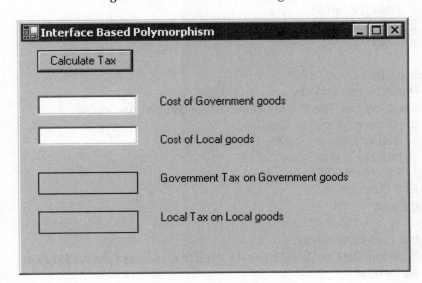

Figure 19.17 The Solution Explorer.

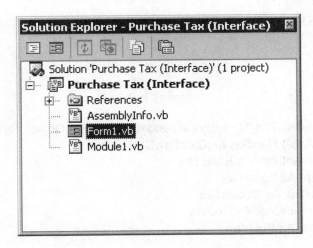

Listing 19.8

```
Module Module1
    Public Interface IFindTax
        Function CalcTax(ByVal ItemCost As Double) As Double
    End Interface

    Public Class BasicTax
        Implements IFindTax
        Function CalcTax(ByVal pItemCost As Double) As Double _
        Implements IFindTax.CalcTax
            Dim totalTax As Double
            totalTax = pItemCost * 0.1
            Return totalTax
        End Function
    End Class

    Public Class LocalTax
        Implements IFindTax
        Function CalcTax(ByVal pItemCost As Double) As Double _
        Implements IFindTax.CalcTax
            Dim totalTax As Double
            totalTax = pItemCost * 0.15
            Return totalTax
        End Function
    End Class

    Public Class ObtainTax
        Function GetTax(ByVal pTax As IFindTax, ByVal pCost As Double) _
        As Double
            Dim totalTax As Double
            totalTax = pTax.CalcTax(pCost)
            Return totalTax
        End Function
    End Class
End Module
```

Listing 19.9

```
Private Sub btnCalcTax_Click(ByVal sender As System.Object, ByVal e As _
System.EventArgs) Handles btnCalcTax.Click
    Dim governmentItem As BasicTax
    Dim localItem As LocalTax
    Dim calcTheTax As ObtainTax
    Dim governmentCost As Double
    Dim localCost As Double
```

Listing 19.9 (cont.)

```
governmentItem = New BasicTax()
localItem = New LocalTax()
calcTheTax = New ObtainTax()
governmentCost = CDbl(txtGovernment.Text)
localCost = CDbl(txtLocal.Text)
lblGovernment.Text = "£" & CStr(calcTheTax.GetTax(governmentItem, _
governmentCost))
lblLocal.Text = "£" & CStr(calcTheTax.GetTax(localItem, localCost))
End Sub
```

There is a lot of similarity in the GUI and coding for the last two programs and you are left to study the execution of the code yourself. The following description will again concentrate upon the polymorphism exhibited by the program.

The last two program statements of Listing 19.9 contain a message sent to the instance of the *ObtainTax* class (as represented by the object reference *calcTheTax*. They both are repeated below:

```
calcTheTax.GetTax(governmentItem, governmentCost))
```

```
calcTheTax.GetTax(localItem, localCost))
```

These messages invoke the *GetTax* function method:

```
Function GetTax(ByVal pTax As IFindTax, ByVal pCost As Double) As Double
    Dim totalTax As Double
    totalTax = pTax.calcTax(pCost)
    Return totalTax
End Function
```

The first formal parameter of this method is *pItem* declared *ByVal* and it is of type *IFindTax*.

IFindTax is an **interface** (in the last program it was a base class) and this will accept an object that implements *IFindTax* (i.e. the formal parameter is an interface and the actual parameter is an object).

Within the instance of the *ObtainTax* class is a function method called *GetTax*. When invoked this method sends a message that invokes the *CalcTax* method. Which version of the *CalcTax* method is invoked depends upon the object reference that was passed as a parameter (i.e. *pTax*) to the *GetTax* method. Of course this reference could be an instance of the *BasicTax* or *LocalTax* class, both of which implement the *IFindTax* interface. The mechanics that these classes have for their respective *CalcTax* method are different – one calculates the tax at 10%, the other at 15%.

Figure 19.18 illustrates the execution and passing of the object reference when the government tax is calculated and Figure 19.19 illustrates the execution when the local tax is calculated.

Figure 19.18 Calculating the government tax.

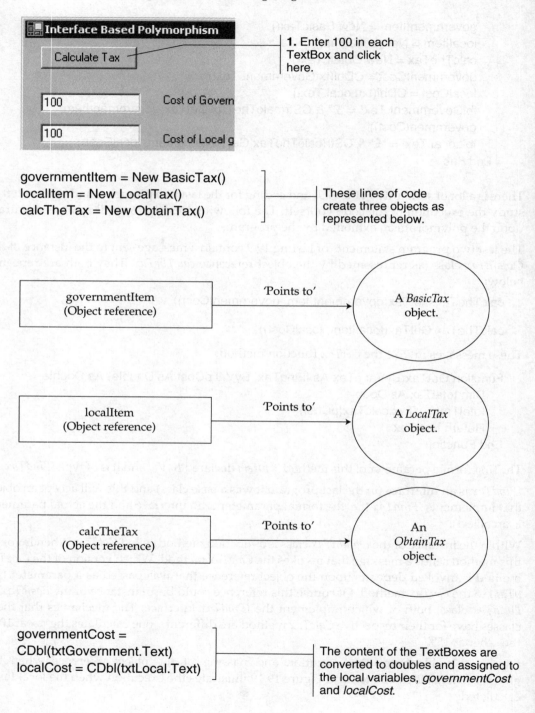

```
governmentItem = New BasicTax()
localItem = New LocalTax()
calcTheTax = New ObtainTax()
```

These lines of code create three objects as represented below.

| governmentItem (Object reference) | → 'Points to' → | A *BasicTax* object. |

| localItem (Object reference) | → 'Points to' → | A *LocalTax* object. |

| calcTheTax (Object reference) | → 'Points to' → | An *ObtainTax* object. |

```
governmentCost =
CDbl(txtGovernment.Text)
localCost = CDbl(txtLocal.Text)
```

The content of the TextBoxes are converted to doubles and assigned to the local variables, *governmentCost* and *localCost*.

Figure 19.18 (cont.)

lblGovernment.Text = "£" & CStr(calcTheTax.GetTax(governmentItem, governmentCost))

The object reference
governmentItem is passed to *pTax*.
pTax now has reference to the
same object. Therefore, *pTax*
references an instance of
the *BasicTax* class.

The content of the
actual parameter
governmentCost is
passed to the **formal**
parameter *pCost*.

Function GetTax(ByVal pTax As IFindTax, ByVal pCost As Double) As Double

> **NOTE:** An actual parameter that is an object can be passed to a formal parameter that is an interface, providing the class of the object implements the interface.

This message (which is part of the code within *GetTax*) invokes the *calcTax* method, passing the content of the actual parameter *pCost*. The object that receives this message is the object referenced by *pTax*. Of course *pTax* was passed the object reference *governmentItem* that 'points to' an instance of the *BasicTax* class. Consequently, the *calcTax* method within the instance of the *BasicTax* class is invoked. The amount of the tax calculated is returned to be stored in the local variable *totalTax*.

totalTax = pTax.CalcTax(pCost)

This message invokes
this function, which is
within an instance of
the *BasicTax* class.

The content of the
double type variable
pCost is passed to
pItemCost.

Function CalcTax(ByVal pItemCost As Double) As Double Implements IFindTax.CalcTax

totalTax = pItemCost * 0.1
Return totalTax

The content of this double is returned to the message that invoked
CalcTax, which in turn returns it to the message that called it. At
which point £10 is displayed in the label.

Figure 19.18 (cont.)

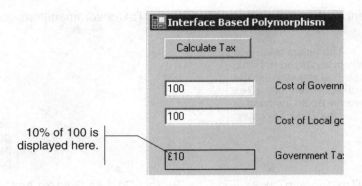

10% of 100 is displayed here.

When the code has returned from all of the methods (that is when every message is complete) the next line of code to execute is the one below, which also sets off a sequence of messages that invoke methods.

lblLocal.Text = "£" & CStr(calcTheTax.GetTax(localItem, localCost))

A copy of the object reference *localItem* is passed to *pTax*. *pTax* now has reference to the **same** object. However, this time it is an instance of the *LocalTax* object.

The content of the double type variable localCost is passed to *pCost*.

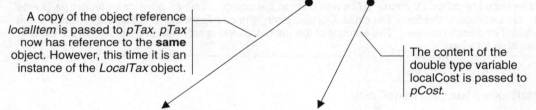

Function GetTax(ByVal pTax As IFindTax, ByVal pCost As Double) As Double

This message (which is part of the code within *GetTax*) invokes the *CalcTax* method, passing the content of *pCost*. The object that receives the message is the object referenced by *pTax*. Of course, *pTax* was passed the object reference *localItem* that 'points to' an instance of the *LocalTax* class. Consequently, the *CalcTax* method within the instance of the *LocalTax* class is invoked. The amount of the tax calculated (which will be 15%) is returned to be stored in the local variable *totalTax*.

totalTax = pTax.CalcTax(pCost)

This message invokes this function.

The content of the double type variable *pCost* is passed to *pItemCost*.

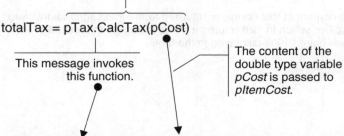

Function CalcTax(ByVal pItemCost As Double) As Double Implements FindTax.CalcTax

Figure 19.18 (cont.)

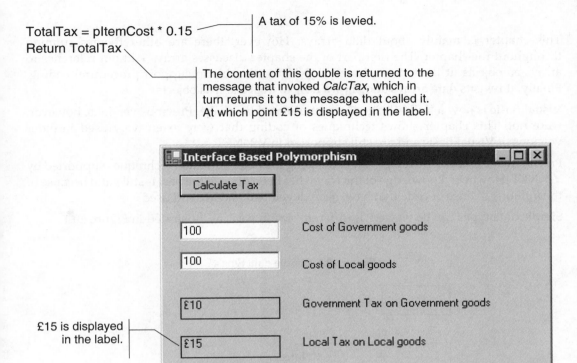

TotalTax = pItemCost * 0.15
Return TotalTax

A tax of 15% is levied.

The content of this double is returned to the message that invoked *CalcTax*, which in turn returns it to the message that called it. At which point £15 is displayed in the label.

£15 is displayed in the label.

NOTE: Polymorphism has been illustrated by this example because the following message has invoked one of two copies of the *CalcTax* method, one calculated tax at 10% and the other at 15%. Which one was chosen was dependent upon the object reference used. Again this choice occurred at runtime.

totalTax = pTax.CalcTax(pCost)

PRACTICAL ACTIVITY 19.5

Implement the program as represented by the GUI of Figure 19.16 and Listings 19.8 and 19.9, and single step through the program.

20 Data arrays

This chapter is mainly about data arrays. However, there are other themes running throughout the chapter. The first part of the chapter discusses arrays without reference to arrays as objects. It then shows how VB .NET is still able to support procedural coding. Finally, it revisits data arrays and shows how to treat them as objects.

Visual Basic is now a 'fully-fledged' object-oriented language. Previous versions, however, were not. This chapter shows techniques of coding that were extensively used in older versions of Visual Basic and are still supported in VB .NET.

I recommend that you develop your code using the object-oriented techniques supported by VB .NET. However, knowledge of the way it has been done in the past is still valid because of the millions of lines of code that have been developed and are still used.

Simple data types can be viewed as different size 'boxes', as illustrated in Figure 20.1.

Figure 20.1 Simple data types.

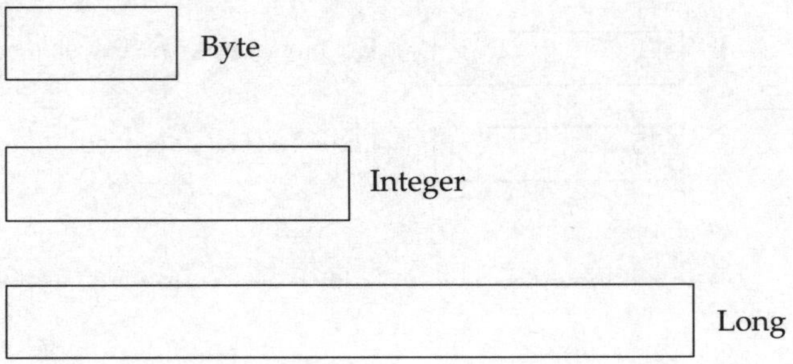

Byte

Integer

Long

Such data types have an important role in programs but they are limited in the way they can represent data. Data arrays are an example of a structured data type that imposes structure upon data items. Once this structure is in place the data is more easily processed.

> **NOTE**: Data arrays provide a convenient means for storing data items of the same data type.

An array is an ordered set of items of the same type. Each member of the array is referred to as an element. Every element has the same data type and the same name, with the addition of an identifying index number. An example of an array structure is shown in Figure 20.2.

The second element of the array is identified as *numbers(1)* and the third element of the array as *numbers(2)* and so on.

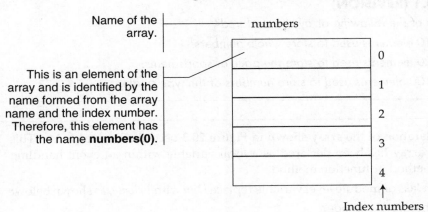

Figure 20.2 An array structure.

Name of the array.

numbers

This is an element of the array and is identified by the name formed from the array name and the index number. Therefore, this element has the name **numbers(0)**.

0

1

2

3

4

Index numbers

Declaring arrays

The basic building blocks of an array are the simple data types found in the VB .NET language and it is possible to have an array of one of these data types, for example, an array of integers, an array of longs and an array of singles, etc. The declaration of a five-element array of integers, identified by the name *numbers* is shown in Figure 20.3.

NOTE: It is also possible to have an array of arrays, an array of objects and an array of user-defined types. This chapter only deals with arrays of simple data types.

Figure 20.3 Declaring an *Integer* array.

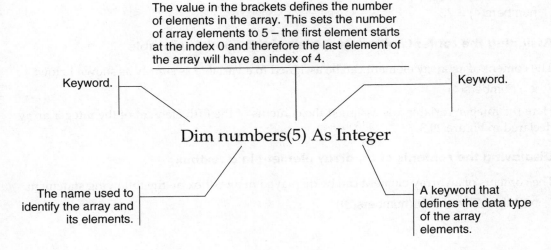

The value in the brackets defines the number of elements in the array. This sets the number of array elements to 5 – the first element starts at the index 0 and therefore the last element of the array will have an index of 4.

Keyword.

Keyword.

Dim numbers(5) As Integer

The name used to identify the array and its elements.

A keyword that defines the data type of the array elements.

QUESTION 20.1 (REVISION)

How would each of the following arrays be declared?

1. *An array of 10 elements used to store whole numbers.*
2. *An array of 20 elements used to store the price of sports items.*
3. *An array of 100 elements used to store numbers of the type single.*

NOTE: The declaration of the array shown in Figure 20.3 used the keyword *Dim*. This implies that the array has been declared as a local variable within an event handling procedure, submethod or function method.

To declare it as a class or module level variable replace *Dim* with *Private*, as shown below:

    Private numbers(5) As Integer

Elements as variables

Every element of an array can be treated in exactly the same as any other variable of the same type. For example an element can be assigned to, read from, and processed in the ways 'allowed by' the data type.

Assigning a value to an array element

The following VB .NET statements assign integers to every element of the array declared in Figure 20.3.

    numbers(0) = 3
    numbers(1) = 32
    numbers(2) = 23
    numbers(3) = 300
    numbers(4) = 73

Assigning the contents of an array element to another variable

The content of an array element can be assigned to a variable as simply as shown below:

    x = numbers(4)

Here the integer variable x is assigned the contents of the fifth element of the integer array declared in Figure 20.3.

Displaying the contents of an array element in a textbox

The contents of an array element can be displayed in a textbox by the following statement.

    txtOutput.Text = CStr(numbers(3))

A textbox named *txtOutput* has its *Text* property set to the value of the *numbers* array's fourth element (note the use of the conversion function).

NOTE: These three examples of accessing the elements of an array show that array elements behave exactly like variables. Indeed they are just variables with a slightly more complex identifier. However, it is this added complexity (i.e. the index number) that allows these data structures to be easily manipulated by program code.

NOTE: An array is an example of a static data structure. The size of a static data structure is fixed. If the array declared in Figure 20.3 were used in a program it would be capable of storing 5 integers. Hopefully this size would be suitable for the functioning of the program. However, if there proved a need for six integers to be stored then this array would not be suitable. Unfortunately, the size of the array is fixed, so the source code would have to be altered and recompiled.

Static data structures are extremely useful for many applications but they do have their drawbacks, as described above. For applications that require data structures to 'grow' with their application VB .NET also offers *ReDim* and collections. Use the VB .NET help to learn about *ReDim*. Collections are covered in the next chapter. It is also possible to create an array of any size and of any type at runtime using the *CreateInstance* method.

Operations on static data structures

The four basic operations that can be carried out on static data structures are:

1. **Initialization**: This loads the data structure with some appropriate starting data.
2. **Assignment**: This stores new information in the data structure replacing the data that was already there.
3. **Rearrangement**: This involves moving the information about in the data structure to, for example, put a list of names in alphabetical order.
4. **Retrieval**: This simply means reading the information in the data structure. It does not mean remove the data!

NOTE: The six operations that can be carried out on dynamic data structures are the four that can be carried out on static data structures plus two others (insertion and deletion).

Dynamic data structures grow with the addition of information. Items of information that are added to the data structure are described as being **inserted**.

Dynamic data structures also shrink with the removal of information. Items of information that are removed from the data structure are described as being **deleted**. Deletion of information from a computer system usually removes all trace of the information. Once the information is removed it cannot be retrieved.

Using arrays

The following specification (and the VB .NET program that implements it) has been designed to illustrate all the four basic operations that can act on data arrays.

SPECIFICATION 20.1

Write a program that reads 5 integers from the keyboard, sorts them into numeric order and displays them. Also only allow the entry of the figures 0 to 9 in the textboxes used for user input.

IMPORTANT: The steps recommended for the implementation of the specification are:

1. *Build and set the properties of the GUI.*
2. *Design the code using N-S charts.*
3. *Produce a data table.*
4. *Derive a simple test plan.*
5. *Convert the design to code and run.*
6. *Test the runtime against the test plan.*

*However, from this point onwards **only** the building of the GUI and the program listings will be covered. This is merely to save space in the book; the missing steps have been covered but are not reproduced. They are still recommended steps that you should endeavour to follow.*

The GUI for Specification 20.1

The graphical user interface suitable for Specification 20.1 is shown in Figure 20.4.

Figure 20.4 A suitable GUI for Specification 20.1.

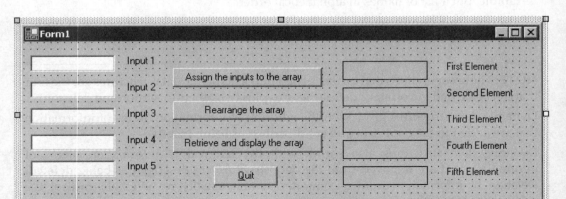

The GUI shown in Figure 20.4 consists of five textboxes, four buttons and fifteen labels. Ten of the labels are used to guide the user with user-friendly information; they are the labels that contain the string Input 1 through to Input 5 and First Element through to Fifth Element. These ten labels and their properties will not be discussed because they will not be used by any of the code attached to this form. Of course the text property of each of these labels will have to be set to the string values as suggested by the GUI (e.g. Input 1 and First Element).

The controls used by the program code are listed in table 20.1. The table has entries that indicate the setting for various proprieties of these controls. Only the properties that are altered are shown not properties that are left at their default value.

> **NOTE**: All 'positional property' settings are **not** listed; set these by dragging the controls to the right size and position.

Table 20.1 Property settings for the GUI.

Control	Property	Setting
TextBox1	Name TabIndex Text	txtInput1 0 <empty>
TextBox2	Name TabIndex Text	txtInput2 1 <empty>
TextBox3	Name TabIndex Text	txtInput3 2 <empty>
TextBox4	Name TabIndex Text	txtInput4 3 <empty>
TextBox5	Name TabIndex Text	txtInput5 4 <empty>
Button1	Name Text TabIndex	btnAssign Assign the inputs to the array 5
Button2	Name Text TabIndex	btnRearrange Rearrange the array 6
Button3	Name Text TabIndex	btnRetrieve Retrieve and display the array 7
Button4	Name Text TabIndex	btnQuit &Quit 8

Table 20.1 (cont.)

Label1	Name Text Border Style TextAlign	lblOutput1 <empty> Fixed Single MiddleCenter
Label2	Name Text Border Style TextAlign	lblOutput2 <empty> Fixed Single MiddleCenter
Label3	Name Text Border Style TextAlign	lblOutput3 <empty> Fixed Single MiddleCenter
Label4	Name Text Border Style TextAlign	lblOutput4 <empty> Fixed Single MiddleCenter
Label5	Name Text Border Style TextAlign	lblOutput5 <empty> Fixed Single MiddleCenter

Listing 20.1 shows the code attached to the GUI of Figure 20.4 (i.e. the class listing for the form – remember that a form is a 'specialized type' of class, but a class nevertheless).

Listing 20.1 The code 'attached' to Figure 20.5.

```
Private Const cMIN As Integer = 0
Private Const cMAX As Integer = 5
Private numbers(cMAX) As Integer

Private Sub btnAssign_Click(ByVal sender As System.Object, ByVal e As _
System.EventArgs) Handles btnAssign.Click
    If (txtInput1.Text = "") Or (txtInput2.Text = "") _
    Or (txtInput3.Text = "") Or (txtInput4.Text = "") _
    Or (txtInput5.Text = "") Then
        MsgBox("A zero length string is present in an input text box!")
    Else
        numbers(0) = CInt(txtInput1.Text)
        numbers(1) = CInt(txtInput2.Text)
        numbers(2) = CInt(txtInput3.Text)
        numbers(3) = CInt(txtInput4.Text)
        numbers(4) = CInt(txtInput5.Text)
    End If
End Sub
```

Please note that this is one line of code. It uses the 'line splitter', which is the space and underscore.

Listing 20.1 (cont.)

```vb
Private Sub btnReArrange_Click(ByVal sender As System.Object, ByVal e As _
System.EventArgs) Handles btnReArrange.Click
    Dim i As Integer
    Dim pass As Integer
    Dim temp As Integer
    Dim noSwitches As Boolean
    pass = 0
    Do
        pass = pass + 1
        noSwitches = True
        For i = cMIN To ((cMAX - 1) - pass)
            If numbers(i) > numbers(i + 1) Then
                noSwitches = False
                temp = numbers(i)
                numbers(i) = numbers(i + 1)
                numbers(i + 1) = temp
            End If
        Next I
    Loop Until noSwitches
End Sub


Private Sub btnRetrieve_Click(ByVal sender As System.Object, ByVal e As _
System.EventArgs) Handles btnRetrieve.Click
    lblOutput1.Text = CStr(numbers(0))
    lblOutput2.Text = CStr(numbers(1))
    lblOutput3.Text = CStr(numbers(2))
    lblOutput4.Text = CStr(numbers(3))
    lblOutput5.Text = CStr(numbers(4))
End Sub


Private Sub btnQuit_Click(ByVal sender As System.Object, ByVal e As _
System.EventArgs) Handles btnQuit.Click
    Close()
    End
End Sub

Private Sub Form1_Load(ByVal sender As System.Object, ByVal _
e As System.EventArgs) Handles MyBase.Load
    Dim i As Integer

    For i = cMIN To (cMAX - 1)
        numbers(i) = 1
    Next I
    txtInput1.Text = CStr(numbers(0))
```

471

Listing 20.1 (cont.)

```
txtInput2.Text = CStr(numbers(1))
txtInput3.Text = CStr(numbers(2))
txtInput4.Text = CStr(numbers(3))
txtInput5.Text = CStr(numbers(4))
lblOutput1.Text = CStr(numbers(0))
lblOutput2.Text = CStr(numbers(1))
lblOutput3.Text = CStr(numbers(2))
lblOutput4.Text = CStr(numbers(3))
lblOutput5.Text = CStr(numbers(4))
End Sub
```

The code for the GUI

The application consists of:

- A declaration of a five-element array and two constants in the declarations section of the form. Consequently, these have form-level scope that makes them available to all the code 'attached' to the form. Please note, as the form is in fact a class the array and both constants can also be regarded as a class level variable and class level constants respectively.

- Five-event handling procedures.

> **NOTE:** The validation of user input through the textboxes is not described here – this was covered in a previous chapter. When you implement this application you must remember to attach appropriate code to fully verify the user input.

Declaration of a five-element array

The declaration of the array is shown in Figure 20.5. It can be seen that the declaration of the array has been achieved using the constants.

> **NOTE:** A constant is a named item that **retains** a constant value throughout the execution of a program, as compared to a variable whose values can change during execution. Constants can be used in code in place of actual values (literal values). An advantage of using constants is that they improve the readability of code, also just **one** change to the declaration of a constant will reflect throughout the program in **all** the places the constant is used.
>
> It is common practice for all constant identifiers to be declared as all capitals. It is also good programming practice to prefix every programmer-defined constant with a lower case **c**. Then when a constant is seen in program code it cannot be confused with a variable. Also a programmer-defined constant cannot be confused with a system constant (i.e. one that 'belongs' to VB. NET) that uses all capitals.

Figure 20.5 Declaring a five-element array with form level scope.

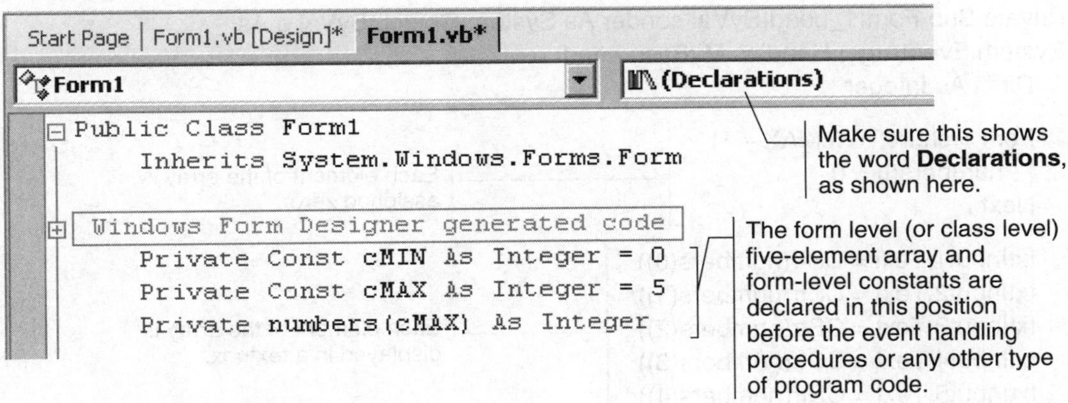

Start Page | Form1.vb [Design]* | **Form1.vb***

Form1 ▾ | **(Declarations)**

```
Public Class Form1
        Inherits System.Windows.Forms.Form

    Windows Form Designer generated code
        Private Const cMIN As Integer = 0
        Private Const cMAX As Integer = 5
        Private numbers(cMAX) As Integer
```

Make sure this shows the word **Declarations**, as shown here.

The form level (or class level) five-element array and form-level constants are declared in this position before the event handling procedures or any other type of program code.

```
Private Const cMIN As Integer = 0
Private Const cMAX As Integer = 5
Private numbers(cMAX) As Integer
```

The first line defines an *Integer* constant *cMIN* with a *Private* access modifier that fixes its scope to the form; this constant has its value fixed to 0 by the assignment symbol (i.e. the equals sign). The second line defines an *Integer* constant *cMAX* that is assigned the value 5; it has the same scope as the *cMIN* constant. The third line declares a five *Integer* array with a *Private* access modifier that fixes its scope to the form. The elements start with an index of 0 and end with an index of 4. It is a five-element array because the brackets of the array declaration contain *cMAX* which has the value of 5.

The five event handlers

Four of the five event handlers for this application have been chosen to reflect the four basic operations that can be carried out on static data structure, namely initialization, assignment, rearrangement and retrieval. These are described on the following pages. The event handling procedure for quitting the application has been discussed before.

Initialization

The code for initializing the data array is shown in Listing 20.2 and is followed by its description trace table. When a form is loaded during the execution of a Windows application a form *Load* event occurs. This event has been used to illustrate the basic operation of initialization. The code within this event assigns zero to all the elements of the array, it also displays these zeros in the input textboxes and the output labels.

Listing 20.2 The *Form1_Load* event

```
Private Sub Form1_Load(ByVal sender As System.Object, ByVal e As _
System.EventArgs) Handles MyBase.Load
    Dim i As Integer
```

```
    For i = cMIN To (cMAX – 1)
        numbers(i) = 0
    Next i
```
Each element of the array is assigned zero.

```
    txtInput1.Text = CStr(numbers(0))
    txtInput2.Text = CStr(numbers(1))
    txtInput3.Text = CStr(numbers(2))
    txtInput4.Text = CStr(numbers(3))
    txtInput5.Text = CStr(numbers(4))
```
Each element of the array is displayed in a textbox.

```
    lblOutput1.Text = CStr(numbers(0))
    lblOutput2.Text = CStr(numbers(1))
    lblOutput3.Text = CStr(numbers(2))
    lblOutput4.Text = CStr(numbers(3))
    lblOutput5.Text = CStr(numbers(4))
End Sub
```
Each element of the array is displayed in a label.

The *For .. Next* loop contains *(cMAX – 1)*, which ensures that the index of the array within the loop never exceeds the index of the last element of the array – which is four. Of course, *cMAX* minus one is four because the value of *cMAX* is five.

Description trace for the *Form1_ Load (..)* event handler

Statement	Description
For i = cMIN To (cMAX – 1)	The range is from *cMIN* to *cMAX–1*, which is 0 to 4. The first time through the loop the variable *i* is set at 0 (i.e. the value of *cMIN*).
numbers(i) = 0	The first element of the array is assigned 0. It is the first element because the statement *numbers(i)* is effectively *numbers(0)* because *i* is set to 0.
For i = cMIN To (cMAX – 1)	*i* is incremented by 1 to store the value 1.
numbers(i) = 0	The second element of the array is assigned 0. It is the second element because the statement *numbers(i)* is effectively *numbers(1)* because *i* is set to 1.
For i = cMIN To (cMAX – 1)	*i* is incremented by 1 to store the value 2
numbers(i) = 0	The third element of the array is assigned 0. It is the third element because the statement *numbers(i)* is effectively *numbers(2)* because *i* is set to 2.
For i = cMIN To (cMAX – 1)	*i* is incremented by 1 to store the value 3

numbers(i) = 0	The fourth element of the array is assigned 0. It is the fourth element because the statement *numbers(i)* is effectively *numbers(3)* because *i* is set to 3.
For i = cMIN To (cMAX – 1)	*i* is incremented by 1 to store the value 4
numbers(i) = 0	The fifth (and last) element of the array is assigned 0. It is the fifth element because the statement *numbers(i)* is effectively *numbers(4)* because *i* is set to 4.
When i is set to 4 it is the last time around the loop because the top of the range for the *For .. Next* loop is *(cMAX – 1)*, i.e. (5 – 1), which is obviously 4. Therefore the next statement executed is after the loop and it is described below.	
txtInput1.Text = CStr(numbers(0))	The content of the first element of the array *numbers(0)* is converted to a string and copied to the *Text* property of the textbox *txtInput1*. Therefore, the textbox displays zero.
The next three statements do something similar.	
txtInput1.Text = CStr(numbers(4))	The content of the last element of the array *numbers(4)* is converted to a string and copied to the *Text* property of the textbox *txtInput5*. Therefore, the textbox displays zero.
lblOutput1.Text = CStr(numbers(0))	The content of the first element of the array *numbers(0)* is converted to a string and copied to the *Text* property of the label *lblOutput1*. Therefore, the label displays zero.
The next three statements do something similar.	
lblOutput1.Text = CStr(numbers(0))	The content of the last element of the array *numbers(4)* is converted to a string and copied to the *Text* property of the label *lblOutput5*. Therefore, this label also displays zero.

Figure 20.6 shows the values that would be stored in the array after it has been initialized.

Figure 20.6 The contents of the array after it has been initialized.

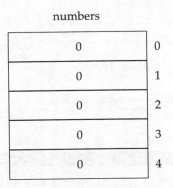

Assignment

The code for assigning values to the data array from the input **textboxes** is shown in Listing 20.3 – the code is 'attached' to the click event of the button *btnAssign*. There are two possible routes through this code because it has been designed to ensure that a zero length

475

string entry is **not** allowed in any of the textboxes. Validation of user input must also be included, of course, but this is left to you to incorporate. Because there are two possible routes there are two description trace tables.

Listing 20.3 Assigning values to a data array.

```
Private Sub btnAssign_Click(ByVal sender As System.Object, ByVal e As
System.EventArgs) Handles btnAssign.Click
    If (txtInput1.Text = "") Or (txtInput2.Text = "") _          One line.
    Or (txtInput3.Text = "") Or (txtInput4.Text = "") _
    Or (txtInput5.Text = "") Then
        MsgBox("A zero length string is present in an input text box!")
    Else
        numbers(0) = CInt(txtInput1.Text)
        numbers(1) = CInt(txtInput2.Text)
        numbers(2) = CInt(txtInput3.Text)
        numbers(3) = CInt(txtInput4.Text)
        numbers(4) = CInt(txtInput5.Text)
    End If
End Sub
```

Figure 20.7 shows the runtime when a user mistakenly attempts to enter a zero length string. The appropriate description trace table follows this figure.

Figure 20.7 The response when a user enters a zero length string.

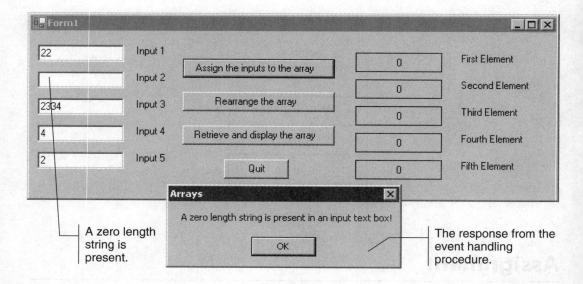

Description trace for the *btnAssign_Click(..)* event handling procedure

The following description trace describes the execution of the event handling procedure if one of the input textboxes contains a zero-length string, i.e. if the textbox contains no text.

Statement	Description
If (txtInput1.Text = "") Or (txtInput2.Text = "") Or (txtInput3.Text = "") Or (txtInput4.Text = "") Or (txtInput5.Text = "") Then	If the *Text* property of one or more of the input textboxes contains a zero length string then this test returns *True*. Consequently, the statements between the keywords *Then* and *Else* are executed.
MsgBox("A zero length string is present in an input text box!")	The string *A zero length string is present in an input text box!* is displayed in a message box. **Note** the use of *MsgBox* instead of *MessageBox.Show*. *MsgBox* is from earlier versions of Visual Basic and still works in this version of VB .NET. It is included here as extra information about VB.

The next description trace describes what happens if all the inputs are integers.

Statement	Description
If (txtInput1.Text = "") Or (txtInput2.Text = "") Or (txtInput3.Text = "") Or (txtInput4.Text = "") Or (txtInput5.Text = "") Then	There are no zero length strings and the outcome from this conditional test is *False*. Consequently, the statements between the keywords *Else* and *End If* are executed.
numbers(0) = CInt(txtInput1.Text)	The value entered by the user into the textbox *txtInput1* is obtained from its *Text* property and converted to an *Integer* and assigned to the first element *numbers(0)* of the array.
Something similar happens for the next three statements.	
numbers(4) = CInt(txtInput5.Text)	The value entered by the user into the textbox *txtInput5* is obtained from its *Text* property and converted to an integer and assigned to the last element *numbers(4)* of the array. Once this statement executes the event handling procedure has complete its execution.

Figure 20.8 shows the runtime after the user enters data and clicks the [Assign the inputs to the array] button. Figure 20.9 shows the values stored in the *numbers* array after the steps as represented by Figure 20.8. Figure 20.10 shows the runtime after the user clicks the [Retrieve and display the array] button (following on from the steps of Figure 20.8).

Figure 20.8 A typical runtime.

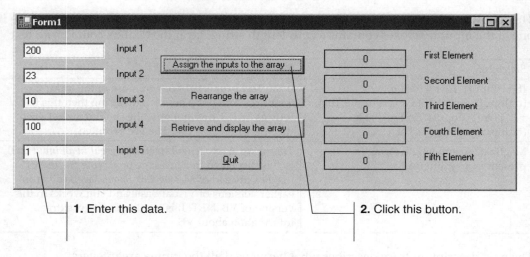

1. Enter this data.

2. Click this button.

Figure 20.9 The state of the array **after** the execution of the *btnAssign_Click(..)* event handling procedure.

numbers

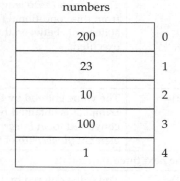

200	0
23	1
10	2
100	3
1	4

Figure 20.10 After the user clicks the **Retrieve and display the array** button.

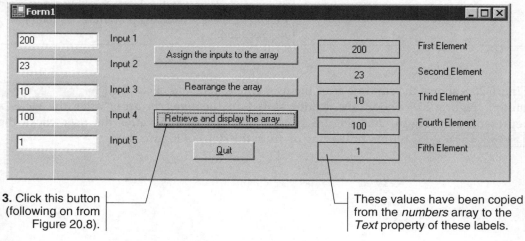

3. Click this button (following on from Figure 20.8).

These values have been copied from the *numbers* array to the *Text* property of these labels.

Rearrangement – the bubble sort

The code for rearranging the values in the data array into numeric order is shown in Listing 20.4 – the code is 'attached' to the click event of the button *btnReArrange*. This code is based on a well-known algorithm known as the **bubble sort**.

> **NOTE**: VB .NET supplies a programmer with powerful methods for sorting. It is highly unlikely that you would want to use your own bubble sort program in the way described here. Implementing algorithms is fundamental to the development of programming skills, however, and a bubble sort algorithm is a standard that all programmers should understand and know how to implement.

Listing 20.4 The bubble sort.

```
Private Sub btnReArrange_Click(ByVal sender As System.Object, ByVal e As _
System.EventArgs) Handles btnReArrange.Click
    Dim i As Integer
    Dim pass As Integer
    Dim temp As Integer
    Dim noSwitches As Boolean
    pass = 0
    Do
        pass = pass + 1
        noSwitches = True
        For i = cMIN To ((cMAX - 1) - pass)
            If numbers(i) > numbers(i + 1) Then
                noSwitches = False
                temp = numbers(i)
                numbers(i) = numbers(i + 1)
                numbers(i + 1) = temp
            End If
        Next i
    Loop Until noSwitches
End Sub
```

The bubble sort

The rearrangement event handling procedure takes a five-element *Integer* array as its input and rearranges the data into numeric order. Figure 20.11 illustrates the bubble sort process, the array structure and the local variables used.

Figure 20.11 11 The bubble sort process.

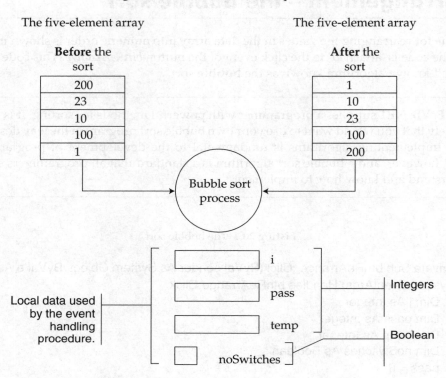

The five-element array

The five-element array

Before the sort

After the sort

The array holds the data before and after the bubble sort. The local data are used for the reasons described in Table 20.2.

Table 20.2 Description of local data.

Local data	What it is used for
i	Used as the index for the *For .. Next* loop and to identify individual elements of the array.
pass	To count the number of passes through the *Do .. Until* loop.
temp	Used to assist in switching the content of the array elements.
noSwitches	If there are no switches on a pass through the *Do..Until* loop then *noSwitches* is set to True. If there is switching of elements then the *noSwitches* is set to False. Consequently, the *Do .. Until* loop is executed until there are no switches, which implies that the array is sorted.

The bubble sort works in the following way:

- On the first pass through the loop the content of the first element is compared to see if it is larger than the content of the second element and if it is then they are switched.

- The content of the second element is then compared with the content of the third element and switched if the content of the second element is larger than the third.

- This is repeated until the content of the fourth element is compared with the fifth element.

- Upon completion of the first pass, the largest number in the array will be in the fifth element position. In fact, the biggest number is guaranteed to be in this position!

The first pass through the loop is illustrated by Figure 20.12.

Figure 20.12 First pass through the loop.

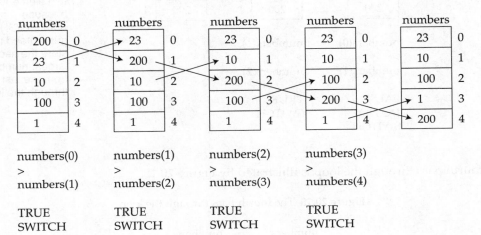

numbers(0)
>
numbers(1)

TRUE
SWITCH

numbers(1)
>
numbers(2)

TRUE
SWITCH

numbers(2)
>
numbers(3)

TRUE
SWITCH

numbers(3)
>
numbers(4)

TRUE
SWITCH

The second pass through the loop is illustrated by Figure 20.13.

Figure 20.13 Second pass through the loop.

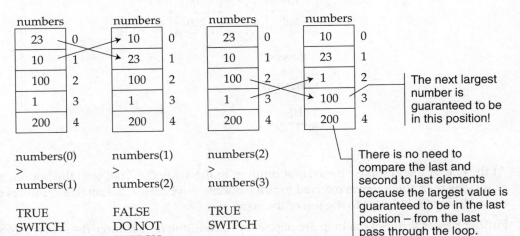

numbers(0)
>
numbers(1)

TRUE
SWITCH

numbers(1)
>
numbers(2)

FALSE
DO NOT
SWITCH

numbers(2)
>
numbers(3)

TRUE
SWITCH

The next largest number is guaranteed to be in this position!

There is no need to compare the last and second to last elements because the largest value is guaranteed to be in the last position – from the last pass through the loop.

481

The third pass through the loop is illustrated by Figure 20.14.

Figure 20.14 The third pass through the loop.

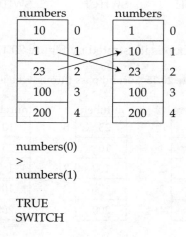

numbers			numbers			numbers		
10	0		10	0		10	0	
23	1		23	1		1	1	
1	2		1	2		23	2	
100	3		100	3		100	3	
200	4		200	4		200	4	

numbers(0)
>
numbers(1)

FALSE
DO NOT
SWITCH

numbers(1)
>
numbers(2)

TRUE
SWITCH

There is no need to compare these two elements because *numbers(3)* is guaranteed to store the second largest number – from the last pass through the loop.

The fourth pass through the loop is illustrated by Figure 20.15.

Figure 20.15 The fourth pass through the loop.

numbers			numbers		
10	0		1	0	
1	1		10	1	
23	2		23	2	
100	3		100	3	
200	4		200	4	

numbers(0)
>
numbers(1)

TRUE
SWITCH

At the end of the first pass the largest number in the array (i.e. 200) is at the bottom of the array. The rearrangement is referred to as the bubble sort because the smaller numbers in the array slowly 'bubble up' to the top of the array.

Further passes through the loop are necessary to continue to rearrange the array. However, on the next pass element four need not be compared with element five because the largest number is already in the fifth element position. After the next pass the largest element will be in the fourth element position, consequently, the third pass will not need to compare the third element with the fourth element because the second largest number will be in the fourth position. Therefore the number of comparisons reduces for every pass through the loop. This is why the range of the *For .. Next* loop is reduced every time the *Do .. Loop* is repeated. This is achieved by incrementing the local variable *pass* and subtracting it from $(cMAX - 1)$, i.e. *For i = cMIN To ((cMAX - 1) - pass)*.

The array is sorted when there are no more switches during a pass through the loop, i.e. when *noSwitches* is *True*.

Description trace for the *btnReArrange _Click()* event handling procedure

The following description trace describes the execution of the rearrangement code when run against the array data, as shown in Figure 20.9.

Statement	Description
pass = 0	Initializes the local variable *pass* to zero
The *Do Loop .. Until* loop is entered.	
pass = pass + 1	Increments *pass* by one – keeps a running total of the number of passes through the *Do* loop. The *pass* variable is used to ensure that the number of comparisons are reduced each time there is a pass through the *Do .. Until* loop.
noSwitches = True	Initializes the Boolean variable *noSwitches* to *True*, which indicates that there is yet to have been a switch.
The *For .. Next* loop is entered – a loop within a loop!	
For i = cMIN To ((cMAX – 1) – pass)	*cMIN* has the value 0 and *((cMAX –1) –pass)* has the value 3, consequently there will be four iterations through the *For .. Next* loop resulting in four comparisons between the elements of the array.
If numbers(i) > numbers(i + 1) Then	Compares the contents of first element with the content of the second element (i.e. is 200 > 23) and *True* is the outcome. Consequently, the *Then* part of the *If .. Then* selection is executed.
noSwitches = False	*False* is assigned to *noSwitches* to indicate that there **will** be a switch. This means that when the comparisons controlled by the *For .. Next* loop have all been completed there will be a further pass through the *Do .. Until Loop* because its condition (i.e. Until *noSwitches*) is *False*.
temp = numbers(i)	The contents of the first element *numbers(i)* are 'saved' in the local variable *temp*.
numbers(i) = numbers(i + 1)	The contents of the second element *numbers(i+1)* are copied to the first element *numbers(i)*.
numbers(i + 1) = temp	The contents of the *temp* variable are *copied* to the second element. The result is that the content of element one and two have been switched.
There will be 3 more passes through the *For .. Next* loop. With each pass switching (or otherwise) the content of the elements being compared. When the *For .. Next* loop is complete, the condition of *Until noSwitches* results in the *Do .. Until Loop* being re-entered and the statement *pass = pass + 1* is executed. The description trace is picked up from this point.	

pass = pass + 1	The value of the variable counting the number of passes through the *Do* loop is increased by one to the value 2.
noSwitches = True	There will be another 'batch of comparisons' around the *For .. Next* loop and therefore it is necessary to set *noSwitches* to *True* to indicate that there has yet to have been any switches.
For i = cMIN To ((cMAX − 1) − pass)	*cMIN* has the value 0 and *((cMAX −1) −pass)* now has the value 2 because the value of the local variable *pass* is now 2 (not 1 as for the last pass) Consequently, there will be three iterations through the *For .. Next* loop resulting in three comparisons between the elements of the array. There is no need for four comparisons because the largest number is guaranteed to be in the last element position.
If numbers(i) > numbers(i + 1) Then	Compares the first element with the second element of the array etc.

Eventually the passes through the loop will result in a completely sorted array. The final pass through the loop will not result in any switches in element content. On this pass *noSwitch* will **not** be set to *False* (inside the *If .. Then* selection) because the *Then* part of the selection will not be executed. Consequently, the condition of the *Do .. Until* Loop will be *True* and the loop and hence the event handling procedure will end.

NOTE: Every pass through the array is guaranteed to place the next largest number in its correct place. It should be noted that a pass could put more than one number in its correct place. The number of passes through the array is dependent upon the order of the original array. The bubble sort is an acceptable method for ordering an array. It is inefficient for large arrays however.

QUESTION 20.2 (DEVELOPMENT)

The description trace for the btnReArrange _Click event was not fully complete. You complete it!

Single step through the program and observe how the variables change value.

Retrieval

If the user clicks the **Retrieve and display the array** button immediately after pressing the **Assign the inputs to the array** button then the output appears as shown in Figure 20.16.

Figure 20.16 Output on the GUI after the user clicks the **Assign inputs to the array** and **Retrieve and display the array** buttons.

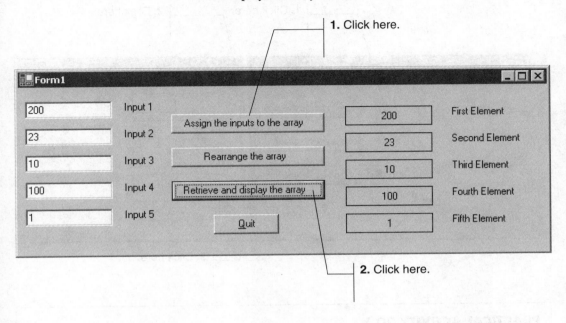

1. Click here.

2. Click here.

Description trace for the *btnRetrieve_Click* event handling procedure

Statement	Description
lblOutput1.Text = CStr(numbers(0))	The content of the first element *numbers(0)* (i.e. 200) is converted to a string and assigned to the *Text* property of the label *lblOutput*.
Something similar happens for the next three statements.	
lblOutput5.Text = CStr(numbers(4))	The content of the last element *numbers(4)* (i.e. 1), is converted to a string and assigned to the *Text* property of the label *lblOutput*.

The output of the GUI after the user clicks the **Assign the inputs to the array** button, and then Rearrange the array followed by **Retrieve and display the array** is shown in Figure 20.17.

Figure 20.17 The display after rearrangement.

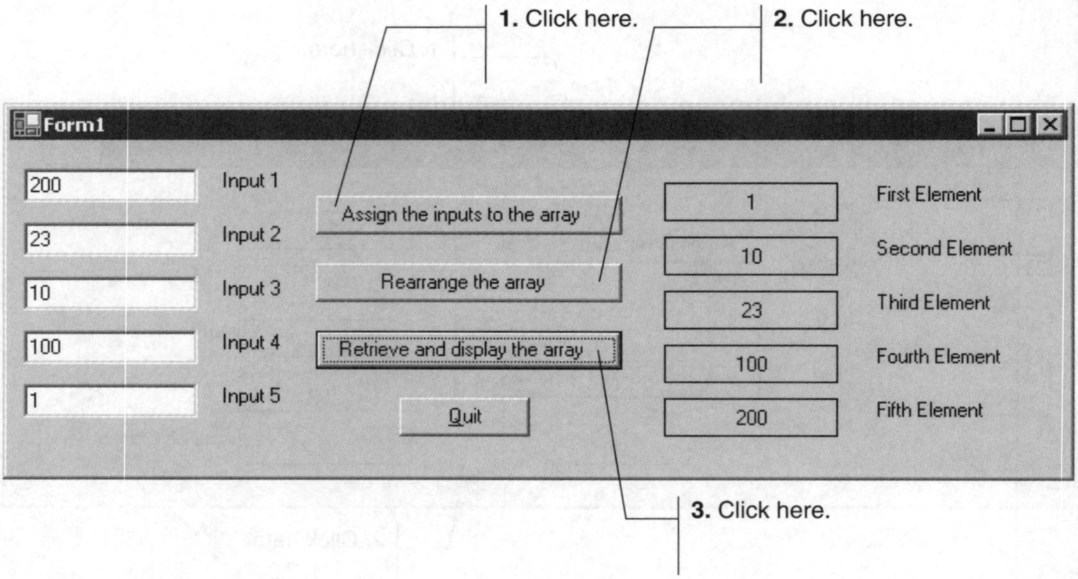

PRACTICAL ACTIVITY 20.1

a) Implement Specification 20.1.

b) Amend the application developed so that it will work for a six-element integer array.

PRACTICAL ACTIVITY 20.2

Amend the *btnAssign_Click()* event handler so that the statements after the *Then* part of the selection construct are exchanged with the statements after the *Else* part of the construct. **Hint**: use the *Not* logical operator.

PRACTICAL ACTIVITY 20.3

Rewrite the program developed for Practical Activity 20.1 so that the array is sorted with the smallest number is in the last element and the largest number in the first element (i.e. the 'opposite way around.')

A matrix array

The one-dimensional arrays considered so far have essentially been a sequence of elements, with each element being accessed by its index (subscript) number. However, it is possible to have a two-dimensional array (a matrix array). Such an array is not a sequence of elements, but it is a matrix that requires more than one number to index each of its elements.

Consider the use of a matrix array data structure for the following specification.

SPECIFICATION 20.2

A small class of five students take four examinations. Write a program that will read the mark obtained by each student, in each of the examinations. The program should also display a matrix of the students' marks against the examination number.

The data structure used for the implementation of the above specification is illustrated in Figure 20.18.

Figure 20.18 A matrix array suitable for Specification 20.2.

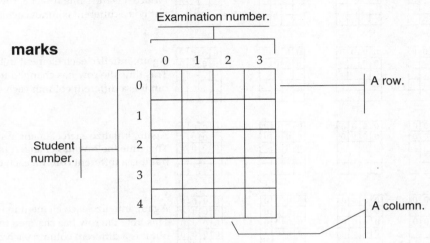

Figure 20.18 is a matrix array with 20 elements. Each element is capable of storing an integer. Every element is accessed by the name of the array (marks) and two index numbers – one for the row and the other for the column.

The marks of student one for the 1st examination will be in array element *marks(0, 0)*. Similarly, the marks of student three for the fourth examination will be in element *marks(2, 3)*. The relationship between an element and its identifier is shown in Figure 20.19.

Figure 20.19 Identifying an element.

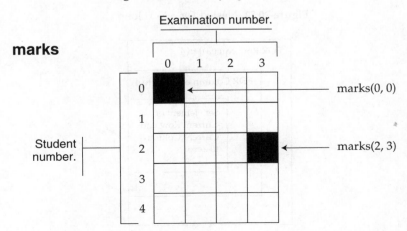

Nested *For .. Next* loops

Matrix arrays are manipulated using **nested** *For .. Next* loops. Setting each row and column in turn can initialize the elements of the matrix array. This is illustrated by Figure 20.20.

Figure 20.20 Initializing a matrix array.

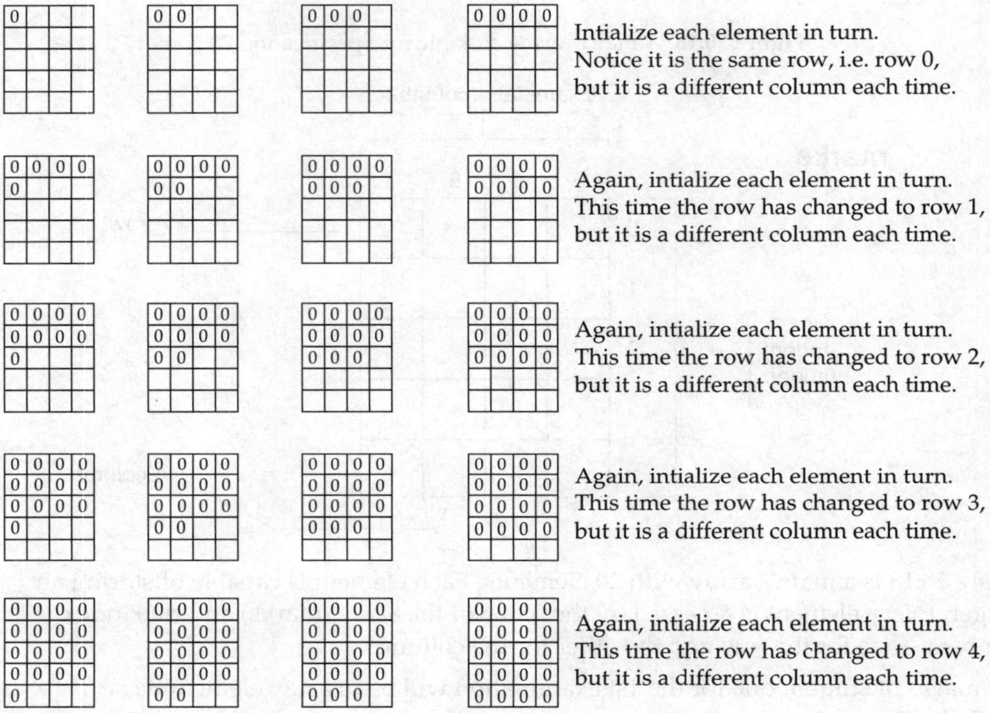

Intialize each element in turn.
Notice it is the same row, i.e. row 0,
but it is a different column each time.

Again, intialize each element in turn.
This time the row has changed to row 1,
but it is a different column each time.

Again, intialize each element in turn.
This time the row has changed to row 2,
but it is a different column each time.

Again, intialize each element in turn.
This time the row has changed to row 3,
but it is a different column each time.

Again, intialize each element in turn.
This time the row has changed to row 4,
but it is a different column each time.

The initializing of the elements in the order shown in Figure 20.20 is achieved by nested *For .. Next* loops as illustrated in Figure 20.21.

Figure 20.21 Nested *For .. Next* loops.

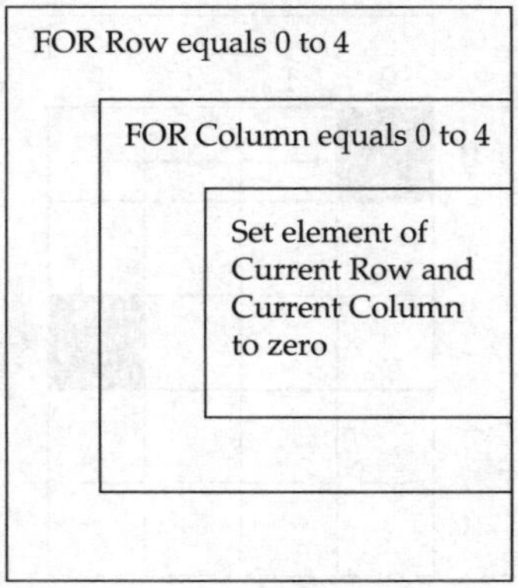

FOR Row equals 0 to 4

FOR Column equals 0 to 4

Set element of
Current Row and
Current Column
to zero

The outer loop sets the row to 0 and the inner loop selects the columns in turn. Consequently, the first row is set to zero. On exit from the inner loop control is passed back to the outer loop where the row is changed to 1. The inner loop is then entered and each of the columns is then selected in turn. This is repeated until the matrix is full of zeros.

Listing 20.5 shows a Console application implementation of Specification 20.2.

Listing 20.5 Implementing Specification 20.2.

```
Module Module1
    Private Const cMIN As Integer = 0
    Private Const cROW As Integer = 5
    Private Const cCOLUMN As Integer = 4
    Private marks(cROW, cCOLUMN) As Integer

    Sub Main()
        Call initializeArray()
        Call displayMarks()
        Call readMarks()
        Call displayMarks()
    End Sub

    Private Sub initializeArray()
        Dim row As Integer
        Dim column As Integer
        For row = cMIN To (cROW - 1)
            For column = cMIN To (cCOLUMN - 1)
                marks(row, column) = 0
            Next column
        Next row
    End Sub

    Private Sub displayMarks()
        Dim row As Integer
        Dim column As Integer

        For row = cMIN To (cROW - 1)
            For column = cMIN To (cCOLUMN - 1)
                Console.Write(marks(row, column) & Space(4))
            Next column
            Console.WriteLine()
        Next row
        Console.Write("PRESS ENTER TO CONTINUE ... ")
        Console.ReadLine()
    End Sub
```

Listing 20.5 (cont.)

```
Private Sub readMarks()
    Dim row As Integer
    Dim column As Integer
    For row = cMIN To (cROW - 1)
        For column = cMIN To (cCOLUMN - 1)
            Console.Write("Please enter a student mark ")
            marks(row, column) = CInt(Console.ReadLine())
        Next column
    Next row
End Sub
End Module
```

> **NOTE:** With every new release, Visual Basic has moved towards true object-oriented programming. However, it is still able to support the development of procedural code. The code shown in Listing 20.5 is procedural in nature; consequently, there is no mention of classes, objects or messaging.
>
> Procedural coding is now becoming a dated approach to the design and development of code. Nevertheless, there are many lines of useful code that is procedural in nature and an understanding of procedural coding is still a useful skill. It is worth remembering that whatever paradigm of coding is used it still has to be converted to machine code!
>
> However, I strongly recommend that you develop your main skills in object-oriented design and object-oriented programming.

Listing 20.5 consists of four 'self-contained' units of code known as sub procedures. These sub procedures are: *Main()*, *initializeArray()*, *displayMarks()*, and *readMarks()*. At the launch of the Console application the first sub procedure to execute is *Main()*. Within *Main()* there are **calls** to invoke the execution of other sub procedures. Whenever there is a *Call* of another sub procedure the called sub procedure executes and when it is finished control is passed back to the sub procedure that did the calling. Consequently, the order of execution of Listing 20.5 is as listed below.

a) Execute *Main()*
b) Call *initializeArray()*
c) Execute all the program statements in *initializeArray()*
d) Return to *Main()*
e) Call *displayMarks()*
f) Execute all the program statements in *displayMarks()*
g) Return to *Main()*
h) Call *readMarks()*
i) Execute all the program statements in *readMarks()*
j) Return to *Main()*
k) Call *displayMarks()*
l) Execute all the program statements in *displayMarks()*
m) Return to *Main()*
Execution Ends

Description of Listing 20.5

The declaration of the matrix array is detailed in Figure 20.22.

Figure 20.22 Declaration of a matrix array.

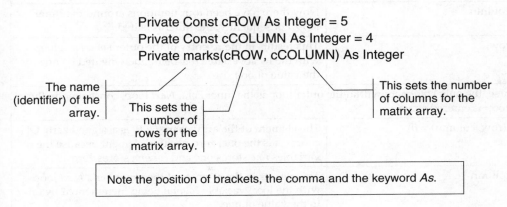

```
Private Const cROW As Integer = 5
Private Const cCOLUMN As Integer = 4
Private marks(cROW, cCOLUMN) As Integer
```

The name (identifier) of the array.

This sets the number of rows for the matrix array.

This sets the number of columns for the matrix array.

Note the position of brackets, the comma and the keyword *As*.

Description trace for *initializeArray()*

Statement	Description
This sub procedure is called (invoked) by the *Call initializeArray()* statement in the *Main()* sub procedure.	
For row = cMIN To (cRow – 1)	The local variable *row* is set to the value 0 (i.e. to the value of the constant *cMIN*) and the **outer** *For .. Next* loop is entered.
For column = cMIN To (cColumn – 1)	The local variable *column* is set to the value 0 (i.e. to the value of the constant *cMIN*) and the **inner** *For .. Next* loop is entered.
marks(row, column) = 0	The element of the array *marks(0, 0)* is assigned zero. Of course it is the zero, zero position element because both the variables *row* and *column* are zero.
Next column	This results in the re-entry of the **inner** *For .. Next* loop with the local variable *column* being incremented by one to the value of one.
marks(row, column) = 0	The element of the array *marks(0, 1)* is assigned zero. Of course it is the zero, one position element because the variables *row* stores zero and *column* stores one.
Next column	This results in the re-entry of the **inner** *For .. Next* loop with the local variable column being incremented by one to the value of two.
marks(row, column) = 0	The element of the array *marks(0, 2)* is assigned zero. Of course it is the zero, two position element because the variables *row* stores zero and *column* stores two.

491

Next column	This results in the re-entry of the **inner** *For .. Next* loop with the local variable *column* being incremented by one to the value of three.
marks(row, column) = 0	The element of the array *marks(0, 3)* is assigned zero. Of course it is the zero, three position element because the variables *row* stores zero and column stores three.
Next column	Now there have been four iterations around the **inner** loop, consequently, the **inner** is exited.
Next row	This results in the re-entry of the outer *For .. Next* loop with the local variable *row* being incremented by one to the value of one.

Of course, the only statement within the outer loop is the inner *For .. Next* loop, consequently the inner loop is entered again.

marks(row, column) = 0	The element of the array *marks(1, 0)* is assigned zero. Of course it is the one, zero position element because the variables *row* stores one and *column* stores zero.
Next column	This results in the re-entry of the **inner** *For .. Next* loop with the local variable *column* being incremented by one to the value of one.
marks(row, column) = 0	The element of the array *marks(1, 1)* is assigned zero. Of course it is the one, one position element because the variables *row* stores one and *column* stores one.
Next column	This results in the re-entry of the **inner** *For .. Next* loop with the local variable *column* being incremented by one to the value of two.
marks(row, column) = 0	The element of the array *marks(1, 2)* is assigned zero. Of course it is the one, two position element because the variables *row* stores one and *column* stores two.

You complete the remainder of the description trace

QUESTION 20.3 (REVISION)
Produce the description trace tables for the following sub procedures: displayMarks(), readMarks() and Main().

PRACTICAL ACTIVITY 20.4
Implement Specification 20.2, i.e. enter and run Listing 20.5.

PRACTICAL ACTIVITY 20.5
Amend the last program so that a small class of six students take five examinations. Write another sub procedure that will find and display the overall average mark obtained by each student.

PRACTICAL ACTIVITY 20.6

Implement Specification 20.2 as a Windows application. Obviously this will involve the development of a suitable GUI.

PRACTICAL ACTIVITY 20.7

Develop a class with behaviour that will sort the content of an *Integer* array. The method that implements the behaviour must be able to receive the array as a parameter, sort it, and return it to the object requesting this sort service. The sort must be implemented using the bubble sort algorithm.

Test the class using a Console application and also a Windows application.

PRACTICAL ACTIVITY 20.8

Develop a class with behaviour that implements the functionality of all the procedures shown in Listing 20.5 except, of course, for *Main()*.

Test the class using a Console application and also a Windows application.

Arrays as objects

This chapter to date has treated arrays as an ordered set of simple data types, e.g. an array of integers. However, VB .NET allows for arrays to be treated as objects.

Constructing an array

Let's again consider an array of five integers. Figure 20.3 showed that we could declare such an array as shown below:

```
Dim numbers(5) As Integer
```

Treating an array as an object allows us to (alternatively) declare and allocate an array as shown below:

```
Dim numbers As Integer()
numbers = New Integer(5) {}
```

The first line of this alternative declares *number* as an array where each element is capable of storing an integer. However, it has not specified a size for the array.

The second line defines the size of the array and it does so by treating the variable *number* as an object reference to an integer array object. It constructs an instance (i.e. an object) using the

493

keyword *New* (this is the same technique as used to construct objects of other types of classes).

The braces ({ and }) that occur on the second line are referred to as the initialize list and are used to set the initial values of the array elements. When the braces are empty each element of an integer array is set to zero.

It is possible to allocate a size to an array at its declaration as shown below:

```
Dim numbers As Integer() = New Integer(5) {}
```

The example below shows how to initialize an array with values other than zero.

```
Dim numbers As Integer()
numbers = New Integer(5) {2,5,3,7,8}
```

Members of the *Array* class

All arrays have access to the members of the *System.Array* class. Examples of such members are shown in Table 20.3.

Table 20.3 Members of the *System.Array* class.

Member	Description
Length	A **public property** that gets the total number of elements in all the dimensions of the Array.
Rank	A **public property** that gets the number of dimensions of the array .
Clear	A **public method** that sets a range of elements in the Array to zero, to false, or to a null reference (Nothing in Visual Basic), depending on the element type.
CopyTo	A **public method** that copies all the elements of the current one-dimensional Array to the specified one-dimensional Array starting at the specified destination Array index.
GetLength	A **public method** that gets the number of elements in the specified dimension of the Array.
GetUpperBound	A **public method** that gets the upper bound of the specified dimension in the Array.
Reverse	A **shared and overloaded public method** that reverses the order of the elements in a one-dimensional array or reverses the order of the elements in a portion of the Array.
Sort	A shared and overloaded public method that sorts the elements in one-dimensional array.

Specification 20.1 will be implemented again but this time it will treat the five-element array as an object and use appropriate members of the *System.Array* class to perform the necessary actions.

The same GUI as shown in Figure 20.4 will be used and the event handling procedures attached to the following buttons will remain unchanged.

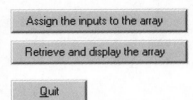

However, the changes to the code are described below.

For Listing 20.1 the declaration of the constants and the array is as follows (repeated here for convenience):

```
Private Const cMIN As Integer = 0
Private Const cMAX As Integer = 5
Private numbers(cMAX) As Integer
```

The following one line replaces these three lines:

```
Private numbers As Integer() = New Integer(5) {}
```

Now, *numbers* is an object of type *Array* and has members that indicate its upper and lower index number as well as the total length of the array. Consequently, there is no need for the constants.

The *For .. Next* loop used in the *Form_Load(..)* event handling procedure of Listing 20.1 is repeated below:

```
For i = cMIN To (cMAX – 1)
    numbers(i) = 0
Next I
```

This is replaced by the following *For .. Next* loop:

```
For i = numbers.GetLowerBound(0) To numbers.GetUpperBound(0)
    numbers(i) = 0
Next i
```

It can be seen that *GetLowerBound(0)* is used to set the starting value of the variable *i*.

GetUpperBound(0) is used to set the last value of the variable *i*.

This is used to specify the dimension of the array for which the upper index number is obtained. Of course in this case it is only a one-dimensional array so the value is set to zero.

Of course this *For .. Next* loop is not really required now as the array elements were initialized to zero at its declaration. However, the purpose of these two members of the Array class (*GetLowerBound(0)* and *GetUpperBound(0)*) should now be obvious.

The event handling procedure attached to the [Rearrange the array] button (as shown by Listing 20.1) is repeated below for convenience:

495

```
Private Sub btnReArrange_Click(ByVal sender As System.Object, ByVal e As _
System.EventArgs) Handles btnReArrange.Click
    Dim i As Integer
    Dim pass As Integer
    Dim temp As Integer
    Dim noSwitches As Boolean
    pass = 0
    Do
        pass = pass + 1
        noSwitches = True
        For i = cMIN To ((cMAX − 1) − pass)
            If numbers(i) > numbers(i + 1) Then
                noSwitches = False
                temp = numbers(i)
                numbers(i) = numbers(i + 1)
                numbers(i + 1) = temp
            End If
        Next I
    Loop Until noSwitches
End Sub
```

The following event handling procedure replaces this code:

```
Private Sub btnReArrange_Click(ByVal sender As System.Object, _
ByVal e As System.EventArgs) Handles btnReArrange.Click
    Array.Sort(numbers)
End Sub
```

The program statement *Array.Sort(numbers)* does the job of the bubble sort that we covered earlier in this chapter. Just one statement replacing numerous lines of code!

PRACTICAL ACTIVITY 20.9

Amend the program shown in Listing 20.1 with the object-oriented aspects of arrays just discussed and run the program. It operation should not have changed.

PRACTICAL ACTIVITY 20.10

Amend the program developed for Practical Activity 20.9 so that the array is sorted in the reverse order.

Hint: Consider the shared and overloaded public method *Reverse*.

PRACTICAL ACTIVITY 20.11

Implement Specifications 20.3 through to 20.5.

SPECIFICATION 20.3

Write a program that:

- Creates an array of twelve.
- Fills the array with multiples of two.
- Finds the sum of the content of all the elements of the array and display this sum on the VDU.

SPECIFICATION 20.4

Write a program that:

- Creates an array of ten elements.
- Asks the user to enter numbers to be stored in the array. Displays the largest number stored in the array.

SPECIFICATION 20.5

Write a program that:

- Asks the user for the size of an array.
- Creates an array of five elements.
- Asks the user to enter numbers to be stored in the array. Displays all the numbers greater than fifty and their position in the array (i.e. the index number).

Passing an array as a parameter

If you wished to pass an array as a parameter to a method then you can pass it *ByVal* or *ByRef*.

If you pass it *ByRef* then any processing of the array by the method is reflected back to the actual parameter.

If you pass it *ByVal* then any processing of the array by the method is **not** reflected back to the actual parameter.

However, passing it *ByVal* copies the entire array content from the actual to the formal parameter and for large arrays this can be slow. Choosing to pass an array *ByRef* only copies the relatively small reference to the array – this is a much faster process.

21 Collections

Collections allow for the management of a group of objects.

> **NOTE**: Objects can also be managed by creating an array of objects. However, by comparison to collections arrays are relatively inflexible structures. Nevertheless object arrays allow for the objects to be sequentially processed and it is possible to have empty elements of an array. Consequently arrays are useful for creating and working with a fixed number of strongly typed objects.

Before we describe collections and how to use them let's briefly look at arrays of objects.

How to create an array of objects

An array of an object type is declared and used in the same way as an array of any type. Individual elements of an array of objects are accessed by the name of the array and the index number. The implementation of Specification 21.1 will be used to illustrate an array of objects.

> **SPECIFICATION 21.1**
>
> *Write a program that will represent four dice each capable of throwing a number between 1 and 6. Upon the click of a button all four are thrown and the sum of their values are displayed in a label.*

The GUI used to implement Specification 21.1 is shown in Figure 21.1.

Figure 21.1 The GUI for Specification 21.1.

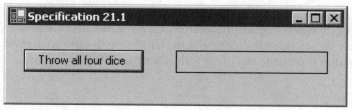

The class that represents a die is shown in Listing 21.1 and the code 'attached' to the Throw all four dice button is shown in Listing 21.2.

Listing 21.1 The *Die* class.

```
Public Class Die
    Private Shared seed As Integer
    Private dieSide As Integer

    Public ReadOnly Property DieValue()
        Get
            Return dieSide
        End Get
    End Property

    Public Sub ThrowDie()
        Dim die As Random
        If seed = 0 Then
            seed = Second(Now)
        End If
        seed = seed + 1
        If seed = Integer.MaxValue Then
            seed = 0
        End If
        die = New Random(seed)
        dieSide = die.Next(1, 7)
    End Sub
End Class
```

Listing 21.2 The code attached to the button.

```
Private Sub btnFourDice_Click(ByVal sender As System.Object, ByVal e As _|
System.EventArgs) Handles btnFourDice.Click
    Dim dice(4) As Die
    Dim sum As Integer
    Dim i As Integer
    sum = 0
    For i = 0 To 3
        dice(i) = New Die()
    Next i
    For i = 0 To 3
        dice(i).ThrowDie()
    Next i
    For i = 0 To 3
        sum = sum + dice(i).DieValue
    Next
    lblSumOfDice.Text = "The sum of all four dice is " & CStr(sum)
End Sub
```

Description of Listing 21.1

```
Private Shared seed As Integer
```

A variable declared with the *Shared* modifier is a *Shared* variable and a *Shared* variable identifies one storage location. Regardless of how many instances of a class are created, there is only ever **one** copy of a *Shared* variable. The lifetime of a *Shared* variable is from the start of the program until the program terminates. A *Shared* variable is initialized to the default value of its type, which in this case is zero.

```
Private dieSide As Integer
```

This is a class level variable used to store the value of the random number that represents the throw of the die. It is a *Private* and therefore 'hidden' variable. Access to the value stored in this variable is via the property *DieValue* that is 'created' using the read-only property procedure declared within the class and shown below:

```
Public ReadOnly Property DieValue)
    Get
        Return dieSide
    End Get
End Property
```

```
Public Sub Throw Die()
    Dim MyDie As Random
    If Seed = 0 Then
        seed = Second(Now)
    End If
    seed = seed + 1
    If seed = Integer.Max Value Then
        seed = 0
    End If
    myDie = New Random(seed)
    dieSide = myDie.Next(1,7)
End Sub
```

This method generates a random number between 1 and 6 and stores the value in the variable *dieSide* (the property procedure *DieValue()* is able to access this variable).

Description trace for *ThrowDice()*

Statement	Description
If seed = 0 Then	When the program starts and the *first* instance of the *Die* class is constructed the value of the variable *seed* will be zero. This test is therefore *True* and the statement within the selection construct is executed.
seed = Second(Now)	*Now* is a function that returns the date and the time. For example, #25/3/2002 12:06:52 PM#. *Second* is a function that extracts the value stored in the seconds field of the current time and date. For the example of the date and time shown above it can be seen that *seed* will be set to the value 52.
seed = seed + 1	The value of seed is incremented by one to 53.
If seed = Integer.MaxValue Then	This ensures that *seed* does not exceed the maximum value of an integer type (as represented by *Integer.MaxValue*). In this case the conditional test if false so the statement within the selection construct is not executed.
myDie = New Random(seed)	This creates an instance of the *Random* class using the *seed* value of 53. This will generate a specific pseudo random sequence of numbers.
dieSide = myDie.Next(1, 7)	The message *myDie.Next(1, 7)* invokes the method *Next* and this returns a random number from 1 to 6.

If the program is **not** terminated then the next time a *ThrowDice* method of a particular instance of the *Die* class is executed then the statements will execute as follows:

If seed = 0 Then	The *seed* value is 53 as it is a shared variable. Consequently it still has this value from the last time the *ThrowDice* method was invoked. The test is *false* and the statement within the selection construct is **not** executed.
seed = seed + 1	The value of *seed* is incremented by one to 54. This will ensure that the next instance of the *Random* object will generate a different pseudo random sequence of numbers.
If seed = Integer.MaxValue Then	This ensures that seed does not exceed the maximum value of an integer type (as represented by *Integer.MaxValue*). In this case the conditional test if false so the statement within the selection construct is not executed.
myDie = New Random(seed)	This creates an instance of the *Random* class using the *seed* value of 54. This will generate a specific pseudo random sequence of numbers.
dieSide = myDie.Next(1, 7)	The message *myDie.Next(1, 7)* invokes the method *Next* and this returns a random number from 1 to 6.

NOTE: The statement *seed = Second(Now)* is used to create one of 60 possible different seeds to be used when creating an instance of the *Random* class.

The statement *seed = seed + 1* is used to ensure that the next instance of *Random* class has a different seed value than the previous instance of the *Random* class.

Description of Listing 21.2.

The local variables used by the event handling procedure will be described first.

Dim dice(4) As Die

This declaration has created a four-element array where each element is capable of storing an *object reference* to a *Die* object that will be used with in the program – as illustrated below:

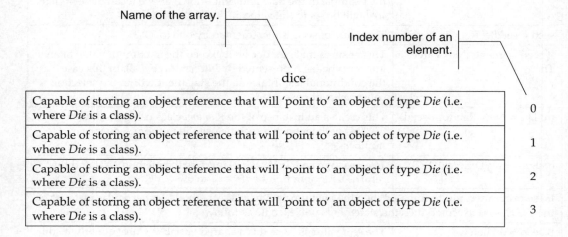

Name of the array.

Index number of an element.

dice

Capable of storing an object reference that will 'point to' an object of type *Die* (i.e. where *Die* is a class).	0
Capable of storing an object reference that will 'point to' an object of type *Die* (i.e. where *Die* is a class).	1
Capable of storing an object reference that will 'point to' an object of type *Die* (i.e. where *Die* is a class).	2
Capable of storing an object reference that will 'point to' an object of type *Die* (i.e. where *Die* is a class).	3

Dim sum As Integer

This variable is used to store the sum of the values thrown for all the dice.

Dim i As Integer

The variable i is used by the deterministic loop to access each element of the array in turn.

Description trace for Listing 21.2

Statement	Description
sum = 0	Initializes the variable to zero.
For i = 0 To 3	Enters the loop for the first time with *i* set at 0.
dice(i) = New Die()	An instance of the *Die* class is constructed. The object reference to this instance of the *Die* class is stored in element zero of the array, that is, *dice(0)* 'points to' this object i.e. the first element of the array is assigned the object reference to an instance of the *Die* class.
Next i	*i* is incremented by 1 to 1 and the loop is re-entered.
dice(i) = New Die()	An instance of the *Die* class is constructed. The object reference to this instance of the *Die* class is stored in element one of the array, that is, *dice(1)* 'points to' this object, i.e. the second element of the array is assigned the object reference to **another** instance of the Die class.
Next i	*i* is incremented by 1 to 2 and the loop is re-entered.
dice(i) = New Die()	An instance of the *Die* class is constructed. The object reference to this instance of the *Die* class is stored in element two of the array, that is, *dice(2)* 'points to' this object i.e. the third element of the array is assigned the object reference to a **third** instance of the *Die* class.
Next i	*i* is incremented by 1 to 3 and the loop is re-entered.
dice(i) = New Die()	An instance of the *Die* class is constructed. The object reference to this instance of the *Die* class is stored in element three of the array, that is, *dice(3)* 'points to' this object i.e. the fourth element of the array is assigned the object reference to a **fourth** instance of the *Die* class.

Figure 21.2 illustrates the relationship between the array and the *Die* objects. The loop has executed four times as specified by the deterministic loop. Consequently, the second deterministic loop is entered.

Statement	Description
For i = 0 To 3	The second loop is entered for the first time with *i* set at 0.
dice(i).ThrowDie()	This message invokes the *ThrowDie* method of the object reference by the first element of the array. This instance now stores a value for the throw of the die in its variable *dieSide*.
Next i	*i* is incremented by 1 to 1 and the loop is re-entered.
dice(i).ThrowDie()	This message invokes the *ThrowDie* method of **another** object that is referenced by the second element of the array. This instance now stores a value for the throw of the die in its variable *dieSide*. This variable is also an instance variable and consequently it is totally **independent** from the instance variable of the object 'pointed at' by the first element of the array.
Next i	*i* is incremented by 1 to 2 and the loop is re-entered.
dice(i).ThrowDie()	This message invokes the *ThrowDie* method of the **third** object that is referenced by the third element of the array. This instance now stores a value for the throw of the die.

Next i	*i* is incremented by 1 to 3 and the loop is re-entered.
dice(i).ThrowDie()	This message invokes the *ThrowDie* method of the **fourth** object that is referenced by the fourth element of the array. This instance now stores a value for the throw of the die.

The loop has executed four times as specified by the deterministic loop. Consequently, the third deterministic loop is entered.

sum = sum + dice(i). DieValue	The value of the property *DieValue* for the first instance of the *Die* class is added to sum, i.e. the value of the first die thrown is added to the sum
Next i	*i* is incremented by 1 to 1 and the loop is re-entered.
sum = sum + dice(i). DieValue	The value of the property *DieValue* for the second instance of the *Die* class is added to sum, i.e. the value of the second die thrown is added to the sum.
Next i	*i* is incremented by 1 to 2 and the loop is re-entered.
sum = sum + dice(i). DieValue	The value of the property *DieValue* for the third instance of the *Die* class is added to sum, i.e. the value of the third die thrown is added to the sum.
Next i	*i* is incremented by 1 to 3 and the loop is re-entered.
sum = sum + dice(i).DieValue	The value of the property *DieValue* for the fourth instance of the *Die* class is added to sum, i.e. the value of the fourth die thrown is added to the sum

The loop has executed four times as specified by the deterministic loop. Consequently, the next statement to execute is as shown next.

lblSumOfDice.Text = "The sum of all four dice is " & CStr(sum)	The sum of all the dice is displayed in the label. An example is shown below.

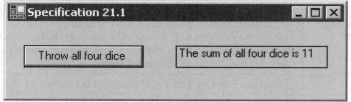

The end of the program execution

Figure 21.2 The relationship between the array elements and the four *Die* objects.

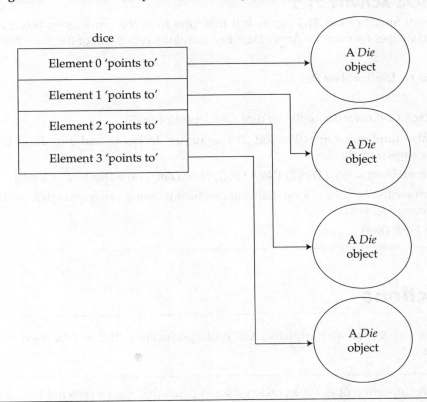

NOTE: It is worth emphasizing that the elements of the array **do not** store the objects. They store the references to the objects, that is, each element 'points to' an object.

Development Question 21.1 also considers this relationship between the elements of an array and the objects it points to.

PRACTICAL ACTIVITY 21.1

Implement Specification 21.1 as represented by the GUI of Figure 21.1 and Listings 21.1 and 21.2.

QUESTION 21.1 (DEVELOPMENT)

What is the effect of the inserting the assignment statements (shown below) after the following segment of code from Listing 21.2?

```
For i = 0 To 3
    dice(i) = New Die()
Next i
```

```
dice(1) = dice(0)
dice(2) = dice(0)
dice(3) = dice(0)
```

Alter and run the code. Single step through the program and observe how the values of the variables change.

PRACTICAL ACTIVITY 21.2

Implement Specification 21.1 again, but this time treat the array as an object and use appropriate members of the Array class to control the repetition of the *For .. Next* loop.

Hint 1:

Dim dice As Die() = New Die(3) {}

Hint 2:

For i = dice.GetLowerBound(0) To dice.GetUpperBound(0)

Try to also implement Specification 21.1 again by declaring and allocating the array object as shown by this line:

Dim dice As Die() = New Die(3) {New Die(), New Die(), New Die(), New Die()}

Then remove the *For .. Next* loop that contains the following program statement (remove this statement as well):

dice(i) = New Die()

Collections

Collections are objects. The implementation of Specification 21.2 will be used to illustrate collections.

NOTE: A Collection object is an ordered set of items that can be referred to as a unit.

SPECIFICATION 21.2

Write a program that will allow a user to choose how many dice they would like to use in a game. Then throw all the dice and sum the value of each dice displaying the result in a label. There must be a least three dice.

A typical runtime for the program that implements Specification 21.2 is shown in Figure 21.3. Listing 21.3 shows the code attached to the GUI; it uses the same *Die* class as developed for Specification 21.1. Figure 21.4 shows the solution explorer for this program.

Figure 21.3 A typical runtime for Specification 21.2.

1. When the user clicks on to the **Register the number of Dice** button the following InputBox appears.

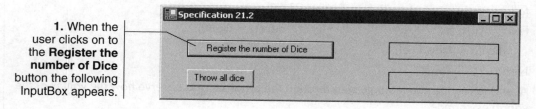

Figure 21.3 (cont.)

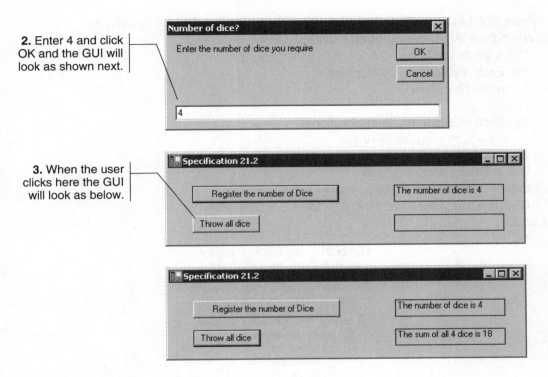

2. Enter 4 and click OK and the GUI will look as shown next.

3. When the user clicks here the GUI will look as below.

Listing 21.3 The code attached to the GUI.

```
Private myDiceCollection As New Collection()
Private myDie As Die

Private Sub btnNumberOfDice_Click(ByVal sender As System.Object, ByVal e As _
System.EventArgs) Handles btnNumberOfDice.Click
    Dim i As Integer
    Dim numberOfDice As Integer
    numberOfDice = InputBox ("Enter the number of dice you require ", "Number of dice? ")
    If numberOfDice < 3 Then
        numberOfDice = 3
    End If
    For i = 1 To numberOfDice
        myDie = New Die()
        myDiceCollection.Add(myDie)
    Next i
    lblShowNumber.Text = "The number of dice is " & CStr(numberOfDice)
End Sub
```

Listing 21.3 (cont.)

```
Private Sub btnThrowDice_Click(ByVal sender As System.Object, ByVal e As _
System.EventArgs) Handles btnThrowDice.Click
    Dim sum As Integer
    For Each myDie In myDiceCollection
        myDie.ThrowDie()
    Next
    For Each myDie In myDiceCollection
        sum = sum + myDie.DieValue
    Next
    lblSumOfDice.Visible = True
    lblSumOfDice.Text = "The sum of all " & _
    CStr(myDiceCollection.Count) & " dice is " & CStr(sum)
End Sub
```

Figure 21.4 The Solution Explorer.

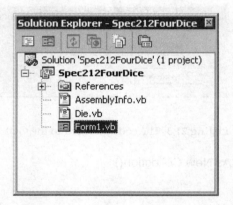

Description of Listing 21.3

The following class variables are described first.

Private myDiceCollection As New Collection()

This declares and constructs (i.e. creates) an object of type *Collection* and this object is referenced by the class variable *myDiceCollection*.

Private myDie As Die

This declares a class level variable of type *Die* (i.e. class *Die*) that is capable of storing an object reference to an instance of the *Die* class.

> **NOTE:** Instances of both of these class level variables can be accessed by all code 'attached' to an instance of the GUI.

The local variables declared inside the *btnNumberOfDice_Click()* event handling procedure are described next.

> Dim i As Integer

This local variable *i* is used as the index of the *For .. Next* loop.

> Dim numberOfDice As Integer

This local variable *numberOfDice* is used to store the number of dice entered by the user and it is used to dictate the number of dice to be used in the program.

Description trace for the *btnNumberOfDice_Click* event handling procedure

Statement	Description
numberOfDice = InputBox("Enter the number of dice you require ", "Number of dice? ")	This displays an InputBox that asks the user how many dice they require for the program. An example is shown below.

If numberOfDice < 3 Then numberOfDice = 3 End If	This selection construct is used to ensure that if a user enters a number less than 3 the program will set the variable *numberOfDice* to at least three. In this case the user has entered three so the statement within the construct is not executed.
For i = 1 To numberOfDice	This sets the value of the variable *i* to 1
myDie = New Die()	This creates an instance of the *Die* class.
myDiceCollection.Add(myDie)	The instance of the *Die* class just created is added to the Collection as represented by the variable *myDiceCollection*. The *Add* method of the *Collection* class is used to add the *Die* object to the collection.
Next i	The loop is entered again
myDie = New Die()	This creates another instance of the *Die* class.
myDiceCollection.Add(myDie)	The instance of the *Die* class just created is also added to the Collection.
Next i	The loop is entered again.
myDie = New Die()	This creates yet another instance of the *Die* class.
myDiceCollection.Add(myDie)	The instance of the *Die* class just created is also added to the Collection.

The object as referenced by *myDiceCollection* now contains three *Die* objects. The adding of these objects is achieved using the *Add(myDie)* message which invokes the *Add* method of the instance of the *Collection* class.

lblShowNumber.Text = "The number of dice is " & CStr(numberOfDice)	This statement displays the number of dice to be used during this execution of the program as shown below:

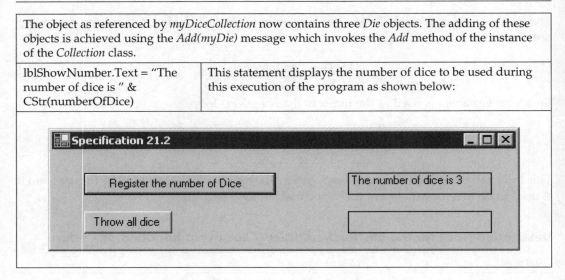

NOTE: The use of the *Add* method associated with the *Collection* class allows for any number of objects to be added to an object of the *Collection* class.

Description trace for the *btnThrowDice_Click* event handling procedure

Statement	Description
For Each myDie In myDiceCollection	The *For Each* construct allows every object within the *Collection* object to be accessed in turn. After the keyword *Each* is a variable whose type, is the type the object, stored in the *Collection*, in this case it is of type *Die* (i.e. of type class *Die*). Following this is the keyword In which is in turn followed by the object reference (*myDiceCollection*) to the instance of the *Collection* class.
myDie.ThrowDie()	This message invokes the *ThrowDie()* method of the **first** entry in the *Collection* object. This first entry is an instance of the *Die* class. Consequently, the object *myDie* generates a number between 1 and 6 and stores this 'within' itself.
Next	This causes a move to the next object within the *Collection* class object.
myDie.ThrowDie()	This message invokes the *ThrowDie()* method of the **second** *Die* object within the Collection object. Consequently, the second *myDie* object generates a number between 1 and 6.
Next	This causes a move on to the next object in the class.
myDie.ThrowDie()	This message invokes the *ThrowDie()* method of the **third** *Die* object in the Collection object. Consequently, the third *myDie* object generates a number between 1 and 6.

There are no more objects in the collection so the program leaves the *For Each* construct and carries on with the rest of the program statements	
For Each myDie In myDiceCollection	The *For Each* construct is again used to allow every object within the Collection object to be accessed in turn.
sum = sum + myDie.DieValue	The value of the property *DieValue* of the **first** object in the Collection object is added to the local variable *sum*.
Next	This causes a move on to the next object in the collection object.
sum = sum + myDie.DieValue	The value of the property *DieValue* of the **second** object in the Collection is added to the local variable *sum*.
Next	This causes a move on to the next object in the collection.
sum = sum + myDie.DieValue	The value of the property *DieValue* of the **third** object in the Collection is added to the local variable *sum*.
There are no more objects in the collection so the program leaves the *For Each* construct and carries on with the rest of the program statements.	
lblSumOfDice.Visible = True	The label displaying the sum of the dice values is made visible.
lblSumOfDice.Text = "The sum of all " & CStr(myDiceCollection.Count) & " dice is " & CStr(sum)	The value of the sum generated by the addition of all the dice values is displayed in a label along with number of the dice used.
	The number of dice used is equal to the number of dice objects held within the collection object. This number is found by sending the message *myDiceCollection.Count*.
	This message is to the instance of the Collection object referenced by the object variable *myDiceCollection* and the message accesses the *Count* property that returns the number of objects within the object, in this case three. An example of GUI is shown below.

Specification 21.2

Register the number of Dice   The number of dice is 3

Throw all dice   The sum of all 3 dice is 10

PRACTICAL ACTIVITY 21.3

Implement Specification 21.2 as represented by the GUI of Figure 21.3 and Listing 21.3. Remember that the *Die* class also has to be part of the solution as illustrated by Figure 21.4. This *Die* class is the same as Listing 21.1.

PRACTICAL ACTIVITY 21.4

Add another two buttons to the GUI developed during Practical Activity 21.3 so it looks like the GUI shown in Figure 21.5 and attach the event handling procedures shown in Listings 21.4 and 21.5.

NOTE: It is worth reminding you that the event handling procedures have a name derived from the control (object) name and the event. Consequently, when you use the programs listed in this book it assumes that you have named the objects as appropriate to the code. Remember the rule: always name your controls (objects) before you start to code!

Figure 21.5 The amended GUI.

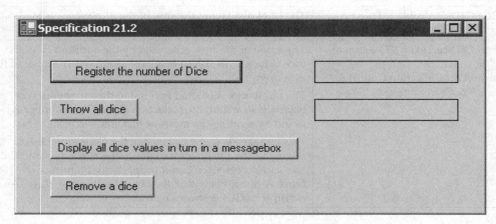

Listing 21.4 The event handling procedures attached to the Display all dice values . . . button.

```
Private Sub btnValuesOfEachDice_Click(ByVal sender As System.Object, ByVal e As
System.EventArgs) Handles btnValuesOfEachDice.Click
    Dim myCount As Integer = 1
    For Each myDie In myDiceCollection
        MessageBox.Show("The value of dice " & CStr(myCount) & " is " & _
        CStr(myDie.DieValue))
        myCount = myCount + 1
    Next
End Sub
```

Listing 21.5 The event handling procedures attached to the Remove a dice button.

```
Private Sub btnRemove_Click(ByVal sender As System.Object, _
ByVal e As System.EventArgs) Handles btnRemove.Click

    If myDiceCollection.Count > 0 Then
        myDiceCollection.Remove(1)
        lblShowNumber.Text = "The number of dice is " & CStr(myDiceCollection.Count)
        lblSumOfDice.Visible = False
    End If
End Sub
```

The code shown in Listing 21.4 uses the *For Each* construct to access each *Die* object in the Collection object and display its value in a MessageBox.

The code shown in Listing 21.5 uses two methods of the Collection class, namely, *Remove* and *Count*.

The message *myDiceCollection.Remove(1)* invokes the *Remove* method which removes one *Die* object from the Collection object.

The message *myDiceCollection.Count* accesses the *Count* property of the Collection object and displays the number of dice in a label along with an appropriate string. The *If .. Then* selection construct is present to ensure that there is no attempt to remove a *Die* object when the Count is zero (i.e. when there are no *Die* objects within the Collection object).

Setting the *Visible* property of the *lblSumOfDice* label to false stops it displaying outdated information.

Table 21.1 describes examples of methods and properties of the *Collection* class.

Table 21.1 Examples of methods and properties of the *Collection* class.

Method/Property	Description
Count	A read-only property that returns an integer containing the number of objects in a collection.
Item	Returns a specific member of a Collection object either by position or by key.
Add	A method that adds a member to a Collection object.
Remove	A method that removes a member from a Collection object.

NOTE: An important difference between collections and arrays are that Collections are one-based whereas arrays are zero based. This means that the first member of a collection is at position 1 not position 0.

How to add, remove and retrieve items from a collection

How to add to a collection

Adding items to a *Collection* is achieved by sending an appropriate message that invokes the *Add* method of the instance of the Collections class. The syntax for the message is shown below:

objectCollectionName.Add(Item, Key)

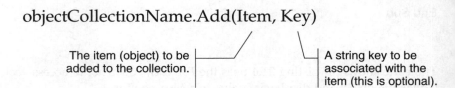

The item (object) to be added to the collection.

A string key to be associated with the item (this is optional).

> **NOTE**: The key has to be a string. However, other types are allowed provided they are converted to a string. For example, if the key was an integer it needs to be converted to a string using either the *CStr* function or the *ToString* method.

The full syntax for the *Add* method is shown below:

```
Public Sub Add(ByVal Item As Object, Optional ByVal Key _
As String, Option ByVal {Before|After} As Object = Nothing)
```

Description of the Syntax is shown in Table 21.2.

Table 21.2 Description of the syntax.

Parameter	Description
Item	This parameter is required (i.e. it is not optional) and it can be an object of any type.
Key	This is an optional parameter that needs to be a unique string expression that specifies a key string that can be used instead of a positional index to access a member of the collection.
Before	This is an optional parameter that specifies a relative position in the collection. The item to be added is placed in the collection before the item identified by the *Before* argument. If *Before* is a numeric expression, it must be a number from 1 to the value of the collection's *Count* property. If *Before* is a string expression, it must correspond to the key string specified when the member being referred to was added to the collection.

Table 21.2 (cont.)

After	This is an optional parameter that specifies a relative position in the collection. The member to be added is placed in the collection after the member identified by the *After* argument. If *After* is a numeric expression, it must be a number from 1 to the value of the collection's *Count* property. If *After* is a String expression, it must correspond to the key string specified when the member referred to was added to the collection.
Note: You cannot specify both *Before* and *After*.	

NOTE: An error will occur if the Before or After argument do not refer to an existing member of the collection. Also when adding a new member if the specified Key value matches the key for an existing member of the collection an error will occur. Both of these will throw an *ArgumentException* exception type – see Chapter 22 on Structured error handling.

How to remove from a collection

The full syntax for the *Remove* method is shown below:

```
Public Overloads Sub Remove(ByVal {Key As String | Index As Integer})
```

Description of the Syntax is shown in Table 21.3.

Table 21.3 Description of the syntax.

Parameter	Description
Key	A unique String expression that specifies a key string that can be used to access a member of the collection that is to be removed.
Index	An expression that specifies the position of a member of the collection. If *Index* is a numeric expression it must be a number from 1 to the value of the collection's *Count* property. If *Index* is a string expression it must correspond to the *Key* argument specified when the member referred to was added to the collection.
Note: You cannot specify both *Key* and *Index*.	

NOTE: An *ArgumentException* exception type error will occur if a key is invalid or not specified.

An *IndexOutOfRangeException* exception type error will occur if the index does not match an existing member of the collection.

The implementation of Specification 21.3 will illustrate the use of the methods *Add* and *Remove*.

SPECIFICATION 21.3

Write a program that will define a Collection of customers. Customers can be added and removed from the Collection by the click of appropriate buttons. All of the customers are displayed in a ListBox and the code to achieve this is also attached to an appropriate button.

The GUI for Specification 21.3 is shown in Figure 21.6 and the listings are shown in Listing 21.6 and 21.7.

Figure 21.6 The GUI for Specification 21.3.

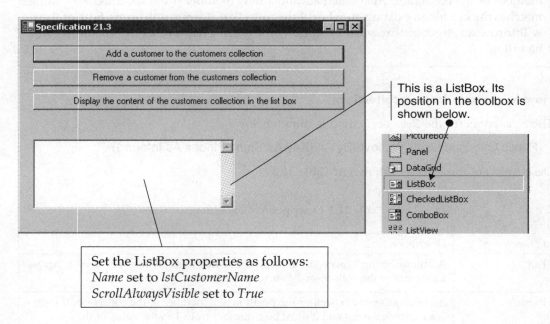

Listing 21.6 The *Customer* class.

```
Public Class Customer
    Private customerName As String
    Sub New(ByVal pName As String)
        customerName = pName
    End Sub
    ReadOnly Property Name()
        Get
            Name = customerName
        End Get
    End Property
End Class
```

516

The code of Listing 21.6 shows the definition of a class that has a constructor that takes a string parameter that is used to set an instance of the class level variable *customerName*. A read-only property procedure allows access to this *Private* class variable.

Listing 21.7 The code attached to the GUI.

```vb
Private customers As New Collection()

Private Sub btnAddCustomer_Click(ByVal sender As System.Object, _
ByVal e As System.EventArgs) Handles btnAddCustomer.Click

    Dim newName As String

    newName = InputBox("Name of new customer: ", " Add a customer")

    If newName <> "" Then
        customers.Add(New Customer(newName), newName)
    End If
End Sub

Private Sub btnDisplayCustomers_Click(ByVal sender As System.Object, _
ByVal e As System.EventArgs) Handles btnDisplayCustomers.Click

    Dim aCustomer As Customer

    lstCustomerName.Items.Clear()
    For Each aCustomer In customers
        lstCustomerName.Items.Add(aCustomer.Name)
    Next
End Sub

Private Sub btnRemoveCustomer_Click(ByVal sender As System.Object, _
ByVal e As System.EventArgs) Handles btnRemoveCustomer.Click

    Dim customerName As String
    customerName = InputBox _
    ("Name of new customer you wish to remove: ", "Remove a customer")

    If customerName <> "" Then
        customers.Remove(customerName)
    End If
End Sub
```

The first line of Listing 21.7 creates a collection object referenced by *customers*.

The code within the *btnAddCustomer_Click* event handling procedure uses an InputBox to ask the user for the name of the customer. It then uses the *Add* method of the collection class to add members to the *customers* object. The line of code responsible for adding to the *customers* object is detailed in Figure 21.7.

Figure 21.7 Adding to the collection. This illustrates the creating of an instance of the *Customer* class 'in line'. Of course, it could have been constructed just before this *Add* method and its object reference could have been used as a parameter to the *Add* method.

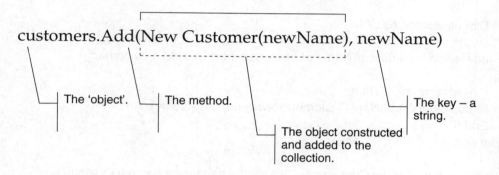

Figure 21.8 shows a sample runtime of the program.

Figure 21.8 A sample runtime.

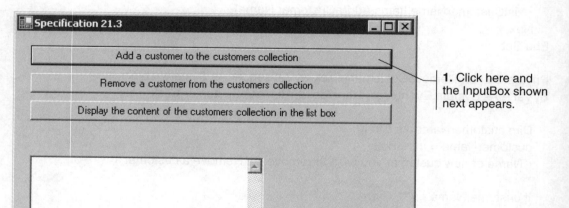

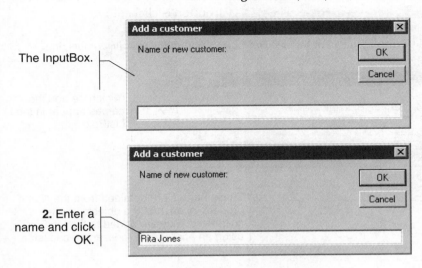

Figure 21.8 (cont.)

The InputBox.

2. Enter a name and click OK.

Assuming that the user continues to add names as illustrated by Figure 21.8 then the *customers* collection will contain objects as illustrated by Figure 21.9.

Figure 21.9 The *customers* collection object after instances the *Customer* class have been added.

The *customers* collection	
Object	*Key*
All instances of the Customer class	The key was chosen to be the same as the value passed as a parameter to the Customer class constructor method
 RRitaJones	"Rita Jones"
 RitaJones	"Cara Jones"
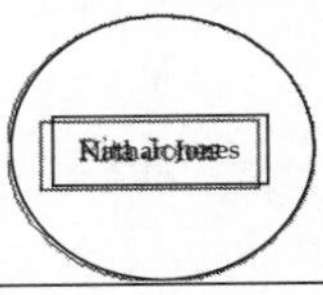 RithJones	"Nathan Jones"
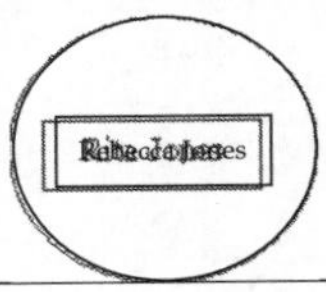 RebeccaJones	"Rebecca Jones"

Figure 21.10 shows the GUI after all of the objects as represented by Figure 21.9 have been added and after the [Display the content of the customers collection in the list box] button is clicked.

Figure 21.10 The GUI displaying all of the *customer* objects within the *customers* collection.

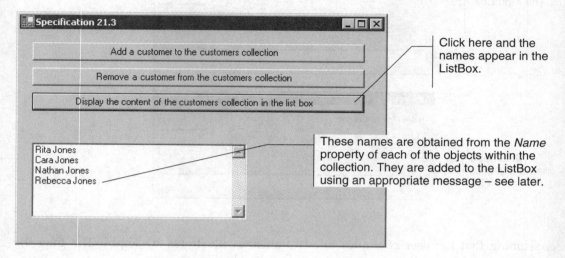

The code within the *btnDisplayCustomers_Click* event handler, clears the content of the *ListBox* using the message *lstCustomerName.Items.Clear()*, it then uses the *For Each* construct to add the content of the *Name* property of the objects within the *customers* collection to the *ListBox* using the following message, *lstCustomerName.Items.Add(aCustomer.Name)*.

Figure 21.11 shows a runtime that removes an object from the collection.

Figure 21.11 Removing an object from the collection.

Figure 21.11 (cont.)

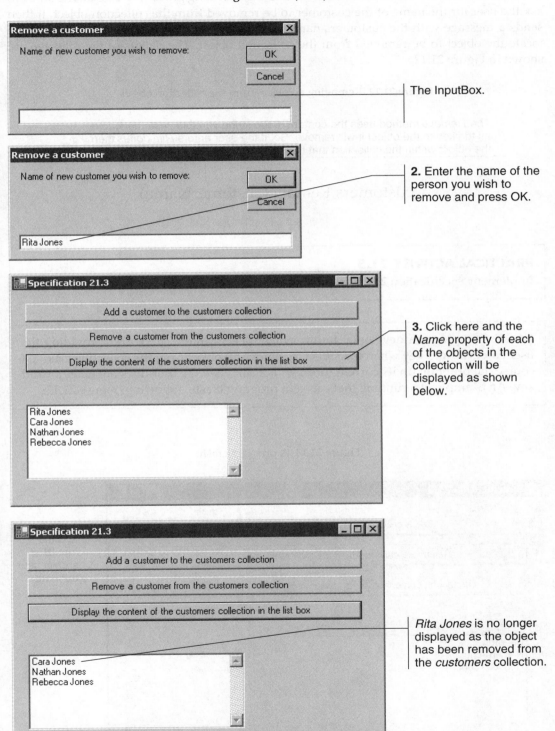

The InputBox.

2. Enter the name of the person you wish to remove and press OK.

3. Click here and the *Name* property of each of the objects in the collection will be displayed as shown below.

Rita Jones is no longer displayed as the object has been removed from the *customers* collection.

The code within the *btnRemoveCustomer_Click* event handling procedure uses an InputBox to ask the user for the name of the customer to be removed from the collection object. It then sends a message with the customers name as a parameter. This name is used as a key to locate the object to be removed from the collection object. The details of the message are shown in Figure 21.12.

Figure 21.12 Removing an object from the collection object.

> The *Remove* method uses the content of the string variable *customerName* as the key to the object it will remove. So, if the user enters *Rita Jones* then the object within the collection that has this as the key is removed.

customers.Remove(customerName)

PRACTICAL ACTIVITY 21.5

Implement Specification 21.3 as represented by Figure 21.6 and Listings 21.6 and 21.7.

NOTE: The program developed to implement Specification 21.3 works providing the user enters a valid key when they wish to remove an object from the collection class. Of course the program (in its current form) will crash when the user does not enter a valid key. An example of a runtime that causes a program crash is shown in Figure 21.13.

Figure 21.13 A program crash.

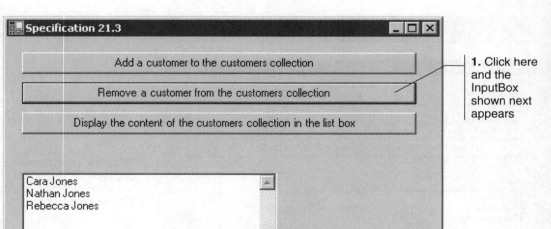

1. Click here and the InputBox shown next appears

Figure 21.13 (cont.)

2. Enter *Paul Lever* and click OK. Of course there is no object within the collection with this key so the program will throw an exception as shown by the dialog box.

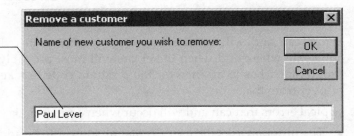

Dialog box describing the exception thrown.

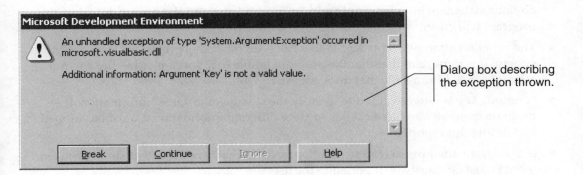

NOTE: Of course it is important that a program is not allowed to crash in this manner. VB .NET uses a structured mechanism to deal with errors that result when a program executes. This is the theme of the next chapter.

22 Structured error handling

Errors can and will occur when a program executes. The task of a programmer is to anticipate where and when the errors will most probably occur. When errors happen the programmer has to arrange for the program code to take appropriate steps to report and recover from the error.

Typical errors that can and will occur when a program is executed are outlined below:

- The program asks the user to enter an integer to be added to a running total and the user accidentally enters a letter instead of a figure (e.g. *3w* instead of 12). It is an obvious statement but you cannot add *3w* to an integer and if steps are not taken the program will crash.

- The program attempts to read a file that has been mistakenly removed from the file system. It is important that that the program is able to report a missing file and not attempt to read from a file that does not exist.

- A unique key is often required to identify the storage of different information. If a program generates an identical key to store different information it must be stopped and its attempt reported.

- If a program attempts to read from a floppy drive that is not ready or simply broken then it must obviously be reported to the user.

Errors and exceptions

The terms error and exception are used interchangeably. When an error occurs during the execution of a program an **exception object** is created and the program attempts to find an **exception handler** to deal with this object and consequently the error that caused its creation.

An exception handler is a block of code that reports the error and then allows the program to resume its normal flow.

Throwing an exception

The phrase **'throwing an exception'** is often used to indicate that the program has encountered an error and reacted by creating an exception object that contains information about the error that occurred.

> **NOTE**: Resource failure, incorrect program logic and user error are the main factors that cause errors and thus exceptions.
>
> These errors relate to how the code undertakes a specific task and not to the purpose of the task.

The *Try-Catch-Finally* construct

A *Try-Catch-Finally* construct is used to catch an exception. This construct is put around any code where the possibility of an exception exists. The structure of a *Try-Catch-Finally* is shown below:

Try

    ' Code that might cause an exception is placed here
    ' between the keywords *Try* and *Catch*

Catch

    ' Code to deal with the exception is placed here
    ' between the keywords *Catch* and *Finally*

Finally

    ' Code to perform any cleanup is placed here
    ' between the keywords *Finally* and *End Try*

End Try

> *Finally* is often not present, in which case, code that deals with the exception appear between the keywords *Catch* and *End Try*.

The exception object

The exception object is derived from the exception class and Table 22.1 lists some of its members that can be invoked (messaged) at runtime.

Table 22.1 Some members of the exception class.

Member	Description
Message	This is a public property that that describes the current exception.
Source	This is a public property that gets or sets the name of the application or the object that causes the error.
TargetSite	This is a public property that gets the method that 'threw' the current exception.
ToString	This is a public method that creates and returns a string representation of the current exception.

PRACTICAL ACTIVITY 22.1

Use the VB .NET help to look up other members of the exception class.

SPECIFICATION 22.1

*Amend the program developed to meet Specification 21.3 from the last chapter so that clicking onto the Remove a customer .... button does **not** cause a crash (as illustrated by Figure 21.13 from the last chapter).*

To implement Specification 22.1 requires an amendment to the *btnRemoveCustomer_Click* event handler. The amendment is shown in Listing 22.1.

Listing 22.1 Amendment to the *btnRemoveCustomer_Click* event handler.

```
Private Sub btnRemoveCustomer_Click(ByVal sender As _
System.Object, ByVal e As System.EventArgs) _
Handles btnRemoveCustomer.Click

    Dim customerName As String
    customerName = InputBox("Name of new customer you wish to remove: ", _
    "Remove a customer")
    If customerName <> "" Then
        Try
            customers.Remove(customerName)
        Catch
            MessageBox.Show("The name you have entered is not a customer ", _
            "Not a customer", MessageBoxButtons.OK, MessageBoxIcon.Error)
        End Try
    End If
End Sub
```

NOTE: The *Finally* section was not used in this example. However, it is important to note that there has to be at least one *Catch* or one *Finally* section present within a *Try .. End Try* construct. There can also be more than one *Catch* section for each *Try .. End Try* construct.

Description trace for the amended *btnRemoveCustomer_Click* event handler when an exception is NOT thrown

Statement	Description
customerName = InputBox("Name of new customer you wish to remove: ", "Remove a customer")	The user enters *Rita Jones*, which 'is' a key to an object within the collection.
If customerName <> "" Then	Something has been entered so this is true; consequently, the selection construct is entered.
customers.Remove(customerName)	This program statement between the *Try* and *Catch* keywords is executed and the object with the key *Rita Jones* is removed from the collection.
The event handler ends its execution. The statement between the keywords *Catch* and *End Try* is not executed because an exception was not thrown. That is, there was no error in the execution of the program.	

Description trace for the amended *btnRemoveCustomer_Click* event handler when an exception IS thrown

Statement	Description
customerName = InputBox("Name of new customer you wish to remove: ", "Remove a customer")	The user enters *Philip Jones*, which is **not** a key to an object within the collection.
If customerName <> "" Then	This is true so the selection construct is entered.
customers.Remove(customerName)	This program statement between the *Try* and *Catch* keywords is executed and it throws an exception because the key is **not** found in the collection object. However, rather than crash the program executes the statement between the keywords *Catch* and *End Try*.
MessageBox.Show("The name you have entered is not a customer ", "Not a customer", MessageBoxButtons.OK, MessageBoxIcon.Error)	The MessageBox informs the user that the name they entered is not a customer and the program does not crash. An example of the MessageBox is shown in Figure 22.1. The arrowed lines show the relationship between the arguments of the *Show* method and the MessageBox runtime.

Figure 22.1 Catching an exception.

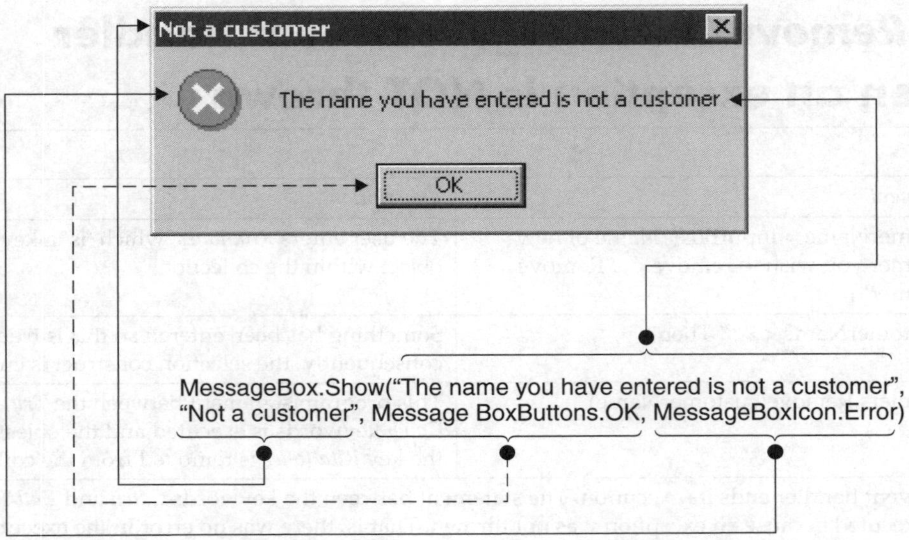
Not a customer
The name you have entered is not a customer
OK
MessageBox.Show("The name you have entered is not a customer", _
"Not a customer", Message BoxButtons.OK, MessageBoxIcon.Error)

> **PRACTICAL ACTIVITY 22.2**
> Make the amendments as shown by Listing 22.1 and run the program to observe the effect.

Obtaining more information about the type of exception

It is often useful to obtain information about what caused the exception and this can be achieved by declaring an object reference of the exception class as illustrated by a further amendment to the *btnRemoveCustomer_Click* event handler as shown in Listing 22.2. The amendment is shown in bold.

Listing 22.2 A further amendment to the *btnRemoveCustomer_Click* event handler.

```
Private Sub btnRemoveCustomer_Click(ByVal sender As System.Object, _
ByVal e As System.EventArgs) Handles btnRemoveCustomer.Click
    Dim customerName As String
    customerName = InputBox _
    ("Name of new customer you wish to remove: ", "Remove a customer")
    If customerName <> "" Then
```

Listing 22.2 (cont.)

```
    Try
        customers.Remove(customerName)
    Catch myError As ArgumentException
        MessageBox.Show _
        ("The name you have entered is not a customer that is the " _
        & myError.Message, "Not a customer", MessageBoxButtons.OK, _
        MessageBoxIcon.Error)
    End Try
  End If
End Sub
```

Declaring *myError* as an object reference to the *ArgumentException* class allows for the code within the *Catch* to use a property of *myError* namely *Message*.

> **NOTE**: The variable *myError* is declared as a type *ArgumentException* and is 'automatically given' an object reference to the exception object created by the error.

This property (*Message*) holds information on the type of exception that occurred when the name entered by the user did not match any of the keys within the collection object. The effect of entering an incorrect name is illustrated in Figure 22.2.

Figure 22.2 Catching an exception and displaying a message.

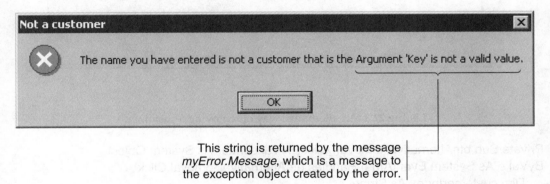

This string is returned by the message *myError.Message*, which is a message to the exception object created by the error.

> **PRACTICAL ACTIVITY 22.3**
>
> Make the amendments as shown by Listing 22.2 and run the program to observe the effect.

Another way of removing an object from the collection and another type of exception

To demonstrate another way to remove an object from a collection and to also demonstrate another exception type a button will be added to the GUI developed during the last chapter. This is illustrated in Figure 22.3 and the event handler attached to this button is shown in Listing 22.3.

Figure 22.3 An alternative way of removing an object from a collection class.

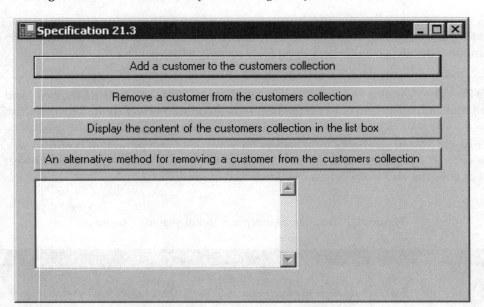

Listing 22.3 An alternative way of removing a customer.

```
Private Sub btnAlternativeRemoval_Click(ByVal sender As System.Object, _
ByVal e As System.EventArgs) Handles btnAlternativeRemoval.Click
    Dim customerIndex As String
    customerIndex = InputBox _
    ("Enter the index position of the customer you wish to remove: ", _
    "Remove a customer")
    If customerIndex <> "" Then
        Try
            customers.Remove(CInt(customerIndex))
```

Listing 22.3 (cont.)

```
Catch myError As IndexOutOfRangeException
    MessageBox.Show _
    (myError.Message, "Not a customer", MessageBoxButtons.OK, _
    MessageBoxIcon.Error)
    End Try
  End If
End Sub
```

When the code of Listing 22.3 is executed the user supplies a number and providing this number is within the range of the collection object then the object within the collection that has the corresponding index number is removed. However, if the number is outside the range an exception is thrown and the code within the *Catch* is executed. Figures 22.4, 22.5 and 22.6 show some typical runtimes.

Figure 22.4 A Typical runtime. For this example an exception is **not** thrown.

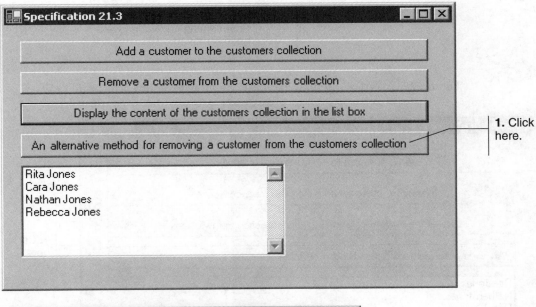

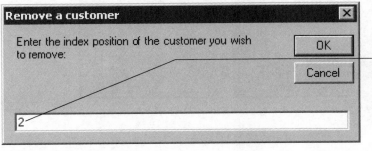

Figure 22.4 (cont.)

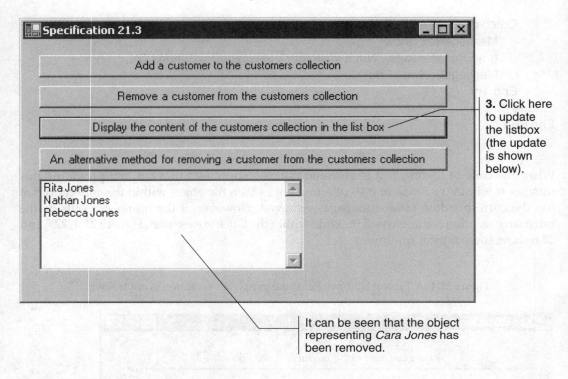

3. Click here to update the listbox (the update is shown below).

It can be seen that the object representing *Cara Jones* has been removed.

Figure 22.5 A Typical runtime. For this example an exception is thrown.

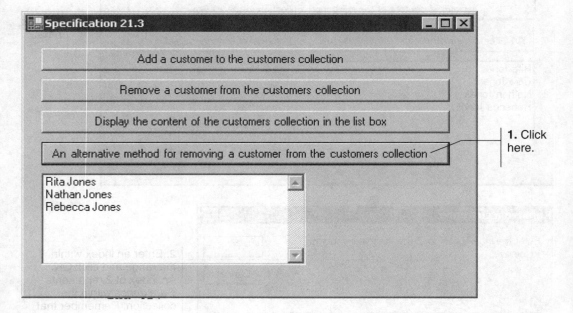

1. Click here.

Figure 22.5 (cont.)

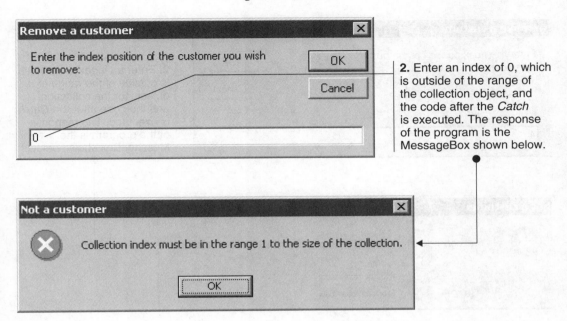

2. Enter an index of 0, which is outside of the range of the collection object, and the code after the *Catch* is executed. The response of the program is the MessageBox shown below.

Figure 22.6 For this runtime example an exception is thrown.

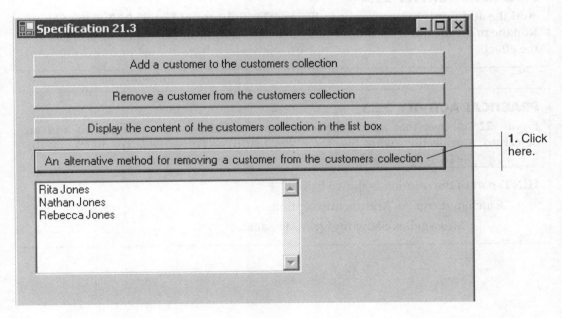

1. Click here.

Figure 22.6 (cont.)

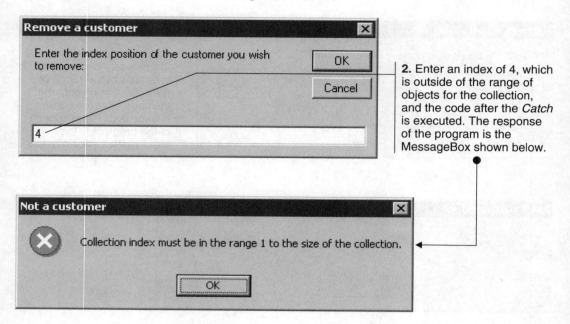

2. Enter an index of 4, which is outside of the range of objects for the collection, and the code after the *Catch* is executed. The response of the program is the MessageBox shown below.

PRACTICAL ACTIVITY 22.4

Add the additional button shown in Figure 22.3 and 'attach' Listing 22.3 to the button. Run the program and enter index numbers within and outside of the range and observe the effect.

PRACTICAL ACTIVITY 22.5

Figure 22.7 shows that an exception is thrown if there is an attempt to add an object to a collection with the same key. Add a *Try .. End Try* block to the

| Add a customer to the customers collection |

button to catch this error.

HINT: part of the solution is shown below:

    Catch myError As ArgumentException

        MessageBox.Show(myError.Message)

Figure 22.7 An error occurs.

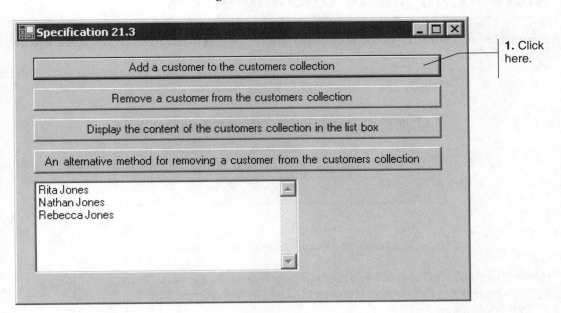

1. Click here.

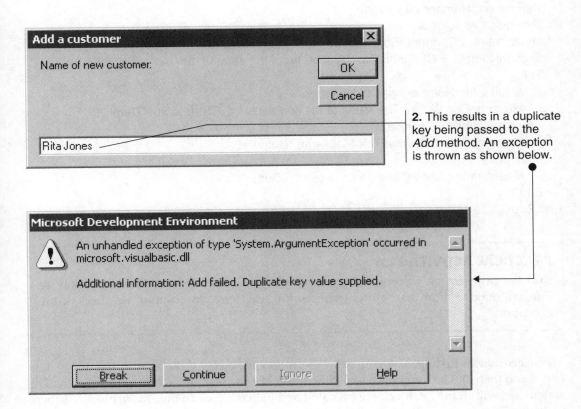

2. This results in a duplicate key being passed to the *Add* method. An exception is thrown as shown below.

More examples of catching errors

Figure 22.8 and Listing 22.4 show a demonstration program that catches an attempt to divide by zero.

Figure 22.8 A simple GUI to demonstrate a divide by zero.

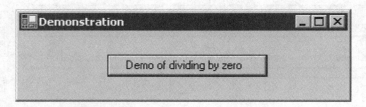

Listing 22.4 Code 'attached' to the button.

```
Private Sub btnZeroDivisionDemo_Click(ByVal sender As System.Object, _
ByVal e As System.EventArgs) Handles btnZeroDivisionDemo.Click
    Dim firstNumber As Integer
    Dim secondNumber As Integer
    Dim result As Integer
    firstNumber = CInt(InputBox("Please enter the first number", "Demo"))
    secondNumber = CInt(InputBox("Please enter the second number", "Demo"))
    Try
        result = firstNumber / secondNumber
        MessageBox.Show("The result of the divison is " & CStr(result), "Demo")
    Catch myError As Exception
        MessageBox.Show(myError.Message, "Demo")
    Finally
        MessageBox.Show("The demo is over", "Demo")
    End Try
End Sub
```

PRACTICAL ACTIVITY 22.6

Run the program as represented by Figure 22.8 and Listing 22.4. Enter a variety of integers making sure that you enter a zero at least once to observe the effect of the exception.

The execution of Listing 22.4 will be in the following order if the user enters valid data (e.g. 4 and then 2). The numbers are obtained from the user by the first two lines of code. The statements within the *Try* block are executed and then the code in the *Finally* block. As there was no exception the code within the *Catch* block is **not** executed.

However, if the user enters zero for the second number the *Catch* block is entered and then the *Finally* block.

PRACTICAL ACTIVITY 22.7

Run the program as represented by Figure 22.8 and Listing 22.4 again. However, this time enter non-integers. For example enter a letter instead of a figure and observe what happens. Figure 22.9 shows a typical example of what happens if the user does not enter an integer.

Figure 22.9 Another exception is thrown when the user does not enter an integer.

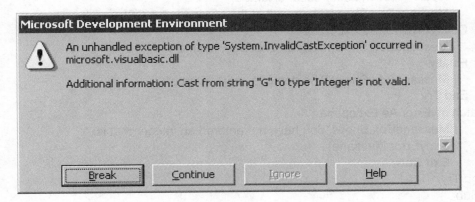

The GUI shown in Figure 22.10 is an amendment to the GUI of Figure 22.8 and Listing 22.5 shows the code 'attached' to the additional button. This code illustrates how to stop the program crashing when the user does not enter an integer.

Figure 22.10 Amendment to catch the entering of a non-integer.

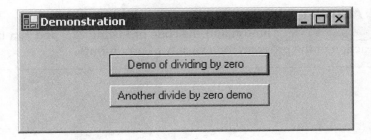

Listing 22.5 The code 'attached' to the additional button.

```
Private Sub btnAnotherDemo_Click(ByVal sender As System.Object, ByVal e As
System.EventArgs) Handles btnAnotherDemo.Click
    Dim firstNumber As Integer
    Dim secondNumber As Integer
    Dim result As Integer

    Try
        firstNumber = CInt(InputBox("Please enter the first number", "Demo"))
        secondNumber = CInt(InputBox("Please enter the second number", "Demo"))
        Try
            result = firstNumber / secondNumber
            MessageBox.Show("The result of the divison is " & CStr(result), "Demo")
        Catch myError As Exception
            MessageBox.Show(myError.Message, "Demo")
        Finally
            MessageBox.Show("The demo is over", "Demo")
        End Try
    Catch myError As Exception
        MessageBox.Show("You have not entered an integer that is: " _
        & myError.Message)
        Exit Sub
    End Try
End Sub
```

The code shown in Listing 22.5 contains two *Try .. End Try* constructs. One construct is nested inside another. The inner construct catches the exception thrown when a divide by zero is attempted. The outer construct catches the exception thrown when the user enters a non-integer. The code in the Catch segment of the outer construct contains the statement *Exit Sub* (shown in bold font). When the user enters a non-integer the program reports this and then exits the sub (which in this case is the event handler for the button).

PRACTICAL ACTIVITY 22.8

Add the | Another divide by zero demo | button and the code of Listing 22.5 and run the program. Observe the action of the program for a variety of user inputs.

PRACTICAL ACTIVITY 22.9

Replace the *Exit Sub* statement within the *Catch* segment of the outer construct with the following message and observe what happens when the user enters a non-integer.

     btnAnotherDemo.PerformClick()

NOTE: One final comment on exception handling: do not use the *Try Catch Finally* construct to implement design algorithms. This construct must be reserved for catching errors!

23 Strings

String data type

A variable of the *String* data type stores a sequence of unsigned 2-byte numbers ranging in value from 0 through to 65535. Each number represents a single Unicode character. A string can contain up to approximately 2 billion (2^{31}) Unicode characters. Figure 23.1 illustrates the concept of a string.

Figure 23.1 A string.

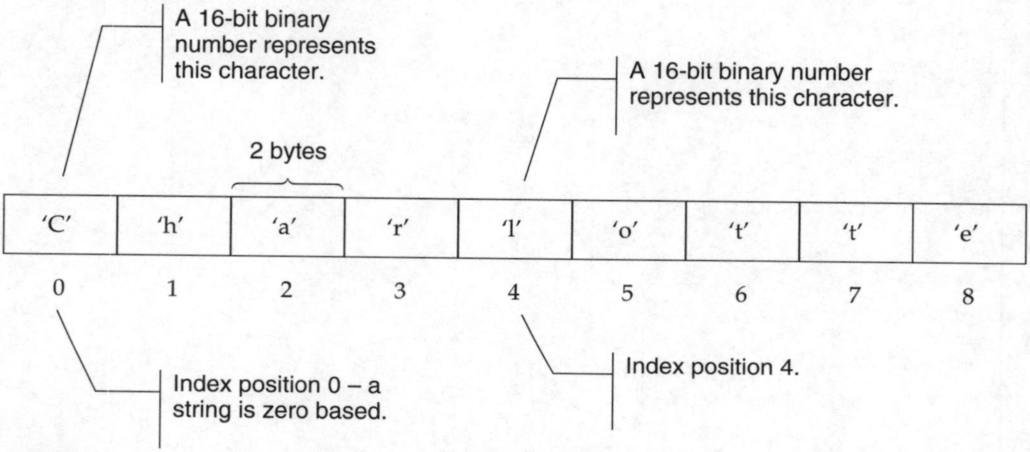

NOTE: An index is associated with a string and it defines the position of a character within the string. It is 'counted' starting from the first character in the string, which is index position zero – a string index is said to be zero-based.

The letters, figures and symbols used on a standard American keyboard correspond to a number between 0 and 127 (which are the same as the ASCII character set). The numbers between 128 and 255 represent characters such as Latin-based alphabet letters, accents, currency symbols, and fractions. The remaining numbers are used for a wide variety of symbols, e.g. worldwide textual characters, mathematical and technical symbols.

Creating ('constructing') a string

A string variable represents an instance of the string class and like all objects it can be created using a constructor. However, it is possible to just declare an instance of a string class without explicitly constructing it. In other words a string is treated like a simple data type.

NOTE: It is worth noting that the declaration of an Integer also creates an instance of the Integer class, likewise with all other simple data types.

Treating strings as simple data types (likewise Integers) is simply a pragmatic approach to programming. Once a string variable is declared it can be treated as an object or as a simple data type variable.

Manipulation of strings

The *String* class exposes numerous methods to facilitate the comparison and manipulation of strings. However, it is worth noting that the Visual Basic .NET language also has inherent methods 'kept' from previous non-object oriented versions of VB that duplicate many of these functionalities.

NOTE: I recommend that you treat strings as objects and use the methods exposed by the *String* class. Both approaches will be shown in this chapter and again for pragmatic reasons. However, the emphasis will be upon the **shared** and **instance** methods of the *String* class. The non-object oriented ways of manipulating strings are to ensure backward compatibility.

SPECIFICATION 23.1

Ask a user to enter a string using an InputBox and display the string and the middle characters of the string in a MessageBox. Attach the code to a button.

The implementation of Specification 23.1 will be achieved using a function inherent in the VB .NET language. The runtime is shown in Figure 23.2 and the program is shown in Listing 23.1.

Listing 23.1 Finding the middle of a string.

```
Private Sub btnDisplayMiddle_Click(ByVal sender As System.Object, ByVal e As _
System.EventArgs) Handles btnDisplayMiddle.Click
    Dim myString As String
    Dim middleString As String

    myString = InputBox("Please enter a string ", " String Manipulation")
    middleString = Mid(myString, 4, 3)
    MessageBox.Show("The full string is:" & myString)
    MessageBox.Show("The middle of the string is: " & middleString)
End Sub
```

Figure 23.2 The runtime for finding the middle of a string.

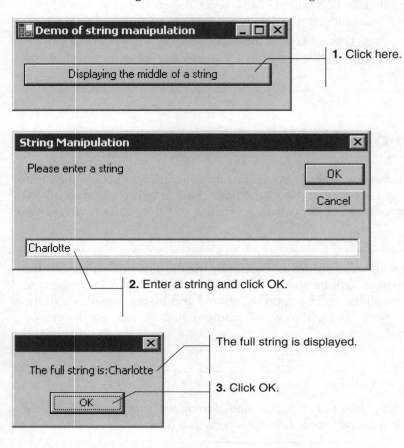

The function responsible for finding the middle of the string is detailed in Figure 23.3.

PRACTICAL ACTIVITY 23.1

Implement Specification 23.1 as represented by Listing 23.1 and Figure 23.2.

Specification 23.1 will now be implemented using a method of the *String* class, namely, *Substring*. The code is shown in Listing 23.2 and the amended GUI that demonstrates the operation of this method is shown in Figure 23.4.

Figure 23.3 The *Mid* function.

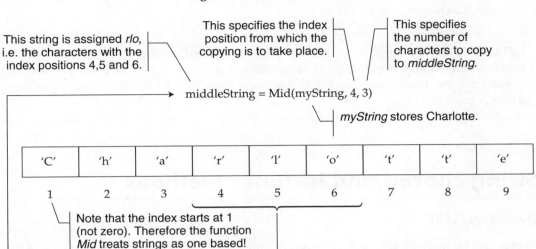

This string is assigned *rlo*, i.e. the characters with the index positions 4,5 and 6.

This specifies the index position from which the copying is to take place.

This specifies the number of characters to copy to *middleString*.

middleString = Mid(myString, 4, 3)

myString stores Charlotte.

'C'	'h'	'a'	'r'	'l'	'o'	't'	't'	'e'
1	2	3	4	5	6	7	8	9

Note that the index starts at 1 (not zero). Therefore the function *Mid* treats strings as one based!

Listing 23.2 Using a method of the *String* class.

```
Private Sub btnAlternative_Click(ByVal sender As System.Object, ByVal e As
System.EventArgs) Handles btnAlternative.Click
    Dim myString As String
    Dim middleString As String

    myString = InputBox("Please enter a string ", " String Manipulation")
    middleString = myString.Substring(3, 3)
    MessageBox.Show("The full string is:" & myString)
    MessageBox.Show("The middle of the string is: " & middleString)
End Sub
```

Figure 23.4 The amended GUI.

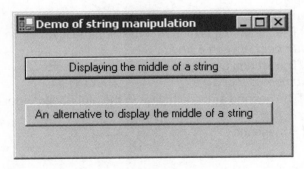

The difference between Listing 23.1 and 23.2 is shown in bold in Listing 23.2. Instead of using the *Mid* function, a message that invokes the *Substring* method is used. This is a message to the string object asking it to return the middle of the string it stores. The returned string is

543

assigned to the string *middleString*. Remember the string *myString* is an object even though a constructor has not been explicitly used.

> **IMPORTANT**: The *Substring* method works on the basis that a string object is **zero based**. Consequently, to obtain the same runtime as shown in Figure 23.2 the parameters to *Substring* are 3 and 3 **not** 4 and 3 as they were with the *Mid* function (that treats the string as one based).

String shared and instance methods

Shared methods

Strings can be manipulated using **shared** methods that do not require an instance of the *String* class. These methods 'belong' to the *String* class and can be qualified with the name of the class (that is, *String*). Listing 23.3 illustrates the use of a shared method (shown in bold). The GUI to which this program is 'attached' is shown in Figure 23.5.

Listing 23.3 Comparing strings.

```
Private Sub btnCompare_Click(ByVal sender As System.Object, ByVal e As
System.EventArgs) Handles btnCompare.Click
    Dim firstString As String
    Dim secondString As String
    Dim message As String
    Dim selector As Integer

    firstString = txtFirstString.Text
    secondString = txtSecondString.Text
    selector = String.Compare(firstString, secondString)          A program
    Select Case selector                                          comment.
        Case Is < 0 ' Number between 1 and 5, inclusive.
            message = "The first string is higher in the alphabetic order"
        Case Is = 0 ' Number between 6 and 8.
            message = "The strings are the same"
        Case Is > 0 ' Number is 9 or 10.
            message = "The second string is higher in the alphabetic order"
    End Select
    lblDifference.Text = message
End Sub
```

Figure 23.5 The GUI used to compare strings.

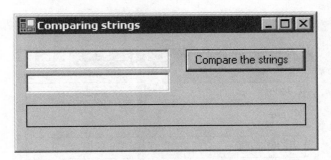

The line of code of interest in Listing 23.3 is repeated in Figure 23.6.

Figure 23.6 A shared method.

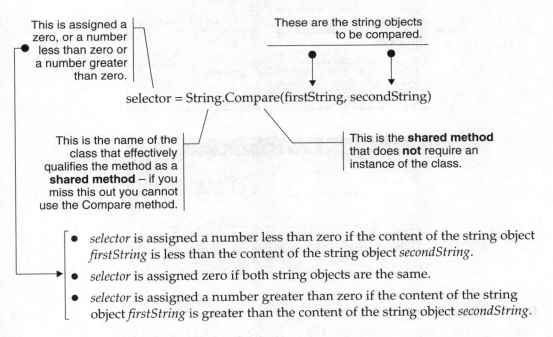

- *selector* is assigned a number less than zero if the content of the string object *firstString* is less than the content of the string object *secondString*.
- *selector* is assigned zero if both string objects are the same.
- *selector* is assigned a number greater than zero if the content of the string object *firstString* is greater than the content of the string object *secondString*.

NOTE: Lowercase *a* is less than lowercase *b* because its 'Unicode number' is less. Uppercase *A* is less than Uppercase *B* for the same reasons.

QUESTION 23.1 (REVISION)

Is uppercase A less than or greater than lowercase a?

Figure 23.7 shows examples of runtimes for the 'compare strings' program.

Figure 23.7 Examples of runtime.

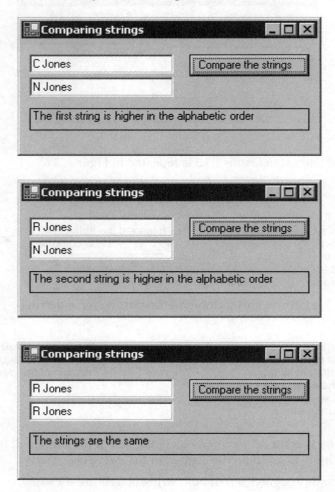

PRACTICAL ACTIVITY 23.2

Implement the program as represented by Figure 23.7 and Listing 23.3.

Use the program to answer Question 23.1.

Consider the runtime shown in Figure 23.8; it shows that when the user enters *PHILIP JONES* (all uppercase) and *Philip Jones* (mixed case) the program does **not** indicate that they are the same.

They are not regarded as the same because the *Compare* method used is case sensitive. If we wished to ignore the case of the strings then another version (overloaded version) of the *Compare* method is used. The version of the *Compare* method that can be used to ignore the case of the strings is shown in Figure 23.9.

Figure 23.8 Another runtime example.

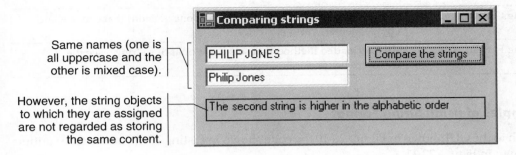

Same names (one is all uppercase and the other is mixed case).

However, the string objects to which they are assigned are not regarded as storing the same content.

Figure 23.9 Another version of the *Compare* method.

This version takes another parameter (argument) referred to as **ignoreCase**. This argument is of the *Boolean* type. If this argument is *True* then the case of the strings are ignored when making the comparison.

String.Compare(firstString, secondString, True)

NOTE: It is worth remembering that an object or class can be sent the same message and perform a different service. In this case the message is *String.Compare* and the service supplied for this message is dependent upon the parameters sent with the message. This is achieved using overloading.

PRACTICAL ACTIVITY 23.3

Amend the program developed during Practical Activity 23.2 by replacing the program statement.

selector = String.Compare(firstString, secondString)

with:

selector = String.Compare(firstString, secondString, True)

Rerun the program again, enter the strings *PHILIP JONES* and *Philip Jones* and observe the effect on the display in the label.

Other examples of shared string methods are described in Table 23.1.

Table 23.1 Examples of *Shared String* methods.

Shared Method	Description
String.Copy	Creates a new instance of a String with the same value as a specified String, e.g.
	MyStr2= String.Copy(myStr1)

Table 23.1 (cont.)

String.Concat	An **overloaded** method (i.e. more than one version) that concatenates (joins together) various Strings.
String.Format	An **overloaded** method that sets the format of a string – see the examples below.

Examples of using *String.Format*

Attach to the GUI shown in Figure 23.10 the code shown in Listing 23.4. An example runtime is shown in Figure 23.11.

Figure 23.10 Demonstration of formatting.

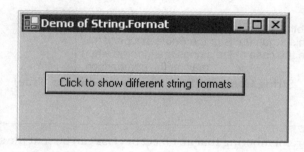

Listing 23.4 Demonstration of formatting.

```
Private Sub btnFormatDemo_Click(ByVal sender As System.Object, ByVal e As
System.EventArgs) Handles btnFormatDemo.Click
    Dim myNumber As Single

    myNumber = 3.14159
    MessageBox.Show("Without formatting " & myNumber)
    MessageBox.Show("With formatting " & String.Format("{0:n3}", myNumber))
    MessageBox.Show("With formatting " & String.Format("{0:n2}", myNumber))
End Sub
```

Figure 23.11 A example runtime.

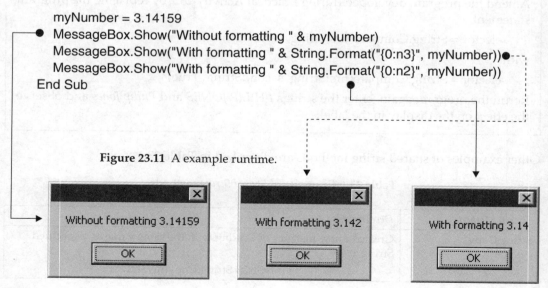

Figure 23.12 takes a closer look at the *String.Format* method used in listing 23.4.

Figure 23.12 A close look at *String.Format*.

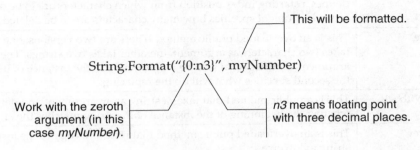

PRACTICAL ACTIVITY 23.4

Enter and run the program as represented by Figure 23.10 and Listing 23.4.

PRACTICAL ACTIVITY 23.5 (DEVELOPMENT)

Write a program that asks for the names of customers and then display an alphabetical list of their names. There are numerous ways to do this, however, use the bubble sort algorithm (covered in a previous chapter) and the shared *Compare* method. This is just an exercise so limit the number of customers to four.

Instance methods

Table 23.2 lists examples of instance methods; these are methods that require to be qualified by a string **instance** (not the class name).

Table 23.2 Examples of *String instance* methods.

Instance method	Description
Equals	An Overloaded public method that determines whether two *String* objects have the same value.
Insert	Inserts a *String* within an instance of a *String* at a specified index position.
LastIndexOf	An overloaded public method that takes a character as an argument and begins searching at the last character position of the instance of the String and proceeds backwards towards the beginning until either the character is found or the first character position has been examined. It then reports the index position. The search is case-sensitive
PadLeft	An overloaded public method that right-aligns the characters in an instance of a string padding on its left with spaces or a specified character for a specified total length. There are two methods one takes an integer as an argument and pads with a number of spaces equal to the integer. The other takes an integer and a character and pads with the character a number of times equal to the integer.

Table 23.2 (cont.)

Remove	This is a public method that takes two integers arguments: the first argument defines a starting index position from which characters are to be deleted. The second argument specifies how many characters are to be deleted.
Replace	This is an overloaded public method. There are two versions: one version takes two characters as argument, the other takes two strings. The first argument specifies what is to be replaced within the instance of the string and the second specifies what will do the replacing.
StartsWith	This is a public method that takes a string as an argument and determines whether the beginning of the instance of the string matches the argument.
ToLower	This is an overloaded public method that returns a copy of the instance of a string in lowercase.
Trim	This is an overloaded public method. There are two versions: one does not take an argument and this removes all occurrences of white spaces (e.g. the code for a spacebar) from the beginning and end of the instance of a string. The other version takes a character array as an argument to specify the characters to be removed.

NOTE: There are many more examples of methods and you are advised to view their meaning using the VB .NET help. Look under String Members.

Examples of string instance methods in action

Illustrating examples of string instance methods will be achieved by implementing Specification 23.2.

NOTE: The implementation of Specification 23.2 will use collections; make sure you understand collection before you proceed. Collections were covered in Chapter 21.

SPECIFICATION 23.2

Write a program that asks for the name and title of customers, e.g. Mr Jones, Ms Smith, etc. Add each customer to a collection. Attach code to a button that will display all the customers with the title Mr and another button that will display the customers with the title Ms.

The GUI for the program that implements Specification 23.2 is shown in Figure 23.13 and the code 'attached to' the GUI is shown in Listing 23.5. The class for the customers that form the items of the collection is shown in Listing 23.6. The Solution Explorer for the solution is shown in Figure 23.14.

Figure 23.13 The GUI for Specification 23.3.

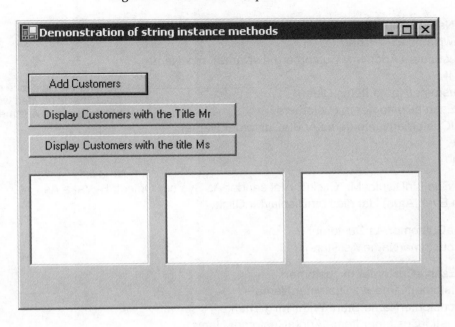

Figure 23.14 The Solution Explorer.

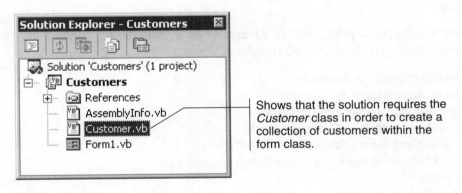

Shows that the solution requires the *Customer* class in order to create a collection of customers within the form class.

Listing 23.5 Code attached to the GUI of Figure 23.13.

Creates a collection object that is available throughout the form.

```
Private customers As New Collection()
Private Sub btnAddCustomers_Click(ByVal sender As System.Object, ByVal e As _
System.EventArgs) Handles btnAddCustomers.Click

    Dim newName As String
    Dim aCustomer As Customer
```

551

Listing 23.5 (cont.)

```
newName = InputBox("Name of new customer: ", " Add a customer")
If newName <> "" Then
   customers.Add(New Customer(newName), newName)
End If
lstCustomerName.Items.Clear()
For Each aCustomer In customers
   lstCustomerName.Items.Add(aCustomer.Name)
Next
End Sub
```

Note how an instance of a *Customer* is created within the brackets of the *Add* method.

```
Private Sub btnDisplayMr_Click(ByVal sender As System.Object, ByVal e As _
System.EventArgs) Handles btnDisplayMr.Click

   Dim aCustomer As Customer
   Dim customerName As String

   For Each aCustomer In customers
      customerName = aCustomer.Name
      If customerName.StartsWith("Mr") Then
         lstMrCustomer.Items.Add(aCustomer.Name)
      End If
   Next
End Sub

Private Sub btnDisplayMrs_Click(ByVal sender As System.Object, ByVal e As _
System.EventArgs) Handles btnDisplayMrs.Click

   Dim aCustomer As Customer
   Dim customerName As String
   For Each aCustomer In customers
      customerName = aCustomer.Name
      If customerName.StartsWith("Ms") Then
         lstMsCustomer.Items.Add(aCustomer.Name)
      End If
   Next
End Sub
```

Listing 23.6 Code for the *Customer* class.

```
Public Class Customer
   Private customerName As String

   Sub New(ByVal pName As String)
      customerName = pName
   End Sub
```

Listing 23.6 (cont.)

```
    ReadOnly Property Name()
        Get
            Name = customerName
        End Get
    End Property
End Class
```

An example runtime is shown in Figure 23.15 after the name of six customers have been entered and both display buttons have been clicked.

Figure 23.15 An example runtime.

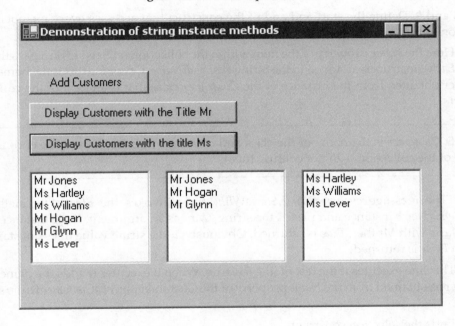

The code for selecting and then adding *Mr Jones, Mr Hogan* and *Mr Glynn* to the second ListBox is listed with line numbers in Figure 23.16, followed by a description.

Figure 23.16 Listing with line numbers.

```
1.    Private Sub btnDisplayMr_Click(ByVal sender As System.Object, _
      ByVal e As System.EventArgs) Handles btnDisplayMr.Click

2.        Dim aCustomer As Customer
3.        Dim customerName As String
```

Figure 23.16 (cont.)

```
4.        For Each aCustomer In customers
5.            customerName = aCustomer.Name
6.            If customerName.StartsWith("Mr") Then
7.                lstMrCustomer.Items.Add(aCustomer.Name)
8.            End If
9.        Next
10.   End Sub
```

Line 1: This is the signature of the button event handling procedure.

Line 2: This defines an object reference of the type added to the *customers* collection.

Line 3: This defines a *String* instance called *customerName*.

Lines 4 and 9: Define the start and end of the construct that accesses every member of the collection in turn.

Line 5: Here the *Name* property of the item within the collection referred to on a pass through the *For Each* construct is assigned to the String *customerName*. Of course this is the name of the customer obtained from the instance of the **Customer** class that is an item of the **collection** *customers*.

NOTE: *Customer* is the name of the class and *customers* (this has an s at the end) is the name of the collection – do not confuse them.

Line 6: The message *customerName.StartsWith("Mr")* invokes the *StartsWith* method of the *customerName* instance and passes the string *"Mr"* as an argument. If the instance of the string starts with *Mr* then *True* is returned. Obviously, if the string value does not start with *Mr* then *False* is returned.

Line 7: This line executes if the test of line 6 is true. When it executes it adds the name of the customer as obtained from the *Name* property of the Customer object *aCustomer* to the second ListBox.

Line 8: Ends the selection construct.

Line 10: Ends the event handler.

QUESTION 23.2

Figure 23.17 shows another runtime that has apparently ignored some of the customers with a Mr title. Why?

Answer: *The program is case sensitive!*

Figure 23.17 Another runtime where some customers are apparently ignored.

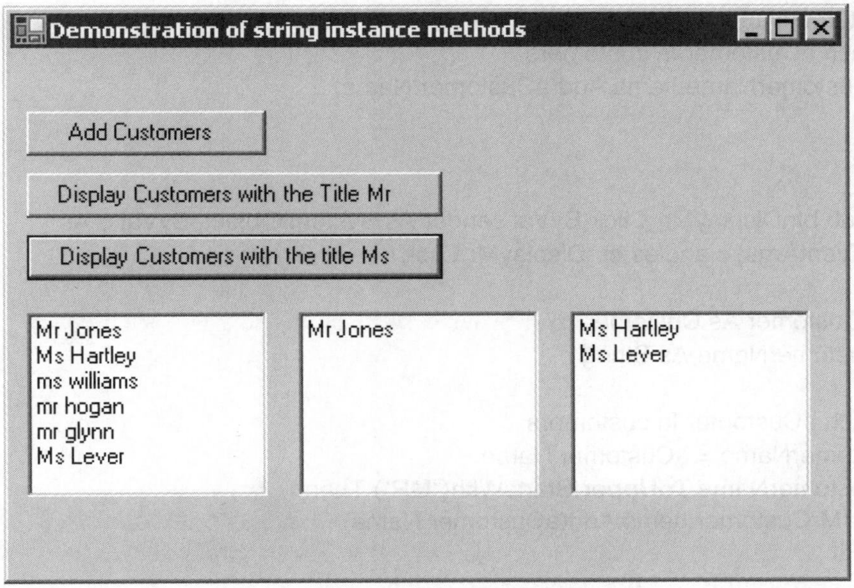

PRACTICAL ACTIVITY 23.6

Enter and run the program as represented by Figure 23.13 and Listing 23.5.

Enter the names as suggested by the first listbox of Figures 23.15 and 23.17 and observe the output in the second and third listboxes. Make sure you enter the strings exactly as they appear. Every entry of a new customer will require a click of the Add Customer button.

The problem of case sensitivity is overcome as shown by Listing 23.7. The amendments are shown in bold. Figure 23.18 shows the runtime after the amendments are made.

Listing 23.7 Amendments to remove case sensitivity.

```
Dim customers As New Collection()

Private Sub btnAddCustomers_Click(ByVal sender As System.Object, ByVal e As _
System.EventArgs) Handles btnAddCustomers.Click
    Dim newName As String
    Dim aCustomer As Customer
    newName = InputBox("Name of new customer: ", " Add a customer")
    If newName <> "" Then
        customers.Add(New Customer(newName), newName)
    End If
```

Listing 23.7 (cont.)

```
lstCustomerName.Items.Clear()
For Each aCustomer In customers
    lstCustomerName.Items.Add(aCustomer.Name)
Next
End Sub

Private Sub btnDisplayMr_Click(ByVal sender As System.Object, ByVal e As _
System.EventArgs) Handles btnDisplayMr.Click

    Dim aCustomer As Customer
    Dim customerName As String

    For Each aCustomer In customers
        customerName = aCustomer.Name
        If customerName.ToUpper.StartsWith("MR") Then
            lstMrCustomer.Items.Add(aCustomer.Name)
        End If
    Next
End Sub

Private Sub btnDisplayMrs_Click(ByVal sender As System.Object, ByVal e As _
System.EventArgs) Handles btnDisplayMrs.Click

    Dim aCustomer As Customer
    Dim customerName As String

    For Each aCustomer In customers
        customerName = aCustomer.Name
        If customerName.ToUpper.StartsWith("MS") Then
            lstMsCustomer.Items.Add(aCustomer.Name)
        End If
    Next
End Sub
```

PRACTICAL ACTIVITY 23.7

Make the amendments as shown by Listing 23.7 and run the program with inputs as specified by the first ListBox shown in Figure 23.18. Observe the output.

PRACTICAL ACTIVITY 23.8 (DEVELOPMENT)

Amend the program so that the outputs in the second and third ListBox are all in uppercase.

Figure 23.18 The runtime after the amendments are made.

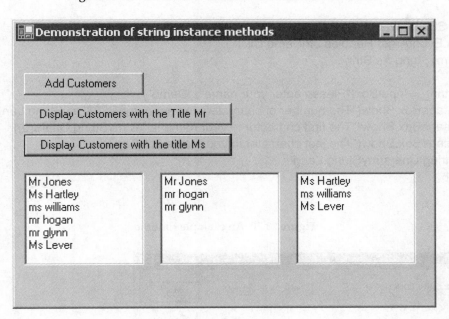

Public properties of the *String* class

Two Public properties of the *String* class are *Length* and *Chars*.

Length returns the numbers of characters in an instance of a string and *Chars* returns the character at a specified character position for an instance of a string. Figure 23.19 and Listing 23.8 illustrates a simple use of both *Length* and *Chars*. Figure 23.20 shows an example runtime.

Figure 23.19 The GUI.

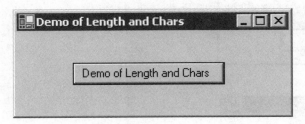

Listing 23.8 A simple use of *Length* and *Chars*.

```
Private Sub btnDemo_Click(ByVal sender As System.Object, ByVal e As _
System.EventArgs) Handles btnDemo.Click
    Dim myString As String

    myString = InputBox("Please enter your name", "Demo")
    MessageBox.Show("The number of characters in your name is " & myString.Length)
    MessageBox.Show("The first character in your name is " & myString.Chars(0))
    MessageBox.Show("The last character in your name is " & _
    myString.Chars(myString.Length - 1))
End Sub
```

Figure 23.20 An example runtime.

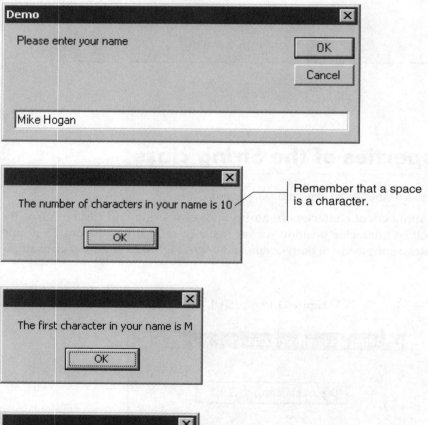

Remember that a space is a character.

PRACTICAL ACTIVITY 23.9

Enter, run and observe the program as represented by Figure 23.19 and Listing 23.8.

More examples of string manipulation

All of the following examples are shown as code segments. You are advised to implement each of the examples as a simple windows application. It will require that you add appropriate code and controls to observe the effect of each segment of code (see Practical Activity 23.10).

Obtaining part of a string – a substring

In this example the variable *mySecondString* is assigned *Jones*.

```
Dim myFirstString As String
Dim mySecondString As String

myFirstString = "Philip Jones"
mySecondString = myFirstString.SubString(7,5)
```

Searching for strings within your strings

In this example the index position of the character 'a' is returned. The index position for 'a' is 3:

```
Dim myString As String
Dim myInteger As Integer

myString = "Rita Jones"
myInteger = myString.IndexOf("a")
```

In this example the index position of the first character of the string 'Jones' is returned. The index position for 'Jones' is 5:

```
Dim myString As String
Dim myInteger As Integer

myString = "Rita Jones"
myInteger = myString.IndexOf("Jones")
```

Concatenating strings

The first three strings are joined together (concatenated) by the *String.Concat* method and assigned to the fourth string *myFourthString*:

```
Dim myFirstString As String
Dim mySecondString As String
```

```
Dim myThirdString As String
Dim myFourthString As String

myFirstString = "Nathan"
mySecondString = "Gordon"
myThirdString = "Jones"
myFourthString = String.Concat(myFirstString, mySecondString, myThirdString)
```

Trimming characters from a string

Here the *Trim* method has taken an argument that specifies the character to be trimmed from the beginning and end of a string:

```
Dim myFirstString As String
Dim mySecondString As String

myFirstString = "#1024#"
mySecondString = myFirstString.Trim("#")
```

For the following code segment the # symbol in the centre of the string is **not** removed:

```
Dim myFirstString As String
Dim mySecondString As String

myFirstString = "#10#24#"
mySecondString = myFirstString.Trim("#")
```

Removing characters from a string

This removes the space after *Nancy* as well as the string *Jones*. Therefore *mySecondString* is assigned *Nancy*:

```
Dim myFirstString As String
Dim mySecondString As String

myFirstString = "Nancy Jones"
mySecondString = myFirstString.Remove(5,6)
```

For this example *mySecondString* is assigned *Nans*:

```
Dim myFirstString As String
Dim mySecondString As String

myFirstString = "Nancy Jones"
mySecondString = myFirstString.Remove(3,7)
```

Replacing characters in a string

For this example *mySecondString* is assigned *Rita Jones* as the *Hartley* part of the *myFirstString* is replaced by *Jones* and assigned to *mySecondString*:

```
Dim myFirstString As String
Dim mySecondString As String
```

```
myFirstString = "Rita Hartley"
mySecondString = myFirstString.Replace("Hartley","Jones")
```

Inserting a string within a string

Here the string *ili* is inserted within the string *Php Jones* at index position 2. The result stored in *mySecondString* is *Philip Jones*:

```
Dim myFirstString As String
Dim mySecondString As String

myFirstString = "Php Jones"
mySecondString = myFirstString.Insert(2, "ili")
```

Concatenating an array of strings together

```
Dim myFamily(2) As String Dim
Dim firstNames As String

myFamily(0) = "Cara"
myFamily(1) = "Nathan"
myFamily(2) = "Rebecca"

firstNames = String.Join(" and ", myFamily)
MessageBox.Show("The names of my children are " & firstNames)
```

The output from this code segment is shown below:

The names of my children are Cara and Nathan and Rebecca

OK

Replacing the and with a comma as shown below gives a different output also shown below:

```
Dim myFamily(2) As String
Dim firstNames As String

myFamily(0) = "Cara"
myFamily(1) = "Nathan"
myFamily(2) = "Rebecca"
firstNames = String.Join(", ", myFamily)
MessageBox.Show("The names of my children are " & firstNames)
```

The names of my children are Cara, Nathan, Rebecca

OK

Splitting a string into a string array

```
Dim myFamily(2) As String
Dim firstNames As String

firstNames = "Cara, Nathan, Rebecca"
myFamily = firstNames.Split(","c)

MessageBox.Show("The names of my children are " & _
myFamily(0) & myFamily(1) & myFamily(2))
```

The output from this code segment is shown below:

PRACTICAL ACTIVITY 23.10

Implement as appropriate the segments of code described on the previous pages. I recommend that you attach the code to the click event of a button and display the resulting string in either a label or MessageBox.

24 Events

An event is a signal that informs an application that something has happened. For example, when a user clicks a button a Click event is raised that invokes a procedure that handles the event.

> **NOTE**: Most of the programs developed throughout this chapter leave the *Name* property of controls with their default value. For example, the first button placed on a form will have its *Name* property set to *Button1* and the second to *Button2* and so on. They will not be changed for the programs used, this is for pragmatic reasons to ensure that the emphasis of the chapter is upon events and their handling. Of course for proper software applications all controls should have their name property set to reflect the purpose they have within the application.

Event handling procedures

These are procedures that are called when a corresponding event occurs. Any valid sub method can be used as an event handling procedure. However, you cannot use a function as an event handler.

Event senders

Any object capable of raising an event is known as an event source. Forms, controls, and user-defined objects are examples of event senders.

Naming convention for event handling procedures

VB .NET uses a standard naming convention for event handlers that combines the name of the event sender, an underscore, and the name of the event. For example, the click event of a button named *Button1* would be named *Sub Button1_Click*.

> **NOTE**: It is possible to define event handlers that do not adopt this naming convention. In fact it is possible to use any valid sub method name, however, it is recommended that you adopt the naming convention.
>
> However, when an event procedure services a number of **different** events a sensible name that reflects its purpose should be chosen.

Associating events with event handling procedures

An event handling procedure can be associated with an event by using the *Handles* keyword. Consider the click event of a Button whose *Name* property is set at its default (*Button1*). The button when clicked simply displays *Hello World* in a MessageBox. This event handling procedure is shown in Listing 24.1. The GUI is shown in Figure 24.1.

Listing 24.1 A button click event handling procedure.

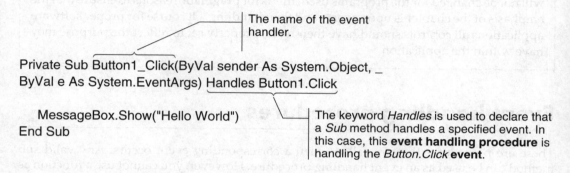

```
Private Sub Button1_Click(ByVal sender As System.Object, _
ByVal e As System.EventArgs) Handles Button1.Click

    MessageBox.Show("Hello World")
End Sub
```

The name of the event handler.

The keyword *Handles* is used to declare that a *Sub* method handles a specified event. In this case, this **event handling procedure** is handling the *Button.Click* **event**.

NOTE: Do not confuse the terminology: an event handling procedure handles an event.

Figure 24.1 The GUI.

Figure 24.2 The GUI with an additional button.

It is possible to add another button to the form and arrange for this button to be handled by the event handling procedure shown in Listing 24.1. The GUI of Figure 24.2 and an appropriate amendment to Listing 24.1 shows how this is achieved. The amended code is shown in Listing 24.2 with the amendment shown in bold.

Listing 24.2 The amended code.

```
Private Sub Button1_Click(ByVal sender As System.Object, ByVal e As _
System.EventArgs) Handles Button1.Click, Button2.Click

    MessageBox.Show("Hello World")
End Sub
```

A comma and the name of another **event** to be handled by this **event handling procedure** are added to the signature.

When the buttons on the GUI of Figure 24.2 are clicked they both display a MessageBox containing the words *Hello World*, as shown by Figure 24.3. That is, they both invoke the same event handling procedure.

Figure 24.3 Runtime for the simple program.

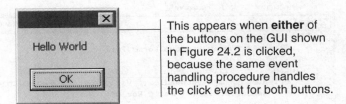

This appears when **either** of the buttons on the GUI shown in Figure 24.2 is clicked, because the same event handling procedure handles the click event for both buttons.

PRACTICAL ACTIVITY 24.1

Enter and execute the program as represented by Figure 24.1 and Listing 24.1.

PRACTICAL ACTIVITY 24.2

Amend the GUI developed during Practical Activity 24.1 and add an extra button as shown by Figure 24.2. Then add the extra code, as shown by the bold text of Listing 24.2, to the *Button1_Click* event handling procedure. Run the program and observe the effect of clicking on both buttons.

How to associate events with a sub method

This is shown by the sequence of steps in Figure 24.4.

Figure 24.4 Associating events with a sub method.

Step 1: Start a new Windows application and call it Associating Events.

Step 2: Add the following sub method to Form1.

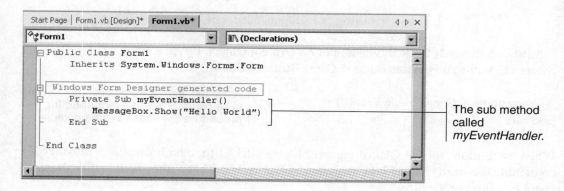

The sub method called *myEventHandler*.

Step 3: Add the arguments as shown.

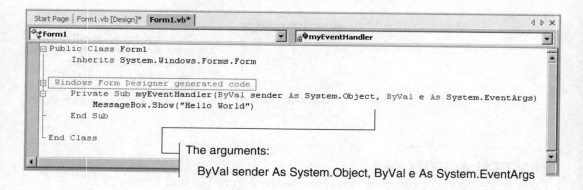

The arguments:

ByVal sender As System.Object, ByVal e As System.EventArgs

Step 4: Add two Buttons and two PictureBoxes, and load appropriate bitmaps into the PictureBoxes as illustrated next.

Step 5: Associate the *click event* of each of these four objects with the sub method *myEventHandler*. This is achieved using the *Handles* keyword followed by a comma-separated list of the events to be handled, as next.

Figure 24.4 (cont.)

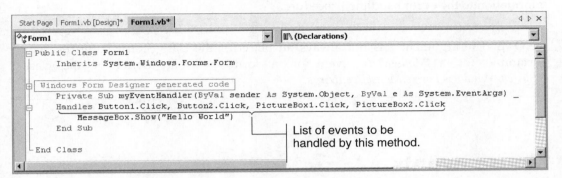

List of events to be handled by this method.

PRACTICAL ACTIVITY 24.3

Enter and execute the program as represented by Figure 24.4. Clicking on all of the objects should result in the display of *Hello World* in a MessageBox.

PRACTICAL ACTIVITY 24.4 (DEVELOPMENT)

Amend the program developed during Practical Activity 24.3 so that the event handler executes when the buttons are clicked and the PictureBoxes are double clicked.

Hint:

PictureBox1.DoubleClick, PictureBox2.DoubleClick

PRACTICAL ACTIVITY 24.5 (DEVELOPMENT)

Amend the program again so that the event handler executes when the cursor enters the space of the two buttons.

Hint:

Handles Button1.MouseEnter, Button2.MouseEnter, _

PictureBox1.DoubleClick, PictureBox2.DoubleClick

The arguments of an event handling procedure

An event handling procedure has two arguments, they are:

- A pass by value argument called *sender* declared as *System.Object*.
- A pass by value argument called *e* that is often declared as *System.EventArgs*.

Both of these arguments are objects and consequently they have members that can supply information to the event handling procedure.

> **NOTE**: The argument e is not always an object of the class *System.EventArgs*. For example for a *MouseMove* event on a form, e is an object of the class *System.Windows.Forms.MouseEventArgs*.

Mouse events

Mouse events enable an application to respond to the location and state of the mouse. The location of the cursor (controlled by the mouse) is defined by the x and y co-ordinates of the object receiving the mouse event. The state of the mouse is defined by which button on the mouse is pressed when the mouse event occurs. Also the status of three keyboard keys can be defined when a mouse event occurs.

The six mouse events are described in Table 24.1.

Table 24.1 Mouse events.

Event	Description
MouseDown	Occurs when the cursor is over a control and **any** mouse button is pressed.
MouseEnter	Occurs when the cursor enters the control.
MouseHover	Occurs when the cursor hovers over the control.
MouseLeave	Occurs when the cursor leaves the control.
MouseMove	Occurs when the cursor is moved over the control.
MouseUp	Occurs when the cursor is over the control and **any** mouse button is released.

> **NOTE**: A control can recognize a mouse event when the cursor is over the control. A form can also recognize a mouse event when the cursor is over any part of the form that does not contain a control.

When a *MouseMove* event occurs it invokes an event handling procedure that takes two arguments (parameters) as illustrated in Figure 24.5.

Figure 24.5 The parameters passed to a *MouseMove* event procedure.

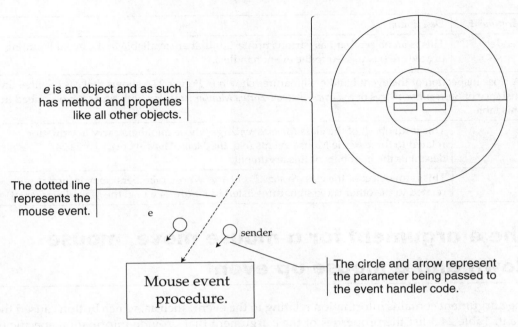

Figure 24.6 illustrates the heading, to all six mouse event handling procedures, to which a **form** will respond.

Figure 24.6 The heading of six mouse event procedures.

```
Private Sub Form1_MouseDown(ByVal sender As Object, ByVal e As_
System.Windows.Forms.MouseEventArgs) Handles MyBase.MouseDown

Private Sub Form1_MouseEnter(ByVal sender As Object, _
ByVal e As System.EventArgs) Handles MyBase.MouseEnter

Private Sub Form1_MouseHover(ByVal sender As Object, _
ByVal e As System.EventArgs) Handles MyBase.MouseEHover

Private Sub Form1_MouseLeave(ByVal sender As Object, _
ByVal e As System.EventArgs) Handles MyBase.MouseLeave

Private Sub Form1_MouseMove(ByVal sender As Object, ByVal e As_
System.Windows.Forms.MouseEventArgs) Handles MyBase.MouseMove

Private Sub Form1_MouseUp(ByVal sender As Object, ByVal e As_
System.Windows.Forms.MouseEventArgs) Handles MyBase.MouseUp
```

The arguments (parameters) to all six mouse events are described in Table 24.2.

Table 24.2 The arguments to mouse events.

Argument	Description
sender	This is an object that has various properties that are available to the event handling procedure (i.e. passed to the event handler).
A close inspection of the event handler signatures shown in Figure 24.6 shows that e is of either an instance of *System.EventArgs* or *System.Windows.Forms.MouseEventArgs* both types are described in this table.	
e	This is an object of the class *MouseEventArgs* whose members carry information related to three of the Mouse events (e.g. the *MouseMove* event) – Table 24.3 describes the members of this argument.
e	This is an object of the class *System.EventArgs* whose members carry information related to the other three signatures listed in Figure 24.6 (e.g. the *MouseLeave* event).

The e argument for a mouse move, mouse down and a mouse up event

The *e* argument contains information relating to the event, such as, which button caused the event. Table 24.3 list the properties of the *e* argument that provide information specific to these events.

Table 24.3 The properties of the *e* argument for Mouse move, down and up events.

Argument	Description
Button	This is a *read-only property* that indicates which mouse button was pressed.
Clicks	A *read-only property* that indicates the number of times the mouse button was pressed and released.
Delta	Another *read-only property* that supplies a count of the number of detents the mouse wheel has rotated.
X	This indicates the X co-ordinate of the cursor when the mouse event occurred – a *read-only property*.
Y	This indicates the Y co-ordinate of the cursor when the mouse event occurred – a *read-only property*.

How to access the properties of the e argument

The following example shows how to access the *Button* property of the *e* argument for a mouse move, mouse up or mouse down event.

The Button Argument is accessed via:

e.Button

This can have the value of either *Left*, *Right* or *Middle* depending upon the mouse button actually pressed or if no button is clicked then it can have the value *None* (for a mouse move event).

NOTE: The syntax *e.Button* is what you would expect when accessing the property of an object, this is because *e* is an object!

SPECIFICATION 24.1

Change the background colour of a form to red when the left button on a mouse is clicked and change the colour to blue if the right button is clicked.

Listing 24.3 shows the code that implements this specification. Figure 24.7 shows the sequence of actions necessary to attach this code to the **Form1**, *MouseDown* event.

Figure 24.7 Attaching code the *MouseDown* event of a Form.

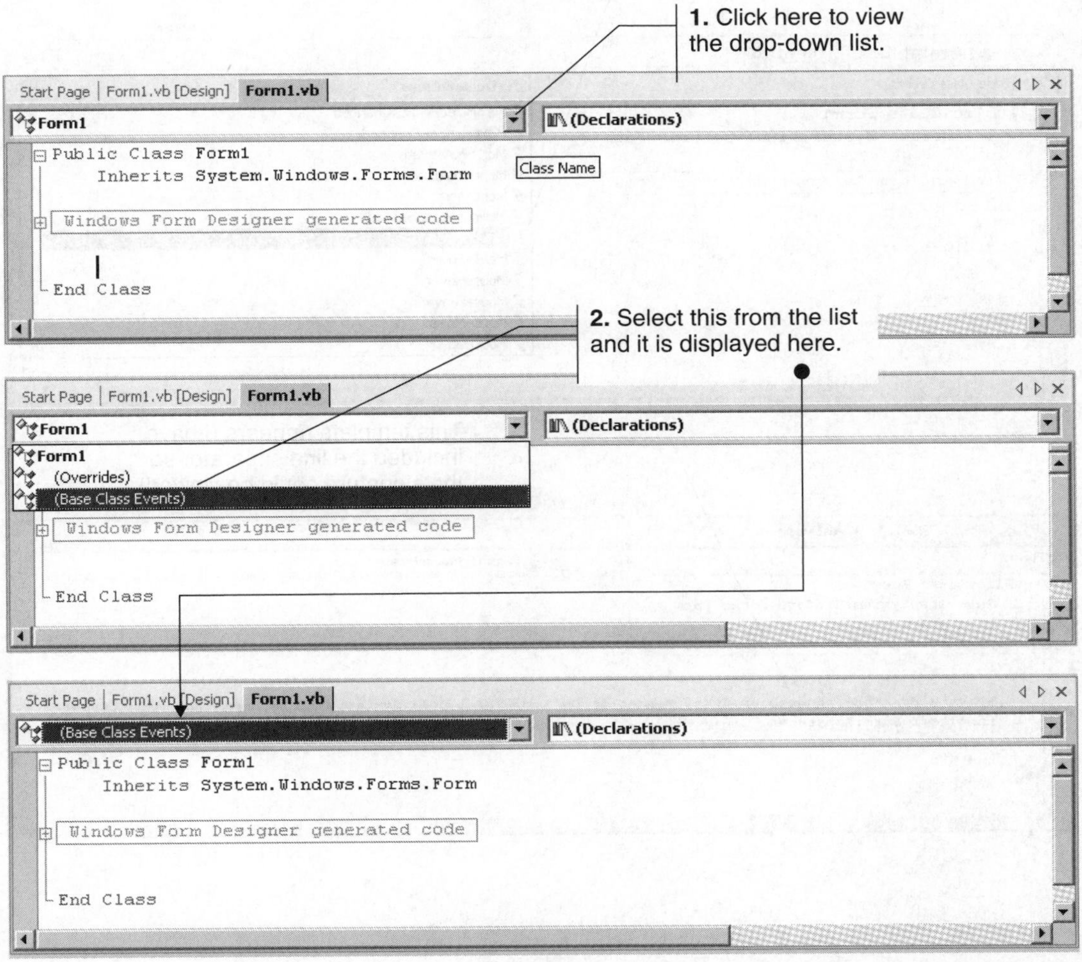

1. Click here to view the drop-down list.

2. Select this from the list and it is displayed here.

Figure 24.7 (cont.)

3. Click here to view the
drop-down list.

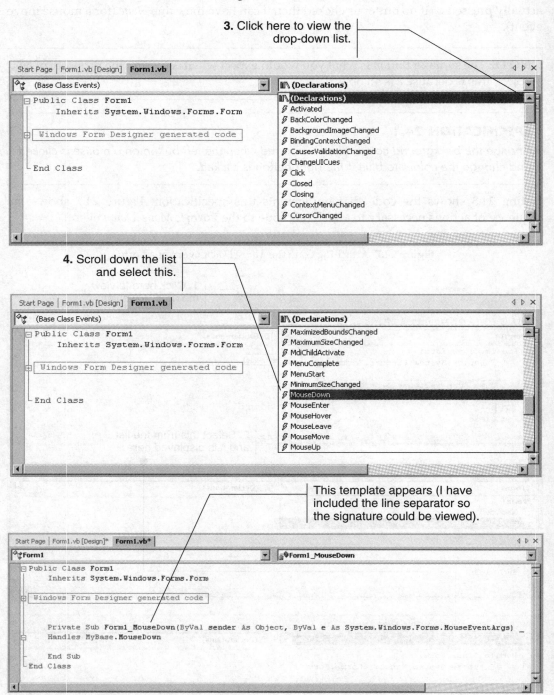

4. Scroll down the list
and select this.

This template appears (I have
included the line separator so
the signature could be viewed).

Figure 24.7 (cont.)

```
Start Page | Form1.vb [Design] | Form1.vb                                    ◁ ▷ ✕

Form1                                    ▼  (Declarations)                          ▼

Public Class Form1
     Inherits System.Windows.Forms.Form

Windows Form Designer generated code

     Private Sub Form1_MouseDown(ByVal sender As Object, ByVal e As System.Windows.Forms.MouseEventArgs) _
     Handles MyBase.MouseDown
         If e.Button = MouseButtons.Left Then
             Me.BackColor = Color.Red
         ElseIf e.Button = MouseButtons.Right Then
             Me.BackColor = Color.Blue
         End If
     End Sub
End Class
```

5. The code is entered.

Listing 24.3 Implementing Specification 24.1.

```
Private Sub Form1_MouseDown(ByVal sender As Object, ByVal e As _
System.Windows.Forms.MouseEventArgs) Handles MyBase.MouseDown
    If e.Button = MouseButtons.Left Then
        Me.BackColor = Color.Red
    ElseIf e.Button = MouseButtons.Right Then
        Me.BackColor = Color.Blue
    End If
End Sub
```

Description trace for the *Form1_MouseDown* event

Statement	Description
Assume the user presses the **left** mouse button while the cursor is over the form.	
e.Button = MouseButtons.Left	The event handling procedure obtains details of the mouse button pressed from the *e.Button* property and in this case it contains a value that indicates that the left mouse button was pressed. This is compared to the visual basic constant for the left mouse button, namely, *MouseButtons.Left*. In this case the comparison returns True, consequently, the code following this test between the keywords *Then* and *ElseIf* is executed.
Form1.BackColor = Color.Red	The background colour of the form is changed to red.
Assume the user presses the **right** mouse button while the cursor is over the form.	

573

e.Button = MouseButtons.Left	The event handling procedure obtains details of the mouse button pressed from *e.Button* and in this case it contains a value that indicates that the right mouse button was pressed. This is compared to the visual basic constant for the left mouse button, namely, *MouseButtons.Left*. In this case the comparison returns False and the test after the *ElseIf* is executed.
e.Button = MouseButtons.Right	This returns true because the right button was pressed, therefore, the code between the keywords *ElseIf* and *EndIf* is executed.
Form1.BackColor = Color.Blue	The background colour of the form is changed to blue.

PRACTICAL ACTIVITY 24.6

Attach the code of Listing 24.3 to the *MouseDown* event of Form1.

● Click the left button and observe the result.

● Click the right button and observe the result.

PRACTICAL ACTIVITY 24.7

Attach the code of Listing 24.4 to the *MouseUp* event of Form1. Set the *Name* property of the form to *frmDemo* and the *Text* property of the form to *Demonstration*.

● Click and release the left button and observe the result.

● Click and release the right button and observe the result.

● Click and release the middle button and observer the result.

Listing 24.4 The *MouseUp* event handler.

```
Private Sub Form1_MouseUp(ByVal sender As Object, ByVal e As
System.Windows.Forms.MouseEventArgs) Handles MyBase.MouseUp
    Select Case e.Button
        Case MouseButtons.Left
            MessageBox.Show("You have released the left Button")
        Case MouseButtons.Right
            MessageBox.Show("You have released the right Button")
        Case MouseButtons.Middle
            MessageBox.Show("You have released the middle Button")
    End Select
    MessageBox.Show(sender.ToString())
End Sub
```

The last program statement of Listing 24.4 displays information about the object responsible for raising the event. The information it supplies is shown in the MessageBox of Figure 24.8. Of course, this information could be used to decide upon the processing of the event handler.

Figure 24.8 The information supplied by the *sender* argument.

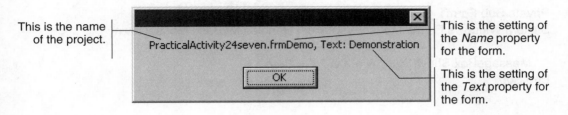

This is the name of the project.

PracticalActivity24seven.frmDemo, Text: Demonstration

OK

This is the setting of the *Name* property for the form.

This is the setting of the *Text* property for the form.

PRACTICAL ACTIVITY 24.8

Amend Listing 24.4 so that the last line only displays the setting of the *Name* property of the form.

Hint: use members of the string class to obtain the string between the full stop and comma of the string shown in Figure 24.8 (refer to Chapter 23).

Being able to isolate the *Name* property of an object that raises an event is very useful.

PRACTICAL ACTIVITY 24.9

Implement Specification 24.2.

SPECIFICATION 24.2

Write a program that displays the x and y coordinates of the cursor when the mouse is clicked over a form.

NOTE: To implement Specification 24.2 requires that the *MouseDown* event is used and **not** the *Form1.Click* event as you may suspect. This is because the *MouseDown* event passes in an argument *e*, which is an instance of the *System.Windows.Forms.MouseEventArgs* class, and this *e* has access to the members shown in Table 24.3. Whereas the form click event has access to the members of the *System.EventArgs* class, and the x and y coordinates are **not** members of the class *System.EventArgs*.

The event handling procedure that implements Specification 24.2 is shown in Listing 24.5 and an example of output when the form is clicked, near its top-left corner, is shown in Figure 24.9.

Listing 24.5 Displaying X and Y when a form is clicked.

```
Private Sub Form1_MouseDown(ByVal sender As Object, ByVal e As _
System.Windows.Forms.MouseEventArgs) Handles MyBase.MouseDown

    MessageBox.Show("X = " & e.X & " Y = " & e.Y)
End Sub
```

Figure 24.9 An example when the form is clicked near its top left corner.

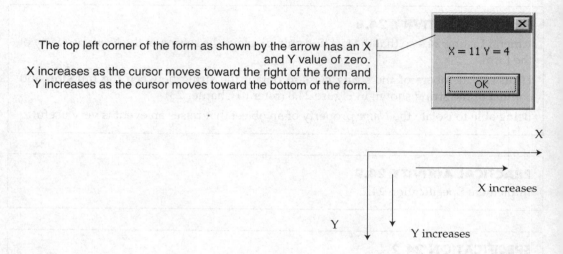

The top left corner of the form as shown by the arrow has an X and Y value of zero.
X increases as the cursor moves toward the right of the form and Y increases as the cursor moves toward the bottom of the form.

X = 11 Y = 4

X

X increases

Y

Y increases

PRACTICAL ACTIVITY 24.10

Implement Specification 24.3 and note what is displayed in the MessageBox when the form is clicked at various positions.

SPECIFICATION 24.3

Write a program that continually displays the x and y coordinates of the cursor, in a label, when the mouse is moved over a form.

The event handler that implements Specification 24.3 is shown in Listing 24.6 and an example of output when the cursor is moved over the form near the top left corner is shown in Figure 24.10. It can be seen from Listing 24.6 that the code was 'attached' to the *MouseMove* event.

Listing 24.6 The *MouseMove* event handling procedure.

Private Sub Form1_MouseMove(ByVal sender As Object, ByVal e As _
System.Windows.Forms.MouseEventArgs) Handles MyBase.MouseMove

   Label1.Text = "X = " & e.X & " Y = " & e.Y
End Sub

Figure 24.10 An example runtime for the *MouseMove* event.

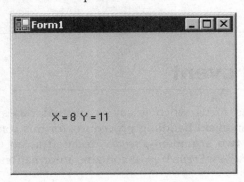

PRACTICAL ACTIVITY 24.11

Place a PictureBox on to a form and load it with a suitable icon. At runtime have the PictureBox move to the position of the cursor when the mouse button is clicked.

Hint:

   PictureBox1.Top = e.Y

   PictureBox1.Left = e.X

Keyboard events

In a windows environment, at any one time, one of the objects on the screen will have the **focus** and this will be indicated by the objects appearance. For example, when a button has the focus the edge of the button appear to be in shadow (or a dotted line surrounds the text), as shown in Figure 24.11.

Figure 24.11 Button1 is in focus.

This button has
the focus.

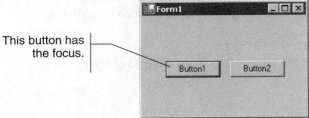

> **NOTE**: The control (object) that has the focus responds to the keyboard input.

There are three keyboard events and they are: *KeyDown*, *KeyUp* and *KeyPress*.

> **NOTE**: Key events occur in the following order:
> 1. *KeyDown*
> 2. *KeyPress*
> 3. *KeyUp*

The *KeyPress* event

The control that has the focus when a key is pressed raises a *KeyPress* event. This causes the execution of an event handling procedure, for this controls the *KeyPress* event. This procedure receives two arguments; *sender* declared as an *Object* and *e* declared as *System.Windows.Forms.KeyPressEventArgs*. *e* contains information related to the event as shown in Table 24.4.

Table 24.4 Properties of the *KeyPressEventArgs* argument *e*.

Property	Description
Handled	Gets or sets a value indicating whether the *KeyPress* event was handled. True if the event is handled; otherwise, False.
KeyChar	Gets the character corresponding to the key pressed.

> **SPECIFICATION 24.4**
> *Write a program that will only allow a TextBox to receive the entry of figures from 0 to 9. The entry of any other character is reported in a MessageBox.*

The event handling procedure that implements Specification 24.4 is shown in Listing 24.7 and an example of the runtime is shown in Figure 24.12.

Listing 24.7 Implementing Specification 24.4.

```
Private Sub TextBox1_KeyPress(ByVal sender As Object, ByVal e As _
System.Windows.Forms.KeyPressEventArgs) Handles TextBox1.KeyPress

    If e.KeyChar < "0" Or e.KeyChar > "9" Then
        MessageBox.Show("Only the figures 0 to 9 are allowed entry")
        e.Handled = True
    End If
End Sub
```

Figure 24.12 An example runtime.

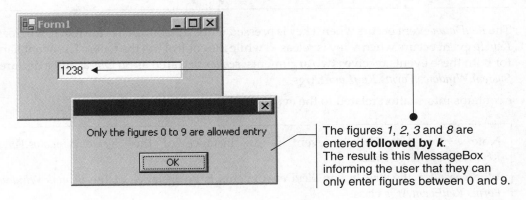

The figures *1, 2, 3* and *8* are entered **followed by** *k*.
The result is this MessageBox informing the user that they can only enter figures between 0 and 9.

Description trace for the *TextBox1_KeyPress* event

Statement	Description
Assume the user enters the figure *1*.	
If e.KeyChar < "0" Or e.KeyChar > "9" Then	The event handler obtains details of the key pressed from *e.KeyChar* and in this case it contains a value that indicates that figure *1* was pressed.
	This figure is not outside the range as defined by the test of the selection construct. Consequently, the test is False and the code within the selection construct is **not** executed.
	The textbox displays the figure *1*.
Assume the user enters the character *k*.	
If e.KeyChar < "0" Or e.KeyChar > "9" Then	The test is True so the code within the selection construct is executed.
MessageBox.Show("Only the figures 0 to 9 are allowed entry")	The MessageBox is displayed as shown in Figure 24.12.
e.Handled = True	Setting this to true indicates that the *KeyPress* event was handled.
	If the event is not handled it is sent to Windows for default processing. The letter k is then displayed in the TextBox and of course we do not want this to happen.

PRACTICAL ACTIVITY 24.12

Implement Specification 24.4 as represented by Listing 24.7. Run and observe the program when the user enters *1238k*.

Remove the program statement *e.Handled = True* from the event handler and execute the program and again enter *1238k*. What is the difference in the response of the program?

The *KeyDown* and the *KeyUp* events

The *KeyDown* event occurs when a key is pressed while the control has the focus, whereas the *KeyUp* event occurs when a key is released while the control has the focus. The event handler for both these events receives two arguments; *sender* declared as an *Object* and *e* declared as *System.Windows.Forms.**KeyEventArgs***.

e contains information related to the events as shown in Table 24.5.

Note *e* for the *KeyPress* event is an instance of the *System.Windows.Forms.KeyPressEventArgs* class.

Whereas *e* for the *KeyUp* and *KeyDown* events is an instance of the *System.Windows.Forms.KeyEventArgs* class.

They are obviously different and consequently have different members (compare Table 24.4 with Table 24.5).

Table 24.5 Properties of the *KeyEventArgs* argument *e*.

Property	Description
Alt	Gets a value indicating whether the Alt key was pressed.
Control	Gets a value indicating whether the Ctrl key was pressed.
Handled	Gets or sets a value indicating whether the event was handled.
KeyCode	Gets the keyboard **code**.
KeyData	Gets the key data.
KeyValue	Gets the keyboard **value**.
Modifiers	Gets the modifier flags. This indicates which combinations of modifier keys (Ctrl, Shift, and Alt) were pressed.
Shift	Gets a value indicating whether the Shift key was pressed.

SPECIFICATION 24.5

*An application consists of one form that contains two buttons. Arrange for the pressing of the F9 function key to quit the application **regardless** of which control has the focus.*

Both buttons and the form can respond to a *KeyDown* event. At runtime one of the buttons will have the focus and it will respond to the *KeyDown* event. However which of the buttons has the focus (when the user presses F9 to quit the application) will be unknown. Therefore at first sight it appears that the *End* statement (this quits the application) needs to be attached to *KeyDown* event for all the controls on the form. This will work but a better way exists. Set the *KeyPreview* Property of the form to *True* and place the End statement in the *KeyDown* event of the form.

Setting the *KeyPreview* Property to *True* ensures that the form responds to the keyboard events **before** the control that has the focus. This makes it easy to provide a common response to a specific keystroke.

NOTE: When the *KeyPreview* property of a form is set to *True* it does not stop the control that has the focus from responding to the *KeyDown* event. The control does respond but it does so **after** the forms *KeyDown* event. Of course in this case the application quits so . . .

The event handler that implements Specification 24.5 is shown in Listing 24.8. Figure 24.13 shows the setting of the *KeyPreview* property to *True*.

Figure 24.13 Setting *KeyPreview* to *True*.

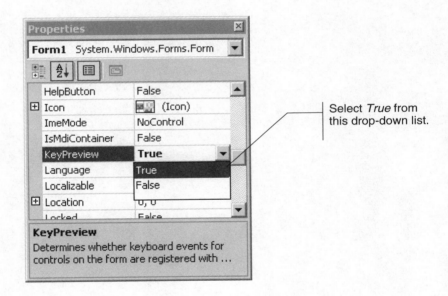

Select *True* from this drop-down list.

Listing 24.8 Using a function key to quit an application.

```
Private Sub Form1_KeyDown(ByVal sender As Object, ByVal e As _
System.Windows.Forms.KeyEventArgs) Handles MyBase.KeyDown

    If e.KeyCode = Keys.F9 Then
        End
    End If
End Sub
```

PRACTICAL ACTIVITY 24.13

Implement Specification 24.5.

Remember to set *KeyPreview* to true.

PRACTICAL ACTIVITY 24.14

Place a button on a form and attach the following code to its *KeyDown* event.

MessageBox.Show ("Button1 is responding")

Attach the following code to the Form *KeyDown* event.

MessageBox.Show ("The form is responding")

Set the *KeyPreview* property of the form to *True* and run the program. Press a key on the keyboard and observe the result.

Now set the *KeyPreview* property of the form to *False* and run the program again. Press a key on the keyboard and observe the result. What is the difference in the runtimes?

25 Dialog boxes

A number of dialog boxes are available within VB .NET that enable you to develop a common user interface as seen in many Windows applications. Examples of such dialog boxes are the:

- MessageBox
- Color
- Font
- OpenFile.

The MessageBox has been used throughout the book and its coverage will not be extended in this chapter. All the others in the list above will be considered. There are two others not covered in this chapter, namely, the SaveFile and Print dialog boxes. However, the principles for the use of dialogs are similar so you are left to discover the operation of the Save and Print dialog boxes. The OpenFile dialog box is considered in Chapter 27.

The Color dialog box

The operation of the Color dialog box will be shown by the implementation of Specification 25.1.

> **SPECIFICATION 25.1**
> *Use a Color dialog box to set the background colour of a textbox.*

Figure 25.1 shows the GUI for implementing Specification 25.1 (set the *MultiLine* property of the TextBox to *True*). The code attached to the GUI is shown in Listing 25.1. An example runtime is shown in Figure 25.2.

Figure 25.1 The GUI for Specification 25.1.

1. Set the *Name* property to *btnColour*. Set the *Text* property to *Set Colour*.

2. Set the *MultiLine* property of the textbox to *True* and drag to an appropriate size. Set the *Name* property to *txtColorDemo*.

Listing 25.1 The event handler attached to the Set Colour button.

```
Private Sub btnColour_Click(ByVal sender As System.Object, ByVal e As _
System.EventArgs) Handles btnColour.Click
   Dim myColourDialog As ColorDialog

   myColourDialog = New ColorDialog()
   myColourDialog.ShowDialog()
   txtColorDemo.BackColor = myColourDialog.Color
End Sub
```

Figure 25.2 An example runtime.

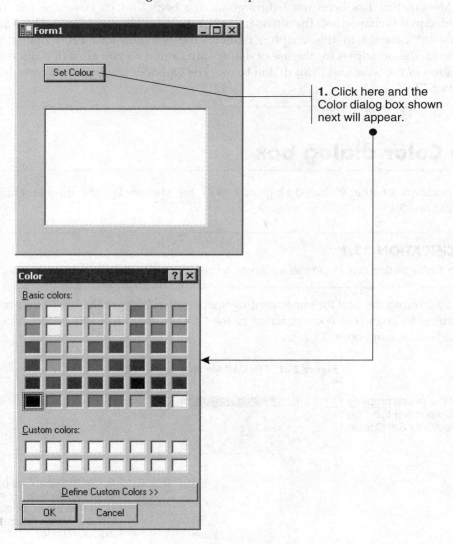

1. Click here and the Color dialog box shown next will appear.

Figure 25.2 (cont.)

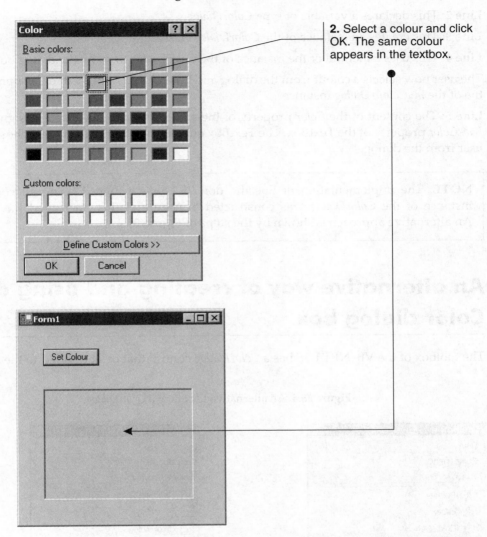

2. Select a colour and click OK. The same colour appears in the textbox.

The code of Listing 25.1 appears in Figure 25.3 with line numbers to aid in its description.

Figure 25.3 The program with line numbers.

1. Private Sub btnColour_Click(ByVal senderAs System Object, ByVal e As_
   System.EventArgs) Handles btnColour.Click
2.   Dim myColourDalog As ColorDialog

3.   myColourDialog = New ColorDialog()
4.   myColourDialog.ShowDialog()
5.   txtColorDemo.BackColor = myColourDialog.Color
6. End Sub

Line 1: This is the signature of event handling procedure.

Line 2: This declares a variable of type *ColorDialog*.

Line 3: This creates an instance of the *ColorDialog* class.

Line 4: This uses a method of the instance of the *ColorDialog* to show the dialog box.

The user now selects a colour from the dialog and this colour is assigned to *Color* property of the of the *myColourDialog* instance.

Line 5: The content of the *Color* property of the *myColourDialog* instance is assigned to the *BackColor* property of the TextBox. The TextBox now has a colour equal to that chosen by the user from the dialog.

NOTE: The implementation of Specification 25.1 was achieved using all code. An instance of the *ColorDialog* was constructed in code and then messaged (i.e. used). An alternative approach is shown by the steps of Figure 25.4.

An alternative way of creating and using a Color dialog box

The toolbox of the VB .NET IDE has a *ColorDialog* control that can be added to the *tray*.

Figure 25.4 An alternative to coding a *ColorDialog*.

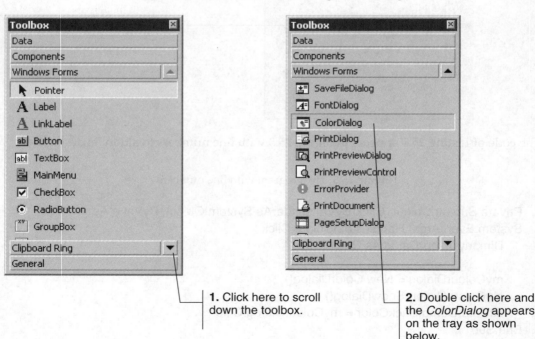

1. Click here to scroll down the toolbox.

2. Double click here and the *ColorDialog* appears on the tray as shown below.

Figure 25.4 (cont.)

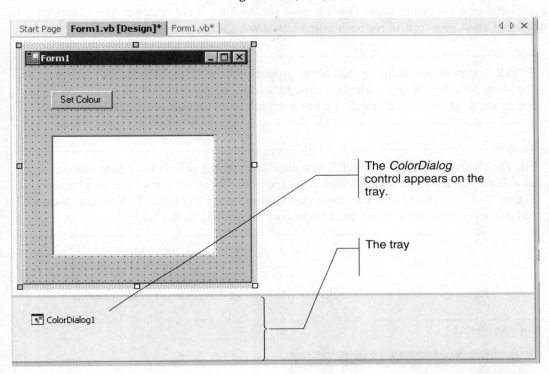

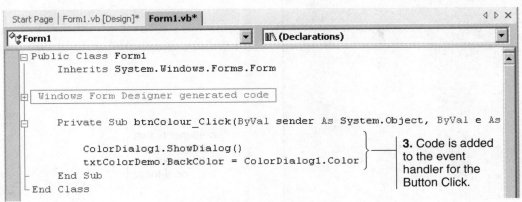

The code added to the button click event handler is shown in Listing 25.2.

Listing 25.2 The event handling procedure.

```
Private Sub btnColour_Click(ByVal sender As System.Object, ByVal e As _
System.EventArgs) Handles btnColour.Click

   ColorDialog1.ShowDialog()
   txtColorDemo.BackColor = ColorDialog1.Color
End Sub
```

587

It can be seen from Listing 25.2 that, compared with Listing 25.1, there was no need to declare a variable of type *ColorDialog*. There is also no need for a constructor. The *ColorDialog* is available because a control representing a *ColorDialog* was placed on the tray.

NOTE: It is possible to change the *Name* property of the *ColorDialog* in the same way as the *Name* property of any control is changed using the Properties window. However, for the example shown in Listing 25.2 it has been left at its default setting of *ColorDialog1*.

NOTE: The tray is new to VB .NET; in a previous version of VB (VB6) components such as a *Timer* were placed on the form. They are now placed on the tray as can be seen in Figure 25.4. To ensure that the tray is understood refer to Figure 25.5, which shows a number of components including a timer control present on the tray.

Figure 25.5 What the tray looks like when it contains a number of components.

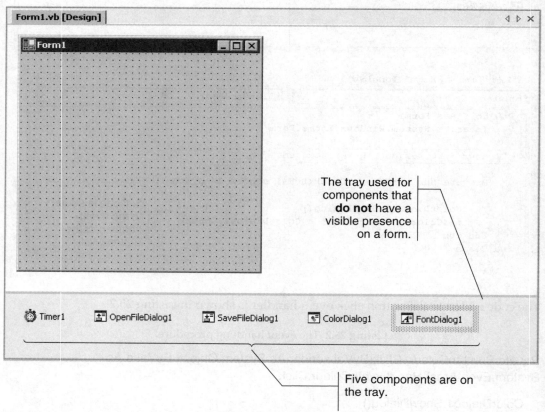

PRACTICAL ACTIVITY 25.1

Implement Specification 25.1 twice using both approaches covered in this chapter: one using just code and the other using a *ColorDialog* control placed in the tray (together with the appropriate code).

PRACTICAL ACTIVITY 25.2

Amend the application developed during Practical Activity 25.1 with the addition of another button to set the Foreground colour of the textbox. This colour is set using the *ColorDialog*. You decide on which of the alternative approaches to use.

During the runtime define and use custom colours.

The Font dialog box

Implementing Specification 25.2 will show the operation of the Font dialog box.

SPECIFICATION 25.2

Use a Font dialog box to set the font of the text displayed in a Textbox.

Figure 25.6 shows the GUI for implementing Specification 25.2 (set the *MultiLine* property of the textbox to *True*). The code attached to the GUI is shown in Listing 25.3. An example runtime is shown in Figure 25.7.

Figure 25.6 The GUI for implementing Specification 25.2.

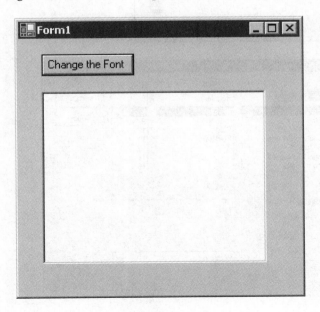

Listing 25.3 The code attached to the button.

```
Private Sub btnFont_Click(ByVal sender As System.Object, ByVal e As _
System.EventArgs) Handles btnFont.Click
    Dim myFontDialog As FontDialog

    myFontDialog = New FontDialog()
    myFontDialog.ShowDialog()
    txtFontDemo.Font = myFontDialog.Font
End Sub
```

This code constructs an instance of the *FontDialog*, then uses the *ShowDialog()* method to show the font dialog box. The user then selects an appropriate font setting from the Font dialog box. The last line assigns the content of the *Font* property of the instance of the *FontDialog* to the *Font* property of the textbox.

Figure 25.7 An example runtime.

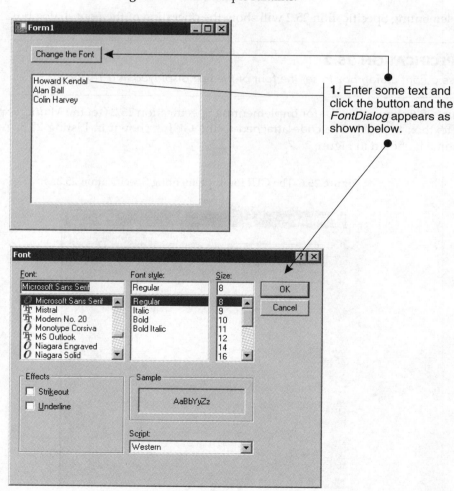

1. Enter some text and click the button and the *FontDialog* appears as shown below.

Figure 25.7 (cont.)

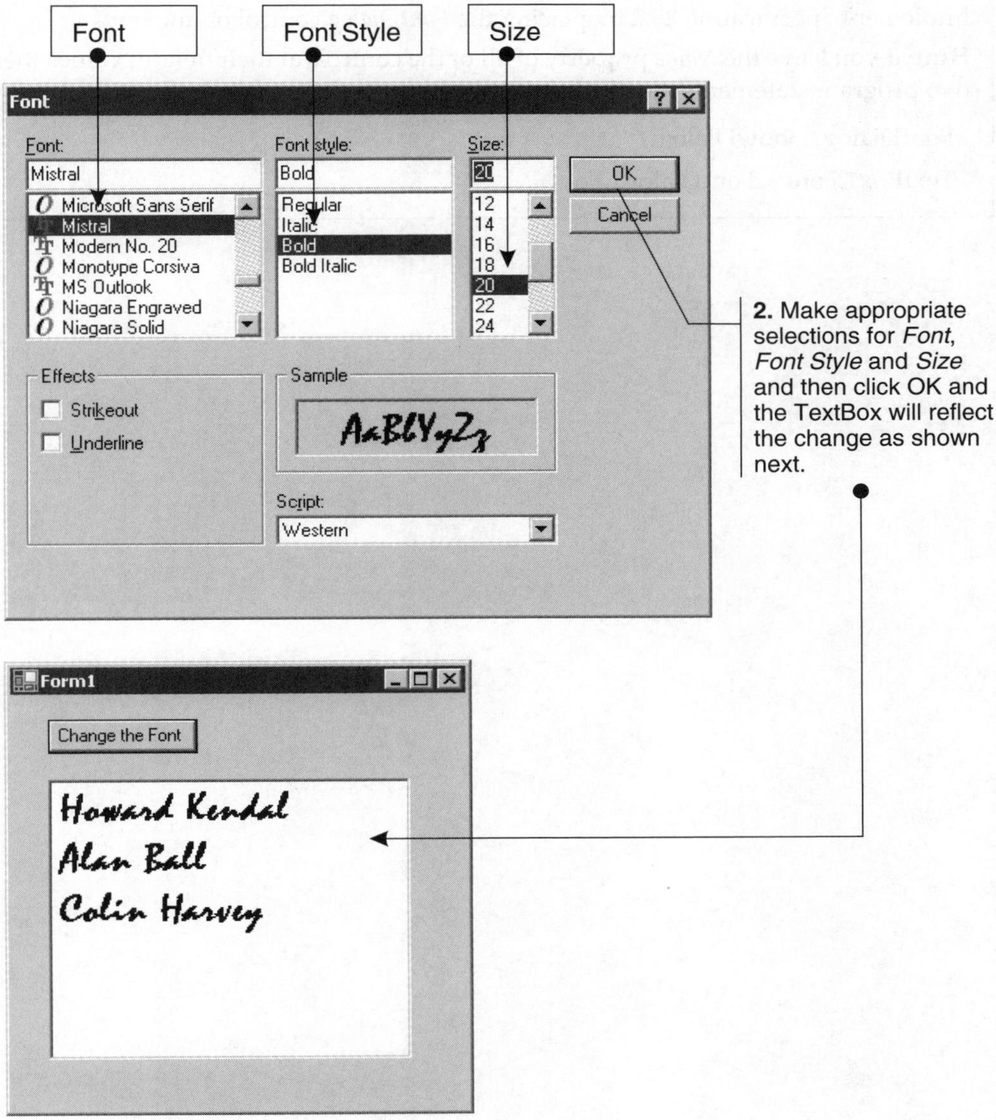

2. Make appropriate selections for *Font*, *Font Style* and *Size* and then click OK and the TextBox will reflect the change as shown next.

PRACTICAL ACTIVITY 25.3

Implement Specification 25.2 as represented by Figure 25.6 and Listing 25.3. Remember to set the *MultiLine* property of the textbox to true.

NOTE: Of course there is an alternative approach to using the *FontDialog*, and it involves putting the *FontDialog* control in the tray.

PRACTICAL ACTIVITY 25.4

Implement Specification 25.2 by placing the *FontDialog* control on the tray.

Hint: if you leave the *Name* property of all of the controls at their default values then the two program statements required are:

FontDialog1.ShowDialog()

TextBox1.Font = FontDialog1.Font

26 Creating menus

Menus are a commonplace feature of Window applications. This chapter shows how to create menus.

Figure 26.1 shows how to create a simple menu.

Figure 26.1 Creating a simple menu.

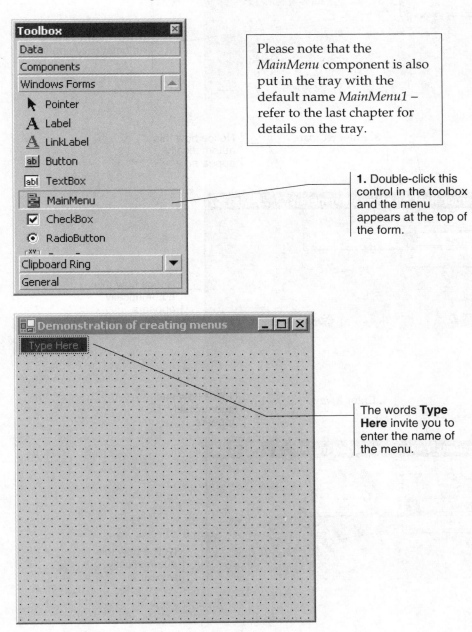

Please note that the *MainMenu* component is also put in the tray with the default name *MainMenu1* – refer to the last chapter for details on the tray.

1. Double-click this control in the toolbox and the menu appears at the top of the form.

The words **Type Here** invite you to enter the name of the menu.

Figure 26.1 (cont.)

2. Enter *&File* – the ampersand in front of the word *File* will result in the letter *F* being underlined. An underlined letter in a menu can be accessed by pressing the Alt key at the same time as the underlined letter.

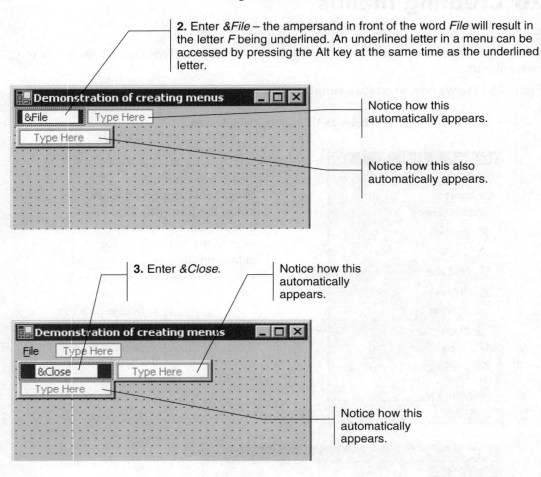

Notice how this automatically appears.

Notice how this also automatically appears.

3. Enter *&Close*.

Notice how this automatically appears.

Notice how this automatically appears.

4. Enter *&New*.

Notice how this automatically appears.

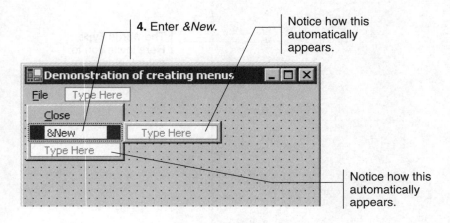

Notice how this automatically appears.

Figure 26.1 (cont.)

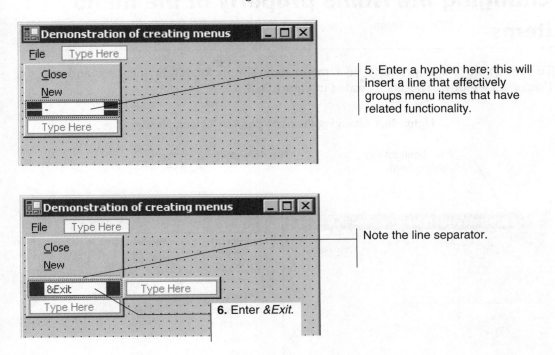

5. Enter a hyphen here; this will insert a line that effectively groups menu items that have related functionality.

Note the line separator.

6. Enter *&Exit*.

Figure 26.2 shows what the menu looks like at runtime.

Figure 26.2 The menu at runtime.

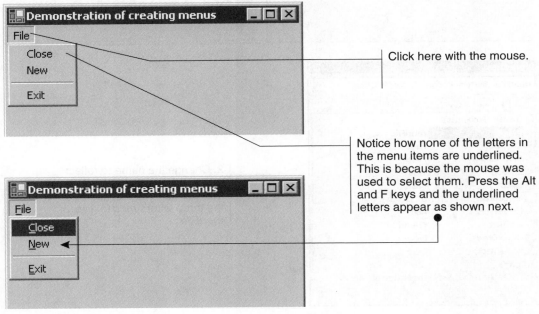

Click here with the mouse.

Notice how none of the letters in the menu items are underlined. This is because the mouse was used to select them. Press the Alt and F keys and the underlined letters appear as shown next.

Changing the *Name* property of the menu items

To change the *Name* property of a menu item simply highlight the item and use the Properties window. This is illustrated in Figure 26.3.

Figure 26.3 Changing the name property of menu items.

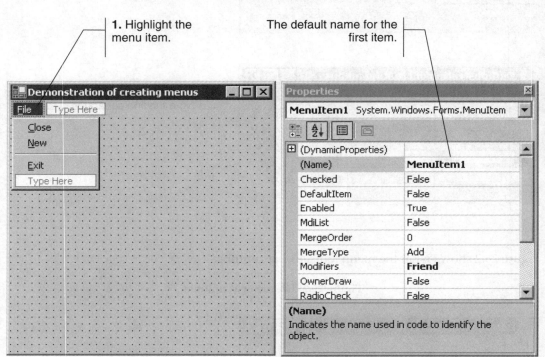

1. Highlight the menu item.

The default name for the first item.

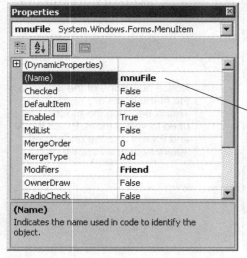

2. Change the name to reflect the purpose of the menu. Note how the name is prefixed by the three letters *mnu* to give *mnuFile*.

Figure 26.3 (cont.)

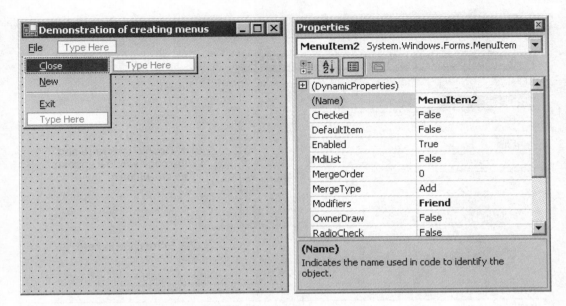

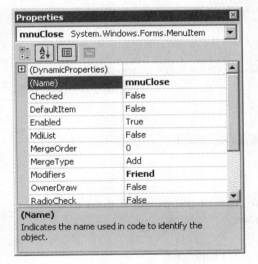

Again, highlight the menu item and set the name in the Properties window.

Attaching an event handling procedure to a menu item

To attach an event handler to a menu item simply double-click on the menu item and the code window will appear with the cursor positioned within the template for the event handler. This is illustrated in Figure 26.4.

Figure 26.4 Attaching an event handler to a menu item.

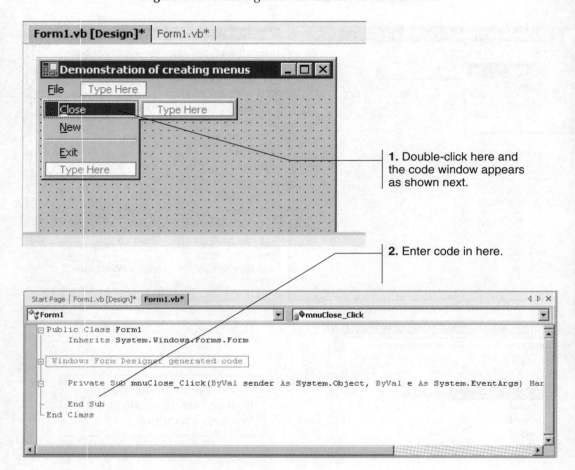

Listing 26.1 shows code to be added to the Close item of the menu; it does not do any processing, it just demonstrates that the event handler is working.

Listing 26.1 A menu item event handler.

```
Private Sub mnuClose_Click(ByVal sender As System.Object, ByVal e
As System.EventArgs) Handles mnuClose.Click
    MessageBox.Show _
    ("Demonstration: You have just clicked the Close Item of the menu")
End Sub
```

Figure 26.5 shows the runtime when the user selects the Close item from the menu.

Figure 26.5 The runtime when the user selects *Close*.

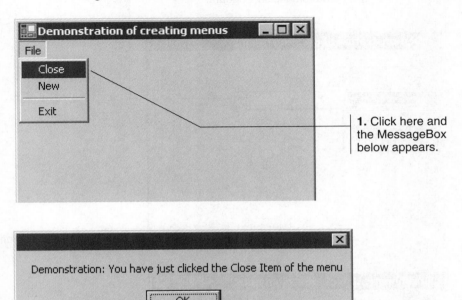

1. Click here and the MessageBox below appears.

PRACTICAL ACTIVITY 26.1

Create the menu as shown by Figure 26.1 and add the event handler of Listing 26.1. Run and observe the response when the Close item is clicked.

Creating submenus

Figure 26.6 shows how to create a submenu; it adds a submenu to the *New* item of the menu created during Practical Activity 26.1.

Figure 26.6 Creating a submenu.

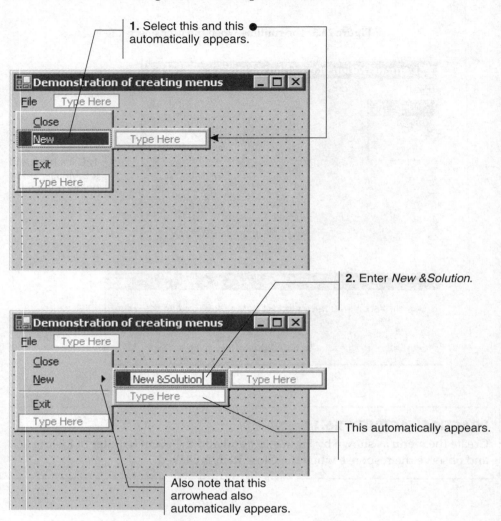

1. Select this and this automatically appears.

2. Enter *New &Solution*.

This automatically appears.

Also note that this arrowhead also automatically appears.

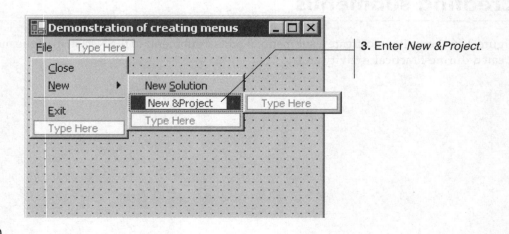

3. Enter *New &Project*.

The runtime for the menu after the completion of the steps outlined by Figure 26.6 is shown in Figure 26.7.

Figure 26.7 The runtime showing submenus.

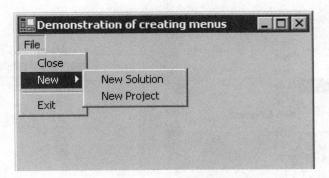

PRACTICAL ACTIVITY 26.2

Add the submenus as represented by Figure 26.7 to the menu you developed in Practical Activity 26.1. Set the *Name* property of the menu items as appropriate (using the prefix *mnu* in all cases). Add a MessageBox to the event handler of each menu item and have it display a simple message that indicates which menu item was clicked, e.g. *You have just clicked the Exit item* and so on.

Adding a shortcut to a menu item

Figure 26.8 shows how to add a shortcut to the *New Project* menu item, which will enable the actions of the menu event handler to be invoked by keystrokes.

Figure 26.8 Adding a shortcut.

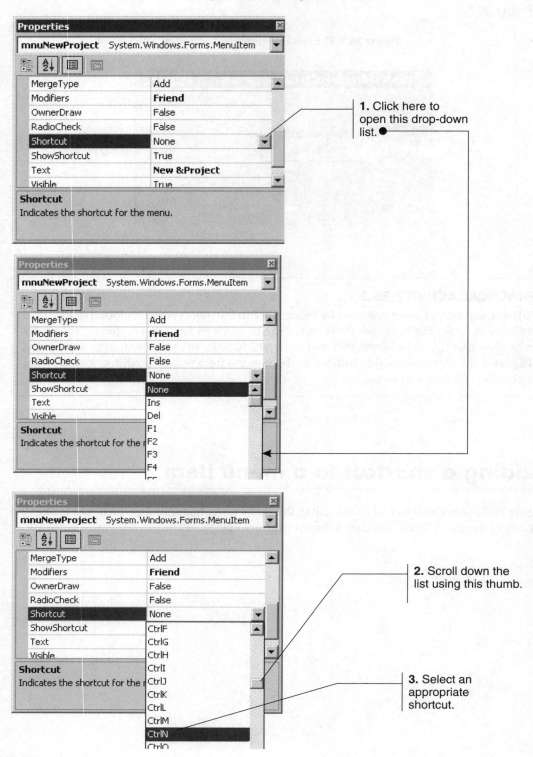

Figure 26.8 (cont.)

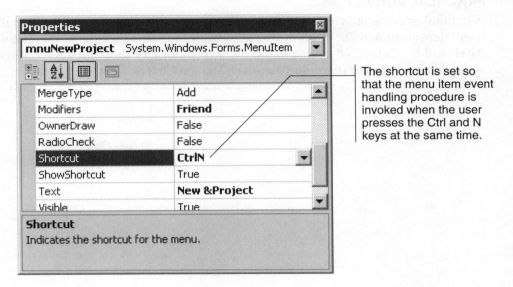

The shortcut is set so that the menu item event handling procedure is invoked when the user presses the Ctrl and N keys at the same time.

NOTE: The shortcut is not visible against the menu item at design time. However, it is visible at runtime as shown by Figure 26.9.

Figure 26.9 The shortcut at runtime.

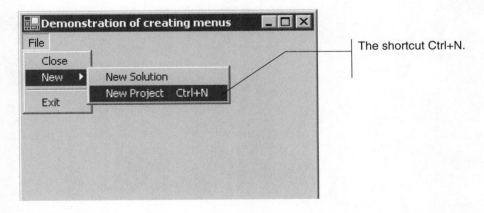

The shortcut Ctrl+N.

NOTE: The event handler attached to the *New Project* menu item can now be invoked by a mouse click on the menu item and by appropriate keystrokes.

PRACTICAL ACTIVITY 26.3

Add the shortcut as shown by Figure 26.8. Run the program and invoke the *New Project* menu item event handler by all three methods, e.g. a mouse click on the menu item, by Alt+P and by Ctrl+N. Of course to use the accelerator and short cut keys will require appropriate keystrokes preceding the Alt+P and the Ctrl+N.

27 Files

There are many ways to access files using VB .NET: this chapter looks at some of the many types of file access. The emphasis of the chapter is on the principles of file access. The beginning of the chapter looks at relatively primitive file access, with more sophisticated types of access at the end of the chapter.

All of the programs to date have been examples of interactive programs. That is, all of the input data has been received from the user via the keyboard and all the output displayed on the VDU for the user to read. Whereas this has been a useful mechanism for learning the VB .NET language, very few commercial software systems are totally interactive.

Consider the issuing of payslips to the employees of a company. Part of the program will involve reading each employee record (e.g. hours worked, rate of pay per hour, etc.) and then calculating the gross pay, etc. If the company has 200 employees then implementing the solution as an interactive program, taking its data from the keyboard, would be very inefficient. The computer would remain idle most of the time, waiting for the user to enter the details at the keyboard. The more employees there are in the company the greater the idle time.

A much more sensible arrangement is for the details on all the employees to be entered into a file using appropriate software (e.g. an editor). Consequently, the details on all of the employees can be in place before the program that issues wage slips is run. The computer would then not suffer from the idle time associated with an interactive process. Instead the program would read the employee details from the file – this is a much faster process.

The outputs from programs are also sent to files where they are stored for future reference.

Input and output files are stored on magnetic media (or other storage media) and their contents are brought into silicon memory (RAM) from where they are processed by the CPU. Once the data is processed it is returned to magnetic media (files) from the RAM. This is illustrated in Figure 27.1.

Figure 27.1 The relationship between files and memory.

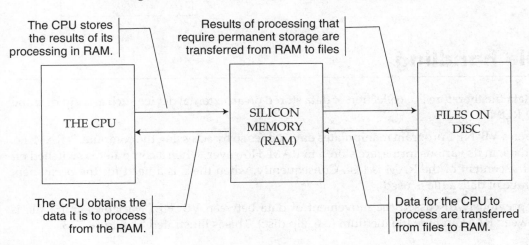

605

The transfer of data between files and RAM is between files and program variables (variables are data allocated regions of RAM). Variables that deal with data supplied to and from files are often referred to as buffer variables. The relationship between program variables and a file is shown in Figure 27.2.

Figure 27.2 The relationship between program variables and a file.

MEMORY

Program Instructions

Program instructions are responsible for transferring the data between program variables and files.
Files are the supplier of data to variables where they are processed.
Files are also the receiver of data, from variables, and are used for permanent storage.

Program variables

Data is transferred between the program variable and the file stored on magnetic media.

File of data (e.g.magnetic media)

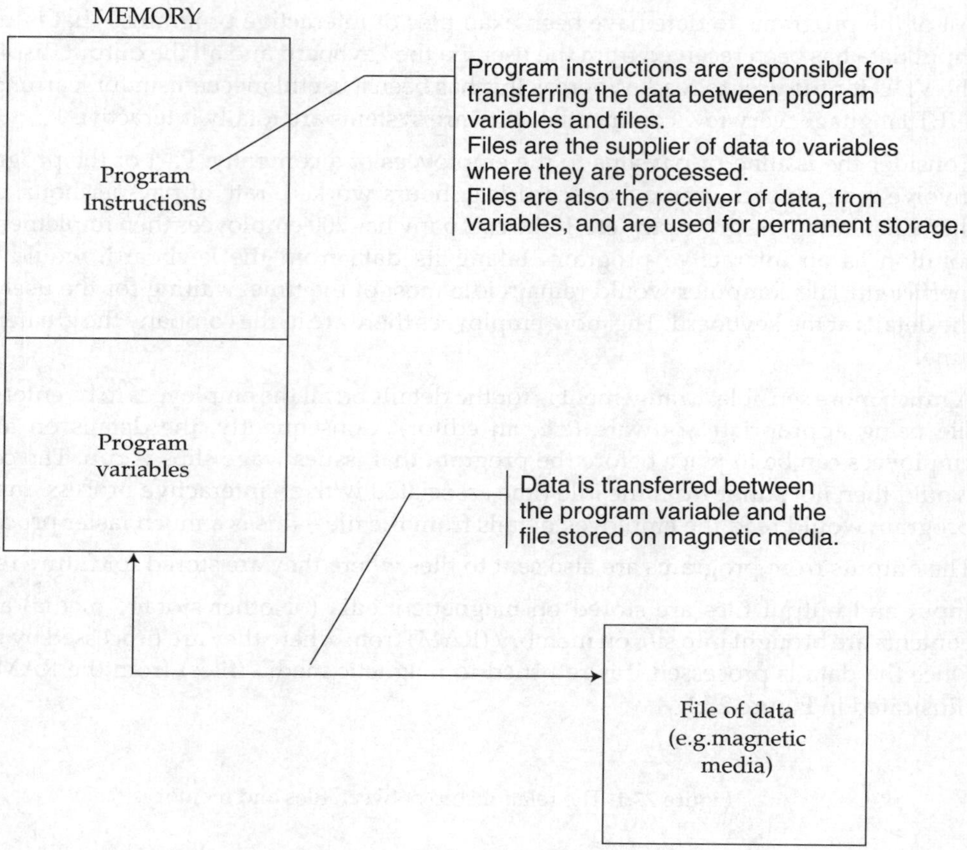

File handling

A **data** file therefore is a collection of data stored on an external device such as a zip disc and CD-ROM.

When a VB .NET program manipulates data it does so by accessing the computer's RAM, i.e. all data, in its various forms, are stored in RAM. However, when a computer is switched off all the content of the RAM is lost. Consequently, when there is a need for the permanent storage of data a file is used.

As previously discussed the movement of data between VB .NET variables and a file is between RAM and the file medium (e.g. zip disc). This is illustrated by Figure 27.3.

Figure 27.3 Movement of data.

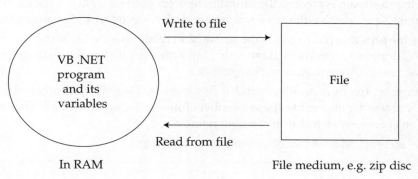

Streams

Object oriented programs use streams for data transfer between programs and files. A stream can be considered as a narrow conduit through which data are moved between the VB .NET program variables and the file. There are two main types of streams: input streams and output streams, as illustrated by Figures 27.4 and 27.5.

Figure 27.4 An input stream.

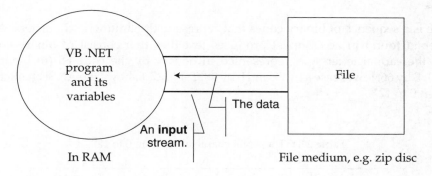

Figure 27.5 An output stream.

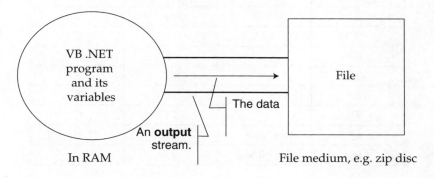

> **NOTE:** Once a stream is created the program references the stream not the file. From the programmer's perspective the stream is where data is stored to and received from.
>
> Of course the program has to create the stream and relate it to the file in the first place but once this is done the access is to the stream. However, despite this the term stream access and file access are often used interchangeably.
>
> Furthermore a stream is an object and it has members just like all other objects. The syntax for accessing and using these members follows the syntax for all 'object access'; namely, object reference full stop member name, i.e.
>
> objectReference.Member or objectReference.Member()

Types of file

There are two fundamental types of files:

1. Text files.

2. Binary files.

Text files

A text file is a sequence of binary codes that represent alphanumeric characters. An editor (e.g. notepad found in accessories) produces text files that consist of binary codes. For example, the capital letter A is represented in denary by the code 65 (in binary this is 01000001), B by 66, lower case a by 97 and b by 98. Table 27.1 shows the ANSI character set for codes from 0 to 127.

Table 27.1 The ANSI character set from 0 to 127.

Code	Character	Code	Character
0		64	@
1		65	A
2		66	B
3		67	C
4		68	D
5		69	E
6		70	F
7		71	G
8	See Note 1	72	H
9	See Note 2	73	i

Table 27.1 (cont.)

Code	Character	Code	Character
10	See Note 3	74	J
11		75	K
12		76	L
13	See Note 4	77	M
14		78	N
15		79	O
16		80	P
17		81	Q
18		82	R
19		83	S
20		84	T
21		85	U
22		86	V
23		87	W
24		88	X
25		89	Y
26		90	Z
27		91	[
28		92	\
29		93	]
30		94	^
31		95	_
32	[space]	96	`
33	!	97	a
34	"	98	b
35	#	99	c
36	$	100	d
37	%	101	e
38	&	102	f
39	'	103	g
40	(	104	h
41	)	105	i
42	*	106	j
43	+	107	k
44	,	108	l
45	-	109	m

Table 27.1 (cont.)

Code	Character	Code	Character
46	.	110	n
47	/	111	o
48	0	112	p
49	1	113	q
50	2	114	r
51	3	115	s
52	4	116	t
53	5	117	u
54	6	118	v
55	7	119	w
56	8	120	x
57	9	121	y
58	:	122	z
59	;	123	{
60	<	124		
61	=	125	}
62	>	126	~
63	?	127	N/A

Note 1: The value 8 has no graphical representation but depending on the application it may affect the display of text by causing a **backspace**.
Note 2: The value 9 has no graphical representation but depending on the application it may affect the display of text by causing a **Tab**.
Note 3: The value 10 has no graphical representation but depending on the application it may affect the display of text by causing a **Line feed**.
Note 4: The value 13 has no graphical representation but depending on the application it may affect the display of text by causing a **Carriage return**.

NOTE: Use the on-line help to view the ANSI character set for the codes between 128 and 255.

Text files are a sequence of ANSI characters. Figure 27.6 shows text, as it would appear on the VDU in a text editor (e.g. notepad). It also shows the sequence of ANSI characters that represent this text.

Figure 27.6 Text and its ANSI representation.

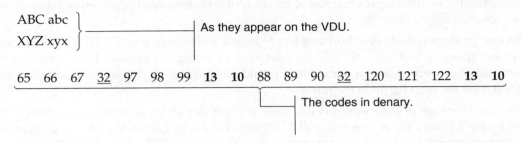

Six of the ANSI codes shown may not at first be apparent (these six characters have either been underlined or shown in bold). The ANSI code 32 represents the space that occurred in the text. The ANSI codes 13 and 10 (carriage return and line feed) mark the end of a line of text. Line feed moves on to the next line and carriage return moves to the beginning of the line.

NOTE: Historically, the terms line feed and carriage return come from the old line printers that were similar to typewriters.

End of file markers

The windows operating system and VB .NET are able to identify the end of a text file (and other types of file) by an 'end of file marker'. This is a useful mechanism that allows code to identify when it is at the end of the text, so it can, for example, count characters in a file or stop reading the file when it reaches the end. If the end of the file can be located then it is possible to append (add) another file to the end of the current file. The **concept** of an end of file marker is illustrated in Figure 27.7.

Figure 27.7 A file and its 'end of file marker' (concept).

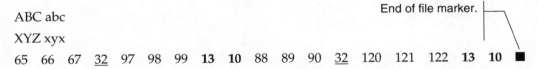

How the end of the file is marked is not that important, what is important is that VB. NET code is able to detect it – more on this later.

Binary files

Programs write data to binary files and programs read data from binary files. In this respect they are no different to a text file. However, whereas the information stored in a text file is in the form of ANSI codes, in a binary file the information is stored in the internal format of the computer system. So, for example, a file that stores integer type variables stores the data in the same format as it is stored in the computer's memory (i.e. in '32 bit chunks' – the length of an integer variable).

611

Access times to binary files can be quicker because there is no need to convert between ANSI codes and the internal representation of the computer system. Also, representing data as text can result in larger files.

An integer storing thirty one thousand five hundred and twenty one (31521) is stored in four bytes of memory and will only take up four bytes of storage in a binary file, whereas if the same number were stored in a text file it would require more bytes of storage space – one ANSI code for each figure in the number.

The disadvantage of binary files is that their content cannot be viewed in an editor. If the content of a binary file is sent to the VDU all you will see is 'gobbledegook' – the operating system interprets the binary information as though it were ANSI codes, which it is not.

NOTE: A text editor does not enter information in a binary file; a running program does.

File system (or folder system)

Files (text or binary) are stored on discs in a file system. A file system is a logical representation of a physical disc or discs. For a VB .NET program to read and write to and from a file it has to 'connect' with the file system.

Consider a computer that has three drives A:, C: and D:. This computer stores files on each disc and each file is identified by an absolute path name – which is a **combination** of the drive letter of the disc, the file name and path to it through all the sub directories (folders) from the root directory. An example of a file system that applies to drive C: is shown in Figure 27.8. Figure 27.9 shows a file system as represented by Windows Explorer.

Figure 27.8 A file system for drive C:.

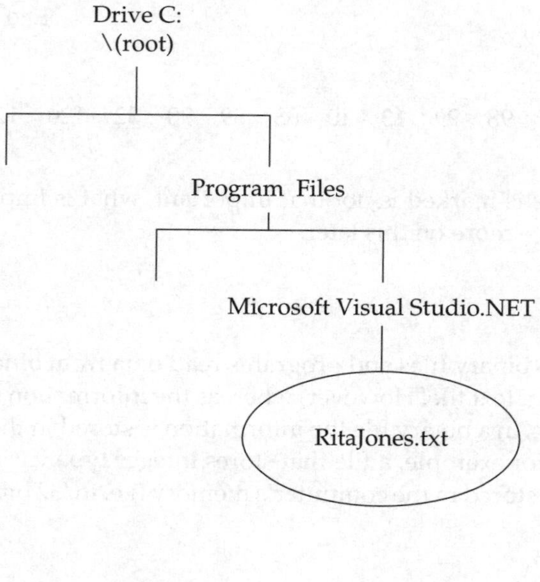

Drive C:
\(root)

Program Files

Microsoft Visual Studio.NET

RitaJones.txt

The ellipse represents a file (named RitaJones.txt) stored in the Microsoft Visual Studio.NET folder (directory). This file is identified and located by its path name. The absolute path to this file is shown below:

c:\Program Files\Microsoft Visual Studio.NET\RitaJones.txt

VB .NET code needs to know where a file is located in the file system and this is achieved by referencing its path name using appropriate program statements. These statements form a stream between the program and the file.

Figure 27.9 Windows Explorer and a file system.

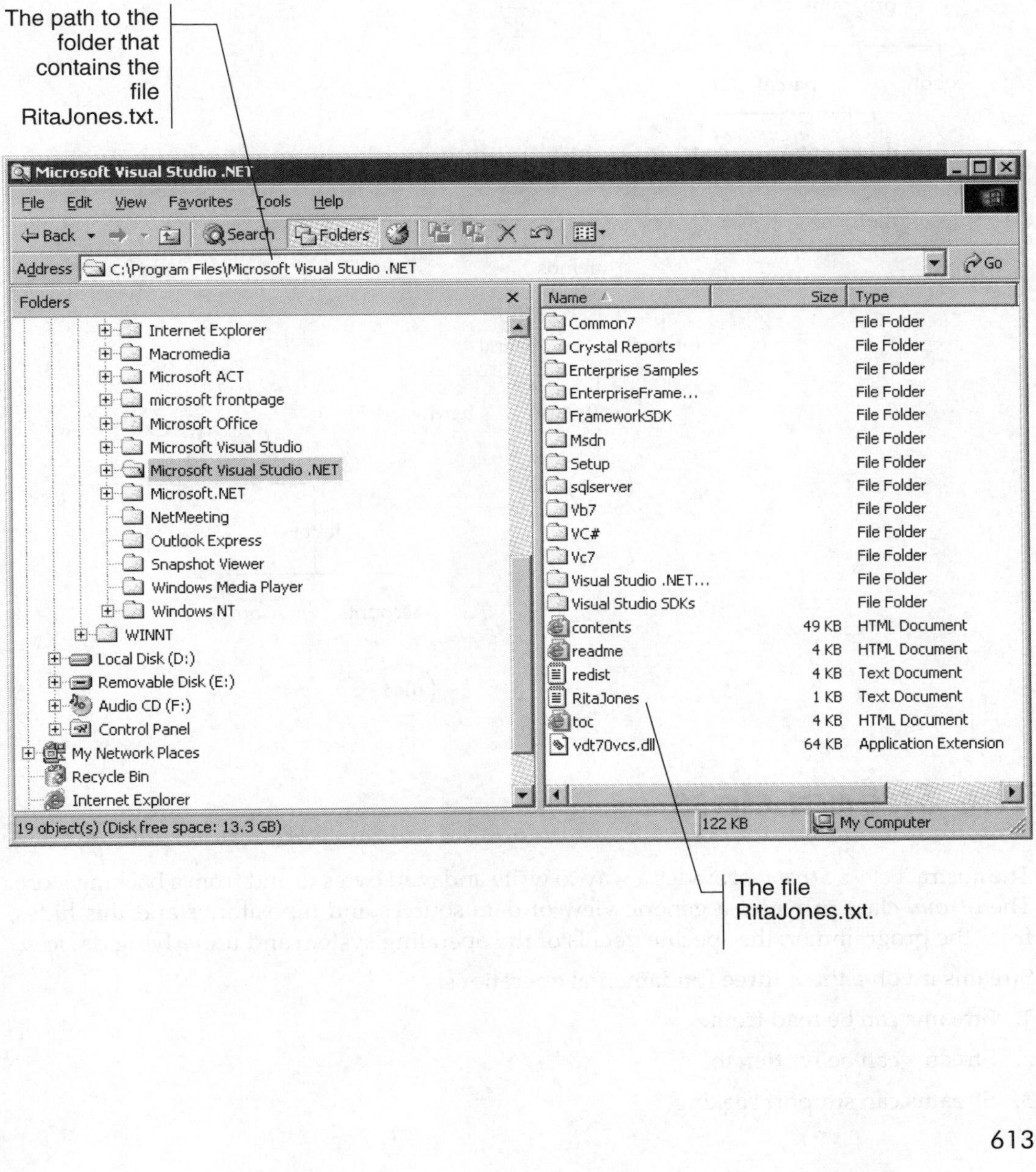

The path to the folder that contains the file RitaJones.txt.

The file RitaJones.txt.

QUESTION 27.1(REVISION)

For the file system shown in Figure 27.10, what are the absolute path names to file1, file2 and file3 (do not forget the root)?

Figure 27.10 A file system.

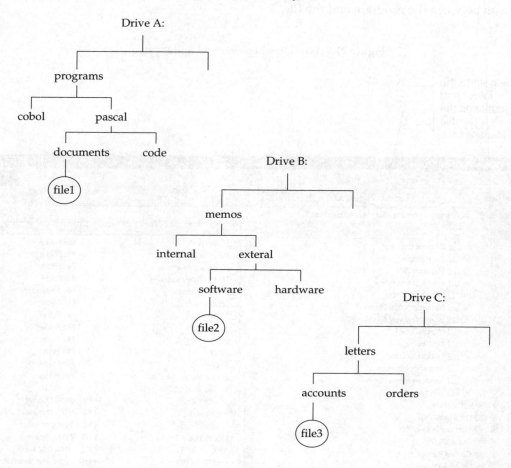

The *Stream* class

The abstract class *Stream* provides a way to write and read bytes to and from a backing store. The *Stream* class provides a generic view of data sources and repositories and this hides, from the programmer, the specific details of the operating system and underlying devices.

Streams involve these **three** fundamental operations:

1. Streams can be read from.
2. Streams can be written to.
3. Streams can support seeking.

Reading from a stream is the transfer of data from the stream into a data structure, such as an array of bytes.

Writing to a stream is the transfer of data from a data structure into a stream.

Seeking is the querying and modifying of the current position within a stream. For example, read from the middle of the stream (i.e. file), or seek the second to last character in a stream (i.e. file) and overwrite it.

> **NOTE**: A stream can link program code to files, to areas of memory for backups and to networks. This chapter deals with streams that link variables with files.

> **NOTE**: The ability to Seek depends on the kind of backing store a stream has. For example, network streams have no unified concept of a current position, and therefore typically do not support seeking.

When associated with files a stream acts as a 'representation' of the file. This means to access the file, we actually access the stream and the details of the file (i.e. the hardware and software links arranged by the operating system) are hidden from the programmer. This is extremely useful because all files can be treated as streams and consequently a consistent form of access is achieved.

Although the stream hides the details of the underlying data source (or repository) knowledge of these data sources and stores is obviously beneficial. However, just considering access to a stream will suffice. But what happens if the stream is connected to a data source that cannot have its contents written to? Or if the data source is a network that cannot have seek applied? The stream class has properties that can be accessed and these properties indicate the capabilities of the stream. These properties are:

- *CanRead*
- *CanWrite*
- *CanSeek.*

If you wish to write to a stream you can test it first by accessing the *CanWrite* property. This property will be true if the stream supports writing; otherwise it will be false.

Asynchronous and synchronous file I/O

A stream supports both synchronous and asynchronous file input and file output. Synchronous I/O generally means that the reading (or writing) of a file starts and finishes and during the period of the reading (or writing) the program did not compete with any other type of operation. With asynchronous I/O the reading (or writing) begins and the program is able to complete other tasks at the same time (concurrently).

> **NOTE**: Only synchronous file I/O is covered in this chapter.

Abstract classes and hierarchies

The *Stream* class is an abstract class that 'belongs' to the *System.IO* namespace. It is not possible to have an instance (i.e. object) of the *Stream* class. The *Stream* class however can be inherited from and three classes that inherit from the stream class are:

- *FileStream*
- *BufferedStream*
- *MemoryStream*.

The *FileStream* class

This class is used primarily for the creation of *FileStream* objects based on file paths. The *FileStream* class can open a file in one of two modes, either synchronously or asynchronously – it defaults to opening files synchronously.

The *BufferedStream* class

An instance of the *BufferedStream* class supplies a buffer, which is simply a block of bytes in memory used to cache data. Using a buffered stream reduces the number of calls to the (disc) operating system and consequently improves read and write performance.

A buffer can be used for either reading or writing, but never both simultaneously.

The *Read* and *Write* methods of *BufferedStream* automatically maintain the buffer, which again hides the details of the file.

The *MemoryStream* class

This provides a way to create streams that have memory as a backing store instead of a disk or a network connection.

The *System.IO* namespace

The *System.IO* namespace contains types (i.e. classes) that allow synchronous and asynchronous reading and writing on data streams and files.

Examples of classes within this namespace are listed below with a brief description.

- **Directory**: This class exposes behaviour to create, edit, and delete folders, as well as maintain the drives on your system.
- **File**: Aids in the creation of FileStream objects and provides behaviour for the creation, copying, deletion, moving and opening of files.
- **StreamReader**: Offers behaviour that enables the reading of a sequential stream of **characters** from a file.

- **StreamWriter**: Offers behaviour that enables the writing of a sequential stream of **characters** to a file.

> **NOTE**: The *StreamReader* and *StreamWriter* classes both use UTF-8 encoding by default. UTF-8 encoding handles Unicode characters correctly, which ensures that localized versions of the operating system are consistent with each other.
>
> It is also possible to detect a file's encoding automatically with *StreamReader*, or you can specify it as a parameter on a constructor.

- **BinaryReader**: Offers behaviour used for reading strings and elementary data types, i.e. it deals with binary files.
- **BinaryWriter**: Offers behaviour used for writing strings and elementary data types, i.e. it deals with binary files.

> **NOTE**: It is important to note the difference between both *BinaryReader/BinaryWriter* and *StreamReader/StreamWriter*.
>
> *BinaryReader* and *BinaryWriter* deal with data in binary (i.e. the internal format of the variables) whereas *StreamReader* and *StreamWriter* deals with characters.

> **NOTE**: The following programs are implemented using the *FileStream* class. A later program in this chapter will use another class that belong to the *System.IO* namespace. However, it is not feasible in a relatively short book to write about all of the classes. This chapter deals with the main principles of file access; you are left to discover other types of access with the assistance of VB .NET help.

Reading from a file

> **SPECIFICATION 27.1**
> *Write a program that will read a text file and display its content in a textbox.*

The program of Listing 27.1 reads from a file named test.txt and displays its contents in a textbox (i.e. it implements Specification 27.1). The contents of the file test.text and the runtime of the program are shown in Figures 27.12 and 27.13.

> **VERY IMPORTANT**: The event handling procedure shown in Listing 27.1 creates an instance of the *FileStream* class. This class belongs to the namespace *System.IO* and in order to be able to use any of the classes in this namespace requires the use of the keyword *Imports* followed by the namespace as shown in Figure 27.11.

Figure 27.11 How to use namespaces.

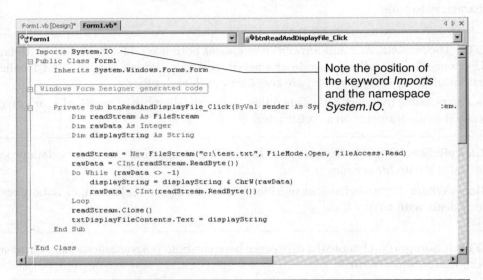

Note the position of the keyword *Imports* and the namespace *System.IO*.

Instead of using *Imports* you could use the namespace within the code as shown below. However, what would be the point; it just involves more typing. The screenshot below emphasizes this point.

Note nothing is actually being imported. The keyword *Imports* followed by the namespace is actually nothing more than an alias. Normally for large applications to be able to use classes requires that they be registered with the solution (use the help to read about this). *System.IO* does not require registering, however, as it is 'automatically' available to all solutions.

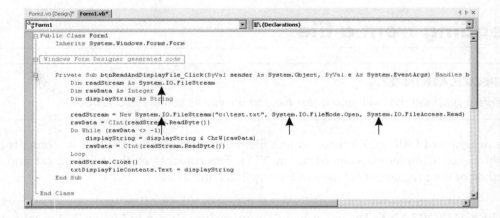

When the keyword *Imports* is not used then the namespace has to be used in numerous places within the code. The arrows on the above screenshot show examples of where the namespace has to be used.

Listing 27.1 Reading from a file.

```
Private Sub btnReadAndDisplayFile_Click(ByVal sender As System.Object, ByVal e As _
System.EventArgs) Handles btnReadAndDisplayFile.Click
    Dim readStream As FileStream
    Dim rawData As Integer
    Dim displayString As String

    readStream = New FileStream("c:\test.txt", FileMode.Open, FileAccess.Read)
    rawData = CInt(readStream.ReadByte())
    Do While (rawData <> -1)
        displayString = displayString & ChrW(rawData)
        rawData = CInt(readStream.ReadByte())
    Loop
    readStream.Close()
    txtDisplayFileContents.Text = displayString
End Sub
```

Figure 27.12 File contents shown in Notepad. Notepad is a Windows accessory suitable for creating text files.

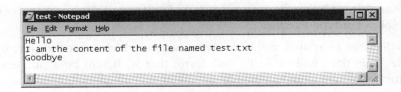

Figure 27.13 The program runtime .

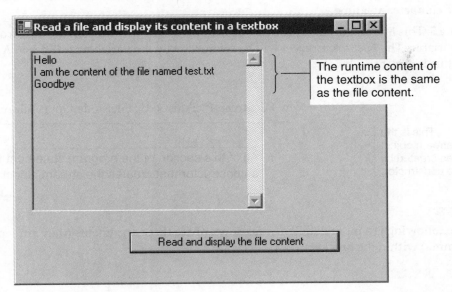

The runtime content of the textbox is the same as the file content.

619

Listing 27.1 is repeated below in Figure 27.14 with line numbers to aid its description.

Figure 27.14 With line numbers.

```
1       Private Sub btnReadAndDisplayFile_Click(ByVal sender As System.Object, _
        ByVal e As System.EventArgs) Handles btnReadAndDisplayFile.Click
2           Dim readStream As FileStream
3           Dim rawData As Integer
4           Dim displayString As String

5           readStream = New FileStream("c:\test.txt", FileMode.Open, FileAccess.Read)
6           rawData = CInt(readStream.ReadByte())
7           Do While (rawData <> -1)
8               displayString = displayString & ChrW(rawData)
9               rawData = CInt(readStream.ReadByte())
10          Loop
11          readStream.Close()
12          txtDisplayFileContents.Text = displayString
13      End Sub
```

Line 1: This line is the signature of the event handling procedure.

Line 2: The variable *readStream* is declared as type *FileStream*. This means that *readStream* can reference an object of type *Filestream*.

Line 3: This declares a variable *rawData* of type Integer, which is used to store the data read from the file. This data will be in its raw form, that is, it will be a numeric value that represents the characters stored in the file.

Line 4: Here a string variable named *displayString* is declared. This string is used to store all of the data read from the file. The data is read one character at a time and the string is built up one character at a time.

Line 5: This line creates the *FileStream* object that will be used to pass the data from the file to a variable. The *FileStream* object will be referenced by the variable *readStream*. A breakdown of this line is given below:

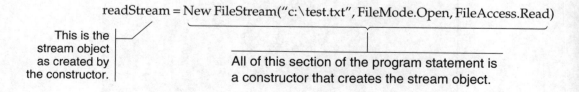

The following is a more detailed breakdown of the **three** arguments (they are separated by a comma) within the brackets:

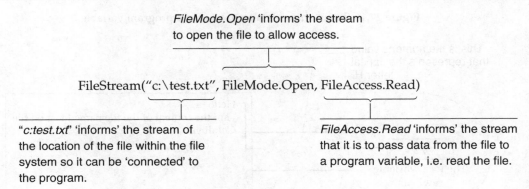

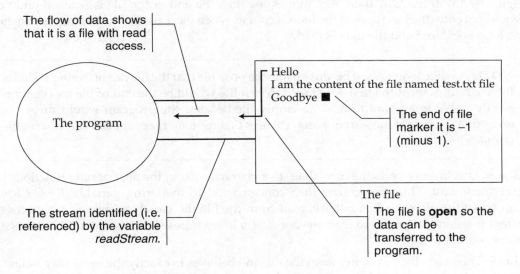

Consequently, after the execution of this program statement the relationship between the program and the file is as shown in Figure 27.15.

Figure 27.15 The relationship between the test.txt file and the program.

Line 6: This is a message to the instance of the *FileStream* class that invokes the *ReadByte* method. The method returns to the local variable *rawData* the numeric value that represents the first character in the file (note *CInt* has been used to explicitly convert a byte to an integer). This character is the letter H and reference to Table 27.1 shows that this has the value 72. This process is illustrated in Figure 27.16.

Figure 27.16 Transferring data from a file to a program variable.

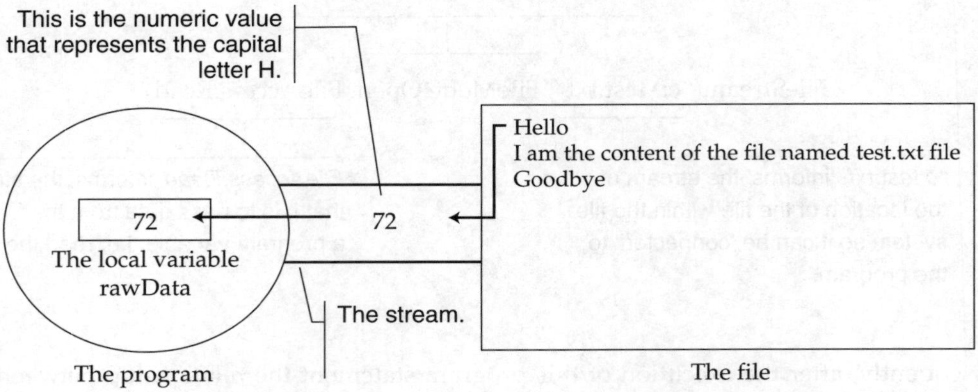

Line 7: The test of the *While* Loop compares the value stored in the variable *rawData* to see if it not equal to minus one (-1). Minus one is used as the end of a file marker (refer to Figure 27.15). If the 'raw data' was minus one then the end of the file is reached and you would not enter the loop to read the file. Of course, when the 'raw data' is not minus one then the loop is entered and the data is read.

> **NOTE**: A while loop is used because it may be possible that the file has no content. Under these circumstances the first value read from a file would be the end of file marker. It is not desirable to attempt to read an empty file because the program would throw an exception. Testing at the start of a loop ensures that the loop is never executed when a file is empty.

Line 8: This line converts the 'raw data' to a character using the appropriate function (i.e. *ChrW(rawData)*). This character is then concatenated to the string variable *displayString*. Consequently, after the first letter is read from the file the variable *displayString* stores *H*. After the second letter is read from the file *displayString* stores *He* and so on until it stores the entire content of the file.

Line 9: This reads the next letter from the file and behaves in exactly the same way as line 6. Of course it is responsible for reading all of the letters of the file except for the first letter (this was achieved by line 6).

> **NOTE**: Lines 7, 8 and 9 will be executed a number of times, dependent upon the content of the file.

Line 10: This marks the end of the loop.

Line 11: Whenever a stream is opened to allow access to a file it takes up system resources (i.e. memory space). It is important to release these resources to allow them to be used by other programs. So when the file has been read and its contents allocated to the program, the stream connecting the file to the program is closed; this releases the resources.

Close() is a method of the *FileStream* class that closes the *FileStream* instance and releases the resources.

Line 12: The string *displayString* has a copy of its content transferred to the *Text* property of the TextBox. Consequently, the file content is displayed in the textbox as shown by Figure 27.13.

Description trace for Listing 27.1 when reading test.txt

Statement	Description
readStream = New FileStream("c:\test.txt", FileMode.Open, FileAccess.Read)	Creates the stream (i.e. object of type *FileStream*) to allow the for the reading of the file test.txt.
rawData = CInt(readStream.ReadByte())	This will transfer *72* (the numeric representation of H) to the local variable *rawData*.
Do While (rawData <> -1)	This is true so the loop is entered.
displayString = displayString & ChrW(rawData)	*H* is concatenated to the string *displayString*.
rawData = readStream.ReadByte()	This will transfer *101* (the numeric representation of e) to the variable *rawData*.
Do While (rawData <> -1)	Again this is true so the loop is entered.
displayString = displayString & ChrW(rawData)	*e* is concatenated to the string – it now stores *He*.
rawData = CInt(readStream.ReadByte())	This will transfer *108* (the numeric representation of l) to the variable *rawData*.
Do While (rawData <> -1)	Again this is true so the loop is entered.
displayString = displayString & ChrW(rawData)	*l* is concatenated to the string – it now stores *Hel*.
rawData = CInt(readStream.ReadByte())	This will transfer *108* (the numeric representation of l) to the variable *rawData*.
Do While (rawData <> -1)	Again this is true so the loop is entered.
displayString = displayString & ChrW(rawData)	*l* is concatenated to the string – it now stores *Hell*.
rawData = CInt(readStream.ReadByte())	This will transfer *111* (the numeric representation of o) to the variable *rawData*.
Do While (rawData <> -1)	Again this is true so the loop is entered.
displayString = displayString & ChrW(rawData))	*o* is concatenated to the string – it now stores *Hello*.

Description trace for Listing 27.1 (cont.)

rawData = CInt(readStream.ReadByte())	This will transfer 13 (the numeric representation of carriage return) to the variable *rawData*.
Do While (rawData <> -1)	Again this is true so the loop is entered.
displayString = displayString & ChrW(rawData)	Carriage return is concatenated to the string – it now stores *Hello* plus *carriage return*.
rawData = CInt(readStream.ReadByte())	This will transfer 10 (the numeric representation of line feed) to the variable *rawData*.
Do While (rawData <> -1)	Again this is true so the loop is entered.
displayString = displayString & ChrW(rawData)	Line-feed carriage return is concatenated to the string – it now stores *Hello* plus carriage return plus *line-feed*.
rawData = CInt(readStream.ReadByte())	This will transfer 73 (the numeric representation I) to the variable *rawData*.
This will continue until the last character from the file is read which will be the *e* of *Goodbye*.	
Do While (rawData <> -1)	Again this is true so the loop is entered.
displayString = displayString & ChrW(rawData)	The last character is concatenated to the string – it now stores the entire content of the file.
rawData = CInt(readStream.ReadByte())	This will transfer - 1 (minus one the end-of-file-marker) to the variable *rawData*.
Do While (rawData <> -1)	This time this conditional test is **false** (because −1 does equal −1) so the loop is NOT entered and the next statement to execute is the one following the loop.
readStream.Close()	The stream is closed, releasing resources.
txtDisplayFileContents.Text = displayString	The content of the string which now stores the content of the file (except for the end of file marker) is copied to the *Text* property of the textbox.

PRACTICAL ACTIVITY 27.1

Run the program of Listing 27.1. Remember the program is reading a file called test.txt that resides on the root of the C: drive. Consequently, you must also create this file using notepad. The TextBox of the GUI shown in Figure 27.13 has a particular 'look' because various properties were set. To achieve this 'look' set the properties as shown by Table 27.2; the table also shows some default properties for the Button and the Form.

Table 27.2 The property setting for GUI shown in Figure 27.12.

Control	Property	Setting
Form	Text	Read a file and display its content in a textbox
Button	Name	btnReadAndDisplayFile
	Text	Read and display the file content
TextBox	Name	txtDisplayFileContents
	ReadOnly	True
	Scrollbars	Vertical
	MultiLine	True

QUESTION 27.2 (DEVELOPMENT)

Use the VB .NET help facility to read about the following properties of the textbox: ReadOnly, Scrollbars and Multiline.

SPECIFICATION 27.2

Write a program that will find and display the size of a file and use this size to read the entire file content and again display the content in a textbox. Also display the absolute path of the file in a label.

To implement Specification 27.2 the same file will be used (test.txt). This file contains 59 characters; this includes all of the obvious characters such as *H* in *Hello*, etc., but added to this there are also all of the space characters plus the carriage-return and line-feed characters. There are 59 characters, providing you end your typing after the 'e' of *Goodbye*!

NOTE: Whenever you are presented with a specification it is usual to use the VB .NET help to assist in the decision as to what class and its members should be used to implement the specification. There are a number of classes that could be used to implement Specification 27.2. However, for the time being we will stick with the *FileStream* class. Figure 27.17 shows a help screen from the VB .NET help that shows some members that will be used to implement Specification 27.2.

Figure 27.17 Help on the *FileStream* class.

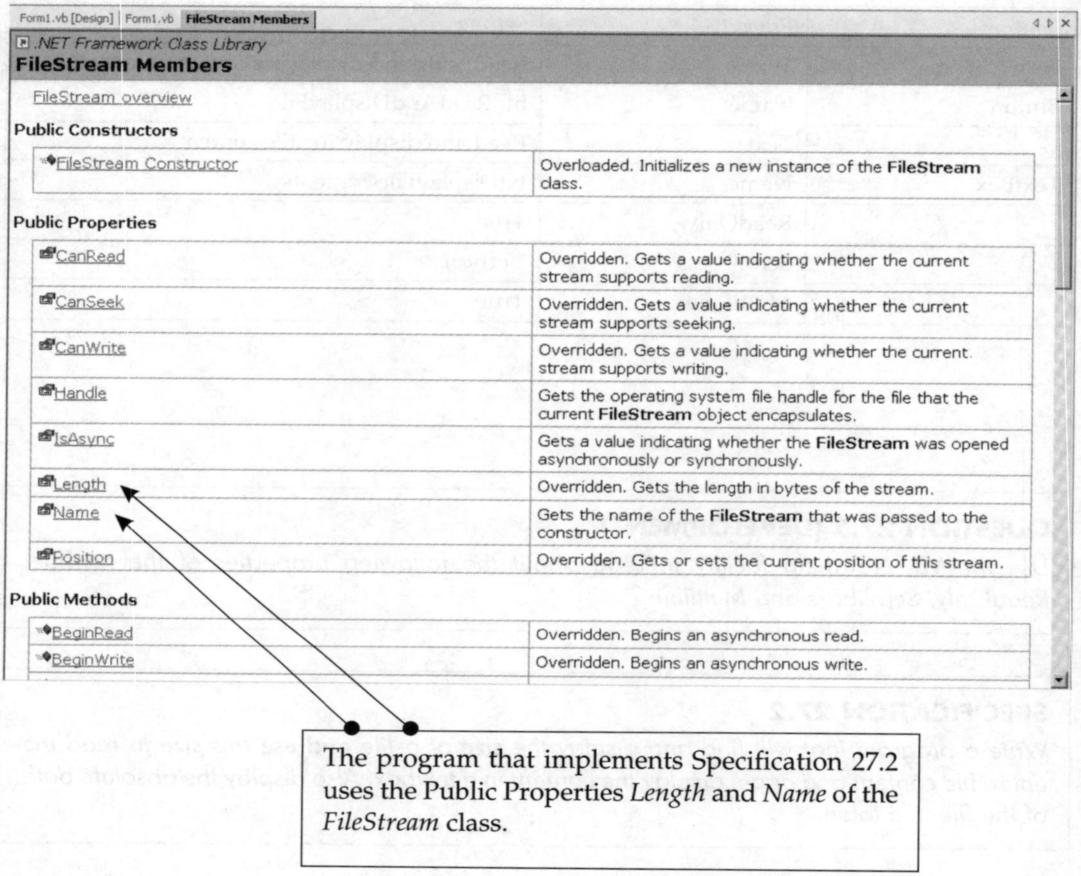

Form1.vb [Design] | Form1.vb | **FileStream Members**

.NET Framework Class Library
FileStream Members

FileStream overview

Public Constructors

FileStream Constructor	Overloaded. Initializes a new instance of the **FileStream** class.

Public Properties

CanRead	Overridden. Gets a value indicating whether the current stream supports reading.
CanSeek	Overridden. Gets a value indicating whether the current stream supports seeking.
CanWrite	Overridden. Gets a value indicating whether the current. stream supports writing.
Handle	Gets the operating system file handle for the file that the current **FileStream** object encapsulates.
IsAsync	Gets a value indicating whether the **FileStream** was opened asynchronously or synchronously.
Length	Overridden. Gets the length in bytes of the stream.
Name	Gets the name of the **FileStream** that was passed to the constructor.
Position	Overridden. Gets or sets the current position of this stream.

Public Methods

BeginRead	Overridden. Begins an asynchronous read.
BeginWrite	Overridden. Begins an asynchronous write.

The program that implements Specification 27.2 uses the Public Properties *Length* and *Name* of the *FileStream* class.

The listing that implements Specification 27.2 is shown in Figure 27.19 with line number for ease of reference. The runtime of the program is shown in Figure 27.18, which is the GUI of Figure 27.13 amended by the addition of another button and two labels.

Figure 27.18 The runtime.

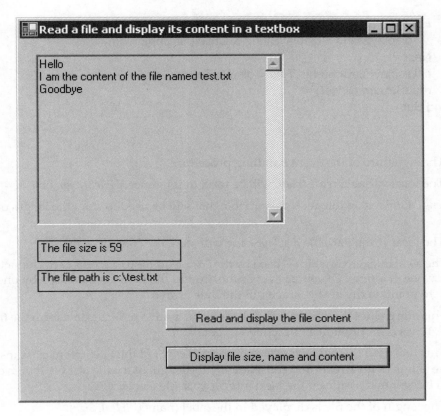

Figure 27.19 Implementation of Specification 27.2.

```
1.   Private Sub btnDisplayFileSizeNameAndContent_Click(ByVal sender As _
     System.Object, ByVal e As System.EventArgs) Handles _
     btnDisplayFileSizeNameAndContent.Click
2.      Dim readStream As FileStream
3.      Dim lengthOfFile As Integer
4.      Dim displayString As String
5.      Dim i As Integer

6.      readStream = New FileStream("c:\test.txt", FileMode.Open, FileAccess.Read)
7.      lengthOfFile = CInt(readStream.Length)
8.      lblFileSize.Text = "The file size is " & CStr(lengthOfFile)
9.      lblAbsolutePath.Text = "The file path is " & readStream.Name
10.     Dim fileContents(lengthOfFile) As Byte
11.     readStream.Read(fileContents, 0, lengthOfFile)
```

Figure 27.19 (cont.)

```
12.        For i = 0 To (lengthOfFile - 1)
13.            displayString = displayString & ChrW(fileContents(i))
14.        Next
15.        txtDisplayFileContents.Text = displayString
16.        readStream.Close()
17.    End Sub
```

Line 1: The signature of the event handling procedure.

Line 2: The local variable *readStream* will be used to reference a *FileStream* object.

Line 3: *lengthOfFile* is an integer local variable that will be used to store the length of the file test.txt.

Line 4: The local string variable *displayString* will store the content of the file.

Line 5: The local integer variable *i* is used by the *For .. Next* loop to access each character of the Byte array one at a time. Of course every time around the loop *i* is increased by one, which causes it 'to point' to the next character in the Byte array.

Line 6: This line creates the stream object that will be used to pass the data from the file to the program. It has been previously described in detail.

Line 7: This line used the public instance property *Length* of the FileStream class instance to obtain the length of the stream and consequently the length of the file test.txt. It then converts this to an integer and assigns it the local integer variable *lengthOfFile*.

Line 8: The length of the file is displayed in the label (named *lblFileSize*).

Line 9: This accesses the *Name* property of the stream object with the message *readStream.Name* and concatenates it with the literal string *The file path is* and then assigns this 'joined' string to the *Text* property of the label *lblAbsolutePath*.

Line 10: This line declares an array of bytes equal to the size of the file.

NOTE: It is not regarded as good programming practice to declare a variable in the middle of a program in this way. However, as this program is used for illustrative purposes it can be excused. As an aside, VB .NET allows for the declaration of a variable within a construct such as a loop and this variable will only have a scope for that loop, i.e. this variable can only be accessed by the program statements within the loop and only exists when the loop is executing, i.e. its lifetime is for the duration of the loop.

Line 11: This line uses the public instance method *Read* of the *FileStream* class instance to transfer the entire content of the stream to a 'byte buffer'. This mechanism is illustrated in Figure 27.20. The entire content of the file is transferred via the stream to the *Byte* array *fileContents*, starting at position zero in the stream (i.e. at the *H* of *Hello*). The *Read* method takes as its arguments the byte array *fileContents*, the starting point *0* and the length of the file (*lengthOfFile*) – this enables it to read all the file.

Figure 27.20 Illustration of the *Read* method of the *FileStream* class.

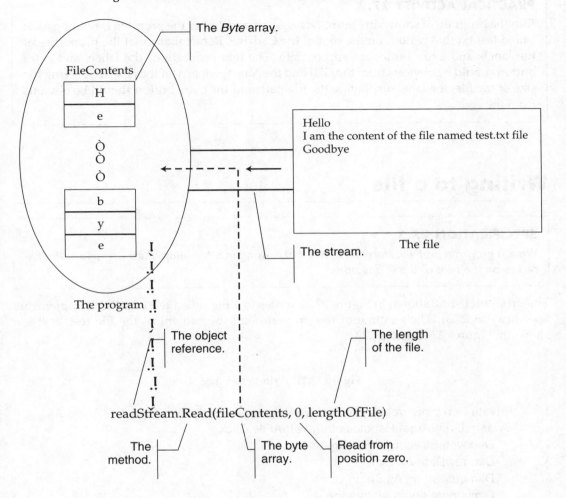

The *Byte* array.

FileContents

| H |
| e |
| Ò |
| Ò |
| Ò |
| b |
| y |
| e |

Hello
I am the content of the file named test.txt file
Goodbye

The file

The stream.

The program

The object
reference.

The length
of the file.

readStream.Read(fileContents, 0, lengthOfFile)

The
method.

The byte
array.

Read from
position zero.

Lines 12, 13 and 14: These lines form a *For .. Next* loop with line 13 being the program statement within the loop. The loop is executed a number of times equal to the size of the file. The *lengthOfFile - 1* is the maximum value of *i* because the stream starts at zero. Each element of the byte array has its content converted to a character and concatenated to the string *displayString*. When the loop has completed all its iterations the string variable *displayString* stores the entire content of the *Byte* array. Consequently, it stores the content of the file.

Line 15: Copies the content of the string *displayString* to the *Text* property of the TextBox.

Line 16: This uses the public instance method *Close()* to release system resources.

QUESTION 27.3 (REVISION)

Produce a description trace table for the listing shown in Figure 27.19.

PRACTICAL ACTIVITY 27.2

Run the program of shown in Figure 27.19. Again remember the program is reading a file called test.txt that resides on the root of the C: drive. Remember to set the properties of the labels and extra button as appropriate. The text property of the labels and extra button should be obvious from the GUI and the *Name* property of the label displaying the size of the file, the label displaying the file path and the extra button should be obvious from the code.

Writing to a file

SPECIFICATION 27.3

Write a program that will store the content of a string in a file named test1.txt. Have the file reside on the root of the C directory.

The program listing shown in Figure 27.21 writes to a file called test1.txt (i.e. it implements Specification 27.3). The runtime of the program and the content of the file test1.text are shown in Figures 27.22 and 27.23.

Figure 27.21 Writing to a file.

```
1.     Private Sub btnSaveInAFile_Click(ByVal sender As System.Object, ByVal e As _
       System.EventArgs) Handles btnSaveInAFile.Click
2.         Dim writeStream As FileStream
3.         Dim rawData As Byte
4.         Dim dataString As String
5.         Dim stringLength As Integer
6.         Dim i As Integer

7.         writeStream = New FileStream("c:\test1.txt", FileMode.Create, FileAccess.Write)
8.         dataString = txtDataInput.Text
9.         stringLength = dataString.Length
10.        For i = 0 To (stringLength - 1)
11.            rawData = CByte(Asc(dataString.Chars(i)))
12.            writeStream.WriteByte(rawData)
13.        Next
14.        writeStream.Close()
15.    End Sub
```

Figure 27.22 The runtime for writing to a file.

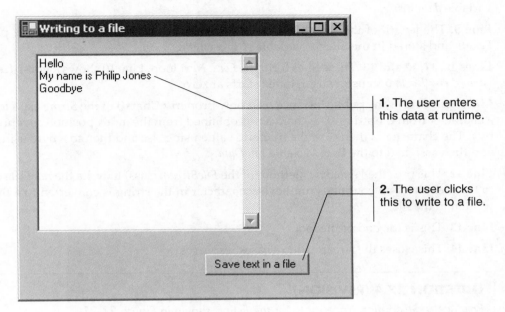

1. The user enters this data at runtime.

2. The user clicks this to write to a file.

Figure 27.23 The file content as shown by Notepad.

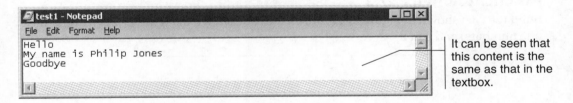

It can be seen that this content is the same as that in the textbox.

Line 1: The signature of the event handling procedure.

Line 2: Declares a variable *writeStream* that will reference an object of the class *FileStream*.

Line 3: Declares a *Byte* variable *rawData* that will be used to send each character of the string to the file *test1.txt*.

Line 4: *dataString* is a string variable whose content will be saved in the file *test1.txt*.

Line 5: An integer variable *stringLength* that is used to hold the size of the string *dataString*.

Line 6: Used as the index for the *For .. Next* loop, that allows access to each character of the string (*dataString*) in turn.

Line 7: This is similar to line 5 shown in Figure 27.14. However, here the object reference is *writeStream* and the constructor *FileStream* has different arguments. The first argument is the path of the file to be written to (i.e *"c:\test1.txt"*). The second argument (*FileMode.Create*) creates the file test1.txt at the root of the C: drive. The third argument (*FileAccess.Write*) results in a Stream that sends data from the program to the file.

Line 8: This reads what the user enters in the TextBox of the GUI and assigns it to the string variable *dataString*.

Line 9: The length of the string (*dataString*) is obtained from the public instance property *Length* and stored in the integer variable *stringLength*.

Lines 10, 11, 12 and 13: These lines form the *For .. Next* loop. Line 10 shows *i* 'going from' 0 to (*stringLength - 1*) because a string index starts at zero.

Line 11: This uses the public instance read only property **Chars()** of the *String* class to obtain a character from the string. The character is obtained from the index position as represented by *i*. The character is then cast to a numeric value using *Asc* and then to a byte using *CByte* and then assigned to the Byte variable *rawData*.

Line 12: This uses the *WriteByte* method (of the *FileStream* class) to write the *rawData* content to the file. The loop continues until every character in the string is converted to a Byte and written to the file.

Line 13: This is the end of the loop.

Line 14: This closes the stream and releases resources.

QUESTION 27.4 (REVISION)

Produce a description trace table for the listing shown in Figure 27.21.

PRACTICAL ACTIVITY 27.3

Build the GUI shown in Figure 27.22, attach the code shown in Figure 27.21 (without the line numbers) and run it.

Appending to a file

SPECIFICATION 27.4

Write a program that will append the content of a string to a file named test1.txt that already has content. Append means add data to the file content (usually at the end of the file).

The program shown in Figure 27.24 appends to a file called test1.txt (i.e. it implements Specification 27.4). A typical runtime of the program is shown in Figure 27.25; it can be seen that the program is attached to a button that has been added to the GUI shown in Figure 27.22. The contents of the file test1.text before and after the append program is run, is also shown in Figure 27.25.

Figure 27.24 Appending to a file.

```
1.      Private Sub btnSaveInAFile_Click(ByVal sender As System.Object, ByVal e As _
        System.EventArgs) Handles btnSaveInAFile.Click
2.          Dim writeStream As FileStream
3.          Dim rawData As Byte
4.          Dim dataString As String
5.          Dim stringLength As Integer
6.          Dim i As Integer

7.          writeStream = New FileStream("c:\test1.txt", FileMode.Append, FileAccess.Write)
8.          dataString = txtDataInput.Text
9.          stringLength = dataString.Length
10.         For i = 0 To (stringLength - 1)
11.             rawData = CByte(Asc(dataString.Chars(i)))
12.             writeStream.WriteByte(rawData)
13.         Next
14.         writeStream.Close()
15.     End Sub
```

Figure 27.25 A typical runtime.

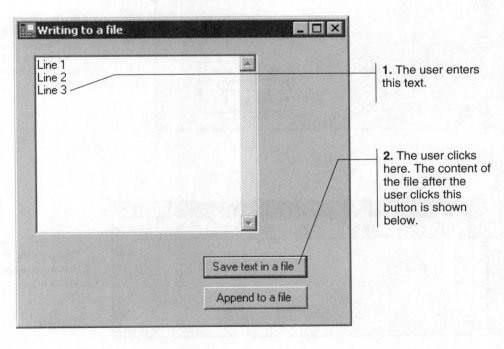

Figure 27.25 (cont.)

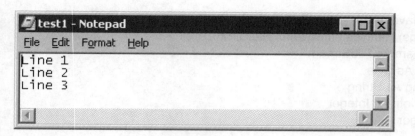

The content of the textbox is saved in the file.

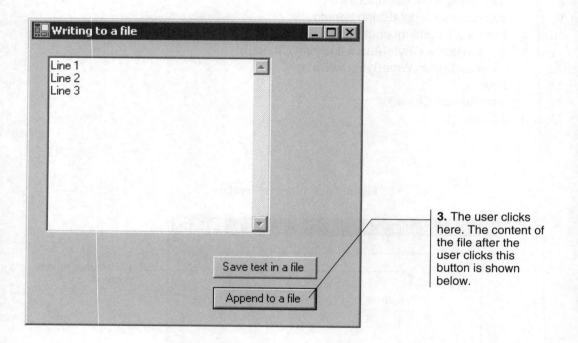

3. The user clicks here. The content of the file after the user clicks this button is shown below.

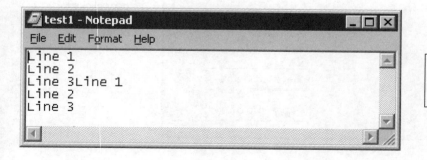

The content of the textbox is appended to the file.

An inspection of the listings of Figures 27.21 and 27.24 shows that they are identical apart from the program statements shown on lines seven. Both these lines are repeated below for your convenience to allow for direct comparison. The first statement is from Figure 27.21 and the second from Figures 27.24. The differences between the statements are shown in bold.

writeStream = New FileStream("c:\test1.txt", **FileMode.Create**, FileAccess.Write)

writeStream = New FileStream("c:\test1.txt", **FileMode.Append**, FileAccess.Write)

Both statements are identical apart from the second argument in the constructor. The first statement has *FileMode.Create* as its second argument, whereas, the second statement has *FileMode.Append*, as its second argument. Of course, the listing shown in Figure 27.5 is the code required to append to a file that already exists, consequently, it is obvious that the file mode should be *Append* as defined by the second argument *FileMode.Append*.

PRACTICAL ACTIVITY 27.4

Amend the GUI developed during Practical Activity 27.3 and attach the code shown in Figure 27.24 and run the application. Of course, remember that you will be appending data to a file so make sure the file actually stores data before you append so you can observe the effect of appending.

Seeking from a stream

Consider a file that stores all the capital letters of the alphabet stored on one line. This file is illustrated in Figure 27.26.

Figure 27.26 A file storing the alphabet.

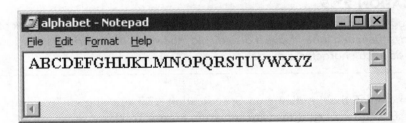

When a Stream is 'connected' to this file each character in the file is effectively at an indexed position within the stream. The relationship of the Stream and the index position of each character are shown in Figure 27.27.

When the stream is created using an appropriate constructor there is effectively a pointer to the first index position within the stream. This is illustrated by Figure 27.28.

Every time a byte (character) is read from the stream the pointer automatically points to the next position. Every stream has a *Position* property, which stores the index number of the 'pointer'. This property can be read to see where the pointer is currently pointing. This property can also be set to move the position of the 'pointer'.

Figure 27.27 The relationship of a file content to its 'index number'.

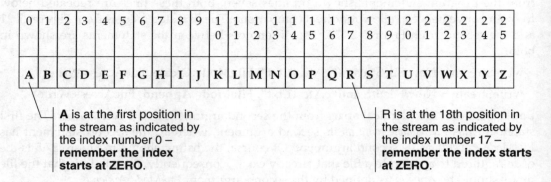

0	1	2	3	4	5	6	7	8	9	10	11	12	13	14	15	16	17	18	19	20	21	22	23	24	25
A	B	C	D	E	F	G	H	I	J	K	L	M	N	O	P	Q	R	S	T	U	V	W	X	Y	Z

A is at the first position in the stream as indicated by the index number 0 – **remember the index starts at ZERO**.

R is at the 18th position in the stream as indicated by the index number 17 – **remember the index starts at ZERO**.

Figure 27.28 The stream and its 'pointer' at its creation using an appropriate constructor.

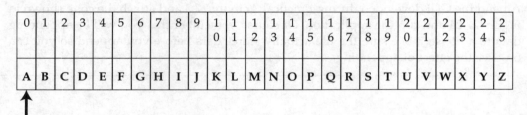

0	1	2	3	4	5	6	7	8	9	10	11	12	13	14	15	16	17	18	19	20	21	22	23	24	25
A	B	C	D	E	F	G	H	I	J	K	L	M	N	O	P	Q	R	S	T	U	V	W	X	Y	Z

'Points'í to the first position within the stream. **At the time of its creation the *Position* property of the stream is set at zero.**

SPECIFICATION 27.5

Write a program that reads the alphabet file one character at a time on the click of a button and displays them in a label. Have it also display the value of the streams Position property in a label as each character is read.

The code and GUI that implements Specification 27.5 are shown in Figure 27.29 and Listing 27.2. Examples of runtimes are shown in Figure 27.30.

NOTE: The GUI of Figure 27.29 and the operation of its code have no practical use for manipulating files. It is used here to illustrate the how streams and the *Position* property work when streams are read.

Figure 27.29 Reading a stream.

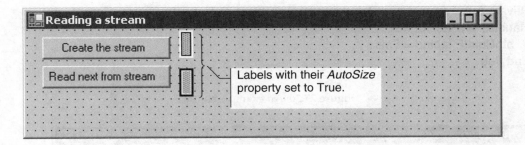

Listing 27.2 The code attached to the GUI of Figure 27.25.

```
Private readStream As FileStream
Private Sub btnNext_Click(ByVal sender As System.Object, ByVal e As _
System.EventArgs) Handles btnNext.Click
    Dim rawData As Integer
    Dim character As Char
    Dim pointerValue As Integer

    rawData = readStream.ReadByte()
    If rawData <> -1 Then
        character = Chr(rawData)
        pointerValue = readStream.Position
        lblDisplayCharacter.Text = "The character just read is " & character
        lblDisplayPosition.Text = "The pointer is now pointing to position " & _
        CStr(pointerValue)
    Else
        lblDisplayCharacter.Text = "Thats it the end of the file"
        readStream.Close()
        lblDisplayPosition.Text = "No longer a valid pointer the stream is closed"
        btnNext.Enabled = False
        btnCreateStream.Enabled = True
    End If
End Sub

Private Sub btnCreateStream_Click(ByVal sender As System.Object, ByVal e As _
System.EventArgs) Handles btnCreateStream.Click
    lblDisplayCharacter.Text = ""
    readStream = New FileStream("c:\alphabet.txt", FileMode.Open, FileAccess.Read)
    lblDisplayPosition.Text = _
    "The position of the 'pointer' at the creation of the stream is " & readStream.Position
    btnNext.Enabled = True
    btnCreateStream.Enabled = False
End Sub
```

Listing 27.2 (cont.)

```
Private Sub Form1_Load(ByVal sender As Object, ByVal e As System.EventArgs) _
Handles MyBase.Load
    btnNext.Enabled = False
End Sub
```

Figure 27.30 An example runtime.

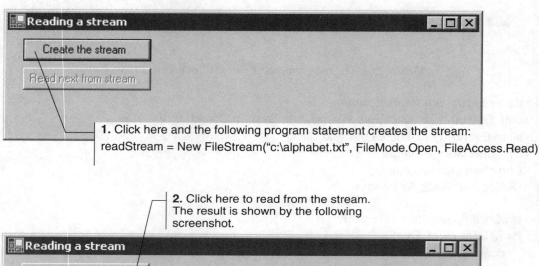

1. Click here and the following program statement creates the stream:
readStream = New FileStream("c:\alphabet.txt", FileMode.Open, FileAccess.Read)

2. Click here to read from the stream.
The result is shown by the following
screenshot.

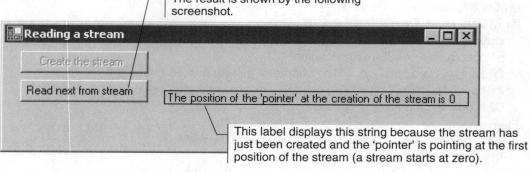

This label displays this string because the stream has
just been created and the 'pointer' is pointing at the first
position of the stream (a stream starts at zero).

The first character at
position zero is read and
then displayed in this label.

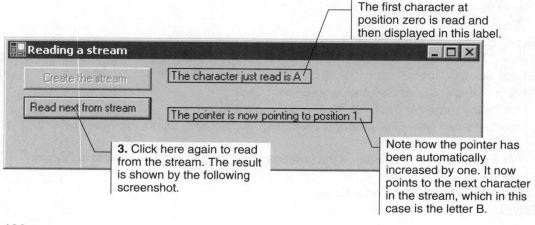

3. Click here again to read
from the stream. The result
is shown by the following
screenshot.

Note how the pointer has
been automatically
increased by one. It now
points to the next character
in the stream, which in this
case is the letter B.

Figure 27.30 (cont.)

The second character at position one is read and then displayed in this label.

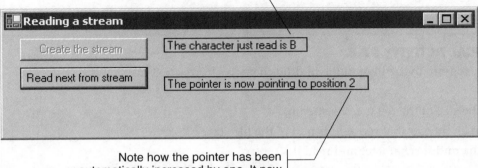

Note how the pointer has been automatically increased by one. It now points to the next character in the stream, which in this case is the letter C.

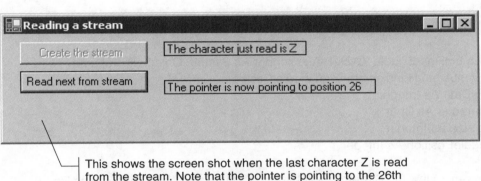

This shows the screen shot when the last character Z is read from the stream. Note that the pointer is pointing to the 26th position. At the 26th position is the end of file marker (–1). The code has been arranged so that it cannot read beyond this marker as shown by the next screenshot.

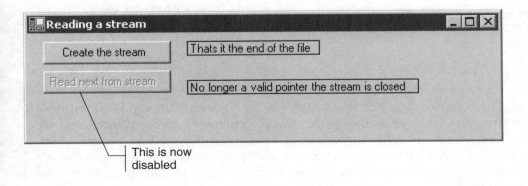

This is now disabled

PRACTICAL ACTIVITY 27.5

Enter and run the program represented by Figure 27.29 and Listing 27.2. Keep clicking the button until you see the last screen shot of Figure 27.30. After each click consider what is happening to the 'pointer'.

PRACTICAL ACTIVITY 27.6

Write a program that will read the middle character from a text file.

Hint:

- Find the size of the file (i.e. the stream).
- Obtain an integer that represents half of the file size.
- Seek the middle character and read it.

The answer is shown in Listing 27.3 – try to do it yourself first without looking at the code.

Listing 27.3 Finding the middle character.

```
Private Sub btnReadMiddle_Click(ByVal sender As System.Object, ByVal e As
System.EventArgs) Handles btnReadMiddle.Click
    Dim rawData As Integer
    Dim character As Char
    Dim fileSize As Integer
    Dim middlePosition As Integer

    readStream = New FileStream("c:\alphabet.txt", FileMode.Open, FileAccess.Read)
    fileSize = readStream.Length
    middlePosition = fileSize \ 2
    readStream.Position = middlePosition
    rawData = readStream.ReadByte()
    character = Chr(rawData)
    lblDisplayCharacter.Text = "The character in the middle of the file is " & character
End Sub
```

The 'pointer' to the stream is set to the middle position and the content is read from this position.

NOTE: The examples of file access in this chapter have used a relatively 'low-level view' of file structures and 'file pointers'. This was to concentrate on the principles of file access. There are many better and efficient classes within VB .NET for accessing files. Regardless of which file access class you use, your program will create streams, which are objects and you will then use the members of these objects to manipulate the streams and hence the files.

The OpenFile dialog box

The operation of the OpenFile dialog box will be shown by the implementation of Specification 27.6.

SPECIFICATION 27.6

Use an OpenFile dialog box to display the contents of a file in a TextBox.

Figure 27.31 shows the GUI for implementing Specification 27.6 (set the *MultiLine* property of the TextBox to *True*). The code attached to the GUI is shown in Listing 27.4. An example runtime is shown in Figure 27.33; for the program to work it must read an appropriate file. Create this file using notepad and save it as *MyFile.txt*. Figure 27.32 shows the content of the file in Notepad.

Figure 27.31 The GUI for implementing Specification 27.6.

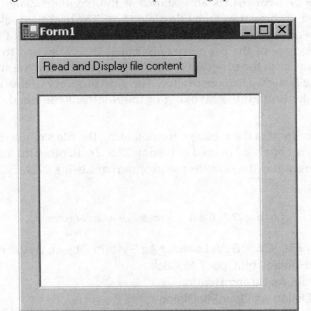

NOTE: Listing 27.4 has been designed to show you a simple use of an OpenFile dialog box. It is **not** a robust program. More code needs to be added in order to ensure that it is a robust program – a *Try Catch* construct to begin with. However, this would distract from how to use the OpenFile dialog box – feel free to improve the design; Chapter 22 deals with error handling.

Listing 27.4 The code attached to the button.

```
Private Sub btnOpenFile_Click(ByVal sender As System.Object, ByVal e As _
System.EventArgs) Handles btnOpenFile.Click
    Dim myReadStream As StreamReader
    Dim myOpenFileDialog As OpenFileDialog
    Dim myFileName As String

    myOpenFileDialog = New OpenFileDialog()
    myOpenFileDialog.ShowDialog()
    myFileName = myOpenFileDialog.FileName
    myReadStream = New StreamReader(myFileName)
    txtDisplayFileContent.Text = myReadStream.ReadToEnd()
    myReadStream.Close()
End Sub
```

The code of Listing 27.4 constructs an instance of the *OpenFileDialog* class, then uses the *ShowDialog()* method to show the Open File dialog box. The user then selects an appropriate file setting from the dialog and this then sets the *FileName* property of this instance of the *OpenFileDialog*. The value of the property *FileName* is then assigned to the string variable *myFileName*. A stream from the program to the file is created using the string *myFileName* as an argument to the *StreamReader* constructor. The *Text* property of the TextBox is assigned the content of the file through the invoking of the *ReadToEnd* method. The stream is then closed.

It is common practice to pass the message for obtaining the file's name to the constructor as an argument. This is highlighted in bold in Listing 27.5. To all other intents and purposes the operation of this program is the same as the program of Listing 27.4.

Listing 27.5 Passing a message as an argument.

```
Private Sub btnOpenFile_Click(ByVal sender As System.Object, ByVal e As
System.EventArgs) Handles btnOpenFile.Click
    Dim myReadStream As StreamReader
    Dim myOpenFileDialog As OpenFileDialog

    myOpenFileDialog = New OpenFileDialog()
    myOpenFileDialog.ShowDialog()
    myReadStream = New StreamReader(myOpenFileDialog.FileName)
    txtDisplayFileContent.Text = myReadStream.ReadToEnd()
    myReadStream.Close()
End Sub
```

Message passed as an argument to the constructor.

Figure 27.32 The content of *MyFile.txt*.

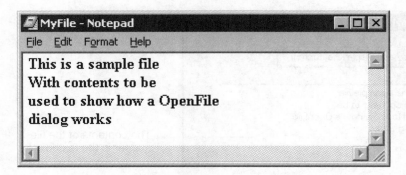

Figure 27.33 An example runtime.

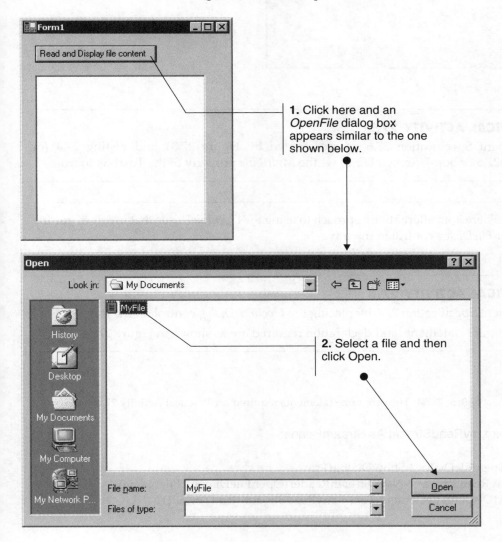

1. Click here and an *OpenFile* dialog box appears similar to the one shown below.

2. Select a file and then click Open.

Figure 27.33 (cont.)

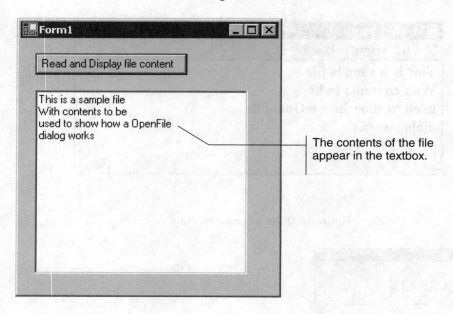

The contents of the file appear in the textbox.

PRACTICAL ACTIVITY 27.7

Implement Specification 27.6 as represented by Figure 27.31 and Listing 27.4 (or Listing 27.5 or both). Remember to set the *MultiLine* property of the TextBox to true.

NOTE: There is an alternative approach to using the *OpenFileDialog* that involves putting the *OpenFileDialog* control in the tray.

PRACTICAL ACTIVITY 27.8

Implement Specification 27.6 by placing the *OpenFileDialog* control on the tray.

The program statements and declaration required are as shown in Figure 27.34.

Figure 27.34 The program statements required for Practical Activity 27.8

```
Dim myReadStream As StreamReader

OpenFileDialog1.ShowDialog()
myReadStream = New StreamReader(OpenFileDialog1.FileName)
txtDisplayFileContent.Text = myReadStream.ReadToEnd()
```

PRACTICAL ACTIVITY 27.9 (DEVELOPMENT)

Use the *SaveFileDialog* and *StreamWriter* classes to develop a simple application that will store the contents of a TextBox in a file.

QUESTION 27.5 (DEVELOPMENT)

Use the VB .NET help to research the use of the PrintDialog component (class).

Appendix

This appendix deals with the fundamental knowledge required by a computer programmer. If you are familiar with computer hardware and the Windows operating system, and if you have written programs in another language then you might want to skip this appendix. However, if you have the knowledge and experience as just mentioned but have not programmed using objects before then you might want to read this appendix.

Object-oriented programming

When an object-oriented program is executing objects are created, used, and destroyed when finished with. During the execution of an object-oriented program, objects send messages to one another requesting services.

Consider a computer program that plays a simple game of snakes and ladders. Here the program allows a user to click a button to throw a die, the value of the die is then displayed on the Visual Display Unit (VDU) for the user to see and the counter is moved on the board that is also displayed on the VDU. Depending on the value of the die thrown the counter will move to a square, move up a ladder or down a snake. Of course the program will allow for two players and each player will have their own button to click. The winner of the game is first to have their counter arrive on the last square.

The program to implement this game will involve a number of objects, each of which have specialized roles. A programmer will have to decide upon these objects and build classes to represent their behaviour and states. From these classes objects are constructed.

> **NOTE**: The behaviours of an object are the services it can offer other objects (and itself).

Without attempting to write a program to implement a game of snakes and ladders, the interaction of suitable objects that might be used in the design of such a game is considered on the following pages. Suitable objects for such a game might be two players, the board and two die. These objects are shown in Figure A.1.

Figure A.1 Objects suitable for a game of snakes and ladders.

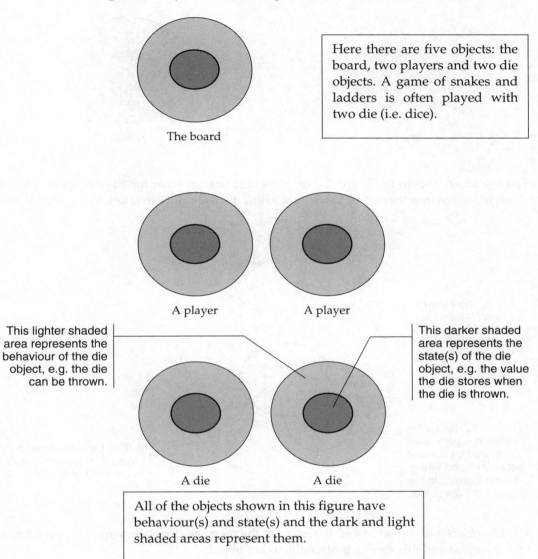

The board

Here there are five objects: the board, two players and two die objects. A game of snakes and ladders is often played with two die (i.e. dice).

A player   A player

This lighter shaded area represents the behaviour of the die object, e.g. the die can be thrown.

This darker shaded area represents the state(s) of the die object, e.g. the value the die stores when the die is thrown.

A die   A die

All of the objects shown in this figure have behaviour(s) and state(s) and the dark and light shaded areas represent them.

During the execution of the snakes and ladders program all of the objects shown in Figure A.1 are created and they message each other requesting services. For example a player object will ask the die to throw itself and generate a random number. The die object because it has this behaviour will generate a random number between 1 and 6 and store this random number in its state. Of course the board object will also want to know the value thrown and it will request this from the die object. The service requested by the board object will return the value of the die state (i.e. the generated random number) to the board object. Once the board object receives this value it moves the counter as appropriate.

All requests for services are achieved by messaging objects; one example is shown in Figure A.2.

Figure A.2 Messaging.

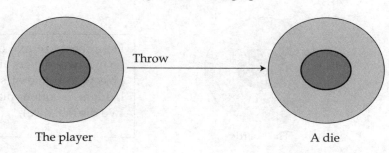

The player   A die

The Die object shown in Figure A.2 receives the message from the Player object. The Die object has behaviour that is able to respond to this message and this is detailed in Figure A.3.

Figure A.3 Responding to a message.

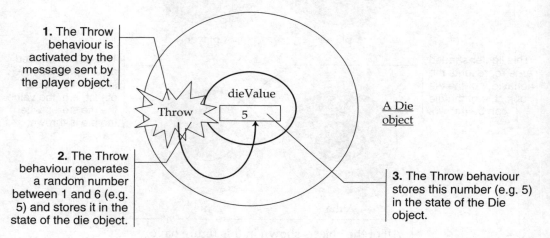

1. The Throw behaviour is activated by the message sent by the player object.

2. The Throw behaviour generates a random number between 1 and 6 (e.g. 5) and stores it in the state of the die object.

3. The Throw behaviour stores this number (e.g. 5) in the state of the Die object.

The Die object had the behaviour to deal with the message. This behaviour is often referred to as a service and this service is offered to other objects.

Of course the board object will require access to state of the Die object and this is detailed in Figure A.4.

Figure A.4 Responding to a message.

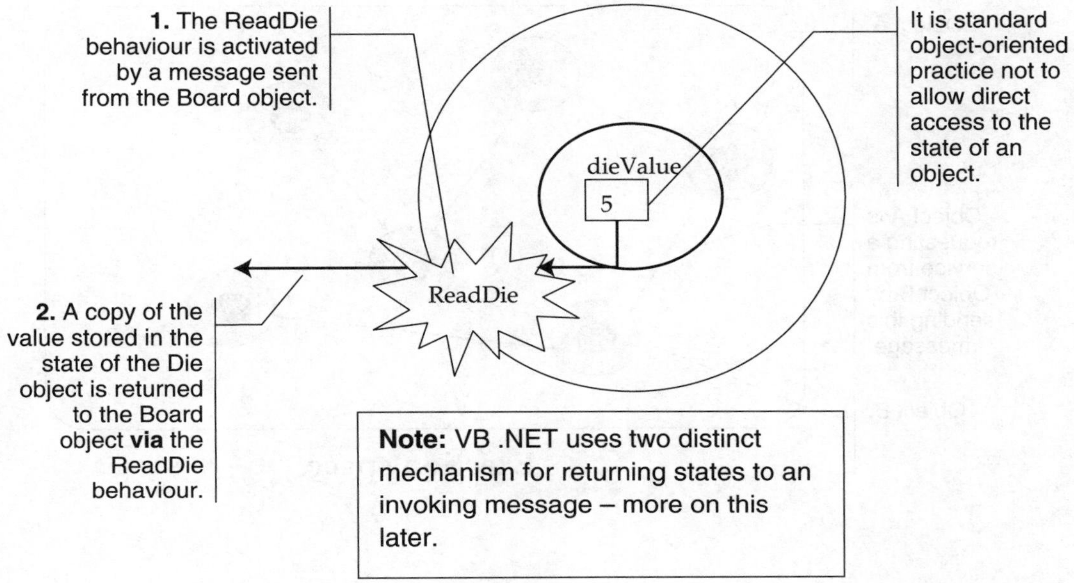

1. The ReadDie behaviour is activated by a message sent from the Board object.

It is standard object-oriented practice not to allow direct access to the state of an object.

dieValue

5

ReadDie

2. A copy of the value stored in the state of the Die object is returned to the Board object **via** the ReadDie behaviour.

Note: VB .NET uses two distinct mechanism for returning states to an invoking message – more on this later.

NOTE: Of course it is possible that the player object will also require to see the value of the die thrown by the die object. Therefore, the player object will also have to send a message that activates the ReadDie behaviour of the die object.

States of an object

States of an object are hidden from other objects. Access to the states of an object is only allowed via the behaviour of the object.

It is possible to allow an object state to be directly accessible to all other objects (i.e. not hidden); however, this is against good programming practice and should not be done.

'Execution space'

When an object-oriented program is executing it can be regarded as existing within an *execution space*, which consists of numerous objects requesting services from one another. This is illustrated by Figure A.5.

Figure A.5 An 'execution space'.

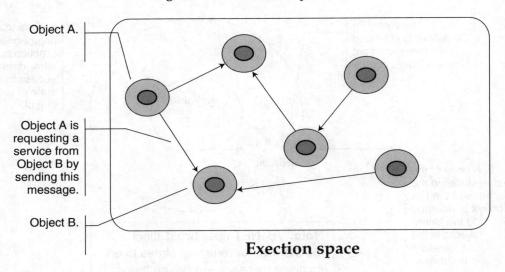

Object A.

Object A is requesting a service from Object B by sending this message.

Object B.

Exection space

Anatomy of an object

All objects have states and behaviours and we have seen an example of this with the Die object. The Die object has two behaviours and one state. Its behaviours were to generate a random number and to allow access to this random number. The state was the random number (i.e. the storing of the random number). This is shown in Figure A.6.

Figure A.6 The Die object.

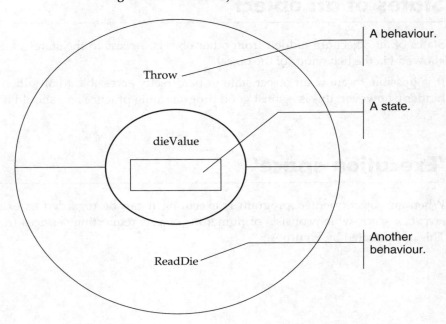

A behaviour.

Throw

A state.

dieValue

Another behaviour.

ReadDie

A class

All objects are constructed from a class. A class is a template from which objects are made. For example, the class for a Die object would look as shown in Figure A.7.

Many independent Die objects can be created from this Die class and each Die object would

Figure A.7 The *Die* Class.

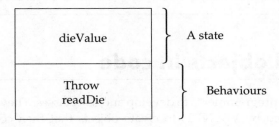

have the same behaviours and states. In this case **each** Die object would have two behaviours (Throw and ReadDie) and one state (dieValue). Although each Die object has the same state (i.e. dieValue) it does not mean that every Die object has the same value stored in this state. As each Die object is independent, each can have a different value within its state. This is illustrated by Figure A.8.

Figure A.8 Relationship between a class and its objects.

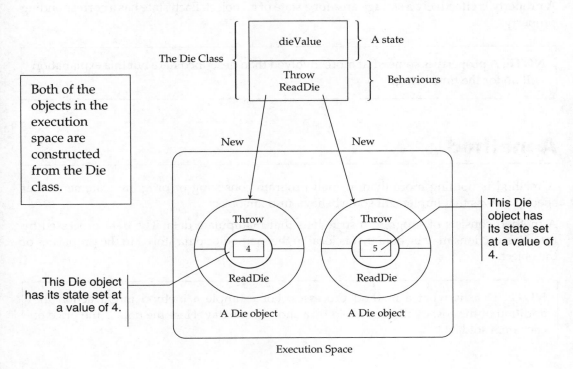

NOTE: Both of the objects shown in Figure A.8 have been created from the Die class. However, each object exits independently within the execution space. Consequently, other objects can message each other independently and each Die object can store their own values in their own states.

NOTE: When an object is created from a class it is said to be an **instance of the class**.

Classes and objects in code

The responsibility of a programmer is to develop and test classes. They then use these classes (or the classes supplied by VB .NET) to create objects that then communicate with one another using messages.

When coding a class using VB .NET behaviour is referred to as a **method**, and a state as a **property**.

A property

A property is effectively a storage area for a state of an object. Each state has a corresponding property.

NOTE: A property is somewhat more involved than described here but this explanation will do for the time being.

A method

A method is nothing more than a small program consisting of program statements that specify actions that implement some behaviour of an object.

A method consists of program instructions that manipulate data. The data processed by these instructions may be data that is local to the method or data stored in the properties of the object.

NOTE: Data is what a method processes. For example a method might action the addition of the cost of all goods sold by a shop in one day. Here the data is the price of each item sold.

A method may arrange the names of its customers into alphabetical order; in this case the data are the names of the customers.

The code that defines a method can be simple or quite complex, involving for example the addition of simple numbers, or the implementation of a complex algorithm.

NOTE: An algorithm is a solution to a problem, e.g. it shows the steps involved in sorting surnames into alphabetical order.

An algorithm is converted to program statements within a method and these statements manipulate data.

Data is stored in variables and these variables can be **local** to the method or they can be used to store the **states** (properties) of an object.

Variables

Variables are named areas of a computer's memory used for the storage of data. Thus data can be the names of customers or the price of an item within a shop.

Variables can be of many types to reflect the types of data that can be processed by a method. Different types of variables take up different amounts of computer memory; for example, a whole number often does not take up as much space as a number with decimal places. Variables of differing types can be manipulated differently. For example variables used to store a number can have their content multiplied together. However, an attempt to multiply the content of variables used to store the names of customers would make no sense and as you would expect it is not allowed.

At this stage of your understanding it is useful to think of variables as different sized boxes that can be processed in differing ways. This is illustrated by Figure A.9.

Figure A.9 Data types represented as different size boxes.

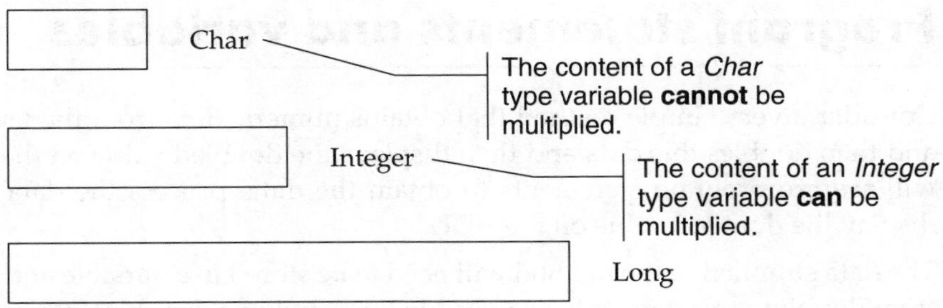

Char — The content of a *Char* type variable **cannot** be multiplied.

Integer — The content of an *Integer* type variable **can** be multiplied.

Long

Identifiers

All variables within a VB .NET program are given an identifier (name). An identifier is formed from alphanumeric characters. Three of the most important rules regarding the formation of an identifier are that it must not contain spaces, it must not start with a number and it must not be a keyword. Examples of legal and illegal identifiers are shown in Table A.1.

Table A.1 Legal and illegal identifiers.

Legal identifiers	Illegal identifiers
FirstNumber	Second number (because it contains a space)
Second_number	2ndnumber (because it starts with a number)
thirdnumber	End (because it is a keyword)

NOTE: A keyword has a special meaning to VB .NET and therefore cannot be used for the name of a variable.

QUESTION A.1 (REVISION)

Which of the following identifiers are legal?

1. *Sum*
2. *sum*
3. *3rdNumber*
4. *Product of Numbers*
5. *While*

Program statements and variables

Consider a very simple method that obtains numeric data from the user via the keyboard and then doubles this data and then displays the doubled value on the VDU. This method will require program statements to obtain the data, process the data (i.e. double it) and display the doubled value on the VDU.

The data supplied to the method will need to be stored in a variable and the result occurring from doubling this data will also need to be stored in a variable. Figure A.10 illustrates this process.

Figure A.10 The execution of a simple method.

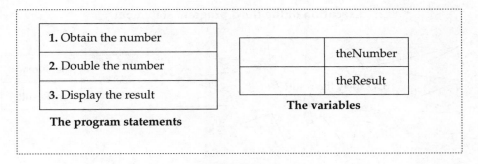

The program statements

1. Obtain the number
2. Double the number
3. Display the result

The variables

theNumber

theResult

Execution of the first program statement

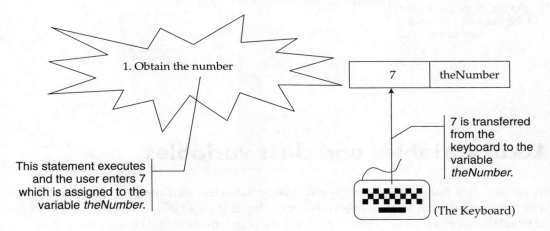

1. Obtain the number

This statement executes and the user enters 7 which is assigned to the variable *theNumber*.

7   theNumber

7 is transferred from the keyboard to the variable *theNumber*.

(The Keyboard)

Execution of the second program statement

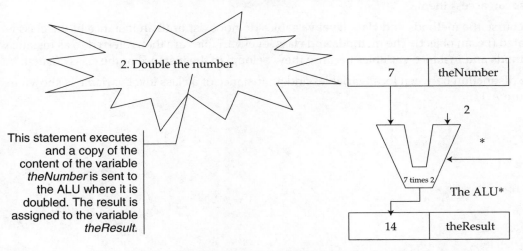

2. Double the number

This statement executes and a copy of the content of the variable *theNumber* is sent to the ALU where it is doubled. The result is assigned to the variable *theResult*.

7   theNumber

2

*

7 times 2

The ALU*

14   theResult

* The purpose of the ALU is explained later in this appendix.

655

Figure A.10 (cont.)

Execution of the third program statement

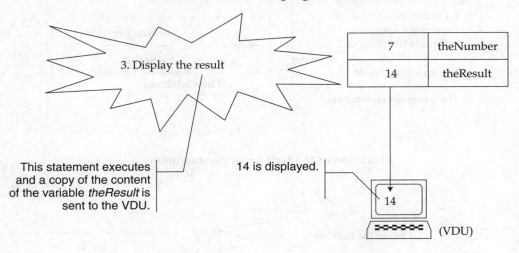

7	theNumber
14	theResult

3. Display the result

This statement executes
and a copy of the content
of the variable *theResult* is
sent to the VDU.

14 is displayed.

14

(VDU)

Local variables and class variables

A method has program statements that manipulate data that reside in variables. These variables can be local level or class level variables. If the variables are declared within the method then they are local variables and only the program statements within the method can access them. However, if the variables are declared within the class declaration area then they are class variables and the program statements of all the methods declared within the class can access them.

Of course the methods and class level variables do not exist until an instance of the class is created (i.e. an object). The methods and class level variables are then referred to as instance methods and instance variables because they 'belong' to the instance of the class created.

The distinction between local variables and an instance of a class level variable is shown in Figure A.11.

Figure A.11 The distinction between a local variable and an instance of a class level variable within an object.

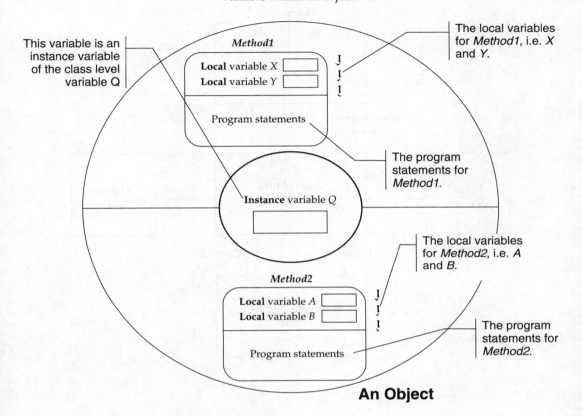

The program statements of *Method1* have access to the *Method1*'s local variables X and Y. However, the program statements of *Method1* do not have access to *Method2*'s local variables A and B.

The program statements of *Method2* have access to the *Method2*'s local variables A and B. However, the program statements *Method2* do not have access to *Method1*'s local variables X and Y.

The program statements of both *Method1* and *Method2* can access the instance variable Q.

Every object created from the class that defined method 1, method 2 and the class level variable Q will have their own copy of the methods and the variable Q. These methods are known as instance methods and the variable is known as an instance variable.

A computer system

A computer system consists of five basic components as illustrated in Figure A.12. Each component is briefly described in the text that follows.

Figure A.12 A Block diagram of a computer system.

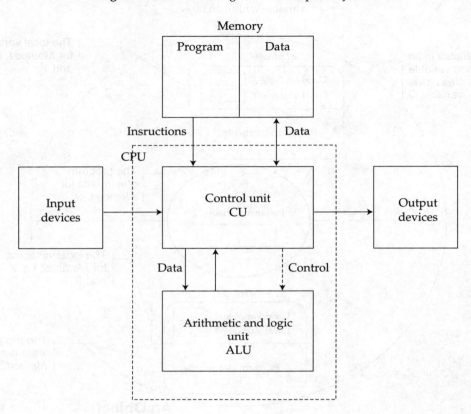

Input devices

A keyboard and a mouse are typical input devices to a computer system. The keyboard supplies the alphanumeric characters requires by an application (program), such as, the names and addresses of customers.

The mouse and its associated cursor are able to activate processes within the application by clicking onto a menu item or button, e.g. activating a spell checker within a word processor.

An application developed with VB .NET also 'sees' the keyboard and the mouse as event generators. These events are used to activate processes (program code) within the application.

Examples of events generated by the mouse are:

- A single click on the mouse button – the *Click* event.
- A double click on the mouse button – the *DoubleClick* event.
- Moving the mouse – the *MouseMove* event.

Examples of events generated by the keyboard are:

- Pressing down a key on the keyboard – the *KeyDown* event.

- Releasing a key on the keyboard – the *KeyUp* event.
- Pressing and releasing a key on the keyboard – the *KeyPress* event.

An event can be associated with a section of code (an event handling procedure) and upon occurrence of an event this code is executed. For example if the user clicks the mouse button the code that handles this click event is executed. The code is an example of a click event handling procedure.

Which particular click event handling procedure executes is dependent upon the position of the cursor on the visual display unit (VDU). For instance, the cursor may be positioned over the spell check icon button in which case the spell checker is executed. Alternatively, the cursor may be positioned over the print icon button in which case a document will be sent to the printer.

There are many more types of events available to applications written in VB .NET and they are dealt with throughout the book as appropriate. What executes in response to an event depends upon the code attached to an event by the computer programmer.

To summarize, input devices supply data to applications running on the computer system and they can also supply events to activate code within the application. This relationship between the application and the input devices is illustrated in Figure A.13.

Figure A.13 Relationship between the application and its input devices.

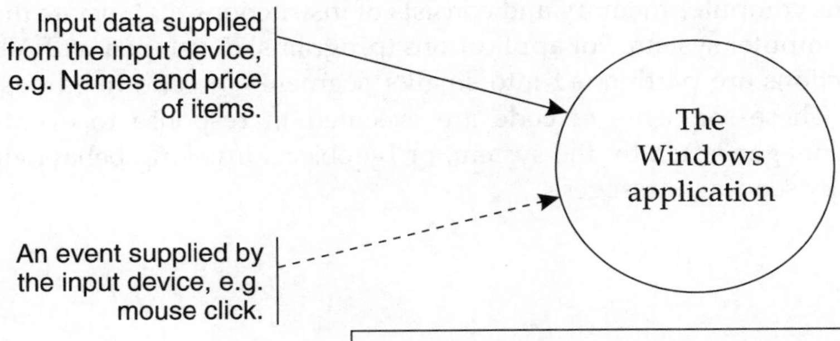

Input data supplied from the input device, e.g. Names and price of items.

An event supplied by the input device, e.g. mouse click.

The Windows application

The circle represents the windows application. The input data is represented by the unbroken arrow and the event by the dotted arrow.

Output devices

Examples of output devices for computer systems are the VDU and the printer. For the development of applications using VB .NET the most important output device is the VDU. Window applications are graphical in nature and users interact with the graphical view using the mouse and keyboard.

The memory

Stores the program instructions (statements) and the data to be manipulated by the program.

The central processing unit (CPU)

The CPU, under direction from the program statements, processes the data.

The control unit (CU)

This is a subsystem of the CPU. It is responsible for the issuing of signals that control the movement of data around the system. It also informs the arithmetic and logic unit (ALU) as to the function it is to perform (i.e. add, subtract, logical NOT, compare, etc.). The control unit receives its instructions from the program statements.

The arithmetic and logic unit (ALU)

This is also a subsystem of the CPU and it is responsible for performing all the arithmetic and logic operations. For example, it will add together numeric data (arithmetic operation) or it will for example mask incoming data to see if a serial modem line is switched on or off (logical operation).

Program

The program is stored in the computer memory and consists of instructions that dictate the activities performed by a computer system. For applications (programs) developed with VB .NET, the program instructions are partitioned into smaller segments of code (methods) contained within objects. These segments of code are executed in response to events generated by the user, events generated by the system, or by objects invoking behaviour (methods) in other objects by sending messages.

Data

Data is stored in the computer memory, usually encapsulated within an object. It is processed by the computer system hardware components that are in turn, controlled by program instructions.

Machine code

The program instructions received by the Control Unit, from the program stored in memory, are in the language of the machine. This language is referred to as machine code.

Machine code is a low level language that controls the architecture of the CPU. It opens pathways for the movement of data between the computer's components and it dictates how data is to be processed by the ALU.

There are vast arrays of different computer systems available. These systems have CPUs that have different architectures. Every type of CPU has its own language. Consequently, a program in the machine language of one CPU will not control the architecture of another CPU type.

Developing software packages in machine code limits their availability to one type of CPU. A programmer experienced in writing programs in one type of machine language requires retraining in the language of another machine. Programs developed in machine code take a long time to produce and are difficult to test and debug.

High level languages

High level languages are converted to machine code by a compiler. Compilers are available for each type of CPU. Consequently, a program developed in a high level language can be used on different types of computer systems. Therefore, high level languages are more **portable** than low level languages.

Productivity is vastly increased if software is developed in a high level language rather than machine code. This productivity is achieved because one line of a high level language is translated into numerous lines of machine code. Also high level language programs are easier to test and debug than machine code programs.

The main advantage of a high level language over machine code is that they are problem oriented. This means that a high level language can represent the solution to a problem in a form that is more understandable to a human.

Machine code programs bear little resemblance to the solution of a problem. This can be best illustrated by the example shown in Table A.2.

Table A.2 Comparison of machine code and a high level language statement.

High level language statement	Machine code
sum = number 1 + number 2	3E01C60200FF

Both the machine code and high level language statement shown in Table A.2 are responsible for the addition of two numbers and the storing of the sum. Obviously, the high level language is more understandable to a human than the machine code.

Assembly language

Low level programs are actually written in an assembly language and these programs are translated to machine code by an assembler. However, assembly language suffers nearly all the problems associated with machine code. Indeed assembly language is nothing more than symbolic machine code. The relationship between high and low level languages is illustrated in Figure A.14.

Figure A.14 Comparison of language levels.

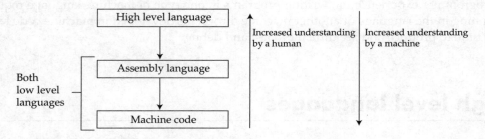

Compilation process

A high level language, such as VB .NET, is a collection of files. These files are generated using the VB .NET integrated development environment. The files consist of classes, program statements and language constructs, such as sequence, selection and repetition.

The VB .NET files are the input to a program referred to as the Compiler. The Compiler 'drives' the computer, which then 'translates' the VB .NET files to produce another file that contains an intermediate language (not quite machine code). This intermediate language, in conjunction with the .NET framework, will then perform the actions of the program. At the end of a successful compilation process two main types of files exist, the original VB .NET files (called the source code) and the Executable file (containing the intermediate language). This process is illustrated in Figure A.15.

Figure A.15 Compilation process.

```
┌─────────────────────┐        ┌─────────────────────┐
│ Visual basic files. │        │      Compiler.      │
└─────────────────────┘        └─────────────────────┘
   Source.

                              Instructions controlling the computer.

              ╭───────────╮
              │ Computer  │   Running the Compiler program.
              ╰───────────╯

        ┌──────────────────────────────────────────────┐
        │ Executable file (intermediate language).     │
        └──────────────────────────────────────────────┘
```

Compile errors

The success of the compilation process is dependent upon the source files being syntactically correct, i.e. correct spelling of declared variables, no keywords words missing, etc. If the source code is incorrect in any way then compilation errors are reported. The programmer, using an editor, amends these errors in the source code. Upon amendment of the compilation errors the VB .NET files are again compiled. This process may be repeated a number of times until all the errors are removed.

Keywords

Many of the words within a VB .NET program have a special meaning to the compiler. They, for instance, tell the compiler where the methods begin and end. Refer to the VB .NET online help facility for a comprehensive list of keywords (refer to the main text on how to use the online help facility).

Runtime

The intermediate language is the machine representation of the activities defined by the VB .NET program and with the assistance of the .NET framework is used to 'drive' the computer system. The input data is processed to produce the output data and the events activate appropriate methods (event handling procedures) within the application as illustrated in Figure A.16.

Figure A.16 The runtime process.

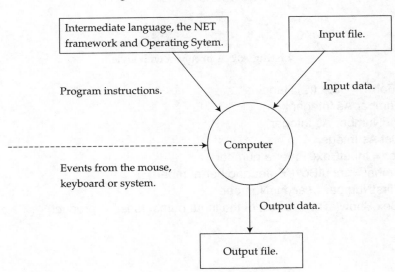

Runtime errors

A successful compilation process does not imply a successful runtime! The executable code, in processing the input data, may attempt to divide by zero. Dividing by zero results in infinity. A runtime error will occur and the program will throw an exception. There are a variety of reasons for runtime errors, as you will discover during your study.

> **NOTE:** A programmer has to arrange for code to catch exceptions thrown by programs and 'gracefully' overcome the error that caused the exception.

Program style

Most software houses adopt layout rules (styles) for their source code. Adopting a consistent style for programs is easier on the eye and gives your programs a professional look. The main advantage of a consistent style is that programmers within the same organization find it easy to debug their colleagues' program – which is an essential activity when producing code. Listing A.1 shows a program with no style. Compare this program to the program shown in Listing A.2. Both programs will compile and perform the same function.

Listing A.1 A program with **no** style.

```
Private Sub Form1_Click (...) Handles ....
    Dim x, y, z As Integer
    x = InputBox("Enter") : y = InputBox("Enter")
    z = x * y : MessageBox.Show("The answer is " & z)
End Sub
```

Listing A.2 A program with style.

```
Private Sub Form1_Click (...) Handles ....
    Dim firstNumber As Integer
    Dim secondNumber As Integer
    Dim product As Integer
    firstNumber = InputBox("Enter a number")
    secondNumber = InputBox("Enter another number")
    product = firstNumber * secondNumber
    MessageBox.Show("The product of the input numbers is " & product)
End Sub
```

The main difference between Listings A.1 and A.2 is that Listing A.2 has one statement per line. Also, the variable identifiers have been chosen to reflect their role in the program. For instance, the variable used to store the first number entered at the keyboard is named *firstNumber* and not *x* as in the first program. Using sensible names for variables is the best way to document code. Also the identifier has the first letter of each word after the first word capitalized (remember that spaces cannot be used in identifiers). You are advised to adopt a consistent style for all of your programs. For the time being, I recommend that you adopt the following rules for code layout:

1. Have only one statement per line.

2. Indent statements (automatically done for you by VB .NET).

3. Use camel casing for identifiers, ensuring that the first letter in each word after the first word is capitalized.

4. Ensure that identifiers reflect the use of the variable within the code.

Index